W9-CUH-563

Peru

BRAZIL

PERU

BOLIVIA

CHILE

ARGENTINA

Pacific Ocean

Atlantic Ocean

Tumbes

Sullana

Chiclayo

Cajamarca

Trujillo

Cordillera Blanca

Rio Huallaga

Iquitos

Rio Marañón

Rio Amazonas

Rio Ucuyali

Pucallpa

LIMA

Huancayo

Ayacucho

Machu Picchu

Cusco

Puerto
Maldonado

South Pacific Ocean

Nasca

Juliaca

*Lake
Titicaca*

Puno

Arequipa

Moquegna

Ilo

Tacna

N

0 km 100

0 miles 62

Paved Roads

Unpaved Roads

Peru Handbook

Published by Footprint Handbooks
6 Riverside Court
Lower Bristol Road
Bath BA2 3DZ. England
T +44 (0)1225 469141
F +44 (0)1225 469461
Email handbooks@footprint.cix.co.uk
Web www.footprint-handbooks.co.uk

ISBN 1 900949 31 8
CIP DATA: A catalogue record for this
book is available from the British Library

In North America, published by
Passport Books, a division of
NTC/Contemporary Publishing Group
4255 West Touhy Avenue, Lincolnwood
(Chicago), Illinois 60646-1975, USA
T 847 679 5500 F 847 679 24941
Email NTCPUB2@AOL.COM

ISBN 0 8442-2187-2
Library of Congress Catalog Card
Number: 98-68297

© Footprint Handbooks Ltd 1999

Footprint Handbooks and the Footprint
mark are a registered trademark of
Footprint Handbooks Ltd.

Credits

Series editor
Patrick Dawson
Editorial
Senior editor: Sarah Thorowgood
Maps: Alex Nott
Production
Typesetting: Jo Morgan, Richard
Ponsford and Ann Griffiths
Maps: Kevin Feeney and Rob Lunn
Proof reading: Rod Gray

Marketing
MBargo, Singapore

Design
Mytton Williams

Photography
Front and back cover: Max Milligan
Colour section: Jamie Marshall, South
American Pictures, Impact, Peru
Embassy

Printed and bound
in Italy by LEGOPRINT

Peru Footprint Handbook

Alan Murphy

Latin American series editor: Ben Box

For my part, I travel not to go anywhere, but to go. I travel for travel's sake. The great affair is to move.

Robert Louis Stevenson

Contents

1

7 **A foot in the door**

2

17 **Essentials**
19 Planning your trip
22 Before you travel
26 Getting there
33 Touching down
43 Where to stay
45 Getting around
54 Keeping in touch
56 Food and drink
58 Shopping
60 Special interest travel
72 Holidays & festivals
73 Health
83 Further reading
85 Useful addresses

3

89 **Lima**
92 Ins and outs
96 Central Lima
108 Suburbs
108 San Isidro
109 Miraflores
109 Barranco
110 Callao
111 Sleeping
116 Eating
120 Bars & nightclubs
121 Entertainment
122 Festivals
125 Sport
127 Transport
130 Directory

4

141 **Cusco & the Sacred Valley**
144 Cusco
169 The Urubamba Valley
170 Pisac
173 Urubamba
176 Ollantaytambo
179 Machu Picchu
183 The Inca Trail
193 Southeast from Cusco

5

197 **Lake Titicaca**
200 Arequipa to Juliaca
201 Juliaca
204 Puno
213 The islands
215 Frontier with Bolivia
219 Puno to Cusco

6

221 **Arequipa**
224 Arequipa
238 Colca Canyon
241 Chivay
243 Cabanaconde
244 Trekking in the Colca Canyon
245 Toro Muerto
245 Cotahuasi Canyon
246 Cotohuasi
247 Trekking in the Cotahuasi Canyon
248 Towards the Valley of the Volcanoes

7

249 **South Coast**
252 Lima to Pisco
255 Pisco
257 Paracas Peninsula and Ballestas Islands
260 Inland from Pisco
261 Ica
264 Ica to Nasca
265 Nasca
269 Nasca Lines
272 South of Nasca
276 Moquegua
279 Ilo
281 Tacna
284 Frontier with Chile

8

285 **Cordillera Blanca**
288 The area
289 Trekking and climbing in the Cordillera Blanca
293 Huaraz
301 North from Huaraz
302 Carhuaz
304 Yungay
307 Caraz
312 Huaraz to Chavín
315 Chavín
316 Chavín de Huantar
317 Callejón de Conchucos
321 Cordillera Huayhuash and Raura

9

325 **North Coast**
328 Lima to Chimbote
333 Sechín

334 Chimbote
336 Trujillo
345 Chan Chán
350 Chiclayo
357 Sipán
359 Túcume
362 Piura
370 North to Ecuador
375 Tumbes
379 Frontier with Ecuador

10

381 **Northern Highlands**
384 From the coast to
        Cajamarca
386 Cajamarca
394 Chachapoyas Region
396 Chachapoyas
399 Around Chachapoyas
401 South of Chachapoyas
402 Kuelap
404 Gran Vilaya
409 East of Chachapoyas
411 North of Chachapoyas
412 East to the Amazon
415 To the coast
416 Jaén

11

419 **Central Highlands**
422 Lima to Huancayo
424 Jauja
425 Huancayo
432 Huancavelica
434 Ayacucho
442 Ayacucho to Cusco
444 East of La Oroya
448 North of La Oroya
449 Cerro de Pasco
451 Huallaga Valley

12

455 **The Amazon Basin**
458 Northern Jungle
463 Pucallpa
467 Iquitos
477 Southern Jungle
478 Manu Biosphere Reserve
483 Puerto Maldonado
487 Tambopata-Candamo
        Reserved Zone

13

491 **Background**
493 **History & politics**
493 Precolombian history
496 Moche culture
497 Inca Dynasty
501 Conquest & after
502 Post independence Peru
504 Political developments
505 1968 coup
506 Peru under Fujimori
509 **Land & environment**
509 Geography
512 Climate
513 Flora & fauna
517 **Culture**
517 People
520 Religion
521 Arts & crafts
526 Music & dance
529 Festivals
530 Literature
533 Fine art & sculpture
537 **Government & the**
        modern country
537 Government
537 Economy
540 Society

14

545 **Footnotes**
547 Basic Spanish for
        travellers
550 Shorts
551 Index
555 Map index
560 Advertisers
563 Coloured maps

A foot in the door

Highlights

One problem above all presents itself when considering a trip to Peru: there's too much choice. It's a big place and there's an awful lot to see, so how on earth do you cram months' worth of essential sightseeing into perhaps only a few weeks? Number one on everyone's itinerary is Cusco and the Sacred Valley of the Urubamba river, where you'll find many of Peru's greatest Inca ruins. But there's a lot more to this country than Inca architecture.

Lake Titicaca Take a spectacular train ride south from Cusco, and you'll find the sparkling sapphire waters of mystical Lake Titicaca, on the border with Bolivia at a breathtaking 3,856 metres above sea level. Visiting the lake's islands is like stepping back in time. You can stay with the local people who have remained unaffected by changes on the mainland and who still hold true to their traditional way of life.

The Southern Highlands In the southern Andes, Ayacucho was once the centre of one of the most influential pre-Incan cultures - and has the ruins to prove it. The city also has no fewer than 33 colonial churches and hosts one of the most impressive Easter celebrations in Latin America. Nearby, in the remote Mantaro valley, is a string of villages producing some of finest handicrafts in Peru, each one renowned for its own particular product.

El Condor Pasa Further south stands the magnificent city of Arequipa, built entirely of volcanic white sillar. This is the home of Santa Catalina convent, perhaps the most fascinating colonial building in the Americas. Surrounded by high walls, it is virtually a city within a city. Inside is a perfectly preserved miniature colonial village, which was until recently closed to the outside world. Arequipa is also the gateway to the Colca Canyon. This remarkable chasm is twice as deep as the Grand Canyon and was thought to be the deepest canyon in the world, until 1994, when the nearby Cotahuasi Canyon was discovered to be even deeper. Visitors flock to the Colca Canyon to enjoy a close encounter with the condor, the largest bird in the world. Every morning they ride the warm thermals and have a good look at the latest group of awe-struck tourists.

Adventure Sports In the northern Andes is the Cordillera Blanca, a mecca for hikers the world over. However if that's not your cup of *mate de coca*, then you can try white water rafting, mountain biking, skiing or simply enjoy the architectural splendour of the 2,500 year-old fortress temple of Chavin de Huantar, one of Peru's most important pre-columbian sites. There's also the white-knuckle bus ride through the Canon del Pato, probably the most thrilling and terrifying journey you'll ever experience.

A Site to Behold In the north-east, where the Andean mountains drop to meet the vast Amazonian jungle, lie countless precolumbian sites, built by the mysterious cloud people, considered by some to be descended from the Vikings. The most visited of these, Kuelap, is the greatest pre-Columbian fortress in the Americas, and of such immense proportions that it makes the Great Pyramid at Giza seem like something out of legoland.

The Amazon River The mighty Amazon begins its long 6,500 kilometre journey high up in the Peruvian Andes, then joins the Ucayali to become the earth's longest river. Standing on its banks is the city of Iquitos, accessible only by air or river. Made famous during the rubber boom of the late 19th century, it is now the main starting point for tourists wishing to explore Peru's northern jungle. From jungle lodges you can experience some of the most exotic wildlife in the world, including the strange, prehistoric-looking pink dolphins, found only on remote Amazon and Orinoco tributaries.

Left: Taquile Island, Lake Titicaca. Visiting the islands of Lake Titicaca is like stepping back in time: no traffic, no pollution, no stress, just peace and quiet and fantastic scenery.

Below: a huge carpet of jungle covers two thirds of Peru. The only way to explore this mysterious and unexplored green world is by a myriad of slow, meandering rivers.

Left and above: fiestas at Taquile Island and in Lima. Fiestas are a fundamental part of life in Peru, which is why Peruvians really know how to put on a good party. Whether it's a more solemn and overtly religious affair or a wild knees-up notable for its excessive drinking and eating, you can't fail to be impressed by the sheer energy and enthusiasm.

The Road to Ruins

To most people, Peruvian history starts with the Incas, but they were very much the **Pre-Inca** new kids on the block in historical terms. Before them came several equally influen- **Civilizations** tial cultures whose advanced architectural and artistic styles and techniques were copied by South America's last great indigenous civilization. Most of these magnifi- cent pre-Inca sites are found along Peru's long stretch of desert coast.

Etched into the dust of the southern coastal desert are the Nasca Lines: huge figures **The Nasca Lines** of animals and geometric patterns, some of them up to 100 metres across. These giant representations of a monkey, killer whale and humming bird, among others, are visible only from the air and have puzzled scientists for many years. They were made by the highly developed Nasca civilisation between 200 BC and AD 600 and to this day no one knows for sure how or why they drew them. The Nasca Lines remain one of the continent's great mysteries.

The elegant colonial city of Trujillo, on Peru's northern coast, is the base for visiting **Around Trujillo** Chan Chan, the largest adobe city in the world. The crumbling ruins of the imperial city, which cover 28 square kilometres, consist of nine great compounds built by suc- cessive dynasties which ruled this part of the country before the arrival of the Incas. Only a few kilometres from Trujillo are the massive adobe pyramids of Huaca del Sol and Huaca de la Luna and farther afield are yet more impressive pre-Inca sites. If all the archeology gets too much, you can always relax at Huanchaco, a fishing village on the coast and a favourite hang-out for surfers.

If the Trujillo area seems full of archaeological treasures, then the desert around **Around Chiclayo** Chiclayo, 200 kilometres further north, is bursting at the seams. At the twin pyramid complex of Sipan, excavations over the past decade have uncovered some of the fin- est examples of pre-Columbian jewellery, pottery and textiles yet found on the continent (now on display in Lima's museums). Further north lie the impressive ruins of Tucume, a vast city built over one thousand years ago, consisting of 26 pyramids, platform mounds, walled citadels, residential compounds and a ceremonial centre.

Sacred Valley of the Incas

Everyone who visits Peru inevitably comes to Cusco, one of the most fascinating cit- **The Inca Capital** ies anywhere in the world. The Spanish built their colonial churches and houses on top of the original Inca foundations, and this startling mix of architectural styles is still much in evidence. Cusco may have become famous as the ancient capital of the Inca Empire, but today it is equally famous among travellers as the "gringo capital" of South America. The city itself has enough to hold the interest of even the most demanding of tourists for at least a week, and after a hard day's sightseeing or souve- nir shopping in the teeming markets, there's a multitude of good restaurants, cafes, bars and nightclubs in which to unwind.

Cusco is also the ideal base from which to explore the Urubamba Valley, or Sacred **Machu Picchu** Valley of the Incas, as it is more commonly known, which runs west all the way to Machu Picchu and beyond. Peru's best known archaeological site is the main attrac- tion for visitors, and rightly so. This ancient citadel, the only major Inca find to escape 400 years of looting and destruction, remains the most spectacular sight in all the

Left: *it may be the oldest cliché in the book, but a visit to Machu Picchu is a must. No amount of hype or build-up can prepare you for that first, unforgettable sight.*

Americas - no matter how many times you see it. Machu Picchu can be visited in a day, by train from Cusco, but the best way to appreciate it is at the end of the four-day Inca Trail. If you attempt just one trek in your life, then this should be it. Much of the trail is along prefectly-preserved Inca paved road, through Inca tunnels and up and down huge Inca staircases. It passes other Inca ruins along the way and runs through sections of beautiful cloudforest, all with the permanent backdrop of snow-capped mountain ranges. Simply breathtaking.

Around Cusco Aside from Machu Picchu, there are many other sites of interest in the Cusco area. For a good example of Inca masonry, check out the ruined ceremonial centre of Sacsayhuaman (see page 4) on a hill in the northern outskirts of the city. The impressive walls are made from massive stones weighing up to 130 tons and fitted together with absolute perfection. Every year on 24 June, Sacsayhuaman plays host to the Inca summer solstice festival of Inti Raymi, one of the biggest celebrations in all of Peru.

Pisac and Ollantaytambo The Sacred Valley between Cusco and Machu Picchu is lined with a string of fascinating little Andean towns, each with its own particular appeal. Standing at the eastern end of the Urubamba Valley is Pisac, famous for its lively market and superb Inca fortress set on the mountainside high above the town. West from Pisac, on the Cusco-Machu Picchu rail line, is the well-preserved Inca town of Ollantaytambo. A flight of terraces leads up above the town to an unfinished Inca temple representing some of the finest Inca architecture in the country.

Manu Biosphere Reserve

Unexplored Rainforest Amazingly, 60 percent of Peru is jungle, even though less than six percent of its population lives there. Because the physical barrier of the Andes has prevented Peru from integrating the tropical lowlands, much of its jungle is intact. In short, Peru boasts some of the best untouched rainforest in the world. Located in the country's southernmost department of Madre de Dios, and accessible from Cusco, is Manu Biosphere Reserve, one of the largest protected areas of rainforest and arguably the most pristine conservation unit in the world. The reserve itself is over half the size of Switzerland, and much of it is completely unexplored. It starts high up in the Andes and goes down through elfin, cloud and montane forest into the vast lowland rainforest of the Amazon, and is, quite simply, the best place on earth for seeing jungle wildlife.

Birds and Insects The variety of birds is astounding; the reserve holds more than 1,000 species - significantly more than the whole of Costa Rica and over one tenth of all the birds on earth. Manu also holds the world record for the number of plant species - 15,000 and counting - not to mention millions of insects species, of which only a tiny percentage have ever been studied by science.

Unique Wildlife In many other jungle areas you'll be lucky to see anything more than birds or insects. In Manu you're guaranteed to see so many monkeys - 13 different species in all - that you can almost become bored of them. Besides the countless multi-coloured macaws, turtles and capybara (a strange hybrid of a guinea pig and a hippopotamus), Manu offers a unique opportunity to see tapirs, peccaries, sloths, giant anteaters, seven metre-long black caimans, giant otters - even the occasional jaguar.

Remote Tribes But it's not just the animals which are protected in Manu. The reserve is home to several Indian tribes, a few of which have had no direct contact with the outside world. One of these, the Mashco Piro, aggressively defend their territory, so don't be too surprised if a poison-tipped arrow comes your way during a hard day's animal watching!

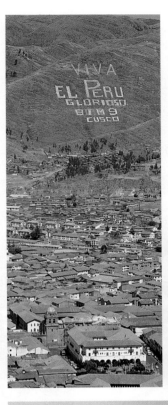

Previous page: men of Taquile Island dressed in traditional costume pass the time of day. **Left**: view of Cusco. "Long live glorious Peru" reads the hillside message, and cities don't get any more glorious than Cusco, the ancient Inca capital which has become the "gringo" capital of South America. **Below**: gold mask from Sipan. The Spanish not only came, saw and conquered, but also took away a fair amount. They left enough to fill Lima's many fine museums, though, in particular the Gold Museum.

Above: jungle lodge in Manu. Visiting a jungle is a unique and enjoyable experience . Lodges like this provide the opportunity to see strange, exotic creatures without sacrificing many of your creature comforts. **Left**: Nasca pot. The desert around Nasca is one vast museum. Not only are there massive animal figures etched in the sand, but also mummified bodies and thousands of pieces of beautiful Nasca pottery just lying around. **Next page**: market at Cusco. Visitors to Peru become addicted to markets. These wonderfully stimulating events tempt unsuspecting tourists with their irresistible sights, sounds and smells.

Essentials

2

Essentials

19	**Planning your trip**		**48**	Car
19	Where to go		**51**	Motorcycling
20	When to go		**52**	Cycling
21	Festivals		**53**	Hitchhiking
21	Adventure tourism		**54**	**Keeping in touch**
21	Finding out more		**54**	Postal services
22	**Before you travel**		**54**	Telephone services
25	Money		**55**	Internet
26	**Getting there**		**55**	Media
26	Air		**56**	**Food and drink**
31	Road and boat		**58**	**Shopping**
33	**Touching down**		**60**	**Special interest travel**
33	Airport information		**60**	Adventure sport
35	Tourist information		**69**	Cultural tourism
37	Special interest groups		**69**	Birdwatching
38	Rules, customs & etiquette		**72**	**Holidays & festivals**
39	Responsible tourism		**73**	**Health**
40	Safety		**73**	Before travelling
43	**Where to stay**		**76**	Staying healthy
45	**Getting around**		**80**	Other risks and serious diseases
45	Air		**83**	When you get home
46	Train		**83**	**Further reading**
47	Bus		**85**	**Useful addresses**

Planning your trip

Where to go

The variety which Peru can offer the visitor is enormous. It may be a tourist brochure cliché, but there really is something for everyone. The problem is, if you're on a tight schedule, how to fit it all in. Obviously people's tastes differ, but the suggested itineraries below should give an idea of what you can cover comfortably in the time available.

Getting around the country can be a difficult task, and this is to be expected in a country whose geography is dominated by the Andes, one of the world's major mountain ranges. Great steps have been taken to improve major roads and enlarge the paved network linking the Pacific coast with the Highlands. But it is worth taking some time to plan an overland journey in advance, checking which roads are finished, which have roadworks and which will be affected by the weather. Peru also, unfortunately, suffers more than its fair share of natural disasters, such as the devastating El Niño of 1997/98. This can have dramatic effects on overland travel.

Useful addresses and websites which will allow you to check up on local conditions in advance are listed under **Finding out more** (page 21) and **Tourist information** (page 35). See also **Getting around** (page 45).

If you only have a couple of weeks, travelling by air is the sensible option. It allows access to most major regions and means you can spend more time at your destination and less getting there. On the downside, though, air travel reduces the amount of local colour compared to what can be seen when going by bus, car or bike. But irrespective of what you choose to see and how you get there, don't attempt too much. Just take it easy and give yourself time to appreciate one of the most beautiful and fascinating countries on Earth.

The southern circuit If time is limited, it makes sense to focus on the southern part of the country, which features many of the top attractions. First-time visitors should, under no cicumstances, miss out Cusco and Machu Picchu, the most precious jewels in Peru's tourist crown. A two-week trip could include Lima, Arequipa, Lake Titicaca, Cusco and Machu Picchu, combining air, rail and road travel. This covers the most important and popular sites in the southern part of the country. One of the main drawbacks in such an itinerary is that it allows insufficient time in the Sacred Valley of the Incas, near Cusco, where you could easily spend a week seeing archaeological sites and Quechua villages, hiking, or just relaxing.

Adding an extra week or two to the basic itinerary would allow you to see much more of Cusco (which is a difficult city to drag yourself away from anyway). This would also leave time to explore the Colca Canyon from Arequipa, or, from Puno, the shores and islands of Lake Titicaca. You could also spend a week in the jungle visiting the unique and wonderful Manu National Park, which is accessible from Cusco by air or road and boat. Another option would be to spend a few days in Lima visiting its fascinating museums, which give you an overview of what you'll be seeing later. And in the meanwhile, you can experience the capital's great nightlife.

Those with more than a few weeks to spare, could spend a week on the southern coast, taking in the Paracas peninsula (near Pisco), with its marine birdlife, and the incredible Nasca Lines.

The Central Highlands A trip to the Central Andes from Lima can be done fairly quickly, calling at Huancayo, Huancavelica and Ayacucho in a minimum of a week to ten days, combined perhaps with a flight to Cusco. The spectacular train journey from Lima up to Huancayo is well worth the time and effort. Alternatively, the route from Cusco to the Central

Essentials

Highlands (via Ayacucho-Huancavelica-Huancayo) is rewarding, either by flying Cusco-Ayacucho, or, for the hardy, by bus. But note that this is an area in which road conditions must be checked in advance. Obviously the more time you allow, the greater the variety of sights to see, especially in the Mantaro Valley near Huancayo, and the places of historical interest around Ayacucho. These are also two of the best places for handicrafts.

Northern routes A two-week trip is possible to a number of places, but as elsewhere in Peru, this would do scant justice to the variety on offer. Huaraz, in the Cordillera Blanca, is only seven hours by road from Lima and is the country's climbing and trekking centre. Hiking or climbing in the Cordillera and neighbouring areas can easily be linked with the coastal archaeological sites near the colonial city of Trujillo (eg Chan Chán).

Alternatively, or additionally, the Cajamarca area includes the pleasant city itself, plus thermal baths, archaeological and more recent historical sites and beautiful countryside. To get there from Huaraz, you have to return to the coast for flights or bus services (via Cajabamba or Pacasmayo). Cajamarca then gives access to the more remote Chachapoyas region, which contains a bewildering number of pre-Hispanic archaeological sites. Access is by air, or by road from the southwest through Celendín.

There is also a more northerly road route through Bagua from Chiclayo, itself rich in archaeological sites (eg Sipán and Túcume). If planning to explore any of these places without rushing through them, four days to a week should do, except Chachapoyas where a week minimum would be a good idea (maybe not that much if flying in and out).

You can break up a tour of archaeology and mountains with some surfing at Puerto Chicama (north of Trujillo) and there are many more beaches in the far north near Piura and Tumbes. Tumbes also has some wildlife parks, such as coastal mangroves, unlike those in other parts of the country.

The jungle Peru's eastern jungle include zones with some of the highest levels of biodiversity in the world, in particular Manu National Park. This provides wonderful opportunities for watchers of birds, butterflies and animals and for plant lovers. A trip to the jungle can be done as part of a visit to Cusco (see above) or as a basic item on its own, for example to Iquitos or to the wildlife reserves near Puerto Maldonado. Flying both ways is the only viable option if short of time. Going overland to the Amazon Basin is possible and adventurous, but will not give much scope for more than the journey itself if you do not plan properly and allow enough time.

When to go

Peru's high season is from June to August, which is the best time for hiking the Inca Trail or trekking and climbing elsewhere in the country. At this time the days are generally clear and sunny, though nights can be very cold at high altitude. The highlands can be visited at other times of the year, though during the wettest months from November to April some roads become impassable and hiking trails can be very muddy. For a more detailed description of conditions in the Cordillera, see page 61.

On the coast, the summer months from December to April are best for swimming. During the rest of the year, a blanket of cloud, the *garúa*, hangs over the coast from the south to about 200 kilometres north of Lima. At this time only the northern beaches near Tumbes are warm enough to provide pleasant swimming.

The best time to visit the jungle is during the dry season, from April to October. During the wet season, November to April, it only rains for a few hours at a time, which is not enough to spoil your trip, but enough to make some roads virtually impassable.

Festivals

Every bit as important as knowing where to go and what the weather will be like, is Peru's festival calendar. At any given time of the year there'll be a festival somewhere in the country, at which time even the sleepiest little town and village is transformed into a wild orgy of drinking, dancing and water throwing (or worse). Not all festivals end up as massive unruly parties – some are solemn and ornate holy processions – but they all draw people from miles around. So it helps a great deal to know about these festivals and when they take place.

Many of the major *fiestas*, such as *Carnaval* (throughout February) and *Semana Santa* (March/April), take place during the wet season. June and July are also big months for *fiestas*, particularly in Cusco, which spends the whole of June in celebration. Accommodation can be very hard to find at this time in Cusco.

For a list of the major national holidays and festivals, see page 72. For a detailed list of local festival dates, see under each town in the main travelling text. For a description of some of the main festivals and their historic roots, see under **Culture**, on page 529.

Adventure tourism

This is very much up and coming in Peru. Some activities such as rafting, mountain biking and paragliding are in the hands of a few enthusiastic specialists. Andinismo and trekking, on the other hand, are recovering the popularity of former years. There is still, however, broad potential for both rarely trodden short excursions and major expeditions. For a more detailed description of the various options, see Adventure sports, page 60.

Finding out more

Tourism promotion and information is handled by *PromPerú*, Edificio Mitince, Calle Uno (sin número), 13th and 14th floor, San Isidro, T(01)2243279/2243118/2243395, F2243323, E postmaster@promperu.gob.pe. W www.rcp.net.pe/promperu; www.peruonline.net; www.promperu.org. PromPerú and the European Commission have set up AL-TUR, which supports local tourism initiatives. These projects are listed in the relevant destinations. For more details, E alter@promperu.gob.pe.

PromPerú has offices in every major centre and freely gives out information. Outside Peru, tourist information can be obtained from Peruvian Embassies and Consulates.

An excellent source of information is the South American Explorers' Club in Lima (see page 137). Also useful is the Latin American Travel Adviser (see page 35). There are numerous tour operators taking travellers to Peru. Many cater to the growing interest in adventure sports. We give a representative list (together with their specialism) under useful addresses on page 85.

Some useful email numbers and websites include:
Perú Guide, www.peruguide.com/menu.htm, E postmaster@miraflores.gob.pe.
Directorio Turístico Nacional, www.travelupdate.limaperu.net/directur.
Canatur (Cámara Nacional de Turismo), www.si.com.pe/CANATUR/epaises.htm.
Guía Turística, ekeko.rcp.net.pe/turifax.
Peruvian Touring Center, www.ptcenter.com/ptc.html.
Magic Peru, www.magicperu.com.
Perú, Imagen y Turismo, ekeko.rcp.net.pe/rcp/rcp-peru.html.
Travel Update (Travel news), www.travelupdate.limaperu.net.

Before you travel

Essentials

Getting in **Visas** No Visa is necessary for countries of Western Europe, Asia, North or South America or citizens of Australia, New Zealand or South Africa. Travellers from Fiji and India do need Visas. Tourist cards are obtained on flights arriving in Peru or at border crossings. The tourist card allows you up to a maximum of 90 days in Peru. The form is in duplicate and you give up the original on arrival and the copy on departure. This means you need to keep the copy as you will need to give it to the officials when you leave. A new tourist card is issued on re-entry to Peru but extensions are obtained with your current tourist card so you just take it and your passport to immigration when asking for extensions. If your tourist card is lost or stolen, apply to get a new one at **Immigraciónes**, Av Huaraz y Av. España, Breña, between 0930 to 0300, Monday to Friday. It shouldn't cost anything to replace your tourist card if you replace it in Lima.

Tourist visas for citizens of countries not listed above cost £8.40 or equivalent, for which you require a valid passport, a departure ticket from Peru, two colour passport photos, one application form and proof of economic solvency. All foreigners should be able to produce on demand some recognizable means of identification, preferably a passport.

You must present your passport when reserving tickets for internal, as well as, international travel. An alternative is to photocopy the important pages of your passport – including the immigration stamp, and legalize it by a 'Notario público', which costs US$1.50. This way you can avoid showing your passport.

Peru embassies and consulates

Australia, 9 Floor, 197 London Circuit, Canberra City, ACT 2601, T(6162)2572953, F(6162)25775198.
Canada, 130 Albert Street, Suite 1901 Ottawa, Ontario KAIP 5G4, T(1613)2881777, F(1613)2323062. Consulates: Toronto, Montreal and Vancouver.
France, 50, Avenida Kleber, Paris 75116, T(331)47043453, F(331)47559830.
Germany, Godesberger Allee 125-127, 53175 Bonn, T(49228)373045, F(49228)379475. Consulate in Berlin, Schadowtrasse, 6, 10117 Berlin, T(4930)2291455, F(4930)2292857.

Israel, 37, Revov Ha-Marganit Shikun Vatikim, 52 584 Ramat Gan, T(9723)6135591, F(9723)7512286.
Sweden, Brunnsgatan 21-B, 111 38 Estocolmo, T(468)4110019, F(468)205592.
Switzerland, Thunstrasse No 36, CH-3005, Berne, T(4131)3518555, F(4131)3518570.
UK, 52 Sloane Street, London SW1X 9SP, T(0171)2351917, F(0171)2354463.
USA, 1700 Massachusetts Avenue, NW, Washington DC 200036, T(1202)8339860 al 833-9869, F(1202)7850933; Consulates: Chicago, Houston, Los Angeles, Miami, New York, Paterson, Puerto Rico, San Francisco.

For further listings of Peru embassies and consulates world-wide, see page 85

We have received no reports of travellers being asked for an onward ticket at Tacna, Aguas Verdes, Yunguyo or Desaguadero. If you do not have one on arrival at the border, you may be forced to pay US$15 minimum for an out-going bus ticket. The best bet is to buy a bus ticket, Tacna-Arica if travelling to Chile, and Puno-La Paz if going to Bolivia, at the Ecuadorean border, eg Machala. Alternatively, a Tumbes-Guayaquil ticket will do. Travellers arriving by air report no onward flight checks at Lima airport.

Remember that it is your responsibility to ensure that your passport is stamped in and out when you cross frontiers. The absence of entry and exit stamps can cause serious difficulties: seek out the proper migration offices if the stamping process is not carried out as you cross. Also, do not lose your entry card; replacing one causes a lot of trouble, and possibly expense.

You should always carry your passport in a safe place about your person, or if not going far, leave it in the hotel safe. If staying in Peru for several weeks, it is worth while registering at your Embassy or Consulate. Then, if your passport is stolen, the process of replacing it is simplified and speeded up.

Renewals and extensions When you arrive in Peru through any of the borders you can get up to 90 days on your tourist card. You are allowed a maximum of three 30-day extensions for up to 180 days (6 months) total in Peru before you are required to leave the country. Travellers have reported problems in Iquitos in getting extensions or even a 30-day visa when entering Peru; it is almost impossible to get more than 30 days at the Iquitos entrance. The first 30 to 90 days of your visa are free; the extensions cost US$20 and US$7 (for forms) each time you want to extend. If you let your tourist visa expire, you can be subject to a fine of US$20 per day. Whether you are fined the full amount is up to the discretion of the immigration officer you are dealing with (be nice to this person!). You can extend your visa in Lima, Cusco, Puno, Puerto Maldanado and Iquitos, but Lima is where the main immigration office is and often in other areas it is more of a headache to extend than to just leave the country. If you are in the Puno or Tacna areas when your visa is about to expire, it may be easier to cross the border and return and get a new 90 days on your visa without paying for extensions.

Business visas If a visitor is going to receive money from Peruvian sources, they must have a business visa: requirements are a valid passport, two colour passport photos, return ticket and a letter from an employer or Chamber of Commerce stating the nature of business, length of stay and guarantee that any Peruvian taxes will be paid. The visa costs £18.90 (or equivalent). On arrival business visitors must register with the Dirección General de Contribuciones for tax purposes.

Student visas To obtain a one year student visa you must have: proof of adequate funds, affiliation to a Peruvian body, a letter of recommendation from your own and a Peruvian Consul, a letter of moral and economic guarantee from a Peruvian citizen and four photographs (frontal and profile). You must also have a health check certificate which takes four weeks to get and costs US$10. Also, to obtain a student visa, if applying within Peru, you have to leave the country and collect it in La Paz, Arica or Guayaquil from Peruvian immigration (it costs US$20).

Duty-free allowance When travelling into Peru you can bring 20 packages of cigarettes (400 cigarettes), 50 cigars or 500 grams of tobacco, three litres of alcohol and new articles for personal use of gifts valued at up to US$300. There are certain items that are blacked out and therefore cannot be brought in duty-free: this includes computers (but laptops are OK). The value added tax for items that are not considered duty-free but are still intended for personal use is generally 20%. Personal items necessary for adventure sports such as climbing, kayaking and fishing are duty-free. Most of the customs rules aren't a worry for the average traveller but anything that looks like it's being brought in for resale could give you trouble. This means don't bring your tripod and 5 lenses in boxes or packages.

Export ban It is illegal to take items of archaeological interest out of Peru. This means that any pre-colombian pottery or Inca artifacts cannot leave Peru, including various gold work and 'worry dolls' from Nasca. If you are purchasing extremely good replicas make sure the pieces have the artist's name on them or that they have a tag which shows that they are not originals. It is very important to realize that no matter how simple it seems, it is not worth your time to try and take anything illegal out of the country - this includes drugs. The security personnel and customs officials are much smarter than you and are experts at their job. It's best to understand that this is a foolhardy idea and save yourself the wasted time, money and energy of 10 years in jail.

Customs

Essentials

What to take Everybody has their own list. Obviously what you take depends on where you are intending going and also what your budget is. Over the years, a selection of those most often mentioned by travellers follows - pick and choose as you wish:

air cushions for slatted seats; inflatable **travel pillow** for neck support; **strong shoes** (and remember that footwear over nine and a half English size, or 42 European size, is difficult to obtain); a small **first-aid kit** and handbook; fully **waterproof top clothing**; **waterproof treatment** for leather footwear; **wax earplugs** (which are almost impossible to find outside large cities) and airline-type **eye mask** to help you sleep in noisy and poorly curtained hotel rooms; **sandals** (rubber-thong Japanese-type or other – can be worn in showers to avoid athlete's foot); a **polyethylene sheet** two metres x one metre to cover possibly infested beds and shelter your luggage; **polyethylene bags** of varying sizes (up to heavy duty rubbish bag size) with ties; a **toilet bag** you can tie round your waist; if you use an **electric shaver**, take a rechargeable type; a **sheet sleeping-bag** and pillow-case or separate pillow-case – in some countries they are not changed often in cheap hotels; a one and a half metre piece of **100% cotton** can be used as a towel, a bedsheet, beach towel, makeshift curtain and wrap; a **mosquito net** (or a hammock with a fitted net); a **straw hat** which can be rolled or flattened and reconstituted after 15 minutes soaking in water; a **clothes line**; a **nailbrush** (useful for scrubbing dirt off clothes as well as off oneself); a **vacuum flask**; a **water bottle**, a **small dual-voltage immersion heater**; a small dual-voltage (or battery-driven) **electric fan**; a light nylon waterproof **shopping bag**; a universal bath- and basin-**plug** of the flanged type that will fit any waste-pipe (or improvise one from a sheet of thick rubber); **string**; **velcro**; **electrical insulating tape**; large **penknife** preferably with tin and bottle openers, scissors and corkscrew – the famous Swiss Army range has been repeatedly recommended (for knife sharpening, go to a butcher's shop); **alarm clock** or watch; **candle**; **torch** (flashlight) – especially one that will clip on to a pocket or belt; **pocket mirror**; **pocket calculator**; an **adaptor and flex** to enable you to take power from an electric-light socket (the Edison screw type is the most commonly used). Remember not to throw away spent batteries containing mercury or cadmium; take them home to be disposed of, or recycled properly.

Useful medicaments are given at the end of the 'Health' section, page 74); to these might be added some lip salve with sun protection, and pre-moistened wipes (such as 'Wet Ones'). Always carry toilet paper. Natural fabric sticking plasters, as well as being long-lasting, are much appreciated as gifts. Dental floss can be used for backpack repairs, in addition to its original purpose. **Never** carry firearms. Their possession could land you in serious trouble. Contact lens solution is readily available in pharmacies and boticas in all major towns.

Vaccinations Before you travel make sure the medical insurance you take out is adequate. Have a check up with your doctor, if necessary and arrange your immunisations well in advance. Try ringing a specialist travel clinic if your own doctor is unfamiliar with health in Latin America. You should be protected by immunisation against typhoid, polio, tetanus and hepatitis A. A yellow fever vaccination certificate is only required if you are coming from infected areas of the world or, for your own protection, if you are going to be roughing it in the Peruvian jungle. Check malaria prophylaxis for all lowland rural areas to be visited and particularly if you will be on the borders of Bolivia, Brazil, Colombia or Ecuador. Vaccination against cholera is not necessary, but occasionally immigration officials might ask to see a certificate. For a full and detailed description of necessary vaccinations and all matters relating to health, see **Health** section on page 74.

Money

The new sol or nuevo sol (S/.) is divided into 100 centimos. In 1991, the new sol replaced the inti at S/. 1 = one million intis. Bills that are in circulation are S/. 200, S/. 100, S/. 50, S/. 20, S/. 10 and the coins are S/. 5, S/. 2, S/. 1 and 50, 20, 10 and 5 centimo pieces. Inti notes are not accepted as currency at all; they are valuable only as souvenirs. Try to break down notes whenever you can as there is a country-wide change shortage (or so it seems) and it will make life simpler if you get change whenever you can; it is difficult to get change in shops and museums and sometimes impossible from street vendors or cab drivers. In **December 1998**, the exchange rate was US$1 = S/. 3.15 Some prices such as airline tickets are quoted in dollars; you can pay in soles or dollars but it is generally easiest to pay dollars when the price is in dollars and in soles when the price is in soles. This will save you from losing on exchange rates.

NB: No one, not even banks, will accept dollar bills that are ripped, taped, stapled or torn. Do not accept torn dollars from anyone; simply tell them you would like another bill. As well, ask your bank at home to only give you nice, crisp, clean dollars and keep your dollars neat in your money belt or wallet so they don't accidentally tear.

Warning There are some forgeries of dollars and soles around in Peru. Always check your money when you change it – even at the bank (the only fake bill I have received was from a bank). Hold the bills up to the light, check the watermark and the line down the side of the bill in which the amount of the money is written. There should be tiny flecks of paper in (not on) the money. Check to see that the faces are clear, and as well the paper should not feel smooth like a photocopy but rougher and fibrous. US forgeries are generally quite obvious to detect. There are also posters in many restaurants, stores and banks explaining exactly what to look for in forged sol notes.

Visa (the most common card), MasterCard, American Express and Diners Club are accepted in various locations in Peru. There is an 8-12% commission for all credit card charges. Often, it is cheaper to use your credit card to get money out of an ATM rather than to pay for your purchases. Of course, this depends on your interest rate for cash advances on your credit cards – ask your bank about this. Another option is to put extra money on your credit cards and use them as a bank card. Most banks are affiliated with Visa /Plus system; examples are Banco de Credito, Banco Weise and Interbank. Banco Latino is affiliated with Mastercard/Cirrus system so now it is possible to get money with both major card systems. Credit cards are not commonly accepted in smaller towns so go prepared with cash. Make sure you carry the phone numbers that you need in order to report your card lost or stolen. As well, some travellers have reported problems with their credit cards being 'frozen' by their bank as soon as a charge from a foreign country occurs. To avoid this problem, notify your bank that you will be making charges in Peru (and other countries).

There are no restrictions on foreign exchange. Banks are the best place to change travellers' cheques into soles; most charge no commission, but often give a poor rate for changing cheques into soles. They will also change cheques into dollars cash at 5% commission. The services of the Banco de Crédito have been repeatedly recommended. *Casas de cambio* are good for changing dollars cash into soles. There is no difference in the exchange rate given by banks and *casas de cambio*. Always count your money in the presence of the cashier.

US dollars are the most useful currency (take some small bills), and Deutsche marks can be changed in all large towns. Other currencies carry high commission fees. For changing into or out of small amounts of dollars cash, the street changers

Currency

Essentials

Credit cards

Credit card assistance
Thomas Cook/
Mastercard
Viajes Laser, Calle Espinar,
331, Lima, T4490134/137.
American Express
Jr Belén 1040, Lima (same
building as Lima Tours)

Exchange

Money matters

Low-value US dollar bills should be carried for changing into local currency if arriving in a country when banks or casas de cambio *are closed. They are also useful for shopping. If you are travelling on the cheap it is essential to keep in funds; watch weekends and public holidays carefully and never run out of local currency. Take plenty of local currency, in small denominations, when making trips into the interior.*

It's best to stick to well-known and well-accepted brands of travellers' cheques such as American Express, Visa and MasterCard. Thomas Cooke cheques are reasonably well known as well. This will avoid suspicious looks or flat out "no's" from storeowners who believe you may have forged your travellers' cheques.

give the best rates, avoiding paperwork and queuing, but you should take care: check your soles before handing over your dollars, check their calculators, etc, and don't change money in crowded areas. If using their services think about taking a taxi after changing, to avoid being followed. Many street changers congregate near an office where the exchange 'wholesaler' operates; these will probably be offering better rates than elsewhere on the street.

Soles can be exchanged into dollars at the banks at Lima airport, and you can change soles for dollars at any border. Dollars can also be bought at the various frontiers.

American Express will sell travellers' cheques against an Amex card and give out emergency money, but only in Lima. They are also very efficient in replacing stolen cheques, though a police report is needed. Travel agents are allowed to accept foreign currencies in payment for their services, and to exchange small amounts. Try to avoid changing travellers' cheques outside the main cities: commission is high and it is often a difficult process. Travellers have reported great difficulty in cashing travellers' cheques in the jungle area, even Iquitos, and other remote areas. Always sign travellers' cheques in blue or black ink or ballpen.

Money transfer It is possible to have US dollars or Deutsche marks sent from your home country. Take the cheque to the banks and ask for a *liquidación por canje de moneda extranjera*. You will be charged 1% commission in dollars or soles. Money can also be transferred between banks. A recommended method is, before leaving, to find out which local bank is correspondent to your bank at home, then when you need funds, telex your own bank and ask them to telex the money to the local bank (confirming by fax). Give exact information to your bank of the routing number of the receiving bank. Cash in dollars, local currency depending on the country can be received within 48 banking hours, but more often it takes five working days.

Alternatively, use Western Union to send or receive money worldwide; they have agencies in all the major towns and cities. Their main offices in Lima are: Avenida Petit Thouars 3595, San Isidro, T4220014; Avenida Larco 826, Miraflores. Details of the provincial offices are given under the relevant sections.

Getting there

Air

From Europe There are direct flights to Lima with Amsterdam (KLM), Frankfurt (Lufthansa), Rome (Alitalia) and Madrid (Iberia). Though there are no direct flights from London, cheap options are available with Iberia via Madrid, and KLM via Amsterdam. Alternatively,

Essentials

Cost of living

Living costs in the provinces are significantly lower than in Lima. For a lot of low income Peruvians, many items are simply out of their reach to buy. Peru is still a reasonably priced place for travellers – more expensive than Ecuador and Bolivia but less expensive than Chile, Argentina and Brazil. In late 1998, the South American Explorers Club estimated a per person per day budget of US$10-US$15 for low budget travellers and US$20 to US$25 per day for medium budget travellers – this could be higher depending how many days you stay in Lima. For Hotel prices, see **Where to stay** (page 43) and for restaurant prices, see **Food and drink** (page 57).

Essentials

you can fly standby to Miami, then fly the airlines shown below. Aeroflot fly to Peru from Moscow via Shannon and Havana and the flight can be joined either in Moscow, or in Shannon, but it is *vital* to check that these services are in operation when you want to travel. To avoid paying Peru's 18% tax on international air tickets, take your used outward ticket with you when buying your return passage.

From USA and Canada

Miami is the main gateway to Peru but New York Newark, Los Angeles and Houston are now strong contenders. Direct flights are available through Miami with American, United and AeroPerú, through Newark and Houston with Continental, through Atlanta with Delta, through New York with Lan Chile and American and through Los Angeles with AeroPerú, Lan Chile and Varig. Daily connections can be made from almost all major North American cities. American now flies daily direct to Cusco from New York, Miami and Dallas, with a brief stop in Lima where passengers from Dallas and Miami board the flight from JFK and continue to Cusco (see also under Cusco Ins and Outs, page 144). AeroPerú offers discounts on internal flights when you buy a Miami-Lima return ticket, eg US$250 for unlimited flights (check in advance for restrictions).

From Latin America

There are regular flights, in many cases daily, to Peru from most South and Central American countries. Lloyd Aéreo Boliviano (LAB) and Lacsa generally have the cheapest flights. Tickets for LAB leaving Lima bought outside of Peru are generally cheaper than tickets bought in Peru. Other airlines to check are AeroPerú, Copa, Seata, Lan Chile and Servivensa.

Air passes

Sometimes it is possible to get discounts with AeroPerú internal flights in the form of an airpass when an AeroPerú international flight is purchased. If you can, check with a travel agent to see what discounts national airlines in Peru are giving because occasionally there are discounts in Peru that are a better deal than the airpasses. Generally, AeroPerú airpasses not purchased in conjunction with an international ticket are not a better deal. You will end up paying the 18% Peruvian tax when you actually go to use the tickets – this results in you spending more than what the regular price would have been. Also, just because you have an airpass doesn't give you priority on the plane. You still need to reconfirm and be at the airport in good time.

Iberia and its partner, Aerolíneas Argentinas, offer Latin American Circular Fares. Available from the UK only, the fares are for circular routes (no back-tracking) in North, Central and South America. There are two zones, mid-Atlantic and South Atlantic, and a flat fare applies to each: mid-Atlantic £847 high season, £680 low; South Atlantic £968 high, £793 low. Two free stopovers are allowed, plus Caracas on mid-Atlantic routes, or Buenos Aires on South Atlantic routes. Additional stops are £35 each. Fares are valid for three months (extensions and business class available). Check with JLA for up-to-date details (see page 85).

Baggage allowance   There is always a weight limit for your baggage. With European carriers, this is generally 2 bags per person of checked luggage weighing up to 20kg for regular class and 30kg for first class. American carriers generally allow 2 bags totalling up to 64kg per person regardless of ticket class. The American airlines are usually a bit more expensive but if you are travelling with a 40kg bag of climbing gear, it may be worth looking into. Many airlines will let you pay a penalty for overweight baggage – often this is US$5 per kilo – but this usually depends on how full the flight is. Check first before you assume you can bring extra luggage. AeroPerú doesn't generally allow excess baggage on its flights even with a penalty, so double check with them before you fly. Internal carriers have a weight limit of 20kg per person so keep this in mind if you plan to take any internal flights.

Prices and discounts   **1.**   To fly from Europe to South America, it is generally cheapest to fly through Madrid with Iberia or Amsterdam with KLM. Fares will vary seasonally and from destination to destination. Check with a travel agent to determine when the high seasons are and which airlines are giving specials.

2.   Most airlines offer discounted fares of one sort or another on scheduled flights. These are not offered by the airlines direct to the public, but through agencies who specialize in this type of fare. For a list of these agencies, see **Tours and tour operators**, page 85. The very busy seasons are 7 December – 15 January and 10 July – 10 September. If you intend travelling during those times, book as far ahead as possible. Between February and May and September to November special offers may be available.

3.   Other fares fall into three groups, and are all on scheduled services:

a. Excursion (return) fares with restricted validity eg 5-90 days. Carriers are introducing flexibility into these tickets, permitting a change of dates on payment of a fee.

b. Yearly fares: these may be bought on a one-way or return basis. Some airlines require a specified return date, changeable upon payment of a fee. To leave the return completely open is possible for an extra fee. You must fix the route in advance. Some of the cheapest flexible fares now have six months validity.

c. Student (or Under 26) fares Do not assume that student tickets are the cheapest. Though they are often very flexible, they are usually more expensive than a. or b. above. Some airlines are flexible on the age limit, others strict. One way and returns available, or 'Open Jaws' (see below). **NB** If you foresee returning home at a busy time (eg Christmas or Easter), a booking is advisable on any type of open-return ticket.

4.   For people intending to travel a linear route and return from a different point from that which they entered, there are 'Open Jaws' fares, which are available on student, yearly, or excursion fares.

5.   Many of these fares require a change of plane at an intermediate point, and a stopover may be permitted, or even obligatory, depending on schedules. Simply because a flight stops at a given airport does not mean you can break your journey there – the airline must have traffic rights to pick up or set down passengers between points A and B before it will be permitted. This is where dealing with a specialized agency will really pay dividends. There are dozens of agencies that offer the simple returns to Lima at roughly the same (discounted) fare. On multi-stop itineraries, the specialized agencies can often save clients hundreds of pounds.

6.   Although it's a little more complicated, it's possible to sell tickets in London for travel originating in Latin America at substantially cheaper fares than those available locally. This is useful for the traveller who doesn't know where they will end up, or who plans to travel for more than a year. Because of high local taxes a one-way ticket from Latin America is more expensive than a one-way in the other direction, so it's always best to buy a return. Taxes are calculated as a percentage of the full IATA fare; on a discounted fare the tax can therefore make up as much as 30-50% of the price.

Essentials

7. Travellers starting their journey in continental Europe can try Uniclam-Voyages, 63 rue Monsieur-le Prince, 75006 Paris for charters. The Swiss company, Balair (owned by Swissair) has regular charter flights to South America. For cheap flights in Switzerland, Globetrotter Travel Service, Renweg, 8001 Zürich, has been recommended. Also try Nouvelles Frontières, Paris, T(1)41415858; and Hajo Siewer Jet Tours, Martinstr 39, 57462 Olpe, Germany, T(02761)924120. The German magazine *Reisefieber* is useful.

8. If you buy discounted air tickets *always* check the reservation with the airline concerned to make sure the flight still exists. Also remember the IATA airlines' schedules change in March and October each year, so if you're going to be away a long time it's best to leave return flight coupons open.

In addition, check whether you are entitled to any refund or re-issued ticket if a discounted air ticket is lost or stolen. Some airlines require the repurchase of a ticket before you can apply for a refund, which will not be given until after the validity of the original ticket has expired. The Iberia group, for example, operate this costly system. Travel insurance in some cases covers lost tickets.

9. Note that some South American carriers change departure times of short-haul or domestic flights at short notice and, in some instances, schedules shown in the computers of transatlantic carriers differ from those actually flown by smaller, local carriers. If you book, and reconfirm, both your transatlantic and onward sectors through your transatlantic carrier you may find that your travel plans have been based on out-of-date information. The surest solution is to reconfirm your outward flight in an office of the onward carrier itself.

Road and boat

To enter Peru, a ticket out of the country may be required. If you have to buy a bus ticket, be warned: they are not transferable or refundable. Lima can be reached from all continental capitals and many major cities in neighbouring countries. If coming from Bolivia, there are frequent bus services from La Paz to Puno and from there to Cusco (see page 215). If travelling south from Ecuador, there are frequent services from Quito and Guayaquil to Lima and the major cities on the north coast.

International buses

Driving To enter Peru by private vehicle, you must have an international driving licence – especially with a number. If you don't have a number on your licence, improvise. (It has been reported that a UK driving licence is acceptable.) You also need the registration document in the name of the driver, or, in the case of a car registered in someone else's name, a notarized letter of authorization.

A great deal of conflicting information surrounds what documents are required in addition to the vehicle's registration. According to the RAC in the UK there are three recognized documents for taking a vehicle into South America: a *carnet de passages* issued by the Fedération Internationale de l'Automobile (FIA – Paris), a *carnet de passages* issued by the Alliance Internationale de Tourisme (AIT-Geneva), and the *Libreta de Pasos por Aduana* issued by the Federación Interamericana de Touring y Automóvil Clubs (FITAC). Officially, Peru requires either *carnet*, the *libreta* and, for caravans and trailers, an inventory. The consulate in London says that a *libreta* is necessary, but if you cannot obtain one a written declaration that the car will leave Peru, authorized at a Peruvian consulate before leaving your home country, will do instead.

Motorists report that a 90-day transit permit for vehicles is available at land borders without a *carnet de passages*, contrary to what officials may say. *Formulario 015*, which can be requested at the border, entitles visitors to bring a vehicle into Peru duty free for three months, it is not extendable, but it is free (one correspondent was charged US$35 anyway). In view of this confusion, contact the Peruvian automobile

Essentials

club and get their advice. In general, motorists in South America seem to fare better with a *carnet de passages* than without it.

The *libreta*, a 10-page book of three-part passes for customs, should be available from any South American automobile club member of FITAC; cost seems to be US$200, half refundable. The *carnet de passages* is issued only in the country where the vehicle is registered (in the UK it costs £65 for 25 pages, £55 for 10 pages, valid 12 months, either bank indemnity or insurance indemnity, half of the premium refundable value of the vehicle and countries to be visited required), available from the RAC or the AA. In the USA the AAA seems not to issue the *carnet*, although the HQ in Washington DC may give advice. It is available from the Canadian Automobile Association, 1775 Courtwood Crescent, Ottawa, K2C 3JZ, T(613)2267631, F(613)2257383, for Canadian and US citizens, cost C$450; full details obtainable from the CAA. See also Getting around (page 48).

Boat Enquiries regarding passages should be made through agencies in your own country, or through John Alton of Strand Cruise and Travel Centre, Charing Cross Shopping Concourse, The Strand, London WC2N 4HZ, T(0171)8366363, F(0171)4970078. In Switzerland, contact Wagner Frachtschiffreisen, Stadlerstrasse 48, CH-8404 Winterthur, T(052)2421442, **F**2421487. In the USA, contact Freighter World

Cruises, 180 South Lake Ave, Pasadena, CA 91101, T(818)4493106, or Travltips Cruise and Freighter Travel Association, 163-07 Depot Road, PO Box 188, Flushing, NY 11358, T(800)8728584.

The *Nordwoge* Shipping Company carries seven passengers on a 70-day round trip Felixstowe, Bilbao, Panama Canal, Buenaventura, Guayaquil, **Callao**, Arica (or Iquique), San Antonio, Valparaíso, Talcahuano, Antofagasta, Guayaquil, Buenaventura, Panama Canal, Bilbao, various Northern European ports and Felixstowe, £5,300 per person. Chilean Line's *Laja* and *Lircay* sail New Orleans, Houston, Tampico, Cristóbal, Panama Canal, Guayaquil, Callao, Antofagasta, San Antonio, Arica, **Callao**, Buenaventura, Panama Canal, Cristóbal and New Orleans; a 48-day round trip for US$4,800-5,280 per person.

Touching down

Airport information

The Jorge Chávez Airport is located deep in the district of Callao. Passengers arriving from international flights will find the *aduana* (customs) process to be relatively painless and efficient. Items such as laptops, bicycles, cameras, hiking and climbing equipment etc are exempt from taxes and should be regarded as personal effects that will not be sold or left in Peru. All customs agents should be satisfied by this and allow you to pass. Once outside and past the gate separating arriving passengers from the general public, you're subject to the inevitable mob of taxi drivers all vying to offer you their services. Fares depend on where you pick up the taxi and how well you are at bargaining.

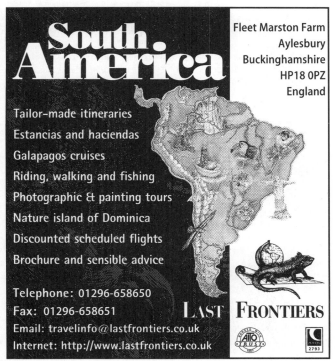
Essentials

Touching down

Tourist Protection Bureau (Indecopi) 24-hr hotline for travellers' complaints, T2247777, T/F7888 (dial 01 first from outside Lima), or toll free on (0800)42579 (not from pay phones), E tour@indecopi.gob.pe. This is run by the Tourist Bureau of Complaints and will help with complaints regarding customs, airlines, travel agencies, accommodation, restaurants, public authorities or if you have lost, or had stolen, documents. There is an office in every town as well as kiosks and information stands in airports and public buildings. They are very effective.

Tourist Police Museo de la Nación, J Prado 2465, 5th Floor, San Borja, T4769896, F4767708. You should come here if you have had property stolen. They are friendly, helpful and speak English and some German. Open daily 0800-2000.

Official time 5 hrs behind GMT.

IDD code 51.

Business hours Shops: 0900 or 1000-1230 and 1500 or 1600-2000. In the main cities, supermarkets do not close for lunch and Lima has some that are open 24 hrs. Some are closed on Saturday and most are closed on Sunday. **Banks** Most banks around the country are open 0930 to 1200 and 1500 to 1800. Banks in Lima generally do not take a siesta so are open throughout the lunch hours. Many banks in Lima and Cusco have Saturday morning hours from 0930 to 1230. Offices: 0830-1230, 1500-1800 all year round. Some have continuous hours 0900-1700 and most close on Saturday. Government Offices: Monday-Friday 0830-1130, January to March. The rest of year Monday-Friday 0900-1230, 1500-1700, but this changes frequently.

Voltage 220 volts AC, 60 cycles throughout the country, except Arequipa (50 cycles).

Weights & measures The metric system of weights and measures is compulsory.

Transport into Lima

Taxis No taxis use meters, so make sure you fix the price before getting in and insist on being taken to the hotel of your choice, not the driver's. Always make sure you have the exact fare, or enough to include the change as a small tip (though this is not expected).

An official taxi from the desk outside Arrivals costs US$10 to the city centre (US$15 at night), and US$15 to Miraflores. A taxi from inside the airport gates costs US$8-9 to the centre and US$12-13 to San Isidro/Miraflores. Check if the fare includes the US$1.50 entry toll.

A cheaper option is to take a taxi from outside the airport gates, though this can seem a daunting prospect at night, especially if travelling alone. The airport exit for pedestrians is at the lefthand corner of the parking area. A taxi from outside the gates costs US$4-5 to the centre, and US$6-7 to San Isidro/Miraflores. The VW 'beetles' tend to be the cheapest. **NB** It's best to flag down a passing taxi. Those standing waiting may be working with local thieves.

Buses There is a service called Airport Express, every 20 minutes to Miraflores from the national exit. These comfortable micro buses cost US$4.50 per person, but they only operate during the day. Local buses and colectivos run between the airport perimeter and the city centre and suburbs. Their routes are given on the front window: 'Tacna' for the centre, 'Miraflores' for Miraflores, and 'Brasil' for South American Explorers Club. Outside the pedestrian exit are the bus, colectivo and taxi stops, but there is more choice for buses at the roundabout by the car entrance. At busy times (which is anytime other than very late at night or early morning) luggage may not be allowed on buses.

Car hire All hire companies have offices at the airport. (For addresses in Lima, see page 128.)

There are no hotels within walking distance of the airport. The larger, more expensive **Finding** hotels have their own buses at the airport, and charge for transfer. Some of the **accommodation** cheaper *hostales* and *pensiones* also provide transport to and from the airport; eg Familia Rodríguez (see Accommodation on page 111). Alternatively, the tourist booth beyond passport control in Arrivals will make local reservations, or you can call the hotel direct. The **Prohotel** agent is very helpful with hotel bookings of all classes. You will be bombarded on arrival by people touting for hotel business, representatives of travel agencies and taxi drivers. Be firm and don't let yourself be bullied.

There are bank machines all over the airport accepting Visa, MasterCard and the Plus and **Airport facilities** Cirrus systems. There are three banks at the airport: *Banco Continental* is located outside the international terminal in a separate building. All travellers' cheques are accepted. Hours are Monday-Friday 0800-2000, Saturday 0900-1500. *Banco del Comercio*, next door to Banco Continental changes American Express travellers' cheques only. *Banco Sur*, with locations scattered throughout the lower level, does not offer any banking services whatsoever. Its only function at the airport is to collect the international or domestic airport tax that must be paid in order to get through the gate.

There are two *Casas de Cambio* (money changing desks). One is located near the American Airlines check-in counter and the other a bit further towards the domestic wing of the airport. They are open 24 hours and change the following travellers' cheques: Visa, Citicorp, MasterCard, Thomas Cook and American Express.

Although public telephones are everywhere in and around the airport, there is also a Telefónica del Peru office open 0700-2300 seven days a week. Fax service is available.

There are two post offices, one on the lower level (open Monday-Saturday 0700-2100) and another on the second which offers more services, open to the public 24 hours, seven days a week.

On the second level there are various cafés and restaurants, some accepting major credit cards. Food tends to be pricey and not very good.

It is recommended to arrive at the airport 2½ hours before international flights and **Airport** 1½ hours before domestic flights. It is quite possible that you'll be first in line, but this **departure** seems a small price to pay to avoid possible hassle. Cars entering the parking lot are **information** subject to a document check of the driver only, but those entering by the pedestrian walkway to the far right of the airport are not. Regardless of what a taxi driver says, vehicles are allowed up to fifteen minutes inside the compound free of charge. Security has become much more relaxed in the past couple of years and spot luggage and passport checks are very rare.

There is a US$25 departure tax for international flights which is almost never **Airport depar-** included in the price of your ticket. For national flights (at all airports in Peru), the **ture tax** airport tax is US$3.50. These taxes are payable in dollars or soles. Tickets purchased in Peru will also have an 18% IGV tax but this should be included in the price of the ticket. **NB** It is very important to reconfirm your flights when flying internally in Peru or leaving the country. This is generally done 48-72 hours in advance and can be done by phoning or visiting the airline office directly or, sometimes, by going to a travel agent for which you may have to pay a service charge. If you do not reconfirm your internal flight, you may not get on the plane. See also Customs, page 23.

Tourist information

Tourist offices throughout Peru are operated by PromPerú, see Finding out more, **Tourist board** page 21. They give out tourist information, make reservations and staff are helpful with advice, including on which parts of the country it is safe to visit. Some former

Useful addresses

Apavit (Asociación Peruana de Agencias de Viaje y Turismo), Antonio Roca 121, Santa Beatriz, Lima, T4337610.
Apotur (Asociación Peruana de Operadores de Turismo), T/F4468773, T4331111/4332021, F4227779, E apotur@amauta.rcp.net.pe.

Apta (Asociación Peruana de Operadores de Turismo de Aventura), Benavides 212, of 1203, Miraflores, T4478078.
Agotur (Asociación de Guías Oficiales de Turismo), Jr Belén 1030, Lima, T4245113.

state tourism offices in large cities have been taken over by former employees within a private organization called Infotur. (For tourist office addresses in Lima, see page 137).

South American Explorers' Club This non-profit, educational organization functions primarily as an information network for Peru and South America and is and is the most useful organization for travellers in the continent. They have offices in Lima, Quito and the USA. Full details are given in the Lima section (page 137).

The Latin American Travel Advisor The Latin American Travel Advisor is a complete travel information service offering a comprehensive quarterly newsletter (free sample available), country reports sent by email or fax, and a wide selection of travel maps. They provide up-to-date, detailed and reliable information concerning travel conditions in 17 South and Central American countries including Peru. Individual travel planning assistance is available for subscribers. Credit card payments for fax or mail orders. Contact PO Box 17-17-908, Quito, Ecuador; USA and Canada toll-free F(888)215-9511, international F(593)2562566. E lata@pi.pro.ec, W http://www.amerispan.com/lata/.

Guide books For information on Bradt Publications' Backpacking Guide Series, other titles and imported maps and guides, contact 41 Nortoft Road, Chalfont St Peter, Bucks SL9 0LA, UK, T/F(01494)873478. Relevant to this Handbook are *Backpacking and Trekking in Peru and Bolivia,* by Hilary Bradt (7th edition, 1997) and *Central and South America by Road,* by Pam Ascanio (1996). An excellent guide to Cusco and the Sacred Valley is Peter Frost's *Exploring Cusco,* which can be found in Lima and Cusco bookshops.

A very useful book, highly recommended, aimed specifically at the budget traveller is *The Tropical Traveller,* by John Hatt (Penguin Books, 3rd edition, 1993). Ask for the free and helpful *Peru Guide* published in English by Lima Editora (T4440815), available at travel agencies or other tourist organizations. Business travellers are advised to get *Hints to Exporters: Peru,* from DTI Export Publications, PO Box 55, Stratford-upon-Avon, Warwickshire, CV37 9GE.

Maps It is a good idea to get as many as possible in your home country before leaving, especially if travelling by land. A recommended series of general maps is that published by International Travel Map Productions (ITM), 345 West Broadway, Vancouver BC, V5Y 1P8, Canada, T(604)8793621, F(604)8794521, compiled with historical notes, by the late Kevin Healey. Relevant to this Handbook are South America North West (1:4M) and Amazon Basin (1:4M). Another map series that has been mentioned is that of New World Edition, Bertelsmann, Neumarkter Strasse 18, 81673 München, Germany, *Südamerika Nord, Südamerika Sud* (both 1:4M).

A good map of the Lima area is available from street sellers in the centre of Lima, or in better bookshops (published by Lima 2000, US$10, or US$14 in booklet form). Other maps can be bought from street vendors in Colmena and Plaza San Martín, Lima. 'Westermanns Monatshefte; folio Ecuador, Peru, Bolivien' has excellent maps of Peru, especially the archaeological sites. A cheaper, less accurate, and less discreet map is published by Cartográfica Nacional for US$3-4. The **Instituto Geográfico Nacional** in Lima sells a selection of good, accurate country and regional maps (see page 124).

Special interest groups

If you are in full-time education you will be entitled to an International Student Identity Card, which is distributed by student travel offices and travel agencies in 77 countries. The ISIC gives you special prices on all forms of transport (air, sea, rail etc), and access to a variety of other concessions and services. If you need to find the location of your nearest ISIC office contact: The ISIC Association, Box 9048, 1000 Copenhagen, Denmark T(+45)33939303.

Students can obtain very few reductions in Peru with an international student's card, except in and around Cusco. To be any use in Peru, it must bear the owner's photograph. An ISIC card can be obtained in Lima from San Martín 240, Barranco, T774105, for US$20. *Intej*, Avenida San Martín 240, Barranco, T4774105/4772864, F4774105, W www.istc.org can extend student cards.

Student travellers

As with most underdeveloped countries, facilities for the disabled traveller are sadly lacking. Wheelchair ramps are a rare luxury and getting a wheelchair into a bathroom or toilet is well nigh impossible, except for some of the more upmarket hotels. Pavements are often in a poor state of disrepair. Disabled Peruvians obviously have to cope with these problems and mainly rely on the help of others to get on and off public transport and generally move around. For general advice see *Nothing Ventured: Disabled People Travel the World* (Rough Guides, 1991). A company offering tours specifically designed for disabled travellers is Apumayo Expeditions, T(084)246018 Cusco, T(1)4442320 Lima, E apumayo@mail.cosapidata.com.pe (see also Cusco, Tour agencies).

Disabled travellers

Movimiento Homosexual-Lesbiana (MHOL), Calle Mariscal Miller 828, Jesús María, T433-5519/433-6375. English from 1630 on. Great contact about the gay community in Lima.

Gay & Lesbian travellers

People contemplating overland travel in South America with children should remember that a lot of time can be spent waiting for buses, trains, and especially for aeroplanes. You should take reading material with you as it is difficult, and expensive to find. Travel on trains, while not as fast or at times as comfortable as buses, allows more scope for moving about. Some trains provide tables between seats, so that games can be played.

Travelling with children

Food Food can be a problem if the children are not adaptable. It is easier to take food with you on longer trips than to rely on meal stops where the food may not be to taste. Avocados are safe, easy to eat and nutritious; they can be fed to babies as young as six months and most older children like them. A small immersion heater and jug for making hot drinks is invaluable, but remember that electric current varies. Try and get a dual-voltage one (110v and 220v). In restaurants, you can normally buy children's helpings, or divide one full-size helping between two children.

Fares On all long-distance buses you pay for each seat, and there are no half-fares if the children occupy a seat each. For shorter trips it is cheaper, if less comfortable, to seat small children on your knee. Often there are spare seats which children can occupy after tickets have been collected. In city and local excursion buses, small children generally do not pay a fare, but are not entitled to a seat when paying customers are standing. On sightseeing tours you should *always* bargain for a family rate – often children can go free. (In trains, reductions for children are general, but not universal.)

All civil airlines charge half for children under 12, but some military services don't have half-fares, or have younger age limits. Note that a child travelling free on a long excursion is not always covered by the operator's travel insurance; it is adviseable to pay a small premium to arrange cover.

Hotels In all hotels, try to negotiate family rates. If charges are per person, always insist that two children will occupy one bed only, therefore counting as one tariff. If rates are per bed, the same applies. In either case you can almost always get a reduced rate at cheaper hotels. Occasionally when travelling with a child you will be refused a room in a hotel that is 'unsuitable'. On river boat trips, unless you have very large hammocks, it may be more comfortable and cost effective to hire a two berth cabin for two adults and a child.

Travel with children can bring you into closer contact with local families and, generally, presents no special problems – in fact the path is often smoother for family groups. Officials tend to be more amenable where children are concerned and they are pleased if your child knows a little Spanish. Moreover, even thieves and pickpockets seem to have some of the traditional respect for families, and may leave you alone because of it! For more detailed advice, see *Travel with Children* by Lonely Planet (3rd ed, 1995).

Rules, customs and etiquette

Clothing Most Latin Americans, if they can afford it, devote great care to their clothes and appearance. It is appreciated if visitors do likewise. How you dress is mostly how people will judge you. This is particularly important when dealing with officials. Buying clothing locally can help you to look less like a tourist. Women should pack one medium- to long-length skirt and men might want to consider bringing a smart sweater or jacket. Nice sweaters and wool shawls can be easily purchased in Peru and make good additions to your wardrobe.

In general, clothing is less formal in the tropical lowlands, where men and women do wear shorts. In the highlands, people are far more conservative, though wearing shorts is considered acceptable on hiking trails. Men should not be seen bare-chested in populated areas.

Courtesy Politeness – even a little ceremoniousness – is much appreciated in Peruvian society. So much so, in fact, that business cards can prove useful. Men should always remove any headgear and say "con permiso" when entering offices, and shake hands with other men. Women or men meeting women usually greet each other with one kiss on the cheek. When introduced, Peruvians will probably expect to greet visitors in the same way. Always say "Buenos días" (until midday) or "Buenas tardes" and wait for a reply before proceeding further.

Always remember that the traveller from abroad has enjoyed greater advantages in life than most Latin American minor officials, and should be friendly and courteous at all times. Never be impatient and do not criticize situations in public (the officials may know more English than you think and they can certainly interpret gestures and facial expressions). In some situations, however, politeness can be a liability. Most Latin Americans are disorderly queuers. In commercial transactions (buying a meal, goods in a shop, etc) politeness should be accompanied by firmness, and always ask the price first.

Politeness should also be extended to street traders. Saying "No, gracias" with a smile is better than an arrogant dismissal. Whether you give money to beggars is a personal matter, but your decision should be influenced by whether a person is begging out of need or trying to cash in on the tourist trail. In the former case, local people giving may provide an indication. Giving money to children is a separate issue, upon which most agree: don't do it. There are occasions where giving food in a

Environmental organizations & Publications

Green Flag International aims to work with travel industry and conservation bodies to improve environments at travel destinations and also to promote conservation programmes at resort destinations. Provides a travellers' guide for 'green' tourism as well as advice on destinations; T(UK)01223 890250.

Tourism Concern aims to promote a greater understanding of the impact of tourism on host communities and environments; E tourconcern@gn.apc.org.

Centre for Responsible Tourism (CRT), Coordinates a North American network and advises on North American sources of information on responsible

tourism; CRT, PO Box 827, San Anselmo, California 94979, USA.

Centre for the Advancement of Responsive Travel (CART) has a range of publications available as well as information on alternative holiday destinations; UK T(01732)352757. The Good Tourist by Katie Wood and Syd House (Mandarin Paperbacks, 1991), addresses issues surrounding environmental impacts of tourism, suggests ways in which damage can be minimised, suggests a range of environmentally sensitive holidays and projects.

restaurant may be appropriate, but first inform yourself of local practice.

In Peru it is common for locals to throw their garbage, paper, wrappers and bottles into the street. Sometimes when asking a local where the garbage is, they will indicate to you that it is the street. This does NOT give travellers the right to apply the "when in Rome" theory. There are trash bins in public areas in many centres and tourists should use them. If there isn't a garbage around, put the garbage in your pocket. You will always find trash bins in bathrooms.

Time-keeping

Peruvians, as with most Latin Americans, have a fairly 'relaxed' attitude towards time. They will think nothing of arriving an hour or so late on social occasions. If you expect to meet someone more or less at an exact time, you can tell them that you want to meet "en punto" or specify "la hora inglesa" (English time).

Tipping

In most of the better restaurants a 10% service charge is included in the bill, but you can give an extra 5% as a tip if the service is good. The most basic restaurants do not include a tip in the bill, and tips are not expected. Taxi drivers are not tipped - bargain the price down, then pay extra for good service if you get it. Tip cloakroom attendants and hairdressers (very high class only), US$0.50-$1; railway or airport porters, US$0.50; car wash boys, US$0.30; car 'watch' boys, US$0.20. If going on a trek or tour it is customary to tip the guide, as well as the cook and porters.

Responsible Tourism

It is usually assumed that tourism only has an adverse impact on the environment and local communities at the more excessive end of the travel industry such as the Spanish Costas and Bali. However, travellers can have an impact at almost any density and this is especially true in areas 'off the beaten track' where local people may not be used to western conventions and lifestyles, and natural environments may be very sensitive.

Environmental legislation is increasingly being enacted to control damage to the environment, and in some cases this can have a bearing on travellers. The establishment of National Parks may involve rules and guidelines for visitors and these should always be followed. In addition there may be local or national laws controlling behaviour and use of natural resources (especially wildlife) that are being increasingly enforced. The Convention on International Trade in Endangered Species

Essentials

of Wild Fauna and Flora (CITES), aims to control the trade in live specimens of endangered plants and animals and also 'recognizable parts or derivatives' of protected species. The full list of protected wildlife varies, so if you feel the need to purchase souvenirs and trinkets derived from wildlife, it would be prudent to check whether they are protected. Peru is a signatory of CITES, as are most European countries, the USA and Canada. Importation of CITES protected species into these countries can lead to heavy fines, confiscation of goods and even imprisonment. Information on the status of legislation and protective measures can be obtained from Traffic International, UK office T(01223)277427, E traffic@wcmc.org.uk.

Safety

The following notes on personal safety should not hide the fact that most Peruvians, particularly outside those areas affected by crime or terrorism, are hospitable and helpful.

Protecting money and valuables   Keep all documents secure and hide your main cash supply in different places or under your clothes. The following means of concealing cash have all been recommended: extra pockets sewn inside shirts and trousers; pockets closed with a zip or safety pin; moneybelts (best worn below the waist rather than outside or at it or around the neck); neck or leg pouches; a thin chain for attaching a purse to your bag or under your clothes; and elasticated support bandages for keeping money and cheques above the elbow or below the knee.

You should keep cameras in bags (preferably with a chain or wire in the strap to defeat the slasher) or briefcases. Also take spare spectacles (eyeglasses) and don't wear wrist-watches or jewellery. If you wear a shoulder-bag in a market, carry it in front of you. Backpacks are vulnerable to slashers: a good idea is to cover the pack with a sack (a plastic one will also keep out rain and dust) with maybe a layer of wire netting between, or make an inner frame of chicken wire. It's best to use a pack which is lockable at its base. Make photocopies of important documents and give them to your family, embassy and travelling companion, this will speed up replacement if documents are lost or stolen and will still allow you to have some ID while getting replacements.

Avoiding con-tricks   Ignore mustard smearers and paint or shampoo sprayers, and strangers' remarks like "what's that on your shoulder?" or "have you seen that dirt on your shoe?" Furthermore, don't bend over to pick up money or other items in the street. These are all ruses intended to distract your attention and make you easy for an accomplice to steal from. If someone follows you when you're in the street, let him catch up with you and 'give him the eye'.

Be wary of 'plainclothes policemen', insist on seeing identification and know that you have the right to write it all down. Do not get in a cab with any police officer, real or not, tell them you will walk to the nearest police station. The real police only have the right to see your passport (not your money, tickets or hotel room) but before handing anything over, ask why they need to see it and make sure you understand the reason. Do not hand over your identification freely and insist on going to the station first.

Hotel security   It is best, if you can trust your hotel, to leave any valuables you don't need in their safe-deposit box. But always keep an inventory of what you have deposited. If you don't trust the hotel, change to a hotel you feel safe in. If there is no alternative, lock everything in your pack and secure that in your room (some people take eyelet-screws for padlocking cupboards or drawers). If you lose your valuables, always report it to the police and note details of the report – for insurance purposes.

You need to take care everywhere, particularly in poor areas of cities, as this is where **Dangerous** most theft takes place. While you should take local advice about being out at night, **places** do not assume that daytime is safer than nighttime. If walking after dark, walk in the road, not on the pavement/sidewalk. If attacked, remember your assailants may well be armed, and try not to resist. You should also be on your guard during festivals at markets when streets are crowded. Outside the July-August peak holiday period, there is less tension, less risk of crime, and more friendliness. A friendly attitude on your part, smiling even when you've thwarted a thief's attempt, can help you out of trouble. In addition, do not be discourteous to officials. If someone tries to bribe you, insist on a receipt.

Be especially careful arriving to or leaving from bus and train stations. Stations are **Public transport** obvious places to catch people (tourists or not) with a lot of important belongings. Do not set your bag down without putting your foot on it, even to just double check your tickets or look at your watch; it will grow legs and walk away. Daypacks are easy to grab and run with and are generally filled with your most important belongings. Take taxis to stations, when carrying luggage, before 0800 and after dark (look on it as an insurance policy). Never accept food, drink, sweets or cigarettes from unknown fellow-travellers on buses or trains; they may be drugged, and you would wake up hours later without your belongings. Avoid staying in hotels too near to bus companies, as drivers who stay overnight are sometimes in league with thieves. Also avoid restaurants near bus terminals if you have all your luggage with you, it is hard to keep an eye on all your gear when eating. On trains, one large bag is easier to watch, and lock to a rack (more than once), than lots of small ones. Try to find a travel companion if alone, as this will reduce the strain of watching your belongings all the time.

Although certain illegal drugs are readily available, anyone found carrying even the **Drugs** smallest amount is automatically assumed to be a drug trafficker. If arrested on any charge the wait for trial in prison can take up to a year and is particularly unpleasant. Unfortunately, we have received reports of drug-planting, or mere accusation of drug-trafficking by the PNP on foreigners in Lima, with US$1,000 demanded for release. If you are asked by the narcotics police to go to the toilets to have your bags searched, insist on taking a witness. **Drugs use or purchase is punishable by up to 15 years' imprisonment**.

Tricks employed to get foreigners into trouble over drugs include slipping a packet of cocaine into the money you are exchanging, being invited to a party or somewhere involving a taxi ride, or simply being asked on the street if you want to buy cocaine. In all cases, a plain clothes 'policeman' will discover the planted cocaine – in your money or at your feet in the taxi – and will ask to see your passport and money. He will then return them, minus a large part of your cash. Do not get into a taxi, do not show your money, and try not to be intimidated. Being in pairs is no guarantee of security, and single women may be particularly vulnerable. Beware also of thieves dressed as policemen asking for your passport and wanting to search for drugs; searching is only permitted if prior paperwork is done.

It is not known how many followers and sympathizers Sendero Luminoso has, but **Terrorism** the military now seems to have taken control of most departments. The Central Highlands suffered much of the violence, but with the reestablishment of military control, there has been much improvement. People have been travelling through the area, mostly with favourable reports. It is still essential to inform yourself of the latest situation before going. There are many checkpoints, which present no problem, but it's safer to travel only by day. Avoid travel in the Huallaga Valley, which includes areas near Tingo María, as well as jungle areas east of Ayacucho. This is an important region for terrorism and cocaine growing and trafficking. The road between Nasca and Cusco can be dangerous due to banditry and should be avoided. Keep yourself informed and always ask locals and other travellers about the conditions up ahead. While in Lima, you can check in at the South American Explorers Club, T425-0142, for latest travel updates. Also recommended is *The Latin American Travel Advisor*, published by Latin American Travel Consultants (see page 35).

Women travellers
Generally women travellers should find visiting Peru an enjoyable experience. However, machismo is alive and well here and you should be prepared for this and try not to over-react. When you set out, err on the side of caution until your instincts have adjusted to the customs of a new culture.

It is easier for men to take the friendliness of locals at face value; women may be subject to much unwanted attention. To help minimize this, do not wear suggestive clothing and do not flirt. By wearing a wedding ring, carrying a photograph of your 'husband' and 'children', and saying that your 'husband' is close at hand, you may dissuade an aspiring suitor. If politeness fails, do not feel bad about showing offence and departing. When accepting a social invitation, make sure that someone knows the address and the time you left. Ask if you can bring a friend (even if you do not intend to do so).

If, as a single woman, you can befriend a local woman, you will learn much more about the country you are visiting as well as finding out how best to deal with the barrage of suggestive comments, whistles and hisses that will invariably come your way. Travelling with another *gringa* may not exempt you from this attention, but at least should give you moral support.

Unless actively avoiding foreigners like yourself, don't go too far from the beaten track. There is a very definite 'gringo trail' which you can join, or follow, if seeking company. This can be helpful when looking for safe accommodation, especially if arriving after dark (which is best avoided). Remember that for a single woman a taxi at night can be as dangerous as wandering around on her own. Travelling by train is a good way to meet locals, but buses are much easier for a person alone; on major routes your seat is often reserved and your luggage can usually be locked in the hold. A good rule is always to act with confidence, as though you know where you are going, even if you do not. Someone who looks lost is more likely to attract unwanted attention.

Police
Whereas in North America and Europe, we are accustomed to law enforcement on a systematic basis; in general law enforcement in Latin America is achieved by periodic campaigns. Be aware that there are some police scams and that you are required to carry some identification even if it is just a photocopy of your passports. The tourist police in Lima are excellent and you should report any incidences to them. The office in Lima is floor five of the Museo de la Nación on Av Javier Prado and Avación; they are open seven days a week, all hours. Dealings with the tourist police in Cusco have produced mixed reviews; you should double check all reports written by the police in Cusco actually state your complaint. There have been some mix-ups, and insurance companies seldom honour claims for 'lost' baggage.

In the event of a vehicle accident in which anyone is injured, all drivers involved are automatically detained until blame has been established, and this does not usually take less than two weeks.

Never offer a bribe unless you are fully conversant with local customs. Wait until the official makes the suggestion, or offer money in some form which is apparently not bribery, eg "In our country we have a system of on-the-spot fines (*multas de inmediato*). Is there a similar system here?" Do not assume that an official who accepts a bribe is prepared to do anything else that is illegal. You bribe him to persuade him to do his job, or to persuade him not to do it, or to do it more quickly, or more slowly.

You do not bribe him to do something which is against the law. The mere suggestion would make him very upset. If an official suggests that a bribe must be paid before you can proceed on your way, be patient (assuming you have the time) and he may relent.

Where to stay

Accommodation is plentiful throughout the price ranges and finding a hotel room to suit your budget should not present any problems, especially in the main tourist areas and larger towns and cities. The exception to this is during the Christmas and Easter holiday periods, Carnival and Independence celebrations at the end of July, when all hotels seem to be crowded. It's advisable to book in advance at these times and during school holidays and local festivals (see Holidays and festivals, page 72).

As tourism continues to grow in Peru, so the choice of accommodation increases, especially at the top end of the range. There are now many top class hotels available in Lima and the main tourist centres, such as Cusco, Arequipa, Nasca, Iquitos and Trujillo. In less visited places the choice of better class hotels may be limited.

Accommodation, as with everything else, is more expensive in Lima, where good budget hotels are few and far between and, therefore, tend to be busy. The best value accommodation can be found in the busiest tourist centres, especially Cusco, which is full of excellent value hotels throughout the range. Accommodation also tends to be more expensive in the north than in the south. Remote jungle towns such as Iquitos and Puerto Maldonado also tend to be more expensive than the norm. And if you want a room with air conditioning expect to pay around 30% extra.

All hotels and restaurants in the upper price brackets charge 18% IGV and 10% service on top of prices (neither is included in prices given in the accommodation listings, unless specified). The more expensive hotels also charge in dollars according to the parallel rate of exchange at midnight. Most lower grade hotels only charge the 18% IGV but some may include a service charge.

By law all places that offer accommodation now have a plaque outside bearing the letters **H** (Hotel), **Hs** (Hostal), **HR** (Hotel Residencial) or **P** (Pensión) according to type. A hotel has 51 rooms or more, a hostal 50 or fewer, but the categories do not describe quality or facilities. Generally speaking, though, a *pensión* or *hospedaje* will be cheaper than a hotel or *hostal*. Most mid-range hotels have their own restaurants serving lunch and dinner, as well as breakfast. Few budget places have this facility, though many now serve breakfast. Many hotels have safe parking for motor cycles. Also note that in cheaper hotels water may be scarce in the middle of the day.

Prices given in the accommodation listings are for two people sharing a double room with bathroom (shower and toilet). Where possible, prices are also given per person, as some hotels charge almost as much for a single room. If travelling alone, it's usually cheaper to share with others in a room with three or four beds. If breakfast is included in the price, it will almost invariably mean continental breakfast. Prices are for the busy seasons (June-August, Christmas and Holy Week). During the low season, when many places may be half empty, it's often possible to bargain the room rate down.

Most places are friendly and helpful, irrespective of the price, particularly smaller *pensiones* and *hospedajes*, which are often family-run and will treat you as another member of the family.

L1 (over US$200) to **A2** (US$61-80) Hotels in these categories are usually only found in Lima and the main tourist centres. They should offer pool, sauna, gym, jacuzzi, all business facilities (including email), several restaurants, bars and often a casino. Most will provide a safe box in each room.

Hotel prices and facilities

Essentials

A3 (US$46-60) and **B** (US$31-45) The better value hotels in these categories provide more than the standard facilities and a fair degree of comfort. Most will include breakfast and many offer 'extras' such as cable TV, minibar, and tea and coffee making facilities. They may also provide tourist information and their own transport. Service is generally better and most accept credit cards. At the top end of the range, some may have a swimming pool, sauna and jacuzzi.

C (US$21-30) and **D** (US$12-20) Hotels in these categories range from very comfortable to functional, but there are some real bargains to be had. At these prices you should expect your own bathroom, constant hot water, a towel, soap and toilet paper, TV, a restaurant, communal sitting area and a reasonably sized, comfortable room with a/c (in tropical regions).

E (US$7-11) Usually in this range you can expect some degree of comfort and cleanliness, a private bathroom with hot water and perhaps continental breakfast thrown in. Again, the best value hotels in this price range will be listed in the travelling text. Many of those catering for foreign tourists in the more popular regions offer excellent value for money in this range and many have their own restaurant and offer services such as laundry, safe deposit box, money exchange and luggage store.

G (up to US$4-6) and **F** (US$3) A room in this price range usually consists of little more than a bed and four walls, with barely enough room to swing the proverbial cat. If you're lucky you may have a window, a table and chair, and even your own bathroom, though this tends to be the exception rather than the rule. Anywhere that provides these facilties, as well as being clean and providing hot water, will normally be recommended in our hotel listings. Cheaper places don't always supply soap, towels and toilet paper. In colder (higher) regions they may not supply enough blankets, so take your own or a sleeping bag. Some places include a meagre breakfast in their price.

Advice and suggestions The cheapest (and often the nastiest) hotels can be found around bus and train stations. If you're just passing through and need a bed for the night, then they may be okay. The better value accommodation is generally found on and around the main plaza (though not always).

Reception areas in hotels may be misleading, so it is a good idea to see the room before booking. Many hoteliers try to offload their least desirable rooms first. If you're shown a dark box without any furniture, ask if there's another room with a window or a desk for writing letters. The difference is often surprising. **NB** The electric showers used in many hotels (basic up to mid-range) are a health and safety nightmare. Avoid touching any part of the shower while it is producing hot water and always get out before you switch it off.

When booking a hotel from an airport, or station by phone, always talk to the hotel yourself; do not let anyone do it for you (except an accredited hotel booking service). You will be told the hotel of your choice is full and be directed to a more expensive one.

NB Hotels are checked by the police for drugs, especially the rooms of foreigners. Make sure they do not remove any of your belongings. You do not need to show them money. Cooperate, but be firm about your rights.

Cockroaches These are ubiquitous and unpleasant, but not dangerous. Take some insecticide powder if staying in cheap hotels – Baygon (Bayer) and Boric acid have been recommended. Stuff toilet paper in any holes in walls that you may suspect of being parts of cockroach runs.

Toilets Except in the most upmarket hotels and restaurants, most Peruvian toilets are at best adequate and at worst require a strong stomach and the ability to hold your breath for a long time. Many hotels, restaurants and bars have inadequate water supplies.

Almost without exception used toilet paper or feminine hygiene products should not be flushed down the pan, but placed in the receptacle provided. This applies even in quite expensive hotels. Failing to observe this custom will block the pan or drain, which can be a considerable health risk. It is quite common for people to stand on the toilet seat (facing the wall – easier to balance), as they do in Asia. If you are concerned about the hygiene of the facility, put paper on the seat.

Youth hostels The only International Youth Hostel (Associación Peruana de Albergues Turísticos Juveniles) in Lima is on Av Casimiro Ulloa 328, Miraflores, Lima, T446-5488, F444-8187, E hostel@mail.cosapidata.com.pe. It has information about Youth Hostels all around the world. For information about International Student Identity Cards (ISIC) and lists of discounts available to cardholders contact INTEJ on Av San Martin 240, Barranco, Lima, T477-4105.

Camping This presents no problems in Peru, especially along the coast. There can, however, be problems with robbery when camping close to a small village. Avoid such a location, or ask permission to camp in a backyard or *chacra* (farmland). Most Peruvians are used to campers, but in some remote places, people have never seen a tent. Be casual about it, do not unpack all your gear, leave it inside your tent (especially at night) and never leave a tent unattended.

Obey the following rules for 'wild' camping: (1) arrive in daylight and pitch your tent as it gets dark; (2) ask permission to camp from the parish priest, or the fire chief, or the police, or a farmer regarding his own property; (3) never ask a group of people – especially young people; (4) never camp on a beach (because of sandflies and thieves). If you can't get information from anyone, camp in a spot where you can't be seen from the nearest inhabited place, or road, and make sure no one saw you go there.

Camping gas in little blue bottles is available in the main cities. Those with stoves designed for lead-free gasoline should use *ron de quemar*, available from hardware shops (*ferreterías*). White gas is called *bencina*, also available from hardware stores. If you use a stove system that requires canisters make sure you dispose of the empty canisters properly. It is very sad and unsightly to go on a hike and find blue gas canisters and toilet paper strewn about. Keep in mind as well that you are responsible for the trash that your group, guide or muledriver may drop and it is up to you to say something and pick up the trash. Often the garbage that is on the trails is blamed on locals and this is not usually the case – low-impact travelling is everyone's responsibility and while you are picking up your own trash, consider picking up an extra piece or two.

Getting around

Air Peru is a big country and it can take days to cover the vast distances between some of the main tourist destinations. If you're on a tight schedule, then by far the best option is to fly. It is possible to travel by air in Peru between all major centres and many towns that are almost impossible to get to by road. There are two main national carriers that service the most travelled routes – Tumbes, Piura, Lima, Arequipa, Cusco, Juliaca, Puerto Maldanado, Pucallpa and Iquitos; they are AeroContinente and AeroPerú. Both airlines generally cost the same, between US$79 and US$99 one-way anywhere in the country. For shorter flights it may cost a bit less; as well, it is not unusual for the prices to go up in the high season (over Christmas and northern hemisphere summer). AeroPerú is also an international carrier and generally has better and more reliable service than AeroContinente. For more remote areas in the north such as Tarapota, Chachapoyas, Cajamarca and Tocache and jungle cities such as Huanuco,

Domestic airlines

Aero Continente
Av Jose Pardo 651
Miraflores
T/F 445-0535/242-1964
www.aerocontinente.com.pe

AeroPerú
Av Jose Pardo 602
Miraflores
T241-0606, F447-0553
www3.rcp.net.pe/AEROPERU

Aerolca
www.peruhot.com/nazcaline/hotel.htm

AeroCóndor
Av Juan de Arona 781
San Isidro
T442-5215/442-5663, F221-5783
E acondor@ibm.net

TdobleA
Av Jose Pardo 640
Office T2
Miraflores
T242-1980/445-4342, F446-1585

Satipo, Tingo Maria and Atalaya check with AeroCóndor and TdobleA. Both airlines have regular flights to many out of the way places. It is also good to check with Fuerza Aerea, the military airline, for flights to remote areas as they run regular cargo flights and will take passengers. In Spring 1999, a subsidiary of Lan Chile, Lan Perú, will operate domestic flights to all major centres. For more information try the Lan Chile W www.lanchile.com.

In general, if you are interested in flying to a city or town, check with all the airlines as new routes are always being added and others deleted. As well, often travel agents will only sell tickets for certain airlines and have no information about routes other companies run; in fact, you will often be told that absolutely no one flies to the place you want to go when actually there are companies that have had regular flights for years to exactly where you are heading. Prices for tickets should be the same whether sold by the airline or an agent.

It is common for flight times to change, earlier or later, or be cancelled because of weather delays especially in the wet season. Do not be surprised or perturbed by this, often there is nothing the airline can do. Always give yourself an extra day between national and international flights to allow for any schedule changes. Flights are often overbooked so it is **very important** to reconfirm your tickets within 72 hours of your flight and be at the airport well in advance. By law, the clerk can start to sell reserved seats to stand-by travellers 20 minutes before the flight.

Internal flight prices are given in US dollars but can be paid in soles and the price should include the 18% IGV. Tickets are not interchangeable between companies but sometimes exceptions will be made in the case of cancellations. Do check with companies as to whether there are specials happening. If the price sounds too good to be true double check your ticket to make sure you are not being sold a ticket for Peruvian nationals; these tickets are often half price but you need to show Peruvian ID to get on the plane.

If you are trying to cut down travel time by flying for part of your trip, you can save a lot of money by only flying nationally. This means cross the border over land on your own and then pick up an internal flight. For information about airline addresses see Lima section.

To save time and hassle, travel with carry-on luggage only (48cm x 24cm x 37cm). This will guarantee that your luggage arrives at the airport when you do.

Train   The main passenger rail line runs from Arequipa to Juliaca, where the line splits, to Cusco and to Puno. The Cusco-Puno journey is the most popular with travellers. It runs during the day, allowing you to enjoy the marvellous scenery, and is a safer and more comfortable option than travelling by overnight. The journey to Arequipa from Cusco or Puno, however, is slow and arduous, and not much cheaper than the cost of a flight. There are also passenger services from Cusco to Machu Picchu, and from Huancayo to Huancavelica. Details of services are given in the text.

For information: **ENAFER (Empresa Nacional de Ferrocarriles)**, E enafer@amauta.rcp.net.pe, T(511)4289440/4276620/4289448, F(511)4280905.

There are in all 2,121 kilometres of railway (1993). Two rail lines run up the slopes of the Andes to the Sierra. These railways, once British owned, run from Lima in the centre and the ports of Matarani and Mollendo in the south. From Lima a railway runs to La Oroya, at which point it splits, one section going to Cerro de Pasco and the other to Huancavelica, via Huancayo. The spectacular train ride from Lima to Huancayo is back on line after seven long years. Starting in August of 1998, the Lima-Huancayo train has run monthly on the last weekend of each month. There is talk of increasing trips to twice a month but check at the train station or at the South American Explorers' Club for more details. (See also Lima Ins and outs.)

NB Train schedules are cut in the rainy season, sometimes to two or three times a week, occasionally they are cancelled for weeks or months.

Peru's road network is being upgraded and better roads mean better bus services **Road network** and improved conditions for drivers. Peru, however, is no different from other Latin American countries in that travelling by road at night or in bad weather should be treated with great care. It is also true that there are many more unpaved than paved roads, so overland travel is not really an option if you only have a few weeks' holiday.

Few roads in Peru, except for the Pan-American and Central Highways, the roads connecting Huaraz and Caraz with Pativilca, and Pacasmayo with Cajamarca, and the Puno-Desaguadero road to Bolivia are paved. The Pan-American Highway runs north-south through the coastal desert and is mostly in good condition, though the terrible El Niño of 1998 caused considerable damage in the far north, and sections are still under repair. In the south, the road which runs into the Sierra to Arequipa is much improved. From Arequipa the road to Puno on Lake Titicaca is partially paved but in poor condition. The Puno-Cusco road is now fully paved and makes for a fast, comfortable journey. The Central Highway from Lima to Huancayo is mostly well-paved. It continues (mostly paved) to Pucallpa in the Amazon basin. Also paved and well-maintained is the direct road from Lima north to Huaraz.

All other roads in the mountains are of dirt, some good, some very bad. Each year they are affected by heavy rain and mud slides, especially those on the eastern slopes of the mountains. Repairs are limited to a minimum because of a shortage of funds. This makes for slow travel and frequent breakdowns. Note that some of these roads can be dangerous or impassable in the rainy season. Check beforehand with locals (not with bus companies, who only want to sell tickets) as accidents are common at these times. Detailed accounts of major and minor road conditions are given in the travelling text.

Services along the coast to the north and south as well as inland to Huancayo, **Bus** Ayacucho and Huaraz are very good. The roads are paved and there are imperial service buses to major centres. Many bus companies have direct (imperial) service and regular (local) service and the difference between the two is often great. Many buses have bathrooms, movies and reclining seats; if any or all of these services are important to you, ask before you buy your ticket. Ormeño and Cruz del Sur are the two bus lines generally thought to have the best service with the most routes. There are many smaller but still excellent bus lines that run only to specific areas.

With the nicer companies or imperial service you will get a receipt for your luggage, it will be locked under the bus and you shouldn't have to worry about it at stops because the storage is not usually opened. On local buses there will be lots of people getting on and off the buses and loading and unloading bags so it's best to watch your luggage and it provides you with a good excuse to get off the bus and stretch anyway. Do not put your day bag above your head inside the bus; keep it at your feet or beside you. It is too easy for someone to grab your bag and get off without your realizing. If you decide to get off the bus at a stop, take all of your carry-on items with you. Tickets for imperial service buses can cost up to double that of the local service bus.

For long journeys be sure to take water and possibly a bit of food, although it is always possible to buy food at the stops along the way. For mountain routes, have a blanket or at least a jacket handy as the temperature at night can drop quite low. Night buses along the coast and into main highland areas are generally fine. Once you get off the beaten track, the quality of buses and roads deteriorates and you may want to stick to the day buses. Attacks on buses are extremely sporadic and not centred around any certain area.

If your bus breaks down and you have to get on another bus, you will probably have to pay for the ticket but keep your old ticket as some bus companies will give refunds. The back seats tend to be the most bumpy and the exhaust pipe is almost always on the left hand side of the bus.

It is best to try to arrive at your destination during the day; it is safer and easier to find accommodation. **NB** Prices of tickets are raised 60-100% during Semana Santa (Easter), Fiestas Patrias (Independence Day) – July 28 and 29 and Navidad (Christmas). Prices will usually go up a few days before the holiday and possibly remain higher a few days after. Tickets also sell out during these times so if travelling during these times, buy your ticket as soon as you know what day you want to travel.

(For bus company addresses, see Lima, Bus companies, page 128). For more information: *Cruz del Sur*, W www.protelsa.com.pe/cruzdelsur, T(511)4241005; *Ormeño*, W www.ascinsa.com. pe/ORMENO, E gorrmeno@ascinsa.com.pe, T(511)4275679/ 4271710, F(511)4263810.

Trucks and colectivos Colectivos usually charge twice the bus fare and leave only when full. They go almost anywhere in Peru. Most firms have offices; book one day in advance. They pick you up at your hotel or in the main plaza. Trucks are not always much cheaper than buses. They charge three quarters of the bus fare, but are wholly unpredictable. They are not recommended for long trips, and comfort depends on the load.

Taxis Taxi prices are fixed in the highland towns and cost around US$0.80 for anywhere in the urban areas. Fares are not fixed in Lima although some drivers work for companies that do have standard fares. Ask locals what the price should be and **always** set the price beforehand.

Taxis at the airport are often a bit more expensive but ask locals what the price should be as taxi drivers may try to charge you three times the correct price. Many taxi drivers work for commission from hotels and will try to convince you to go to that hotel. Feel free to choose your own hotel and go there. If you walk away from the arrivals gate a bit, the fares should go down to a price that is reasonable. In 1998, the price from the airport to Miraflores was about US$7.

Car **Toll roads** Toll roads in Peru include: Aguas Verdes-Tumbes, many on the Pan-American Highway between Tumbes and Lima, Pativilca-Huaraz, Lima-Pucusana, Ica-Nasca, Lima (highway around city), and Variante-Pacasmayo; these vary from US$1.50 to US$0.50. Ecuador to Chile/Bolivia on main roads comes to about US$17. Motorcycles are exempt from road tolls: use the extreme righthand lane at toll gates.

Motoring information The Touring and Automobile Club of Peru have offices in most provincial cities offer help to tourists and particularly to members of the leading motoring associations. They give news about the roads and hotels along the way, although for the most up-to-date information try the bus and colectivo offices.

They sell a very good road map at US$5 (Mapa Vial del Perú, 1:3,000,000, Ed 1980, reliable information about road conditions) and route maps covering most of Peru (Hoja de Ruta, detail maps 1:1,000,000), which are very good but have no information on road conditions. Good maps are available from the South American Explorers Club, who will give good advice on road conditions (see page 137). Buy maps separately or in packages of eight. Cuadernos de Viaje are travel notebooks covering all Peru with valuable information and maps, in Spanish.

Touring y Automóvil Club del Perú
Avda César Vallejo 699
Lince
Lima
T(511)4403270
F(511)4225947
E touring@hys.com.pe
W www.hys.com.pe/tacp.

Essentials

Fuel Gasoline is sold as 'extra' (84 octane), US$2.05 a gallon, and 'importada' (95 octane), US$2.50-2.75 a gallon, found in Lima, the coastal towns and Arequipa. Unleaded fuel (90 and 97 octane SP) is sold on the coast for US$2.25-US$2.55 a gallon. Fuel in remote jungle areas can be double the price of urban areas. Diesel costs US$1.15 a gallon. Filling stations are called *grifos*. Always make sure your fuel tank is full when branching off a major highway, fill up whenever possible and make sure you do not put in diesel or kerosene by mistake.

Traffic and parking In Lima never trust the green light. Peruvian drivers tend to regard traffic lights as recommendations, at most. No-parking signs are painted at the roadside and illegally parked cars are towed away. Do not leave your vehicle on the street in Lima, always put it in a car park (called *playas*), which usually charge US$0.50 per hour. If you want to sleep in your car, check with the local tourist police first. They may allow you to park near their office.

General hints Roads go to very high altitudes in Peru – make sure that the spark is properly adjusted and consider use of smaller carburettor jets if driving much at altitude. Avoid mountain travel between November and April. Take two planks of wood in case your car gets stuck in soft soil when allowing other vehicles to pass. Never travel off the main roads without being self-sufficient. If you need mechanical assistance in the mountains ask for the nearest mining or road construction camp. 4WD is not necessary, but it does give you greater flexibility in mountain and jungle territory, although you may not get far in Amazonas, where roads are frequently impassable.

Wherever you travel you should expect from time to time to find roads that are badly maintained, damaged or closed during the wet season, and delays because of floods, landslides and huge potholes. Don't plan your schedules too tightly. If you have to drive at night, do not go fast; many local vehicles have poor lights and street lighting is bad.

The disadvantages of travelling in your own vehicle include the difficulties of getting insurance, theft, finding guarded parking lots, maintenance on appalling roads and nervous exhaustion. These may outweigh the advantages of mobility and independence.

Spares Imported car spares are available and cheaper than in neighbouring countries. Makes with well-established dealerships are the easiest to obtain (eg Volvo, Peugeot, VW). VW Beetles, Toyota Coronas and Datsun Stanzas are assembled in Peru and are therefore easier to get spares and service for. Most towns can supply a mechanic of sorts, and probably parts for Bosch fuel injection equipment. Watch the mechanics like a hawk, since there's always a brisk market in spares, and some of yours may be highly desirable. That apart, they enjoy a challenge, and can fix most things, eventually.

Preparation Preparing the car for the journey is largely a matter of common sense: obviously any part that is not in first class condition should be replaced. It's well worth installing extra heavy-duty shock-absorbers (such as Spax or Koni) before starting out, because a long trip on rough roads in a heavily laden car will give heavy wear. Fit tubes on 'tubeless' tyres, since air plugs for tubeless tyres are hard to find, and if you bend the rim on a pothole, the tyre will not hold air.

Take spare tubes, and an extra spare tyre. Also take spare plugs, fan-belts, radiator hoses and headlamp bulbs. Even though local equivalents can easily be found in cities, it is wise to take spares for those occasions late at night or in remote areas when you might need them.

You can also change the fanbelt after a stretch of long, hot driving to prevent wear (eg after 15,000 kilometres/10,000 miles). If your vehicle has more than one fanbelt, always replace them all at the same time (make sure you have the necessary tools if doing it yourself).

If your car has sophisticated electrics, spare 'black boxes' for the ignition and fuel injection are advisable, plus a spare voltage regulator or the appropriate diodes for the alternator, and elements for the fuel, air and oil filters if these are not a common type. (Some drivers take a spare alternator of the correct amperage, especially if the regulator is incorporated into the alternator.)

Dirty fuel is a frequent problem, so be prepared to change filters more often than you would at home. In a diesel car you will need to check the sediment bowl often, too. An extra in-line fuel filter is a good idea if feasible (although harder to find, metal canister type is preferable to plastic), and for travel on dusty roads an oil bath air filter is best for a diesel car.

It is wise to carry a spade, jumper cables, tow rope and an air pump. Fit tow hooks to both sides of the vehicle frame. A 12 volt neon light for camping and repairs will be invaluable. Spare fuel containers should be steel and not plastic, and a siphon pipe is essential for those places where fuel is sold out of the drum. Take a 10 litre water container for self and vehicle.

Security Apart from the mechanical aspects, spare no ingenuity in making your car secure. Use a heavy chain and padlocks to chain doors shut, fit security catches on windows, and remove interior window winders (so that a hand reaching in from a forced vent cannot open the window). All these will help, but none is foolproof. Anything on the outside – wing mirrors, spot lamps, motifs etc – is likely to be stolen. So are wheels if not secured by locking nuts.

Try never to leave the car unattended except in a locked garage or guarded parking space. Remove all belongings and leave the empty glove compartment open when the car is unattended. Also lock the clutch or accelerator to the steering wheel with a heavy, obvious chain or lock. Street children will generally protect your car fiercely in exchange for a tip. Be sure to note down key numbers and carry spares of the most important ones (but don't keep all spares inside the vehicle).

Documents See Getting there, page 31.

Insurance Insurance for the vehicle against accident, damage or theft is best arranged in the country of origin, but it is getting increasingly difficult to find agencies who offer this service. It is very expensive to insure against accident and theft, especially as you should take into account the value of the car increased by duties calculated in real (ie non devaluing) terms.

If the car is stolen or written off you will be required to pay very high import duty on its value. Get the legally required minimum cover, which is not expensive, as soon as you can, because if you should be involved in an accident and are uninsured, your car could be confiscated. If anyone is hurt, do not pick them up (you may become liable). Seek assistance from the nearest police station or hospital if you are able to do so.

Car hire The minimum age for renting a car is 25. Car hire companies are given in the text. They do tend to be very expensive, reflecting the high costs and accident rates. Hotels and tourist agencies will tell you where to find cheaper rates, but you will need to check that you have such basics as spare wheel, toolkit and functioning lights etc.

Car hire insurance Check exactly what the hirer's insurance policy covers. In many cases it will only protect you against minor bumps and scrapes, not major accidents, nor 'natural' damage (eg flooding). Ask if extra cover is available. Also find out, if using a credit card, whether the card automatically includes insurance. Beware of being billed for scratches which were on the vehicle before you hired it.

People are generally very amicable to motorcyclists and you can make many friends by returning friendship to those who show an interest in you.

Motorcycling

Essentials

The machine It should be off road capable. A recommended choice would be the BMW R80/100/GS for its rugged and simple design and reliable shaft drive, but a Kawasaki KLR 650s, Honda Transalp/Dominator, or the ubiquitous Yamaha XT600 Tenere would also be suitable. A road bike can go most places an off road bike can go at the cost of greater effort.

Preparations Fit heavy duty front fork springs and the best quality rebuildable shock absorber you can afford (Ohlins, White Power). Fit lockable luggage such as Krausers (reinforce luggage frames) or make some detachable aluminium panniers. Fit a tank bag and tank panniers for better weight distribution. A large capacity fuel tank (Acerbis), +300 mile/480 kilometres range is essential if going off the beaten track.

A washable air filter is a good idea (K&N), also fuel filters, fueltap rubber seals and smaller jets for high altitude Andean motoring. A good set of trails-type tyres as well as a high mudguard are useful. Get to know the bike before you go, ask the dealers in your country what goes wrong with it and arrange a link whereby you can get parts flown out to you. If riding a chain driven bike, a fully enclosed chaincase is useful. A hefty bash plate/sump guard is invaluable.

Spares You should reduce service intervals by half if driving in severe conditions. A spare rear tyre is useful but you can buy modern tyres in Lima at least. Take oil filters, fork and shock seals, tubes, a good manual, spare cables (taped into position), a plug cap and spare plug lead. A spare electronic ignition is a good idea, try and buy a second hand one and make arrangements to have parts sent out to you.

A first class tool kit is a must and if riding a bike with a chain then a spare set of sprockets and an 'o' ring chain should be carried. Spare brake and clutch levers should also be taken as these break easily in a fall. Parts are few and far between, but mechanics are skilled at making do and can usually repair things. Castrol oil can be bought everywhere and relied upon.

Take a puncture repair kit and tyre levers. Find out about any weak spots on the bike and improve them. Get the book for international dealer coverage from your manufacturer, but don't rely on it. They frequently have few or no parts for modern, large machinery.

Clothes and equipment A tough waterproof jacket, comfortable strong boots, gloves and a helmet with which you can use glass goggles (Halycon) which will not scratch and wear out like a plastic visor. The best quality tent and camping gear that you can afford and a petrol stove which runs on bike fuel is helpful.

Security Try not to leave a fully laden bike on its own. An Abus D or chain will keep the bike secure. A cheap alarm gives you peace of mind if you leave the bike outside a hotel at night. Most hotels will allow you to bring the bike inside (see accommodation listings in the travelling text for details). Look for hotels that have a courtyard or more secure parking and never leave luggage on the bike overnight or whilst unattended.

Documents Passport, International Driving Licence, bike registration document are necessary. Riders fare much better with a *carnet de passages* than without it.

Cycling At first glance a bicycle may not appear to be the most obvious vehicle for a major journey, but given ample time and reasonable energy it most certainly is the best. It can be ridden, carried by almost every form of transport from an aeroplane to a canoe, and can even be lifted across your shoulders over short distances. Cyclists can be the envy of travellers using more orthodox transport, since they can travel at their own pace, explore more remote regions and meet people who are not normally in contact with tourists.

Choosing a bicycle The choice of bicycle depends on the type and length of expedition being undertaken and on the terrain and road surfaces likely to be encountered. Unless you are planning a journey almost exclusively on paved roads – when a high quality touring bike such as a Dawes Super Galaxy would probably suffice – a mountain bike is strongly recommended.

The good quality ones (and the cast iron rule is **never** to skimp on quality) are incredibly tough and rugged, with low gear ratios for difficult terrain, wide tyres with plenty of tread for good road-holding, cantilever brakes, and a low centre of gravity for improved stability. Although touring bikes, and to a lesser extent mountain bikes, and spares are available in the larger cities, remember that most indigenous manufactured goods are shoddy and rarely last. Buy everything you possibly can before you leave home.

Bicycle equipment This should include: a small but comprehensive tool kit (to include chain rivet and crank removers, a spoke key and possibly a block remover), a spare tyre and inner tubes, a puncture repair kit with plenty of extra patches and glue, a set of brake blocks, brake and gear cables and all types of nuts and bolts, at least 12 spokes (best taped to the chain stay), a light oil for the chain (eg Finish-Line Teflon Dry-Lube), tube of waterproof grease, a pump secured by a pump lock, a Blackburn parking block (a most invaluable accessory, cheap and virtually weightless), a cyclometer, a loud bell, and a secure lock and chain. *Richard's Bicycle Book* makes useful reading for even the most mechanically minded.

Luggage and equipment Strong and waterproof front and back panniers are a must. When packed these are likely to be heavy and should be carried on the strongest racks available. Poor quality racks have ruined many a journey for they take incredible strain on unpaved roads. A top bag cum rucksack (eg Carradice) makes a good addition for use on and off the bike. A Cannondale front bag is good for maps, camera, compass, altimeter, notebook and small tape-recorder. Other recommended panniers are Ortlieb – front and back – which is waterpoof and almost 'sandproof', Mac-Pac, Madden and Karimoor. 'Gaffa' tape is excellent for protecting vulnerable parts of panniers and for carrying out all manner of repairs.

All equipment and clothes should be packed in plastic bags to give extra protection against dust and rain. Also protect all documents, etc carried close to the body from sweat. Always take the minimum clothing. It's better to buy extra items en route when you find you need them. Generally it is best to carry several layers of thin light clothes than fewer heavy, bulky ones. Always keep one set of dry clothes, including long trousers, to put on at the end of the day. The incredibly light, strong, waterproof and wind resistant goretex jacket and overtrousers are invaluable. Training shoes can be used for both cycling and walking.

Useful tips Wind, not hills is the enemy of the cyclist. Try to make the best use of the times of day when there is little. Mornings tend to be best but there is no steadfast rule. Take care to avoid dehydration, by drinking regularly. In hot, dry areas with limited supplies of water, be sure to carry an ample supply. For food, carry the staples (sugar, salt, dried milk, tea, coffee, porridge oats, raisins, dried soups, etc) and supplemented these with whatever local foods can be found in the markets.

Give your bicycle a thorough daily check for loose nuts or bolts or bearings. See that all parts run smoothly. A good chain should last 2,000 miles (3,200 kilometres) or more but be sure to keep it as clean as possible – an old toothbrush is good for this – and to oil it lightly from time to time. Remember that thieves are attracted to towns and cities, so when sight-seeing, try to leave your bicycle with someone such as a café owner or a priest. Country people tend to be more honest and are usually friendly and very inquisitive. However, don't take unnecessary risks; always see that your bicycle is secure (most hotels will allow bikes to be kept in rooms).

In more remote regions dogs can be vicious; carry a stick or some small stones to frighten them off. Traffic on main roads can be a nightmare; it is usually far more rewarding to keep to the smaller roads or to paths if they exist. Most towns have a bicycle shop of some description, but it is best to do your own repairs and adjustments whenever possible.

Most cyclists agree that the main danger comes from other traffic. A rearview mirror has been frequently recommended to forewarn you of vehicles which are too close behind. You also need to watch out for oncoming, overtaking vehicles, unstable loads on trucks, protruding loads etc. Make yourself conspicuous by wearing bright clothing and a helmet.

Organizations and publications The Expedition Advisory Centre, administered by the Royal Geographical Society, 1, Kensington Gore, London SW7 2AR has published a useful monograph entitled *Bicycle Expeditions*, by Paul Vickers. Published in March 1990, it is available direct from the Centre, price £6.50 (postage extra if outside the UK). In the UK there is also the Cyclist's Touring Club, CTC, Cotterell House, 69 Meadrow, Godalming, Surrey GU7 3HS, T(01483)417217, E cycling@ctc.org.uk, for touring, and technical information.

Hitchhiking in Peru is not easy, owing to the lack of private vehicles on the roads, and requires a lot of patience. It can also be a risky way of getting from A to B, but with common sense, it can be an acceptable way of travelling for free (or very little money) and a way to meet a range of interesting people.

For obvious reasons, a lone female should not hitch by herself. Besides, you are more likely to get a lift if you are with a partner, be they male or female. The best combination is a male and female together. Three or more and you'll be in for a long wait. Your appearance is also important. Someone with matted hair and a large tattoo on their forehead will not have much success. Remember that you are asking considerable trust of someone. Would you stop for someone who looked unsavoury?

Positioning is also key. Freight traffic in Peru has to stop at the police *garitas* outside each town and these are the best places to try (also toll points, but these are further from towns). Make sure there is plenty of room behind you for a vehicle to stop, as well as enough distance in front for a driver to make their assessment of you. A cardboard sign setting out your destination in big letters is always helpful – and don't forget to add the word "please" (in Spanish, of course).

NB Drivers usually ask for money but don't always expect to get it. In mountain and jungle areas you usually have to pay drivers of lorries, vans and even private cars; ask the driver first how much he is going to charge, and then recheck with the locals. Readers report that mining trucks are especially dirty to travel in, so avoid them if possible.

Hitchhiking

Essentials

Keeping in touch

Points of contact Details of organizations which can help sort out problems or give advice, such as the South American Explorers Club, British Council and Alliance Francaise, or addresses of embassies and consulates, can be found in the Lima section (page 134).

Language The official language is Spanish. Quechua, the language of the Inca empire, has been given some official status and there is much pride in its use, but despite the fact that it is spoken by millions of people in the Sierra who have little or no knowledge of Spanish, it is not used in schools. Another important indigenous language is Aymara, used in the area around Lake Titicaca. English is not spoken widely, except by those employed in the tourism industry (eg; hotel, tour agency and airline staff). Some basic Spanish for travellers will be found in the Footnotes section on page 547.

Postal services **Parcels** Sending parcels and mail can be done at any post office but Correo Central on the Plaza de Armas in Lima is the best place. The office is open Monday to Friday from 0800 to 1800. Stamps, envelopes and cloth sacks (to send bigger parcels in) can all be bought there. It costs US$1 to mail a letter anywhere in the Americas and US$1.20 to the rest of the world. You can also mail letters 'expresso' for about US$0.50 extra and they will arrive a little more quickly. Don't put tape on envelopes or packages, wait until you get to the post office and use the glue they have. It is very expensive to mail large packages out of Peru so it is best not to plan to send things home from here. For emergency or important documents, DHL and Federal Express are also options in Lima (check in city of Lima section for addresses).

Receiving mail To receive mail, letters can be sent to Poste Restante/General Delivery (*lista de correos*), your embassy, or, for cardholders, American Express offices. Remember that there is no W in Spanish; look under V, or ask. For the smallest risk of misunderstanding, use title, initial and surname only. If having items sent to you by courier (eg DHL), do not use poste restante, but an address such as a hotel: a signature is required on receipt. Try not to have articles sent by post to Peru – taxes can be 200% of the value.

Telephone services The telephone company in Peru is Telefónica del Perú. This company had a monopoly on phone service which ended in August 1998. In the near future there will be competition, and new companies emerging which may improve service and rates for the entire country.

There are offices in all large and medium-sized towns. Overseas calls made through the operator cost on average US$12 for three minutes (minimum). Collect calls can now be made (most of the time) to North America and some European

Essentials

countries at the Telefónica offices throughout the country, though the best place to try is Lima (see Lima, Telecommunication, page 132).

Telephone dialling codes will be found on the inside front cover

Local, national and international calls can be made from public phone boxes with coins or phone cards which can be bought at Telefónica offices and grocery stores (though cards don't work everywhere). Telephone directories found in most hotel rooms have a useful map of Lima and show itineraries of the buses. Faxes can also be sent abroad from major Telefónica offices: US$2.80 per page to USA; US$4.75 per page to Europe; US$5 per page to Israel. To receive faxes costs US$0.70 per page.

The internet craze has definitely hit Peru. You can find internet access in all important centres especially those with high tourism. Many hotels and Spanish schools have email access through their personal addresses. This may not allow you to surf the net but will allow you to send and receive messages. It is possible to get web supported email addresses through hotmail.com, yahoo.com, backpacker.com and many others; keep this in mind as an easy and cheap way to keep in touch! Internet cafés are listed in the travelling text under each town.

Internet and Email

Essentials

There are a number of sites which provide regular new updates:
El Comercio www.elcomercio.com.pe/
Expreso www.hsur.com/expreso/expreso.htm
Gestión www.gestion.com.pe/
La República www.rcp.net.pe/LaRepublica
Perú Home Page/Red Científica Peruana ekeko.rcp.net.pe/index2.htm

Newspapers Lima has several daily papers. *El Comercio* is good for international news and has a near monopoly on classified ads, *La República* takes a more liberal-left approach, and the others are *La Nación*, *Expreso*, *Ojo*, *El Mundo* and *El Peruano*, which inlludes a parliamentary gazette. *Síntesis* and *Gestión* are business dailies. Gaining in popularity are the sensationalist papers, written in raunchy slang and featuring acres of bare female flesh on their pages. The main provincial cities have at least one newspaper each.

Media

Magazines The most widely read magazine is the weekly news magazine *Caretas*, which gives a very considered angle on current affairs and is often critical of government policy. *Lima Times* is an excellent bi-monthly magazine with many years under its belt. Available at bookstores, street kiosks and at their office on Pasaje Los Pinos 156 #B6 in Miraflores near Parque Kennedy; US$3. *The Lima Herald* is a weekly publication which is good for the latest news in Peru, business and stock reports and various articles dealing with travel/tourism. Look for it at bookstores, street kiosks and larger grocery stores; US$0.30. A bi-monthly magazine called *Rumbos* (English and Spanish together) is a good all-round what's happening in Peru magazine. Monthlies include *Business*, *Proceso Económico*, *Debate* and *Idede*. There is a monthly magazine in English, the *Lima Times*, with useful information and articles, and a weekly economic and political report, the *Andean Report*.

Radio Radio is far more important in imparting news to Peruvians than newspapers, partly due to the fact that limited plane routes make it difficult to get papers to much of the population on the same day. There are countless local and community radio stations which cover even the most far-flung places. The most popular stations are Radioprogramas del Perú, which features round-the-clock news, and Cadena Peruana de Noticias.

A shortwave (world band) radio offers a practical means to brush up on the language, keep abreast of cureent events, sample popular culture and absorb some of the richly varied regional music. International broadcasters such as the BBC World

Service, the Voice of America, Boston (Mass)-based Monitor Radio International (operated by *Christian Science Monitor*) and the Quito-based Evangelical station, HCJB, keep the traveller informed in both English and Spanish.

Compact or miniature portables are recommended, with digital tuning and a full range of shortwave bands, as well as FM, long and medium wave. Detailed advice on radio models (£150 for a decent one) and wavelengths can be found in the annual publication, *Passport to World Band Radio* (Box 300, Penn's Park, PA 18943, USA). Details of local stations is listed in *World TV and Radio Handbook* (WTRH), PO Box 9027, 1006 AA Amsterdam, The Netherlands, US$19.95. Both of these, free wavelength guides and selected radio sets are available from the BBC World Service Bookshop, Bush House Arcade, Bush House, Strand, London WC2B 4PH, UK, T(0171)2572576.

Food and drink

Peruvian cuisine

Not surprisingly for a country with such a diversity of geography and climates, Peru boasts the continent's most extensive and varied menu. In fact, Peru is rivalled in Latin America only by Mexico in the variety of its cuisine. One of the least expected pleasures of a trip to Peru is the wonderful food on offer, and those who are willing to forego the normal traveller's fare of pizza and fried chicken are in for a tasty treat.

Peruvian cuisine varies from region to region, but basically can be divided into coastal, highland and tropical.

Coastal cuisine

Not surprisingly, the best coastal dishes are those with seafood bases, with the most popular being the jewel in the culinary crown, *ceviche*. This delicious dish of white fish marinated in lemon juice, onion and hot peppers can be found in neighbouring countries, but Peruvian is best. Traditionally, *ceviche* is served with corn-on-the-cob, *cancha* (toasted corn), yucca and sweet potatoes. Another mouth-watering fish dish is *escabeche* – fish with onions, hot green pepper, red peppers, prawns (*langostinos*), cumin, hard eggs, olives, and sprinkled with cheese. For fish on its own, don't miss the excellent *corvina*, or white sea bass. You should also try *chupe de camarones*, which is a shrimp stew made with varying and somewhat surprising ingredients. Other fish dishes include *parihuela*, a popular bouillabaisse which includes *yuyo de mar*, a tangy seaweed, and *aguadito*, a thick rice and fish soup said to have rejuvenating powers.

They don't just eat fish on the coast. A favourite northern coastal dish is *seco de cabrito*, roasted kid (baby goat) served with the ubiquitous beans and rice, or *seco de cordero* which uses lamb instead. Also good is a *ají de gallina*, a rich and spicy creamed chicken, and duck is excellent. People on the coast are referred to as *criollos* (see page 517) and *criollo* cooking has a strong tradition and can be found throughout the country. Two popular examples are *cau cau*, made with tripe, potatoes, peppers, and parsley and served with rice, and *anticuchos*, which are shish kebabs of beef heart with garlic, peppers, cumin seeds and vinegar.

Highland cuisine

The staples of highland cooking, corn and potatoes, date back to Inca times and are found in a remarkable variety of shapes, sizes and colours.

Two good potato dishes are *Causa* and *carapulca*. *Causa* is made with yellow potatoes, lemons, pepper, hard-boiled eggs, olives, lettuce, sweet cooked corn, sweet cooked potato, fresh cheese, and served with onion sauce. Another potato dish is *papa a la huancaina*, which is topped with a spicy sauce made with milk and cheese. The most commonly eaten corn dishes are *choclo con queso*, corn on the cob with cheese, and *tamales*, boiled corn dumplings filled with meat and wrapped in banana leaf.

Meat dishes are many and varied. *Ollucos con charqui* is a kind of potato with dried meat, *sancochado* is a meat and all kinds of vegetables stewed together and seasoned with ground garlic and *lomo a la huancaína* is beef with egg and cheese sauce. A dish almost guaranteed to appear on every restaurant menu is *lomo saltado*, a kind of stir-fried beef with onions, vinegar, ginger, chilli, tomatoes and fried potatoes, served with rice. *Rocoto relleno* is spicy bell pepper stuffed with beef and vegetables, *palta rellena* is avocado filled with chicken salad, *Estofado de carne* is a stew which often contains wine and *carne en adobo* is a cut and seasoned steak. Others include *fritos*, fried pork, usually eaten in the morning, *chicharrones*, deep fried chunks of pork ribs and chicken, and *lechón*, suckling pig. And not forgetting that popular childhood pet, *cuy* (guinea pig), which is considered a real delicacy.

Very filling and good value are the many soups on offer, such as *yacu-chupe*, a green soup which has a basis of potato, with cheese, garlic, coriander leaves, parsley, peppers, eggs, onions, and mint, and *sopa a la criolla* containing thin noodles, beef heart, bits of egg and vegetables and pleasantly spiced. And not to be outdone in the fish department, *trucha* (trout) is delicious, particularly from Lake Titicaca.

Tropical cuisine The main ingredient in much jungle cuisine is fish, especially the succulent, dolphin-sized *paiche*, which comes with the delicious *palmito*, or palm-hearts, and the ever-present yucca and fried bananas. Other popular dishes include *sopa de motelo* (turtle soup), *sajino* (roast wild boar) and *lagarto* (caiman). *Juanes* are a jungle version of *tamales*, stuffed with chicken and rice.

Desserts and fruits The Peruvian sweet tooth is evident in the huge number of desserts and confections from which to choose. These include: *cocada al horno* – coconut, with yolk of egg, sesame seed, wine and butter; *picarones* – frittered cassava flour and eggs fried in fat and served with honey; *mazamorra morada* – purple maize, sweet potato starch, lemons, various dried fruits, sticks of ground cinnamon and cloves and perfumed pepper; *manjar blanco* – milk, sugar and eggs; *maná* – an almond paste with eggs, vanilla and milk; *alfajores* – shortbread biscuit with *manjar blanco*, pineapple, peanuts, etc; *pastelillos* – yuccas with sweet potato, sugar and anise fried in fat and powdered with sugar and served hot; and *zango de pasas*, made with maize, syrup, raisins and sugar. *Turrón*, the Lima nougat, is worth trying. *Tejas* are sugar candies wrapped in wax paper; the pecan-flavoured ones are tastiest.

The various Peruvian fruits are wonderful. They include bananas, the citrus fruits, pineapples, dates, avocados (*paltas*), eggfruit (*lúcuma*), the custard apple (*chirimoya*) which can be as big as your head, quince, *papaya*, mango, guava, the passion-fruit (*maracuyá*) and the soursop (*guanábana*). These should be tried as juices or ice cream – an unforgettable experience.

Eating out The high-class hotels and restaurants serve international food and, on demand, some native dishes, but the best places to find native food at its best are the taverns (*chicherías*) and the local restaurants (*picanterías*).

Lunch is the main meal, and apart from the most exclusive places, most restaurants have a set lunch menu, called *menú* or *menú económico*. The set menu has the advantage of being ready and is served almost immediately and it is usually cheap; as little as US$1.75-3.50 for a three course meal. But don't leave it too late – most Peruvians eat lunch around 1230-1300. There are many Chinese restaurants (*chifas*) in Peru which serve good food at reasonable prices. For really economically-minded people the *Comedores populares* found in the markets of most cities offer a standard three course meal for as little as US$1 (see **Health**, page 76).

For those who wish to eschew such good value, the menu is called *la carta*. An *a la carte* lunch or dinner costs US$5-8, but can go up to about US$80 in a first-class

Essentials

restaurant, with drinks and wine included. Middle and high-class restaurants add 11% tax and 17% service to the bill (sometimes 18% and 13% respectively). This is not shown on the price list or menu, so check in advance. Lower class restaurants charge only 5% tax, while cheap, local restaurants charge no taxes. Dinner in restaurants is normally about 1900 onwards, but choice may be more limited than lunchtime. For a full list of restaurants, see under **Places to eat** for each town. Peruvians tend to ask guests for dinner at 2000.

The situation for vegetarians is improving, and you should have no problem finding a vegeatarian restaurant in the main tourist centres, especially Cusco and Arequipa and, of course, Lima. Elsewhere, choice may be rather limited. Many restaurants now have a small selection of vegetarian options. Vegetarians and people with allergies should be able to list (in Spanish) all the foods they cannot eat. By saying "no como carne" (I don't eat meat), people may assume that you eat chicken and eggs. Restaurant staff will often bend over backwards to get you exactly what you want but you need to request it.

Drink Peru's most famous drink is *pisco*, a grape brandy made in the Ica valley, used in the wonderful pisco sour, a deceptively potent cocktail which also includes egg whites and lime juice. Other favourites are *chilcano*, a longer refreshing drink made with *guinda*, a local cherry brandy, and *algarrobina*, a sweet cocktail made with the syrup from the bark of the carob tree, egg whites, milk, pisco and cinnamon.

Peruvian wine is acidic and not very good. The best of a poor lot are the Ica wines Tacama and Ocucaje, and both come in red, white and rosé, sweet and dry varieties. Tacama blancs de blancs and brut champagne have been recommended, also Gran Tinto Reserva Especial. Viña Santo Tomás, from Chincha, is reasonable and cheap, but Casapalca is not for the discerning palate.

Peruvian beer is very good, especially the *Cusqueña* and *Arequipeña* brands of lager. Peruvians will argue long into the night over which is the best, but I can't tell the difference. A good dark beer is Trujillo Malta. In Lima, the *Cristal* and *Pilsener* are both pretty good and served everywhere. Those who fancy a change from the ubiquitous pilsner type beers should look out for the sweetish 'maltina' brown ale.

Chicha de jora is a strong but refreshing maize beer, usually homemade and not easy to come by, and *chicha morada* is a soft drink made with purple maize. Coffee in Peru is usually execrable. It is brought to the table in a small jug accompanied by a mug of hot water to which you add the coffee essence. If you want coffee with milk, a mug of milk is brought. Those who crave a decent cup of coffee will find recommended places listed in the café section of each town, though these are few and far between. There are many different kinds of herb tea: the commonest are *manzanilla* (camomile) and *hierbaluisa* (lemon grass).

Bars Bars as we understand them in Europe or North America are not prevalent in Peru. Other than in the poorer working class districts, most people seem to do their drinking in restaurants, *peñas*, discos or at *fiestas*. In saying that, there are some very good bars/pubs in Cusco and, particularly, in Barranco, an attractive seaside suburb of Lima which boasts perhaps the best nightlife in the country (see page 120).

Shopping

Almost everyone who visits Peru will end up buying a souvenir of some sort from the vast array of arts and crafts (*artesanía*) on offer. The best, and cheapest, place to shop for souvenirs, and pretty much anything else in Peru, is in the myriad street markets which can be found absolutely everywhere. The country also has its share of shiny, modern shopping centres, especially in the capital, but remember that the high overheads are reflected in the prices.

Bartering is an accepted method of determining prices in Peru. This can be an **Bartering** exciting and new approach to shopping that many people have little experience with. There is no way to know how much to offer; however, generally places that have more tourists tend to have slightly higher prices. Often you can get a greater discount when buying quantity. With the fun of bartering also comes the responsibility of it. It is not necessary to get the lowest price possible. Ask around and you will get an idea of what the price should be – this applies to everything from weavings to the price of a taxi. Keep in mind, these people are making a living not playing a game and often one sol means a lot more to them than it does to you. You want the *fair* price not the lowest one.

Since so many artesans have come from the Sierra to Lima, it is possible to find any kind of **What to buy** handicraft in the capital. The prices are often the same as in the highlands, and the quality is high. Good buys are: silver and gold handicrafts; Indian hand-spun and hand-woven textiles; manufactured textiles in Indian designs; llama and alpaca wool products such as ponchos, rugs, hats, blankets, slippers, coats and sweaters; *arpilleras* (appliqué pictures of Peruvian life), which are made with great skill and originality by women in the shanty towns; and fine leather products which are mostly hand made. Another good buy is clothing made from high quality Pima cotton, which is grown in Peru.

The *mate burilado*, or engraved gourd found in every tourist shop, is cheap and one of the most genuine expressions of folk art in Peru. These are cheaper if bought in the villages of the Mantaro Valley near Huancayo in the Central Highlands. The Mantaro Valley is generally renowned for its folk culture, including all manner of *artesanía* (see Huancayo, page 428).

Alpaca clothing, such as sweaters, hats and gloves, is cheaper in the Sierra, especially in Puno. Another good source is Arequipa, where alpaca cloth for suits, coats, etc (mixed with 40% sheep's wool) can be bought cheaply from factories. However, although Lima is more expensive, it is often impossible to find the same quality of goods elsewhere. **NB** Geniune alpaca is odourless wet or dry, wet llama 'stinks'.

One of the very best places in Peru to look for *artesanía* is Ayacucho in the Central Highlands. Here you'll find excellent woven textiles, as well as the beautifully intricate *retablos*, or Saint Mark's boxes (see page 439). Cusco is one of the main weaving centres and a good place to shop for textiles, as well as excellent woodcarvings (see page 144). Also recommended for textiles is Cajamarca. The island of Taquile on Lake Titicaca is a good place to buy *ch'uspas* (bags for coca leaves), *chumpis* (belts) and *chullos* (knitted conical hats).

For a more detailed look at Peruvian arts and crafts, see under Arts and crafts on page 521.

Photography   Pre-paid Kodak slide film cannot be developed in Peru and is also very hard to find. Kodachrome is almost impossible to buy. Some travellers (but not all) have advised against mailing exposed films home. Either take them with you, or have them developed, but not printed, once you have checked the laboratory's quality. Note that postal authorities may use less sensitive equipment for X-ray screening than the airports do.

Developing black and white film is a problem. Often it is shoddily machine-processed and the negatives are ruined. Ask the store if you can see an example of their laboratory's work and if they hand-develop.

Exposed film can be protected in humid areas by putting it in a balloon and tying a knot. Similarly keeping your camera in a plastic bag may reduce the effects of humidity.

Specialist interest travel

Adventure sports

Climbing It is now considered safe again to travel throughout the Cordilleras Blanca and Huayhuash. Climbers are starting to pick up again on unfinished routes and ambitions harboured during the troubles.

The attractions are obvious. The Cordillera Blanca is an ice climber's paradise. It takes just one or two days to reach the snowline on most mountains in this, the most intensive grouping of glaciated peaks in South America. The statistics are impressive: more than 50 summits between 5,000 and 6,000 metres; over 20 surpassing 6,000 metres; 663 glaciers; and there are no peak fees. It is not unusual for climbers to reach three or more 6,000 metres summits, climbed Alpine style, over a three-week trip. The degree of difficulty ranges between **Pisco** (5,752 metres), an excellent acclimatizer or novice's mountain, **Copa** (6,173 metres), of moderate difficulty, and the tremendous challenges such as **Alpamayo** (5,957 metres), **Artesonraju** (6,025 metres), **Quitaraju** (6,036 metres) and **Ranrapalca** (6,162 metres). Huaraz, the main climbing centre of the Cordillera Blanca (see page 293), has a growing infrastructure and is home to the Peruvian Mountain Guide Association (see below).

The Huayhuash (see page 321) is a little more remote and Chiquián, northwest of the range, and Cajatambo to the south, have few facilities for climbers. It is possible to contact guides, *arrieros*, porters and cooks in Chiquián, although it is best to enquire in Huaraz first. Mules may need to be brought down from villages higher up. The Huayhuash has some of the most spectacular ice walls in Peru. The **Jirishancas** and **Yerupajas** (Grande and Chico) are the most popular and demanding.

The Cordilleras Vilcabamba and Vilcanota (see page 194) have the enticing peaks of **Salkantay** (6,271 metres) and **Ausangate** (6,398 metres), but Cusco is not developed for climbing. This is one of the genuine attractions of Peruvian Andinismo – there is always another mountain slightly more remote to feed the appetite. **Huagurunchu** (5,730 metres), for instance in the central Andes, is barely known and **Corupana**, Peru's third highest at 6,425 metres, is hardly ever climbed.

Rock climbing In the *quebradas*, where the rock is most solid (frost-shattered higher up) is becoming more popular, particularly in the **Quebrada de Llaca**, near Huaraz, and for beginners at **Monterrey** (see page 291). To get to Quebrada de Llaca, take a camioneta from Jirón Caraz (one block behind Raimondi) for Marian and **Monterrey**, US$1. At Marian, take a path leading off from the football pitch to Quebrada de Llaca.

Equipment Technical equipment such as rope, harness, double boots, ice hammers, helmets, crampons, carabiners, pitons, chocks and ice screws can all be hired in Huaraz quite cheaply, but they can be of poor quality.

Peruvian Mountain Guide Association (AGMP) Founded in 1980, it is housed in the *Casa de Guías* and is a member of the International Union of Guide Associations (UIAGM). It regulates and trains guides and the three classes of porter, which are: 1) those with some ice climbing experience, who are most useful; 2) those who carry loads only on paths, who are less useful; and 3) *arrieros* (mule drivers), cooks and camp guardians.

The AGMP also sets prices and organizes rescues, though don't rely on this. One criticism of the organization is that some of the guides only have experience on the most popular mountains such as Alpamayo and Huascarán and that its influence does not extend much beyond the Cordillera Blanca and Huayhuash. However, its continued development is a positive step.

Peru has some outstanding circuits around the Nevados. The best known are the **Llanganuco to Santa Cruz loop** (see page 305), the **Ausangate circuit** and a strenuous trek around the Huayhuash (see page 322). See also **Treks from Caraz** (page 310), **Treks from Carhuaz** (page 303) and **Trekking in the Cordillera Blanca** (page 289).

The other type of trekking for which Peru is justifiably renowned is walking among ruins, and, above all, for the **Inca Trail** (see page 183). However, there are many other walks of this type in a country rich in archaeological heritage. Some of the best are: the valley of the Río Atuen near Leimebamba and the entire **Chachapoyas region** (see page 394); **Huamachuco to Gran Pajatén**; the **Tantamayo** ruins above the Marañón; the **Cotahuasi canyon** (see page 245); and beyond Machu Picchu to **Vilcabamba** (see page 189).

Most walking is on clear trails well trodden by campesinos who populate most parts of the Peruvian Andes. If you camp on their land, ask permission first and, of course, do not leave any litter. Tents, sleeping bags, mats and stoves can easily be hired in Huaraz and Cusco but check carefully for quality.

Conditions for trekking and climbing May to September is the dry season in the Cordillera. October, November and April can be fine, particularly for trekking. Most bad weather comes from the east and temperatures plummet around twilight. The optimum months for extreme ice climbing are from late May to mid July. In early May there is a risk of avalanche from sheered neve ice layers. It is best to climb early in the day as the snow becomes slushy later on.

After July successive hot sunny days will have melted some of the main support (compacted ice) particularly on north facing slopes. On the other hand, high altitude rock climbs are less troubled by ice after July. On south facing slopes the ice and snow never consolidates quite as well.

Email addresses and websites
Guía Turística ekeko.rcp.net.pe/turifax. matriza.htm.
Caminante www.hsclperu.com/ caminante.
APTAE(Asociación Peruana de Turismo de Aventura y Ecoturismo) E apotur@ amauta. rcp.net.pe, T/F(511)4460422.
Adventure Travel near Lima hermes. pucp. edu.pe/~airepuro
www.geocities.com/thetropics/shores/ 8717
www.iaxis.com.pe/explorperu;
www.geocities.com/Yosemite/7363
www.geocities.com/Yosemite/4685
www.geocities.com/TheTropics/shores/ 8719
www.geocities.com/Yosemite/4166/ index.html
www.geocities.com/

Essentials

Trekking

Essentials

Yosemite/4166/atordoya.html
www.geocities.com/Yosemite/4166/aaulima.html
www.geocities.com/Yosemite/4166/drakonc.html
Club Andino Peruano E club_andino@geocities.com.

Skiing Without the aid of lifts, skiing in Peru is largely for the high altitude enthusiast. Pastoruri, at 5,000 metres, has the only piste and holds a championship during *Semana del Andinismo* at the end of the November to June season. Pisco, Vallunaraju and Caullaraju are also used for skiing. Huascarán and Copa have been tackled by experienced ski-mountaineers and the eastern flank of Coropuna also has potential. There is, however, a high possibility of crevasses on Copa and Huascarán from November to March. Those thinking of skiing the more difficult peaks should have some technical climbing experience and a guide is recommended. The *Casa de Guías* has the names of at least eight people with skiing experience; they are not instructors but have taken groups to most peaks.

Most agencies in Huaraz hire out equipment for between US$12-15 per day, which includes skis, boots, poles and clothing. Snowboards can be hired for US$12.

Rafting If you have never tried the sport you may be wondering what all the fuss is about. Rafting can best be described as about as much fun as you can legally have with a large rubber inflatable toy. It is an adrenaline buzz, rushing down a river, paddling 'for your life' as an expert guide screams commands. An adventure beyond description and one best experienced with only the most professional of outfitters.

Peru has some of the finest rivers in the World from which to choose. Several of them are up there in the World's Top Ten whitewater rivers. Not only is the adrenaline a large part of the adventure, one of the joys of rafting is that with specialist rafts you can access spectacular places that are only accessible by river. Desert canyons, impenetrable jungle gorges, rare wildlife and exotic rock formation are all part of a rafting trip and Peru has it all on a scale beyond comparison with anywhere in the world.

Peru has the World's deepest canyon (the Cotahuasi in Southern Peru), the source of the world's greatest river (the Apurimac is the true Source of the Amazon), rivers that flow through the World's most biologically diverse region (the Amazon) with the World's highest birdcount as well as the World's largest Macaw lick (the Río Tambopata and Río Madre de Dios) and probably the World's highest concentration of Condors (the Río Colca).

On top of all this, Peru has World class whitewater rapids of all different levels of difficulty available in sub-tropical weather conditions with almost year-round availability. A whitewater rafting trip in Peru is a must for travellers looking for the perfect way to get off the Gringo Trail and really experience a bit of what wild Peru has to offer as well as catering to any adrenaline junkies looking for the ultimate thrill.

Choosing an agency Before you leap in the first raft that floats by, a word of warning and a bit of advice will help you ensure that your rafting "Trip of a lifetime" really is as safe, as environmentally friendly and as fun as you want it to be. Basically, the very remoteness and amazing locations that make Peruvian rivers so attractive mean that dealing with an emergency (should it occur) can be difficult, if not impossible. As the sport of rafting has increased in popularity over the last few years, so too have the number of accidents (including fatalities), yet the rafting industry seems to remain virtually unchecked and the operators responsible for these accidents (who have given the industry a bad name) are still allowed to operate.

If you are keen on your rafting and are looking to join a rafting expedition of some length, then it is definitely worth signing up in advance before you set foot in Peru. Some of the rivers mentioned below will have fewer than two or three scheduled departures a year and the companies that offer them only accept foreign bookings well in advance as they are logistically extremely difficult to organize. If it's just a day trip or possibly an overnighter, then you can just turn up a few days in advance and chances are there will be space on a trip departing shortly.

How do you choose your operator? As mentioned before, any company can offer rafting and as yet there is no government body that controls the quality or experience of your operator. However all operators are required by law to put up a bond of US$10-25,000 as a guarantee should anything go wrong. Do not even think of going with a company that cannot offer this. As with many of Peru's adventure options, it simply boils down to 'you pay for what you get' and at the end of the day, it's your life. Rafting is an inherently dangerous sport and doing it in Peru with the wrong operator can quite seriously endanger your life. If price is all that matters, bear in mind the following comments: the cheaper the price, the less you get, be it with safety cover, experience of guides, quality of equipment, quantity of food, emergency back up and environmental awareness.

Basic requirements All companies are required by law to issue you with a Boleta de Venta whenever you part with your hard earned cash. This ensures that taxes get paid, so that the government can build the very roads along which you are travelling to the river or provide the running water and the whitewashed school in that pretty village you just passed. Avoiding taxes is a serious offence in Peru but the temptation particularly with a cash economy like tourism only creates unfair competition and dirty dealing. Worst of all, with no Boleta de Venta or Factura you will have no come back should anything go wrong on your trip. Always demand your receipt!

Often on trips you will be required to sign a disclaimer and show proof that your travel insurance will cover you for whitewater rafting. If you are unsure about it, and are planning to go rafting, it is worth checking with your insurance before you leave as some policies have an additional charge. When signing up for a trip, ask what insurance your rafting operator has, just in case. It might be quite interesting!

Guides When signing up you should ask about the experience of the guides or even if possible get to meet them. The internationally recognized Swiftwater Technician certificate is the industry standard worldwide, but as such I think there is only one guide who holds this qualification and he's Swiss. Whilst at present there is no exam or qualification required to become a river guide, certain things are essential of your guide.

Firstly find out his command of English (or whatever language; there are a few German speaking guides available), which is essential if you are going to understand his commands. Find out his experience; how many times has he done this particular stretch of river. Many Peruvian Guides have worked overseas in the off season from Chile to Costa Rica, Europe and New Zealand. The more international experience your guide has, the more aware he will be of International safety practices.

All guides should have some experience in rescue techniques. Whilst most guides own a rescue knife, some pulleys and a few slings, do they really know how to safely extract a raft from a rock or a swimmer from dangerous location? All guides must have a knowledge of First Aid. Ask when they last took a course and what level they are at (a Wilderness First Aid course is the best available though once again maybe one or two guides hold this basic qualification in the whole of Peru).

Equipment Good Equipment is essential for your safe enjoyment of your trip. If possible ask to see some of the gear provided. Basic essentials include self-bailing rafts for all but the calmest of rivers. Check how old your raft is and where it was made (the best rafts are made in Llanelli, South Wales at the Avon factory). Paddles should be of plastic and metal construction (locally made wooden ones have been know to snap regularly and give nasty blisters). Helmets should always be provided and fit correctly (again home made fibre glass copies are an accident waiting to happen).

Life-jackets must be of a lifeguard recognized quality and be replaced regularly as they have a tendency to lose their flotation. Local made jackets look the business but in fact are very poor floaters. Some of the rivers are surprisingly cold, so find out if your company provides wetsuits, or at least quality splash jackets, as the wind can cause you to chill rapidly. On the longer trips, dry bags are provided, but what state are these in? How old are they? Do they leak? There is nothing worse than a soggy sleeping bag at the end of a day's rafting. Are tents provided? And, most importantly (for the jungle), do the zips on the mosquito net work and is it rainproof? Do the company provide mosquito netting dining tents, tables and chairs? These apparent luxuries are very nice when camping for some time at the bottom of a sandfly infested canyon!

Ask to see the First aid kit and find out what is in there and most importantly do they know how to use it? When was it last checked? Updated? Pretty basic stuff but if someone used all the lomotil you could come unstuck.

Food and hygiene After a tough day on the river, the last thing you want to do is get sick from the food. Good, wholesome food is relatively cheap in Peru and can make all the difference on a long trip. Once again you pay for what you get. Ask if there's a vegetarian option. On the food preparation, simple precautions will help you stay healthy but seem to be ignored by many companies. Are all vegetables soaked in Iodine before serving? Do the cooks wash their hands and is there soap available for the clients? Are the plates, pots and cutlery washed in Iodine or simply swilled in the river? (Stop and think how many villages upstream use that river as their main sewage outlet). These are simple ways to avoid getting sick.

Environmental concerns Sadly, on the Apurimac, on certain beaches, a completely uncaring attitude by many of the companies has left a pile of pink toilet paper and quantities of human excrement that make the Inca Trail look like a safe haven. Ask your company whether they provide a toilet tent? A lighter for burning the paper? Or at the very least a trowel to go dig a hole. Simple rules to follow: always defecate below the high-water mark so at least in the rainy season it will wash clean, always bury it good and deep and watch out when burning the paper so as not to start a fire. A toilet tent is probably the best way forward. On the Apurimac, rafting trips of four instead of three days give you a wider range of beaches to choose from thus avoiding the worst offenders.

If your company does not, make it your responsibility to encourage other members of the group to keep the campsites clean. Some campsite are rubbish tips. Surely all waste brought in can just as easily be taken out save perhaps the organic waste that should be disposed of in a suitably inconspicuous way. When camping, is a campfire really necessary? On some rivers, the drift wood supplies are critically low, forcing even the locals to cut down trees. An environmental disaster waiting to happen. Is it really necessary for companies to cook using wood when gas or kerosene is so readily available?

Safety Above all it is your safety on the river that is important. Some companies are now offering safety kayaks as standard as well as safety catarafts on certain rivers. This is definitely a step in the right direction but one that is open to misuse. Sometimes safety kayakers have little or no experience of what they are required to do and are merely along for the ride, sometimes they are asked to shoot video (rendering the safety cover useless). A safety cataraft is a powerful tool in the right hands but weigh it down with equipment and it is of little use. All companies should carry at the very least a 'wrap kit' consisting of static ropes, carabiners, slings and pulleys should a raft unfortunately get stuck. But more importantly, do the guides know how to use it? Ask a simple question like How do you set up a Z-drag? Panic if your guide says "What's a z-drag?"!

So if all this doom and gloom has not put you off, you are now equipped to go out there and find the company that offers what you are looking for at a price you think is reasonable. Bear in mind a basic day's rafting in the USA can cost between US$75-120. In Peru you might get the same for just US$25 but ask yourself what you're getting for so little. It's your life, after all.

The Río Urubamba Cusco is probably the 'rafting capital' of Peru. It has more whitewater runs on offer than anywhere else in Peru. The Urubamba is probably the most popular day run in the whole of Peru. The following variations are possible:

Huambutio-Pisac (all year availability Grade 2): a scenic half day float with a few rapids to get the adrenaline flowing right through the heart of the Sacred Valley of the Incas. Fits in perfectly with a day trip to Pisac Market. A sedate introduction to rafting for all ages.

Ollantaytambo-Chilca (all year availability, Grade 3): a fun half day introduction to the exciting sport of whitewater rafting with a few challenging rapids and beautiful scenery nearby the Inca Fortress of Ollantaytambo. This trip also fits in perfectly with the start of the Inca Trail. Try to go early in the morning as a ferocious wind picks up in the late morning.

Huaran Canyon (all year, Grade3 +): short section of fun whitewater that is occasionally rafted and used as site of the Peruvian National Whitewater Championships for kayaking and rafting.

Santa Maria to Quillabamba (May-December, Grade 3-4): a rarely rafted two-day high jungle trip. A long way to go for some fairly good whitewater but mediocre jungle.

Chuquicahuana (December-April, Grade 5): a technically demanding one-day trip for genuine adrenaline junkies only available in the rainy season.

Kiteni-Pongo Manaiqui: this was made famous by Michael Palin's BBC series. An interesting jungle gorge but logistically hard to reach and technically pretty average except in the rainy season.

The Río Apurimac The Río Apurimac is technically the true source of the Amazon. It cuts a 2,000 metres deep gorge through incredible desert scenery and offers probably some of the finest whitewater rafting sections on the Planet.

Puente Hualpachaca-Puente Cunyac (May-November, Grade 4-5): three or four days of non stop whitewater adventure through an awesome gorge just five hours' drive from Cusco. Probably the most popular multi-day trip, this is one definitely to book with the experts as there have been fatalities on this stretch. Due to the amount of people rafting this river, some of the campsites are filthy, but the whitewater is superb. This is an adventure worth doing.

Canoeing the Source: high up in the Andes at the very start of the mighty Amazon river is a beautiful section that is brilliant for trying the fun new sport of 'Duckies', or inflatable kayaking. Three days of awesome scenery, Inca ruins and much more.

The Abyss: below Puente Cunyac is a section of rarely run whitewater, this extreme expedition involves days of carrying rafts around treacherous rapids and rarely gets done.

Choquequirao: another rarely run section, this 10-day adventure involves a walk in with mules, a chance to visit the amazing ruins of Choquequirao and raft huge rapids in an imposing sheer sided canyon all the way to the jungle basin. Definitely only for the experts.

Tambopata June-October, Grade 3-4. Most expeditions to the Tambopata-Candamo Reserved Zone either start or end in Cusco. This offers a great jungle adventure for those looking to get away from the standard organized packages. Four days of whitewater followed by two days of gently meandering through virgin tropical rainforest where silent rafts make perfect wildlife watching platforms, then a visit to the World's largest Macaw Clay lick and a short flight out from Puerto Maldonado. Definitely book in advance with the experts as this is a true expedition through one of the remotest places in the whole of South America.

Arequipa 1. Río Cotahuasi (May-June, Grade 4-5): a recent addition to Peruvian whitewater rivers, the Cotahuasi was only first fully explored in 1994. Since then fewer than six further expeditions have been led down through what is now recognized as the World's deepest canyon. A total expedition including a long drive in past Corupuna mountain, a two-day trek around the spectacular Sipia Falls (where the river drops 150 metres in to an inpenetrable gorge) followed by six days of non-stop technical whitewater. The scenery is out of this world including Pre-Inca Huari culture terracing and ruins all in an incredibly deep desert canyon. Probably the best whitewater river on offer in Peru. Only a handful of operators offer this trip and only one or two depart each year. Once again book early and only with companies who have the experience.

2. Río Colca (June, Grade 4-5): possibly even harder than the Cotahuasi, this rarely run expedition river has had its fair share of casualties in the past. At present (July, 1998) it is virtually unrunnable due to a landslide practically cutting off the whole river and causing a huge lake to form. Be prepared for rocks falling off the cliffs almost continuously, sandflies, storms and out of this world whitewater.

3. Río Majes (all year, Grade 2-3): where the Colca emerges from its gorge it becomes the Río Majes and some day trips can be organized from Arequipa. Good freshwater shrimp make up for the pretty average whitewater.

Huaraz Río Santa (year round, Grade 2-3): not particularly special whitewater in attractive surroundings. Good for first-timers. Most agencies in Huaraz organize half day tours on the Río Santa. The river is highest during the May to October rainy season, but trips are most popular during the dry season. It is possible to go from Jangas to Caraz, a two day trip, with camping overnight, with *Andean Sports Tours* in Huaraz.

Around Lima Río Canete (December-February only, Grade 3+): the valley of Lunahuaná is home to a handful of whitewater companies that operate only during the Lima summer. A fun weekend out but watch the sandflies.

Agencies There are several agencies in Lima, Huaraz, Cañete, Arequipa and Cusco. Details are given in the main travelling text.

Kayaking Peru offers outstanding whitewater kayaking for all standards of paddlers form novice to expert. Many first descents remain unattempted due to logistical difficulties though they are slowly being ticked off by a dedicated crew of local and internationally renowned kayakers. For the holiday paddler, you are probably best joining up with a raft company who will gladly carry all your gear (plus any non paddling companions) and provide you with superb food whilst you enjoy the river from an unladen kayak. There is a surprising selection of latest model kayaks available in Peru for hire from about US$10-20 a day.

For complete novices, some companies offer two to three day kayak courses on the Urubamba and Apurimac that can be booked locally. For expedition paddlers, bringing your own canoe is the best option though it is getting increasingly more expensive to fly with your boats around Peru. A knowledge of Spanish is virtually indispensable.

This is still a fledgling sport in Peru, but one that looks like it is going to take off in the future. Every year a few hardy souls brave the Panamaerican highway en route form Alaska or Tierra del Fuego, but for the more recreational biker, Peru has miles and miles of superb trail, dirt road and outstanding single track throughout the Andes that are still waiting to be discovered. The problem is finding the routes as virtually no detailed maps exists.

Your answer lies in a few hardy souls who have slowly been researching routes and putting together itineraries that offer some of the most mouth-watering mountain biking any where in the world: 80 kilometres rough road descents; 40 kilometres single tracks from 4,200 metres to 2,800 metres in just two hours; Andes to the Amazon in three days and other adventures.

If you are planning a cycling holiday in Peru and are serious about your biking then definitely bring your own bike. They are relatively easy to box and fly with though recently AeroPeru have introduced a US$50 charge for bikes on internal flights so go with Aero Continente.

If you just fancy a day's ride, there are very few good quality bikes available in Peru for hire unless you join part of an official tour. Cheap Peruvian Mountain bike copies can be found for as little as US$5 a day but if you want anything remotely nice to cycle be prepared to pay US$20 at least and to join a tour. Besides, it's easy to get lost in the Peruvian Andes and water can be hard to find and your guide will know where all the best single track is.

Mountain biking

Agencies In Huaraz, Julio Olaza at *Mountain Bike Adventures* (see page 298) hires out bikes and leads tours. A typical circuit is Huaraz-Recuay-Chavín-Huari-San Luis-Chacas-Punta Olympica which lasts two days; or returning through Quebrada Llanganuco, lasting six days. Camping gear is needed and a deposit of US$500 or passport/airline ticket.

'Vuelo Libre' is just taking off in Peru. Flying from the coastal cliffs is easy and the thermals are good. The Callejón de Huaylas is more risky owing to variable thermals, crosswinds and a lack of good landing sites, but there is a strong allure to flying at 6,000 metres in front of the glaciers of Huascarán. Launch sites near Huaraz are the Puca Ventana near the Mirador, or from Churup-Pitec. A better site is Cayasbamba near Caraz, at 3,000 metres.

Parapenting & hang gliding

The area with the greatest potential is the Sacred Valley of Cusco which has excellent launch sites, thermals and reasonable landing sites. 45 kilometres from Cusco is Cerro Sacro (3,797 metres) on the Pampa de Chincheros with 550 metres clearance at take-off. It is the launch site for cross-country flights over the Sacred Valley, Sacsayhuamán and Cusco. Particularly good for parapenting is the Mirador de Urubamba, 38 kilometres from Cusco, at 3,650 metres, with 800 metres clearance and views over Pisac.

From Lima, Pasamayo (430 metres) is a good launch zone, as are the 80 metres high cliffs of the Costa Verde, which are suitable for beginners. Other possibilities are flights over the Mantaro Valley from near Huancayo (580 metres clearance, launching at 4,000 metres), Cumbemayo (850 metres elevation) over the Valle de Cajamarca, or from Majes (850 metres) over the valley at the mouth of the Colca canyon, with the possibility of seeing condors.

The season in the Sierra is May to October, with the best months being August and September. Some flights in Peru have exceeded 6,500 metres.

Surfing   Peru is a top internationally renowned surfing destination. Its main draws are the variety of wave and the all year round action. Point Break, Left and Right Reef Break and waves up to six metres can all be found during the seasons; September to February in the north and March to December in the south, though May is often ideal south of Lima.

Ocean swells are affected by two currents; the warm El Niño in the north and the cold Humboldt current in the south arriving from Antartica. Pimentel, near Chiclayo, is the dividing point between these two effects but a wet suit is normally required anywhere south of Piura.

The biggest wave is at Pico Alto (sometimes six metres in May), south of Lima, and the largest break is 800 metres at Chicama, near Trujillo. There are more than 30 top surfing beaches. **North of Lima** these are: Chicama and Cabo Blanco (both highly recommended); Pimentel; Pacasmayo/El Faro; and Máncora. **South of Lima** the best beaches are: Punta Hermosa, Punta Rocas (right reef break) and Pico Alto (best in May), the pick of the bunch; Señoritas (left reef break); San Bartolo; Caballeros (right reef break); La Isla (point break); El Huaico (left reef break); Los Muelles; Cerro Azul.

International competitions are held at Pico Alto (Balin Open in May) and Punta Rocas (during the summer months). A surfing magazine *Tablista* is published in December and July and there are forecasts in the US *International Surf Report*. (See also Lima Sports section, page 127).

Diving   The chill of the Humboldt current puts many people off diving in the Peruvian waters. Diving off the Paracas peninsula is rewarding, as is the warmer tropical ocean off Tumbes with larger fish. It is also practiced in the Bahía de Pucusana. The best season for visibility is March to November because the rivers from the mountains don't deposit silt in the sea. It can be cheap to do a PADI course in Peru; less than US$200 for a month's course, two weeks of theory, four dives in a pool, four in the ocean (see Lima Sports page 127).

Fishing   There is excellent deep-sea fishing off Ancón, north of Lima, and at the small port of Cabo Blanco, north of Talara (see page 371). In that part of the Andes easily reached from La Oroya, the lakes and streams have been stocked with trout, and fly fishing is quite good. For details about the best rainbow trout fishing in Peru (near Juliaca and in Lakes Arapa and Titicaca) write to Sr José Bernal Paredes, Casilla 874, Arequipa.

Swimming   Between December and April the entire coast of Peru offers good bathing, but during the rest of the year only the northern beaches near Tumbes provide pleasantly warm water. There are many bathing resorts near Lima (do not swim at, or even visit, these beaches alone). The current off the coast can be very strong, making it too dangerous to swim in places.

Cave diving   This is not yet widely known in Peru, but there is an organization which can provide information; *Centre of Subterranean Explorations of Peru (CEESPE)*, Avenida Brasil 1815, Jesús María, Lima, T4634722, Sr Carlos Morales is very helpful.

A cave which has attracted international expeditions is the *Gruta de Huagapo*, or 'The Cave that Weeps', located in the Valle de Palcaymo 30 kilometres northwest of Tarma in the Department of Junín, at 3,572 metres (see page 446).

Yachting   Yacht clubs in Lima are: *Club Regatas de Lima*, 494 García y García, T4292994; *Yacht Club Ancón*, Malecón San Martín, T4883071; *Club Regatas Unión*, Gálvez s/n, T4290095.

Cultural tourism

This covers more esoteric pursuits such as archaeology and mystical tourism. Several of the tour operators listed on page 85 offer customised packages for special interest groups. Local operators offering these more specialized tours are listed in the travelling text under the relevant location.

Federico Kaufmann-Doig is a great source of information on Peruvian archaeology, for serious students and archaeologists. He has worked on various sites in Peru and is currently engaged on a three year project in the Kuelap area. He is the director of the Instituto de Arqueología Amazónica, T4490243, or (home) T4499103. His book, *Historia del Perú: un nuevo perspectivo*, in two volumes (*Pre-Inca*, and *El Incario*) is available at better bookshops. The Instituto Nacional de Cultura, in the Museo de la Nación (see page 104), should be contacted by archaeologists for permits and information. The Museo Nacional de Antropología y Arqueología in Pueblo Libre (see page 104) is the main centre for archaeological investigation and the Museo de la Nación holds exhibitions.

For more information, try these websites: *Universidad de Trujillo* (www.unitru.edu.pe; dcastillo@chanchan.unitru.edu.pe). *Arqueología del Perú* (www.geocities.com/ Athens/ Acropolis/9071). For specialized shamanic healing tours, contact K'vichy Light International, Avda Sol 814, oficina 219, Cusco, T/F(084) 221166/264107, E Kvichy@amauta.edu.pe.

Birdwatching

Peru is the number one country in the world for birds. Its varied geography and topography, and its wildernesses of so many different life zones have endowed Peru with the greatest biodiversity and variety of birds on earth. 18.5% of all the bird species in the world and 45% of all neotropical birds occur in Peru. This is why Peru is number one for birds on the continent dubbed 'the bird continent' by professional birders. There is no better destination for a birding trip.

A birding trip to Peru is possible during any month of the year. Birds breed all year round in Peru, but there is a definite peak in breeding activity - and consequently birdsong - just before the rains come in October, and this makes it rather easier to locate many birds between September and Christmas.

Rainwear is recommended for the mountains, especially during the rainy season between December and April. But in the tropical lowlands an umbrella is the way to go. Lightweight hiking boots are probably the best general footwear, but wellingtons are preferred by many neotropical birders for the lowland rainforests.

Apart from the usual binoculars, a telescope is helpful in many areas, whilst a tape recorder and shotgun microphone can be very useful for calling out skulking forest birds, although experience in using this type of equipment is recommended, particularly to limit disturbance to the birds.

If your experience of Neotropical birding is limited, the potential number of species **The birds** which may be seen on a three or four week trip can be daunting. A four week trip can produce over 750 species, and some of the identifications can be tricky! You may want to take an experienced bird guide with you who can introduce you to, for example, the mysteries of foliage-gleaner and woodcreeper identification, or you may want to 'do it yourself' and identify the birds on your own. There is no single field-guide or book that covers all the birds of Peru, and some species are not illustrated anywhere. However, taking a combination of a few books will ensure that 99% of your sightings can be identified. Those listed on page 84 are recommended.

The key sites Details of the following sites are given in the main travelling text: **Paracas National Reserve** (page 257); **Lomas de Lachay** (page 330); **Huascarán Biosphere Reserve** (page 288); **Tambopata-Candamo Reserved Zone** (page 487); **Iquitos** (page 467); **Manu Biosphere Reserve** (page 478). Some of the other birding hot-spots of Peru are listed below, but there are many more. A great three-to four-week combination is about 16 days in Manu, then two or three days in the highlands at Abra Malaga and two or three days in the Huascarán Biosphere Reserve. A trip into the Marañon Valley (Chiclayo-Cajamarca) can be substituted for Manu; this allows access to some of the most sought-after endemics, but would produce far fewer species. More information on the birds of Peru is given in the **Flora and fauna** section on page 513.

Maracpomacocha & the Central Highway Maracpomacocha is an area of high Puna grass-and-bog-land about four hours drive east of Lima along the Central Highway. This is high altitude birding at its extreme: a giddy 4,500 metres above sea-level. As well as regular high Andean species such as Ground-tyrants, Seed-snipes and Sierra-finches, the main reason for birding is twofold: Diameded Sandpiper-plover, the almost mythical wader of the mineral-rich bogs, and White-bellied Cinclodes, perhaps the prettiest and one of the rarest of the furnarids. Both can be seen here, with a little luck. Other highlights include Giant coot on the lake at Maracpomacocha and the smart Black-breasted Hillstar, a hummingbird endemic to Peru. To reach this area, a car is essential and, if you are camping overnight, make sure that your radiator has anti-freeze (something that car-hire firms in Lima tend to forget, being in the Atacama desert!). There is no accommodation at Maracpomacocha.

Along the Central Highway from the Maracpomacocha turnoff, the well-paved road continues another 120 kilometres to **Lake Junín**, where, with prior arrangement, it is possible to hire a boat to see the endemic Junín Flightless Grebe. The lake is a fantastic place to see all the highland waterbirds and raptors, and the surrounding fields abound with Sierra-finches and Ground-tyrants. Only very basic accommodation is available at Junín, so camping is perhaps the best option. See also page 448.

180 kilometres further along the Central Highway is **Huánuco**, the base for exploring the Carpish Tunnel area (see also page 451). About an hour's drive north-east of Huánuco, the road passes through the Carpish range, and birding either side of the tunnel can be very productive. Powerful Woodpecker, Sickle-winged Guan and large mixed feeding flocks appear out of the mist in the epiphite-laden cloud-forest.

Chiclayo-Cajamarca circuit Starting at the coastal city of Chiclayo (see page 350), a tough but rewarding trip can be made into the deep Marañon Valley and its environs. On this route, some of Peru's birds can be found: legendary species such as Marvellous Spatuletail, Marañon Crescent-chest, Long-whiskered Owlet and Buff-bridled Inca Finch, to name but a few. Many of the species to be found along this circuit have been seen by only a handful of ornithologists.

Arequipa Using the city as a base, it is possible to see many of the specialities which inhabit the arid scrub and Polylepis woodland of the Andean west slope. The best road to bird is the one to Laguna Salinas. This large salt lake regularly holds three species of Flamingo; Chilean, Andean and Puna. It is also a good place to see Andean Avocet and Puna Plover. In the dry season, you may have to hike out towards the middle of the lake, but do not forget your sunglasses as the glare from the salt is fierce.

Between Arequipa and Laguna Salinas, birding the Polylepis-clad slopes and arid scrub can produce various earthcreepers and canasteros not found elsewhere, and this is one of only two places for Tamarugo Conebill.

Amazon
Earth's Greatest Wilderness

Explore the mighty Amazon River and rainforest.
Join expert naturalists adept at spotting and
interpreting wildlife. Ascend into the treetops of
the rainforest on the spectacular ACEER Canopy
Walkway System. Experience three comfortable
and secluded jungle lodges including the Amazon
Center for Environmental Education and Research.

8-Day Rainforest Expeditions Depart Monthly
Priced all-inclusive with international airfare from Miami U.S.A.

Optional extensions to Cusco/Machu Picchu
Ask about our special Rainforest Workshops

ADVANCED RESERVATIONS REQUIRED.
CONTACT US FOR AVAILABLE DATES
AND CURRENT PRICING.

Essentials

One of the main reasons for birders to visit the Arequipa area is to make the trip to Cruz del Condor, in the Colca Canyon (see page 238).

Machu Picchu and Abra Malaga Machu Picchu (see page 179) may be a nightmare for lovers of peace and solitude, but the surrounding bamboo stands provide excellent opportunities for seeing the Inca Wren. A walk along the railway track near Puente Ruinas station can produce species which are difficult to see elsewhere. This is *the* place in Peru to see White-capped Dipper and Torrent Duck.

From Ollantaytambo (see page 176), it is only two hours' drive to one of the most accessible Polylepsis woodlands in the Andes, whilst the humid temperate forest of Abra Malaga is only 45 minutes further on. In the Polylepsis some very rare birds can be located without too much difficulty, including Royal Cinclodes and White-browed Tit-spinetail (the latter being one of the ten most endangered birds on earth). The humid temperate forest is laden with moss and bromeliads, and mixed species flocks of multi-coloured tanagers and other birds are common.

Holidays and festivals

Festivals Two of the major festival dates are *Carnaval*, which is held over the weekend before **Ash Wednesday**, and *Semana Santa* (Holy Week), which ends on **Easter Sunday**. Carnival is celebrated in most of the Andes and **Semana Santa** throughout most of Peru. Accommodation and transport is heavily booked at these times and prices rise.

Another important festival is *Fiesta de la Cruz*, held on the first of **May** in much of the central and southern highlands and on the coast. In Cusco, the entire month of **June** is one huge *fiesta*, culminating in *Inti Raymi*, on **24 June**, one of Peru's prime tourist attractions.

The two main festivals in Lima are *Santa Rosa de Lima*, on **30 August**, and *Señor de los Milagros*, held on several dates throughout **October**.

Another national festival is *Todos los Santos* (All Saints) on **1 November**, and on **8 December** is *Festividad de la Inmaculada Concepción*.

A full list of local festivals is listed under each town.

National holidays Aside from the festivals listed above, the main holidays are: **1 January**, New Year; **6 January**, *Bajada de Reyes*; **1 May**, Labour Day; **28-29 July**, Independence (Fiestas Patrias); **7 October**, Battle of Angamos; **24-25 December**, *Navidad*.

NB Most businesses such as banks, airline offices and tourist agencies close for the official holidays while supermarkets and street markets may be open. This depends a lot on where you are so ask around before the holiday. Sometimes holidays that fall during mid-week will be moved to the following Monday. If you are going to spend a holiday in a certain area, find out what the local customs and events are. Often there are parades, processions, special types of food or certain traditions (like yellow underwear at New Year's) that characterize the event. This will allow you to delve into the customs of the country you are travelling in. The high season for foreign tourism in Peru is June through September while national tourism peaks on certain holidays, Navidad, Semana Santa and Fiestas Patrias. Prices rise and accommodation and bus tickets are harder to come by. If you know when you will be travelling buy your ticket in advance.

Health

For anyone travelling overseas health is a key consideration. With the following advice and sensible precautions the visitor to Peru should remain as healthy as at home. Most visitors return home having experienced no problems at all apart from some travellers' diarrhoea.

The health risks, especially in the lowland tropical areas, are different from those encountered in Europe or the USA. It also depends on where and how you travel. There are clear differences in risks for the business traveller, who stays in international class hotels in large cities and the backpacker trekking in remote areas, and there is huge variation in climate, vegetation and wildlife. There are no hard and fast rules to follow; you will often have to make your own judgment on the healthiness or otherwise of your surroundings.

There are English (or other foreign language) speaking doctors in most major cities who have particular experience in dealing with locally-occurring diseases, but don't expect good facilities away from the major centres. Your Embassy representative will often be able to give you the name of local reputable doctors and most of the better hotels have a doctor on standby. If you do fall ill and cannot find a recommended doctor, try the Outpatient Department of a hospital – private hospitals are usually less crowded and offer a more acceptable standard of care to foreigners.

Before travelling

Take out medical insurance. Make sure it covers all eventualities especially evacuation to your home country by a medically equipped plane, if necessary. You should have a dental check up, obtain a spare glasses prescription, a spare oral contraceptive prescription (or enought pills to last) and, if you suffer from a chronic illness (such as diabetes, high blood pressure, ear or sinus troubles, cardio-pulmonary disease or nervous disorder) arrange for a check up with your doctor, who can at the same time provide you with a letter explaining the details of your disability in English and if possible Spanish and/or Portuguese. Check the current practice in countries you are visiting for malaria prophylaxis (prevention). If you are on regular medication, make sure you have enough to cover the period of your travel.

More preparation is probably necessary for babies and children than for an adult and **Children** perhaps a little more care should be taken when travelling to remote areas where health services are primitive. This is because children can be become more rapidly ill than adults (on the other hand they often recover more quickly). Diarrhoea and vomiting are the most common problems, so take the usual precautions, but more intensively.

Breastfeeding is best and most convenient for babies, but powdered milk is generally available and so are baby foods in most countries. Papaya, bananas and avocados are all nutritious and can be cleanly prepared. The treatment of diarrhoea is the same for adults, except that it should start earlier and be continued with more persistence. Children get dehydrated very quickly in hot countries and can become drowsy and uncooperative unless cajoled to drink water or juice plus salts.

Upper respiratory infections, such as colds, catarrh and middle ear infections are also common and if your child suffers from these normally take some antibiotics against the possibility. Outer ear infections after swimming are also common and antibiotic eardrops will help. Wet wipes are always useful and sometimes difficult to find in South America, as, in some places are disposable nappies.

Essentials

Medical supplies

You may like to take some of the following items with you from home:

Sunglasses
ones designed for intense sunlight

Earplugs
for sleeping on aeroplanes and in noisy hotels

Suntan cream
with a high protection factor

Insect repellent
containing DET for preference

Mosquito net
lightweight, permethrin-impregnated for choice

Tablets
for travel sickness

Tampons
can be expensive in some countries in Latin America

Condoms

Contraceptives

Water sterilizing tablets

Antimalarial tablets

Anti-infective ointment eg Cetrimide

Dusting powder for feet etc
containing fungicide

Antacid tablets
for indigestion

Sachets of rehydration salts
plus anti-diarrhoea preparations

Painkillers
such as Paracetamol or Aspirin

Antibiotics
for diarrhoea etc

First Aid kit
Small pack containing a few sterile syringes and needles and disposable gloves. The risk of catching hepatitis etc from a dirty needle used for injection is now negligible, but some may be reassured by carrying their own supplies – available from camping shops and airport shops.

Medicines There is very little control on the sale of drugs and medicines in Peru. You can buy any and every drug in pharmacies without a prescription. Be wary of this because pharmacists can be poorly trained and might sell you drugs that are unsuitable, dangerous or old. Many drugs and medicines are manufactured under licence from American or European companies, so the trade names may be familiar to you. This means you do not have to carry a whole chest of medicines with you, but remember that the shelf life of some items, especially vaccines and antibiotics, is markedly reduced in hot conditions.

Buy your supplies at the better outlets where there are refrigerators, even though they are more expensive and check the expiry date of all preparations you buy. Immigration officials occasionally confiscate scheduled drugs (Lomotil is an example) if they are not accompanied by a doctor's prescription.

What to take Self-medication may be forced on you by circumstances so the following text contains the names of drugs and medicines which you may find useful in an emergency or in out-of-the-way places.

Vaccination and immunisation Smallpox vaccination is no longer required anywhere in the world. Neither is cholera vaccination recognized as necessary for international travel by the World Health Organisation – it is not very effective either. Nevertheless, some immigration officials are demanding proof of vaccination against cholera following the outbreak of the disease which originated in Peru in 1990-91 and subsequently affected most surrounding countries. Although very unlikely to affect visitors, the cholera epidemic continues making its greatest impact in poor areas where water supplies are polluted and food hygiene practices are insanitary.

Vaccination against the following diseases are recommended:
Yellow Fever This is a live vaccination not to be given to children under nine months of age or persons allergic to eggs. Immunity lasts for 10 years, an

International Certificate of Yellow Fever Vaccination will be given and should be kept because it is sometimes asked for. Yellow fever is very rare in Peru, but the vaccination is practically without side effects and almost totally protective.

Typhoid A disease spread by the insanitary preparation of food. A number of new vaccines against this condition are now available; the older TAB and monovalent typhoid vaccines are being phased out. The newer, eg Typhim Vi, cause less side effects, but are more expensive. For those who do not like injections, there are now oral vaccines.

Poliomyelitis Despite its decline in the world this remains a serious disease if caught and is easy to protect against. There are live oral vaccines and in some countries injected vaccines. Whichever one you choose it is a good idea to have booster every three to five years if visiting developing countries regularly.

Tetanus One dose should be given with a booster at six weeks and another at six months and 10 yearly boosters thereafter are recommended. Children should already be properly protected against diphtheria, poliomyelitis and pertussis (whooping cough), measles and HIB all of which can be more serious infections in Peru than at home. Measles, mumps and rubella vaccine is also given to children throughout the world, but those teenage girls who have not had rubella (german measles) should be tested and vaccinated. Hepatitis B vaccination for babies is now routine in some countries. Consult your doctor for advice on tuberculosis inoculation: the disease is still widespread in Peru.

Infectious Hepatitis Is less of a problem for travellers than it used to be because of the development of two extremely effective vaccines against the A and B form of the disease. It remains common, however, in Peru. A combined hepatitis A & B vaccine is now available – one jab covers both diseases.

Other vaccinations Might be considered in the case of epidemics eg meningitis. There is an effective vaccination against rabies which should be considered by all travellers, especially those going through remote areas or if there is a particular occupational risk, eg for zoologists or veterinarians.

Further information on health risks abroad, vaccinations etc may be available from a local travel clinic. If you wish to take specific drugs with you such as antibiotics these are best prescribed by your own doctor. Beware, however, that not all doctors can be experts on the health problems of remote countries. More detailed or more up-to-date information than local doctors can provide are available from various sources. **Further information**

In the UK there are hospital departments specializing in tropical diseases in London, Liverpool, Birmingham and Glasgow and the Malaria Reference Laboratory at the London School of Hygiene and Tropical Medicine provides free advice about malaria, T(0891)600350. In the USA the local Public Health Services can give such information and information is available centrally from the Centre for Disease Control (CDC) in Atlanta, T(404)3324559.

There are additional computerized databases which can be assessed for destination-specific up-to-the-minute information. In the UK there is MASTA (Medical Advisory Service to Travellers Abroad), T(0171)6314408, F(0171)4365389, Tx8953473 and Travax (Glasgow, T(0141)9467120, ext 247). Other information on medical problems overseas can be obtained from the book by Dawood, Richard (Editor) (1992) *Travellers' Health: How to stay healthy abroad*, Oxford University Press 1992, £7.99. We strongly recommend this revised and updated edition, especially to the intrepid traveller heading for the more out of the way places. General advice is also available in the UK in *Health Information for Overseas Travel* published by the Department of Health and available from HMSO, and *International Travel and Health* published by WHO, Geneva.

Essentials

Staying healthy

Intestinal upsets   The commonest affliction of visitors to Peru is probably traveller's diarrhoea. Diarrhoea and vomiting is due, most of the time, to food poisoning, usually passed on by the insanitary habits of food handlers. As a general rule the cleaner your surroundings and the smarter the restaurant, the less likely you are to suffer.

Foods to avoid Uncooked, undercooked, partially cooked or reheated meat, fish, eggs, raw vegetables and salads, especially when they have been left out exposed to flies. Stick to fresh food that has been cooked from raw just before eating and make sure you peel fruit yourself. Avoid raw food, undercooked food (including eggs) and reheated food. Food that is cooked in front of you and offered hot all through is generally safe. Wash and dry your hands before eating – disposable wet-wipe tissues are useful for this.

Shellfish are always a risk eaten raw (as in *ceviche*) and at certain times of the year some fish and shellfish concentrate toxins from their environment and cause various kinds of food poisoning. The local authorities notify the public not to eat these foods. Do not ignore the warning.

Heat treated milk (UHT) pasteurized or sterilized is becoming more available in Peru as is pasteurized cheese. On the whole matured or processed cheeses are safer than the fresh varieties and fresh unpasteurized milk from whatever animal can be a source of food poisoning germs, tuberculosis and brucellosis. This applies equally to ice cream, yoghurt and cheese made from unpasteurized milk, so avoid these homemade products – the factory made ones are probably safer.

Tap water in Peru is unsafe to drink. Filtered or bottled water is usually available and safe, although you must make sure that somebody is not filling bottles from the tap and hammering on a new crown cap. If your hotel has a central hot water supply this water is safe to drink after cooling. Ice for drinks should be made from boiled water, but rarely is so stand your glass on the ice cubes, rather than putting them in the drink. The better hotels have water purifying systems. Stream water, if you are in the countryside, is often contaminated by communities living surprisingly high in the mountains.

Travellers'   This is usually caused by eating food which has been contaminated by food
diarrhoea   poisoning germs. Drinking water is rarely the culprit. Sea water or river water is more likely to be contaminated by sewage and so swimming in such dilute effluent can also be a cause.

Infection with various organisms can give rise to travellers' diarrhoea. They may be viruses, bacteria, eg Escherichia coli (probably the most common cause worldwide), protozoal (such as amoebas and giardia), salmonella and cholera. The diarrhoea may come on suddenly or rather slowly. It may or may not be accompanied by vomiting or by severe abdominal pain and the passage of blood or mucus when it is called dysentery.

How do you know which type you have caught and how to treat it?
If you can time the onset of the diarrhoea to the minute ('acute') then it is probably due to a virus or a bacterium and/or the onset of dysentery. The treatment in addition to rehydration is Ciprofloxacin 500 mg every 12 hours; the drug is now widely available and there are many similar ones.

If the diarrhoea comes on slowly or intermittently ('sub-acute') then it is more likely to be protozoal, ie caused by an amoeba or giardia. Antibiotics such a Ciprofloxacin will have little effect. These cases are best treated by a doctor as is any outbreak of diarrhoea continuing for more than three days. Sometimes blood is passed in ameobic dysentery and for this you should certainly seek medical help. If this is not available then the best treatment is probably Tinidazole (Fasigyn) one tablet four times a day for three days. If there are severe stomach cramps, the following drugs may help but are not very useful in the management of acute diarrhoea: Loperamide (Imodium) and Diphenoxylate with Atropine (Lomotil) They should not be given to children.

Any kind of diarrhoea, whether or not accompanied by vomiting, responds well to the replacement of water and salts, taken as frequent small sips, of some kind of rehydration solution. There are proprietary preparations consisting of sachets of powder which you dissolve in boiled water or you can make your own by adding half a teaspoonful of salt (3.5 grammes) and four tablespoonsful of sugar (40 grammes) to a litre of boiled water.

Thus the lynch pins of treatment for diarrhoea are rest, fluid and salt replacement, antibiotics such as Ciprofloxacin for the bacterial types and special diagnostic tests and medical treatment for the amoeba and giardia infections. Salmonella infections and cholera, although rare, can be devastating diseases and it would be wise to get to a hospital as soon as possible if these were suspected.

Fasting, peculiar diets and the consumption of large quantities of yoghurt have not been found useful in calming travellers' diarrhoea or in rehabilitating inflamed bowels. Oral rehydration has on the other hand, especially in children, been a life saving technique and should always be practised, whatever other treatment you use. As there is some evidence that alcohol and milk might prolong diarrhoea they should be avoided during and immediately after an attack.

Diarrhoea occurring day after day for long periods of time (chronic diarrhoea) is notoriously resistent to amateur attempts at treatment and again warrants proper diagnostic tests (most towns with reasonable sized hospitals have laboratories for stool samples). There are ways of preventing travellers' diarrhoea for short periods of time by taking antibiotics, but this is not a foolproof technique and should not be used other than in exceptional circumstances. Doxycycline is possibly the best drug. Some preventatives such as Enterovioform can have serious side effects if taken for long periods.

Paradoxically **constipation** is also common, probably induced by dietary change, inadequate fluid intake in hot places and long bus journeys. Simple laxatives are useful in the short-term and bulky foods such as maize, beans and plenty of fruit are also useful.

High altitude

Spending time at high altitude in Peru, especially in the tropics, is usually a pleasure – it is not so hot, there are no insects and the air is clear and spring like. Travelling to high altitudes, however, can cause medical problems, all of which can be prevented if care is taken.

On reaching heights above about 3,000 metres, heart pounding and shortness of breath, especially on exertion are a normal response to the lack of oxygen in the air. A condition called acute mountain sickness (*Soroche*) can also affect visitors. It is more likely to affect those who ascend rapidly, eg by plane and those who over-exert themselves (teenagers for example). Soroche takes a few hours or days to come on and presents with a bad headache, extreme tiredness, sometimes dizziness, loss of appetite and frequently nausea and vomiting.

Insomnia is common and is often associated with a suffocating feeling when lying in bed. Keen observers may note their breathing tends to wax and wane at night and their face tends to be puffy in the mornings – this is all part of the syndrome. Anyone can get this condition and past experience is not always a good guide: the author, having spent years in Peru travelling constantly between sea level and very high

Essentials

altitude never suffered symptoms, then was severely affected whilst climbing Kilimanjaro in Tanzania.

The treatment of acute mountain sickness is simple – rest, painkillers, (preferably not aspirin based) for the headache and anti sickness pills for vomiting. Oxygen is actually not much help, except at very high altitude. Various local panaceas – Coramina glucosada, Effortil, Micoren are popular and mate de coca (an infusion of coca leaves widely available and perfectly legal) will alleviate some of the symptoms.

To **prevent** the condition: on arrival at places over 3,000 metres have a few hours rest in a chair and avoid alcohol, cigarettes and heavy food. If the symptoms are severe and prolonged, it is best to descend to a lower altitude and to reascend slowly or in stages. If this is impossible because of shortage of time or if you are going so high that acute mountain sickness is very likely, then the drug Acetazolamide (Diamox) can be used as a preventative and continued during the ascent. There is good evidence of the value of this drug in the prevention of soroche, but some people do experience peculiar side effects. The usual dose is 500 mg of the slow release preparation each night, starting the night before ascending above 3,000 metres.

Watch out for **sunburn** at high altitude. The ultraviolet rays are extremely powerful. The air is also excessively dry at high altitude and you might find that your skin dries out and the inside of your nose becomes crusted. Use a moisturiser for the skin and some vaseline wiped into the nostrils. Some people find contact lenses irritate because of the dry air. It is unwise to ascend to high altitude if you are pregnant, especially in the first three months, or if you have a history of heart, lung or blood disease, including sickle cell.

A more unusual condition can affect mountaineers who ascend rapidly to high altitude – **acute pulmonary oedema**. Residents at altitude sometimes experience this when returning to the mountains from time spent at the coast. This condition is often preceded by acute mountain sickness and comes on quite rapidly with severe breathlessness, noisy breathing, coughing, blueness of the lips and frothing at the mouth. Anybody who develops this must be brought down as soon as possible, given oxygen and taken to hospital.

A rapid descent from high places will make sinus problems and middle ear infections worse and might make your teeth ache. Lastly, don't fly to altitude within 24 hours of Scuba diving. You might suffer from 'the bends'.

Heat and cold Full acclimatization to high temperatures takes about two weeks. During this period it is normal to feel a bit apathetic, especially if the relative humidity is high. Drink plenty of water (up to 15 litres a day are required when working physically hard in the tropics), use salt on your food and avoid extreme exertion. Tepid showers are more cooling than hot or cold ones. Large hats do not cool you down, but do prevent sunburn. Remember that, especially in the highlands, there can be a large and sudden drop in temperature between sun and shade and between night and day, so dress accordingly. Warm jackets or woollens are essential after dark at high altitude. Loose cotton is still the best material when the weather is hot.

Insects These are mostly more of a nuisance than a serious hazard and if you try, you can prevent yourself entirely from being bitten. Some, such as mosquitos are, of course, carriers of potentially serious diseases, so it is sensible to avoid being bitten as much as possible.

Sleep off the ground and use a mosquito net or some kind of insecticide. Preparations containing Pyrethrum or synthetic pyrethroids are safe. They are available as aerosols or pumps and the best way to use these is to spray the room thoroughly in all areas (follow the instructions rather than the insects) and then shut the door for a while, re-entering when the smell has dispersed. Mosquito coils release insecticide as they burn slowly. They are widely available and useful out of doors. Tablets of insecticide which are placed on a heated mat plugged into a wall socket are probably the most effective. They fill the room with insecticidal fumes in the same way as aerosols or coils.

You can also use insect repellents, most of which are effective against a wide range of pests. The most common and effective is diethyl metatoluamide (DET). DET liquid is best for arms and face (care around eyes and with spectacles – DET dissolves plastic). Aerosol spray is good for clothes and ankles and liquid DET can be dissolved in water and used to impregnate cotton clothes and mosquito nets. Some repellents now contain DET and Permethrin, insecticide. Impregnated wrist and ankle bands can also be useful.

If you are bitten or stung, itching may be relieved by cool baths, antihistamine tablets (care with alcohol or driving) or mild corticosteroid creams, eg. hydrocortisone (but take great care: never use if there's any hint of infection). Careful scratching of all your bites once a day can be surprisingly effective. Calamine lotion and cream have limited effectiveness and antihistamine creams are not recommended – they can cause allergies themselves.

Bites which become infected should be treated with a local antiseptic or antibiotic cream such as Cetrimide, as should any infected sores or scratches.

When living rough, skin infestations with body lice (crabs) and scabies are easy to pick up. Use whatever local commercial preparation is recommended for lice and scabies.

Crotamiton cream (Eurax) alleviates itching and also kills a number of skin parasites. Malathion lotion 5% (Prioderm) kills lice effectively, but avoid the use of the toxic agricultural preparation of Malathion, more often used to commit suicide.

Ticks They attach themselves usually to the lower parts of the body often after walking in areas where cattle have grazed. They take a while to attach themselves strongly, but swell up as they start to suck blood. The important thing is to remove them gently, so that they do not leave their head parts in your skin because this can cause a nasty allergic reaction some days later. Do not use petrol, vaseline, lighted cigarettes etc to remove the tick, but, with a pair of tweezers remove the beast gently by gripping it at the attached (head) end and rock it out in very much the same way that a tooth is extracted.

Certain tropical flies which lay their eggs under the skin of sheep and cattle also occasionally do the same thing to humans with the unpleasant result that a maggot grows under the skin and pops up as a boil or pimple. The best way to remove these is to cover the boil with oil, vaseline or nail varnish so as to stop the maggot breathing, then to squeeze it out gently the next day.

Sunburn The burning power of the tropical sun, especially at high altitude, is phenomenal. Always wear a wide brimmed hat and use some form of suncream lotion on untanned skin. Normal temperate zone suntan lotions (protection factor up to seven) are not much good; you need to use the types designed specifically for the tropics or for mountaineers or skiers with protection factors up to 15 or above. These are often not available in Peru. Glare from the sun can cause conjunctivitis, so wear sunglasses especially on tropical beaches, where high protection factor sunscreen should also be used.

Prickly heat This very common intensely itchy rash is avoided by frequent washing and by wearing loose clothing. It's cured by allowing skin to dry off through use of powder and spending two nights in an airconditioned hotel!

Athletes foot   This and other fungal skin infections are best treated with Tolnaftate or Clotrimazole.

Other risks and more serious diseases

Remember that rabies is endemic throughout Latin America, so avoid dogs that are behaving strangely and cover your toes at night from the vampire bats, which also carry the disease. If you are bitten by a domestic or wild animal, do not leave things to chance: scrub the wound with soap and water and/or disinfectant, try to have the animal captured (within limits) or at least determine its ownership, where possible, and seek medical assistance at once.

The course of treatment depends on whether you have already been satisfactorily vaccinated against rabies. If you have (this is worthwile if you are spending lengths of time in developing countries) then some further doses of vaccine are all that is required. Human diploid vaccine is the best, but expensive: other, older kinds of vaccine, such as that derived from duck embryos may be the only types available. These are effective, much cheaper and interchangeable generally with the human derived types. If not already vaccinated then anti rabies serum (immunoglobulin) may be required in addition. It is important to finish the course of treatment whether the animal survives or not.

AIDS   AIDS (*SIDA*) is increasing but is not wholly confined to the well known high risk sections of the population, ie homosexual men, intravenous drug abusers and children of infected mothers. Heterosexual transmission is now the dominant mode and so the main risk to travellers is from casual sex. The same precautions should be taken as with any sexually transmitted disease.

The Aids virus (HIV) can be passed by unsterilized needles which have been previously used to inject an HIV positive patient, but the risk of this is negligible. It would, however, be sensible to check that needles have been properly sterilized or disposable needles have been used. If you wish to take your own disposable needles, be prepared to explain what they are for. The risk of receiving a blood transfusion with blood infected with the HIV virus is greater than from dirty needles because of the amount of fluid exchanged. Supplies of blood for transfusion should now be screened for HIV in all reputable hospitals, so again the risk is very small indeed.

Catching the AIDS virus does not always produce an illness in itself (although it may do). The only way to be sure if you feel you have been put at risk is to have a blood test for HIV antibodies on your return to a place where there are reliable laboratory facilities. The test does not become positive for some weeks.

Malaria   In Peru malaria is theoretically confined to jungle zones, but is now on the increase again. Mosquitos do not thrive above 2,500 metres, so you are safe at altitude. There are different varieties of malaria, some resistant to the normal drugs. Make local enquiries if you intend to visit possibly infected zones and use a prophylactic regime.

Start taking the tablets a few days before exposure and continue to take them for six weeks after leaving the malarial zone. Remember to give the drugs to babies and children also. Opinion varies on the precise drugs and dosage to be used for protection. All the drugs may have some side effects and it is important to balance the risk of catching the disease against the albeit rare side effects.

The increasing complexity of the subject is such that as the malarial parasite becomes immune to the new generation of drugs it has made concentration on the physical prevention from being bitten by mosquitos more important. This involves the use of long sleeved shirts or blouses and long trousers, repellants and nets.

Clothes are now available impregnated with the insecticide Permethrin or Deltamethrin or it is possible to impregnate the clothes yourself. Wide meshed nets impregnated with Permethrin are also available, are lighter to carry and less claustrophobic to sleep in.

Prophylaxis and treatment If your itinerary takes you into a malarial area, seek expert advice before you go on a suitable prophylactic regime. This is especially true for pregnant women who are particularly prone to catch malaria. You can still catch the disease even when sticking to a proper regime, although it is unlikely. If you do develop symptoms (high fever, shivering, headache, sometimes diarrhoea), seek medical advice immediately. If this is not possible and there is a great likelihood of malaria, the treatment is:

Chloroquine, a single dose of four tablets (600 mg) followed by two tablets (300 mg) in six hours and 300 mg each day following.

Falciparum type of malaria or type in doubt: take local advice. Various combinations of drugs are being used such as Quinine, Tetracycline or Halofantrine. If falciparum type malaria is definitely diagnosed, it is wise to get to a good hospital as treatment can be complex and the illness very serious.

The main symptoms are pains in the stomach, lack of appetite, lassitude and yellowness of the eyes and skin. Medically speaking there are two main types. The less serious, but more common is Hepatitis A for which the best protection is the careful preparation of food, the avoidance of contaminated drinking water and scrupulous attention to toilet hygiene. The other, more serious, version is Hepatitis B which is acquired usually as a sexually transmitted disease or by blood transfusions. It can less commonly be transmitted by injections with unclean needles and possibly by insect bites. The symptoms are the same as for Hepatitis A. The incubation period is much longer (up to six months compared with six weeks) and there are more likely to be complications.

Infectious hepatitis (jaundice)

Hepatitis A can be protected against with gamma globulin. It should be obtained from a reputable source and is certainly useful for travellers who intend to live rough. You should have a shot before leaving and have it repeated every six months. The dose of gamma globulin depends on the concentration of the particular preparation used, so the manufacturer's advice should be taken. The injection should be given as close as possible to your departure and as the dose depends on the likely time you are to spend in potentially affected areas, the manufacturer's instructions should be followed.

Gamma globulin has really been superceded now by a proper vaccination against Hepatitis A (Havrix) which gives immunity lasting up to 10 years. After that boosters are required. Havrix monodose is now widely available as is Junior Havrix. The vaccination has negligible side effects and is extremely effective. Gamma globulin injections can be a bit painful, but it is much cheaper than Havrix and may be more available in some places.

Hepatitis B can be effectively prevented by a specific vaccine (Engerix) – three shots over six months before travelling. If you have had jaundice in the past it would be worthwhile having a blood test to see if you are immune to either of these two types, because this might avoid the necessity and costs of vaccination or gamma globulin. There are other kinds of viral hepatitis (C, E etc) which are fairly similar to A and B, but vaccines are not available as yet.

This can still occur and is carried by ticks. There is usually a reaction at the site of the bite and a fever. Seek medical advice.

Typhus

Intestinal worms These are common and the more serious ones such as hookworm can be contracted from walking barefoot on infested earth or beaches.

Various other tropical diseases can be caught in jungle areas, usually transmitted by biting insects. They are often related to African diseases and were probably introduced by the slave labour trade. Leishmaniasis (Espundia) is carried by sandflies and causes a sore that will not heal or a severe nasal infection. Wearing long trousers and a long sleeved shirt in infected areas protects against these flies. DET is also effective. Epidemics of meningitis occur from time-to-time. Be careful about swimmimg in piranha or caribe infested rivers. It is a good idea not to swim naked: the Candiru fish can follow urine currents and become lodged in body orifices. Swimwear offers some protection.

Leptospirosis Various forms of leptospirosis occur throughout Latin America, transmitted by a bacterium which is excreted in rodent urine. Fresh water and moist soil harbour the organisms which enter the body through cuts and scratches. If you suffer from any form of prolonged fever consult a doctor.

Snake bites This is a very rare event indeed for travellers. If you are unlucky (or careless) enough to be bitten by a venomous snake, spider, scorpion or sea creature, try to identify the creature, but do not put yourself in further danger. Snake bites are very frightening, but in fact rarely poisonous – even venomous snakes bite without injecting venom.

What you might expect if bitten are: fright, swelling, pain and bruising around the bite and soreness of the regional lymph glands, perhaps nausea, vomiting and a fever. Signs of serious poisoning would be the following symptoms: numbness and tingling of the face, muscular spasms, convulsions, shortness of breath and bleeding. Victims should be got to a hospital or a doctor without delay.

Commercial snake bite and scorpion kits are available, but usually only useful for the specific type of snake or scorpion for which they are designed. Most serum has to be given intravenously so it is not much good equipping yourself with it unless you are used to making injections into veins. It is best to rely on local practice in these cases, because the particular creatures will be known about locally and appropriate treatment can be given.

Treatment of snake bite Reassure and comfort the victim frequently. Immobilise the limb by a bandage or a splint or by getting the person to lie still. Do not slash the bite area and try to suck out the poison because this sort of heroism does more harm than good. If you know how to use a tourniquet in these circumstances, you will not need this advice. If you are not experienced do not apply a tourniquet.

Precautions Avoid walking in snake territory in bare feet or sandals – wear proper shoes or boots. If you encounter a snake stay put until it slithers away, and do not investigate a wounded snake. Spiders and scorpions may be found in the more basic hotels, especially in the Andes. If stung, rest and take plenty of fluids and call a doctor. The best precaution is to keep beds away from the walls and look inside your shoes and under the toilet seat every morning.

Certain **tropical sea fish** when trodden upon inject venom into bathers' feet. This can be exceptionally painful. Wear plastic shoes when you go bathing if such creatures are reported. The pain can be relieved by immersing the foot in extremely hot water for as long as the pain persists.

Dengue fever This is increasing worldwide including in South and Central American countries and the Caribbean. It can be completely prevented by avoiding mosquito bites in the same way as malaria. No vaccine is available. Dengue is an unpleasant and painful disease. Symptoms are a high temperature and body pains, but at least visitors are spared the more serious forms (haemorrhagic types) which are more of a problem for local people who have been exposed to the disease more than once. There is no specific treatment for dengue – just pain killers and rest.

This is a chronic disease, very rarely caught by travellers and difficult to treat. It is transmitted by the simultaneous biting and excreting of the Reduvid bug, also known as the Vinchuca or Barbeiro. Somewhat resembling a small cockroach, this nocturnal bug lives in poor adobe houses with dirt floors often frequented by opossums. If you cannot avoid such accommodation, sleep off the floor with a candle lit, use a mosquito net, keep as much of your skin covered as possible, use DET repellent or a spray insecticide. If you are bitten overnight (the bites are painless) do not scratch them, but wash thoroughly with soap and water.

Chagas' disease (South American Trypanosomiasis)

When you get home

Remember to take your antimalarial tablets for six weeks after leaving the malarial area. If you have had attacks of diarrhoea it is worth having a stool specimen tested in case you have picked up amoebas. If you have been living rough, blood tests may be worthwhile to detect worms and other parasites. If you have been exposed to bilharzia (*schistosomiasis*) by swimming in lakes etc, check by means of a blood test when you get home, but leave it for six weeks because the test is slow to become positive. Report any untowards symptoms to your doctor and tell the doctor exactly where you have been and, if you know, what the likelihood of disease is to which you were exposed.

The above information has been compiled for us by Dr David Snashall, who is presently Senior Lecturer in Occupational Health at the United Medical Schools of Guy's and St Thomas' Hospitals in London and Chief Medical Adviser to the British Foreign and Commonwealth Office. He has travelled extensively in Central and South America, worked in Peru and in East Africa and keeps in close touch with developments in preventative and tropical medicine.

Further reading

Many general books contain information on Peru: *The Cambridge Encylopedia of Latin America and the Caribbean*, edited by Simon Collier, Thomas E Skidmore and Harold Blakemore (2nd edition 1992); *The Penguin History of Latin America*, Edwin Williamson (1992); and *The Discovery of South America*, J H Parry (1979).

There are many periodicals which specialize in Peru: consult a good library for those which cover your particular interest. Consistently interesting is *South American Explorer*, published quarterly by the South American Explorers Club. Also highly recommended is the *Peru Reader* (Stark, Degregori and Kirk, eds, 1995) which, besides literature, also contains history, culture and politics and is an excellent introduction to these topics; the anthology ranges from the precolonial to the present. Anyone interested in the Sapnish conquest should read John Hemming's excellent *The Conquest of the Incas* (1983).

History and culture Other recommended books on Peru's history and culture are: *The Ancient Civilizations of Peru*, J. Alden Mason, (1991); *The Prehispanic Cultures of Peru*, Justo Caceres Macedo (1988); *Chachapoyas; The Cloud People*, Morgan Davis (1988); *The City of Kings: A guide to Lima*, Carolyn Walton (1987) *Lima monumental*, Margarita Cubillas Soriano (1993); *Pyramids of Túcume*, Thor Heyerdahl, Daniel H Sandweiss & Alfredo Narváez (Thames & Hudson, 1995).

Literature A detailed account of Peruvian literature and its finest writers is given in the **Literature** section on page 530. The following novels are also recommended: *The Bridge of San Luis Rey*, Thornton Wilder (Penguin books, 1941); *At Play in the Fields of the Lord*, Peter Matthiessen (1965); *The Vision of Elena Silves*, Nicholas Shakespeare (1989). Two good travel books are: *Cut Stones and Crossroads: a Journey in Peru*, Ronald Wright (Viking, 1984); and *Inca-Kola*, Matthew Parris (1990).

Many sources have been used in the preparation of this survey; special acknowledgement must be given to: James Higgins, *A History of Peruvian Literature* (Liverpool monographs in Hispanic studies 7, 1987); *The Peru Reader*, ed Orin Starn, Carlos Iván Degregori and Robin Kirk (Duke University Press, 1995); Jean Franco, *Spanish American Literature since Independence* (London and New York, 1973); Gerald Martin, *Journeys through the Labyrinth* (London and New York, 1989); Gordon Brotherston, *The Emergence of the Latin American Novel* and *Latin American Poetry* (Cambridge University Press, 1977 and 1975); Darío Villanueva and José María Viña Liste, *Trayectoria de la novela hispanoamericana actual* (Madrid, 1991).

Climbing and trekking *Touching the Void*, Joe Simpson, is an excellent falling off a mountain guide; *Climbing in the Cordillera Blanca*, David Sharman, is an excellent route and general information guide; *The High Andes. A Guide for Climbers*, John Biggar (Castle Douglas, Kirkcudbrightshire; Andes, 1996), contains two chapters on Peru.

Serious walkers are advised to get Hilary Bradt's *Backpacking and Trekking in Peru and Bolivia* (see page 36). *The Peruvian Andes*, by Philipe Béaud, is a good guide, describing 100 climbs and 40 treks in Spanish, French and English. John Richter's *Yurak Yunka* can be obtained from the South American Explorers' Club or from *Lima 2000* bookshop, J Bernal 271, Lima. For an account of the Andean Inca road, see Christopher Portway, *Journey Along the Andes* (Impact Books, London, 1993).

Rafting A recommended read is Joe Kane's *Running the Amazon* (The Bodley Head, 1989); as is *Rafting the Amazon*, Francois Ordendaal. There are a number of magazine articles on rafting in Peru: Kurt Casey, 'Cotahuasi Canyon – an Ultimate Peruvian Adventure', in *American Whitewater* (July/August, 1995); in the same edition is 'Paddling the Inca Trail' by John Foss, an account of runs on the Ríos Colca, Apurímac and Urubamba; by the same author are: 'Diarios de Cotahuasi', in *Caretas* magazine, 6 July 1995; and 'Rio Cotahuasi: the World's Deepest Canyon – Really!' in *South American Explorer*, Spring 1996 edition.

Wildlife and environment Peter Frost et al (Edited by Jim Bartle), *Machu Picchu Historical Sanctuary*, with superb text and photos on all aspects of the Inca Trail and the endangered ecosystem of the sanctuary.

Recommended for bird watchers are: *Birds of the High Andes* (1990) by Nils Krabbe and Jon Fjeldsa, which covers all Peruvian birds that occur above 3,000 metres - a large proportion of the birds likely to be seen in the Andes; *Birds of South America* Volumes 1 & 2 (1989 and 1994), by Robert Ridgely and Guy Tudor, helps tremendously with the passerines (especially volume 2); *A guide to the Birds of Colombia* by Steve Hilty and William Brown (1986), covers the vast majority of the Amazonian species likely to be seen; *An Annotated checklist of Peruvian Birds* by Ted Parker, Susan Parker and Manuel Plenge (1982), is slightly outdated but still useful, it lists all Peruvian birds by habitat type; *The Birds of the Department of Lima* by Maria Koepcke (1983), is useful for the coast.

For the whole period of the Conquest John Hemming's *The Conquest of the Incas* is invaluable; he himself refers us to Ann Kendall's *Everyday Life of the Incas*, Batsford, London, 1978. Also *Oro y tragedia* by Manuel Portal Cabellos, excellent on the division of the empire, civil war, the conquest and *huaqueros*.

Useful addresses

Argentina, Avenida del Libertador 1720; 1425 Capital Federal, T(541)8022000, F(541)8025887. Consulates: Córdoba, La Plata.

Bolivia, Edificio Alianza, Mezanine, Fernando Guachalla y 6 de Agosto, Sopocachi, La Paz, T(5912)353550, F(5912)367640. Consulate: Santa Cruz.

Brazil, Avenida Das Naçes, Lote 43, 70428 900 Brasília DF, T(5561)2429933, F(5561)2435677. Consulates: Rio de Janeiro, So Paulo, Manaus.

Chile, Avenida Andrés Bello 1751, Providencia, Santiago, T(562)2356451, F(562)2358139.

Colombia, Carrera 10 No 93-48, Bogotá, T(571)2189212, F(571)6235102.

Costa Rica, Del Auto Mercado de los Yoses 300 mts, Sur y 75 mts, Oeste, San José, T(506)2259145, F(506)2530457.

Ecuador, Avenida Amazonas No 1429 y Colón, Edificio España. Quito, T(5932)554161, F(5932)562349.

Guatemala, Segunda Avenida 9-67 Zona 9, Guatemala, Guatemala 01009, T(5022)318558, F(5022)343744.

Hong Kong, 10th Floor Wong Chung Ming Commercial House, 16 Wyndham Street, Central Hong Kong, T(852)28682622, F(852)28400733.

Italy, Via Po, 22, 00198 Roma, T(396)8416556, F(396)85354447. Consulate in Milan, Via Giacosa 31; 20127 Milan, T(392)26821276, F(392)26821752.

Japan, 4-4-27 Higashi, Shibuya-Ku, Tokio 150, T(813)34064240, F(813)34097589.

Korea, Namhan Building, Sixth Floor, 76-42 Hannam-Dong, Yongsan-Ku, Se£l, T(822)7935810, F(822)7973736.

Malaysia, Peti Nro. 18, Wisma, Selangor Dredoing, 6th, Floor, South Block 142 – A Jalan Ampang, 50450 Kuala Lumpur, PO Box 18, T(603)2633034/26330, F(603)2633039.

Mexico, Paseo de la Reforma 2601, Lomas Reforma, CP 11020 Mexico DF, T(525)5702443, F(525)2590530.

Singapore, 390, Orchard Road No 12-03, Singapore 0923, Palais Renaissance, T(65)7388595/7388740, F(65)7388601.

South Africa, Infotech Building, Suite 202, 1090 Arcadia Street 0083, Hatfield, Pretoria, T(2712)3422390, F(2712)3424449.

Spain, Principe de Vergara No 36, 5o Derecha, 28001 Madrid, T(341)4314242, 4314424, F(341)5776861. Consulate in Barcelona, Avenida Diagonal Nro 441, Barcelona 08036, T(343)4103833, F(343)4192847.

Uruguay, Soriano 1124, Montevideo, T(5982)921046, F(5982)921194.

Venezuela, Centro Empresarial Andrés Bello, Torre Oeste, Piso 7, Sector Maripérez, Caracas, T(582)7937974, F(582)7936705.

Peruvian Embassies & Consulates

Adventure Travel Centre, 131-135 Earls Court Road, London SW5 9RH. Organizes short tours as well as longer expeditions.

Amazonas Explorer, in Cusco, PO Box 722, T/F(084)236826. In the UK: Riverside, Black Tar, Llangwm, Haverfordwest,Pembs, Wales, SA62 4JD, E info@amazonas- explorer. com, W www.amazonas-explorer.com. Experienced in leading trekking, kayaking, rafting and mountain biking expeditions throughout South America.

Amerindia, Steeple Cottage, Easton, Winchester, Hants SO21 1EH, England, T(44)1962779317, F779458, E pkellie@yachtors.u-net.com. In the USA: 7855 NW 12th Street, Suite 221, Miami, Florida 33126, T(1305)5999008/2472925, F5927060, E tumbaco@gate.net. Standard country tours, as well as customised nature, cultural and adventure tours for groups.

Aracari, Sara Bampfylde, #3, 68 Princes Square, London W2 4NY, T(0171)2299881,

Tours and tour operators

Essentials

F2299883, E postmaster@aracari.com, W www.aracari.com. Regional tours throughout Peru, also 'themed' and activity tours.

Cox & Kings Travel, Gordon House, 10 Greencoat Place, London SW1P 1PH, T(0171)8735001, F6306038, E Cox.Kings@coxkings.sprint.com.

Dragoman Camping/Hotel Adventures, Camp Green, Debenham, Stowmarket, Suffolk IP14 6LA, T(01728)861133, F861127, E aito@dragoman.co.uk, W www.dragoman.co.uk. Overland camping and/or hotel journeys throughout South and Central America.

Encounter Overland, 267 Old Brompton Road, London SW5 9JA, T(0171)3706845, E adventure@encounter.co.uk, W www.encounter.co.uk.

eXito Latin American Travel Specialists, 5699 Miles Avenue, Oakland, CA 94618, USA, T(1)8006554053 (toll free), F(510)6554566, E exito@wonderlink.com.

Exodus Travels, 9 Weir Road, London SW12 0LT, T(0181)6755550, F6730779, E sales@exodustravels.co.uk, W www.exodustravels.co.uk. Experienced in adventure travel, including cultural tours and trekking and biking holidays.

Explore Worldwide, 1 Frederick Street, Aldershot, Hants GU11 1LQ, T(01252)319448, F(01252)343170, E info@explore.co.uk, W www.explore.co.uk. Highly respected operator with offices in Eire, Australia,New Zealand, USA and Canada who run two to five week tours in more than 90 countries worldwide including Peru.

Guerba Expeditions, Wessex House, 40 Station Road, Westbury, Wiltshire BA13 3JN, T(01373)826611, F858351, E info@guerba.demon.co.uk. Specializes in adventure holidays, from canoeing safaris to wilderness camping.

Hayes & Jarvis, 152 King Street, London W6, T(0181)7480088. Long established operator offering tailor-made itineraries as well as packages.

High Places, Globe Works, Penistone Road, Sheffield S6 3AE, T(0114)2757500, F2753870, E highpl.globalnet.co.uk.

International Expeditions, One Environs Park, Helena, AL 35080, USA, T(205)4281700, (1)8006334734 (toll free), F4281714, E amazon.letravel.com,

W www.ietravel.com/intxp. Eight day Amazon voyages, with optional five day extension in the Sacred Valley. In the UK*Wildlife Discovery*, Lesbourne House, South Road, Reigate, Surrey RH2 7JS, T(01737)223903, F241102.

Journey Latin America, 12-13 Heathfield Terrace, Chiswick, London W4 4JE, T(0181)747-8315, E sales@journeylatinamerica.co.uk. The world's leading tailor-made specialist for Latin America, running escorted tours throughout the region, they also offer a wide range of flight options.

KE adventure Travel, 32 Lake Road, Keswick, Cumbria CA12 5DQ, T(017687)73966, F74693, E keadventure@enterprise.net, W www.keadventures.com. Specialist in adventure tours, including three-week cycling trips in and around Cusco.

Ladatco Tours, T USA (305)8548422 or F(305)2850504. Based in Miami, run 'themed' explorer tours based around the Incas, mysticism etc.

Last Frontiers, Fleet Marston Farm, Aylesbury, Buckinghamshire HP18 0PZ, T(01296)658650, F(01296)658651, E epaine@lastfrontiers.co.uk, W http://www. lastfrontiers.co.uk. South American specialists offering tailor-made itineraries as well as discounted air fares and air passes.

Lost World Adventures, 112 Church Street, Decatur, GA 30030, T(800)999 0558, E info@lostworldadventures.com. In Peru *Viracocha Turismo*, Av Vasco Nunnex de Balboa 191, Miraflores, Lima, T445 3986, F447 9074. Cultural and mystical tours. Also hiking, rafting, birdwatching for the outdoor types.

Naturetrek, Chautara, Bighton, Alresford, Hants, SO24 9RB, T(01962)733051, F736426/733368, E sales@naturetrek.co.uk, W www.naturetrek.co.uk. Birdwatching tours throughout the continent, also botany, natural history tours, treks and cruises.

Nomadic Thoughts, 23 Hopefield Ave, London NW6 6LJ, T(0181)9601001, F960-1006. Specialize in tailor-made itineraries.

South American Experience, 47 Causton Street, Pimlico, London SW1P 4AT, T(0171)976 5511, F976 6908. Apart from booking flights and accommodation, also

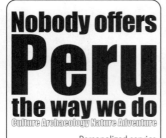

offer tailor-made trips.

South American Tours, Hanauer Landstrasse 208-216, D-60314, Germany, T(0049) 6940 58970, F (0049) 694 40432, E sat.fra@t-online.de. For holidays, business travel, or special packages. Has own office in San Isidro, Lima.

Sol International, 13780 SW 56 Street, Suite 107, Miami, Fl 33175, T(800)766-5657, F(305)382-9284, E solint@cwixmail.com. Offers personalized service to provide custom itineraries to suit all budgets.

STA Travel, Priory House, 6 Wrights Lane, London W8 6TA, T(0171)3616100, F9389570, W www.statravel.co.uk.

Tambo Tours, PO Box 60541, Houston, Texas 77205, USA, T1-888-246-7378, E tambo@ tambotours.com. Customized trips to the Amazon and archaeological sites of Peru for groups and individuals . Daily departures.

Trailfinders, 48 Earl's Court Road, London W8 6EJ, T(0171)9383366.

Tucan/The Imaginative Traveller, 14 Barley Mow Passage, London W4 4PH, UK, F(0181)7423045, E info@imaginative-traveller.com, W imaginative-traveller. com. Offer adventure tours and overland expeditions.

Wildland Adventures, 3516 NE 155 Street, Seattle, WA 98155, USA, T(800)345 4453, F(800)365 0686, E info@wildland.com, http://www.wildland.com. Specializes in cultural and natural history tours to the Andes and Amazon.

Useful Websites **Destinations**
Arequipa: www.interplace.com.pe/aqpweb; www.aqplink.com/; www.andys.com/peru5.html; www.tardis.de.ac.uk/~angus/Gallery/Photos/SouthAmerica/Peru/index.html
Cusco: csweb.sxu.edu/van/picts/peru.html; www.cbc.org.pe/CMUNDO.HTM; www.tardis.de.ac.uk/~angus/Gallery/Photos/SouthAmerica/Peru/index.htm; expedia.msn.com/daily/fullcircle/peru/best-things.htm
Machu Picchu: fox.nstn.ca/~nstn/833/machupg.html; expedia.msn.com/daily/fullcircle/peru/best-things.htm
Machu Picchu Library: geog.gmu.edu/gess/classes/students/studgeog411/miked/library.html
Inca trail: www.tardis.de.ac.uk/~angus/Gallery/Photos/SouthAmerica/Peru/IncaTrail.html
Maratón Camino Inca: ekeko.rcp.net.pe/maraton
Manu: vif27.icair.ica.org.nz/Locations/contents.htm
ekeko.rcp.net.pe/MANU/6.htm
Nasca lines: ekeko.rcp.net.pe/turifaxf/nasca/index.htm
www.magicperu.com/MariaReiche
Puno/Lake Titicaca: www.incacorp.com/taquile
www.andrys.com/indox.html
vif27.icair.iac.org.nz/gallery/inca.htm
www.tardis.de.ac.uk/~angus/Gallery/Photos/SouthAmerica/Peru/index.html
Trujillo: www.unitru.edu.pe
Ecotourism
Señal Verde: www.geocities.com/RainForest/Vines/9624/index.htm
Folklore
Cultures of the Andes: www.best.com/%7Egibbons
Quechua: www.best.com/%7Egibbons
www.nalejandria.com/00/rol/katia/cursoque.htm
Textiles: www.rain.org/~pjenkin/civiliz/civiliza.html
Gastronomy
Cevichería Virtual: www.geocities.com/TheTropics/4100/
Cocina Internacional con Sabor Peruano: ekeko.rcp.net.pe/cocina/index.htm
Perú Gourmet: ekeko.rcp.net.pe/per.gourmet/PERUG.HTM

Lima

3

Lima

92 Ins and outs

94 History

96 Central Lima

108 Beaches & Suburbs

108 San Isidro

109 Miraflores

109 Barranco

110 Callao

111 Sleeping

116 Eating

120 Bars & nightclubs

121 Entertainment

122 Festivals

122 Shopping

125 Sport

127 Transport

130 Directory

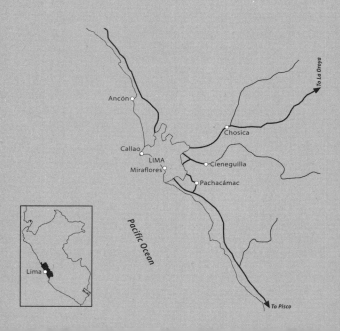

The well-established cliché is to call Lima a city of contradictions, but it's difficult to get beyond that description. Here you'll encounter grinding poverty and conspicuous wealth in abundance. The eight million inhabitants of this great, sprawling metropolis will defend it to the hills and, in their next breath, tell you everything that's wrong with it. If the grim squalour of the poorer districts and constant begging of street children gets too much at least the visitor has the option of heading for Miraflores or San Isidro, whose chic shops, bars and restaurants would grace any major European city.

Lima's image as a place to avoid or quickly pass through is enhanced by the thick grey blanket of cloud that descends in May and hangs around for the next seven months, seemingly perched on top of the many skyscrapers. Wait until the blanket is pulled aside in November to reveal bright blue skies and the visitor would see a very different place. This is beach weather for all Limeños, when weekends become a very crowded raucous mix of sun, sea, salsa and ceviche at the city's more popular coastal resorts.

While Lima has the ability to incite frustration, fear and despair in equal measure it can also, given the chance, entertain, excite and inform. It boasts some of the finest museums and historical monuments in the country and the best cuisine and nightlife. Scratch beneath that coating of grime and decay and you'll find one of the most vibrant and hospitable cities anywhere.

Ins and outs

Climate
Only 12° south of the equator, you would expect a tropical climate, but Lima has two distinct seasons. The winter is from May to November, when a damp *garúa* (sea mist) hangs over the city, making everything look greyer than it is already. It is damp and cold, 8° to 15°C. The sun breaks through around November and temperatures rise as high as 30°C. Note that the temperature in the coastal suburbs is lower than the centre because of the sea's influence. You should protect yourself against the sun's rays when visiting the beaches around Lima, or elsewhere in Peru.

Getting there
For fuller details see under transport, page 127

All international flights land at Jorge Chávez Airport, some 16 kilometres northeast of the centre of Lima. It is a little further to Miraflores and Barranco. Transport into town is easy if a bit expensive. A cheaper option which involves some effort after a long flight, is to take a taxi into town from outside the airport perimeter fence.

If you are arriving by bus, most of the recommended companies have their terminals a little to the south of the centre of Avda Carlos Zavala and Jr Montevideo. In theory it is possible to walk to your hotel but this is a dangerous area and you should take a taxi. The train station is at the back of the Río Rímac, some 200 metres from the cathedral. Most of the hotels are to the west.

Getting around
Lima is not really a city that can be visited on foot although the central hotels are fairly close to the main sites. Miraflores is about 5 kilometres south of the centre. Many of the better hotels and restaurants are located here and in neighbouring San Isidro. Transport between the centre and suburbs is not a problem.

Bus: the Lima public transportation system, at first glance very intimidating, is actually quite good. There are three different types of vehicles that will stop whenever

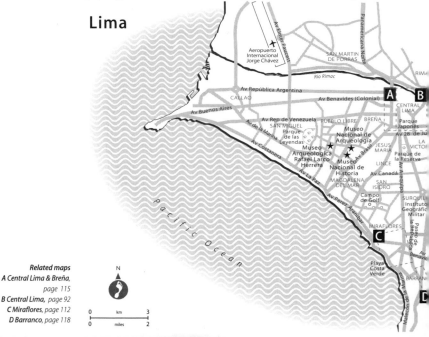

Lima

Related maps
A Central Lima & Breña,
page 115
B Central Lima, page 92
C Miraflores, page 112
D Barranco, page 118

N

0   km   3
0   miles   2

flagged down: buses, *combis*, and *colectivos*. They can be distinguished by size; big and long, mid-size and mini-vans, respectively. Fare for most buses is US$0.30 while *combis* and *colectivos* charge US$0.35. **NB** On public holidays, Sundays and from 2400 to 0500 every night, a small charge is added to the fare. Always try to pay with change to avoid hassles, delays and dirty looks from the *cobrador* (driver's assistant). **NB** Routes on any public transportation vehicle are posted on *windshields* with coloured stickers. Destinations written on the side of any vehicle should be ignored.

Buses between Lima centre and Miraflores: Avda Arequipa runs 52 blocks between the downtown Lima area and Parque Kennedy in Miraflores. There is no shortage of public transport on this avenue. When heading towards downtown from Miraflores the window sticker should say "Wilson/Tacna". To get to Parque Kennedy from downtown look on the windshield for "Larco/Schell/Miraflores," "Chorrillos/ Huaylas" or "Barranco/Ayacucho".

Via Expresa: Lima's only urban freeway runs from Plaza Grau in the centre of town, to the northern tip of the district of Barranco. This six lane thoroughfare, locally known as *El Zanjón* (the Ditch), with a separate bus lane in the middle is by far the fastest way to cross the city. In order from Plaza Grau the 8 stops are: 1) Avda Mexico; 2) Avda Canada; 3) Avda Javier Prado; 4) Corpac; 5) Avda Aramburu; 6) Avda Angamos; 7) Avda Ricardo Palma, for Parque Kennedy; 8) Avda Benevides. Buses in the centre for the *Via Expresa* can be caught at Avda Tacna, Avda Wilson (Garsilaso de la Vega), Avda Bolivia and Avda Alfonso Ugarte. These buses when full, are of great interest to highly skilled pickpockets who sometimes work in groups. If you're standing in the aisle be extra careful.

Taxi Colectivos: regular automobiles make this a faster, more comfortable option than normal public transportation. There are only 3 routes: 1) back and forth between all of Avda Arequipa and Avda Tacna; 2) starting at Plaza San Martín going through Callao; 3) *Via Expresa* to Chorrillos, picked up in between the Sheraton Hotel and Plaza Grau. Look for the coloured sticker posted on the windshield. These cars will stop at any time to pick people up. When full (usually 5 or 6 passengers) they will only stop for someone getting off, then the process begins again to fill the empty space.

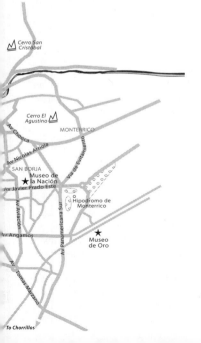

Taxis: to drive a taxi in Lima, or for that matter, anywhere in Peru, simply requires a windshield sticker that says "Taxi". Meters are not used, therefore the fare should be agreed upon before you get in. Tips are not expected. The cheapest option is always the VW Bug/Beetle but they, more often than not, are on the verge of falling apart. The South Korean company Daewoo introduced their model 'Tico' a few years back which quickly replaced the VW Bug as the taxi of choice. They are quick and clean but most importantly, they have seatbelts that work. However it's still rare to find a driver who actually *uses* his.

The following are taxi fares for some of the more common routes, give or take a sol. From downtown Lima to: Parque Kennedy (Miraflores), US$2.10. Gold Museum, US$2.50. Museo de la Nacion, US$1.75. South

Impressions of Lima

Ever since the earthquake of 1746 all but razed the city to the ground, descriptions of Lima have tended towards the unfavourable.

Take the German naturalist and traveller, Alexander Von Humboldt, for instance, who considered life in the city to be tedious with few diversions and described driving round the capital in 1802 thus: "the filthyness of the streets, strewn with dead dogs and donkeys, and the unevenness of the ground make it impossible to enjoy." Charles Darwin, who made a short visit in 1839 during his historic research trip on the Beagle, was no less graphic in his appraisal. He found it "in a wretched state of decay; the streets are nearly unpaved and heaps of filth are piled up in all directions where black vultures pick up bits of carrion."

Rather more complimentary was Jean Jacques Tschudi, the Swiss naturalist who made extensive explorations in Peru. He wrote: "The impression produced at first sight of Lima is by no means favourable,

for the periphery, the quarter which the stranger first enters, contains none but old, dilapidated and dirty homes; but on approaching the vicinity of the principal square, the place improves so greatly that the miserable appearance it presents at first sight is easily forgotten."

The French feminist, Flora Tristan, who was Paul Gauguin's grandmother, came to Peru in 1834. She travelled extensively in the country and wrote a fascinating account of her experience, 'Peregrinations of a Pariah', in which she painted Lima in a most favourable light: "The city has many beautiful monuments", she wrote, "The homes are neatly constructed, the streets well marked out, are long and wide." Paul Gauguin himself spent his early formative years in Lima, where he was brought by his parents who were fleeing Napoleon Bonaparte's France. Towards the end of his life Gauguin wrote a collection of memoirs in which he included his impressions of Lima.

American Explorers Club, US$1.25. Archaeology Museum, US$1.60. Immigration, US$1.25. From Miraflores (Parque Kennedy) to: Gold Museum, US$2.10. Museo de la Nacion, US$1.75. South American Explorers Club, US$2.50. Archaeology Museum, US$2.65. Immigration, US$2.50. For prices to and from the airport, see **Touching down** (page 33).

Official taxi companies, registered with the Municipality of Lima are without a doubt the safest option but cost much more than just picking one up in the street. Hourly rates possible: Taxi Real, T4706263. Taxi Seguro, T4387210. Moli Taxi, T4790030. Taxi Phono, T4226565 Willy (Alfonso) Garcia, T/F4527456 (cellular 9755871). Fluent English, frequently contracted by foreign tour agencies, US$10 hourly. Highly recommended.

History

Lima, originally named *La Ciudad de Los Reyes*, The City of Kings, in honour of the Magi, was founded on Epiphany in 1535 by Francisco Pizarro. From then until the independence of the South American republics in the early 19th century, it was the chief city of Spanish South America. The name Lima, a corruption of the Quechua name *Rimac* (speaker), was not adopted until the end of the 16th century.

At the time of the Conquest, Lima was already an important commercial centre. It continued to grow throughout the colonial years and by 1610, the population was 26,000, of whom 10,000 were Spaniards. This was the time of greatest prosperity. The commercial centre of the city was just off the Plaza de

Armas in the Calle de Mercaderes (first block of Jr de la Unión) and was full of merchandise imported from Spain, Mexico and China. All the goods from the mother country arrived at the port of Callao, from where they were distributed all over Peru and as far away as Argentina.

At this time South American trade with Spain was controlled by a monopoly of Sevillian merchants and their Limeño counterparts who profited considerably. It wasn't until the end of the 18th century that free trade was established between Spain and her colonies, allowing Peru to enjoy a period of relative wealth. Much of this wealth was reinvested in the country, particularly in Lima where educational establishments benefitted most of all.

Ever since **Francis Drake** made a surprise attack on Callao on the night of 13 February 1579, plans were made to strengthen the city's defences against the threat from English pirates. However, an argument raged over the following century between Spain and Lima as to what form the defences should take and who should pay. Finally, it was agreed to encircle the city with a wall, which was completed by 1687.

Life for the white descendants of the Spaniards was good, although *criollos* (Spaniards born in the colonies) were not allowed to hold public office in Peru. The Indians and those of mixed blood were treated as lesser citizens. Their movements were strictly controlled. They weren't allowed to live in the city centre; only in areas allocated to them, referred to as *reducciones*.

Earthquakes and wars

There were few cities in the Old World that could rival Lima's wealth and luxury, until the terrible earthquake of 1746. The city's notable elegance was instantly reduced to dust. Only 20 of the 3,000 houses were left standing and an estimated 4,000 people were killed. Despite the efforts of the Viceroy, José Manso de Velasco, to rebuild the city, Lima never recovered her former glory.

During the 19th century man-made disasters rather than natural ones wreaked havoc on the capital and its people. The population dropped from 87,000 in 1810 to 53,000 in 1842, after the wars of Independence, and the city suffered considerable material damage during the Chilean occupation which followed the War of the Pacific.

Towards the 20th century

Lima was built on both banks of the Rimac river. The walls erected at the end of the 17th century surrounded three sides while the Rimac bordered the fourth. By the time the North American railway engineer, Henry Meiggs, was contracted to demolish the city walls in 1870, Lima had already begun to spread outside the original limits. Meiggs reneged on his contract by leaving much of the wall intact in the poor area around Cercado, where the ruins can still be seen.

By the beginning of the 20th century the population had risen to 140,000 and the movement of people to the coastal areas meant that unskilled cheap labour was available to man the increasing numbers of factories. Around this time, major improvements were made to the city's infrastructure in the shape of modern sanitation, paved streets, new markets and plazas. For the entertainment of the burgeoning middle classes, a modern race track was opened in what is now the Campo de Marte, as well as the municipal theatre, the Teatro Segura. At the same time, the incumbent president, José Pardo, dramatically increased government expenditure on education, particularly in Lima.

Large-scale municipal improvements continued under the dictatorship of Augusto Leguía and the presidency of Oscar Benavides, who focussed on education for the masses, housing facilities for workers and low cost restaurants in the slum areas which were now growing up around Lima.

Street names

Several blocks, with their own names, make up a long street, a jirón (often abbreviated to Jr). The visitor is greatly helped by the corner signs which bear both names, of the jirón and the name of the block. The new and old names of streets are used interchangeably: remember that Colmena is also Nicolás de Piérola, Wilson is Inca Garcilaso de la Vega, and Carabaya is also Augusto N Wiese.

Modern Lima

Lima (*Phone code*: 01) continues to struggle to live up to its former reputation as the City of Kings. It is now very dirty and seriously affected by smog for much of the year, and is surrounded by 'Pueblos Jóvenes', or shanty settlements of squatters who have migrated from the Sierra. Villa El Salvador, a few miles southeast of Lima, may be the world's biggest 'squatters' camp' with 350,000 people building up an award-winning self-governing community since 1971. They pay no taxes to the government but when a school is built the government will pay for the roof.

Over the years the city has changed out of recognition. Many of the hotels and larger business houses have moved to the fashionable seaside suburbs of Miraflores and San Isidro, thus moving the commercial heart of the city away from the Plaza de Armas. Amidst the traditional buildings which still survive soar many skyscrapers which have changed the old skyline.

Half of the town-dwellers of Peru now live in Lima. The metropolitan area contains eight million people, nearly one third of the country's total population, and two-thirds of its industries.

Sights in Central Lima

When Alberto Andrade Carmona became Mayor of Lima in 1995, he began a campaign to return the historical centre to its original beauty. This meant ejecting the *ambulantes* (street sellers), constant cleaning of the streets and sidewalks, and full rehabilitation of the Plaza de Armas and Plaza San Martín. He also mounted a security force called *Serenazgo* to enforce public safety and order. These men are easily recognizable by their dark blue jump-suits, long night sticks, and riot gear. The municipality of Lima has also begun a costly and tedious balcony restoration project, soliciting businesses and citizens to take on the financial responsibility of a balcony in need. Although many buildings in the centre are not maintained, their architectural beauty and importance is still quite visible and well worth seeing.

Plaza de Armas

One block south of the Río Rímac lies the Plaza de Armas, which has been declared a World Heritage by Unesco. The plaza used to be the city's most popular meeting point and main market. Before the building of the Acho bullring in the 1760s, bullfights were traditionally held here.

Around the great Plaza de Armas stand the **Palacio de Gobierno**, the **Cathedral**, the **Archbishop's Palace**, the **Municipalidad** and the **Club Unión**. In the centre of the plaza is a bronze fountain dating from 1650.

Palacio de Gobierno Palacio de Gobierno (Government Palace), on the north side of the Plaza, stands on the site of the original palace built by Pizarro. When the Viceroyalty was founded it became the official residence of the representative of the crown. Despite the opulent furnishings inside, the exterior remained a poor sight throughout colonial times, with shops lining the front facing the plaza. The façade was remodelled in the second half of the 19th century, then transformed in 1921, following a terrible fire. In 1937, the palace was totally rebuilt.

The changing of the guard is at 1200. Any tour agency can offer a tour of the Palace by submitting a formal request. It must be organized a few days ahead of time. Tours by appointment, contac Sheila Cuadros, at the department of public relations in the palace, T4615922 (home). ■ Cost US$20 per person.

The Cathedral stands on the site of two previous buildings. The first, finished **The Cathedral** in 1555, was partly paid for by Francisca Pizarro on the condition that her father, the *Conquistador*, was buried there. A larger church, however, was soon required to complement the city's status as an Archbishopric. In 1625, the three naves of the main building were completed while work continued on the towers and main door. The new building was reduced to rubble in the earthquake of 1746 and the existing church, completed in 1755, is a reconstruction on the lines of the original.

The interior is immediately impressive, with its massive columns and high nave. Also of note are the splendidly carved stalls (mid-17th century), the silver-covered altars surrounded by fine woodwork, mosaic-covered walls bearing the coats of arms of Lima and Pizarro and an allegory of Pizarro's commanders, the 'Thirteen Men of Isla del Gallo'. The assumed remains of Francisco Pizarro lie in a small chapel, the first on the right of the entrance, in a glass coffin, though later research indicates that they reside in the crypt.

There is a **Museo de Arte Religioso** in the cathedral, with free guided tours (English available, give tip), ask to see the picture restoration room. ■ *The cathedral is open to visitors Monday-Saturday 1000, 1300 and 1500-1700. All-inclusive entrance ticket is US$2, students US$1. A recommended guide for the Cathedral is Patricia Cerrillo, T5424019, English/German/French. Also Julio Torres, T4756044.*

Next to the cathedral is the **Archbishop's Palace**, rebuilt in 1924, with a **Archibishop's** superb wooden balcony. **The Municipalidad de Lima** holds art exhibits in its **Palace &** gallery; T4276080 ext 510. Just behind the Municipalidad is **Pasaje Ribera el** **Municipalidad** **Viejo**, which has been restored and now is a pleasant place to hang out with several good cafés with huge terraces.

Around the centre

The Jr de La Unión, the main shopping street, runs to the Plaza de Armas. It has been converted into a pedestrian precinct which teems with life in the evening. In the two blocks south of Jr Unión, known as Calle Belén, several shops sell souvenirs and curios. The shops nearer to the best hotels are more expensive.

From the plaza, passing the Government Palace on the left, straight ahead is the **Desamparados** Station of the Central Railway. The name, which means "the helpless ones", comes from the orphanage and church that used to be nearby.

The Puente de Piedra, behind the Palacio de Gobierno is a Roman-style stone bridge built in 1610. Until about 1870 it was the only bridge strong enough to take carriages across the river Rímac to the district of the same name. Though this part of the city enjoyed considerable popularity in Colonial times, it could no longer be considered fashionable.

Lima

Lima Centre

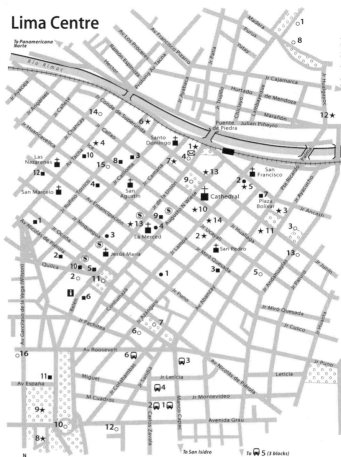

Lima

N

0 metres 100
0 yards 109

Related maps
Central Lima & Breña,
page 115

■ **Sleeping**
1. Crillón
2. Familia Rodríguez
3. Gran Hotel Savoy
4. Granada
5. Grand Bolivar
6. Hostal Belén
7. Hostal España
8. Hostal Roma
9. Hostal San Martín & El Plaza
10. Pensión Ibarra
11. Sheraton

● **Eating**
1. Heydi
2. Machu Picchu
3. Natur
4. Raimondi

🚌 **Buses**
1. Buses to Pisco, Ica & Nasca
2. Civa & Mariscal Cáceres
3. Movil Tours
4. Ormeño
5. Transportes León de Huánuco
6. Transportes Rodríguez

★ **Sights**
1. Casa Aliaga
2. Casa de la Rada & L'Eau Vive restaurant
3. Casa de Las Trece Monedas
4. Casa La Riva
5. Casa Pilatos / Casa de Cultura
6. Casa de Oquendo

7. Municipalidad de Lima
8. Museo de Arte
9. Museo de Arte Italiano
10. Museo Banco Central de la Reserva
11. Museo del Tribunal de la Santa Inquisición
12. Museo Taurino/Plaza de Acho
13. Palacio de Gobierno
14. Palacio de Torre Tagle

○ **Others**
1. Alameda de Los Descalzos & Convento de Los Descalzos
2. American Express, Lima Tours
3. Congress

4. Correo Central and Museum
5. Mercado Central
6. Panteón de los Próceres & Old Universidad de San Marcos
7. Parque Universitario
8. Paseo de Aguas
9. Plaza de Armas
10. Plaza Grau
11. Plaza San Martín
12. Polvos Azules
13. Santo Tomas School
14. Santuario de Santa Rosa
15. Teatro Municipal & Teatro AAA
16. US Embassy

A fashion for passion

A unique form of women's dress worn by Lima's upper class mestizas – women born in the colonies of Spanish origin – in the 18th century was the saya and manto. Both were of Moorish origin. The saya was an overskirt of dark silk, worn tight at the waist with either a narrow or wide bottom. The manto was like a thick, black veil fastened by a band at the back of the waist where it joined the saya. It was brought over the shoulders and head and drawn over the face so closely that only a small, triangular space was left uncovered, sufficient for one eye to peep through. This earned them the title Las Tapadas, or "covered ones".

The fashion was created by Lima's mestizas in order to compete in the flirting stakes with their Spanish-born counterparts, whose tiny waists and coquettish fan-waving was turning men's heads. The tapadas, though veiled, were by no means modest. Their skirts were daringly short, revealing their appealingly tiny feet, and necklines plunged to scandalously low levels. The French feminist, Flora Tristan, was much taken with this brazen show. She commented: "I am sure it needs little imagination to appreciate the consequences of this time-honoured practice."

One consequence of this fashion, which ensured anonymity, was that Lima's mestizas could freely indulge in romantic trysts with their lovers. Often, however, they were content with some playful flirting – sometimes with their unwitting husbands. Another consequence of their anonymity was political. Many tapadas used their afternoon strolls to pass notes and messages to the organizers of the independence movement. This romantic and political intrigue usually took place on the Paseo de Aguas, a popular walkway of pools and gardens built by the Viceroy.

"Tapado con saya y manto" (After a Bonnafé lithograph)

Lima

The **Alameda de los Descalzos** was designed in the early 17th century as a restful place to stroll and soon became one of the most popular meeting places. People of all social classes would gather here for their Sunday walk, some up to the cross at the top of **Cerro San Cristóbal**. Travellers today would be ill-advised to follow in their footsteps as this can be a dangerous area to wander around alone. Worth visiting on the Alameda de los Descalzos, though, is the **Convento de los Descalzos** (see under **Churches** below). Near the Alameda is the **Paseo de Aguas**, which was also popular for a Sunday stroll in days gone by.

On Jr Hualgayoc is the bullring in the **Plaza de Acho**, famous for once being the largest in the world and the first in the Spanish America, inaugurated on 20 January 1766. Limeños have always been great enthusiasts of bullfighting and in 1798 a royal decree had to be passed forbidding fights on Sundays as people were failing to attend mass. Next to the bullring is the **Museo Taurino** (see Museums below).

July is the month when the most famous fighters come from Spain for the *Fiestas Patrias*. The season is also from October to the first week of December. Famous *toreros* practise in the Lima ring, the oldest in the Americas, and fighting bulls are of Spanish stock.

Wedged between Avda Abancay and Jr Ayacucho is **Plaza Bolívar**, from where General José de San Martín proclaimed Peru's independence. The plaza is dominated by the equestrian statue of the Liberator. Behind lies the Congress building which occupies the former site of the **Universidad de San Marcos**, the first University in the Americas. Founded by the Dominicans in 1551, students first began to use this building in 1574. The University now occupies other premises away from the city centre.

The newer parts of the city are based on **Plaza San Martín**, south of Jr de la Unión, with a statue of San Martín in the centre. The plaza has been restored and is now a nice place to sit and relax. One and a quarter kilometres west is the **Plaza Dos de Mayo**. About one kilometre due south of this again is the circular **Plaza Bolognesi**, from which many major *avenidas* radiate.

Barrio Chino   Behind the Congress, next to the *Mercado Central* or Central Market, it is Lima's Chinatown, or *barrio chino*, located within the district of Barrios Altos.

Peru is home to the largest population of first-generation Chinese in all of Latin America. The current statistic stands at around 200,000. Some of the first immigrants arrived at the port of Callao in 1849 from the Chinese provinces of Canton and Fukien to work the coastal fields, replacing the black slaves given their freedom by then-president Ramón Castilla in 1851. More Chinese began to arrive, settling in the north; Chiclayo, Trujillo and the jungle town of Iquitos. Chinese people, born in Peru (referred to as "Tu-San") adds up to more than 1,000,000.

On the seventh block of Jr Ucalayi is the locally famous *Portada China*, the arch that stretches across the street and is the gateway to Chinatown. It was a gift from the Chinese government officially inaugurated by Lima mayor Alberto Andrade in July of 1997. The temple of Kuan Kong, at Jr Huanta 962, was built more than 140 years ago to honour the mythical Chinese warrior of the same name. Mystical consultations on love, careers and health are offered by Sr Germán Ku; by pre-arranged visits only (T4263759), a donation of US$7 is requested, open 0900-1300 and 1500-1800. For authentic Chinese cuisine, see Eating in Central Lima, on page 118).

Colonial Mansions

At Jr Ucayali 363, is the **Palacio Torre Tagle**, the city's best surviving specimen of secular colonial architecture. It was built in 1735 for Don José Bernardo de Tagle y Bracho, to whom King Philip V gave the title of First Marquis of Torre Tagle. The house remained in the family until it was acquired by the government in 1918. Today, it is still used by the Foreign Ministry, but visitors are allowed to enter courtyards to inspect the fine, Moorish-influenced wood-carving in balconies, wrought iron work, and a 16th-century coach complete with commode. ■*During working hours, Monday-Friday, visitors may enter the patio only.*

Another historic mansion worth visiting is the late 16th century **Casa de Jarava** or **Pilatos** opposite the San Francisco church, Jr Ancash 390. **Casa La Riva**, on Jr Ica 426, has an 18th century porch and balconies, a small gallery with some 20th century paintings. It is run by the Entre Nous Society. **Casa de Oquendo** or **Osambela** is at Conde de Superunda 298. It is said that José de San Martín stayed here after proclaiming independence from Spain. The house is typical of Lima secular architecture with two patios and a broad staircase leading from the first to the upper floor.

Casa Negreiros, at Jr Azángaro 532, once belonged to Don José Balta, one time president of Peru. The patio with Ionic columns is one of the best Neoclassical examples of its type in Lima. **Casa de las Trece Monedas** at Jr Ancash 536 was built in 1787 by Counts from Genoa, it still has the original doors and window grills.

Casa Aliaga, Unión 224, is still occupied by the Aliaga family but has been opened to the public. The house contains what is said to be the oldest ceiling in Lima and is furnished entirely in the colonial style. Don Jerónimo de Aliaga was one of the 13 commanders to arrive with Francisco Pizarro, and all 13 were given land around the main square to build their own houses when Lima was founded in 1535.

Casa Barbieri, Jr Callao, near Jr Rufino Torrico – is a fine old 18th-century town house in the Sevillian style. Ring the bell in the entrance hall for permission to look at the patios. **Casa Museo Prado**, Jr Cusco 448, visitable when Sr Prado is in residence, is a beautifully maintained house with early 19th-century front and, apparently, a 17th-century patio. **Casa de Riva Agüero**, Jr Camaná 457, has the library and archives of the Universidad Católica on the first floor; the second floor has a small folk art museum. A special appointment is needed to visit the rest of the house.

AAA Theatre (Amateur Artists' Association), Jr Ica 323, is in a lovely 18th-century house with an *azaguán*, a covered area between the door and patio, a common feature in houses of this period. **Casa de la Rada**, or **Goyoneche**, Jr Ucayali 358, opposite Palacio Torre Tagle, is an extremely fine mid-18th century town house in the French manner which now belongs to a bank. ■*The patio and first reception room are open occasionally to the public.*

Churches

Church and Monastery are in Plazuela de la Merced, Unión y Huancavelica. **La Merced** The first mass in Lima was said here on the site of the first church to be built. At independence the Virgin of La Merced was made a Marshal of the Peruvian army. The restored colonial façade is a fine example of Baroque architecture. Inside are some magnificent altars and the choir stalls and the vestry's panelled ceiling are also noteworthy. A door from the right of the nave leads into the Monastery where you can see some 18th century religious paintings in the sacristy. The cloister dates from 1546. ■*Open 0800-1200, 1600-2000 every day and its monastery 0800-1200 and 1500-1730 daily.*

Church and Monastery is on the first block of Jr Camaná. Built in 1549, the **Santo Domingo** church is still as originally planned with a nave and two aisles covered by a vaulted ceiling, though the present ceiling dates from the 17th century. The cloister is one of the most attractive in the city and dates from 1603. The second cloister is much less elaborate. A chapel, dedicated to San Martín de Porres, one of Peru's most revered saints, leads off from a side corridor. Between the two cloisters is the Chapter House (1730), which was once the premises of the Universidad de San Marcos. Beneath the sacristy are the tombs of San Martín de Porres and Santa Rosa de Lima (see below). In 1669, Pope Clement presented the alabaster statue of Santa Rosa in front of the altar. ■ *Open 0900-1230, 1500-1800 Monday-Saturday; Sunday and holidays, mornings only. Entrance US$0.75. Basilica de La Veracruz is open lunchtimes. The main hall has some interesting relics.*

San Francisco Church and Monastery, stand on the first block of Jr Lampa, corner of Ancash. The baroque church, which was finished in 1674, was one of the few edifices to withstand the 1746 earthquake. The nave and aisles are lavishly decorated in the Moorish, or Mudejar, style. The choir, which dates from 1673, is notable for its beautifully-carved seats in Nicaraguan hardwood and its Mudejar ceiling. There is a valuable collection of paintings by the Spanish artist, Francisco de Zuburán (1598-1664) which depict the apostles and various saints.

The monastery is famous for the Sevillian tilework and panelled ceiling in the cloisters (1620). The 17th century *retablos* in the main cloister are carved from cedar and represent scenes from the life of San Francisco, as do the paintings. A broad staircase leading down to a smaller cloister is covered by a remarkable carved wooden dome dating from 1625. Next to this smaller cloister is the Capilla de la Soledad where a café is open to the public. The Catacombs under the church and part of the monastery are well worth seeing. This is where an estimated 25,000 Limeños were buried before the main cemetery was opened in 1808. ■ *T4271381. Open daily 0700-1730. Entrance US$1.75, US$0.50 children, guided tours only. A recommended English-speaking guide is José García.*

San Pedro San Pedro Church and Monastery is on the third block of Jr Ucayali. The church, finished by Jesuits in 1638, has an unadorned façade, different from any other in the city. In one of the massive towers hangs a five tonne bell called *La Abuelita* (the grandmother), first rung in 1590, which sounded the Declaration of Independence in 1821. The contrast between the sober exterior and sumptuous interior couldn't be more striking. The altars are marvellous, in particular the high altar, attributed to the skilled craftsman, Matias Maestro. The church also boasts Moorish-style balconies and rich, gilded wood carvings in the choir and vestry, all tiled throughout. The most important paintings in the church are hung near the main entrance.

In the monastery, the sacristy is a beautiful example of 17th century architecture. Also of note are La Capilla de Nuestra Señora de la O and the penitentiary. Several Viceroys are buried below. ■ *Open Monday-Saturday 1100-1700.*

Santuario de Santuario de Santa Rosa is on Avda Tacna, first block. Santa Rosa is the first
Santa Rosa Saint of the Americas and Patron Saint of Lima. Born on 20 April 1586, Rosa of Lima became a member of the third Order of St Dominic and established an infirmary for destitute children and old people in her family home. She died at the age of 31 on 23 August 1617 and was beatified on 16 December 1668. 30 August is her day.

The small but graceful church was built in 1728 and contains the 'Little Doctor' image of Jesus who helped Rosa cure the sick. Beyond the church is a sanctuary where she was born and lived. There is a tiny room where she would allow herself only two hours' sleep each night on a bed of two tree trunks with stones as pillows. A chapel was later built on the site.

The hermitage in the garden was built by Rosa herself and she would retire there to pray alone. The well, into which she threw the key to the padlocked chain around her waist, now receives petitions from the faithful for forgiveness and thanksgivings. ■ *Open 0900-1230 and 1530-1800 daily. Entrance to the grounds is free.*

Las Nazarenas The 18th century Las Nazarenas Church, on Avda Tacna, fourth block, was
Church built around an image of Christ Crucified painted by a liberated slave in the mid 16th century. In the earthquake of 1655, the church collapsed but the

painting on the wall remained intact. This was deemed a miracle and the painting became the most venerated image in Lima. Together with an oil copy of El Señor de los Milagros (Lord of Miracles), the image is encased in a gold frame and carried on a silver litter – the whole weighing nearly a ton – through the streets on 18, 19, and 28 October and again on 1 November (All Saints' Day). ■ *Open Monday-Saturday 0700-1200 and 1700-2030, Sunday 0630-1300 and 1600-2030.*

San Agustín is on the corner of Jr Ica and Jr Camana, west of the Plaza de Armas. Its façade (1720) is a splendid example of churrigueresque architecture. There are carved choir stalls and effigies, and a sculpture of Death, said to have frightened its maker into an early grave. Since being damaged in the last earthquake the church has been sensitively restored, but the sculpture of Death is in storage (to protect tourists of a more nervous disposition). ■ *Open Tuesday-Friday 1630-1730 (ring for entry).*

San Agustín

The 18th century **Jesús María** on the corner of Jr Moquegua and Jr Camana, contains some of the finest paintings and gilded Baroque altars in all of Lima. The church of **Magdalena Vieja**, built in 1557, but reconstructed in 1931, with altar pieces of gilded and carved wood, is particularly fine. It can be seen during a visit to the Museum of Archaeology on Plaza Bolívar in Pueblo Libre (see **Museums** below).

Jesús María

Another church worth seeing for its two beautiful colonial doors is **San Marcelo**, at Avda de la Emancipación, fourth block. The interior is also remarkable, particularly the 18th century gold leaf high altar and pulpit and the religious paintings sited above attractive Sevillian tiles.

San Marcelo

The Convento de Los Descalzos on the Alameda de Los Descalzos in Rímac was founded in 1592 and contains over 300 paintings of the Cusco, Quito and Lima schools which line the four main cloisters and two ornate chapels. The chapel of El Carmen was constructed in 1730 and is notable for its baroque gold leaf altar. A small chapel dedicated to Nuestra Señora de la Rosa Mística has some fine Cusqueña paintings. Opposite, in the chapel dedicated to Señora de los Angeles, Admiral Grau made his last confession before the battle of Angamos.

Convento de Los Descalzos

The museum shows the life of the Franciscan friars during colonial and early republican periods. The cellar, infirmary, pharmacy and a typical cell have been restored. The library has not yet been incorporated into the tour (researchers may be permitted to see specific books on request). ■*Open daily 1000-1300 and 1500-1800 except Tuesday. Entrance is US$1, by guided tour only, 45 minutes in Spanish, but worth it.*

The church of Santo Tomás, on Junín y Andahuaylas, is now a school – Gran Unidad Escolar 'Mercedes Cabello de Carbonera'. It is said to have the only circular cloister in the world apart from St Peter's in Rome, and a fine 17th-century Italian-designed baroque library. Ask the doorman on Andahuaylas to see inside.

Santo Tomás

Lima

Museums

Museo Nacional de Antropología y Arqueología

NB Many museums are closed on Monday

On display are ceramics of the Chimú, Nasca, Mochica and Pachacámac cultures, various Inca curiosities and works of art, and interesting textiles. The museum houses the Raimondi Stela and the Tello obelisk from Chavín, and a reconstruction of one of the galleries at Chavín. It also has a model of Machu Picchu. ■ *Plaza Bolívar in Pueblo Libre, not to be confused with Plaza Bolívar in the centre. T4635070. Open Tuesday-Sunday 0900-1800. Entrance US$1.50. Photo permit US$5. Guides are available. Take any public transportation vehicle with a window sticker saying "Tdo Brasil." Get off at the 21st block called Avda Vivanco. Walk about five blocks down Vivanco. The museum will be on your left. Taxi from downtown Lima US$1.50; from Miraflores US$2.50.*

Museo de la Nación

This is the new anthropological and archaeological museum for the exhibition and study of the art and history of the aboriginal races of Peru. There are good explanations in Spanish on Peruvian history, with ceramics, textiles and displays of almost every ruin in Peru. There is an excellent display of the original treasures of the tomb of the Señor de Sipán, which is highly recommended, with guided tours in English and Spanish. Another exhibition shows artefacts from Batán Grande near Chiclayo (Sicán culture). There's also a reconstruction of the friezes found at Huaca El Brujo, near Trujillo. The museum holds a concert every Sunday and most evenings there is a lecture, or an event in the theatre (see the monthly programme, or newspaper). ■ *Javier Prado Este 2465, San Borja, in the huge Banco de la Nación building. T4769875/4769878. Open Tuesday-Friday 0900-2100, Saturday and Sunday 1000-1900. Entrance US$4 (including the Sipán display), 50 percent discount with ISIC card. From downtown Lima take a combi with a window sticker that says "Javier Prado/Aviacion". Get off at the 21st block of Javier Prado Avda Aviacion. The museum is caddy-corner. From Miraflores take a bus down Avda Arequipa to Avda Javier Prado (27th block), then take a bus with a window sticker saying "Tdo Javier Prado" or "Aviacion." A taxi from downtown Lima or from the centre of Miraflores costs US$2.*

Museo Peruana de Ciencias de la Salud

Museo Peruano de Ciencias de la Salud, now part of the Museo de la Nación, has a collection of ceramics and mummies, plus an explanation of precolumbian lifestyle, divided into five sections: *micuy* (Quechua for food), *hampi* (medicine), *onccoy* (disease), *hampini* (healing) and *causay* (life).

Museo de Oro

Museo de Oro (Gold Museum) is the private collection of Miguel Mujica Gallo. An underground museum contains items which have been exhibited in the world's leading museums. This excellent collection includes precolumbian gold, silver and bronze, ceramics, weavings, mummies, etc. Allow plenty of time to appreciate it fully as it is positively full to bursting with artefacts. The catalogues cost US$20 or US$40 and the complete book US$70. Upstairs is a remarkable arms collection with an impressive exhibition from Spanish colonial times. In the garden are high quality, expensive craft shops. ■ *18th block of Prolongación Avda Primavera (Avda de Molina 1110), Monterrico. T3451271. Open daily (including Sunday and holidays) 1130-1900. Entrance US$3, children half price. No photography allowed. Guide Eder Pena speaks English and Italian; T4665877 (home), 9714851 (cellular). From downtown, take a bus or microbus to the 47th block of Avda Arequipa (Avda Angamos). Get off, cross Avda Angamos and take a colectivo with a window sticker saying "U de Lima". Tell the cobrador you want to get off at the Museo de Oro. From Miraflores walk to 47th block of Avda Arequipa (Avda*

Angamos) and take a bus up Angamos with sticker that says "U de Lima" and say you want to get off at the Museo de Oro.

Museo Arqueológico Rafael Larco Herrera

Museo Arqueológico Rafael Larco Herrera is the Chiclín pottery museum brought from Trujillo. The greatest number of exhibits stem from the Mochica period (AD 400-800). The Cupisnique period, dating back to 1000 BC, and the Nasca, Chimú, and Inca periods are also well represented. There is an erotica section in a separate building. This is a museum for the pottery specialist and it gives an excellent overview on the development of Peruvian cultures. It is more like a warehouse than a museum with few explanations, but the general visitor will enjoy the excellent collection of precolumbian weaving, including a sample of two-ply yarns with 398 threads to the inch. There are also several mummified weavers buried with their looms and a small display of gold pieces. ■*Avda Bolívar 1515, Pueblo Libre. T4611312. Open Monday-Saturday 0900-1800, Sunday 0900-1300. Entrance US$3 (half price for student-card holders), Photography not permitted. Take any bus to the 15th block of Avda Brasil. Then take a bus down Avda Bolívar. Taxi from downtown US$1.50 and from Miraflores US$2.50.*

Museo Arqueológico Amano

This very fine private collection of artefacts from the Chancay, Chimú and Nasca periods, owned by the late Mr Yoshitaro Amano, boasts one of the most complete exhibits of Chancay weaving. It is particularly interesting for pottery and precolumbian textiles, all superbly displayed and lit. ■*Calle Retiro 160 Avda Santa Cruz, 11th block of Avda Angamos Oeste, Miraflores. T4412909. Open by appointment Monday-Friday in the afternoons only. Entrance free (photography prohibited). Take a bus or colectivo to the corner of Avda Arequipa y Avda Angamos and another one to the 11th block of Avda Angamos Oeste. Taxi from downtown US$2; from Parque Kennedy US$1.*

Museo Banco Central de Reserva

This is a large collection of pottery from the Vicus or Piura culture (AD 500-600) and gold objects from Lambayeque, as well as 19th and 20th century paintings. Both modern and ancient exhibitions are highly recommended. ■*Avda Ucayali 291 and Lampa, one block from San Pedro Church, on same side as Torre Tagle Palace, T4276250, ext 2657. Open Tuesday-Friday 1000-1600, Saturday-Sunday 1000-1300. Entrance free. Photography prohibited.*

Museo Nacional de la Cultura Peruana

This extraordinary mock Tiahuanaco façade houses a rather disjointed collection of precolumbian and modern artefacts, including *mate burilado* (carved gourds), *retablos*, textiles, *keros* and *huacos*. There are examples of ceramics and cloth from some Amazonian tribes and a set of watercolours by Pancho Fierro, the 19th century *costumbrista* artist. ■*Avda Alfonso Ugarte 650, Lima. T4235892. Open Tuesday-Friday 1000-1630, Saturday 1000-1400. Entrance US$1. Free guide in Spanish.*

Poli Museum

Poli Museum is one of the best private collections of precolumbian and colonial artefacts in Peru, including material from Sipán. ■*Lord Cochrane 466, Miraflores. T4222437. Guided tours (not in English) by Sr Poli cost US$10 per person irrespective of the size of the group; allow two hours. Call in advance to arrange tours.*

Museo de Arte

The Museo de Arte in the Palacio de la Exposición, was built in 1868 in Parque de la Exposición. There are more than 7,000 exhibits, giving a chronological history of Peruvian cultures and art from the Paracas civilization up to today.

It includes excellent examples of 17th and 18th century Cusco paintings, a beautiful display of carved furniture, heavy silver and jewelled stirrups and also precolumbian pottery. ■*9 de Diciembre 125. T4234732. Open Tuesday-Sunday 1000-1700. Entrance US$1.50 (free on Tuesday). Between April and October, and with special programmes in the holiday season, the cinema shows films and plays almost every night (cheap). See the local paper for details, or look in the museum itself. Free guide, signs in English.*

Museo de Arte Italiano Museo de Arte Italiano is in a wonderful neo-classical building, given by the Italian colony to Peru on the centenary of its independence. Note the remarkable mosaic murals on the outside. It consists of a large collection of Italian and other European works of art, including sculpture, lithographs and etchings. The museum now also houses the Instituto de Arte Contemporáneo, which has many exhibitions. ■*Paseo de la República, second block. T4239932. Open Monday-Friday 0900-1630. Entrance US$1.*

Other museums **Contemporary Folk Art Museum** is recommended. There is a shop in the museum grounds. ■*Saco Olivero 163, between Arenales and third block of Arequipa, Open Tuesday-Friday 1430-1900, Saturday 0830-1200.*

Pinacoteca Municipal contains a large collection of paintings by Peruvian artists. The best of the painters is Ignacio Merino (1817-76). The rooms and furnishings are very ornate. ■*Housed in the Municipal Building on the Plaza de Armas. Open Monday-Friday, 0900-1300.*

Colección Pedro de Osma This is a private collection of colonial art of the Cusco, Ayacucho and Arequipa schools. ■*Avda Pedro de Osma 421, Barranco. T4670915/0019 for an appointment. Entrance US$3. Take bus 2, 54 or colectivo from Avda Tacna. The number of visitors is limited to ten at any one time.*

Museo Nacional de Historia is in a mansion built by Viceroy Pezuela and occupied by San Martín (1821-1822) and Bolívar (1823-1826). It is next to the old Museo de Antropoligía y Arqueología. Take the same buses to get there (see above). The exhibits comprise colonial and early republican paintings, manuscripts, portraits, uniforms, etc. The paintings are mainly of historical episodes. ■*Plaza Bolívar, Pueblo Libre.*

Museo del Tribunal de la Santa Inquisición The main hall, with a splendidly carved mahogany ceiling, remains untouched. The Court of Inquisition was first held here in 1584, after being moved from its first home opposite the church of La Merced. From 1829 until 1938 the building was used by the Senate. In the basement there is an accurate recreation *in situ* of the gruesome tortures. The whole tour is fascinating, if a little morbid. A description in English is available at the desk. ■*Plaza Bolívar, C Junín 548, near the corner of Avda Abancay. Monday-Friday 0900-1300, 1430-1700. Entrance free. Students offer to show you round for a tip; good explanations in English.*

Museo Histórico Militar There are many interesting military relics such as: a cannon brought by Pizarro, a cannon used in the War of Independence, the flag that flew during the last Spanish stand in the fortress, portraits of General Rodil and of Lord Cochrane, and the remains of the small Bleriot plane in which the Peruvian pilot, Jorge Chávez, made the first crossing of the Alps from Switzerland to Italy. He was killed when the plane crashed at Domodossola on 23 September 1910. ■*Parque Independencia, in Real Felipe Fortress, Callao.*

Museo Naval contains a collection of paintings, model ships, uniforms, etc. ■*Avda Jorge Chávez 123, off Plaza Grau, Callao. T4294793. Open Tuesday-Friday 0900-1400, Saturday and Sunday 0900-1600. Entrance US$1.*

Guilt by inquisition

Established by Royal Decree in 1569, the Court of Inquisition was soon to prove a particularly cruel form of justice, even in the context of Spanish rule.

During its existence, the Church meted out many horrific tortures on innocent people. Among the most fashionable methods of making the accused confess their "sins" were burning, dismemberment and asphyxiation, to name but a few. The most common form of punishment was public flogging, followed by exile and the not so appealing death by burning. Up until 1776, 86 people are recorded to have been burned alive and 458 excommunicated.

Given that no witnesses were called except the informer and that the accused were not allowed to know the identity of their accusers, this may have been less a test of religious conviction than a means of settling old scores. This Kafkaesque nightmare was then carried into the realms of surreal absurdity during the process of judgement. A statue of Christ was the final arbiter of guilt or innocence but had to express its belief in the prisoner's innocence with a shake of the head. Needless to say, not too many walked free.

The Inquisition was abolished by the Viceroy in 1813 but later reinstated before finally being proscribed in 1820.

Museo de los Combatientes del Morro de Arica gives the Peruvian view of the famous battle against the Chileans during the War of the Pacific. ■*Cailloma 125, Lima. T4270958. Open Tuesday-Saturday 0930-1530. Entrance US$0.50.*

Museo Miguel Grau is the house of Admiral Grau and has mementoes of the War of the Pacific. ■*Jr Huancavelica 170, Lima. T4285012. Open daily 0900-1400. Entrance free.*

Museo de Historia Natural Javier Prado belongs to Universidad de San Marcos. The exhibits comprise Peruvian flora, birds, mammals, butterflies, insects, minerals and shells. ■*Avda Arenales 1256, Jesús María. T4710117. Open Monday-Friday 0900-1500, Saturday 0900-1700, Sunday 0900-1300. Etnrance US$1 (students US$0.50). Take a colectivo from Avda Tacna.*

La Casa O'Higgins is an interesting colonial house which holds temporary exhibitions from the Universidad de Lima (entry US$1). Bernardo O'Higgins, president of Chile from 1817-23, died here on 24 October 1842. ■*Unión 550.*

Museo Taurino Apart from matadors' relics, the museum contains good collections of paintings and engravings – some of the latter by Goya. ■*Hualgayoc 332, Plaza de Acho Bull Ring (see above), Rímac. T4823360. Open Monday-Saturday 0900-1600. Entrance US$1; students US$0.50. Photography US$2.*

Philatelic Museum Contains an incomplete collection of Peruvian stamps and information on the Inca postal system. There is a stamp exchange in front of the museum every Saturday and Sunday, 0900-1300. You can buy stamps here as well, particularly commemorative issues. ■*Central Post Office, off Plaza de Armas. Open Monday-Friday 0800-1200, 1400-1500. No charge to enter museum; open Monday-Friday 0830-1300 and 1400-1830.*

Museo Teatral contains a collection of mementoes and photographs of people who have appeared on the Lima stage. ■*Teatro Segura, Jr Huancavelica 251, Lima. T4267206. Open during performances.*

Museo de la Electricidad IInaugurated in 1994, this museum describes the history of electricity in Peru and some examples of energy-saving projects. ■*Avda Pedro de Osma 105, Barranco, near the main plaza. T/F4776577.*

Lima

E postmaster@museoelectri.org.pe. Open Monday-Sunday 0900-1700 and until 2400 on Friday and Saturday. Entrance free.

Lima beaches

Most beaches have very strong currents and extreme caution should be exercised. Lifeguards are not always present.

Lima sits next to an open bay, with its two points at La Punta (Callao) and Morro Solar (Chorrillos). During the summer (December-March), beaches get very crowded on weekdays as much as weekends even though all the beaches lining the Lima coast have been declared unsuitable for swimming. A nice stroll on the beach is pleasant during daylight hours, but when the sun goes down, the thieves come out and it becomes very dangerous. Needless to say, camping is a very bad idea.

The *Circuito de Playas*, which begins with Playa Arica (30 kilometres from Lima) and ends with San Bartolo (45 kilometres from Lima), has many great beaches for all tastes. If you want a beach that always is packed with people, there's El Silencio or Punta Rocas. Quieter options are Señoritas or Los Pulpos. Punta Hermosa has frequent surfing and volleyball tournaments.

Suburbs of Lima

San Isidro

The district of San Isidro combines some upscale residential areas, many of Lima's fanciest hotels and important commercial zones with a huge golf course smack in the middle. Along Avda La Republica is **El Olivar**, an old olive grove planted by the first Spaniards which has been turned into a beautiful park. It's definitely worth a stroll either by day or night.

At Avenidas Rosario and Rivera are the ruins of **Huallamarca** – or **Pan de Azúcar** – a restored adobe pyramid of the Maranga culture, dating from about AD 100-500. There is a small site museum on the premises. The Huaca (temple) Juliana located near the intersection of Avenidas Pezet and Belen is a good example of the Lima culture which occupied the area from 200-700 AD.■*Open 0900-1700 daily except for Tuesdays.*

There are many good hotels and restaurants in San Isidro (see under Sleeping, page 113 and Eating, page 116).

West of San Isidro is the rundown seaside resort of **Magdalena del Mar**, inland from which is **Pueblo Libre** (formerly Magdalena Vieja), where the **Museo de Antropología y Arqueología**, the **Museo Arqueológico Rafael Larco Herrera** and the **Museo Nacional de Historia** are found (see under Museums, page 104). In Pueblo Libre is the church of **Santa María Magdalena**, on Jr San Martín, whose plain exterior conceals some fine ornamentation and art inside.

Parque de las Leyendas It is arranged to represent the three regions of Peru: the coast, the mountainous Sierra, and the tropical jungles of the Selva, with appropriate houses, animals and plants and children's playground. Elephants and lions have been introduced so the zoo is no longer purely Peruvian. It gets very crowded at weekends. ■*24th block of Avda de La Marina in Pueblo Libre, between Lima and Callao, T4526913. Open daily 0900-1730. Entrance US$2. There is a handicrafts fair (Feria Artesanal) at the entrance to the park; particularly good insect specimens can be bought here. Take bus 23 or colectivo on Avda Abancay, or bus 135A or colectivo from Avda La Vega.*

At the intersection of Avda Derby and Avda Manuel Olguin in **Monterrico** is the entrance to **Daytona**, Lima's version of a North American amusement park. For *afficionados* of these types of places, Daytona will inevitably be a disappointment, but it's still a fun way to spend a weekend afternoon. There is a wide variety of fast food restaurants to choose from. The go-karts are by far the best attraction. ■*Open daily, Friday and Saturday until late. Entrance is cheap (US$2).*

Miraflores

Miraflores, apart from being a nice residential part of Lima is also home to a bustling mercantile district full of fashionable shops, cafés, discotheques, fine restaurants and five star hotels (see under **Sleeping**, page 111, and **Eating**, page 116). In the centre of all this is the beautiful Parque Central de Miraflores – **Parque Kennedy** – located between Avda Larco and Avda Oscar Benavides (locally known as Avda Diagonal). This extremely well kept park has a small open-air theatre with performances Thursday-Sunday, ranging from Afro-Peruvian music to rock'n'-roll. Towards the bottom of the park is a nightly crafts market open from 1700 to 2300. Just off Avda Diagonal across from the park is Pasaje San Ramon, better known as Pizza Street (Calle da las Pizzas). This small pedestrian walkway is full of outdoor restaurants/bars/discotheques open until the wee small hours of the morning. A very popular place to see and be seen.

At the end of Avda Larco and running along the Malecón (meaning street by the sea) de la Reserva is the newly renovated **Parque Salazar** and the soon to be inaugurated Centro Comercial Larco-Mar; future home of Big Apple Bagels and Hard Rock Café, just to name a few. A few hundred metres to the north is the famous **Parque del Amor** where on just about any night you'll see at least one wedding party taking photos of the newly married couple. Peruvians are nothing if not romantic.

The beach, although not safe to walk at night, has a great view of the whole Lima coastline from Chorrillos to La Punta. *La Rosa Nautica*, a very expensive restaurant/discotheque (see under **Eating in Miraflores**) occupies a pier that juts out from the beach. A Lima dining institution for those willing to part with a nice chunk of change.

On the 12th block of the Malecón Cisneros the **Yitzhak Rabin Memorial Park**, with its beautiful ocean view, is a nice place to relax, read a book, chat or just think about your recent trip to the mountains.

The house of the author, poet and historian **Ricardo Palma** is at Calle General Suarez 189. He is one of Peru's most famous literary figures, best known for his work *Tradiciones Peruanas*, which covers the country's colonial period (see **Literature**, page 530). The house where he lived and died is now a museum, open to the public Monday-Friday 0915-1245 and 1430-1700 (small entrance fee; photography fee US$3).

At the intersection of Calles Borgona y Tarapacá, near the 45th block of Avda Arequipa, is the **Huaca Pucllana** also of the Lima culture; guided tours only.

Barranco

South of Miraflores is **Barranco**, which was already a seaside resort by the end of the 17th century. During the republic it was a holiday centre for rich Limeños and many British and Germans built opulent country houses there. Nowadays, Barranco is something of an intellectual haven where a number of artists have their workshops.

The attractive public library, formerly the town hall, stands on the delightful plaza. Nearby is the interesting *bajada*, a steep path leading down to the beach, where many of Lima's artists live. The old houses are in state of disrepair and many are under restoration. **The Puente de los Suspiros** (Bridge of Sighs), leads towards the Malecón, with fine views of the bay.

Barranco is a quiet, sleepy suburb during the day but comes alive at night when the city's young flock here to party at weekends. Squeezed together into a few streets are dozens of good bars and restaurants (see under Eating, page 116, and Bars & clubs, page 120). No visit to Lima would be complete without a tour of Barranco's 'sights'.

An antique train wagon that discontinued its Barranco-Lima service in 1965 now offers a pleasant, albeit very short ride (6 blocks) down Avda Pedro de Osma to the door of the museum of the same name. There is a video on board describing the train's history. ■*The train runs Tuesday-Sunday at 1000, 1040, 1120, 1200, 1240, 1400, 1440, 1520, 1600, 1620. Tickets can be bought at the Electricity museum, US$0.70.*

The next development on the coast is at **Chorrillos**, a fashionable resort with a cliff promenade, and boating. Beyond Chorrillos is **La Herradura**, another bathing resort with several restaurants.

Callao

Callao has a well earned reputation for theft. It's not recommended to just blindly wander around, day or night

Founded in 1537, Callao quickly became the main port for Spanish colonial commerce in the Pacific. During much of the 16th century Spanish merchants were plagued by threats from English pirates such as Sir Francis Drake and Richard Hawkins who were all too willing to relieve the Spanish armada of its colonial spoils. The harbour was fortified in 1639 in order to prevent such attacks.

In 1746, the port was completely destroyed by a massive wave, triggered by the terrible earthquake of that year. According to some sources, all 6,000 of Callao's inhabitants were drowned. The watermark is still visible on the outside of the 18th century church of Nuestra Señora del Carmen de la Legua which stands near the corner of Avenida Oscar Benavides and the airport road, Avenida Elmer Faucett.

In 1850, the first railway in South America was opened between Lima and Callao. It was used not only as a passenger service but, more importantly, for the growing import-export trade, transporting ore from the mines in the Central Highlands and manufactured goods from the disembarking ships.

Callao (*Population*: 588,600) is now contiguous with Lima. The road between the two is lined by factories. Shipyards, far from sea, load the fishing vessels they build on huge lorries and launch them into the ocean at Callao. The port is still very much a commercially active place. It handles 75 percent of the nation's imports and some 25 percent of its exports. San Lorenzo island, a naval station, protects the roadstead from the south and inland stretches the Rímac valley. The market is between Sáenz Peña and Buenos Aires.

The port's few attractions include **The Club**, the oldest English club on the coast, at Pasaje Ronald, Callao Constitución. There is also an English cemetery.

The **Castillo del Real Felipe** is still a military post, and tourists are allowed to visit it. The **Museo Histórico Militar** is in the old barracks. There is also the **Museo Naval** (see page 106 for both).

The Naval College is at **La Punta**, just beyond Callao, served by municipal buses and colectivos through Callao from Lima. La Punta is on a spit of land stretching out to sea. It was once a fashionable beach resort and is still a pleasant enough residential area, but the water is cool. A yacht club is on the north side. The walk along the seafront between Callao and La Punta has its charms.

Essentials

All hotels and restaurants in the upper price brackets charge 18% VAT and 10% service on top of prices. Neither is included in prices below, unless indicated otherwise. In cheaper hotels water may be scarce in the middle of the day. The more expensive hotels charge in dollars according to the parallel rate of exchange at midnight. More visitors stay in the Miraflores area than in the centre, as it is generally cleaner and safer, but more expensive. Backpackers prefer the cheaper *hostales* in the centre, which has more theft problems and is more chaotic, but which, with care and attention to your belongings, is OK. (Consult the general Security section on page 40.)

Sleeping

L1-2 *Miraflores César*, La Paz y Diez Canseco, T4441212, F4444440. Luxury hotel with pool, gym, sauna and facilities for the handicapped. **L2** *El Condado*, Alcanfores 465, T4443614, F4441981. Luxury hotel with casino and parking. **L2-3** *El Pardo*, Independencia 141, T2410410/4442283, F4442171, E pardohot@si.com.pe. A/c, satellite TV, fax service, pool, gym, good restaurant. Recommended. **L2** *Las Américas*, Avda Benavides 415, T2412820/4447272, F4460355. 5-star, commercial centre, pool, gym, restaurant. **L2** *María Angola*, Avda La Paz 610, T4441280, F4462860. Recommended. **L3** *Ariosto*, Avda La Paz 769, T4441414, F4443955. Friendly. Recommended. **L3** *La Hacienda*, 28 de Julio 511 y Avda Larco, T4444346, F4441942, English spoken, excellent service, breakfast included. **L3** *Palace*, Avda 28 de Julio 1088, T2414050, F2414051. Includes breakfast, very clean, comfortable, friendly, keeps luggage, English-speaking reception.

A1 *Antigua*, Avda Grau 350 at C Francia, T2416116, F2416115, E hantigua@ amauta.rcp.net.pe. A beautiful, small and elegant hotel in a quiet but central location, very friendly service, tastefully furnished and decorated, 35 rooms, gym, cable TV, good restaurant. Recommended. **A2** *Grand Hotel Miraflores*, Avda 28 de Julio 151, T2414647. The hotel discotheque 'Red & Blue' is very popular with young Limeños, also casino, very pleasant. **A2** *José Antonio*, 28 de Julio 398 y C Colón, T/F4456870. Clean, friendly, good restaurant. Recommended. **A2** *Residencial Alemán*, Arequipa 4704, T4456999, F4473950. No sign, comfortable, clean, friendly, quiet, garden, breakfast included, inquire about laundry service. **A3** *El Doral*, Avda José Pardo 486, T4476305, F4468344. Nice rooms with lounge and kitchenette, safe, friendly, pool.

In Miraflores
■ *on maps*
Price codes:
see inside front cover

Lima

Recommended. **A3-2** *Hostal La Castellana*, Grimaldo del Solar 222, T4443530/4662, F4468030. Pleasant, good value, nice garden, safe, restaurant, laundry, English spoken, 10 percent discount for South American Explorers Club (SAEC) members. Recommended. **A3** *Hostal Miramar Ischia*, Malecón Cisneros 1244, T4466969, E ischia@bellnet.com.pe. Overlooking Pacific, includes breakfast, good value restaurant, friendly. Recommended. **A3** *Hostal San Antonio Abad*, Ramón Ribeyro 301, T4476766, T/F4464208. Quiet, secure, very friendly and helpful, free airport transfer. Highly recommended. **A3** *Hostal Torreblanca*, Avda José Pardo 1453, near the seafront, T/F4473363, E torreble@ett.com.pe. Includes breakfast, quiet, safe, laundry, restaurant and bar, friendly, cosy rooms, will help with travel arrangements. Recommended.

B *Colonial Inn*, Cmdte Espinar 310, T2417471, F4457587, E coloinn@telematic.edu.pe. Colonial style, parking, includes breakfast. **B** *Hostal El Ejecutivo*, Avda 28 de Julio 245 y C Porta, T/F2413575. Includes breakfast, payment in dollars, overpriced but clean, tariff negotiable for long stay, safe, luggage can be left. **B** *Hostal*

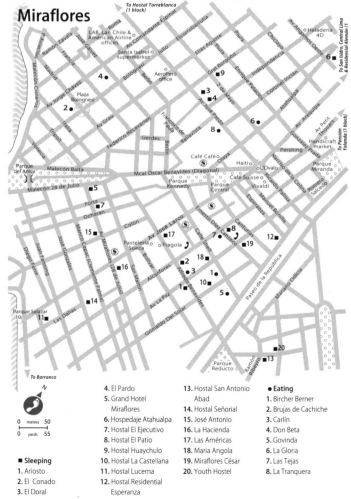

Miraflores

To Hostal Torreblanca (1 block)

To Barranco

0 metres 50
0 yards 55

■ **Sleeping**
1. Ariosto
2. El Conado
3. El Doral
4. El Pardo
5. Grand Hotel Miraflores
6. Hospedaje Atahualpa
7. Hostal El Ejecutivo
8. Hostal El Patio
9. Hostal Huaychulo
10. Hostal La Castellana
11. Hostal Lucerna
12. Hostal Residencial Esperanza
13. Hostal San Antonio Abad
14. Hostal Señorial
15. José Antonio
16. La Hacienda
17. Las Américas
18. Maria Angola
19. Miraflores César
20. Youth Hostel

● **Eating**
1. Bircher Berner
2. Brujas de Cachiche
3. Carlín
4. Don Beta
5. Govinda
6. La Gloria
7. Las Tejas
8. La Tranquera

Huaychulo, Avda Dos de Mayo 494, T/F2313130. Secure, helpful, excellent, German owner-manager also speaks English. Recommended. **B** *Hostal Lucerna*, Las Dalias 276 (parallel with 12th block of Larco), T4457321, F4466050. Friendly, safe, quiet, cosy. Recommended. **B** *Hostal El Patio*, Diez Canseco 341a, T4442107. Includes breakfast, reductions for long stays, clean, comfortable, friendly, English and French spoken. **B** *Hostal Residencial Esperanza*, Esperanza 350, T4442411/4909, F4440834. Café, bar, TV, phone, pleasant, secure. **B** *Hostal Señorial*, José González 567, T4459724, F4445755. Includes breakfast, comfortable, friendly, nice garden. Recommended. **B-C** *Hostal Porta*, C Porta 686 y C Juan Fanning. No sign, ring doorbell, with bathroom, hot water, clean and safe, cable TV, English spoken, spacious rooms.

C *Hospedaje Atahualpa*, Atahualpa 646c, T4476601. Cheaper without private bath, includes breakfast, friendly, hot water, cooking and laundry facilities, clean, taxi service. Recommended. **C-D** *Pensión Yolanda*, Domingo Elias 230, T4457565. Clean, owner speaks English, family house, quiet, safe, reservation required. Highly recommended.

D *Pensión José Luis*, Paula de Ugarriza 727, T4441015, E hsjluis@telematic.edu.pe. All but 3 rooms on roof with private bath, kitchen available, hot water 24 hours, reservation required, very clean and friendly, English-speaking owner, best to reserve in advance. Highly recommended. **D** *Residencial El Castillo Inn*, Diez Canseco 580, T4469501. All rooms with private bath and hot water, family home, use of lounge negotiate for longer stay. **D** per person *Imperial Inn*, C Bolognesi 641, T4452504. Quiet street, great ocean view, near Parque del Amor. **D** per person *Casa de La Sra Jordan*, Porta 724, near Parque del Amor, T4459840. Includes breakfast, 5 rooms, shared baths only, reservations required, family home, friendly, quiet. **D-E** per person *Albergue Turístico Juvenil Internacional*, Avda Casimiro Ulloa 328, San Antonio between San Isidro and Miraflores, T4465488, F4448187. Youth hostel, dormitory accommodation, more for a double, **B** for private room, basic cafeteria, travel information, cooking (minimal) and laundry facilities, swimming pool often empty, extra charge for kitchen facilities, clean and safe, situated in a nice villa. Recommended.

In San Isidro **L1** *Los Delfines*, C Los Eucaliptos 555, T2157000, F2157070/2157071, E reservas@losdelfineshotel.com.pe. The newest and most exclusive hotel in Lima, with state-of-the-art conference hall and all the luxuries and more expected of a 5-star hotel, 207 rooms and suites, has live dolphins on constant display in a tank that is unfortunately too small. **L1** *Oro Verde*, Via Central 150, Centro Empresarial (Avda Camino Real), T4214400, F4214422. Recommended as one of the best in town. **L2** *El Olivar de San Isidro*, Pancho Fierro 194, T4411454, F4411382. Luxury, one of the top 5-star hotels in Lima, modern, restaurant, coffee shop, garden, swimming pool, quiet, popular with business visitors. **L3** *Posada Del Inca*, Avda Libertadores 490, T2224777, F2224345, E posada_ventas@el-olivar.com.pe. Prices include all taxes, cable TV, restaurant, parking, very comfortable, excellent service. Recommended.

A1 *Garden*, Rivera Navarrete 450, T4421771, F4224079, E hgarden@ mail.cosapidata.com.pe. Includes tax and breakfast, good, large beds, shower, small restaurant, travel agency. Recommended. **A2** *Regina's*, Avda Dos de Mayo 1421, T4412541, F4412044. Includes taxes and breakfast, pool. Recommended. **A3** *Limatambo*, Avda Aramburú 1025, T4419615. Tax included, Italian-owned, friendly, secure laundry service, caters to business travellers. **A3** *Sans Souci*, Avda Arequipa 2670, T4226035, F4417824. Breakfast and tax included, front rooms noisy, clean, safe, friendly, good services, garden, garage. **A3** *Residencial Frank*, Los Olivos 225, T4401222. German-Peruvian family, nice garden, laundry service, phone, fax and email, includes breakfast, English spoken.

F *Albergue Juvenil Malka*, Los Lirios 165 (Alt Cuadra 4 Avda Javier Prado Este), T4420162, T/F2225589, E a-mauriz@usa.net. Youth hostel, 20% discount with ISIC card, accommodation for up to 48 people in rooms with 4, 6, 7 and 8 beds, cable TV, laundry, kitchen, games room. Highly recommended.

In Barranco **C** *Hostal Gemina*, Avda Grau 620, T/F4775775. **E** per person *Mochileros Hostal*, Avda Pedro de Osma 135, 1 block from main plaza, T4774506, E backpacker@ amauta.rcp.net.pe. Beautiful house, very clean, friendly English-speaking owner, shared rooms, Irish-type pub on the premises, stone's throw from Barranco nightlife.

In Santa Beatriz **B-C** *Hostal La Posada del Parque*, Parque Hernán Velarde 60, Alt Cuadra 1 y 2 de Avda Petit Thouars, T4332412, F3326927, E monden@telematic.com.pe. Run by Sra Monica Moreno and her husband Leo who both speak good English, a charmingly refurbished old house in a safe area, excellent bathrooms, breakfast US$3 extra, airport transfer for US$12 for 2. Highly recommended as excellent value. **C** *Renacimiento*, Parque Hernán Velarde 52-54. T4332806. A bit run down, quiet, parking, colonial building, very close to national stadium, not all rooms with bathroom, clean, helpful, quiet.

In Lince **C** *Albergue Juvenil Qorpawasi*, Avda J. Pardo de Zela 877, T4712480. Includes breakfast, **E** per person in dormitory. **D** *Hostal Ambassador*, Julio C Tello 650, T4700020. Clean, safe, hot water, changes money for guests. Recommended. **D** *Hostal Lia*, C Las Geranios 166, T4405187. All rooms with bath, clean, secure.

In San Miguel **D-E** per person *Hostal Mami Panchita*, Jr Bolívar 206, corner of Avda San Miguel, T2637203/2630749, E Raymi_travels@perusat.net.pe. Dutch-Peruvian owned, English, French, Spanish and German spoken, includes breakfast, have their own *Raymi* Travel agency.

In Central Lima **L2** *Lima Sheraton*, Paseo de la República 170, T4335844/4333320, F4265920. *Las Palmeras* coffee shop is good, daily buffet breakfast, all you can eat for US$15 per

---

LA POSADA DEL PARQUE HOSTAL

Parque Hernán Velarde No 60
Block 1 and 2 Petit Thouars Ave.
Santa Beatriz Lima 1
e mail: monden@telematic.com.pe
phone: (511) 4332412
Fax: 3326927

Special rates for groups.

Peruvian Mansion in a cul de sac decorated with antiques and popular art, big rooms, private bathrooms with hot water all time, safe box in each room, Deluxe mattress, cable TV. English and French speaking.
Rates in U$: Single 25; Double 30; Triple 45; Quadruple 48. Inc Taxes.
Continental Breakfast 3 U$.
10% discount in room rates when booking by yourself in advance.

WEB PAGE: http://clientes@telematic.com.pe/monden

person, casino. **L3** *Crillón*, Avda Nicolás de Piérola, or Colmena 589, T4283290, F4325920. Good food and service in *Skyroom*, open 1200-2400 Monday-Saturday, Peruvian/international cuisine, buffets and live music at weekends, great view over Lima.

A1 *Grand Hotel Bolívar*, Unión 958, Plaza San Martín, T4287671/4287672, F4287674. Can be negotiated down to **C** out of season, reflecting its sad decline, a palatial but rundown old building, carpets threadbare, leaking ceilings. The staff are still very friendly and helpful though and despite everything still recommended. **A3-B** *Gran Hotel Savoy*, Jr Cailloma 224. 210 rooms, includes taxes and breakfast, restaurant, cafeteria, bar, laundry, airport transfer, recently refurbished. **A3-B** *Hostal San Martín*, Avda Nicolás de Piérola 882, Plaza San Martín, T4285337, F4235744. Includes breakfast served in room, a/c, modern, very clean, secure, friendly, helpful, safe, rooms on street noisy, money changing facilities, Japanese run, good restaurant, good service. Recommended.

B *El Plaza*, Nicolás de Piérola 850, T4286270, F4286274. Very noisy at the front but quiet at the back (except Saturday), convenient, good, safe for luggage, inquire about cheaper rates for tourists, includes breakfast. **B** *Kamana*, Jr Camaná 547, T4267204, F4260790. Modern, TV, phone, comfortable, safe, restaurants, French and some English spoken, very friendly staff.

D *Granada*, Huancavelica 323, T4279033. Includes breakfast, clean, hot water, English spoken, safe, friendly, safety deposit, washing facilities. **D** *Gran Hotel Continental*, Jr Puno 196, T4275890. Owned by Aero Continente who offer good deals to its passengers, large, modern, price includes breakfast. **D** *Hostal Roma*, Jr Ica 326, T4277576, 4260533, F4277572. With bathroom, cheaper without, hot water all day, safe to leave luggage, basic but clean, often full, motorcycle parking (*Roma Tours*, helpful for trips, reservations, flight confirmations, Dante Reyes speaks English). Highly recommended. **D-E** *Hostal de las Artes*, Jr Chota 1460 near Avda España and SAEC, T4330031, E artes@telematic.com.pe; W www.rcp.net.pe/usr/hostaldelasartes. With bathroom, **E** without, **F** per person in dormitory, Dutch owned, English spoken, clean, safe luggage store, friendly, nice colonial building, usually hot water, friendly, book exchange. Recommended. Also owns *Hostal Liceo* around the corner, which is cheaper, much more basic but clean and secure.

E *Hostal Belén*, Belén 1049, just off San Martín, T4278995. Discount for groups of 3 or more but give prior notice, Italian spoken, basic breakfast extra, hot water, basic, clean, friendly. **E** *Hostal Europa*, Jr Ancash 376, T4273351, opposite San Francisco church. Good, clean rooms with shared bathrooms, excellent hot showers, also 6-bed

Central Lima & Breña

- ■ **Sleeping**
  1. Hostal de Las Artes 3. Sheraton
  2. Hostel Iquique
- ● **Eating**
  1. Gigi's
  2. La Choza Náutica Cebichería
  3. Nakasone

Related maps
Central Lima, page 92

0 metres 100
0 yards 109

rooms for **G** per person, great value, friendly, popular with backpackers. Recommended. **E** *Hostal Iquique*, Jr Iquique 758, Breña, round the corner from SAEC (discount for members), T4334724. With bathroom, clean, friendly, use of kitchen, warm water, storage facilities, rooms on the top floor at the back are best. Repeated recommendations. **E** *Familia Rodríguez*, Avda N de Piérola 730, 2nd floor, T4236465. With breakfast, clean, friendly, popular, some rooms noisy, will store luggage, **F** per person in dormitory accommodation with only one bathroom, transport to airport US$9.50, good information, secure. Recommended. **E** *Pensión Ibarra*, Avda Tacna 1402-1502, in high-rise building, T/F427860, T4271035 (no sign). Breakfast extra, discount for longer stay, use of kitchen, balcony with views of the city, clean, friendly, very helpful owner, hot water, full board available. Highly recommended.

F *Hostal España*, Jr Azángaro 105 (no sign), T4279196. **G** per person in dormitory, fine old building, shared bathroom, hot showers possible either very early or very late, friendly, run by a French-speaking Peruvian painter and his Spanish wife, English spoken, motorcycle parking, luggage store (free), laundry service, don't leave valuables in rooms, roof garden with some animals in tiny cages, good café, very popular. **F** *Machu Picchu*, Avda Juan Pablo Fernandini 1015, Breña, Alt 10 Avda Brasil, T4243472/4442435, F4479247. Shared bathrooms, hot water all day, English spoken, secure, kitchen, 6 double rooms, breakfast included, very friendly owners. Highly recommended.

Outside Lima Outside Lima is the 5-star: **A2** *El Pueblo*, Santa Clara, Km 11.2, Vitarte (along the Central Highway), reservations T4441599/2427601. Huge luxurious complex in the country, with restaurants, bars, discos, swimming pool, tennis, shows, shops, you can visit for the day and use the facilities for a small fee.

In Punta *Hostal Luisfer*, in Urb. Miramar, C 7, MZL, Lot 13, T/F2307280 (in Lima call T4464453).
Hermosa Recommended.

Eating

In Miraflores **Expensive**: *Rosa Náutica*, T4470057, built on old British-style pier (Espigón No 4), in
● *on maps* Lima Bay. Delightful opulence, finest fish cuisine, experience the atmosphere by buying an expensive beer in the bar at sunset, open 1230-0200 daily. Highly recommended. *Las Brujas de Cachiche*, C Bolognesi 460, T4445310. An old mansion converted into bars and dining rooms, beautifully decorated, traditional food, best Lomo Saltado in town, live *criollo* music. Highly recommended. *Don Beta*, José Gálvez 667, T4469465. Open 0800-2200 daily, good for seafood. *Carlín*, La Paz 646, T4444134. Open 1200-1600, 1900-2400 daily, cosy, international cuisine. *La Gloria*, C Atahualpa 201, T4466504. Very smart, excellent food and service. *Bohemia*, Avda Santa Cruz 805, on the Plaza Gutiérrez, T4465240. Large menu of international food, great salads and sandwiches. Highly recommended. *Ambrosia*, at *Hotel Miraflores Park Plaza*, Malecón de la Reserva 1035, T2423000. Gourmet cuisine, one of the best in Lima. *Astrid y Gaston*, C Cantuarias 175, T4441496. Excellent local and international cuisine, one of the best. *Don Vito*, C Martín Dulanto 111, T4458156. Italian. *Don Rosalino*, Juan Figari 135. Pizzas. *Las Tejas*, Diez Canseco 340, T4444360. Open 1100-2300 daily, good, typical Peruvian food. *C'est Si Bon*, Cdte Espinar 663, T4469310. Open 1000-2200 daily, French-style.

Mid-range: *Café de Paris*, C Diez Canseco 180, T2422469. Great new French restaurant offering delicious soups, crepes etc, set 3-course meal for US$10, also good coffee. Recommended. *La Tranquera*, Avda Pardo 285, T4475111. Steaks, open 1200-2400 daily. *Martín Fierro*, Malecón Cisneros 1420, T4410199. Argentine, good Sunday buffet. *Silvestre*, Avda Benavides 420. Huge selection of juices and good sandwiches. *Chifa Kun Fa*, C San Martin 459 at Avda Larco, T4478634. Great Peruvian style Chinese food, excellent wan-tan soup. *Super Rueda*, C Porta 133, near the Cine Julieta, T4445609. Mexican food a-la Peru. *El Suche*, Centro Comercial El Suche, C La Paz 646, T2427090. International cuisine, nice ambience. *Cuarto y Mitad*, Malecón de la Marina, T4222075. Popular Grill. *Punta Sal*, C Jorge Chavez 694, T2424524. Good *ceviche*. Also in San Isidro, Avda Conquistadores 948. *El Reydel Pacifico*, Avda José Gálvez 558, T2424700. Open until 2100 on weekdays, 1800 at weekends, popular with locals, good fish soup. *Fuji*, Paseo de la Republica 4090, T4408531. Japanese. *Il Postino*, C Colina 401, T4468381. Great Italian food. *La Trattoria*, C Manuel Bonilla 106, 1 block from Parque Kennedy, T4467002. Italian cuisine, popular, best cheese-cake in Lima. *T.G.I Friday's*, Ovalo Gutiérrez, T2214080. American chain, somewhat modified menu. *Manolo*, Avda Larco 608. Open till 2230 daily, good food, popular. *Whatta Burger*, Grau 120. American-style hamburgers.

Cheap: *Mediterráneo Chicken*, Avda Benavides block 420, T4479337. Open 1200-2300 daily, good chicken and chips chain. *El Parquecito*, C Diez Canseco 150. Good cheap menu. *Pardo's Chicken*, Avda Benavides 730, T4464790. Chicken and chips, very good and popular. There are various small restaurants good for a cheap set meal along C Los Pinos with Avda Schell, at the bottom of Parque Kennedy. C San Ramon, more commonly known as Pizza Street (across from Parque Kennedy) is a pedestrian walkway lined with restaurants specializing in Italian food. Very popular and open all night on weekends.

Expensive: *La Fondue*, in *Hotel Oro Verde*, Via Central 150, T4214400. *La Réserve*, Las **In San Isidro** Flores 326, T4400952. Open 1200-1530, 1930-2400, excellent French, Italian and Peruvian cuisine. *Punta Sal*, Conquistadores 948, T4417431, 0900-1700 daily. *Valentino*, C Manuel Bañon 215, T4416174. One of Lima's best international restaurants, open 1200-1500, 1930-2400. *Chifa Royal*, Avda Prescott 231, T4210874. Excellent Sino-Peruvian food. *Matsuei*, C Manuel Bañon, T4224323. Sushi bar. *José Antonio*, B Monteagudo 200, T2640188. Open 1300-1600, 1930-2400 Monday-Saturday, creole and Peruvian dishes.

Mid-range: *Los Años Locos de San Isidro*, Avda Conquistadores 430, T4420454. Open 1000-2400 Monday-Saturday. *Mi Casa*, Augusto Tamayo 150, T4403780. Japanese, open 1200-1500, 1900-2300 Monday-Saturday. *Lung Fung*, Avda Rep de Panamá 3165, T4418817. Open 1200-1500, 1900-2400 daily, Chinese. *La Casa de España*, C Roma 190, T4703465. Open 1000-1600, 1900-2300 Monday-Saturday, 1000-1600 Sunday, Spanish. *La Carreta*, Rivera Navarrete 740, T4422690. Open 1200-2400 daily, Peruvian and international, good steaks. *Le Bistrot de mes Fils*, Avda Conquistadores 510, T4226308. Cozy French Bistrot, great food. *Segundo Muelle*, Avda Pezet 1455, 2 blocks from Avda Portillo, T2643323. Excellent ceviche, younger crowd. Recommended. *Aromas Peruanos*, Avda Guardia Civil 856, T2241482. Peruvian food. *Mi Casa*, C Augusto Tamayo 150, T4403780. Japanese food. *Sushi Ito*, Avda Miguel Dasso 110, T4400766. *Al Dente*, Avda Dos de Mayo 789, T4419877. Italian.

La Costa Verde, on Barranquito beach, T4772424. Excellent fish and wine, expensive **In Barranco** but recommended as the best by Limeños, Amex accepted, open 1200-2400 daily, Sunday buffet. *Manos Morenas*, Avda Pedro de Osma 409, T4670421. Open 1230-1630, 1900-2300, creole cuisine with shows some evenings (cover charge for shows). *El Buen Gusto*, Avda Grau 323, T4774199. Good for atmosphere, service, selection of meat dishes and desserts. *Abdala*, Avda Grau 340. Local and international food in a casual bar-like atmosphere. *Canta Rana*, Génova 101, T4778934. Open daily 1200-1700, good ceviche but expensive, small portions. *Taco Mex*, Avda Grau 302. Mexican fast food. *Manos Morenas*, Avda Pedro de Osma 409, T4760421. Excellent creole food, nightly shows. Recommended. *Cevichería Barranco*, Avda Panamericana Sur 270, 4 blocks from the main plaza, T4674560. Good.

In Chorrillos *Punta Arenas*, Santa Teresa 455, 1 block from the 1st block of Avda Huaylas, T4670053. Excellent seafood, especially *ceviche*, very good value.

In San Borja *El Piqueo Trujillano*, Avda San Luis 1956-58, T4761993. Open 1130-1830 Monday-Thursday, 1200-2100 Friday-Sunday, creole cooking. *El Molinero*, Avda Rosa Toro 1124, at the 32nd block of Avda Javier Prado Este, T3461082. Great *ceviche*, huge portions, cheap. Recommended.

In Lince *Blue Moon*, Pumacahua 2526, T4701631. Open 1030-0200 daily, expensive Italian bistro.

In Pueblo Libre *Taberna Quierolo*, Avda San Martín 1090, 2 blocks from Museo Nacional de Antropología y Arqueología. Old bar, good seafood and atmosphere, not open for dinner.

In Central Lima *L'Eau Vive*, Ucayali 370, T4275612, across from the Torre Tagle Palace. Run by nuns, open Monday-Saturday, 1230-1500 and 1930-2130, fixed-price lunch menu, Peruvian-style in interior dining room, or à la carte in either of dining rooms that open onto patio, excellent, profits go to the poor, Ave Maria is sung nightly between 2100 and 2200. *Restaurant El Maurito*, Jr Ucayali 212, T4262538. Peruvian/international, good pisco sours. *Chifa Cai*, Carabaya y Ucayali, clean, cheap, good fish dishes, ask about vegetarian if they're not too busy. *Raimondi*, Quesada 110 (no sign), T4277933. Open 1300-1600 daily, Peruvian, good (especially *ceviche*). *Heydi*, Puno 367. Good, cheap seafood, open daily 1100-1900, popular. *El Damero de Pizarro*, Jr de la Unión 543, T4272209. Typical Peruvian food, huge helpings, popular with locals, loud music. *Machu Picchu*, near *Hostal España* on Jr Ancash. Excellent set menus for breakfast (US$1.50, but ask as it's not on the menu) and lunch, huge portions. *Castañuelas Café*, Jr de la Union 873, at the Plaza San Martin, T4266453. Also a discotheque. *Manhatten*, Jr Miro Quesada 253, T4282117. Open Monday-Friday 0800-1900, low end executive-type restaurant, local and international food from US$5-10, good. *La*

Barranco

● **Eating & Bars**

0 métres 200
0 yards 218

1. Abdala
2. Barman's House
3. Canta Rana
4. El Buen Gusto
5. Juanito's Bodega Bar
6. La Noche Bar

Colmena, Avda Nicolas de Pierola 722. Good set lunches. *Cafe Carrara*, Jr Ica 330, attached to *Hostal Roma*. Open daily until 2300, multiple breakfast combinations, pancakes, sandwiches, nice ambience, good. *Cafe-Restaurant Accllahuasy*, Jr Ancash 400, around the corner from *Hostal España*. Open 0700-2300, good. Jr Olaya, on the Plaza de Armas between Jr de la Union and Jr Carabaya, is a small pedestrian walkway with many nice restaurants frequented during lunch hours by executives. A bit on the pricey side but good.

La Choza Náutica*, Jr Breña 102, close to SAEC. Good ceviche and friendly service. **In Breña** Around the corner from the SAEC, on Avda Alfonso Ugarte, is *Nakasone*, chicken and chips, cheap, greasy but good. Also *Chifa Angel*, which is good. *Razato* Avda Arica 298, 3 blocks from Plaza Bolognesi, T4234369. Excellent and cheap Peruvian dishes.

There are many highly recommended *chifas* in the district of Barrios Altos. *Wa Lok*, Jr **In Chinatown** Paruro 864, T4272656. Owner Liliana Com speaks fluent English, very friendly. *Salon Capon*, Jr Paruro 819. *Chun Koc Sen*, Jr Paruro 886, T4275281. *Shanghai*, Jr Andahuaylas 685, T4271560. *Fung Yen*, Jr Ucayali 744, T4276567.

In Miraflores: *Haiti*, Diagonal 160, Parque Kennedy. Open almost round the clock daily, **Cafés** great for people watching. *Vivaldi*, Avda Ricardo Palma 260, 1 block from Parque Kennedy, T4471636. Good, expensive. *Café Suisse*, Avda Larco 111 on Parque Kennedy, T4459797. One of Miraflores' oldest, expensive, good people-watching, very good cakes, European-style food and delicatessen. *Café Café*, Martin Olaya 250, near the Ovalo. Very popular, good atmosphere, over 100 different blends of coffee, good salads and sandwiches, very popular with 'well-to-do' Limeños. Also on the ground floor of the *Roosevelt Suites Hotel* in San Isidro. *Café de la Paz*, C Lima on Parque Kennedy, T4450940. Good outdoor café right on the park, expensive. *El Suche Café Bar*, Avda Alcanfores 471. Great sandwiches and crêpes, pleasant. and snacks, very pricey. *Café 21*, Avda Jose Pardo 4th block (ground floor of the *Las Americas Suites hotel*). Quiet and pleasant. *Café Milenium*, Avda Jose Pardo 4th block (ground floor of the *El Pardo Hotel*). Busy at lunch and at night. *Mangos*, Ovalo Gutiérrez. Good, popular. *Minotauro*, Avda 28 de Julio 192. Café/bookstore, you can rent books for US$0.35 per day.

In San Isidro: *News Café*, Avda Santa Luisa 110, T4216278. Great salads and desserts, popular and expensive. *Café Oro Verde*, Via Central 150 (behind Camino Real Shopping Centre), T4214400. Excellent for coffee, lunch and snacks. *Café Ole*, C Pancho Fierro 115 (1 block from *Hotel Olivar*), T4401186. Huge selection of entrees and desserts.

In Miraflores: *Bircher Berner*, Diez Canseco 487 y Grimaldo del Solar, Miraflores, **Vegetarian** T4444250. Closed Sunday, natural food store inside, slow service, good cheap *menú*. *Govinda*, Shell 634 y Grimaldo del Solar, T4469147. Also sells natural products, good. *El Paraiso*, C Alcanfores 416, 2 blocks from Avda Benavides. Natural foods/snacks, fruit salads and juices. Recommended.

In Central Lima: *Centro Natural Salud y Vigor*, Jr Puno 170. Fruit salads, yoghurt, juices, good variety, friendly. *Natur*, Moquegua 132, 1 block from Jr de la Union, T4278281. The owner, Humberto Valdivia, is also president of the South American Explorers Club's board of directors, the casual conversation, as well as his restaurant is highly recommended. *Comedor San Juan*, Camaná 949, 1 block from Plaza Francia, T4330263. *Centro de Medicina Natural*, Jr Chota 1462, next door to *Hostal de las Artes*, 1 block from Avda 9 de Diciembre, T3303851. Very good. There's a recommended vegetarian restaurant at Jr Ica 316, 2 doors from *Hostal Roma*. Also a good vegetarian *chifa* at Jr Callao 480, at Avda Tacna.

Yoghurt & ice cream *Heladería 4D*, Angamos Oeste 408. Open 1000-0100 daily, good Italian ice cream, at other locations in Monterrico and San Isidro. *Mi Abuela*, Angamos 393. Open 0900-2100 daily, probably the best yogurt in Lima, large selection of natural foods. Highly recommended. *Zugatti*, Avda Larco 361, across from Parque Kennedy. Good Italian gelato. *Yogen Früz*, Avda Larco 799, at C San Martín. Yogurt blended with your choice of fruit, excellent. Also at Jr de la Union 731, in Lima centre.

Bars & nightclubs

Lima has an excellent nightlife, with many places to choose from, all with different styles and themes. Often there is a cover charge ranging from US$3-10 per person. Unfortunately, there are some nightclubs and bars that deny entrance to people solely due to skin colour and assumed economic status. We **only** include here the names of the establishments that **do not** practise this policy.

In Miraflores **Bars**: *Marrakesh*, C Berlin 601. New, good. *Barajo*, Avda Larco 1180. Young crowd, fun. *Media Naranja*, C Schell 130, at the bottom of Parque Kennedy. Brasilian bar with typical drinks and food. *Torero Si Señor*, Avda Angamos Oeste 598. *O'Murphys*, C Schell 627. Great Irish pub (but no relation – Ed), "a must". *Phantom*, Avda Diagonal 344, next to Parque Kennedy, T2427949. Bar, internet café and restaurant in nice modern setting. *Si Señor*, C Bolognesi 706.

Nightclubs: there are many discotheques on Pizza Street by Parque Kennedy. *Tequila Rocks*, C Diez Canseco 146, a half block from Parque Kennedy. Good music, very popular. Recommended. *Mamut*, C Berlin 438, parallel to the 5th block of Avda Jose Pardo. Large and popular, one of Lima's best. *Downtown*, C Los Pinos 162, at the 2nd block of Avda Benavides. *Bauhaus*, C Bellavista 362. Black clothes, crucifixes and Robert Smith make-up compulsory (ie Gothic crowd). *Estatus*, Avda 28 de Julio 540, near Avda Larco. *Red & Blue*, in the *Grand Hotel Miraflores* at 28 de Julio 151. *Mitos*, Avda Benavides 621. Great architectural design, trendy. *La Parada*, C San Martín 587. Popular and recommended. *Siglo XIII*, C Gonzalez Prada 194.

In Barranco **Bars**: *Sargento Pimienta*, Bolognesi 755. Live music, always a favourite with Limeños. *Murdisco*, behind El Caserio, off Pasaje Sánchez Carrion. *Juanitos*, Avda Grau, opposite the park. Barranco's oldest bar, and perfect to start the evening. *El Ekeko*, Avda Grau 266. *La Estacion*, Avda Pedro de Osma 112. Live music, older crowd. *La Posada del Mirador*, near the *Puente de los Suspiros* (Bridge of Sighs). Beautiful view of the ocean, but you pay for the privilege. *Lorelie*, Avda 28 de Julio 205, behind the municipal library. *Democracia*, Avda Bolognesi 660. *Kafe Kistch*, Avda Bolognesi 743. *Barranco Bar*, Avda Grau 298. *Dejavú*, Avda Grau 294. *El Caserio*, Pasaje Sánchez Carrion 110. Great for dancing. Recommended. *Amnesia*, Pasaje Sánchez Carrion. *La Noche*, Avda Bolognesi 307, at Pasaje Sánchez Carrion. A Lima institution. *Florentino*, Avda Grau 689. Also a peña. *Golem*, Avda Salaverry 139. *Los 7 Pecados*, Avda Bolognesi 98. *El Mas Alla*, Pasaje Sánchez Carrion 110. *Dirty Nelly's*, Avda Pedro de Osma 135, inside the *Mochileros Hostal*. Small, cozy, nice and Irish.

Nightclubs: many of the bars in this area turn into discotheques as the evening goes on. *Noctambul*, Avda Grau. Once Lima's most popular discotheque, large and modern. *Decimo Planeta*, Avda Bolognesi 198. *My Place*, C Domeyer 122. *Las Terrazas*, Avda Grau 290.

In San Isidro *Torremolinos*, Avda Conquistadores 183. Older crowd, a good bar (but no Watney's Red Barrel). *Escandelo*, Avda Camino Real 147. *Knights*, Avda Conquistadores 605.

Ceanus Piano Bar, in *Hotel Los Delfines*, C Los Eucaliptos 555. Perfect for a relaxing, if expensive, evening. *Bogart*, Avda Pardo y Aliaga 456. *Tutu Tango*, Avda Camino Real 111.

Mirage, Avda La Marina 1400. *Nuevo Reflejos*, Avda La Marina 1500. *Bertolotto*, **In San Miguel** Malecón Bertolotto 770. *Woodstock*, Malecón Bertolotto 760.

Svago Beach, Complejo Nocturno Costa Verde. **In Chorrillos**

Queirolo Bar, Jr Camana 900 at Jr Quilca. Excellent for local colour, "a must". **In Central Lima**

NB The centre of town, specifically Jr de la Unión has many discotheques. It's best to avoid the nightlife spots on and around the intersection of Avda Tacna, Avda Piérola and Avda de la Vega. These places are on the rough side and the foreigner will most likely receive much unwanted attention.

Entertainment

Alianza Francesa, Avda Arequipa 4595, Miraflores, T2417014. Mon-Sat 1700-2100. **Art galleries** *Ediciones Wu*, C Diez Canseco 150, 2nd Flr, Miraflores, T2420221. Artist Frances Wu's studio is also a gallery of engravings, etchings and other graphics, with an emphasis on Peruvian artists. *La Quinta*, Avda Grau 170, oficina C, Miraflores, T4448816. Contemporary engravings. Old maps of Peru and South America. *Banco Wiese*, Avda Larco 1101, Miraflores, T4452390. Open Mon-Sat 1000-2000. Permanent exhibition of photos and drawings of the excavation at the pre-Inca site of El Brujo. *Asociación Cultural Peruano-Británico*, (John Harriman Gallery), Avda Bellavista 531, Miraflores, T4479760/4468511. Open Mon-Sat 1000-1300, 1600-2000. *Miraflores Municipal Gallery*, corner of Avda Larco and Diez Canseco, Miraflores, T4440540. Open Mon-Sun 1000-2200. *Praxis Arte Internacional*, C San Martin 689, Barranco, T/F4772322. Open Mon-Sat 1700-2100.

The Friday edition of *El Comercio* includes a booklet called *Vistas & Buenos* detailing **Cinemas** the following week's entertainment information. The *'Crónicas'* section of *El Comercio* has a daily entertainment list as well, but not as detailed. Tuesdays are half price at most cinemas for show times throughout the day and night.

There are many good cinemas throughout the city. Most films are in English with subtitles and cost US$2 in the centre and around US$4-5 in Miraflores. Cinemas in the centre tend to have poor sound quality.

In Miraflores: *Ciné Alcazar*, Avda Santa Cruz 814, on the Ovalo Gutiérrez, T4226345. Good choice of quality restaurants within short walking distance. *Ciné Benavides*, Avda Benavides 4981, T4488900. *Ciné El Pacífico*, on the Ovalo by Parque Kennedy, T4456990. Modern and expensive. *Ciné Romeo y Julieta*, Pasaje Porta 115, at the bottom of Parque Kennedy, T4475476.

In San Isidro: *Ciné Orrantia*, Avda Arequipa 2701, T4224407. *Ciné Real*, Avda Camino Real 492, T4223575.

In Monterrico: *Ciné El Polo*, Centro Comercial El Polo, T 434-1980, opposite the US embassy. New, good sound, pricey. *Ciné Mark*, Jockey Plaza Shopping Centre, T4359262. The best in town.

In Santa Beatriz: *Ciné Roma*, C Teniente Fernández 242, 9th block of Avda Arequipa, T4338618.

In central Lima: *Ciné Metro*, Plaza San Martín, T4284954. *Ciné Adán y Eva*, Jr de la Unión 805, T4288460. One of the few downtown theatres of any quality, cheap, too.

Some *Ciné Clubs* are: *El Cinematógrofo*, Pérez Roca 196, T4771961, Barranco. *Filmoteca de Lima*, Avda 9 de Diciembre 125 (better known as Colón), T4234732. *Cooperativa Santa Elisa*, Jr Cailloma 824. *Euroidiomas*, Juan Fanning 520, Miraflores. *La Otra Vida*, Valdelomar 665, Pueblo Libre. *Ciné Club Melies*, Avda Bolívar 635, Pueblo Libre, T4248441. *Raimondi*, Alejandro Tirado 274. *Ciné Club Miraflores*, Avda Larco 770, in the Miraflores Cultural Centre building, T4462649. *Instituto Cultural Peruano-Norte Americano*, Avda Cusco 446, T4283530. *Asociación Cultural Peruano Británico*, Avda Bellavista 531, Miraflores, T4454326. *Centro Cultural de la Universidad Católica del Peru*, Avda Camino Real 1075, San Isidro, T2226899.

Peñas *Museo de Arte* offers courses in various typical Peruvian dances and hosts performances. Check at the museum for schedules. *Hatuchay Peña*, Trujillo 228, across the bridge past the post office, in Rímac, T4330455. *Las Brisas de Titicaca*, Pasaje Walkuski 168, at the 1st block of Avda Brasil near Plaza Bolognesi, T4237405. US$7 entry, a Lima institution. *Sachun*, Avda Del Ejercito 657, Miraflores, T4410123/4414465. Great shows on weekdays as well. *Asi Es Mi Peru*, Avda Aviación 3390, San Borja, T4762419.

The following are all in Barranco: *Manos Morenas*, Avda Pedro de Osma 409, T4670421/4674920. Also a restaurant, older crowd, great shows beginning at 2230. *Las Guitarras*, C Manuel Segura 295 (6th block of Avda Grau), T4772395/4791874. Recommended. *La Esquina del Parque*, Sánchez Carrión y Avda Grau, T4772072. Excellent shows with typical dances from all over Peru. *Los Balcones*, Avda Grau across from main plaza. Good, noisy and crowded. *La Estación de Barranco*, at Pedro de Osma 112, T4775030. Good, family atmosphere, varied shows, US$14 cover charge. *De Rompe y Raja*, Manuel Segura 127, T2473099. *Pericho's*, Avda Pedro de Osma 1st block at the main plaza, T4771311.

Theatre The most professional plays are staged at *Teatro Segura*, Jr Huancavelica 265. Unfortunately, the *Teatro Municipal* completely burned down in August of 1998. Restoration plans are in the works. *Teatro Marsano*, C General Suárez 409. *Teatro Canut*, Avda Petit Thouars 4550, Miraflores, T4225373. *Teatro Auditorio Miraflores*, Avda Larco 1150, T4479378. *Teatro Larco*, Avda Larco 1036, Miraflores T4478310. *Alianza Frances de Miraflores*, Avda Arequipa 4595, T2417014. *Teatro Británico*, C Bellavista 527, Miraflores, T4479760 (details in *Lima Times*). *Teatro Mocha Grana*, C Saenz Peña 107, Barranco, T4770759. *Teatro en mi Casa*, Avda Paseo de los Andes 1147, Pueblo Libre, T4604768.

Festivals

On **18 January** is the anniversary of the *founding of Lima*. **Semana Santa**, or Holy Week, is a colourful spectacle with processions. **28-29 July** is *Independence*, with music and fireworks in the Plaza de Armas on the evening before. **October** is the month of *Our Lord of the Miracles* with impressive processions (see *El Comercio* for dates and routes). On **3 November** is *San Martín de Porres*.

Shopping

Since so many artesans have come from the Sierra to Lima, it is possible to find any kind of handicraft in the capital. The prices are the same as in the highlands, and the quality is high. Among the many items which can be bought in the capital are silver and gold handicrafts of all kinds, Indian hand-spun and hand-woven textiles and manufactured textiles in Indian designs. It is better to buy alpaca pullovers in the

Sierra. However, although Lima is more expensive, it is often impossible to find the same quality of goods elsewhere. You can find llama and alpaca wool products such as ponchos, rugs, hats, blankets, slippers, coats, sweaters, etc. Note that genuine alpaca is odourless wet or dry, but wet llama 'stinks'.

Lima is a good place to buy *arpilleras*, appliqué pictures of Peruvian life (originated in Chile with political designs). These are made with great skill and originality by women in the shanty towns. The fine leather products on sale are mostly hand made. The *mate burilado*, or engraved gourd found in every tourist shop, is cheap and a genuine expression of folk art. These are cheaper in the villages near Huancayo (see page 430). There are also bargains on offer for clothing made from high quality Pima cotton.

Antiques are available in Miraflores on Avda La Paz. Also at: *Forum*, Avda Larco 1150, Miraflores, T4461313. *Porta 725*, C Porta 735, Miraflores, T4476158. Open Monday-Friday 1030-1330, 1530-1930, by appointment only. *El Almacén del Arte*, C Francia 339, Miraflores, T2429274. *Borkas*, C Las Flores 249, San Isidro, T4418306. Open Monday-Friday 0900-1900. **Antiques**

Unfortunately, for a cosmopolitan city of 8 million people, Lima doesn't offer a large selection of bookstores with foreign language books. The best place to find novels in English is **Libreria Mosca Azul**, located next to Parque Salazar on Malecón de la Reserva 713, Miraflores, T4456264. For beautiful but expensive coffee table books, the bookstore chain *Epoca*, has a decent selection with 3 locations: Avda José Pardo 399, T4478907, Miraflores; Avda Comandante Espinar 864 (near Ovalo Gutiérrez), T2422296, Miraflores; and Jr Belén 1072 T4249545, Lima centre near Plaza San Martin. *American Book Center* (ABC Books), on Benavides 455, T4444099, Miraflores. Has few books in English but sells nice coffee table books, a few maps and some magazines in English. Magazines are another story. Whether in downtown Lima or Miraflores, almost all street kiosks sell up to date magazines in English such as Time, Newsweek, People etc. Jr Camana between Parque Francia and Avda Nicolás de Piérola near the Plaza San Martín has many stores selling back issues at cheap prices. For the most recently published magazines and newspapers, try *Mallcco's* on Avda Larco 175, on the Parque Kennedy roundabout, open daily 0800-2100. They have a wide variety of magazines (expensive but the latest releases) and newspapers from England. In front of *Café Haiti* by Parque Kennedy, you'll often see the men with stacks of newspapers for sale. These are taken from arriving international flights so tend to be only a day or two old; bargain hard. The *Hotel Sheraton* sells the New York Times and the Wall Street Journal. Many cafés have various foreign newspapers to browse through while enjoying a cup of coffee or a sandwich. **Bookshops**

Camping stores are few and far between in Lima. It's very much recommended that you bring all gear needed from your home country. *Alpamayo*, Avda Larco 345, Miraflores at Parque Kennedy, T4451671. Sleeping mats, boots, rock shoes, climbing gear, water filters, tents, backpacks etc., very expensive but top quality equipment. *Todo Camping*, Avda Angamos Oeste 350, Miraflores, near Avda Arequipa, T4476279. Open Monday-Saturday 1000-2000, sells 100% deet, bluet gas canisters, lots of accessories, tents, crampons and backpacks. *Camping Center*, Avda Benavides 1620, Miraflores. *Outdoor Peru*, Centro Comercial Chacarilla, store 211, on Avda Caminos del Inca 257, Surco, T3720428. Open 0900-2100, has a decent selection of camping equipment. **Camping equipment**

Silvania Prints, Avda Conquistadores 915, San Isidro, T4226440, also at Avda Diez Canseco 376, Miraflores. Open Monday-Saturday 0930-1800. They sell modern silk-screen prints on Pima cotton with precolumbian designs. *Centro Artesanal 'El* **Handicrafts**

Arte Peruano', Avda Alfonso Ugarte 901-925, T4241978. Open 0900-2000. Ask for Carlos Ramos for especially fine retablos, or Guillermo Arce for fine Cajamarca mirrors in colonial style, they also sell rugs from Ayacucho and San Pedro de Cajas, ceramics from Ayacucho and Cusco and other items (there is a nationwide handicraft association of this name). *La Casa de la Mujer Artesana*, Juan Pablo Ferandini 1550 (Avda Brasil cuadra 15), Pueblo Libre, T4238840, F4234031. Cooperative run by Movimiento Manuela Ramos, excellent quality work mostly from *pueblos jóvenes*, open Monday-Friday 1200-2000. There are vendors on Avda Nicolás de Piérola selling oil paintings of Andean scenes.

Miraflores is the best place for high quality, pricey handicrafts. There are many shops on and around Avda La Paz, and on Petit Thouars, blocks 53/54. Recommended is *Kuntur Wasi*, Ocharan 182, T4440557. Open Monday-Saturday, English-speaking owner very knowledgeable about Peruvian textiles, frequently has exhibitions of fine folk art and crafts, high quality. *Antisuyo*, Jr Tacna 460, Miraflores. Monday-Friday 0900-1930, Saturday 1030-1830, an indigenous cooperative run by an English-woman, sells high-quality handicrafts from all regions, reasonable prices, T4472557 (another outlet in Cusco). *Agua y Tierra*, Diez Canseco 298 y Alcanfores, Miraflores, T4446980. Highly recommended for fine crafts and indigenous art. *Centro Comercial El Alamo*, corner of La Paz and Diez Canseco, Miraflores, 0900-2000. Small shopping centre with excellent selection of jewellery and craft stores. Recommended. *El Arcon*, Centro Comercial, Pasaje El Suche, Avda La Paz 646 #12, Miraflores, T4476149. Open Monday-Friday 1030-2000, Saturday 1030-1400. Superb selection of crafts and antiques. Very pricey but top quality. *Las Pallas*, Cajamarca 212, parallel to 6th block of Avda Grau, Barranco, T4774629. Open Monday-Saturday 0900-1900. Good quality handicrafts. Specializes in Andean amulets, ceremonial offerings, fine textiles, masks and pottery. See *H Stern's* jewellery stores at *Hotels Miraflores César* and *Sheraton*, and at the International Airport.

Alpaca wool for knitting or weaving from *Alpaca III*, Avda Larco 671, Miraflores, T4471623. English spoken, made-to-measure cotton shirts in 24 hours from Sr Hurtado, Jr Carabaya 1108, and in 48 hours from Luz Manrique, Cailloma 328, T4279472. *Alpaca 859*, Avda Larco 859, Miraflores, T4477163. Excellent quality alpaca and baby alpaca products, English and French spoken. *Royal Alpaca*, Centro Comercial, Pasaje El Suche, Avda La Paz 646 #14, Miraflores, T4442150. Recommended for quality (also at the Gold Museum). *La Casa de la Alpaca*, Avda La Paz 665, Miraflores, T4476271. Open Monday-Friday 0930-2100, Saturday 0930-1800.

Maps **Instituto Geográfico Nacional**, Avda Aramburú 1190, Surquillo, T4759960, F4753075. They have an extensive collection of maps for sale or research on the premises. They sell a standard road map of Peru (1:2,000,000) for US$8, which is very good. Also departmental maps at various scales for US$6.50 and satellite maps at 1:100,000 and 1:250,000 for US$8 (not too helpful). They have excellent topos for sale at US$8 as well. Various scales. Recommended. Some maps representing border areas might be harder to get. Geological and political maps are also sold. They have a beautiful 4-sheet map of Peru costing US$33. At the same size and price is a geological map. Both are recommended. Bring your passport and wear long pants (trousers) or you won't be allowed in. **Ingemmet** (Instituto Geológico Minero Y Metalúrgico), Avda Canadá 1470, San Borja, T2253158/2242964/2242965, F2254540, E ingemmet5@ chavin.rcp.net.pe. Sells a huge selection of geographic maps ranging from US$12 to US$112. Also satellite, aeromagnetic, geochemical and departmental mining maps. Aerial photographs are available at **Servicio Aerofotográfico Nacional**, Surco Airforce Base, open Monday-Friday 0800-1400. **Lima 2000**, Avda Arequipa 2625, Lince (near the intersection with Avda Javier Prado), T4403486, F4403480, open Monday-Friday 0900-1300 and 1400-1800. Have an excellent street map of Lima (the only one worth buying), US$10, or US$14 in booklet form.

Parque Kennedy, the main park of Miraflores, hosts a daily crafts market from **Markets** 1700-2300. **Feria Artesanal**, Avda La Marina y Avda Sucre, in Pueblo Libre. This crafts market lines Avda La Marina, starting at the 6th block, and is one of the biggest in Lima. **Artesania Carabaya**, Jr Carabaya 319 at the Plaza de Armas. There are crafts markets on **Avda Petit Thouars** in Miraflores near Parque Kennedy. Avda Petit Thouars runs parallel to Avda Arequipa. Its 54 blocks end at Avda Ricardo Palma, a few blocks from Parque Kennedy. At the 51st block you'll find an unnamed market area with a large courtyard. This is the largest crafts arcade in Miraflores. A few more blocks towards the park is another bazaar, **Artesania Gran Chimú**. It's a bit smaller than its counterpart, but carries the same merchandise. Both of these are open 7 days a week. Just a block from Plaza Grau in the centre of town is **Polvos Azules**, the official black market of Lima. The normal connotations of a 'black market' do not apply here as this establishment is an accepted part of Lima society, condoned by the government and frequented by people of all economic backgrounds. It's good for cameras, hiking boots, music and an extensive selection of walkmans. **NB** This is not a safe area, so be alert and put your money in your front pockets. Lima has 3 supermarket chains: Santa Isabel, E. Wong and Metro. They all are well stocked and carry a decent supply of imported goods (Marmite, Tesco products etc.). The Santa Isabel on Avda Benavides y Avda Alcanfores in Miraflores is open 24 hours.

For camera film try: *Foto Magnum*, Ocoña 190, Lima Centre, T4271599, F4272060, **Photography** open Monday-Friday 0945-1900, Saturday 0900-1400. Also camera accessories. *Laboratorio Color Profesional*, Avda Benevides 1171, Miraflores T4467621. Open Monday-Friday 0900-1900, Saturday 0900-1300. Professional quality developing, fairly priced, touch-ups, repair services, excellent for slide developing, sells top quality equipment, film and accessories, the best you'll find in Lima. Highly recommended. Also *Metro Supermarket*, corner Alfonso Ugarte y Avda Venezuela (2 blocks from South American Explorers Club), T4235533. Open Monday-Saturday 0900-2200, Sunday 0900-2100.

Sport

For those interested in exercise and the massive consumption of beer (at the same **Athletics** time), then the Lima Hash House Harriers is just what you're looking for. This hardcore mix of Peruvians and foreigners meet every 2 weeks at a different location each time. This is an informal group who just want to meet new people, run or walk and drink copious quantities of beer (before, during and after the run). Runs conclude with a not-too-serious ceremony, like singing "Sweet Chariot" while chugging suds out of your shoe, followed by a barbeque. There is a US$5 charge for food and beer. The event usually falls on a Saturday (sometimes Sunday). Meeting time is generally 1430, the run starts at 1500. Contact Marisol Diaz, T4333200.

Association football matches and various athletic events take place at the National Stadium, in the centre of the city on ground given by the British community on the 100th anniversary of Peru's Declaration of Independence. The local soccer derby is Universitario against Alianza Lima (tickets US$2.50-25).

Basketball is played on Mondays and Thursdays at 1900-2100 at Colegio Roosevelt, **Ball games** Avda Las Palmeras 325, Camacho-Monterrico. Contact Chris Akin T4350890 during school hours (0830-1600). Other sports played: the local **softball** league has 8 teams. Games are played on Saturday mornings. **Volleyball** on Tuesdays at 1900-2100; and **indoor football** on Fridays at 1830-2030.

There are 2 bullfight seasons: October to first week in December and during July. They **Bull fighting** are held in the afternoons on Sunday and holidays. Tickets can be bought at Plaza

Acho from 0930-1300 (T4811467), or Farmacia Dezza, Avda Conquistadores 1144, San Isidro, T4408911/3798. Prices range from US$14 to US$90 (see page 99).

Cockfights For those interested in cockfights, contact El Circulo de Aficionados a los Gallos de Pelea, T4422151. Also at Avda Paseo de la República 6500, Barranco at the end of the Via Expresa, T4770934/4418718.

Cycling Most bike shops have free copies of the biking publication called *Boletín Informativo De La Comisión De Ciclismo De Montaña*. Good for what's going on in the Lima biking community. *Best Internacional*, Avda Comandante Espinar 320, Miraflores, T4464044 and Avda Arenales 2246, Lince, T4701704. Open Monday-Saturday 1000-1400, 1600-2000. Sells leisure and racing bikes, also repairs, parts and accessories. *Biclas*, Avda Los Conquistadores, San Isidro, T4400890. Open Monday-Friday 1000-1300, 1600-2000, Saturday 1000-1300. Great bike shop, staff very knowledgeable, tours possible, good selection of bikes, repairs and accessories. Highly recommended. *Willy Pro*, Avda Dos de Mayo 430, San Isidro, T2220289. Open Monday-Friday 0900-1300, 1500-2000. Has a selection of specialized bikes and helpful staff. *Casa Okuyama*, Jr Montevideo 785, Lima, T4283444/4263307. Open Monday-Friday 0900-1300, 1400-1800, Saturday 0900-1300. Repairs, parts, try here for 28 inch tyres. *Cycling*, Avda Benavides 1909, Miraflores, T2710247. *Peru Bike*, C Pedro de Osma 560, Barranco, T4670757. Bike sales, repairs and accessories. *Cicloroni*, C Las Casas 019, San Isidro, 32nd block of Petit Thouars, T2217643/2226358. Open Monday-Saturday 0900-2100, for repairs, parts and accessories, Jorge Miranda (repairs manager) has good information about the Lima biking scene, ask about Saturday and Sunday bike rides. **Contacts**: for information about all aspects of cycling in Lima and Peru, contact Richard Fernandini at 4421402/4411377 during the hours of 0900-1300, 1500-1800. He speaks English. Tito López at 4631747, organizer of the now defunct Lima Bike Touring Club, also gives good information. Also George Schofield, T2311385. Gustavo Prado T2710247. The Peruvian Federation of Biking, Puerta 4 of the National Stadium, T4336646.

Fishing *Todo Pesca*, Avda Benevides 249, Miraflores, T/F4455143. Supplies and accessories. Ask about renting equipment.

Horse racing The Jockey Club of Peru (Hipódromo de Monterrico) has horse races every Tuesday and Thursday at 1800, Saturday and Sunday at 1400. Bets start at US$0.75. For information about Peruvian Paso horses contact the Asociación Nacional de Caballos de Paso at T4476331.

Lima Cricket and The Lima Cricket and Football Club is at C Justo Vigil 200, Magdalena del Mar,
Football Club T2640027/2640028. 7 clay courts, 1 fronton court, 2 squash courts, swimming pool and gymnasium. **Rugby** is also played.

Mountaineering *Asociación de Andinismo de la Universidad de Lima*, Universidad de Lima, Javier Prado
and trekking Este s/n, T4376767. Meetings on Wednesday 1800-2000, offers climbing courses. *Club*
clubs *de Montañeros Américo Tordoya*, Jr Tarapacá 384, Magdalena, T4606101. Meetings Thursday 2000, contact Gonzalo Menacho. Climbing excursions ranging from easy to difficult. *Trek Andes*, Avda Benavides 212, of 1203, Miraflores, T/F4478078. For information contact Percy Tapia. Good advice from Richard Hidalgo, T4482691. Good climbing and hiking equipment shop, *Alpamayo*, at Avda Larco 345, Miraflores, T4451671, F4450370. The owner Sr Enrique Ramírez speaks fluent English. *Asociación Latinoamericana de Deportes de Aventura*, T4486762/9461785. *Patones Trails*, T4501947/2585384. Camping and hiking. *Grupo Cordillera*, T4201822/ 9428063. Tunnelling and other adventure-type excursions. *Club de Ecoturismo*, T4233329.

Contact *Condor adventure*, T2645244, F2217116. Christian Munch (cellular) **Paragliding** T9959595. Fritz Schilter (cellular) T9938353. Alfonso Casabonne (office) T2477315, (home) T4681279.

Lima Polo Club, Avda El Cortijo 700, Monterrico, T4365712. Matches every Saturday **Polo** and Sunday at 1400.

Strokers, Avda Benavides 325, Miraflores, near Avda Larco. Good tables and cues, **Pool halls** fully-stocked bar, popular and friendly. Recommended. *Cassis*, C Independencia 130, Miraflores, at the 4th block of Avda Pardo. 5 tables in perfect condition, bar setting, expensive.

Mundo Submarino, Avda Conquistadores 791, San Isidro, T4417604. Sr Alejandro Pez **Scuba diving** is a professional diver, fluent in German, Italian, English, French and Portuguese and a member of the Peruvian Federation of Skin Divers, he sells new as well as second-hand diving equipment (brand names), rents equipment to certified divers only, great for general information. Recommended. *Kailua Dive Shop*, Avda Conquistadores 969, San Isidro, T/F4414057. Owner Paolo is the definitive authority on diving, he organizes trips, offers certification courses, sells some high quality gear and is a wealth of information, extremely professional. All those interested in diving in Peru **must** stop by his shop. *Peru Divers*, Avda Conquistadores 946, San Isidro, T4413282, F4217814, E perudivers@bellnet.com.pe. Owner Luis (Lucho) Rodriguez, a certified PADI instructor.

*F*ocus, De la Torre Ugarte 320, Lince, T4225644. For repairs. Will pick up and drop off **Surfing** bikes. *Gordo Barreda*, Avda Atahualpa 287, Miraflores, T4459621. Has a decent selection of boards. *Wayo Whiler*, Avda 28 de Julio 287, Barranco, T2470299/2541344. For accessories, gear and repairs. *Billa Bong*, C Ignacio Merino 711, Miraflores, T4218217/2214196. Australian surf wear. *Picante*, Avda Bolívar 133, Miraflores. *O'Neills*, Avda Santa Cruz 851, Miraflores, T4450406. Equipment, clothes, accessories, good information. *Klimax*, Jose Gonzalez 488, Miraflores, T4471685. *Tubos* is a magazine dedicated solely to the Peruvian surfing scene. It's sold at most kiosks and bookstores that carry a magazine selection. Good information given with a visit to the office, at Pasaje Los Pinos 153, near Parque Kennedy, T4455443/2427922, E revistatubosperu@hotmail.com.

Club Las Terrazas, Malecón 28 de Julio 390, near Parque Kennedy. This private club **Tennis** has 12 courts which are available to non-members at US$5 per hour from 0700-1800.

Transport

Car rental: most rental companies have an office at the airport, where you can **Car hire** arrange everything and pick up and leave the car. It's recommended to test-drive car before signing contract as quality varies. Cars can be hired from: *Alamo Rent A Car*, Avda Comandante Espinar 349, Miraflores, T4444122/4443934/4443906, F2417431. *Avis Rent A Car*, Avda Bolognesi 599, T2426631, F2414852. *Dollar Rent A Car*, Avda La Paz 434, oficina 702, Miraflores, T4460876/4445646, Tx4444294. *Budget Car Rental*, Avda Canaval y Moreyra 476, San Isidro, T4419458/4410493, airport, T5751624, F4414174 (24 hrs). *Hertz Rent A Car*, Aristides Aljovin 472, Miraflores, T4444441, F4455479. *Paz Rent A Car*, Cayalti 386, Centro Comercial, Monterrico, T4363941, F4374471, Avda Diez Canseco 319, Miraflores, T4464395, F2424306. *Value Rent A Car*, C Francia 597, Miraflores, T4479798/4479786, F4473021.

Lima

National car rentals: *Avis*, Avda Javier Prado Este 5235, Camacho, T4341111/4340101, F4377813, Avda Grimaldo del Solar 236, Miraflores, T4463156, F4464937, Airport, T5751637 (24 hrs). *Budget* (see above). Dollar, Avda La Paz 438, Miraflores, T4444920/4443050, F4443498, Airport, T5751637 (24 hrs). *First Rent A Car*, Avda El Alamo 243, oficina 305, Centro Comercial, Monterrico, T/F4361943. *Hertz*, Avda Rivera Navarrete 550, San Isidro, T4424475, T/F4424509, Airport, T5751590/5750912 (24 hrs). *Inka's Rent A Car*, C Cantuarias 160, Miraflores, T4455716, T/F4479200, Airport, T5751390 (24 hours).

Air connections For all information on international flight arrivals and departures, airport facilities and transport to and from the Lima airport, see **Touching down** (page 33). For all information on domestic flights, see **Getting around** (page 45). Domestic flight schedules are given under the relevant destinations.

Buses Although Lima is home to a seemingly never-ending list of bus companies, only a small percentage are actually recommended. The following is a concise, user-friendly list of the companies repeatedly recommended for either their service or professionalism. Note that some less reputable companies are included simply because they're the only ones with buses to certain destinations. It's best to buy tickets the day before travelling. Most offer daily service. Confirm that the bus leaves from same place that ticket was purchased. For prices and approximate duration of trip, refer to the destination.

Cruz del Sur: according to sources within this company, the terminal at Jr Quilca 531 in downtown Lima will discontinue the bus service 'sometime in 1999'. It will become strictly a ticketing and information counter. Two new terminals have begun operation: Avda Paseo de la Republica 801, opposite the National Stadium, T3323210/3324000/3323209. This terminal offers 'Ideal' service only, which is basic, but the buses are okay, though some might drive around hoping to fill bus before heading off. They go to: Ica, Arequipa, Cusco, Puno, Chiclayo, Trujillo, Chincha, Cañete, Camana, Ilo, Moquegua, Nasca, Pisco and Juliaca. The other is at Avda Javier Prado 1109, San Isidro, T2256163/2256200/2256027/225/6058/2256086. This terminal offers the 'Imperial' service, which are luxury buses, more expensive and direct, with no chance of passengers in the aisle. They go to: Tumbes, Sullana, Huancayo, Piura, Chiclayo, Trujillo, Huaraz, Jauja, Camana, Arequipa, Moquegua, Ilo, Tacna, Cusco and La Paz (**NB** this service is Imperial only to Arequipa, where you must transfer to an Ideal bus for the remaining leg of the trip).

Ormeño: there is *also* talk of closing the central terminal at: Avda Carlos Zavala 177, Lima Centre, T4275679. Buses to: Arequipa, Ayacucho, Camana, Cañete, Caraz, Carhuaz, Casma, Chiclayo, Chimbote, Chincha, Cusco, Huaraz, Ica, Ilo, Juliaca, Moquegua, Nasca, Pisco, Piura, Puno, Sullana, Tacna, Trujillo and Tumbes. The other terminal is at: Avda Javier Prado Este 1059, Santa Catalina (La Victoria), T4721710. Aside from international destinations, this station offers what they call "Royal Class" service. This consists of super luxurious buses and all that goes with it. They go to: Trujillo, Tumbes, Chiclayo, Ica, Pisco (Hotel Paracas), Arequipa, Tacna and Nasca.

Other companies include: Movil Tours, Jr Montevideo 581, Lima Centre, T4262727/4280740. Very recommended service to Huaraz. Lots of leg room. **Expreso Molina**, Jr Ayacucho 1141, Lima Centre, T4280617. Good service to Ayacucho on newly paved road via Pisco. **Rodríguez**, Avda Roosevelt 354, Lima Centre, T4280506. Huaraz, Caraz, Yungay, Carhuaz. Recommended to arrive in Huaraz and then use local transportation to points beyond. Good. Various levels of bus service. **Mariscal Cáceres**, Avda Carlos Zavala 211, Lima Centre, T4272844. To: Huancayo and Jauja.

Airline offices

Domestic
AeroPerú
head office at
Avda Pardo 602,
Miraflores,
T2410606,
F4470553; and
Avda Garcilaso de
la Vega 870,
T4478255
Aero Continente
Avda Jose Pardo
651, Miraflores,
T/F4450535/2421
964; and Francisco
Masias 528, 8th
Flr, San Isidro,
T4428770/7829
Aero Cóndor
Avda Juan de
Arona 781, San
Isidro,
T4425215/4425663
F2215783
TAA
Avda Jose Pardo
640, oficina T2,
Miraflores,
T2421980/4454342
F4461585
Grupo Ocho
military airline,
T4529560, at the
airport (desk not
always staffed)

International
Aeroflot
Avda
Comandante

Espinar 233,
Miraflores, E
aeroflot@peru.itet
e.com.pe,
T4448717/4448718
*Aerolineas
Argentinas*
Avda Jose Pardo
805, 3rd Flr,
Miraflores,
T2413327/4441387
Aero Mexico
C Aristides Aljovin
472, Miraflores,
T4444441
Air Canada
C Lord Nelson
128A, Miraflores,
T4424541/4428409
Air France
Avda Jose Pardo
601, Miraflores,
T4449285
Air New Zealand
C Aristides Aljovin
472, Miraflores,
T4444441
Alitalia
Avda Camino Real
497, 3rd Flr, San
Isidro,
T4428505/06/07
American Airlines
Avda Juan de
Arona 830, 14th
Flr, San Isidro,
T4428610/4428614
/4428555/4756161
Avianca
Avda Paz Soldan

225, oficina C5,
San Isidro,
E almeydasa@prot
elsa.com.pe,
T2217822
British Airways
C Andalucia 174,
Miraflores,
T4226600/4220889
Continental
C Victor Andreas
Belaunde 147,
Edificio Real,
oficina 101, San
Isidro,
T2214340/2227080
Copa
Avda Dos de
Mayo 755,
Miraflores,
T4449778/4444155
Ecuatoriana
Avda Jose Pardo
231, Miraflores,
T2415219/444051
0/2415210
Iberia
Avda Camino Real
390, 9th Flr, San
Isidro,
T4214616/4214633
KLM
Avda Jose Pardo
805, 6th Flr,
Miraflores,
T2421240/2421241
Lacsa
Avda Dos de
Mayo 755,
Miraflores,

T4460033/446075
8/4469419
Lan Chile
Avda Jose Pardo
805, 5th Flr,
Miraflores,
T2415522
*Lloyd Aereo
Boliviano*
Avda Jose Pardo
231, Miraflores,
T2415219/444051
0/2415210
Lufthansa
Avda Jorge
Basadre 1330, San
Isidro, T4424466
Mexicana
Avda Juan
Fanning 573,
Miraflores,
T2414292
Saeta
C Andalucia 174,
Miraflores,
T4221710/4428256
Servivensa
C Jorge Basadre
1330, San Isidro,
T4424430.
United Airlines
Avda Camino Real
390, 9th Flr, San
Isidro,
T4213365/4381060
Varig
Avda Camino Real
456, 8th Flr, San
Isidro, T4424361

Very good. Service ranges from basic to deluxe. **Transportes Atahualpa**, Jr Sandia 266, Lima Centre, T4275838. Direct to Cajamarca continuing on to Celendin. **CIVA**, Avda Carlos Zavala 211, Lima Centre, T4264926/4285649/4280963. To Cajamarca, Celendin, Chachapoyas and Bagua. **NB** Drivers known to exceed safe speed limits. **Royal Tours**, Avda Paseo de la Republica 565, Lima Centre, T3305346. To Huánuco, Tingo Maria and Pucallpa. **Transportes Leon de Huánuco**, Avda 28 de Julio 1520, La Victoria, T4329088. Daily to Huánuco, Tingo Maria and Pucallpa. **Transportes Chanchamayo**, Avda Manco Capac 1052, La Victoria, T2656850. To Tarma, San Ramón and La Merced.

Warning The area around the terminals on Avda Carlos Zavala is very unsafe at any time of day but much more-so at night. You are strongly advised to take a taxi to and from these terminals. Make sure you see your gear being stored on the correct bus as the place is always very busy. 'Mistakes', intentional or innocent, are not uncommon.

International Services: Ormeño, Avda Javier Prado 1059, Santa Catalina, T4721710, F4263180. To: Bogota (70 hours), Buenos Aires (90 hours), Cali (56 hours), Caracas (100 hours), Guayaquil (29 hours), Mendoza (78 hours), Quito (38 hours), Santiago (54 hours). **NB** A maximum of 20 kilos is allowed per person. Depending on the destination, extra weight penalties range from US$1-3 per kilo. **Caracol**, C Enrique Palacios 954 Miraflores, T4454879. To: Santiago, Buenos Aires, Montevideo, São Paulo (144 hours), Rio de Janeiro, Guayaquil, Caracas, Bogota. **El Rapido**, Avda Rivera Navarrete 2650, Lince, T4229508. Service to Argentina and Uruguay only.

NB For international service, it's cheaper to take a bus to the border, cross and then another to your final destination. The week before and after 28 July (Peruvian independence day) and Semana Santa (Holy Week) are the most travelled times of the year. Bus tickets out of Lima are extremely hard to come by unless purchased in advance. Expect prices to double during these dates and check in earlier than you normally would to avoid possible problems. When entering Peru at either of the six *official* border crossings: Aguas Verdes, La Tina, Tacna, Desaguadero, Yunguyo and Ramon Castilla, you might be asked to show a ticket out of the country though this is not common. If you find yourself in this unlikely and understandably annoying situation, don't automatically assume the worst. It's usually a simple matter of buying a bus ticket that exits Peru (this is not an option at Ramon Castilla), although keep in mind that you won't be able to refund it. For departure dates and times as well as prices, contact the companies directly.

Train The passenger service from Lima to Huancayo, known as the highest train ride in the world, was discontinued in 1991 but due to recent investments, the line has reopened and, as of August 1998, trains are now doing this route at the end of every month, departing on Sunday and returning on Monday, with the likely possibility of more frequent departures in the future. The round trip costs US$20. For a description of the line see page 429.

There is a pleasant trip from Lima to San Bartolomé, east towards the foothills of the Andes departing Lima every Sunday at 0830 and arriving in San Bartolomé at 1045. The return leaves at 1600, pulling into Lima at 1845. The train offers good food at a cheap price as well as bathrooms on board. Sit on the left side for nice views of the Río Rimac. Once in San Bartolomé enjoy typical Peruvian cuisine such as pachamanca, anticuchos and parilladas of all different varieties of meat. There are some nice walks and always plenty of sun no matter what time of year. The round trip cost is US$4.

Departure is from the Desamparados station, Jr Ancash 201, behind the presidential palace (T4289440/4276620/4274387, F4281075). Tickets to Huancayo and San Bartolomé can be purchased at the station Monday-Friday 0800-1600. Siduth Ferrer Herrera, of *Fertur Peru*, is an official ticket agent for the Lima-Huancayo train; address listed under Tourist offices on page 137.

Directory

Banks *Interbank*, Avda Pardo 413/Avda Larco 690, Miraflores, Jr de la Union 600, Lima Centre (main branch). Open Mon-Fri 0900-1800. Also on the corner of Avda Alfonso Ugarte and Avda Venezuela in Metro Supermarket, 2 blocks from South American Explorers Club, open Mon-Sun 0900-2100. Changes TCs (American Express, Mastercard, Visa and Citicorp), sells American Express cheques only, with a 1% commission (Metro branch does not sell cheques). ATM for Visa and Plus system at Avda Pardo and Avda Larco branches. Visa and Plus machine inside Metro available only during store hours. *Banco de Crédito*, Avda Pardo 491/Avda Larco 6th block,

Miraflores, Jr Lampa 499, Lima Centre (main branch). Open Mon-Fri 0900-1800, Sat 0930-1230. TCs (American Express, Visa, Citicorp), can buy cheques with Visa card at main branchs, sell American Express and Visa cheques with ½% commission. ATM for Visa and Plus system at Avda Pardo branch and Avda Larco branch. Visa/Plus bank machine inside downtown branch. *Banco Santander*, Avda Pardo 482/Avda Larco 479, Miraflores, Avda Augusto Tamayo 120, San Isidro (main branch). Open Mon-Fri 0900-1800, Sat 0930-1230. TCs (American Express only), sells American Express cheques with a 1% commission. ATM for Visa and Plus system. *BancoSur*, Avda Pardo 450/Avda Larco 878, Miraflores, Avda Rivera Navarrete 698, San Isidro (main branch). Open Mon-Fri 0900-1800. TCs (Visa, Citicorp, American Express), sells Citicorp and American Express cheques, can make withdrawals on Visa card (Soles and dollars) and Mastercard (Soles only). *Banco de Comercio*, Avda Pardo 272/Avda Larco 265, Miraflores, Jr Lampa 560, Lima Centre (main branch). Open Mon-Fri 0900-1800, Sat 0930-1200. TCs (American Express at Miraflores branch/Citicorp at Lima centre branch), sells American Express cheques, ATM (on Avda Pardo) for Visa and Plus system. *Banco del Nuevo Mundo*, Avda Pardo 175, Miraflores, Avda Paseo de la Republica 3033, San Isidro (main Branch). Open Mon-Fri 0915-1730, Sat 0930-1230. Does not change TCs, sells Citicorp and American Express at main branch only, money orders cost US$5 regardless of amount, ATM for Visa and Plus system at Avda Pardo branch. *Banco Financiero*, Avda Ricardo Palma 278, near Parque Kennedy (main branch). Open Mon-Fri 0900-1800, Sat 0930-1230. TCs (American Express, Thomas Cook), ATM for Visa and Plus system. *Banco Latino*, Avda Larco 337, Miraflores, Avda Paseo de la Republica 3505, San Isidro (main branch). Open Mon-Fri 0830-2000, Sat 0900-1300. TCs (Mastercard, American Express), ATM for Mastercard and Cirrus system at Avda Larco branch/Avda Alfonso Ugarte 1206 (2 blocks from the South American Explorers Club). *Banco de Lima*, Avda Larco 642, Miraflores, Jr Miroquesada 309, Lima Centre. Open Mon-Fri 0915-1800, Sat 0930-1230. TCs (American Express only), no commission to change into Soles, sells American Express cheques, ATM for Visa and Plus system at Avda Larco branch. *Banco Continental*, corner of Avda Larco and Avda Benevides/corner of Avda Larco and Pasaje Tarata, Miraflores, Jr Cusco 286, Lima Centre near Plaza San Martin. Open Mon-Fri 0900-1800, Sat 0930-1230. TCs (American Express, Mastercard at downtown branch), Visa card representative. *Banco Wiese*, Avda Diagonal 176 on Parque Kennedy/Avda Larco 1123, Miraflores, Jr Cusco 245 near Plaza San Martín. Open Mon-Fri 0915-1800, Sat 0930-1230. TCs (American Express, Thomas Cook, Mastercard, Visa at downtown branch), Mastercard representative, ATMs only for account holders.

Exchange houses and street changers There are many *casas de cambio* on and around Jr Ocoña off the Plaza San Martín. On the corner of Ocoña and Jr Camaná you'll no doubt see the large concentration of *cambistas* (street changers) with huge wads of dollars and soles in one hand and a calculator on the other. They should be avoided. Changing money on the street should only be done with official street changers wearing an identity card with a photo. Keep in mind that this card doesn't *automatically* mean that they are legitimate but most likely you won't have a problem. It's safer changing money in Miraflores, specifically around Parque Kennedy and down Avda Larco. Many *cambistas* wear bright yellow vests and an official Miraflores municipality badge with a photo (the night-shift wears a blue vest). There are also those who are independent and are dressed in street clothes, but it's safer to do business with an official money changer. There are a few places on Jr de la Unión at Plaza San Martín that will accept worn, ripped and old bills, but the exchange will be terrible. A repeatedly recommended *casa de cambio* is LAC Dolar, Jr Camaná 779, 1 block from Plaza San Martín, 2nd Flr, T4288127, T/F4273906. Open Mon-Sat 0900-1900, Sun and holidays 0900-1400, good rates, very helpful, safe, fast, reliable, 2% commission on cash and TCs (Amex, Citicorp, Thomas Cook, Visa), will come to your hotel if you're in a group.

American Express Office Avda Belén 1040 in the Lima Tours office, near Plaza San Martín. Official hours are Mon-Fri 0900-1700, Sat 0900-1300, but there is always someone there in case of emergencies. This office does **not** change TCs. Services are as follows: replaces lost or stolen American Express cheques of any currency in the world. Can purchase Amex cheques with Amex card only.

Diners Club Canaval y Moreyra 535, San Isidro, T4414272. Mon-Fri 0900-1330, 1430-1800.

Western Union For telephone consultations call 422-0014. Miraflores branches: Avda Larco 826, Avda José Pardo 138, Avda Benavides 708. Downtown Lima branches: Avda Nicolás de

Lima

Embassies & consulates

NB During the summer, most embassies only open in the morning.

US Embassy Avda Encalada block 17, Monterrico, T4343001, F4343037. Open 0800-1200, for emergencies after hours T4343032, the Consulate is in the same building.

Japanese Embassy and Consulate Avda San Felipe 356, Jesús María (postal address: Apdo 3708, Lima), T4639144/ 4639854. Open 0900-1200.

Australian Consulate Avda Santa Cruz 398, San Isidro, T4415366, F4216253/ 4216254. Services are very limited and everything but the most basic information must come from the closest consulate in Santiago, Chile.

Canadian Embassy Libertad 130, Miraflores, PO Box (Casilla) 18-1126, T4444015, F4444347. Open 0800-1700.

New Zealand All consular affairs handled by the British consulate, contact British Embassy.

South African Consulate Avda Camino Real 1252, 2nd Flr, San Isidro, T4222280, F4427154. Open 0900-1400.

Austrian Embassy Avda Central 643, 5th Flr, San Isidro, T4420503/ 4421807, F4428851. Open 0900-1200.

Belgian Consulate Angamos Oeste 380, Miraflores, T2417556, F2416379. Open 0830-1200.

British Embassy and Consulate Avda Natalio Sánchez 125, 4th Flr at the 5th block of Avda Arequipa in the Pacifico-Washingt on building, T4338923/ 4334738, F4338922. Open 0830-1200.

Danish Consulate General Bernardo Monteguido 201, San Isidro, T2643620/ 2644040, F2643080. Open 0930-1230.

French Consulate Arequipa 3415, San Isidro, T2217598, F2217177, open 0900-1100.

German Embassy Avda Arequipa 4210, Miraflores, PO Box (Casilla) 18-0504, T4224919, F4226475. Open 0900-1200, for visas contact Avda Natalio Sánchez 125, 4th floor in Santa Beatriz, T4240161.

Piérola 760, Jr de la Unión 536, Avda Colmena 724, Jr Carabaya 675. Near South American Explorers Club: Avda Alfonso Ugarte 1212.

Baths Baños Turcos Pardo: men, Avda Pardo 182, Miraflores, women, Avda Pardo 170, T4455046/4461395. Open Monday-Friday 1000-2200, Saturday 0800-2200. *Baños Turcos Windsor*, C Miguel Dasso 156, San Isidro, T4401050. Open Monday-Saturday 1000-2200.

Communications **Post Office** The central post office is on Jr Camaná 195 in the centre of Lima near the Plaza de Armas. Hours are Mon-Fri 0815-2015 and Sat 0900-1330. Poste Restante is in the same building but is considered unreliable. In Miraflores the main post office is on Avda Petit Thouars 5201 in Miraflores (same hours). There are many more small branches scattered around Lima but reliability is questionable. The above two locations should be the only ones considered. For express service, there are a few companies to choose from: *DHL*, Los Castanos 225, San Isidro, T9544345/2212474. *UPS*, Pasaje Tello 241, Miraflores, T2423366. *Federal Express*, Avda Jorge Chávez 475, T2422280, Miraflores, C José Olaya 260, T4451935, Miraflores. *EMS*, next to central post office in downtown Lima, T2254709. For shipping overseas: *Concas Travel*, Avda Alcanfores 345, oficina 101, T2417516, Miraflores, Avda Paz Soldan 225, T4217071, San Isidro. When receiving parcels from other countries that weigh in over 1 kg, they will be automatically sent to one of Lima's two customs post offices. Bring your passport and a lot of patience as the process can (but not always) take a long time: C Teodoro Cardenas 267, Santa Beatriz (12th block of Avda Arequipa); and Avda Tomas Valle, Los Olivos (near the Panamerican Highway). **NB** Long trousers must be worn when going to these offices.

Lima

Irish Consulate Santiago Acuña 135, Urb (neighbourhood) Aurora, Miraflores T4456813, F2423849. Open 0930-1300. *Israeli Embassy and Consulate* Natalio Sánchez 125, 6th Flr, same building as British Embassy, Santa Beatriz, T4334431, F4338925. Open 1000-1300. *Italian Embassy and Consulate* Avda G Escobedo 298, Jesús María, T4632727/2728, F4635717. *Netherlands Embassy and Consulate* Avda Principal 190, Santa Catalina,

T4761069/475653 7F4756536. Open 0900-1200. Norwegian Consulate Canaval y Moreyra 595, T4404048, F4416175. Open 0900-1200. *Spanish Embassy and Consulate* Jorge Basadre 498, San Isidro, T2217704/ 2217207, F4402020. Open 0900-1130. *Swiss Embassy and Consulate* Avda Salaverry 3240, Magdalena, PO Box (Casilla 378), T2640305, F2641319. Open 0830-1100. *Swedish Embassy and Consulate* Camino Real 348, 9th Flr, San Isidro,

T4213400/421342 1F4429547. Open 1000-1200. *Argentine Consulate* Pablo Bermúdez 143, 2nd Flr, Jesús María, T4335709. Open 0800-1300. Bolivian Consulate Los Castaños 235, San Isidro, T4228231 (0900-1330). 24 hrs for visas. Brazilian Consulate José Pardo 850, Miraflores, T4462635. Mon-Fri 0930-1300. *Chilean Consulate* Javier Prado Oeste 790, San Isidro, T4407965. Open 0900-1300, need appointment. *Ecuadorean Consulate*

Las Palmeras 356, San Isidro (6th block of Avda Javier Prado Oeste), T4424184. *Colombian Consulate* Natalio Sánchez 125, 4th Flr, T4338922/3. Mon-Fri 0900-1300. *Paraguayan Consulate* Los Rosarios 415, San Isidro, T4418154. Open 0900-1300. *Uruguayan Consulate* Avda Larco 1013, 2nd Flr, Miraflores, T4479948. Open 0930-1330. *Venezuelan Consulate* Avda Salaverry 3005, San Isidro, T4415948.

Telecommunications There are many Telefónica del Peru offices all over Lima. Most allow collect calls but some don't. All offer fax service (sending and receiving). Payphones have sprung up everywhere in the past few years. Telefónica booths are light blue and green. Some accept coins, some only phone cards and some honour both. Phone cards can often be purchased in the street near these booths. The other kind of phone-booth, painted dark green, is called Telepoint. These do not take coins, only Telepoint phone cards, available where Telefónica cards are sold. Some Telefónica del Peru offices are: Jr Carabaya 937, Lima centre (on the Plaza San Martín); Pasaje Tarata 280, Miraflores (near Avda Alcanfores); Avda Bolivia 347, Lima Centre (at Jr Chota near the South American Explorers Club); C Porta 139, Miraflores (near the bottom of Parque Kennedy). For full details on phone operation, see **Telephones** in **Essentials**, page 54.

Internet & Email services Internet 'Cafes' are springing up all over Lima. *Red Cientifica Peruana*, Avda Larco 770 in the Miraflores Cultural Centre Building, 3rd Flr, Mon-Fri 0800-2200, Sat 0800-1300, T2415696, US$1.75 per hour. *InterAxis*, Pasaje Tarata 277, Miraflores, US$3.50 per hour, 16 computers. *Dragon Fans Internet Axis*, Pasaje Tarata 230, Miraflores. US$2 per hour, T4449325. *Internet Club Peru*, Avda Arequipa 1202-1208, 4th Flr, Santa Beatriz. Mon-Fri 0900-2000, Sat 0900-1600, T4718157, F4717930, E postmast@clubperu.com.pe, US$3.50 per hour, 22 computers. *Internet Cabina Pública*, Jr Washington 1308, Oficina 302, Lima, T4338041/3302523. Mon-Fri 0900-1800, US$1.75 per hour. *Internet Para Viajeros Cabina Publica*, Avda Wilson (Garcilaso de la Vega) 1132, Oficina 203. Mon-Fri 0900-2100, Sat 0900-1800, US$1.75 per hour. *Cyber Sandeg*, Jr de la Unión 553, Oficina 210. US$1.50 per hour.

Lima

Cultural centres *Peruvian-British Cultural Association*, Avda Arequipa 3495, T2217550. English library and British newspapers. Open Mon-Fri 0800-1300 and 1530-1930. *British Council*, Alberto Lynch 110, San Isidro, T2217552. *Teatro Británico* (amateur productions of plays in English), C Bellavista 531, Miraflores, T4454326. Affiliated with the Peruvian-British Cultural Centre. Opera, conferences and exhibitions. *Peruvian-British Chamber of Commerce*, Pasaje Alberto Lynch 110, San Isidro, T2210453. *Instituto Cultural Peruano-Norteamericano*, Jr Cusco 446, Lima Centre, T4283530, with library. Main branch at Avda Arequipa 4798 y Angamos, Miraflores, T2411940. Language tuition, US$80 for 4 weeks, Mon-Fri, 2 hrs a day. *Goethe Institute*, Jr Nasca 722, Jesús María, T4333180. Open 0900-1300 and 1530-1900 (closed Wed and Sat), library, German papers, tea and cakes. *Allianza Francesa*, Avda Garcilaso de la Vega 1550, T4233842, also in Miraflores, Avda Arequipa 4598, T2417014.

American Schools *Colegio Franklin Roosevelt*, the American School of Lima, Monterrico, co-educational: Villa María, La Planicie (for girls); María Alvarado, Lima (girls). **British Schools:** *Markham College*, for boys, is one of only four Headmasters' Conference Schools outside the Commonwealth. *Colegio San Andrés*, for boys, run by the Free Church of Scotland. *Colegio San Silvestre*, a school for girls at Miraflores, is represented in the Association of Headmistresses. *Colegio Peruano-Británico*, San Isidro, co-educational. In La Molina, *Colegio Newton* offers the international baccalaureate. **German School:** *Colegio Peruano Alemán Von Humbolt*, Avda Benavides 3081, Miraflores, T4487000.

Hospitals & **Dentists** *Ribamar Camacho Rodríguez*, Clínica Los Pinos, C Los Pinos 190, 4th Flr, Miraflores,
medical services T4462056. Speaks a little English. Recommended. *Víctor Melly*, Avda Conquistadores 965, San Isidro, T4225757. Cleaning, check-ups, extractions, fillings and crowns. Recommended. *Dr Víctor Aste*, Antero Aspillaga 415, San Isidro, T4417502, T/F4219169 (make appointment). *Dra Ada Lucía Arroyo Torres*, Jr Laredo 196, Centro Comercial Monterrico, T4360942. *Dr Juvenal Gonzalez*, C Victor Maurtua 131, oficina 204, San Isidro, T4217011/4210867/4218936. Recommended for route canals. *Dr Carlos Abugattas*, Avda Benavides 261, oficina 301, Miraflores, T4457305. Good oral surgeon. *Dr Alberto Espinar*, Avda Angamos Oeste 893, oficina 3, T4450113. Highly recommended.

Doctors *Dr José Luis Calderon*, general practitioner at the *Clínica Santa Isabel*. Highly recommended. *Dr Luis Manuel Valdez*, internal medicine at the Clínica Anglo-Americano. Also highly recommended: *Drs Francisco Bravo & Alejandro Morales*, Avda Angamos Oeste 896, Miraflores, T4466250/2416121/4460484. Both dermatologists, excellent, both speak fluent English. *Dr Alejandro Bussalleu Rivera*, Instituto Médico Lince, León Velarde 221, Lince, T4712238. Speaks English, good for stomach problems. Repeatedly recommended. Also good for stomach or intestinal problems, *Dr Raul Morales*, Clínica Padre Luis Tezza, Avda del Polo 570, Monterrico, T4356990/6991 (cellular T9776883). Speaks some English. For traditional Chinese medicine: *Dr José Lui Kam*, Jr Huallaga 767, oficina 307, Lima centre. Acupuncturist, sells medicinal teas. *Dr Chan Tak Luen*, Jr Ucayali 749, 2nd Flr, oficina 4, Lima centre. Open Mon-Sat 1000-1300, 1600-1800. **Acupuncturist/Herbalist.** *Dr Li Ju*, Jr Paruro 887, oficina 202, Lima centre. Mon-Sat 0900-1900. Acupuncturist and Chinese massage.

Hospitals *Clínica Anglo Americano*, Avda Salazar 3rd block, San Isidro. A few blocks from Ovalo Gutiérrez, T2213656. Stocks Yellow Fever for US$17 and Tetanus for US$1.50. *Clínica Internacional*, Jr Washington 1471 y Avda Colón (9 de diciembre), downtown Lima, T4334306. Good, clean and professional, consultations up to US$35, no innoculations. *Clínica San Borja*, Avda Guardia Civil 337, San Borja (2 blocks from Avda Javier Prado Este), T4754000/4753141. *Clínica Ricardo Palma*, Avda Javier Prado Este 1066, San Isidro, T2242224/2242226. *Instituto de Ginecología & Reproducción*, Avda Monterrico (aka Avda Olguin) 1045, Monterrico parallel to Avda Polo, T4342130/4342426. Recommended Gynaecologists are *Dra Alicia Garcia* and *Dr Ladislao Prasak. Instituto de Medicina Tropical*, Avda Honorio Delgado near the Pan American Highway in the Cayetano Heredia Hospital, San Martín de Porres, T4823903/4823910. Cheap consultations, good for check-ups after jungle travel. Recommended. *Hospital del Niño*, Avda Brasil 600 at 1st block of Avda 28 de Julio, Breña, T3300022/3300033. Stocks Yellow Fever for US$17, tetanus shots are free of charge. *Centro Anti-Rabia de Lima*, Jr Austria 1300, Breña, T4256313. Open Mon-Sat 0800-1830. Consultation is about US$0.45. *Clínica de Fracturas San Francisco*, Avda San Felipe 142 at Avda Brasil, Jesus María, T4639855/4632501. *Clínica Padre Luis*

Tezza, Avda El Polo 570, Monterrico, T4356990/4356991/4365570. Top quality clinic specializing in a wide variety of illnesses/disorders etc, expensive. *International Chiropractors Center*, Avda Santa Cruz 555, Miraflores, T2214764, F4409747.

Pharmacy Not too long ago pharmacy chains were introduced in Lima. They're modern, well-stocked, safe, professional and can often be found in grocery stores (E. Wong, Santa Isabel) or attached to gas station mini-marts. Aside from being open 24 hrs a day, some even offer delivery service. *Superfarma*, T2221575/2221577, Avda Benavides 2849, Avda Cmdte. *Espinar/Avda Angamos*, Avda Armendariz 215, Miraflores, Avda Gral Pezet 1491, San Isidro. Boticas Fasa, Avda Javier Prado Este 2030, San Borja, T2653894, F2653799, Avda José Pardo 715, T2421378, Avda Benavides 487, T2424073, Avda Libertadores 594, San Isidro, T4405239, Avda 2 de Mayo 1410, San Isidro, T4401151, Block 15 of Avda Brasil (at Avda Husares de Junín), T3300800. *Santa Isabel supermarket* in Jockey Plaza, Monterrico. *Farmacia Deza*, Avda Conquistadores 1140, San Isidro, T/F4403798. The pharmacy equivalent of a hypermarket, open 24 hrs. *Pharmax*, Avda Salaverry 3100, San Isidro, Centro Comercial El Polo, Monterrico (near the US embassy), T2642282. Another pharmacy/hypermarket place, with imported goods (Jewish foods at Avda Salaverry branch and excellent Italian ice-cream store inside, open 24 hrs).

Asociación Cultural Peruano-Británico, Avda Arequipa 3495, San Isidro, T2217550. US$33 per month, 3 lessons per week at 1½ hrs each, no private classes offered. *Instituto Cultural Peruano-Norteamericano*, Avda Arequipa 4798, Miraflores, T2411940/4283530. US$95 per month, 5 lessons per week at 2 hrs per lesson, no private classes offered. *Instituto de Idiomas (Universidad Católica del Peru)*, Avda Camino Real 1037, San Isidro, T4428761/4426419. US$119 per month, 5 lessons per week at 2 hrs per lesson. *Instituto de Idiomas (Universidad del Pacifico)*, Avda Prescott 333, San Isidro, T4212969. US$290 for 3 months, 3 days per week at 1½ hrs per lesson. Private classes possible for executive (business) level only. *Euroidiomas*, Avda Santa Cruz 111, Miraflores, T4418303. US$25 per hour for private classes. **Independent teachers** (all US$5 per hour): Sra Lourdes Gálvez, T4353910. Highly recommended, also Quechua. *Sra Llorgelina Savastiazagal*, T4382676. Recommended. *Srta Susy Arteaga*, T5340208. For beginners only. *Srta Patty Felix*, T5333713. For beginners only. **Language schools**

In the past few years *lavanderias* (Laundromats) have sprung up all over the city, inundating, for example, the districts of San Isidro and Miraflores. Some charge by piece (expensive) while others by weight. Many have a self-service option. Next day service is the norm if you've left laundry for them to wash. Most of the hotels in the higher price range offer laundry service but tend to be very expensive. *Lava Philip*, Avda Arica 448, Breña. Wash US$2 per basket, Dry US$2, reliable, good, self-serve option, near South American Explorers Club. *Burbujitas*, C Porta 293, Miraflores, T2413592. 4 kg wash and dry US$4.50. *Lavarap*, chain of 6 stores throughout Lima, at Schell 601, Miraflores, T2410759. Self-service option, extra US$1.25 per load if you leave laundry to be picked up, good, not cheap. *Lava Express*, Avda Alcanfores 694, Miraflores, T9350124. *Continental*, Jr Callao 420, Lima Centre, T4269015. *Martinizing Dry Cleaning*, new chain in Lima, T2427595, at: Avda Comandante Espinar 270, Avda Armendariz 255, Miraflores, Avda 2 de Mayo 1225, San Isidro, Avda Benavides 1763 in Surco, also Jockey Plaza. **Laundry**

The *Union Church of Lima (Interdenominational)*, Avda Angamos 1155, Miraflores, Worship Sun 1030, T4411472. *Trinity Lutheran Church of Peru*, Las Magnolias 495, Urb Jardín, San Isidro. *Church of the Good Shepherd*, Avda Santa Cruz 491, Miraflores (Anglican) T4457908. Sun 0800 Holy Communion, 1000 morning service. *International Baptist Church of Lima*, Col Inclán 799, Miraflores, T4757179. Worship Sun 1000. *Iglesia San José*, Dos de Mayo 259, Miraflores. Services in German at 0900. Christian Science Society, 1285 Mayta Capac (near Avda Salaverry), Jesús María. English Benedictine Monastery, Jr Olivares de la Paz, Las Flores (57M minibus from Plaza de Acho). Sunday Mass 0900, weekdays 1900. *Synagogue*, Avda 2 de Mayo 1815, San Isidro, T4400290. *La Iglesia de Santa María Reina*, Ovalo Gutiérrez, Avda Santa Cruz, Miraflores, T4247269, Sun 0930. Catholic Mass in English. **Places of worship**

Visits to the woman's prison in the district of Chorrillos are easy and much appreciated by the inmates, both Peruvian and foreign. You must bring your passport and give the name of someone you're visiting (check at the South American Explorers Club for the current list). You are permitted to bring food, magazines, books etc (but no fruit that ferments). The *Penal de* **Prison visits**

Chorrillos para Mujeres, has its visitors day on Sat for men and Sun for women. Hours are 0900-1600 with the option to leave at 1300. **NB** This is strictly enforced. If you do not leave at 1300, you will *not* be allowed to leave until 1600. Shoes that have any kind of heel are not permitted (also no boots) and women must wear dresses which, if you don't have one, can be rented across the street from the prison. Visits are also possible to the mens prisons of Callao and Lurigancho. Again, contact the SAEC for details.

Tour agencies Lima is busting at the seams with tour and travel agencies. Some are good and reliable, many are not. If possible, use agencies in or close to the area you wish to visit and always shop around. Bargaining ability is a plus. See also *Fertur Peru* in the Tourist Office section. **NB** We have received complaints about agencies, or their representatives at bus offices or the airport arranging tours and collecting money for companies that either do not exist or which fall far short of what is paid for. Do not conduct business anywhere other than in the agency's office and insist on a written contract. *Lima Tours*, Jr Belén, Lima centre, T4245110/7560/6410, F3304487. Highly recommended. Shares an office with American Express (see Banks above), possible move to a new office sometime in 1999. *Explorandes*, C San Fernando 320, T4458683/2429527, F2423496, E Postmast@Exploran.com.pe. Offer a wide range of adventure and cultural tours throughout the country. Also offices in Cusco (see page 165) and Huaraz (see page 299). *Cóndor Travel*, Mayor Armando Blondet 249, San Isidro, T4427305, F4420935, E incoming@condortravel.com.pe. Kinjyo Travel, Las Camelias 290, San Isidro, T4424000/2216025, F4421000, E postmaster@kinjyo.com.pe. Roma Tours, Jr Ica 330, next to *Hostal Roma*, T/F4277572, E resroma@peru.itete.com.pe. Good and reliable. Administrator Dante Reyes is very friendly and speaks English. *Hada Tours*, 2 de Mayo 529, Miraflores, T4468157, F446274, E saleprom@hadatours.com.pe. 20 years of experience. *Solmartur*, C Grau 300, Miraflores, T4441313, F4443060. *Perú Chasquitur*, Mariana de los Santas 183, oficina 201, San Isidro, T4411455/1387, F4411459. *Turismo Pacífico*, Avda Schell 369, oficina 102, Miraflores, T4443464, F4443438. *Setours*, Cdte Espinar 229, Miraflores, T4468786, F4467129. *Tecnitur*, Avda 28 de Julio 572, T/F4466772. *Peruvian's Life*, Diez Canseco 332, Miraflores, T4463246, F4448825. *Andean Tours*, Jr

Shell 319, oficina 305, Miraflores, T4478430, T/F4456097. *Hirca*, Bellavista 518, Miraflores, T2412317/2420275, F4473807. *Irré Tours*, Avda Boulevard 1012, T4758808. Julio speaks good English, arranges trips and guides for small groups. *CanoAndes*, Avda San Martín 455, Barranco, T4770188, F4741288. Rafting and kayaking trips. *Expediciones Viento Sur*, Avda Grau 855, La Punta-Callao, T4291414. Boat trips to islands off the coast of Lima. Contact Alfredo Zavaletta. *Servicios Aéreos*, Los Castaños 462, San Isidro, T2642460, F2641877, E aqpsa-lima@ mail.interplace.com.pe. Comprehensive service. *South American Tours*, Av Miguel Dasso 230, Suite 401, San Isidro, T4227261, F4408149, E 7034998@mcimail.com. *Aracari Travel Consulting*, Malecon Cisneros 1270, T4479003, F4471861, E postmaster@aracari.com. Regional tours throughout Peru, also 'themed' and activity tours.

Private guides All the guides listed below are highly recommended and most are officially registered with AGOTUR (Asociasion De Guias Oficiales De Turismo). They have requested that travellers wait until they arrive in Lima before contacting them. Many have repeatedly received phone calls from all over the world in the middle of the night. All speak English, unless indicated otherwise. *Gladis Araujo*, T4633642, F4484080, cellular 9664780. *Maria Antonieta 'Kika' Caballero*, T3725744, cellular 9709039. *Alejandra Cabieses*, T4456500, cellular 902-5322. *Luzmila 'Lucy' Guerra*, T4440516, cellular 9664820. *Silvia Rodrich*, T4460391/4468185. *Diana Hidalgo*, T4228937, cellular 9957894. *Tino Guzman*, T/F4295779, cellular 968-3776, E tino @amauta.rcp.net.pe (member of South American Explorers Club). *Alberto Gomez*, T4247963, cellular 9981716. *Rudy Borja*, T4811885, F3441362, cellular 9948776. *Hugo Ochoa*, T4499499 ext 5095, cellular 9726117. Also speaks French and German. *Frankie Ochoa*, T4780937, cellular 9677854. *Lilian Alfaro*, T4375744, cellular 9401031. Also speaks French. *Sra Elzinha de Mayer*, T4450676, cellular 9306490. Also speaks Portuguese. *Tessy Torres*, T2411704/4388066, F2424688, cellular 9971307, E perubra@mail.cosapidata.com.pe. Also speaks Portuguese, Italian and French. *Nelida Manrrique*, T4463771, cellular 9606328. Also speaks French and German. *Nila Soto*, T4525483, cellular 9728880. Also speaks Italian. *Freda Zuluoga*, T4750687, cellular 9765281. *Victor Aranda*, T4749814. Also speaks French, German and Italian. Ernesto Riedner, T4452732/2711022, F4466739, cellular 9094224, E eried@mail.cosapidata.com.pe. Also speaks German. *Ina Brodersen*, T4462170, F4471808. Also speaks German. *Silvia De Vetto*, T4452919/ 2424552, F4495336, cellular 9356792. Also speaks German. *Ruben Cuneo*, T2217274, cellular 9464949. Speaks Italian. *Sra Nariko De Kanna*, T4424000/4792238. Speaks Japanese. *Sra Toshie Matsumura De Irikura*, T4765101. Speaks Japanese. Sra Goya, T5785937, cellular 9883773. Speaks Japanese. *Jennie Tang*, T2752676 (am)/4493376 (pm), cellular 9400808. Speaks Chinese Mandarin and Cantonese. For Arabic contact *Sr Said* at the Arabic Center of Lima, T4618144. Fri, Sat and Sun only. *Sra Matin Azham*, T4792238. Speaks Farsi. *Angel Rios*, T4381060/4422040. Speaks Hebrew. *Sr Partab Sing*, T2417078, cellular 9305123, Avda 28 de Julio 674, Miraflores. Speaks Indian languages. *Sra Evelin Kang*, T4442890/4465430. Speaks Korean. *Sr Na*, T4405038, cellular 9925099. Speaks Korean. *Sali Li*, T4454982. Speaks Korean. *Jonie Roh*, T4769336, cellular 9632629. Speaks Korean. For Russian contact the *Russian embassy* at 51-1-264-0038. For Swedish contact *Sr Gunner*, T4765016.

Tourist offices Highly recommended is Siduith Ferrer Herrera, CEO of *Fertur Peru*. Her agency not only offers up to date, correct tourist information on a national level, but also great prices on national and international flights, discounts for those with ISIC and Youth cards and South American Explorers Club members (of which she is one). Other services include flight reconfirmations, hotel reservations and transfers to and from the airport or bus stations and the sale of tickets for the Lima-Huancayo train. For those needing any or all of the services listed above, contact Fertur Peru: Jr Junin 211 (main office) at the Plaza de Armas, T4271958, F4283247, E fertur@correo.dnet.com.pe. Open 0900-1900. **Tourist information** also at: *Hostal España*, Jr Azangaro 105, T4279196, open 0730-1630; Jr de la Unión (a.k.a Belén) 1066, oficina E-2, near the Plaza San Martín, T/F3305412. Open 0900-1800. **NB** This office might close in 1999. The government-run consumer protection and tourist complaint bureau, INDECOPI, is professional, friendly and most of all, effective. Complaints regarding airlines, customs, restaurants, hotels, travel agencies etc. should be registered here. In Lima: T/F2247888/7800. In provinces: 0-800-4-4040, E postmaster@indecopi.gov.pe.

South American Explorers' Club Avda República de Portugal 146, district of Breña (block 13 of Avda Alfonso Ugarte between Avenidas Bolivia and España). T/F4250142, E montague@ amauta.rcp.net.pe; W www.samexplo.org. The SAEC is a non-profit educational organization which functions as a travel resource centre for South America and is widely recognized as the best place to get the most up-to-date information regarding everything from travel advisories to volunteer opportunities. Hours are Mon-Fri 0930-1700 with the first Wed of every month until 2000 (closed on weekends). A yearly membership is currently US$40 per person and US$70 per couple. Services include access to member-written trip reports, a full map room for reference, an extensive library in English and a book exchange. Members are welcome to use the Club's Email services, their PO Box for receiving post and can store luggage as well as valuables in their very secure deposit space. The SAEC sells official maps from the Instituto Geografico Nacional, Club-produced trekking maps, used equipment and a large variety of Peruvian crafts. Note that all imported merchandise sold at the SAEC is reserved for members only, no exceptions. At least once a month, they host presentations on various topics ranging from jungle trips to freedom of the press. The Club also offers a discount in membership fees to researchers, archaeologists and scientists in exchange for information and/or presentations. If you're looking to study Spanish in Peru, hoping to travel down the Amazon or in search of a quality Inca Trail tour company, they have the information you'll need to make it happen. The South American Explorers Club, apart from the services mentioned above, is simply a great place to step out of the hustle and bustle of Lima and bask in the serenity of a cup of tea, a magazine and good conversation with a fellow traveller.

Archaeological information   Federico Kauffmann-Doig is a great source of information on Peruvian archaeology, for serious students and archaeologists. He is the director of the Instituto de Arqueología Amazónica, T4490243, or (home) 4499103. His book, *Historia del Perú: un nuevo perspectivo*, in two volumes (*Pre-Inca*, and *El Incario*) is available at better bookshops. The Instituto Nacional de Cultura, in the Museo de la Nación, should be contacted by archaeologists for permits and information. The Museo Nacional de Antropología y Arquelogía in Pueblo Libre (address above) is the main centre for archaeological investigation and the Museo de la Nación holds exhibitions.

Useful addresses   *Tourist Police*, Museo de la Nación, Javier Prado 2465, 5th Flr, San Borja, T2258699/8698 (24 hrs), F4767708. They are friendly and very helpful, English and some German spoken, open 0800-2000

(open 24 hrs). It is recommended to visit when you have had property stolen. **Immigration:** Avda España 700 y Jr Huaraz, Breña (2 blocks from SAEC), open 0830-1500, but they only allow people to enter until 1400. Visa extensions on 3rd floor given the same day, usually within 30 mins (expensive). Provides new entry stamps if passport is lost or stolen. *Intej*, Avda San Martín 240, Barranco, T4774105. They can extend student cards, change flight itineraries bought with student cards. *National library*, Avda Abancay 4th block, with Jr Miró Quesada, T4287690. Open Mon-Sat 0800-1900.

The *Peruvian Touring and Automobile Club*: Avda César Vallejo 699 (Casilla 2219), Lince, T2212432. Offers help to tourists and particularly to members of the leading motoring associations. Good maps available of whole country; regional routes and the South American sections of the Pan-American Highway available (US$3.50).

NB If you're having car problems and you find yourself on Avda Javier Prado Oeste near the 11th block and you happen to see the familiar logo of the American Automobile Association (AAA), just keep going. Although the logo is exactly the same, the Agrupacion de Asistencia al Automovilista has no affiliation whatsoever with the US organization. What's more, the services that they *do* offer are limited only to the Lima metropolitan area and cost US$100 per month.

Voluntary organizations

There are a number of organizations in and around Lima that welcome volunteers. Some ask the volunteer to show up when they can, other more structured projects might ask for a commitment of at least 3 months. Although some are listed below, the South American Explorers Club is the best place to find out about volunteer opportunities. *Fundacion Peruana Para La Conservacion De La Natureleza*, Parque Blume y C General C?2rdoba, Miraflores, T4422272. Involved in keeping protected areas protected, environmental education, public policy etc. *Pro Natureleza*, Parque Blume y C General Córdoba, Miraflores, T4413800. Rainforest conservation. *Hogar San Francisco de Asis*, C Los Geranios 345, Chaclacayo, T4971868, contact Antony Lazzera. Home for street children. *Zapallel*, Colegio Fe & Alegria 43, Km 37, Panamerican Highway North, Ventanilla, T9802130/9050947, F4715362. Contact Paul McAuley. Volunteers needed to work in a shanty town a short distance from Lima. Cedro, C Roca y Bolona 271, Miraflores, T4470748/4466682, F4460751. Contact Alejandro Menendes (home T4519149). Working with street children in Lima. *Amnesty International*, C Enrique Palacios 735A, Miraflores, T4471360, E postmaster@aminte.org.pe. *Centro Anne Sullivan del Peru*, C Petromila Alvarez 180, Urbanizacion Pando, San Miguel, T2636296, F2631237. Contact Elena Lazarte. Organization assisting children with Downs Syndrome.

Excursions from Lima

Cieneguilla

Cieneguilla, about 20 kilometres east of Lima, on the Lurín river, is a small village in the country, an easy escape from the city and cloud cover of Lima. It is a popular place on Sunday, with good restaurants with gardens and swimming pools. The valley of Lurín is good for birdwatching in the early morning, especially the **Pantanal de Villa**, an ecological wetland reserve which is full of migrating waterfowl during December.

Pachacamac

Pachacámac is in the Lurín valley, 31 kilometres from Lima. When the Spaniards arrived, Pachacámac was the largest city and ceremonial centre on the coast. It was a vast complex of palaces and temple-pyramids, to which pilgrims went to pay homage to the creator-god Pachacámac, a wooden statue of whom is in the site museum.

Hernando Pizarro came to Pachacámac in 1533, having been sent by his brother to speed the delivery of gold from the coast for Atahualpa's ransom. However, great disappointment awaited Pizarro as there was no store of riches. In their desperate search for the promised gold the Spaniards destroyed images, killed the priests and looted the temples.

The ruins encircle the top of a low hill, whose crest was crowned with a **Temple of the Sun**, a large pyramid built in 1350 of sun-baked bricks, now partially restored. Slightly apart from the main group of buildings and hidden from view is the reconstructed **House of the Mamaconas**, where the 'chosen women' were taught to weave and spin fine cloth for the Inca and his court. Further to the north the **Temple of Urpi-Huachac**, who was reputed to be the wife of Pachacámac, is in a state of total ruin.

An impression of the scale of the site can be gained from the top of the Temple of the Sun, or from walking or driving the three kilometre circuit.

■*Open 0900 to 1600; closed 1 May. Entrance US$2 including the small site museum which sells soft drinks. Buses to the ruins run south down the Pan American Highway every few minutes. We recommend going to where Avda Angamos Este crosses the PanAm. Climb the stairs up the bridge and take a combi with a sticker in the window reading "Pachacamac/Lurin". Let the driver know you want to get off at the ruins. For organized tours contact one of the tour agencies listed above.*

Puruchuco On the way to Chosica, up the Rímac valley, turn off at Km 4½ to Puruchuco, to see the reconstructed palace of a pre-Inca Huacho noble. There is a small museum with ceramics and textiles from the lower Rímac or Lima valley and a selection of indigenous plants and animals. ■*Open 0830-1800 daily (closed 1 May and 28 July). Entrance US$1. It's on the Central Highway on the way to Chosica, transport as for Chosica.*

Cajamarquilla

This large adobe pre-Inca city can also be visited. The turnoff (left, at Huachipa) is about six kilometres on from the Puruchuco turn. The site cannot be seen from the road; look for a sign 'Zona Arqueológica' in the middle of a brickyard. Keep on driving through the yard, and Cajamarquilla is at the end of an ill-kept dirt road. ■*Open daily 0900-1700.*

Pucusana Pucusana, 60 kilometres south of Lima, is a pleasant, relaxed fishing village with some good restaurants serving seafood, not cheap, and some basic hotels (in our E range). All are very popular with Limeños from December to March, school holidays, and at weekends. There are plenty of buses from the bus station area in Lima. Robbery is common on the beaches and you are advised to sit on your clothes and other possessions. Do not leave anything unattended when swimming.

To get to Pucusana, get to the Pan American Highway where it crosses Avda Angamos Este. Climb the bridge and take a bus with a window sticker reading "Pucusana".

Ancón 30 kilometres northwest of Lima, Ancón is reached by a double-lane asphalted highway. In the 19th and early 20th centuries, this was the smart seaside resort in Peru, but has now been deserted by the wealthy and in summer is crowded with daytrippers. It has a mix of elegant 19th century houses with wooden balconies and modern apartment blocks. Also bathing, tennis, and a yacht club. The beaches are very small and crowded during January-March holidays.

On the way to Ancón is the pleasant Santa Rosa beach (entrance fee). Beyond Ancón is a Chancay cemetery, from which has come much Chancay weaving and pottery (as seen in the Museo Amano). In the valley of Chillón, north of Callao, are several interesting pre-Inca and Inca ruins; the Templo de la Media Luna y El Paraíso and **Chuquitanta**. For more information contact Dr Richard Holmberg at the Instituto Nacional de Cultura, Callao.

D *Hostal del Pirata*. Antique furniture, good views, excellent seafood.

Cusco & the Sacred Valley

4

Cusco & the Sacred Valley

144 Cusco

169 The Urubamba Valley

170 Pisac

173 Urubamba

176 Ollantaytambo

179 Machu Picchu

183 The Inca Trail

193 Southeast from Cusco

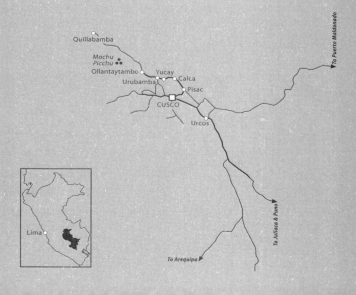

Cusco stands at the head of the Sacred Valley of the Incas and is the jumping off point for the Inca Trail and famous Inca city of Machu Picchu. Not surprising, then, that this is the prime destination for the vast majority of Peru's visitors. In fact, The ancient Inca capital is now the 'gringo' capital of the entire continent. And it's easy to see why. There are Inca ruins aplenty, as well as fabulous colonial architecture, stunning scenery, great 'trekking, river rafting and mountain biking, beautiful textiles and other traditional handicrafts – all within easy reach of the nearest cappuccino or comfy hotel room.

Cusco

Ins and outs

Getting there Most travellers arriving from Lima will do so by air. However, bad weather can cause delays. The airport is to the southeast of the city and the road into the centre goes close to Wanchac station and bus offices. Transport to your hotel is not a problem as representatives are often on hand. For travel information see transport on page

Getting around The centre of Cusco is quite small and is certainly possible to explore on foot. More police patrol the streets, trains and stations than in the past, which has led to an improvement in security, but you still need to be vigilant. Look after your belongings, leaving valuables in safe keeping with hotel management, not in hotel rooms. Places in which to take care are: when changing money on the streets; in the railway and bus stations; the bus from the airport; the Santa Ana market; the San Cristóbal area and at out-of-the-way ruins. Also take special care during Inti Raymi. Avoid walking around alone at night on narrow streets, between the stations and the centre, or in the market areas. Stolen cameras often turn up in the local market and can be bought back cheaply. If you can prove that the camera is yours, contact the police.

NB On no account walk back to your hotel after dark from a bar, nightclub or restaurant; strangle muggings are on the increase. For the sake of your own safety pay the US$1.05 taxi fare!

The Tourist Police are on Calle Saphi, block 1, T221961. If you need a *denuncia* (a report for insurance purposes), which is available from the Banco de la Nación, they will type it out. Always go to the police when robbed, even though it will cost you a bit of time. The Tourist Protection Bureau (Indecopi) has been set up to protect the consumer rights of all tourists and will help with any problems or complaints. They can be

The Sacred Valley

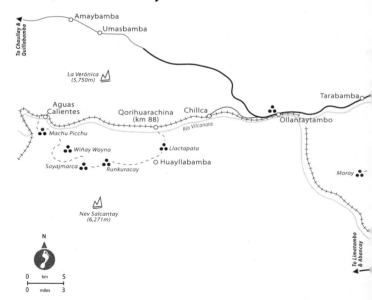

very effective in dealing with tour agencies, hotels or restaurants. They are at Portal Carrizos, Plaza de Armas. T(0800)44040 (24-hour hotline).

Taxis in Cusco are cheap and recommended when arriving by air, train or bus. They have fixed prices: in the centre US$0.70 (after dark US$1.05); to the suburbs US$1.25. Taxis on call are reliable but more expensive, in the centre US$1.25 (El Dorado, T221414). Trips to Sacsayhuamán cost US$10; to the ruins of Tambo Machay US$15-20 (3-4 people); a whole day trip costs US$40. For US$50 a taxi can be hired for a whole day (ideally Sunday) to take you to Cachimayo, Chinchero, Maras, Urubamba, Ollantaytambo, Calca, Lamay, Coya, Pisac, Tambo Machay, Qenqo and Sacsayhuamán.

Recommended taxi drivers: *Angel Salazar*, Saguán del Cielo B-11, T224597 to leave messages. He is English speaking and arranges good tours. *Ferdinand Pinares Cuadros*, Yuracpunco 155, Tahuantinsuyo, T225914. Speaks English, French and German. *Milton Velásquez*, T222638, cellular T680730. He is also an anthropologist and tour guide and speaks English. *David Quispe*, T621947 (cellular). He has a Toyota minibus which holds 10. *Movilidada Inmediate*, T623821 (cellular), run local tours with an English-speaking guide.

To rent a minibus for the day costs US$60 (US$30 for ½-day), including guide (less without guide), maximum 10 people. For transport contact *Orellana Tours*, Garcilaso 206, T243717 (cellular T621758). Also *Explorers Transporte*, C Plateros 345, T233498.

If you wish to explore this area on your own, Road Map (*Hoja de ruta*) No 10 is an excellent guide. You can get it from the *Automóvil Club del Perú*, Avda del Sol 457, next to Banco del Sur, 3rd floor, oficina 305. They have other maps. Motorists beware; many streets end in flights of steps not marked as such. There are very few good maps of Cusco available.

Cusco & the Sacred Valley

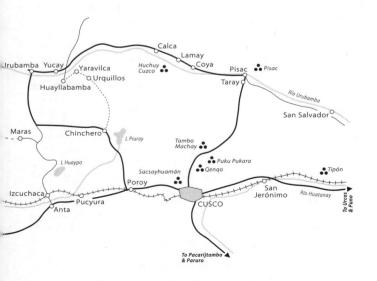

Information and advice

Population: 275,000
Altitude: 3,310 metres
Phone code: 084
Coloured map 5, grid A5

Cusco stands at 3,310 metres, a little lower than Puno, so you should respect the altitude. Two or three hours' rest after arriving makes a great difference. Also avoid smoking, don't eat meat but do eat lots of carbohydrates and drink plenty of clear, non-alcoholic liquid, and remember to walk slowly. *A word of advice for those arriving in Cusco by air. It makes a lot of sense to get down to the Urubamba Valley, at 2,800 metres compared to Cusco's 3,310 metres, and make the most of your first couple of days. There are a few good hotels in Urubamba and Yucay. At this relatively low altitude you will experience no headaches and you can eat and sleep comfortably.*

To see Cusco and the surrounding area properly – including Pisac, Ollantaytambo, Chinchero and Machu Picchu – you need five days to a week, allowing for slowing down because of altitude. Those on a tight itinerary should note that this is a difficult city to leave and many a carefully-planned travelling schedule has been revised in the face of its overwhelming attraction. Anyone interested in seeing more than the inside of a pizzería is advised to purchase Peter Frost's excellent guide, *Exploring Cusco*, which is available throughout the city.

The town

The ancient Inca capital is said to have been founded around 1100 AD. According to the central Inca creation myth, the sun sent his son, Manco Capac and the Moon her daughter, Mama Ocllo, to spread culture and enlightenment throughout the dark, barbaric lands. They emerged from the waters of Lake Titicaca and began their journey in search of the place where they would found their kingdom. When they reached the site of present-day Cusco, Manco plunged his golden staff into the ground in order to test its suitability, and it duly sank deep into the fertile soil. This was the sign they were looking for. They named this place Cusco – meaning "navel of the earth".

Thus was the significance of Cusco and the sacred Urubamba Valley established for many centuries to come. As Peter Frost states in his *Exploring Cusco*: "Cusco was more than just a capital city to the Incas and the millions of subjects in their realm. It was a Holy City, a place of pilgrimage with as much importance to the Quechuas as Mecca has to the Moslems. Every ranking citizen of the empire tried to visit Cusco once in his lifetime; to have done so increased his stature wherever he might travel."

Today, the city's beauty cannot be overstated. It is a fascinating mix of Inca and colonial Spanish architecture: colonial churches, monasteries and convents and extensive precolumbian ruins are interspersed with countless hotels, bars and restaurants that have sprung up to cater for the hundreds of thousands of tourists who flock here to savour its unique atmosphere. Almost every central street has remains of Inca walls, arches and doorways. Many streets are lined with perfect Inca stonework, now serving as the foundations for more modern dwellings. This stonework is tapered upwards (battered); every wall has a perfect line of inclination towards the centre, from bottom to top. The stones have each edge and corner rounded. The curved stonework of the Temple of the Sun, for example, is probably unequalled in the world.

Cusco has developed into a major, commercial centre of 275,000 inhabitants, most of whom are Quechua. The city council has designated the Quechua, Qosqo, as the official spelling. Despite its growth, however, the city is still laid out much as it was in Inca times. The Incas conceived their capital in the shape of a puma and this can be seen from above, with the river Tullumayo forming the spine, Sacsayhuamán the head and the main city

Visitors' Tickets

A combined ticket (Boleto Turístico Unico, or 'BTU') allows entry to the Cathedral, San Blas, Santa Catalina, Museo de Arte Religioso, Museo de Historia Regional, the Piquillacta ruins, Pisac, Chincheros, Ollantaytambo, Sacsayhuamán, Qenqo, Puku Pukara and Tambo Machay.

The combined ticket costs US$10 and is valid for five or 10 days. It can be bought from the INC office at Garcilaso sin número on Plaza Regocijo, Mon-Fri 0700-1800, Sat 0830-1300, or at any of the sites included on the ticket.

There is a 50 percent discount with a green ISIC card, which is only available at the INC office. There is a cheaper version, which costs US$4 and allows entry to Sacsayhuamán, Qenqo, Puka Pukara and Tambo Machay.

Note that all sites are very crowded on Sun. No photographs are allowed in any museums. Many churches are closed to visitors on Sun, and the 'official' opening times are unreliable.

Machu Picchu, the Museo Arqueológico, Santo Domingo-Qoricancha and the church of La Merced are not included on the ticket. Tickets for Machu Picchu and the Inca Trail can be bought at the INC office on San Bernardo, between Mantas and Almagro; opening hours as above.

centre the body. The best place for an overall view of the Cusco valley is from the puma's head – the top of the hill of Sacsayhuamán.

Sights

The heart of the city, as in Inca days, is the Plaza de Armas. It was originally, however, more than twice its present size. The part that remains today was once called the *Aucaypata*, or Square of War. This was the great civic square of the Incas, flanked by their palaces, and was a place of solemn parades and great assemblies. Each territory conquered by the Incas had some of its soil taken to Cusco to be mingled symbolically with the soil of the Aucaypata, as a token of its incorporation into the empire.

Plaza de Armas

As well as the many great ceremonies, the Plaza has also seen its share of executions, among them Túpac Amaru, the last Inca, the rebel conquistador Diego de Almagro the Younger, and Túpac Amaru II, the 18th century indigenous leader.

Around the present-day Plaza are colonial arcades and four churches. To the northeast is the early 17th century baroque **Cathedral**, built on the site of the Palace of Viracocha. The high altar is solid silver and the original altar *retablo* behind it is a masterpiece of native wood carving. In the sacristy are paintings of all the bishops of Cusco and a painting of Christ attributed to Van Dyck. The choir stalls, by a 17th-century Spanish priest, are a magnificent example of colonial baroque art. The elaborate pulpit and the sacristy are also notable. Much venerated is the crucifix of El Señor de los Temblores, the object of many pilgrimages and viewed all over Peru as a guardian against earthquakes. The doors from the Cathedral open into the church of **Jesús María** (1733), which stands to its left as you face it. ■ *The Cathedral is open until 1000 for genuine worshippers – Quechua mass is held 0500-0600. Those of a more secular inclination can visit Monday-Saturday 1400-1730.*

To the right of the cathedral is **El Triunfo** (1536), which was closed in mid-1998. Built on the site of *Suntur Huasi* (the Roundhouse), El Triunfo was the first Christian church in Cusco. It has a fine granite altar and a statue of the Virgin of the Descent, reputed to have helped the Spaniards repel Manco Inca when he besieged the city in 1536. It also has a painting of Cusco during the

Cusco & the Sacred Valley

1650 earthquake – the earliest surviving painting of the city – in a side chapel. In the far right hand end of the church is an interesting local painting of the Last Supper. But this is the Last Supper with a difference, for Jesus is about to tuck into a plate of *cuy*, washed down with a glass of *chicha*, instead of the standard Cusco fare of a slice of pizza and bottle of Cusqueña.

On the southeast side of the plaza is the beautiful **La Compañía de Jesús**, built on the site of the Palace of the Serpents (*Amarucancha*) in the late 17th century. Its twin-towered exterior is extremely graceful, and the interior rich

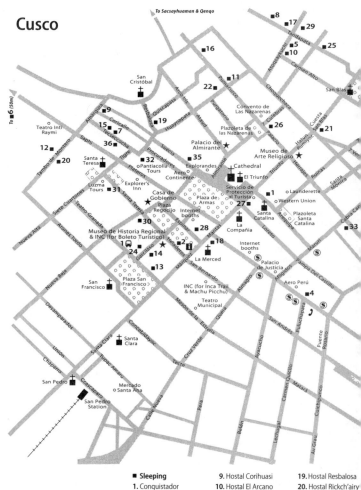

Cusco

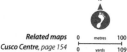

Related maps
Cusco Centre, page 154

| 0 | metres | 100 |
| 0 | yards | 109 |

■ **Sleeping**
1. Conquistador
2. Cusco
3. Don Carlos
4. El Dorado Inn
5. Hospedaje Familiar Inti Quilla
6. Hostal Cahuide
7. Hostal Carlos V
8. Hostal Casa de Campo

9. Hostal Corihuasi
10. Hostal El Arcano
11. Hostal El Arqueólogo
12. Hostal El Balcón
13. Hostal El Solar
14. Hostal Garcilaso
15. Hostal Imperial Palace
16. Hostal Maria Esther
17. Hostal Pakcha Real
18. Hostal Qosqo

19. Hostal Resbalosa
20. Hostal Rickch'airy
21. Hostal San Blas
22. Huaynapata
24. Libertador
25. Los Marqueses
27. Mirador del Inka
28. Monasterio del Cusco
29. Pensión Loreto
30. Posada del Inca

in fine murals, paintings and carved altars. The cloister is also noteworthy, though it has been closed since 1990 for restoration.

Much **Inca stonework** can be seen in the streets and most particularly in the Callejón Loreto, running southeast past La Compañía de Jesús from the main plaza. The walls of the *Acllahuasi* (House of the Chosen Women) are on one side, and of the *Amarucancha* on the other. There are also Inca remains in Calle San Agustín, to the east of the plaza. The famous stone of 12 angles is in Calle Hatun Rumiyoc halfway along its second block, on the right-hand side going away from the plaza.

Churches

La Merced was first built 1534, and rebuilt in the late 17th century. Attached is a very fine monastery with an exquisite cloister. Inside the church are buried Gonzalo Pizarro, half-brother of Francisco, and the two Almagros, father and son. Their tombs were discovered in 1946. The church is most famous for its jewelled monstrance, on view in the monastery's museum during visiting hours. The superb choir stalls, reached from the upper floor of the cloister, can be seen by men only, but you must persuade a Mercedarian friar to let you see them. ■*Calle Márquez. Open 0830-1200, 1430-1730. Entrance US$1.75, students US$1.25. The church was closed for restoration at the time of writing.*

San Francisco, on Plaza San Francisco, three blocks southwest of the Plaza de Armas, this is an austere church reflecting many indigenous influences. Its monastery is being rebuilt and might still be closed. ■*Open 0600-0800, 1800-2000.*

The magnificent **Santa Catalina** church, convent and museum are on Arequipa, opposite C Santa Catalina. ■*Open Monday-Thursday and Saturday 0800-1800, Friday 0800-1900. There are guided tours by English-speaking students; a tip is expected.*

San Pedro, in front of the Santa Ana market, was built in 1688. Its two towers were made from stones brought from an Inca ruin. ■*Open Monday-Saturday 1000-1200, 1400-1700.*

The nuns' church of **Santa Clara** is on Santa Clara, through an arch from Plaza San Francisco. It is

To Piquillacta, Puno & Bolivia

Cusco & the Sacred Valley

Chihuampata

Carmen Bajo

Recoleta

Colla calle

Tullumayo

San Agustín Zetas

Internet Booths

●23

Av de la Cultura

3 ☐ ☐2

Santo Domingo & Temple of the Sun

Museo Arqueológico ★

Amargura

●34 American Airlines Agent

Pampa Para

Av Garcilaso

Huáscar

Manco

Inca

●3

○Centro Qosco

Peruvian Andean Treks ★

Tullumayo

Manco Capac

Avenida Sol

B u s O f f i c e s

Pachacutec

Avenida Pardo

Manu ○Expeditions

Wanchac Station

Centenario

○Manu Nature Tours

To Airport

31. Posada del Sol
32. Royal Inka
33. Royal Inka II
34. Royal Qosco
35. San Agustín Internacional
36. San Agustín Plaza
37. Suecia
38. Suecia II

☐ **Buses**
1. Abancay & Andahuaylas
2. Chincheros
3. Pisac, Calca & Urubamba

unique in South America for its decoration, which covers the whole of the interior, but is virtually impossible to visit.

The smaller and less well-known church of **San Blas**, on Carmen Bajo, has a beautiful carved *mestizo* cedar pulpit, which is well worth seeing. ∎*Open Monday-Saturday 1400-1730.*

Above Cusco, on the road up to Sacsayhuamán, is **San Cristóbal**, built to his patron saint by Cristóbal Paullu Inca. North of it, you can see the 11 doorway-sized niches of the great Inca wall of the Palacio de Colcampata.

Belén de los Reyes, in the southern outskirts of the city, was built by an *indígena* in the 17th century. It has a striking main altar, with silver embellishments at the centre and goldwashed *retablos* at the sides. The church is open 1000-1200, 1500-1700, daily except Thursday and Sunday.

Santo Domingo

A visit to Santo Domingo, southeast of the main plaza, is highly recommended. It was built in the 17th century on the walls of the Qoricancha Temple of the Sun and from its stones. Current excavation is revealing more of the five chambers of the Temple of the Sun, which shows the best Inca stonework to be seen in Cusco. The Temple of the Sun was awarded to Juan Pizarro, the younger brother of Francisco, who willed it to the Dominicans after he had been fatally wounded in the Sacsayhuamán siege.

The baroque cloister has been gutted to reveal four of the original chambers of the great Inca temple – two on the west have been partly reconstructed in a good imitation of Inca masonry. The finest stonework is in the celebrated curved wall beneath the west end of Santo Domingo. This was rebuilt after the 1950 earthquake, at which time a niche that once contained a shrine was found at the inner top of the wall. Below the curved wall was a garden of gold and silver replicas of animals, maize and other plants. Excavations have revealed Inca baths below here, and more Inca retaining walls. The other superb stretch of late Inca stonework is in Calle Ahuacpinta outside the temple, to the east or left as you enter (John Hemming).

∎*Open 0900-1700. Entrance US$0.85. There are guides outside who charge around US$2-3, but Peter Frost's book is just as good.*

Colonial buildings

The **Palacio del Almirante**, just north of the Plaza de Armas on Ataud, is impressive. It houses a museum on Inca artwork. Note the pillar on the balcony over the door, showing a bearded man and a naked woman (thankfully, not the other way round). ∎*Entrance US$1.80.*

Nearby, in a small square on Cuesta del Almirante, is the colonial house of **San Borja**, where Bolívar stayed after the Battle of Ayacucho. **The Casona del Marqués de Valleumbroso,** on San Bernardo y Márquez, three blocks southwest of the Plaza de Armas, was gutted by fire in 1973 and is being restored.

The **Palacio Arzobispal** stands on Hatun Rumiyoc y Herrajes, two blocks northeast of Plaza de Armas. It was built on the site of the palace occupied in 1400 by the Inca Roca and was formerly the home of the Marqueses de Buena Vista. It contains the Museo de Arte Religioso (see below).

Above San Cristóbal church, to the left, is a private colonial mansion, once the home of the infamous explorer and murderer, Lope de Aguirre (see page 461). Also worth a visit is the palace called **Casa de los Cuatro Bustos** at San Agustín 400, which is now the *Hotel Libertador*. The **Convento de las Nazarenas,** on Plaza de las Nazarenas, now houses the offices of Copesco. You can see the Inca-colonial doorway with a mermaid motif, but ask permission to view the lovely 18th century frescos inside. Also on Plaza Nazarenas is **Casa Cabrera**, which is now a gallery and used by Banco Continental.

On the way to the airport on Avda del Sol, 20 minutes' walk from the Plaza de **Other sites**
Armas, there is a statue of the **Inca Pachacútec** placed on top of a lookout
tower, from which there are excellent views of Cusco. Inside are small galleries, a restaurant and a tourist police office. ■*Open 1000-2000. Entrance free.*

The **Astronomical Observatory** is at Km 3 on the road west to Cachimayo
and affords fine views of Cusco and the Sacred Valley. It has a pleasant restaurant where you can enjoy the views while you are dining. ■*Observations are
1830-2300.*

Museo Arqueológico is now housed in an underground site on Avda Sol, in **Museums**
the gardens below Santo Domingo. It contains a first-rate precolumbian collection, Spanish paintings of imitation Inca royalty dating from the 18th century, as well as an excellent collection of textiles. Visitors should ask to see the
forty miniature pre-Inca turquoise figures found at Piquillacta and the golden
treasures, all kept under lock and key but on display. It's a good idea to visit
Santo Domingo before the museum, in order to better understand the limited
information given. ■*Open Monday-Friday 0800-1730, Saturday and Sunday
0800-1400. Entrance US$2.*

    Museo de Arte Religioso, in the Palacio Arzobispal (see above), has a
fine collection of colonial paintings and furniture. The collection includes the
paintings by the indigenous master, Diego Quispe Tito, of a 17th century
Corpus Christi procession that used to hang in the church of Santa Ana, and
you should insist on seeing them (see **Painting and sculpture**, page 533).
■*Open Monday-Saturday, 0830-1200, 1500-1730.*

    Museo de Historia Regional, in the Casa Garcilaso, Jr Garcilaso y
Heladeros, tries to show the evolution of the Cuzqueño school of painting. It
also contains Inca agricultural implements, colonial furniture and paintings,
a small photographic exhibition and mementos of more recent times. ■*Open
0800-1800. A guide is recommended; they are available at the ticket office, and
many of them speak English.*

    Museo de Arte Contemporáneo is in the Casa de Gobierno, on Plaza
Regocijo.

There are some magnificent Inca walls in the ruined ceremonial centre of **Sacsayhuamán**
Sacsayhuamán, on a hill in the northern outskirts. The Incaic stones are
hugely impressive. The massive rocks weighing up to 130 tons are fitted
together with absolute perfection. Three walls run parallel for over 360 metres
and there are 21 bastions.

    Sacsayhuamán was thought for centuries to be a fortress, but the layout
and architecture suggest a great sanctuary and temple to the Sun, which rises
exactly opposite the place previously believed to be the Inca's throne – which
was probably an altar, carved out of the solid rock. Broad steps lead to the altar
from either side. Zig-zags in the boulders round the 'throne' are apparently
'*chicha* grooves', channels down which maize beer flowed during festivals. Up
the hill is an ancient quarry, the Rodadero, which is now used by children as a
rock slide. Near it are many seats cut perfectly into the smooth rock.

    The hieratic, rather than the military, hypothesis was supported by the
discovery in 1982 of the graves of priests, who would have been unlikely to be
buried in a fortress. The precise functions of the site, however, will probably
continue to be a matter of dispute as very few clues remain, due to its steady
destruction.

    The site survived the first years of the conquest. Pizarro's troops had
entered Cusco unopposed in 1533 and lived safely at Sacsayhuamán, until the

Cusco & the Sacred Valley

rebellion of Manco Inca, in 1536, caught them off guard. The bitter struggle which ensued became the decisive military action of the conquest, for Manco's failure to hold Sacsayhuamán cost him the war, and the empire. The destruction of the hilltop site began after the defeat of Manco's rebellion. The outer walls still stand, but the complex of towers and buildings was razed to the ground. From then, until the 1930s, Sacsayhuamán served as a kind of unofficial quarry of pre-cut stone for the inhabitants of Cusco (Peter Frost). The site is about a 30 minute walk from the town centre. Walk up Pumacurco from Plaza de las Nazarenas.

■*Open daily 0700-1730. You can get in earlier if you wish and definitely try to get there before midday when the tour groups arrive. Free student guides are available, but you should give them a tip.*

Other sites near Cusco

Along the road from Sacsayhuamán to Pisac, past a radio station, is the temple and amphitheatre of **Qenqo**. These are not exactly ruins, but rather one of the finest examples of Inca stone carving *in situ*, especially inside the large hollowed-out stone that houses an altar. The rock is criss-crossed by zig-zag channels that give the place its name and which served to course *chicha*, or perhaps sacrificial blood, for purposes of divination.

On the same road is **Cusillyuioc** (K'usilluyuq), a series of caves and Inca tunnels in a hillside. Take a torch/flashlight to find your way around.

The Inca fortress of **Puka Pukara** (Red Fort), was actually more likely to have been a *tambo*, a kind of post-house where travellers were lodged and goods and animals housed temporarily. It is worth seeing for the views alone.

A few hundred metres up the road is the spring shrine of **Tambo Machay**. It is in excellent condition. Water still flows by a hidden channel out of the masonry wall, straight into a little rock pool traditionally known as the Inca's bath. It seems much more likely that the site was a centre of a water cult.

Taking a guide to the sites mentioned above is a good idea and you should visit in the morning for the best photographs. Carry your multi-site ticket, there are roving ticket inspectors. You can visit the sites on foot. It's a pleasant walk through the countryside requiring half a day or more, though remember to take water and sun protection, and watch out for dogs. An alternative is to take the Pisac bus up to Tambo Machay (US$0.35) and walk back. Another excellent way to see the ruins is on horseback, arranged at travel agencies (US$16 per person for five hours). An organized tour (with guide) will go to all the sites for US$6 per person, not including entrance fees. A taxi will charge US$15-20 for three to four people.

NB It is safest to visit the ruins in a group, especially if you wish to see them under a full moon. Take as few belongings as possible, and hide your camera in a bag.

Essentials

Sleeping
■ *on maps*
Price codes:
see inside front cover

Prices given are for the high season in June-August and do not include 28% tax and service, unless stated. When there are fewer tourists hotels may drop their prices by as much as half. Always check for discounts. You should book more expensive hotels well in advance through a good travel agency, particularly for the week or so around Inti Raymi, when prices are greatly increased. Hotel prices, especially in the mid to upper categories, are often lower when booked through tour agencies. On the Puno-Cusco train there are many hotel agents for medium-priced hotels, whose prices can often be negotiated down. It's best to pay the agent for 1 day only and then negotiate with the hotel. Rooms offered at Cusco station are usually cheaper than those offered on the train. Taxis and tourist minibuses meet the train and take you to the hotel of your choice for US$0.50, but be insistent. It is cold in Cusco, and many hotels do not have heating. It is worth asking for an 'estufa', a space heater which some places will provide for an extra charge. The whole city suffers from water shortages, and the cheaper hotels usually only have supplies in the mornings.

L2 *Libertador*, in the Casa de los Cuatro Bustos at C San Agustín 400, T231961, F233152 (Lima T4216666, F4423011), W www.libertador.com.pe. Price includes 28% tax and service and buffet breakfast, excellent food and service, friendly staff, checkout time is 0900, folk music in the restaurant every evening. Recommended. **L3** *Don Carlos*, Avda Sol 602, T226207/224457 (Lima T2240263, F2248581), E dcarloslim@ tci.net.pe. 49 rooms, breakfast extra, full range of services, all rooms with safe, fridge, heating, also rooms with handicapped facilities. **L3** *Monasterio del Cusco*, Palacio 140, T241777, F237111 (in Lima T2210826, F4218283), E reserlima@peruhotel.com. Includes breakfast, beautifully restored Convent of San Antonio Abad, wonderful rooms, courtyards and cloisters (the president has his own suite), good restaurant, set lunch and buffet dinner for US$15. Mixed reports on service but otherwise recommended.

A1 *IncaTambo Hacienda*, at Km 2, close to Sacsayhuamán, T/F222045/222126 (Lima T4462062, T/F2427811. Price includes 28% tax and service, built on the site of Pizarro's original house, cable TV, heating in rooms, full services and facilities, horse riding in 60 hectares of hotel grounds, 25% discount if booked through *Luzma Tours* (see below). **A1** *Posada del Inca*, Portal Espinar 142, T/F233091/227061 (Lima T2224777/ 2212121, F4224345), E posada_cusco@el-olivar.com.pe. Includes tax and service, 40 rooms, includes buffet breakfast, full range of services, excellent service, elevator, comfortable, popular with tour groups, book in advance. Recommended. **A1** *San Agustín Plaza*, Avda Sol 594, T238121/237331, F237375. 26 rooms, includes 18% tax and breakfast, very good, English spoken, very expensive to send fax. **A1** *San Agustín Internacional*, San Agustín y Maruri 390, T231001, F221174. 74 rooms, includes 18% tax and breakfast, more expensive than *Plaza* but higher standard. **A2** *Cusco*, Heladeros 150, T224821, T/F222832. Includes taxes and buffet breakfast, a huge rambling old building, has a certain old fashioned charm but looks like no one has stayed there for years. **A2** *El Dorado Inn*, Avda Sol 395, T233112/231232/23115, F240993, E doratur@telser.com.pe. 54 rooms with full range of facilities, includes breakfast, excellent service, good restaurant, elevator. **A2** *Royal Inka I*, Plaza Regocijo 299, T231067. Price includes taxes and breakfast, bar, dining room, good service. Recommended. **A2** *Royal Inka II*, on the same street. More modern and expensive, good sauna for US$8, but overall not good value. **A3-B** *Hostal Carlos V*, Tecseccocha 490, T223091. Includes tax and breakfast, has charm and character, restaurant, refurbished, pleasant.

B *Conquistador*, Santa Catalina Angosta 149, T224461, F236314. Price includes tax and breakfast, heating, restaurant, safe deposit, parking, laundry. **B-C** *Hostal Casa de*

Campo, Tandapata 296-B (at the end of the street), T244404, F241422, E amauta@ mail.cosapidata.com.pe (or contact via *La Tertulia* café). 20 rooms with bathroom, hot water 24 hours, includes American breakfast and airport/rail transfer with reservations, discount for longer stays and for students at the *Amauta* language school (see below), 15% discount for SAEC members, 10% discount for Handbook owners, safe deposit box, laundry service, meals on request, sun terrace, quiet and relaxing, all rooms have great views, Dutch and English spoken. Recommended. **B** *Hostal El Balcón*, Tambo de Montero 222, T236738, F225352, E balcon@peru.itete.com.pe. With bathroom and breakfast, nice homely atmosphere, very friendly and welcoming, quiet, laundry, sauna, bar, meals on request, English spoken, wonderful views. Recommended. **B** *Pensión Loreto*, Pasaje Loreto 115, Plaza de Armas. With bathroom, discounts possible, clean, very friendly, rooms with Inca walls and electric heaters, a bit dark, cheap laundry service, friendly, comfortable and secure, taxis and other travel can be arranged, Lucio here is a good guide, safe luggage deposit. Recommended. **B** *Los Marqueses*, Garcilaso 256, T232512, F227028. With bathroom, heaters extra, room prices differ, lovely colonial house with a beautiful patio, comfortable. Recommended. **B-C** *Raymi*, Avda Pardo 950, T225141. With bathroom, heater, includes breakfast. Recommended.

C *Hostal Corihuasi*, C Suecia 561, T/F232233. With bathroom and breakfast, colonial house, laundry arranged, hot water, quiet, friendly, electric heaters, good views, popular with tour groups. Recommended. **C** per person *Hostal Garcilaso*, Garcilaso de la

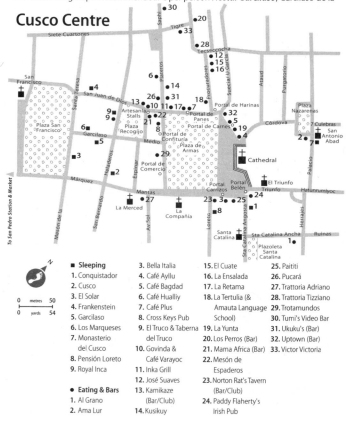

Cusco Centre

■ Sleeping	3. Bella Italia	15. El Cuate	25. Paititi
1. Conquistador	4. Café Ayllu	16. La Ensalada	26. Pucará
2. Cusco	5. Café Bagdad	17. La Retama	27. Trattoria Adriano
3. El Solar	6. Café Hualliy	18. La Tertulia (&	28. Trattoria Tizziano
4. Frankenstein	7. Café Plus	Amauta Language	29. Trotamundos
5. Garcilaso	8. Cross Keys Pub	School)	30. Tumi's Video Bar
6. Los Marqueses	9. El Truco & Taberna	19. La Yunta	31. Ukuku's (Bar)
7. Monasterio	del Truco	20. Los Perros (Bar)	32. Uptown (Bar)
del Cusco	10. Govinda &	21. Mama Africa (Bar)	33. Victor Victoria
8. Pensión Loreto	Café Varayoc	22. Mesón de	
9. Royal Inca	11. Inka Grill	Espaderos	
	12. José Suaves	23. Norton Rat's Tavern	
● Eating & Bars	13. Kamikaze	(Bar/Club)	
1. Al Grano	(Bar/Club)	24. Paddy Flaherty's	
2. Ama Lur	14. Kusikuy	Irish Pub	

0 metres 50
0 yards 54

Vega 233, T233031, T/F222401. With bathroom, safe for luggage, discount if booked through agents, quite good value, helpful. **C** *Hostal Qosqo*, Portal Mantas 115, near the Plaza de Armas. With bathroom, hot water, clean, friendly, helpful, includes breakfast, heating on request at no extra charge. Recommended. **C** *Los Portales*, Matará 322, T223500. Includes airport pickup, tastefully renovated hotel with modern facilities but plenty of character, very clean, very friendly and helpful, English spoken, safe deposit, luggage store. Recommended. **C** *Hostal Q'Awarina*, C Suecia 757. Includes breakfast, great views, great value. **C** *Posada del Sol*, Atoqsaykuchi 296, T/F246394. Includes taxes and breakfast. 10 rooms with bathroom, hot water, communal sitting area, sun patio, kitchen laundry facilities, email facilities for US$1.75 per hour, snack bar, great views. **E** per person in low season. Recommended.

D *California*, Nueva Alta 444, T235770. With bathroom, also dormitories with shared bathroom for **F** per person, hot water 24 hours, includes breakfast, cheaper without, quiet, secure, family atmosphere, stores luggage. Recommended. **D** *El Inca*, Quera 251. **F** in the low season, clean, heating, hot water variable, luggage store, restaurant, includes breakfast, Wilbur speaks English, and is helpful, noisy disco in basement till 0100. But otherwise recommended. **D** *Hostal Amaru*, Cuesta San Blas 541, T225933. With bathroom, cheaper without, hot water 24 hours, laundry, clean, friendly, safe, nice views. Recommended. **D** *Hostal Cahuide*, Saphi 845, T222771. Discount for long stay, hot water, good rooms, quiet, good laundry service, storage facilities, helpful, good value breakfasts. **D** *Hostal El Arqueólogo*, Pumacurco 408, T232569, F235126, E vida@net.cosapidata.com.pe. Includes breakfast, hot water, helpful, French and English spoken, will store luggage, garden, cafeteria and kitchen. Recommended. **D** *Hostal El Solar*, San Francisco 162, T232451. **E** during the low season. Recommended. **D** *Hostal Incawasi*, Portal de Panes 147, Plaza de Armas, T238245. Hot water 0800-0900, 2000-2200, good beds, bargain for long stays, secure, helpful, good value. **D** *Hostal María Esther*, Pumacurco 516, T224382/238627. With bathroom, very comfortable, helpful, includes breakfast, garden. Recommended. **D** *Hostal Samleño*, Carmen Alto 114, T221452, F262979. With bathroom, hot water, breakfast available, laundry service, friendly. Recommended. **D** *Hostal San Blas*, Cuesta San Blas 526, T225781. **F** per person without bathroom, basic, clean, friendly, secure for luggage, includes breakfast. **D** *Huaynapata*, Huaynapata 369, T228034. Small rooms, quieter rooms at the back, clean, family-run, hot water, stores luggage, friendly. Recommended. **D** *Kristina*, Avda Sol 341, T227251. Nice rooms, with private bathroom, hot water, breakfast available, friendly, reliable. Recommended. **D** *Niños Hotel*, C Medoc 442, T/F235183, E ninos@correo.dnet.com.pe. With bathroom, **E-F** per person without, hot water, restaurant, laundry service, luggage store, airport transfer, fax and email service, Dutch, English, German and French spoken, run as part of the Dutch foundation *Niños Unidos Peruanos* and all profits are invested in projects to help street

children. **D** *Suecia II*, Tecseccocha 465, T239757. With bathroom, **E** without, good beds and blankets, clean, good security procedures, breakfast US$1.50 from 0500, beautiful building, good meeting place for trekkers doing the Inca Trail, best to book in advance. Recommended. **D** *Tambo*, Ayacucho 233, T236788. Heating in rooms, laundry facilities, safe for luggage, hot water intermittent, OK restaurant. Recommended.

E *Hostal Bellavista*, Avda Santiago 100, 10 minutes' walk from the plaza (not a safe area at night). With bathroom, **F** without, hot water, very friendly, safe, breakfast available, will store luggage. Recommended. **E** *Hostal Cáceres*, Plateros 368, 1 block from the Plaza de Armas. Hot water, big rooms, luggage store, friendly, laundry service, motorcycle parking in the patio. **E-F** *Hostal Frankenstein*, San Juan de Dios 260, 200 metres from the Plaza de Armas, T236999. New in 1998, with bathroom, slightly cheaper without, hot water 24 hours, German-owned. **E** per person *Hostal Mirador del Inka*, Tandapata 160, T261384. With bathroom, cheaper in dormitory rooms, clean, good-sized rooms, laundry and kitchen facilities, very secure, great views, family run, very friendly. Recommended, especially for families with kids. **E** *Hostal Quipu*, Fierro 495 (not a safe part of town), T236179, F260721. Hot water 24 hours, colonial-style house with attractive courtyard, laundry service, luggage store, safe deposit. **E** per person *Hostal Tahuantinsuyo*, Jr Tupac Yupanqui 204, Urb Tahuantinsuyo (15 minute walk from the Plaza de Armas), T/F261410, E suya@chaski.unsaac.edu.pe. Cheaper without bathroom, includes breakfast, also drinks and snacks available, hot water 24 hours, friendly, lovely atmosphere, very helpful, laundry service and facilities, secure parking for bikes and motorbikes, English, French and Italian spoken, can arrange tours. Recommended.

F per person *El Arcano*, Carmen Alto 288, T/F232703. Cheaper in low season, very clean, hot water 0600-1800, safe to leave luggage, 9 rooms for 1-4 people, very friendly owner, laundry, good beds, toilet paper provided, cheap breakfast. Highly recommended. **F** *Hostal Choquechaca*, Choquechaca 436-B, T237265. Discount for longer stays, hot water all day, 10 rooms with 3 shared bathrooms. Recommended. **F** *Hostal Familiar Carmen Alto*, Carmen Alto 197, 1 block from Choquechaca. Hot water, use of the kitchen, laundry facilities, quiet, secure. Recommended. **F** *Hostal Familiar Casa*, Pasaje España 844, off Pardo, T224152. Shared bathroom, basic rooms, quiet, friendly, safe, hot water in the mornings only, baggage stored for a small fee, laundry. Recommended. **F** per person *Hostal Imperial Palace*, Tecseccocha 492, T223324. Includes breakfast, with bathroom, cheaper without, large and very nice rooms, hot water on request, café, bar, restaurant, a bit cold but well furnished, English spoken, good, very friendly, safe deposit open only 0700-1100. **F** per person *Hostal Kuntur Wasi*, Tandapata 352-A, T227570. Great views, very clean, laundry service costs US$1 per kilo, owner speaks a bit of English and is very helpful and welcoming, water not very warm, but excellent value. **F** per person *Hospedaje Magnolia's*, Plaza San Francisco 122, T233799/243463. With bathroom, cheaper without but hot

water only in shared bathrooms in mornings and evenings only, friendly, secure, towels provided, laundry service, cable TV in lounge. Recommended. **F** per person *Hostal Pakcha Real*, Tandapata 300, San Blas, T237484. Friendly, family run, hot water, cooking and laundry facilities, TV and video lounge, luggage stored, owner Edwin will arrange tours. Recommended. **F** per person *Hostal Pumacurco*, Pumacurco 336, Interior 329, T227739 (3 minutes from the Plaza de Armas). In the newly restored part of a very old colonial house, hot water, owner Betty is very friendly and helpful, some large rooms, clean, secure, washing facilities. **F** *Hostal Resbalosa*, Resbalosa 494, T224839. Clean, hot water in the mornings and evenings, luggage stored, laundry facilities, full breakfast for US$1.50. Recommended. **F** per person *Hostal Rickch'airy*, Tambo de Montero 219, T236606. Shared bathroom, hot water in the morning, laundry service, free luggage store, breakfast available, nice garden with good views, tourist information, owned by Leo who is helpful. Highly recommended. **F** per person *Hospedaje Sol Naciente*, Avda Pardo 510, T228602. Hot water, comfortable, laundry facilities, luggage stored for a small fee, very clean, family-run. **F** *Hostal Unión*, Unión 189, T231580, ½ block from the Santa Ana market. Shared bathroom, hot water 24 hours, basic but clean, secure, laundry facilities, kitchen/café, luggage store, includes breakfast, helpful. Very noisy but recommended. **F** *Imperio*, on C Chaparro. Run by Elena and family, near San Pedro station, be careful at night in this part of town, hot water, friendly, clean, noisy, motorcycle parking, safe to leave luggage. Recommended. **F** per person *Qorichaska*, Nueva Alta 458, T228974. Clean, hot water, will store luggage, cafeteria open till 2100, safe, friendly, great value. Recommended. **F-G** per person *Hospedaje Familiar Inti Quilla*, Atoqsaykuchi 281, T252659. Shared rooms around a pleasant little courtyard, hot water 24 hours, friendly. **F-G** per person *Hostal Luzerna*, Avda Baja 205, near San Pedro train station (take a taxi at night), T232762/237591/227768. Hot water 24 hours, clean, safe to leave luggage, good beds, nice family, with breakfast. Recommended.

G per person *Hostal San Cristóbal*, Quiscapata 242, near San Cristóbal. Dormitory rooms, cooking and clothes-washing facilities, baggage deposit, friendly and reliable, if full Sra Ema de Paredes will let you spread a sleeping bag on the floor. Recommended.

There is a network of local families offering tourist accommodation in 3 categories: *Inti* (room with private bath), *Quilla* (room with shared bathroom), and *Chaska* (rooms with use of family's bathroom). Guests are also invited to participate in family events. Contact: Small Business Association of Family Lodgings, C San Augustin 415, T244036, F233912, E ititoss@mail.cosapidata.com.pe.

Youth hostel: **E** per person *Albergue Municipal*, Quiscapata 240, San Cristóbal, T252506. Dormitories, very clean, helpful staff, luggage store, great views, bar, cafeteria, laundry, safe deposit, discount for members. **E-F** per person *El Procurador*, Coricalle 440, Prolongación Procuradores, T243559. Cheaper without bathroom, includes breakfast, hot water, laundry, motorcycle parking, friendly. Recommended.

Inka Grill, Portal de Panes 115, Plaza de Armas, T262992. According to many the best food in town, very smart decor. Recommended. *El Truco*, Plaza Regocijo 261. Excellent local and international dishes, buffet lunch 1200-1500, nightly folk music at 2045, next door is *Taberna del Truco*, which is open 0900-0100. *Mesón de los Espaderos*, Espaderos y Plaza de Armas, 2nd floor. Good *parrilladas* and other typical local dishes. *Paititi*, Portal Carrizos 270, Plaza de Armas. Live music, good atmosphere, Inca masonry, excellent pizzas but the service is hit or miss, depending on how busy they are. *Roma*, Portal de Panes 105, Plaza de Armas. International cuisine, including seafood and Italian specialities, also features folk music shows nightly. *La Retama*, Portal de Panes 123, 2nd floor. Good food and service.

Eating: expensive
● *on maps*

Cusco & the Sacred Valley

Eating:
mid-range
Al Grano, Santa Catalina Ancha 398, T228032. Authentic Asian dishes for only US$4.50, menu changes daily, excellent food and without doubt the best coffee in town, vegetarian choices, open 1000-2100, closed on Sunday. Highly recommended. *Pucará*, Plateros 309. Peruvian and international food, open 1230-2200, closed on Sunday, nice atmosphere, very good food. Recommended. *Los Tomines*, Triunfo 384. Excellent 4-course set meal for US$5-6. Recommended. *Chez Maggy*, Plateros 339. Opens at 1800, good atmosphere, popular with tourists, pasta, soups, pizzas freshly baked in wood-burning oven. *Pizzería América*, Plateros 316, and *Americana*, at 369, are both highly recommended. *Pizzería Wasi*, Procuradores 347. Good pizzas, also meat dishes, helpful German owner. *Tizziano Trattoria*, Tecseccocha 418. Good Italian food, homemade pasta, excellent value *menú* served Monday-Saturday 1200-1500 and 1800-2300, also vegetarian dishes.

Eating:
cheaper
Kusikuy, Plateros 348, T262870. Open 0800-2300 Monday-Saturday, local, national and international dishes, good service, their set lunch is unbeatable value at only US$2.15. Highly recommended. *Los Candiles*, Plateros 323. Good set lunch for US$2.50. *La Yunta*, Portal de Carnes, Plaza de Armas. Good salads, pancakes and juices, also vegetarian, popular with tourists, same owners as *Instinct Travel Agency*. *José Suaves*, Procuradores 398 (top end), T243024. Huge breakfast with fruit salad, pancakes, eggs and hashbrowns, great value for under US$3, great burgers and chicken wings, also Chinese and vegetarian food, book exchange, they even deliver to your hotel, open 1300-2300 Monday-Saturday, 1800-2300 on Sunday, Canadian owner. Recommended. *Víctor Victoria*, Tigre 130. Israeli and local dishes, highly recommended for breakfast, good value. *El Cuate*, Procuradores 386. Mexican food, great value, big portions. Recommended. *La Ensalada*, on Procuradores. French cuisine, very good value menú, excellent crepes. *Ama Lur*, Plaza de las Nazarenas 159, clean, cheap, varied menu, excellent food, vegetarian dishes available, foreign newspapers and magazines. *El Nevado*, Plateros 345. Good set meals, also good soups and fish.

Cafés
Café Hualliy, Plateros 363. Popular meeting place, especially for breakfast, good for comments on guides, has good snacks and 'copa Hualliy' – fruit, muesli, yoghurt, honey and chocolate cake, also good vegetarian *menú* and set lunch. *Trotamundos*, Portal Comercio 177, 2nd floor. Balcony overlooking the plaza, nice atmosphere, especially at night with open fire, good coffee and cakes, safe salads, best to stick to the simpler dishes. *Café Plus*, Portal de Panes 151, 2nd floor. Delicious cakes, excellent coffee, friendly, good service. *La Tertulia*, Procuradores 50, 2nd floor. Run by Johanna and Alfredo, who also run the *Amauta* Language School downstairs, excellent breakfast buffet is served 0630-1300, includes muesli, homemade bread, yoghurt, eggs, juice and coffee, eat as much as you like for around US$3, superb value, vegetarian buffet served daily 1800-2200, set dinner and salad bar for US$3.50, also fondue and gourmet meals, book exchange, newspapers, classical music, open till 2300. *Café Literario Varayoc*, Espaderos 142. Good meeting place, Dutch owner, excellent coffee, pizzas and chocolate cake. *Ayllu*, Portal de Carnes 208. Open at 0600, classical/folk music, good atmosphere, has a superb range of milk products and wonderful apple pastries, try *leche asada*, good selection for breakfast, great juices, quick service. Next door upstairs is *Café Bagdad*. It has a nice balcony with good views of the plaza, it does a cheap set lunch, good atmosphere, happy hour 1930-2130, German owner Florian Thurman speaks good English, but the service is variable. *One World Café*, Choquechaca 182. Good food, nice atmosphere, book exchange, English/Peruvian owners, US$2.50 for set meal. *Yacumama*, Procuradores 397. Good breakfast, unlimited tea or coffee.

Vegetarian *Govinda*, Espaderos 128, just off the Plaza de Armas. Good value, especially the set meals, but it's now a bit run down and service is poor. *Acuarium*, Cuesta del Almirante 211. Good *menú*. *Frutos*, C Triunfo 393, 2nd floor. Open Monday-Saturday 0630-2200, Thursday 0900-1500, excellent value set lunch. *Auliya*, C Garcilaso 265, on 2nd floor. Beautifully-renovated colonial house, excellent vegetarian food, also stocks a wide range of dried food for trekking.

Bars *Cross Keys Pub*, Plaza de Armas, Portal Confiturías 233 (upstairs). Open 1100-0130, run by Barry Walker of *Manu Expeditions*, a Mancunian and bird expert, darts, cable sports, pool, bar meals, happy hours 1800-1900 and 2100-2130, plus daily half price specials Sunday-Wednesday, great pisco sours, very popular, loud and raucous, great atmosphere. *Los Perros Bar*, Tecseccocha 436. Completely different vibe, great place to chill out on comfy couches, excellent music, owners Tammy and Guillermo are English-speaking and very friendly and welcoming, good coffee, tasty snacks available, books, magazines and board games, open 1500-0100, happy hours on selected drinks 1800-1900 and 2100-2200. *Paddy Flaherty's*, C Triunfo 124 on the corner of the plaza, E paddy@qenqo.unsaac.edu.pe. Irish theme pub, serves cans of Guinness, open 1300-0100. *Tumi's Video Bar*, Saphi 478. Shows 4 movies daily, US$1.80, you can also choose your own video from over 200 titles (in English) and pick a time to watch it, free popcorn served during movies, comfortable seating, drinks and pizzas available, owner Maurice Drews has good local information. *Keros Pub*, on the corner of Procuradores and Plaza de Armas. Café until 1800, good, cheap breakfast, cakes, juices, good view of plaza, bar afterwards with live music every night, happy hour 1900-2200. *Norton Rat's Tavern*, Loreto 115, same entrance as *Hostal Loreto*. Also serves meals, cable TV with BBC and CNN, popular with North Americans.

Bars & nightclubs

Nightclubs *Ukuku's*, Plateros 316. US$1.35 entry, happy hour 0730-0930, very popular, good atmosphere, good mix of music, shows free movies around 1600-1700. *Kamikaze*, Plaza Regocijo 274. *Peña* at 2200, good old traditional rock music, candle-lit cavern atmosphere, entry US$2.50 but usually you don't have to pay. *Mama Africa*, Espaderos 135, 2nd floor. Live music at weekends, very popular, free entry with a pass which you can get on the plaza, free movies on large screen daily at 1630-1700, also has cybercafé. *Uptown*, Suecia 302 on the corner of the plaza. Good music and atmosphere, very popular, happy hours 2100-2200 and 2300-2330.

Folklore There's a regular nightly folklore show at *Centro Qosqo*, Avda del Sol 604, next to *Hotel Don Carlos*, at 1900, entrance fee US$6. Also at *Teatro Inti Raymi*, Saphi 605, nightly at 1845, US$4.50 entry and well worth it. There's a *peña* at *Inka's Restaurant Peña*, Portal de Panes 105, Plaza de Armas. *Teatro Municipal*, C Mesón de la Estrella 149 (T227321 for information 0900-1300 and 1500-1900). This is a venue for plays, dancing and shows, mostly on Thursday-Sunday. Ask for their programmes. They also run classes in music and dancing from January to March which are great value.

Entertainment

On **20 January** is a procession of saints in the *San Sebastián* district of Cusco. **Carnival** in Cusco is a messy affair with flour, water, cacti, bad fruit and animal manure thrown about in the streets. **Easter Monday** sees the procession of *El Señor de los Temblores* (Lord of the Earthquakes), starting at 1600 outside the Cathedral. A large crucifix is paraded through the streets, returning to the Plaza de Armas around 2000 to bless the tens of thousands of people who have assembled there.

Festivals

On **2-3 May** the *Vigil of the Cross*, which takes place at all mountaintops with crosses on them, is a boisterous affair. In **June** is *Corpus* Christi, on the Thursday after Trinity Sunday, when statues and silver are paraded through the streets. This is a colourful event. The Plaza de Armas is surrounded by tables with women selling *cuy* and a mixed grill called *chiriuchu* (*cuy*, chicken, *tortillas*, fish eggs, water-weeds, maize,

Cusco & the Sacred Valley

The festival of Inti Raymi

The sun was the principal object of Inca worship and at their winter solstice, in June, the Incas honoured the solar deity with a great celebration known as Inti Raymi, the sun festival. The Spanish suppressed the Inca religion, and the last royal Inti Raymi was celebrated in 1535.

However, in 1944 a group of Cusco intellectuals, inspired by the contemporary 'indigenist' movement, revived the old ceremony in the form of a pageant, putting it together from chronicles and historical documents. The event caught the public imagination, and it has been celebrated every year since then on 24 Jun, now a Cusco public holiday. Hundreds of local men and women play the parts of Inca priests, nobles, chosen women, soldiers (played by the local army garrison), runners, and the like. The coveted part of the Inca emperor Pachacuti is won by audition, and the event is organized by the municipal authorities.

It begins around 1000 at the Qoricancha – the former sun temple of Cusco – and winds its way up the main avenue into the Plaza de Armas, accompanied by songs, ringing declarations and the occasional drink of chicha. At the main plaza, Cusco's presiding mayor is whisked back to Inca times, to receive Pachacuti's blessing and a stern lecture on good government. Climbing through Plaza Nazarenas and up Pumacurcu, the procession reaches the ruins of Sacsayhuamán at about 1400, where scores of thousands of people are gathered on the ancient stones.

Before Pachacuti arrives the Sinchi (Pachauti's chief general) ushers in contingents from the four Suyus (regions) of the Inca empire. Much of the ceremony is based around alternating action between these four groups of players. A Chaski (messenger) enters to announce the imminent arrival of the Inca and his Coya (queen). Men sweep the ground before him, and women scatter flowers. The Inka takes the stage alone, and has a dialogue with the sun. Then he receives reports from the governors of the four Suyus. This is followed by a drink of sacred chicha, the re-lighting of the sacred fire of the empire, the sacrifice (faked) of a llama, and the reading of auguries in its entrails. Finally the ritual eating of sankhu (corn paste mixed with the victim's blood) ends the ceremonies. The Inca gives a last message to his assembled children, and departs. The music and dancing continues until nightfall.

cheese and sausage). In **early June**, 2 weeks before Inti Raymi (see below) is the highly recommended *Cusqueño beer festival*, held near the rail station, which boasts a great variety of Latin American music. The whole event is well-organized and great fun. In 1998 entry cost US$6.50.

In **mid-June** is *Q'Olloriti*, the ice festival, held at a 4,700 metre glacier. To get there involves a 2 hour walk up from the nearest road at Mawayani, beyond Ocongate, then it's a further exhausting climb up to the glacier. It's a good idea to take a tent, food and plenty of warm clothing. Note that it can be very confusing for those who don't understand the significance of this ancient ritual. Many trucks leave Cusco, from Limacpampa, in the days prior to the full moon in mid-June; prices from US$2 upwards. This is a very rough and dusty overnight journey lasting 14 hours, requiring warm clothing and coca leaves to fend off cold and exhaustion. Several agencies now offer tours (see also page 194).

On **24 June** *Inti Raymi*, the Inca festival of the winter solstice, where locals outnumber tourists, is enacted at 1300 at the fortress of Sacsayhuamán. It lasts 2½ hours, and is in Quechua. Tickets for the stands can be bought a week in advance from the Municipalidad, and cost US$25. Standing places on the ruins are free but get there at about 1030 as even reserved seats fill up quickly, and defend your space. Travel agents who try to persuade you to buy a ticket for the right to film or take photos are being dishonest. On the night before Inti Raymi, the Plaza de Armas is crowded with processions and food stalls. Try to arrive in Cusco 15 days before Inti Raymi. The atmosphere in the town during the build up is fantastic and something is always going on (festivals, parades etc).

On the last Sunday in **August** is the *Huarachicoy festival* at Sacsayhuamán, a spectacular reenactment of the Inca manhood rite, performed in dazzling costumes by boys of a local school.

On **8 September**, the *Day of the Virgin*, is a colourful procession of masked dancers from the church of Almudena, at the southwest edge of Cusco, near Belén, to the Plaza de San Francisco. There is also a fair at Almudena, and a bull fight on the following day. The **8 December** is *Cusco day*, when churches and museums close at 1200. And, on **24 December**, when all good little travellers should be tucked up in bed, is *Santuranticuy*, 'the buying of saints'. This is a huge celebration of Christmas shopping, with a big crafts market in the Plaza de Armas.

Local crafts Cusco is the weaving centre of Peru, and excellent textiles can be found at good value at various places throughout the city and surrounding villages. In the Plaza San Blas and the surrounding area, authentic Cusco crafts still survive and wood workers can be seen in almost any street. Leading artisans who welcome visitors include *Hilario Mendivil*, Plazoleta San Blas 634, who makes biblical figures from plaster, wheatflour and potatoes and *Edilberta Mérida*, Carmen Alto 133, who makes earthenware figures showing the physical and mental anguish of the Indian peasant. *Víctor Vivero Holgado*, at Tandapata 172, is a painter of pious subjects, while *Antonio Olave Palomino*, Siete Angelitos 752, makes reproductions of precolumbian ceramics and colonial sculptures. *Maximiliano Palomino de la Sierra*, Triunfo 393, produces festive dolls and wood carvings, and Santiago Rojas, near San Blas, statuettes. *Luis Aguayo Revollar, Galería de Arte Aguayo*, Cuesta del Almirante 211-256 y Avda Sol 616, T237992, makes fine wood carvings. Note that much of the wood used for picture frames etc is *cedro*, a rare timber not extracted by sustainable means.

Galería Latina, Calle San Agustin 427, T246588, for alpaca sweaters, pottery and traditional folk art. *Museo Inca Art Gallery* is good for contemporary art, run by Amílcar Salomón Zorrilla, it's at Huancaro M-B – L8, T231232 (PO Box 690), telephone between 0900 and 2100. Visit *Nemesio Villasante*, Avda 24 de Junio 415, T222915, for Paucartambo masks, and *Miguel Chacón Ventura*, Portal Confituría 265, Plaza de Armas, for watercolour paintings.

There's a market on the corner of San Andrés and Quera, which is good for local handicrafts. *Mercado Artesanal*, Avda del Sol, block 4, is also good for cheap crafts. *Coordinadora Sur Andina de Artesanía*, C del Medio 130, off Plaza de Armas, has a good assortment of crafts and is a non-profit organization. *Pedazo*, Plateros 334-B, T242967, sells a wide range of local handicrafts. *La Mamita*, Portal de Carnes 244, T246093, is open every day and sells the beautiful ceramics of Pablo Seminario from

Shopping

Cusco & the Sacred Valley

Urubamba (see page 173). *La Pérez*, Urb Mateo Pumacahua 598, Huanchac, T232186/222137, is a big cooperative with a good selection. They will arrange a free pick-up from your hotel. *Artesanía La Paloma*, Cuesta San Blas 552 and Plazuela Santa Catalina 211, is good but expensive. *Sr Aller*, Plaza Santo Domingo 261, sells interesting antiques. *Josefina Olivera*, Santa Clara 501, sells old ponchos and antique mantas, without the usual haggling. *Kaliran*, Cuesta San Blas 522, sells musical instruments and Andean music. Be very careful when buying gold and silver objects and jewellery in and around Cusco – we have received many reports of sharp practices.

General *Santa Ana Market*, opposite Estación San Pedro, is the best market for a variety of goods. The best value is at closing time or in the rain. Take care after dark. The market is said to be the cheapest for slide and print film, eg Fuji US$4.50. Sacks to cover rucksacks are available in the market for US$0.75. A good supermarket is *El Chinito*, on Matará, behind Avda Sol. There's also a supermarket of the same name on Avda Sol, but the choice isn't as good. A couple of good bookshops are *Librería Studium*, Marqués Mantas 239, and *Los Andes*, Portal Comercio 125, Plaza de Armas.

Camping equipment There are several places around the plaza area which rent out equipment but check it carefully as it is common for parts to be missing. An example of prices per day: tent US$3, sleeping bag US$2, stove US$3. A deposit of US$100 is asked, plus credit card, passport or plane ticket. *Soqllaq'asa Camping Service*, owned by English-speaking Louis Aedo, at Plateros 354, T/F222224, is recommended for equipment hire, but, as elsewhere, check the stoves carefully. Upstairs Sra Luzmila Bellota M has a workshop where she makes alpaca wool fleece jackets to order. They cost US$60 upwards, but try bargaining. White gas (*bencina*) costs US$1.50 per litre and can be bought at hardware stores, but check the purity. Stove spirit (*alcohól para quemar*) is available at pharmacies. Blue gas canisters, costing US$5, can be found at some hardware stores and at shops which rent gear. You can also rent equipment through travel agencies. A shop with useful, imported (so expensive) camping gear is *Camping Deportes*, Centro Comercial Ollanta, Avda del Sol 346, shop no 118. It also sells insect repellent, Deet, US$10 for a small bottle.

Transport **Air connections** There are regular daily flights to **Lima**, with AeroPerú and Aero Continente. There are often promotional offers, so shop around. Grupo Ocho (military) flies every Wednesday in a Hercules transport plane (T221206), US$55. Flights are heavily booked on this route in the school holidays (January-February) and national holidays. There are also daily flights to **Arequipa**, with AeroPerú and Aero Continente and to **Juliaca**. There are daily flights to **Puerto Maldonado** with Aero Continente. Grupo Ocho has 2 flights a month via Iberia from which there is a dry season route to Brazil (see under Iñapari, page 490).

There are international flights to/from **La Paz**, daily with AeroPerú. Also with LAB to La Paz, Santa Cruz, Cochabamba and Puerto Suárez. AeroPerú flies to **Santiago**. American Airlines flies to Lima daily from New York (JFK), Dallas and Miami. Passengers from Dallas and Miami then connect with the New York flight at Lima and continue to Cusco. Return flights leave Cusco at 0740, arrive in Lima at 0900 and depart at 1050.

Airport information T222611/222601. A taxi to and from the airport costs US$1.75. combis cost US$0.35 from Plaza San Francisco or US$0.18 from outside the airport car park to the centre. You can book a hotel at the airport through a travel agency, but this is not really necessary. Many representatives of hotels and travel agencies operate at the airport, with transport to the hotel with which they are associated. Take your time to choose your hotel, at the price you can afford. There is a post office, phone booths, restaurant and cafeteria at the airport. Also a Tourist Protection Bureau desk, which can very helpful if your flight has not been reconfirmed (not an uncommon problem). Pay the departure tax at the BancoSur desk.

NB On the Cusco-Lima route there is a high possibility of cancelled flights during the wet season; tourists are sometimes stranded for several days. It is possible for planes to leave early if the weather is bad. Sit on right side of the aircraft for the best view of the mountains when flying Cusco-Lima; it is worth checking in early to get these seats. Make sure you reconfirm 24 hours before your flight departure. In the high season make sure you arrive at the airport 2 hours before departure to avoid problems.

Buses Most bus offices are in C Pachacútec. To **Juliaca**, 344 kilometres, 10 hours, US$8, several buses daily. The road is now fully paved. When the train is not running it is necessary to go by bus, but even buses do not run after heavy rain. Continuing to **Puno**, 44 kilometres from Juliaca, 1 hour, US$0.50. Cruz del Sur and Ormeño (C Pachacútec) both have buses to **La Paz**, US$12.50, 24 hours, depart 1830 and 1900. A tourist bus to Puno in the daytime is worth paying the extra for the views. Check on safety before taking a night bus to Juliaca or Puno.

To **Arequipa**, 521 kilometres, 13-17 hours, US$10-13. The new road leaves the Cusco-Puno road at Sicuani and runs close to the Colca Canyon, via Chivay; it is very rough in parts. Buses travel mostly at night and it's a very cold journey, so take a blanket. See under Arequipa and the relevant sections for the continuation to Nasca and Lima. Most buses to **Lima** go via Arequipa, 36-40 hours (Cruz del Sur at 1600), US$18-22; Civa goes direct, US$27, a very rough and cold trip with frequent stops.

To **Abancay**, 195 kilometres, 7 hours (longer in the rainy season), US$7, several buses and trucks leave daily from Avda Arcopata, eg Transcusal at 0600, 1000, 1300. The road continues to **Andahuaylas**, 135 kilometres, 5½ hours minimum, US$5, and on to **Ayacucho**, 252 kilometres, 12 hours (longer in the wet), US$8-9. Note that the only direct bus to Andahuaylas leaves at 0300. Most companies will claim that they go direct, but you will have to change in Abancay and wait several hours for another. From Limatambo to Abancay the road is mostly paved and in fairly good condition, otherwise road conditions are poor, but the spectacular scenery compensates.

Continuing from Abancay to **Nasca** via Puquío, the road is mostly paved from Puquío to Nasca (155 kilometres, 6 hours) but otherwise in very bad condition; Expresso Cusco, Avda Grau 820, run 3 times a week, US$20, but can take up to 2½ days. There are many military checkpoints, but some stunning scenery. Seek advice before taking this route to the coast.

Buses to the Sacred Valley: to **Pisac**, 32 kilometres, 1 hour, US$0.65; to **Calca**, 18 kilometres, 30 minutes, US$0.10; to **Urubamba** a further 22 kilometres, 45 minutes, US$0.40. Colectivos, minibuses and buses leave from the bus station in a narrow street off Tullumayo whenever they are full, between 0600 and 1600; also trucks and pick-ups. Buses returning from Pisac are often full. The last one back leaves around 2000. An organized tour can be fixed up anytime with a travel agent for US$5 per person. Taxis charge about US$25 for the round trip. To **Chinchero**, 23 kilometres, 45 minutes, US$0.45; to **Urubamba** a further 25 kilometres, 45 minutes, US$0.45 (or US$0.85 Cusco-Urubamba direct). Colectivos, minibuses and buses leave from C Arcopata when full, or from Inticahuarina 305 (between Tullumayo and Ahuacpinta), every 20 minutes; also from the same place as buses to Pisac. Tours can also be arranged to Chinchero, Urubamba and Ollantaytambo with a Cusco travel agency. To Chinchero, US$6 per person; a taxi costs US$25 for the round trip. Usually only day tours are organized for visits to the valley; see under **Tour Agencies**. Using public transport and staying overnight in Urubamba, Ollantaytambo or Pisac will allow much more time to see the ruins and markets.

Cusco & the Sacred Valley

Trains There are 2 stations in Cusco. To **Juliaca**, for the Arequipa and Puno services, trains leave from the Wanchac station on C Pachacútec. When arriving in Cusco, a tourist bus meets the train to take visitors to hotels whose touts offer rooms on the train. **Machu Picchu** trains leave from Estación San Pedro, opposite the Santa Ana market. To Machu Picchu, see page 181.

The train to **Juliaca** leaves at 0800, on Monday, Wednesday, Friday and Saturday, arriving at about 1730; it arrives in Puno at 1900 (sit on the left for the best views). If going to Puno, it is quicker to get off at Juliaca and take a bus or colectivo from there. See under Juliaca (page 202) for details on the splitting of the train and services to **Arequipa** and **Puno**, also for a description of the 3 classes of travel. Trains return from Puno on Monday, Wednesday, Thursday and Saturday at 0700, arriving at 1800. Fares: *Económico*, US$9, Pullman US$19, Inca US$23.

The train to **Arequipa**, leaves on Monday and Friday at 0800 and arrives 24 hours later. It returns from Arequipa on Sunday and Wednesday at 2000-2100. Fares: *Económico*, US$14, Pullman US$30.

Tickets can be bought up to 5 days in advance. The ticket office at Wanchac station is open Monday-Friday 0800-1200 and 1400-1700, Saturday 0800-1200, Sunday 0800-1000. Tickets sell out quickly and there are queues from 0400 before holidays in the dry season. In the low season tickets to Puno can be bought on the day of departure. You can buy tickets through a travel agent, but check the date and seat number. Meals are served on the train; US$6.50 in pullman. Always check on whether the train is running, especially in the rainy season, when services can be reduced or completely cancelled.

Directory **Airline offices** *AeroPerú*, Avda Sol 319, T24001/232684 (toll free 0800-45370 for reconfirmation). *Aero Continente*, Portal de Harinas 181, Plaza de Armas, T240070 (toll free 0800-42420 for reconfirmation). *American Airlines*, Avda Sol 603-A, T226605/225961 (toll free 0800-40350 for reconfirmation). *LAB* (Lloyd Aero Boliviano), Avda Pardo 675, T222990/224715, F222279.

Banks Most of the banks are along Avda del Sol and all have ATMs from which you can withdraw dollars or soles, saving the inconvenience of waiting in a long queue. *Banco de Crédito*, gives cash advances on Visa and changes TCs at 1% commission to soles, 3% to dollars. It has an ATM for Visa. *Interbanc*, Avda Sol y Puluchapata, charges no commission on TCs and has a Visa ATM which gives dollars as well as soles. Next door is *Banco Continental*, also has a Visa ATM and charges US$5 commission on TCs. *Banco del Sur*, Avda Sol 459, changes Amex and Thomas Cook TCs at reasonable rates. *Banco Latino*, on Avda Sol next to the *El Dorado Inn*, has an ATM for Mastercard. *Banco Wiese*, on Maruri between Pampa del Castillo and Pomeritos, gives cash advances on Mastercard, in dollars.

Many travel agencies and *casas de cambio* change dollars. Some of them change TCs as well, but charge 4-5% commission.

The street changers hang around Avda del Sol, blocks 2-3, every day and are a pleasure to do business with. Some of them will also change TCs. In banks and on the street check the notes.

Communications **Post Office:** Avda del Sol, block 5. Open Mon-Sat 0730-2000, 0800-1400 Sun and holidays. *Poste restante* is free and helpful. Sending packages from Cusco is not cheap, reliable or quick. It's much better to wait until Lima. For sending packages or money overseas, *DHL*. Western Union, Avda Sol 393, T244167; *Western Union* also at Sta Catalina Ancha y Angoste.

Telecommunications: Telefónica del Perú, Avda del Sol 386. For telephone and fax, open Mon-Sat 0700-2300, 0700-1200 Sun and holidays. International calls can be made by pay phone or go through the operator – a long wait is possible and a deposit is required. To send a fax costs (per page): US$4.75 to Europe and Israel; US$2.80 to North America. To receive a fax costs US$0.70 per page; the number is (084) 241111. **Email:** *Internet Cusco*, at Galerias UNSAAC, near the top of Avda Sol, T238173. US$1.80 per hour, 20 machines, no problem if you want more than an hour. *Telser*, at Telefónica del Perú, C del Medio 117, T242424. US$2 per hour, 6 machines, difficult to get more than an hour, they have a café if you have to wait; also at Plazoleta Limacpampa, at Avda Tullumayo and Arcopunco, T245505. **Radio messages:** Radio

Tawantinsuyo, Avda del Sol 806. Open Mon-Sat 0600-1900, Sun 0600-1600, messages are sent out between 0500 and 2100 (you can choose the time), in Spanish or Quechua, price per message is US$1. This is sometimes helpful if things are stolen and you want them back. Radio Comercial, Avda del Sol 457, oficina 406, T231381. Open daily 0900-1200, 1600-1900, for making contact with other radio-users in Cusco and the jungle area. This is helpful if you wish to contact people in Manu and costs US$1.50 for 5 mins.

Embassies & consulates *US Agent*, Olga Villa García, Apdo 949, Cusco, T222183 or 233541. *German*, Sra Maria-Sophia Júrgens de Hermoza, San Agustín 307, T235459, Casilla Postal 1128, Correo Central. Open Mon-Fri, 1000-1200, appointments may be made by phone, it also has a book exchange. *French*, C Espinar (M Jean Pierre Sallat, *Farmacia Vallenas* – may let French people leave luggage if going to Machu Picchu). *British*, Dr Raul Delgado de la Flor, *Hotel San Agustín Internacional*, T222322 or 231001 (address above). The Austrian Consul is also there. *Finnish*, Emmel 109, Yanahuara, T223708.

Hospitals & medical services Dentists: *Gilbert Espejo*, T228074. Health: *Hospital Regional*, Avda de la Cultura. Recommended. If lab tests are needed, *Lab Pasteur*, Tullumayo 768 is recommended. *Dr Oscar Tejada* (PO Box 425, Cusco), T233836 or 240449 day or night (cellular T621821) is a member of the International Association for Medical Assistance to Travellers and is prepared to help any visitor in an emergency, 24-hour attention; he charges according to that organization's scales, which are not expensive. *Dr Gustavo Garrido Juárez*, Matará 410, T239761 (cellular T682159), English and French spoken. *Clínica Pardo*, Avda de la Cultura 710, T240387. Open 24 hrs daily, most of the doctors speak English, very quick with test results. Recommended.

Language classes *Exel*, Cruz Verde 336, T235298. Señorita Sori is highly recommended. The school can arrange accommodation with local families. *Amauta*, Procuradores 50, 2nd Flr, T/F241422, PO Box 1164, E amautaa@mail.cosapidata.com.pe. Same owners as *La Tertulia* and *Hostal Casa de Campo*. Spanish classes, one-to-one or in small groups, also Quechua classes and workshops in Peruvian cuisine, dance and music. They have apartments to rent, arrange excursions and can help find voluntary work. They also have a school in Urubamba with accommodation and meals included and pottery and cooking workshops. Spanish classes are run by the *ACUPARI*, the German-Peruvian Cultural Association, San Agustín 307.

Laundry *Lavandería T'aqsana Wasi*, Santa Catalina Ancha 345. Same day service, they also iron clothes, US$1 per kg, good service, speak English, German, Italian and French, open Mon-Fri 0900-2030, Sat 0900-1900. *Lavamatic*, Procuradores 341. Same day service, US$1.20 per kg. There's also a good laundry opposite Suecia II at Tecseccocha 450, fast service, under US$1 per kg. There are several cheap laundries on Procuradores, and also on Suecia and Tecseccocha.

Tour companies & travel agents There are a million and one tour operators in Cusco, most of whom are packed into the Plaza de Armas. The sheer number and variety of tours on offer is bewildering and prices for the same tour can vary dramatically. Always remember that you get what you pay for.

Always check details before making arrangements, shop around and be aware that overcharging and failing to keep to arrangements are common, especially in the high season. Also beware agencies quoting

STUDY SPANISH ...and experience the fascinating Inca culture! ...in both our Cusco and Sacred Valley locations!

Private and Group Lessons
Professional and Survival Spanish
Guest Family or School Accommodations
Quechua Lessons & Cultural Workshops
Volunteer Work Program

Amauta Language School

P.O. Box 1164, Cusco, Perú T/F: 5184-241422
Email: amautaa@mail.cosapidata.com.pe
Website: http://www.telser.com.pe/amauta

prices in dollars then converting to soles at an unfavourable rate when paying. Do not deal with guides who claim to be employed by agencies listed below without verifying their credentials. It is better to deal direct with the agencies. Seek advice from visitors returning from trips for the latest information. Beware also of tours which stop for long lunches at expensive hotels. In and around Cusco, and Machu Picchu, check the standard of your guide's English (or whichever language is required) as some have no more than a memorized spiel.

A day tour Pisac-Ollantaytambo-Chinchero costs US$10-15 per person; a ½-day tour visiting the 4 ruins around Cusco, US$6 per person, not including entrance fees; ½-day city tours cost around US$3-3.50.

The following agencies are those for which we have received favourable reports, which is not to say that those not listed are not recommended. They are divided into their respective categories. Those listed under general tours (expensive and economical) offer a wide range of different tours, including Machu Picchu and the Inca Trail. The more expensive agencies generally offer a higher standard and quality of service. Most of the agencies speak English.

General tours Expensive: *Lima Tours*, Avda Machu Picchu D-24, Urb Mañuel Prado, T228431/235241. Amex representative, gives traveller's cheques against Amex card, but no exchange, also DHL office, to receive a parcel you pay 35% of the marked value of customs tax. *Explorandes*, Portal de Panes 236, Plaza de Armas, T244308, F233784, E expcuzco@ peru.itete.com.pe (in Lima, San Fernando 320, Miraflores, T4450532/4458683, F4454686, E postmast@exploran.com.pe). Offer a wide range of trekking, rafting and cultural tours in and around Cusco and throughout Peru. *Southern Cross Adventures*, Portal de Panes 123, oficina 301, Plaza de Armas, T237649, F239447. Specializes in horseback trips. *APU Expediciones*, Urb Magisterio, 2da etapa, G-3, T/F246377, PO Box 24, E apuexpe@qenqo.rcp.net.pe; www.geocities.com/TheTropics/Cabana/4037. Cultural, adventure and educational tours, packages to Manu and Tambopata, special interest trips, run by Mariella Bernasconi Cilloniz. *Tambo Treks*, Atocsaycuchi 589, Plaza San Blas, T237718. Adventure trips. *Peruvian Andean Treks*, Avda Pardo 705, T225701, F238911, E postmast@patcusco.com.pe. Manager Tom Hendrikson, adventure tour specialists. Kinjyo Travel Service, Portal de Panes 101, Plaza de Armas, T231101, F239044, E ktscus@qenqo.rcp.net.pe. Includes treks to weaving villages. *Destinos Turísticos*, Portal de Panes 123, oficina 101-102, Plaza de Armas, T/F228168/624672, E destinos@telser.com.pe. Luzma Tours, Santa Teresa 399, T/F261327, E lmtrhb@mail.cosapidata.com,pe. Wide range of treks around Cusco, also offers email, fax, phone and photocopying service, can provide ISIC cards, manager Luz-Marina is very helpful. *Andean Adventures*, C Heladeros 157, T263498, F236201, E andeanad@chaski.unsaac.edu.pe. Includes 4-5 day trek on rarely used Inca Trail to Willoc. *Apumayo Expeditions*, C Garcilaso 265 interior 3, T246018 (Lima: T/F4442320), E apumayo@ mail.cosapidata.com.pe. Run rafting and hiking tours in the Cotahuasi canyon. Also run tours

Cusco & the Sacred Valley

designed specifically for disabled travellers, include the Sacred Valley, Paracas Nature Reserve, cultural tours, horse riding and river rafting.

General tours Economical: *Kantu Tours*, Portal Belén 258, T221381, F232012. Good horse treks around Cusco (US$10 for 6 hrs). *Ecotours*, Heladeros 150, T231288. *Eric Adventures*, Plateros 324, T/F228475, E ericadv@net.cosapidata.com.pe. Paragliding course, 2-3 days for US$105. Snow Tours, Portal de Panes 109, or 204, T241313, F240108. *SAS Travel*, Portal de Panes 143, T/F237292, and Espaderos 135.

Inca Trail: *United Mice*, Plateros 348, T221139, F238050. Discount with student card. *Scout Service*, C del Medio 123, T245527.

Manu: *Manu Expeditions*, Avda Pardo 895, T226671, F236706, E Adventure@ ManuExpeditions.com, W www.ManuExpeditions.com. Run by ornithologist Barry Walker of the Cross Keys Pub, highly recommended for trips to Manu and also specialize in birdwatching and horseriding trips. *Manu Nature Tours*, Avda Pardo 1046, T252721, F234793, E mnt@ amauta.rcp.net.pe, www.rcp.net.pe/MANU. Owned by Boris Gómez Luna. Their café next door serves a wide range of excellent coffees. *InkaNatura Travel*, Avda El Sol 821, 2nd flr (same building as ACSS), T243408, F226392 (in Lima: Manuel Bañ on 46, San Isidro, T4402022/4228114, E inkanatur@chavin.rcp.net.pe, www.inkanatura.com). Tours to Manu wildlife centre, also a unique tour into Machiguenga territory including the Pongo de Mainique. *Pantiacolla Tours*, C Plateros 360, T238323, F252696, E pantiac@ mail.cosapidata.com.pe, W www.pantiacolla.com. (For more details of the tours on offer to Manu, see page 482.)

Cusco & the Sacred Valley

Tambopata: *Peruvian Safaris*, Plateros 365, T/F235342 (Lima: Avda Garcilaso de la Vega 1334, T4316330), E safaris@amauta.recp.net.pe. (For more details on tours to Tambopata, see page 487).

River rafting: *Instinct*, Procuradores 107, T233451, T/F238366, E instinct@protelsa.com.pe. Benjamín speaks good English and is recommended, also mountain bike hire. Safety standards on many rafting trips from Cusco are often woefully inadequate. See the rafting section under **Adventure sports** (page 62).

Cultural: *Milla tourism*, Avda Pardo 689, T231710, F231388, E millaturismo@ amauta.rcp.net.pe. Tours of the artists' quarter in San Blas, also contact for details of the Centre for Andean Studies, which offers courses in Spanish, Quechua and Andean culture. *Mystic Inca Trail*, Unidad Vecinal Santiago, bloque 9, dpto 301, T/F221358, E ivanndp@mail.cosapidata.com.pe. Tours of sacred Inca sites and study of Andean spirituality. *Personal Travel Service*, Portal de Panes 123, oficina 109, T244036, F233912, E ititoss@mail.cosapidata.com.pe. Cultural tours in the Urubamba valley.

Tourist offices Official tourist information is at Mantas 188, opposite La Merced church, T263176, open 0800-2000. There is also a tourist information desk at the airport. *Ministry of Tourism*, Avda de la Cultura 734, 3rd floor, T233701/223761. Open Mon-Fri 0800-1300. The University is also a good source of information, especially on archaeological sites. They sell good videos of Cusco and surroundings. For INC tourist offices, see under **Sights** above.

Asociación de Conservación para la Selva Sur (ACSS), Avda Sol 821, 2nd floor (same office as *InkaNatura Travel*), T243408, F226392, E acss@telser.com.pe. For information and free video shows about Manu National Park and Tambopata-Candamo Reserve. They are friendly and helpful and also have information on programmes and research in the jungle area of Madre de Dios, as well as being distributors of the expensive (US$75), but beautiful book on the Manu National Park by Kim MacQuarrie and André Bartschi.

Maps and guidebooks: maps of the city, the Inca Trail and the Urubamba Valley are available at tour companies. There are lots of information booklets on Machu Picchu and the other ruins at the bookshops. The best book on Cusco, the Sacred Valley, Inca Trail, Machu Picchu and other ruins is *Exploring Cusco*, by Peter Frost, which is available in Cusco bookshops. Also recommended for general information on Cusco is *Cusco Peru Tourist Guide*, published by Lima 2000. *The Sacred Center*, by Johan Reinhard, explains Machu Picchu in archaeological terms. *Apus and Incas*, by Charles Brod, describes cultural walks in and around Cusco, and treks in the Cordilleras Vilcabamba, Vilcanota and Urubamba, plus the Manu National Park (2nd edition, Inca Expeditions, 2323 SE 46th Ave, Portland, OR 97215, USA, US$10.95 plus US$1.50 postage, or from bookshops in North America, Europe and Peru).

Useful information Motorcycle mechanics: Eric and Oscar Antonio Aranzábal, Ejercicios 202, Tahuantinsuyo, T223397. Highly recommended for repairs. Also *Autocusa*, Avda de la Cultura 730 (Sr Marco Tomaycouza), T240378/239054. A good bike shop is *Bike Center*, C Concebidayoc 192-B, Cruz Verde.

The Urubamba Valley

The road from Cusco which runs past Sacsayhuamán and on to Tambo Machay (see page 151) climbs up to a pass, then continues over the pampa before descending into the densely populated Urubamba valley – or Sacred Valley – which stretches from Sicuani (on the railway to Puno) to the gorge of Torontoi, 600 metres lower, to the northwest of Cusco. This road then crosses the Urubamba river by a bridge at Pisac and follows the north bank of the river to the end of the paved road at Ollantaytambo. It passes through Calca, Yucay and Urubamba, which can also be reached from Cusco by the beautiful, direct road through Chinchero (see below, page 175). Transport throughout the Urubamba valley is plentiful. For more details, see under Cusco (page 144).

The best time to visit this area is April-May or October-November. The high season is June-September, but the rainy season, from December to March, is cheaper and pleasant enough.

Pisac

Coloured map 5, grid A5   *Pisac, 30 kilometres north of Cusco, is well worth a visit for its superb Inca ruins, high above the town, on the mountainside. Most visitors come to Pisac, though, for its Sunday morning market, described as touristy and expensive. The market comes to life after the arrival of tourist buses around 1000, and is usually over by 1500. Pisac has other, somewhat less crowded, less expensive markets on Tuesday and Thursday morning. It's best to get there before 0900.*

On the plaza are the church and a small interesting Museo Folklórico. The town is worth strolling around, and while you're doing so, look for the fine façade at Grau 485. There are many souvenir shops on Bolognesi. A local fiesta is held on 15 July. On 14 September is the festival of *El Señor de Huanca*, a religious pilgrimage to the shrine, set in a beautiful mountain landscape between Pisac and San Salvador.

Pisac is usually visited as part of a tour from Cusco. You can continue the Sunday morning tour to Pisac along the Urubamba valley to Ollantaytambo, with lunch at Yucay or in Urubamba (see below). Tours from Cusco usually allow only one and a half hours at Pisac. This is not enough time to take in the ruins and splendid scenery. Apart from Sunday when Pisac is crowded, there are very few tourists. If you're not interested in the market, it would be a good idea to ask the driver to do the tour clockwise, Chinchero, Ollantaytambo, then Pisac, thereby missing the crowds.

Sights

The walk up to the ruins begins from the plaza, past the Centro de Salud and a new control post. The path goes through working terraces, giving the ruins a context. The first group of buildings is *Pisaqa*, with a fine curving wall. Climb up to the central part of the ruins, the *Intihuatana* group of temples and rock outcrops in the most magnificent Inca masonry. Here are the *Reloj Solar* ('Hitching Post of the Sun') – now closed because thieves stole a piece from it, palaces of the moon and stars, solstice markers, baths and water channels. From *Intihuatana*, a path leads around the hillside through a tunnel to *Q'Allaqasa*, the 'military area'. Across the valley at this point, a large area of Inca tombs in holes in the hillside can be seen. The end of the site is *Kanchiracay*, where the agricultural workers were housed. Road transport approaches from this end.

The descent takes 30 minutes. At dusk you will hear, if not see, the *pisaca* (partridges), after which the place is named. If lucky you will also see deer.

To appreciate the site fully, allow five or six hours if going on foot. If you do not show your multi-site ticket, or pay US$2.25, on the way up, you will be asked to do so by the warden. Guides charge US$5. The site is open 0700-1730. If you go early (before 1000) you'll have the ruins to yourself. There is transport up to the

Pisac

A market for beads

A major feature of Pisac's popular market is the huge and varied collection of multi-coloured beads on sale. Though commonly called 'Inca beads', this is something of a misnomer. For although the Incas were highly talented potters and decorated their ware with detailed geometric motifs, they are not known to have made ceramic beads.

These attractive items have become popular relatively recently. They used to be rolled individually by hand and were very time-consuming to produce. Now, in a major concession to consumerism, they are machine-made and produced in quantity, then hand-painted and glazed.

Today, the clay beads are produced in countless, often family-run, workshops in Cusco and Pisac. Some are made into earrings, necklaces and bracelets, but many thousands are sold loose.

Inca ruins only on market days. At other times you'll have to walk. It's at least one hour uphill all the way. Horses are available for US$3 per person, but travellers with a couple of dollars to spare should get a taxi from near the bridge up to the ruins and walk back down. A van from the plaza to the ruins costs US$2.50 each way.

Essentials

A2 *Royal Inca Pisa*, Carretera Ruinas Km 1.5, T(084)203064/65/66/67, F203067. Includes taxes and breakfast. Will provide guide for ruins, very nice and pleasant, converted hacienda with pool, sauna and jacuzzi. **D** per person *Pisaq*, Pardo y Arequipa, on the plaza in front of the church and marketplace, T(084) 203062. Recently renovated, run by a young couple, Roman Vizcarra and his wife Fielding Wood from New Mexico, 15 rooms, 3 with private bathroom, price with shared bathroom is **E** per person, hot water 24 hours, clean, pleasant decor, sauna, friendly, knowledgeable, meals available at the hotel's café on the plaza, good homemade pizza. Recommended. **F** *Residencial Beho*, Intihuatana 642. Ask afor a room in the main building, good breakfast for US$1, the owner's son will act as a guide to the ruins at the weekend. *At Km 2.5 on the Pisac-Calca road is the new Hostal-Restaurant Inti Wasi*, T(084)203047, E angelicakiskus.com.pe

Sleeping

Samana Wasi, on the plaza, is reasonable. Good, cheap trout is available in many restaurants. *Doña Clorinda*, C Bolognesi on the corner of the plaza, doesn't look very inviting but cooks very tasty food, also vegetarian, very friendly. The bakery at Mcal Castilla 372 sells excellent cheese and onion *empanadas* for US$0.25, suitable for vegetarians, and good wholemeal bread.

Eating

Calca

18 kilometres beyond Pisac is **Calca** at 2,900 metres. The plaza is divided in two. Urubamba buses stop on one side, and Cusco and Pisac buses on the other side of the dividing strip. Look out for the *api* sellers with their bicycles loaded with steaming kettle and assortment of bottles, glasses and tubs.

It is a two day hike from Cusco to Calca, via Sacsayhuamán, Qenqo, Puka Pukará, Tambo Machay and Huchuy Cusco with excellent views of the Eastern Cordilleras, past small villages and along beautifully built Inca paths. There are many places to camp, but take water. At **Coya**, between Calca and Pisac, the *Fiesta de la Vírgen Asunta* is held on 15-16 August.

Cusco & the Sacred Valley

There are mineral baths (cold) at **Minas Maco**, 30 minutes walk along the Urubamba river, and at **Machacancha**, eight kilometres east of Calca. If you continue past Minas Maco, and bear right up a small footpath leading by a clump of trees, the first house you come to after crossing a small stream and climbing a hill is a precolumbian ruin. Three kilometres beyond Machacancha are the Inca ruins of **Arquasmarca**. The ruins of a small Inca town, **Huchuy Cusco**, are across the Río Urubamba, and up a stiff climb, three to four hours. There is a two-storey house, paved with flat stones, and a large stone reservoir at Huchuy Cusco.

Walter Góngora Arizábal, T202124, is a combi driver who does private trips. He charges around US$30 to Cusco, and US$18 to Pisac, including wait.

Sleeping and eating There are a couple of very basic hotels. One is opposite the market place, 1 block from the plaza, **G** *Hostal Martín*, dirty, cold water only. Also **E** *Hostal Pitusiray*, on the edge of town. There are some basic restaurants around the plaza.

Between Calca and Yucay a bridge crosses the river to the village of **Huayllabamba**. East along the bank of the river, near the community of Urquillos, on a working maize farm is **A1** *Posada-Hacienda Yarivilca*. Also *Albergue Hacienda Urpi Wata*, on the headwaters of the Río Urquillos just below Chinchero. This is also a working farm, with maize and milk/cheese production. *Urpi Wata* will accommodate both backpackers and other guests, and visitors to the farm are welcome at any time. Both hotels are run by Tierras Atlas SA (managing director Scotsman Ken Duncan). Further information in Cusco, at Las Nazarenas 211, T232829; or in Lima: Los Pinos 584, San Isidro, Lima 27, T/F4405476.

Yucay

A few kilometres east of Urubamba, Yucay has two grassy plazas divided by the restored colonial church of Santiago Apóstol, with its oil paintings and fine altars. On the opposite side from Plaza Manco II is the adobe palace built for Sayri Túpac (Manco's son) when he emerged from Vilcabamba in 1558.

In Yucay monks sell fresh milk, ham, eggs and other dairy produce from their farm on the hillside. Behind *Posada del Inca* a steep trail leads up a river valley to the 'Black Lake', at the foot of Nevado San Juan. The circuit continues down to Huayllabamba. It is a day's hike in total.

Sleeping **L3** *Posada del Inca*, on Plaza Manco II de Yucay, T201107/201346, F201345 (Lima T2224777, F4224345), E posada_yucay@el-olivar.com.pe. Price includes taxes and

buffet breakfast, a converted 300-year-old monastery which is like a little village with plazas, lovely gardens, chapel, and many different types of room (one even has its own ghost – ask for room 111 if you want to be spooked), the restaurant serves an excellent buffet lunch, conference centre and a museum with the owner's private collection of pre-Inca ceramics, gold and silver pieces and weavings. Highly recommended. **A3** *Posada del Libertador*, on the same plaza, T201115, T/F201116. Colonial house where Simón Bolívar stayed during his liberation campaign in 1825, price includes taxes and breakfast. The hotel is the contact address and phone number for *Globo de los Andes* – balloon flights over the Sacred Valley. A 45 minute flight costs US$300. Also on the plaza is **B-C** *Hostal Y'Llary*, T201112. With bathroom and breakfast.

Urubamba

Like many places along the valley, Urubamba is in a fine setting with snow-capped peaks in view and enjoys a mild climate. The main plaza, with a fountain capped by a maize cob, is surrounded by buildings painted blue. Calle Berriozabal, on the west edge of town, is lined with pisonay trees. The large market square is one block west of the main plaza. The main road skirts the town and the bridge for the road to Chinchero is just to the east of town.

Altitude: 2,863 metres
Coloured map 5, grid A5

A visit to the ceramics workshop of Pablo Seminario, who uses precolumbian techniques and designs, is highly recommended. A large selection of his work is for sale. He can be found at M Castilla cuadra 9 y Zavala, T201002.

Six kilometres west of Urubamba is the village of **Tarabamba**, where a bridge crosses the Río Urubamba. If you turn right after the bridge you'll come to **Pichingoto**, a tumbled-down village built under an overhanging cliff. Also, just over the bridge and before the town to the left of a small, walled cemetery is a salt stream. Follow the footpath beside the stream and you'll come to **Salinas**, a small village below which are a mass of terraced Inca salt pans which are still in operation. It's a very spectacular sight as there are over 5,000. The walk to the salt pans takes about 30 minutes. Take water as this side of the valley can be very hot and dry.

Ins and outs

Buses run from Urubamba to Calca, Pisac (US$0.80, 1 hour) and Cusco (2 hours, US$1), from 0530 onwards with Caminos del Inca, M Castilla y Mainique. Buses to Cusco via Chinchero leave from the west side of the plaza. El Señor de Huanca combis run to Calca from the petrol station on M Castilla when full between 0700 and 1900. From the opposite side of the street combis run to Ollantaytambo, 45 minutes, US$0.30. Buses to Quillabamba leave from M Castilla outside *Hirano's*.

Essentials

A2 *Valle Sagrado de los Inkas* (ex-*Turistas*, being upgraded), is 5 minutes walk from the centre, T201126/27, F201071. Special rates are also available, 67 comfortable bungalows with gardens, 15 suites and 50 rooms, English-owned, restaurant, bar, disco, 2 pools, also horse riding (eg to Moray), mountain biking, kayaking and rafting.

   A2-3 *Turquesa*, 20 minutes walk from town, towards Yucay. With a small pool, restaurant, buffet on Tuesday, Thursday and Sunday for US$3.50, room service, comfortable, part of the San Agustín chain, reservations at *San Agustín Internacional* in Cusco.

Sleeping

Cusco & the Sacred Valley

D per person *Hostal Urpihuasi*. Without private bathroom, **C** per person with full board, pleasant modern rooms, clean, friendly, small outdoor pool, sauna, quiet and relaxing, recommended (manager Rae Pieraccini runs a project for street children, financed by the hotel's income).

E per person *Hostal Rumichaca*, 3 kilometres west of Urubamba, back from the Rumichaca bus stop. Includes all meals, beautiful location, vegetarian food available, run by Martín and Ada, Martín is also a mountain guide, Ada is a great cook and "does a mean pisco sour", great place to relax.

In the town of Urubamba is **F** *Hostal Urubamba*, on Bolognesi. Basic, pleasant, cold water.

Eating   There are several restaurants on M Castilla such as *Hirano's*, whigh does good food. *La Luna Nueva*, Grau y Mainique. Homemade pasta, good food and atmosphere, live music, recommended. On the main road, before the bridge, are: *Quinta los Geranios*, excellent lunch for US$3 with more than enough food; and *El Maizal*, which is OK. *New World Café*, Jr Comercio y M Castilla, 2 blocks from the plaza. Vegetarian food, American owned, excellent value, daily set menu, good book exchange, great atmosphere.

Local festivals   **May** and **June** are the *harvest months*, with many processions following mysterious ancient schedules. Urubamba's main festival, *El Señor de Torrechayoc*, takes place during the **first week of June**.

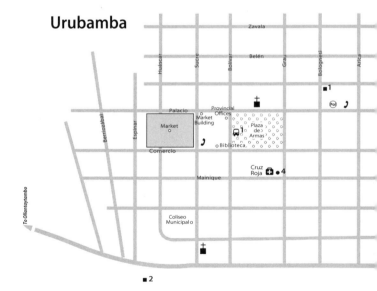

Urubamba

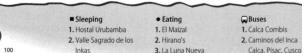

■ Sleeping
1. Hostal Urubamba
2. Valle Sagrado de los Inkas

● Eating
1. El Maizal
2. Hirano's
3. La Luna Nueva
4. Quinta los Geranios

🚌 Buses
1. Calca Combis
2. Caminos del Inca Calca, Pisac, Cusco

Río Urubamba

Banks *Banco de la Nación*, with the Correos behind it, is on the main road, opposite the petrol station at M Castilla. **Directory**

Chinchero

Chinchero (3,762 metres), is northwest from Cusco on a direct road to Urubamba. It has an attractive church built on an Inca temple. The church is only open on Sunday for mass. Opposite the church is a small local museum. Recent excavations there have revealed many Inca walls and terraces. The site is open daily, 0700-1730, and can be visited on the combined entrance ticket (see page 147). The local produce market on Sunday morning is fascinating and very colourful, and best before the tour groups arrive. It's on your left as you come into town. There's also a small handicraft market, also on Sunday, up by the church. Chinchero attracts few tourists, except on Sunday. The town celebrates the day of the Virgin, on 8 September. There's accommodation in town at **F** *Hotel Inca*, with restaurant.

Chinchero to Huayllabamba hike: there is a scenic path from Chinchero to Huayllabamba, a village on the left bank of the Río Urubamba, or Vilcanota, between Yucay and Calca (see above). The hike is quite beautiful, with fine views of the peaks of the Urubamba range, and takes about three to four hours. Follow the old Chinchero-Urubamba dirt road, to the left of the new paved road. Ask the locals when you are not sure. It runs over the pampa, with a good view of Chinchero, then drops down to the Urubamba valley. The end of the hike is about 10 kilometres before the town of Urubamba. You can either proceed to Urubamaba or back to Cusco.

An alternative hike from Chinchero could be by following the Maras-Moray-Pichingoto salt mines route. This brings you to the main Urubamba valley road, about 10-12 kilometres beyond the town of Urubamba. You could also take the more direct main road from Chinchero to Urubamba, with occasional shortcuts, but this route is a lot less interesting.

Moray

This remote but beautiful site lies to the west of the little town of **Maras** and is well worth a visit. There are three 'colosseums', used by the Incas as a sort of open-air crop laboratory, known locally as the greenhouses of the Incas. Peter Frost writes: "There are no great ruined structures here to impress visitors. Moray is more for the contemplative traveller with an affinity for such phenomena as the

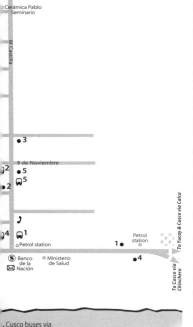

Nasca Lines, the stone rings of Avebury and the menhirs of Brittany." The scenery around here is absolutely stunning, especially in late afternoon, when the light is wonderful; but for photography it's best to arrive in the morning.

Getting there The easiest and most interesting way to get to Moray is from Urubamba via the Pichingoto bridge over the Río Urubamba. The climb up from the bridge is fairly steep but easy, with great views of Nevado Chicón. The path passes by the spectacular Maras salt pans, which are still in production after thousands of years – these are now a fixture on the tourist circuit and can become congested with buses. Moray is about 1½ hours further on. Alternatively, wait for a pickup on the bridge on the Chinchero road. This will take you near to Maras. Walk to Maras (30 minutes) and on through it, bearing left a little, and ask directions to Moray. It's 1½ hours walk in total. Hitching back to Urubamba is quite easy, but there are no hotels at all in the area, so take care not to be stranded. The *Hotel Valle Sagrado de los Inkas* in Urubamba can arrange horses and guide and a pick-up truck for the return, all for US$30-40 per person (see page 173).

At **Tiobamba**, near Maras, a fascinating indigenous market-festival is held on 15 August, where Sacred Valley yellow maize is exchanged for pottery from Lake Titicaca.

Ollantaytambo

Altitude: 2,800 metres
Coloured map 5, grid A5

The attractive little town of Ollantaytambo, at the foot of some spectacular Inca ruins and terraces, is built directly on top of the original Inca town, or Llacta. The Inca canchas (blocks) are almost entirely intact and can be clearly seen. It's an impressive sight and one that shouldn't be missed. The best examples are behind the main plaza.

Entering Ollantaytambo from Pisac, the road is built along the long wall of 100 niches. Note the inclination of the wall: it leans towards the road. Since it was the Incas' practice to build with the walls leaning towards the interiors of the buildings, it has been deduced that the road, much narrower then, was built inside a succession of buildings. The road out of the plaza leads across a bridge, down to the colonial church with its enclosed *recinto*. Beyond is a plaza (and car park) with entrances to the archaeological site.

Ins and outs

The station is 10-15 minutes walk from the plaza. There are colectivos at the plaza for the station when trains are due. Check in advance the time trains pass through here (see also under trains to and from Machu Picchu, page 179). You won't be allowed on the station unless you have previously bought a ticket for the tourist train. The gates are locked and only those with tickets can enter. Once the tourist train has come and gone, tickets are sold for the local train, then you're allowed on the platform. Seats on the train will be occupied, but find a gringo who's getting off at Km 88 for the Inca Trail and take their seat when they get off. Both the tourist and local trains stop on the way to and from Machu Picchu. For those travelling by car and intending to go to Machu Picchu, it is recommended to leave the car at Ollantaytambo railway station, which costs US$1 a day. Ask Wendy Weeks at *El Albergue* for details (see below).

Sights

The **Baño de la Ñusta** (bath of the princess) is of grey granite, and is in a small area between the town and the temple fortress. Some 200 metres behind the

Baño de la Ñusta along the face of the mountain are some small ruins known as Inca Misanca, believed to have been a small temple or observatory. A series of steps, seats and niches have been carved out of the cliff. There is a complete irrigation system, including a canal at shoulder level, some 15 centimetres deep, cut out of the sheer rock face (under renovation).

The flights of terraces leading up above the town are superb, and so are the curving terraces following the contours of the rocks overlooking the Urubamba. These terraces were successfully defended by Manco Inca's warriors against Hernando Pizarro in 1536. Manco Inca built the defensive wall above the site and another wall closing the Yucay valley against attack from Cusco. These are still visible on either side of the valley.

The temple itself was started by Pachacuti, using Colla Indians from Lake Titicaca – hence the similarities of the monoliths facing the central platform with the Tiahuanaco remains. The Colla are said to have deserted half-way through the work, which explains the many unfinished blocks lying about the site. The guide book *Ollantaytambo* by Víctor Angles Vargas is available in Cusco bookshops, and Peter Frost's *Exploring Cusco* is also useful. Ask for Dr Hernán Amat Olazábal, a leading Inca-ologist, at the community museum for further explanation.

■*Open 0700-1730. Admission is by combined entrance ticket, which can be bought at the site. Otherwise it's US$2. If possible arrive very early, 0700, before the tourists. Avoid Sunday afternoons, when tour groups from Pisac descend in their hundreds.*

El Museo Catco is one block from the plaza, T(084)204034. Has displays of textiles as well as ethnographic and archaeological information and findings from local ruins, run by Sra Rosa de Alamo. Open Tuesday-Sunday 1000-1300, 1400-1600, entry US$1.75 (children free).

Recently a 'pyramid' has been identified on the west side of the main ruins of Ollantaytambo. Its discoverers, Fernando and Edgar Elorietta, claim it is the real Pacaritambo, from where the four original Inca brothers emerged to found their empire, contrary to the more popular legend (see page 195). Whether this is the case or not, it is still a first-class piece of engineering with great terraced fields and a fine 750-metre wall aligned with the rays of the winter solstice, on 21 June.

Ollantaytambo

Cusco & the Sacred Valley

The mysterious 'pyramid', which covers 50-60 hectares, can be seen properly from the other side of the river. This is a pleasant, easy one-hour walk, west from the Puente Inca, just outside the town. You'll also be rewarded with great views of the Sacred Valley and the river, with the snowy peaks of the Verónica massif as a backdrop.

Essentials

Sleeping **D** per person *El Albergue*, next to, and access via, the railway station, T/F(084)204014 (or in Cusco at *Manu Expeditions*, T226671). Owned by North American Wendy Weeks, 6 rooms with shared bathrooms, "wonderful showers", charming, very relaxing, homely, with sauna, meals available on request but a bit overpriced at US$10 per person, convenient for Machu Picchu train, good place for information. Highly recommended. **E** *Hostal Chuza*, just below the main plaza in town. Very clean, friendly. Recommended. **E** *Hostal La Ñusta*, next to *Hostal Miranda*. Same owners as the restaurant of the same name on the plaza, shared bathrooms, basic but clean and modern, very friendly and helpful owners, they'll open the restaurant for breakfast if you need to leave early. Recommended. **E-F** *Hostal Miranda*, between the main plaza and the ruins. With shower, basic, very friendly, clean. **G** per person *Alojamiento Yavar*, 1½ blocks from the main plaza. Basic, friendly, no water in the evening, they have information on horse riding in the area, if they're full, they'll let you sleep on the floor for free.

Eating There are several restaurants on the Plaza, such as *La Ñusta*, see above. Also *Bahía*, on the south side of the Plaza. Very friendly, vegetarian dishes on request.

Festivals On **6 January** there is the festival of *Reyes Magos* (the Three Wise Men), with music, dancing, processions. On the Sunday following *Inti Raymi*, there is a colourful festival, the *Ollanta-Raymi*. Around **26 October** there is a two-day, weekend festival with lots of dancing in traditional costume and many local delicacies for sale.

Around Ollantaytambo

Horses can be hired for US$5 a day. A gentle day's ride or hike is to **La Marca**, along the beautiful river valley; ask Wendy Weeks for details. You can also visit the Inca quarry on the other side of the river.

A major excavation project has been carried out since 1977 under the direction of Ann Kendall in the **Cusichaca** valley, 26 kilometres from Ollantaytambo, at the intersection of the Inca routes. Only nine kilometres of this road is passable by ordinary car. The Inca fort, **Huillca Raccay**, was excavated in 1978-80, and work is now concentrated on Llactapata, a site of domestic buildings. Ann Kendall is now working in the Patacancha valley northeast of Ollantaytambo. Excavations are being carried out in parallel with the restoration of Inca canals to bring fresh clean water to the settlements in the valley.

Pinculluna, the mountain above Ollantaytambo, can be climbed with no mountaineering experience, although there are some difficult stretches – allow two to three hours going up. The path is difficult to make out, so it's best not to go on your own. Walk up the valley to the left of the mountain, which is very beautiful and impressive, with Inca terraces after four kilometres.

Machu Picchu

There is a tremendous feeling of awe on first witnessing this incredible sight. The ancient citadel (42 kilometres from Ollantaytambo by rail) straddles the saddle of a high mountain with steep terraced slopes falling away to the fast-flowing Urubamba river snaking its hairpin course far below in the valley floor. Towering overhead is Huayna Picchu, and green jungle peaks provide the back-drop for the whole majestic scene.

Altitude: 2,380 metres
Coloured map 5, grid A5

For centuries it was buried in jungle, until Hiram Bingham stumbled upon it in July 1911. It was then explored by an archaeological expedition sent by Yale. Machu Picchu was a stunning archaeological find. The only major Inca site to escape 400 years of looting and destruction, it was remarkably well pre-served. And it was no ordinary Inca settlement. It sat in an inaccessible loca-tion above the Urubamba gorge, and contained so many fine buildings that people have puzzled over its meaning ever since.

Bingham claimed he had discovered the lost city of Vilcabamba, and for 50 years everyone believed him. But he was proved wrong, and the mystery deepened. Later discoveries have revealed that Machu Picchu was the centre of an extensive Inca province. Many finely preserved satellite sites and high-ways also survive. This is craggy terrain, and the value of a province with no mines and little agricultural land – it was not even self-sufficient – is hard to determine. Bingham postulated it was a defensive citadel on the fringes of the Amazon. But the architecture fails to convince us, and in any case, defense against whom?

The Incas were the first to build permanent structures in this region, which was unusual because they arrived at the tail end of 4,000 years of Andean civilization. 16th-century land titles discovered in the 1980s revealed that Machu Picchu was built by the Inca Pachacuti, founding father of the Inca empire. But they do not tell us why he built it. One reasonable specula-tion is that this area provided access to coca plantations in the lower Urubamba valley. However, the fine architecture of Machu Picchu cannot be explained away simply as a coca-collecting station.

Recent studies have shown that the 'torreón' was an observatory for the solstice sunrise, and that the 'Intihuatana' stela is the centre-point between cardinal alignments of nearby sacred peaks. The Incas worshipped nature: the celestial bodies, mountains, lightning, rainbows, rocks – anything, in fact, that was imbued with 'huaca', or spiritual power. And here Pachacuti found 'huaca' in unusual abundance.

This spiritual component is the key to understanding Machu Picchu. The Bingham expedition identified 75 percent of the human remains as female, and a common belief is that Machu Picchu was a refuge of the Inca 'Virgins of the Sun'. However, the skeletons were re-examined in the 1980s using mod-ern technology, and the latest conclusion is that the gender split was roughly 50/50.

Machu Picchu was deliberately abandoned by its inhabitants – when, we do not know. This may have happened even before the Spanish invasion, per-haps as a result of the Inca civil wars, or the epidemics of European diseases which ran like brushfires ahead of the Spanish in the New World. One theory proposes that the city ran dry in a period of drought, another suggests a devas-tating fire. Or the city may have been evacuated during the period of Inca resistance to the Spanish, which lasted nearly 40 years and was concentrated not far west of Machu Picchu.

Cusco & the Sacred Valley

Huayna Picchu The mountain overlooking the site (on which there are also ruins), has steps to the top for a superlative view of the whole site, but it is not for those who are afraid of heights and you shouldn't leave the path. The climb takes up to 90 minutes but the steps are dangerous after bad weather. The path is open 0700-1300, with the latest return time being 1500; and you must register at a hut at the beginning of the trail.

Machu Picchu

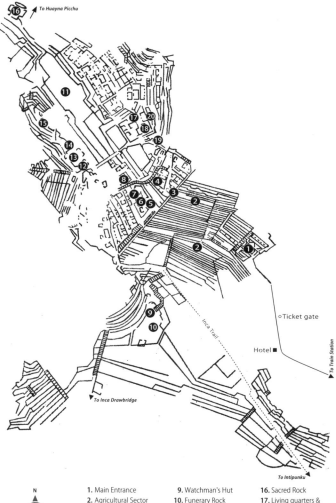

1. Main Entrance	**9.** Watchman's Hut	**16.** Sacred Rock
2. Agricultural Sector	**10.** Funerary Rock	**17.** Living quarters &
3. Dry Moat	**11.** Main Plaza	workshops
4. Ceremonial Baths	**12.** Temple of the 3	**18.** Mortar Buildings
5. Principal Bath	Windows	**19.** "Prison Group" or
6. Temple of the Sun	**13.** Principal Temple	"Condor Temple"
7. Two Fountains	**14.** "Sacristy"	**20.** Intimachay
8. Royal Sector	**15.** Intihuatana (gnomon)	

Cusco & the Sacred Valley

The other trail to Huayna Picchu, down near the Urubamba, is via the Temple of the Moon, in two caves, one above the other, with superb Inca niches inside, which have sadly been blemished by graffiti. To reach the Temple of the Moon from the path to Huayna Picchu, take the second trail to the left – both are marked 'Danger, do not enter'. The danger is in the first 10 minutes, after which it is reasonable, although it descends further than you think it should. After the Temple you may proceed to Huayna Picchu. The round trip takes about four hours. Before doing any trekking around Machu Picchu, check with an official which paths may be used, or which are one way. **NB** Huayna Picchu was closed following a fire in 1997.

The famous Inca bridge is about 45 minutes along a well-marked trail south of the Royal Sector. The bridge – which is actually a couple of logs – is spectacularly sited, carved into a vertiginous cliff-face. East of the Royal Sector is the path leading up to **Intipunku**. It's a 45 minute walk and well worth it for the fine views alone.

Getting there

Air The quickest way to Machu Picchu is by helicopter. While not exactly following in the footsteps of the Incas, it does get you there in only 25 minutes. Flights leave from Cusco airport daily at 0700 and return at 1700. US$80 one way, US$150 return; with *HeliCusco*, C Triunfo 379, 2nd floor, T/F227283/243555 (Lima T4447104, F4467197), E dfhr@amauta.rcp.net.pe; W www.recp.net.pe/helicusco

Trains The train to Machu Picchu runs from San Pedro station in Cusco. It passes through Ollantaytambo and Km 88 (for the start of the Inca Trail) to Aguas Calientes (the official name of this station is 'Machu Picchu'). Trians do not go on to Machu Picchu (officially called 'Puente Ruinas'). The railway continues to Quillabamba, but this section was closed in 1998. There is a paved road between 'Machu Picchu' and 'Puente Ruinas' which is at the foot of the road up to the ruins.

The *Económica* service (local train) leaves San Pedro Monday-Saturday at around 0700 and stops at Ollantaytambo and Km 88. It arrives at Aguas Calientes at 1140. One way costs US$5 irrespective of where you get off, and includes a numbered seat. The train returns from Aguas Calientes at 1650, stops in Ollantaytambo at 1830 and arrives in Cusco at 2130-2200. Seats are not guaranteed on the return journey. Buy your ticket the day before at San Pedro station between 1500 and 1600. Seats can be reserved only if returning the same day. Expect long queues for tickets at Cusco in the high season and during holiday periods. The train is really crowded and you should watch your possessions carefully as bag-slashing is common. Take as little as possible, and no valuables, on the train. When on your way to hike the Inca Trail, equipped with a big backpack, try to be in a group, watching each other's gear.

There are three classes of tourist train: Autovagón, Pullman and Expresso. Pullman and Expresso class have closed doors (only ticket holders are allowed on). Pullman costs US$34 return; Expresso costs US$18.50 return. They leave Cusco daily at 0625, stopping at Ollantaytambo at 0830 and Aguas Calientes at 1000. They return from Aguas Calientes at 1600, arrive in Ollantaytambo at 1740 and get back to Cusco at 2000. Seats can be reserved even if you're not returning the same day.

The *Autovagón* leaves Cusco at 0600 daily. It costs US$55 return, takes only 3 hours one way and returns from Aguas Calientes at 1500. It has toilets, video, snacks and drinks for sale. The train stops in Ollantaytambo at 0745. The return train reaches Ollantaytambo at 1630 and arrives in Cusco at 1830. The same train leave Machu Picchu at 0930 and arrives in Ollantaytambo at 1050, and costs US$25. A new Autovagón runs from Ollantaytambo at 1115 and arrives at Aguas Calientes at 1230. It returns from Aguas Calientes at 1830 and arrives in Cusco at 2145. This service is for visitors arriving by plane; a bus ("cerrojo service") takes you from Cusco to Ollantaytambo and from there by train.

Tickets for Pullman, Expresso and *Autovagón* class trains should be bought at Wanchac station in Cusco, on Avda Pachacutec. They can be bought up to 5 days in advance. These tourist trains do not stop en route to Aguas Calientes. Thee is a new train station for the tourist trains at Aguas Calientes – it is on the outskirts of town, 200 metres from *Machu Picchu Pueblo Hotel* and 50 metres from where buses leave from Machu Picchu.

NB Train schedules are unreliable and long delays are common, especially on the *Económica* train. In the rainy season mudslides often cause cancellations. The entire service is due to be privatized.

Tourist tickets: travellers on an inclusive tour often return by bus from Ollantaytambo, leaving the trains emptier for the return trip to Cusco. There are 2 types of tourist ticket: 1) round trip in the *Autovagón*, round trip in the bus up to the ruins, entrance fee and guide, all for US$110; 2) round trip on the local train, buffet class, round trip in the bus up to the ruins, entrance fee and guide, for US$60. These tickets can be booked through any of the tour agencies in Cusco who will pick you up from your hotel in Cusco and take you to the train station. Tickets for any of the tourist trains guarantee a numbered seat.

Buses Buses leave Aguas Calientes for Machu Picchu every 20 minutes from 0630 and cost US$6 return. The last bus down from the ruins is at 1730.

Essentials

The site is open from 0700 to 1700. Entrance fee is US$10. A second day ticket is half price. It may be possible to pay in dollars, but only clean, undamaged notes will be accepted. You can deposit your luggage at the entrance for US$0.50, though theft has been reported; check for missing items and demand their return. Guides are available at the site, they are often very knowledgeable and worthwhile, and charge US$15 for $2\frac{1}{2}$ hours.

It takes at least a day to fully appreciate the ruins and their surroundings. Monday and Friday are bad days because there is usually a crowd of people on guided tours who are going or have been to Pisac market on Sunday, and too many people all want lunch at the same time. The expensive hotel is located next to the entrance, with a self-service restaurant. Lunch costs US$15, so it's best to take your own food and drink, and take plenty of drinking water. Note that food is not officially allowed into the site.

The ruins are quieter before 0830 for the best views but in any case before the tourist train arrives at 1030. Permission to enter the ruins before 0630 to watch the sunrise over the Andes, which is a spectacular experience, can be obtained from the Instituto Nacional de Cultura (INC) in Cusco, but it is often possible if you talk to the guards at the gate. They are also quieter after 1530, but note that the last bus down from the ruins leaves at 1730. The walk up takes 2-2½ hours, following the zig-zag road. Walking down to Aguas Calientes, if staying the night there, takes 1-1½ hours.

NB Camping is not allowed at Intipunku; guards may confiscate your tent. There is a free campsite down beside the rail tracks at Puente Ruinas station. You are not allowed to walk back along the trail, though you can pay US$4.50 at Intipunku to be allowed to walk back as far as Wiñay-Wayna. You cannot take backpacks into Machu Picchu; leave them at ticket office.

L2 *Machu Picchu Ruinas*, for reservations T(511)2210826/4408043, F4406197, Lima; **Sleeping** T241777, F237111, Cusco; E reserlima@peruhotel.com. Electricity and water 24 hours a day, will accept American Express traveller's cheques at the official rate, restaurant for residents only. The hotel is usually fully booked well in advance, try Sunday night as other tourists find Pisac market a greater attraction. The South American Explorers Club in Lima advise against trying to make your own reservation as this can be very frustrating; they will do it for you. Call them several months in advance with details, including credit card number, T(51-1)4250142.

Lost City of the Incas by Hiram Bingham (available in Lima and Cusco). *A Walking Tour* **Recommended** *of Machu Picchu* by Pedro Sueldo Nava – in several languages, available in Cusco. See **reading** also *The Sacred Center*, by Johan Reinhard. *Exploring Cusco*, by Peter Frost has good information about the site. The Tourist Hotel sells guides, although at a rather inflated price. The South American Explorers Club in Lima has detailed information on walks here, and so have Hilary Bradt's and Charles Brod's books.

The Inca Trail

The wonder of Machu Picchu has been well documented over the years. Equally impressive is the centuries-old Inca Trail that winds its way from the Sacred Valley near Ollantaytambo, taking three to four days.

What makes this hike so special is the stunning combination of Inca ruins, unforgettable views, magnificent mountains, exotic vegetation and extraordinary ecological variety. The government acknowledged this uniqueness in 1981 by including the trail in a 325 square kilometres national park, the Machu Picchu Historical Sanctuary.

Machu Picchu itself cannot be understood without the Inca Trail. Its principal sites are ceremonial in character, apparently in ascending hierarchical order. This Inca province was a unique area of elite access. The trail is essentially a work of spiritual art, like a gothic cathedral, and walking it was formerly an act of devotion.

The trek to the sacred site begins at **Qorihuayrachina** – or Km 88 – at 2,600 metres, which is the disembarkation point for the intrepid trekker. The first ruin is **Llaqtapata**, near Km 88, the utilitarian centre of a large settlement of farming terraces which probably supplied the other Inca trail sites. From here, it is a relatively easy three hour walk to the village of **Huayllabamba**.

A series of gentle climbs and descents leads along the Río Cusichaca, the ideal introduction to the trail. The village is a popular camping spot for tour groups, so it's a better idea to continue for about an hour up to the next site, **Llulluchayoc** – 'three white stones' – which is a patch of green beside a fast-flowing stream. It's a steep climb but you're pretty much guaranteed a decent pitch for the night. If you're feeling really energetic, you can go on to the next camping spot, a perfectly flat meadow, called **Llulluchapampa**. This means a punishing one and a half hour ascent through cloud forest, but it does leave you with a much easier second day. There's also the advantage of relative isolation and a magnificent view back down the valley.

For most people the second day is by far the toughest, though horses can be hired en route to carry your backpack. It's a steep climb to the meadow, followed by an exhausting two and a half hour haul up to the first pass – aptly named **Warmiwañusqa** (Dead Woman) – at 4,200 metres. The feeling of relief on reaching the top is immense and there's the added, sadistic pleasure of watching your fellow sufferers struggling in your wake. After a well-earned break it's a sharp descent on a treacherous path down to the Pacamayo valley, where there are a few flat camping spots near a stream if you're too weary to continue.

Halfway to the second pass, comes the ruin of **Runkuracay**, which was probably an Inca tambo, or post-house. It is no longer permitted to camp here. A steep climb up an Inca staircase leads to the next pass, at 3,850 metres, with spectacular views of Pumasillo (6,246 metres) and the Vilcabamba range. The trail then desends to **Sayacmarca** (Inaccessible town), a spectacular site overlooking the Aobamba valley. Just below Sayacmarca lies **Conchamarca** (Shell town), a small group of buildings standing on rounded terraces – perhaps another tambo.

Inca Trail

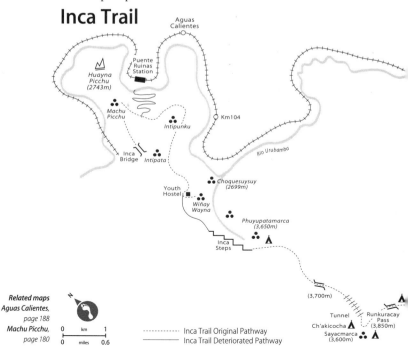

Related maps
Aguas Calientes,
page 188
Machu Picchu,
page 180

A blissfully gentle two hours climb on a fine stone highway, leads through an Inca tunnel and along the enchanted fringes of the cloud forest, to the third pass. This is the most rewarding part of the trail, with spectacular views of the entire Vilcabamba range, and it's worth taking the time to dwell on the wonders of nature. Then it's down to the extensive ruins of **Phuyupatamarca** (Cloud-level town), at 3,650 metres, where adjacent Inca observation platforms offer awesome views of nearby Salcantay (6,270 metres) and surrounding peaks. There is a 'tourist bathroom' here, where water can be collected, but purify it before drinking.

From here an Inca stairway of white granite plunges more than a thousand metres to the spectacularly-sited and impressive ruins of **Wiñay-Wayna** (Forever Young), offering views of newly uncovered agricultural terraces at **Intipata** (Sun place). A trail, not easily visible, goes from Wiñay-Wayna to the newly-discovered terracing. There is a youth hostel at Wiñay-Wayna, with bunk beds (**F** per person), showers and a small restaurant, but the place is in state of disrepair and facilities are appallingly run down. Should you forego the dubious privilege of using the sleeping facilities, there is enough space for a few tents. After Wiñay-Wayna there is no water, and no place to camp, until Machu Picchu.

From here it is a gentle hour's walk through another type of forest, with larger trees and giant ferns, to a steep Inca staircase which leads up to **Intipunku** (Sun gate), where you look down at last upon Machu Picchu, basking in all her reflective glory. Aching muscles are quickly forgotten and even the presence of the functional hotel building cannot detract from one of the most magical sights in all the Americas.

Cusco & the Sacred Valley

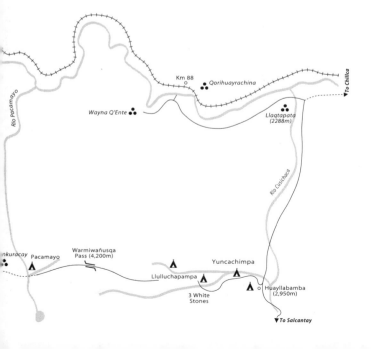

Getting there

Only the local train (*Económica* calss) stops at Km 88, about 3 hours after leaving Cusco. The tourist trains do not stop here. Be ready to get out at Km 88, at the village called Chamana, as it's easy to pass it. If you do not wish to travel on the local train, the simplest method is to go to Ollantaytambo, or Chillca and start walking from there.

From Ollantaytambo it takes about 8 hours to the start of the Inca Trail. Follow the railway in the direction of Machu Picchu until you come to Chillca village where you can cross the river. Sometimes there is a truck going to Chillca. From Chillca to the start of the Trail takes 5 hours. Climb up to a path that runs parallel to the river. This is an original Inca trail (still in use) that leads to Llaqtapata on the Inca Trail. **Warning** It's best not to spend a night on this trail. Theft is possible because you have to sleep near the villages.

Essentials

An entrance ticket for the trail must be bought at Km 88, which costs US$17. There is a 50% discount for students, but note that officials are very strict, only an ISIC card will be accepted as proof of status. It also gives entry to Machu Picchu if you get it stamped there. Guided tours often start at Km 83. Check whether the price includes site entrance.

Equipment It is cold at night, and weather conditions change rapidly, so it is important to take not only strong footwear, rain gear and warm clothing but also food, water, insect repellent, a supply of plastic bags, coverings, a good sleeping bag, a torch/flashlight and a stove for preparing hot food and drink to ward off the cold at night. A stove using paraffin (kerosene) is preferable, as fuel can be bought in small quantities in markets. Camping gas (white gas) is available in hardware stores in Cusco, US$1.50 per litre.

A tent is essential, but if you're hiring one in Cusco, check carefully for leaks. Walkers who have not taken adequate equipment have died of exposure. Caves marked on some maps are little better than overhangs, and are not sufficient shelter to sleep in. You could also take a first-aid kit; if you don't need it the porters probably will, given their rather basic footwear.

All the necessary equipment can be rented in Cusco (see page 165 under **Tour agencies**). Good maps of the Trail and area can be bought from the South American Explorers Club in Lima. If you have any doubts about carrying your own pack, reasonably-priced porters/guides are available, most reliably through Cusco agencies. You can also hire porters in Ollantaytambo – speak to the men in the plaza wearing red ponchos. Expect to pay US$7 a day plus basic foodstuffs. Carry a day-pack nonetheless in case you walk faster than the porters and you have to wait for them to catch you up.

Tours You can do the Inca Trail independently or with a Tour Agency in Cusco who will arrange transport to the start, equipment, food, etc, for an all-in price. Agency tours range from the more expensive, with smaller groups, better equipment and transport arrangements, to cheaper, cost-cutting outfits with large groups and basic gear. Almost everyone reports that things do not go to plan. Most complaints are minor, but do check equipment carefully. Ask around for people who have done the trip and take extra food and water. For a list of recommended agencies in Cusco, see page 165.

NB Prices range from around US$60 per person up to over US$200 for 4 days. Understandably, those on a tight budget will be attracted by lower prices but bear in mind that if a 4 day tour costs much less than US$100-120 then this probably means poor quality equipment, inexperienced guides, under-age and poorly-paid porters or insufficient and inadequate food; or possibly all of these.

Try to camp in groups at night, leave all your valuables in Cusco and keep everything inside your tent, even your shoes. Security has, however, improved in recent years. Avoid the July-August high season and the rainy season from November to April (note that this can change, check in advance). In the wet it is cloudy and the paths are very muddy and difficult. Also watch out for coral snakes in this area (black, red, yellow bands).

General information and advice

Due to regular clean-ups the trail is usually litter free. To keep it this way, please remove all your rubbish, including toilet paper, or use the pits provided. Do not light open fires as they can get out of control. The Earth Preservation Fund sponsors an annual clean-up July-August: volunteers should write to EPF, Inca Trail Project, Box 7545, Ann Arbor, Michigan 48107, USA. Preserving the Inca Trail: in Lima contact APTA, Percy Tapiá, T478078, or Antonio Bouroncle, T450532. In Cusco, different agencies organize the clean-up each year.

The Inca Trail from Km 104

A short Inca trail has recently opened for those who don't want to endure the full hike. Get off the train at Km 104, where a footbridge gives access to the ruins of Chachabamba and the trail which ascends through the ruins of Choquesuysuy to connect with the main trail at Wiñay-Wayna. This first part is a brutal ascent (take water) and the trail is narrow and exposed in parts. It takes about two and a half to three and a half hours to reach Wiñay-Wayna.

The regular train arrives around 0930-1030, but arrange with the conductor to make sure it stops. Entry to the trail is US$12. There is a good hike from Aguas Calientes to Km 104.

Aguas Calientes

One and a half kilometres back along the railway from Puente Ruinas, this is a popular resting place for those recovering from the rigours of the Inca Trail. Most activity is centred around the railway station, on the plaza, or on Avda Pachacútec, which leads from the plaza to the thermal baths.

The baths consist of a communal pool, 10 minutes walk from the town. They are open, 0500-2200, and entry is US$2.50. You can rent towels and bathing costumes for US$0.65 at several places on the road to the baths. There are basic toilets and changing facilities and showers for washing *before* entering the baths. Take soap and shampoo and keep an eye on your valuables.

L2 *Machu Picchu Pueblo Hotel*, Km 110, 5 minutes walk along the railway from the town. For reservations: Jr Andalucia 174, San Isidro, Lima, T(01)4226574, F4224701; in Cusco at Julio C Tello C-13, Urb Santa Mónica, T245314, F244669, E reservas@inkaterra.rom.pe; W www.inkaterra.com.pe. Beautiful colonial-style rooms in village compound surrounded by cloud forest, lovely gardens, pool, restaurant, also campsite with hot showers at good rates, offer tours to Machu Picchy, great buffet breakfasts for US$12. Highly recommended. **A2-3** *Hostal Machu Picchu Inn*, Avda Pachacútec. With bathroom, includes breakfast, good, friendly.

B *Hostal Inka*, at the train station, T211034. Includes breakfast. Recommended.

C *Hostal Ima Sumac*, Avda Pachacútec, 5 minutes before the baths, T211021. Exchanges money.

D *Gringo Bill's* (*Hostal Q'oñi Unu*), Qoya Raymi, third house to the left of the church, T211046. With bathroom, cheaper without, friendly, relaxed, hot water, laundry, money exchange, good but expensive meals served (usually slowly), they offer a US$2 packed lunch to take up to the ruins, luggage stored, good beds, don't stay in the rooms nearest the entrance as they flood during heavy rain. **D-E** *Hostal*

Sleeping
■ *on maps*
Price codes:
see inside front cover

Continental, near the train station. Very clean, good beds, hot showers. **D-E** *Hostal Machu Picchu*, at the station. Clean, basic, quiet, friendly, especially Wilber, the owner's son, with travel information, hot water, nice balcony over the Urubamba, grocery store. Recommended.

E *Hostal El Paroque*, Plaza Manco Capac, T211040. With bathroom, clean, very nice rooms. **E** *Hostal Inti Sumi*, at the top of the hill near the baths. Hot water, clean. **E** per person *Hostal Los Caminantes*, by the railway just beyond the station. With bathroom, **F** per person without, basic, but friendly and clean. **E** *Hostal Pachacútec*, up the hill beyond *Hostal La Cabaña*, T211061. With bathroom, hot water 24 hours, good breakfast, quiet, family-run. Recommended.

Camping: the only official campsite is in a field by the river, just below Puente Ruinas station. Do not leave your tent and belongings unattended.

Eating
● *on maps*

There are many places at the station, including: *El Refugio*, expensive, good food, slow service; *Aiko*, recommended; and *La Chosa Pizzería*, pleasant atmosphere, good value. *Clave de Sol*, Avda Pachacútec 156. Same owner as *Chez Maggy* in Cusco, good cheap Italian food for under US$4, changes money, has vegetarian menu, great atmosphere. Also on this street: *Govinda*, just off the plaza. Vegetarian. *Machu Picchu*. Good, friendly. *Chifa Hong Kong*; and others. *Inka's Pizza Pub*, on the plaza. Good pizzas, changes money, accepts traveller's cheques. Recommended. On C Lloque Yupanqui is *Waisicha Pub*, good music and atmosphere. On the same street is *Indio Feliz*, C Lloque Yupanqui, near the main plaza, T/F211090. Great French cuisine, excellent value and service, set 3-course meal for US$10, good pisco sours. Highly recommended.

Directory

Travel agency, *Información Turística Rikuni*, is at the station, Nydia is very helpful. Also *Qosqo Service*, by the railway. The Post Office at the station sells maps of Machu Picchu. The telephone office is on the plaza. There are lots of places to choose from for exchange. The town has electricity 24 hrs a day.

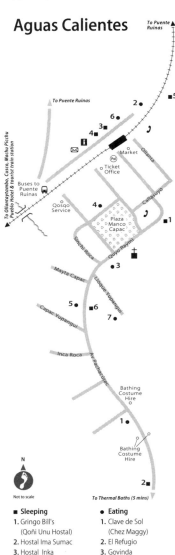

Aguas Calientes

To Puente Ruinas

To Puente Ruinas

To Ollantaytambo, Cusco, Machu Picchu Pueblo Hotel & tourist train station

Buses to Puente Ruinas

Market

Ticket Office

Ollanta

Qosqo Service

Plaza Manco Capac

Callabuyo

Quyo Raymi

Shichi Roca

Mayta Capac

Lloque Yupanqui

Capac Yupangui

Inca Roca

Pachacutec

Bathing Costume Hire

Bathing Costume Hire

N

Not to scale

To Thermal Baths (5 mins)

■ **Sleeping**
1. Gringo Bill's (Qoñi Unu Hostal)
2. Hostal Ima Sumac
3. Hostal Inka
4. Hostal Machu Picchu
5. Los Caminantes
6. Machu Picchu Inn

● **Eating**
1. Clave de Sol (Chez Maggy)
2. El Refugio
3. Govinda
4. Inka's Pizza Pub
5. Machu Picchu
6. Pizzería La Chosa
7. Wasicha Pub

Quillabamba

The railway from Machu Picchu continues for 79 kilometres, through Chaullay, to **Quillabamba** in the Urubamba Valley. There is a Dominican mission here.

Population: 24,000
Altitude: 1,054 metres

The train station at Quillabamba is right on the river. Cross a footbridge put up by the Lions Club and then climb up a 100-odd flight of stairs to reach the town. There are not many attractions for the tourist, but this is a good place to bask in the sun or take a swim in the river, though ask the locals where the safe stretches are, as the current is quite rapid in places. There is also a clean market building and a football stadium. Unless you're here during the high season – June and July – you won't see many other tourists in these parts.

Getting there

See above for train information, but in mid-1998 trains were not running beyond Aguas Calientes. There is an alternative route by road from Ollantaytambo. It passes through Peña, a place of great beauty. Once out of Peña, the road climbs on endless zig-zags and breathtaking views to reach the Abra Málaga pass. At Chaullay, the road meets the railway to Quillabamba, Machu Picchu and Cusco. The road crosses the river at the historic Choquechaca bridge. A minibus leaves Cusco in the morning when full, from C Gen Buendía near Machu Picchu station. Also trucks go in the day-time; 233 kilometres, 6-11 hours, US$4.50.

Sleeping

D *Quillabamba*, Prolongación y M Grau 590, unmarked entrance next to Autoservicio behind the market. Roof terrace restaurant, laundry service. Recommended. *Hostal Don Carlos*, clean, private shower, generally hot water. **F** *Hostal Cusco*, with patio and roof terrace. Recommended. **F** *Hostal Alto Urubamba*, on Dos de Mayo. Clean, good, with or without bathroom, hot water, restaurant. There is other accommodation, **G** and upwards, near the market.

Eating

Pub Don Sebas, Jr Espinar 235 on Plaza de Armas. Good, great sandwiches, run by Karen Molero who is very friendly and always ready for a chat. *El Gordito*, on Espinar. Good place for chicken, US$3. There are many *heladerías*, which are much needed in the heat. The best of these is on the northwest corner of the Plaza de Armas.

Directory

Banks *Banco de Crédito*, is good for TCs.

Huancacalle

From Chaullay you can drive to the village of Huancacalle, the best base for exploring the nearby Inca ruins of **Vitcos**, with the palace of the last four Inca rulers from 1536 to 1572, and **Yurac Rumi**, the impressive sacred white stone of the Incas.

Hans Ebensten of Key West, Florida, writes: "While a visit to the ruins of Vilcabamba Vieja, near Espíritu Pampa, is still a formidable undertaking, involving at least eight days of hiking over rough trails, taking all camping gear, food, etc, the ruins of Vitcos and the Yurac Rumi, the Inca sacred stone, are now easily accessible. Both are well worth the effort of a visit. Vitcos remains romantically overgrown by jungle, much as Dr Hiram Bingham found it (and Machu Picchu) in 1911, but unlike Machu Picchu it has all the documented historical associations which make a visit particularly interesting and rewarding.

The Yurac Rumi, the most sacred site in South America, must be one of the most impressive religious sites in the world; far larger and more intricately and elaborately carved than any descriptions of it. Dr Hiram Bingham was chiefly concerned in stressing the importance of Machu Picchu, and thus in his books and reports dismissed Vitcos and the Yurac Rumi as almost insignificant."

Getting there Huancacalle can be reached from Quillabamba daily by truck and bus, the journey takes 4-7 hours. There is a small hotel at Huancacalle, or alternatively villagers will accept travellers in their very basic homes (take a sleeping bag). The Cobo family permits travellers to put up their tents on their property. Allow plenty of time for hiking to, and visiting the ruins. It takes one hour to walk from Huancacalle to Vitcos, 45 minutes Vitcos-Yurac Rumi, and 45 minutes Yurac Rumi-Huancacalle. Horses can be hired if you wish.

You can also hike up to **Vilcabamba La Nueva** from Huancacalle. It's a three-hour walk through beautiful countryside with Inca ruins dotted around. There is a missionary building run by Italians, with electricity and running water, where you may be able to spend the night.

Espíritu Pampa

Travellers with plenty time can hike from Huancacalle to Espíritu Pampa, the site of the **Vilcabamba Vieja** ruins, a vast pre-Inca ruin with a neo-Inca overlay set in deep jungle at 1,000 metres. The jungle in the area of Vilcabamba

Vilcabamba

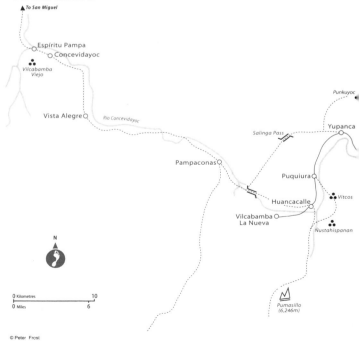

© Peter Frost

Vieja is full of wildlife and worth the trip on its own. At Espíritu Pampa is a sister stone of the Yurac Rumi.

To visit this area you must register with the police in Pucyura. You are advised to seek full information before travelling. Distances are considerable – it is at least 100 kilometres from Chaullay to Espíritu Pampa – the going is difficult and maps appear to be very poor. If you intend to attempt this trip, you should first read *Sixpac Manco: travels among the Incas*, by Vincent R Lee, which is available in Cusco. It contains accurate maps of all the archaeological sites in this area, and describes two expeditions into the region by the author and his party in 1982 and 1984, following in the footsteps of Gene Savoy, who first identified the site in the 1960s. His book, *Antisuyo*, which describes his expeditions here and elsewhere in Peru, is also recommended reading.

Getting there The site is reached on foot or horseback from Pampaconas. From Chaullay, take a truck to Yupanca, Lucma or Pucyura, where you can rent horses or mules and travel through superb country to Espíritu Pampa. You can then continue to Koshireni on the Río San Miguel.

Allow five to eight days if going on foot. The best time of year is May-October. During the wet season it really does rain, so be prepared to get very wet and very muddy. Insect repellent is essential. Also take pain-killers and other basic medicines; these will be much appreciated by the local people should you need to take advantage of their hospitality.

Guides For Vilcabamba Vieja contact Vidal Albertes in Huancacalle, or Paulo Quispe Cusi in Yupanca. Another local guide in Pucyura is Gilberto Quintanilla. Also try Adriel Garay

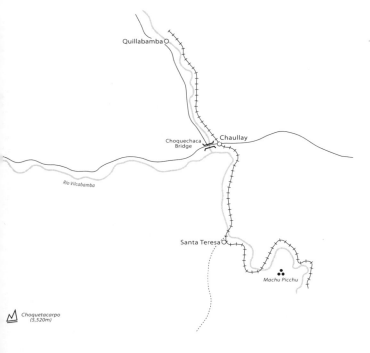

The last Incas of Vilcabamba

After Pizarro killed Atahualpa in 1532 the Inca empire disintegrated rapidly, and it is often thought that native resistance ended there. But in fact it continued for 40 more years, beginning with Manco, a teenage half-brother of Atahualpa.

In 1536, Manco escaped from the Spanish and returned to lead a massive army against them. He besieged Cusco and Lima simultaneously, and came close to dislodging the Spaniards from Peru. Spanish reinforcements arrived and Manco fled to Vilcabamba, a mountainous forest region west of Cusco that was remote, but still fairly close to the Inca capital, which he always dreamed of recapturing.

The Spanish chased Manco deep into Vilcabamba but he managed to elude them and continued his guerrilla war, raiding Spanish commerce on the Lima highway, and keeping alive the Inca flame. Then, in 1544, Spanish outlaws to whom he had given refuge murdered him, ending the most active period of Inca resistance.

The Inca line passed to his sons. The first, a child too young to rule named Sayri Túpac, eventually yielded to Spanish enticements and emerged from Vilcabamba, taking up residence in Yucay, near Urubamba in 1558. He died mysteriously – possibly poisoned – three years later.

His brother Titu Cusi, who was still in Vilcabamba, now took up the Inca mantle. Astute and determined, he resumed raiding and fomenting rebellion against the Spanish. But in 1570, Titu Cusi fell ill and died suddenly. A Spanish priest was accused of murdering him. Anti-Spanish resentment erupted, and the priest and a Spanish viceregal envoy were killed. The Spanish Viceroy reacted immediately, and the Spanish invaded Vilcabamba for the third and last time in 1572.

A third brother, Túpac Amaru was now in charge. He lacked his brother's experience and acuity, and his destiny was to be the sacrificial last Inca. The Spanish overran the Inca's jungle capital, and dragged him back to Cusco in chains. There, Túpac Amaru, the last Inca, was publicly executed in Cusco's main plaza.

The location of the neo-Inca capital of Vilcabamba was forgotten over the centuries, and the search for it provoked Hiram Bingham's expeditions, and his discovery of Machu Picchu. Bingham did also discover Vilcabama the Old, without realizing it, but the true location at Espíritu Pampa was only pinpointed by Gene Savoy in the 1960s, and was not confirmed irrefutably until the work of Vincent Lee in the 1980s.

at *White River Tours*, Plateros, Cusco, or C Bayoneta 739, Cusco, T234575.

Kiteni

You can also go by boat to Kiteni from Koshireni and then by truck to Quillabamba; 12-15 hours, US$5. There is basic accommodation at **G** *Hotel Kiteni*, and several restaurants. At Kiteni you must register on arrival with the police. Take a torch/flashlight as there is no electricity.

Irregular boats go to the Pongo de Mainique, where the river goes through the mountain with a rock wall of several hundred metres on either side, before descending into the jungle, where you can see many varieties of animals, birds, butterflies, snakes etc. This has been described by no less a traveller than Michael Palin (ex-Monty Pyhton) as one of the most spectacular journeys anywhere on earth. It is two days from Quillabamba to Pongo. Seek advice in advance on the river conditions; at certain times it is too high.

Southeast from Cusco

A newly paved road runs southeast from Cusco to Sicuani(see page 219),and on to Puno, on the shores of Lake Titicaca. There are many interesting villages and ruins on this road. Combis run every 15-20 minutes between Cusco and Sicuani (US$1.50), and more frequently to the villages and towns in between.

Tipón ruins, between the villages of Saylla and Oropesa, are extensive and include baths, terraces, irrigation systems and a temple complex, accessible from a path leading from just above the last terrace, all in a fine setting. From the ruins you can go up to more ruins and an amazing Inca road with a deep irrigation channel which leads straight up into a mountain and the further sites of Pucará and Cruzmoco. Allow a full day to see them all. From Tipón village it's an hour's climb to the ruins; or take a taxi.

Oropesa church contains a fine ornately carved pulpit. **Huacarpay**, the well-preserved ruins of the Inca town of Kañaracy, are nearby, reached from a path behind the Albergue. The site is on Lago Muina, with the *Albergue Urpicancha* on the shore, offering accommodation and a restaurant. This is a popular place with locals at weekends.

At **Lucre**, three kilometres from Huacarpay, there is an interesting textile mill, and many unexplored ruins. Ask the local history teacher, Sr Hernán Flores Yávar, for details. About three kilometres from Huacarpay is **C** *El Dorado Inn*, in a converted monastery, some of the rooms are done in a remarkable style and the service is very good.

At **Huambutío**, north of Huacarpay, the road divides; northwest to Pisac (see page 170) and north to Paucartambo, on the eastern slope of Andes.

Paucartambo

This once remote town is on the road to Pilcopata, Atalaya and Shintuya. This is the overland route used by tour companies from Cusco into Manu National Park (see page 480). Consequently, it has become a popular tourist destination. On 16 July, the festival of the *Virgen del Carmen* is a major attraction and well worth seeing. Masked dancers enact rituals and folk tales in the streets. Note that the *Fiesta* dates change and should be checked in advance in Cusco.

Private car hire for a round trip from Cusco on 16 July costs US$30; travel agencies in **Getting there** Cusco can arrange this. A minibus leaves for Paucartambo from Avda Huáscar in Cusco, every other day, US$4.50, 3-4 hours; alternate days Paucartambo-Cusco. Trucks and a private bus leave from the Coliseo, behind Hospital Segura in Cusco; 5 hours, US$2.50.

G *Quinta Rosa Marina*, near the bridge, basic; and **G** *Albergue Municipal Carmen de* **Sleeping** *la Virgen*. Also basic.

From Paucartambo, in the dry season, you can go 44 kilometres to **Tres Cruces**, along the Pilcopata road, turning left after 25 kilometres. Sr Cáceres in Paucartambo will arrange this trip for you. Tres Cruces gives a wonderful view of the sunrise in June and July and private cars leave Paucartambo between 0100 and 0200 to see it. You may be able to get a lift.

You can walk from Paucartambo to the *chullpas* of **Machu Cruz** in about an hour, or to the *chullpas* of **Pijchu** (take a guide). You can also visit the Inca

Cusco & the Sacred Valley

fortress of **Huatojto**, which has fine doorways and stonework. A car will take you as far as Ayre, from where the fortress is a two hour walk.

To Andahuaylillas Further on from Huacarpay, on the road southeast to Puno, are the Huari (pre-Inca) adobe wall ruins of **Piquillacta**, the monkey temple and the wall of Rumicolca. Piquillacta is quite large, with some reconstruction in progress. Buses to Urcos from Avda Huáscar in Cusco will drop you at the entrance on the north side of the complex, though this is not the official entry. Walk through to the official entry and continue to Rumicolca on the other side of the highway. ■*Open daily, 0700-1730.*

Andahuaylillas is a village 32 kilometres southeast from Cusco. It boasts a particularly fine early 17th century church, with beautiful frescoes, a splendid doorway and a gilded main altar. Ask for Sr Eulogio; he is a good guide, but speaks Spanish only. Taxis go there, as does the Oropesa bus (from Avda Huáscar in Cusco) via Tipón, Piquillacta and Rumicolca.

Urcos to Tinqui Beyond Andahuaylillas is **Urcos**. There is accommodation in municipal rooms on the plaza, or better ones in the 'hotel'; ask for directions.

A spectacular road from Urcos crosses the Eastern Cordillera to Puerto Maldonado in the jungle (see page 483). 47 kilometres after passing the snow-line Hualla-Hualla pass, at 4,820 metres, the super-hot thermal baths of Marcapata, 173 kilometres from Urcos, provide a relaxing break (entry US$0.10). 82 kilometres from Urcos, on the road to Puerto Maldonado, at the base of **Nevado Ausangate** (6,384 metres), is the town of **Ocongate**, which has two hotels on the Plaza de Armas.

Tinqui Beyond Ocongate is Tinqui, the starting point for hikes around Ausangate and in the Cordillera Vilcanota. On the flanks of the Nevado Ausangate is *Q'Olloriti*, where a church has been built close to the snout of a glacier. This place has become a place of pilgrimage (see Cusco Local festivals, page 160).

Buses to Tinqui leave Cusco Monday-Saturday at 1000 (six to seven hours, US$3.50) from C Tomasatito Condemayta, near the Coliseo Cerrado. There is accommodation in Tinqui at **G** *Hostal Tinqui Guide*, on the right-hand side as you enter the village, friendly, meals available, the owner can arrange guides and horses.

Hiking around Ausangate The hike around the mountain of Ausangate takes about five days. It is spectacular, but quite hard, with three passes over 5,000 metres, so you need to be acclimatized. Alternatively, a shorter and easier return trek can be made from Ausangate down the beautiful Pitumarca valley to the town of the same name and the Sacred valley. It is recommended to take a guide or *arriero*. *Arrieros* and mules can be hired in Tinqui for US$4 per day. A recommended *arriero* is Enrique Mandura, who also rents out equipment. Make sure you sign a contract with full details. Buy all food supplies in Cusco. Maps are available at the IGM in Lima or the South American Explorers Club. Some tour companies in Cusco have details about the hike (*Luzma Tours*, T/F261327), or check with the Mountain Guide Club, T226844.

Southeast from Urcos **Huaro** has a church whose interior is covered entirely with a colourful mural painting. **Cusipata**, with an Inca gate and wall, is where the ornate bands for the decoration of ponchos are woven. Close by is the Huari hilltop ruin of Llallanmarca.

Between Cusipata and Checacupe a road branches west to **Acomayo**, a pretty village which has a chapel with mural paintings of the 14 Incas. Accommodation is available in *Pensión Aguirre*. To get to Acomayo, take a Cusco-Sicuani bus or truck (US$1, one and a half hours), then a truck or bus to Acomayo (three hours, same price). Alternatively, get off at Checacupe and take a truck on to Acomayo.

From Acomayo, you can walk to Huáscar, which takes one hour, and from there to Pajlia; a climb which leads through very impressive scenery. The canyons of the upper Apurímac are vast beyond imagination. Great cliffs drop thousands of metres into dizzying chasms and huge rocks balance menacingly overhead. The ruins of Huajra Pucará lie near Pajlia. They are small, but in an astonishing position.

The church at **Checacupe** is, according to John Hemming, very fine, with good paintings and a handsome carved altar rail.

Tinta, 23 kilometres from Sicuani, has a church with brilliant gilded interior and an interesting choir vault. F *Casa Comunal*, offers dormitory accommodation, clean with good food. There are frequent buses and trucks to Cusco, or take the train from Cusco.

Continuing to Sicuani, Raqchi is near the site of the Inca Viracocha temple. **Raqchi** Raqchi is also the scene of the region's great folklore festival in mid-June, the *Huiracocha* dance festival. Dancers come to Raqchi from all over Peru and through music and dance they illustrate everything from the ploughing of fields to bull fights.

John Hemming adds: "The Viracocha temple is just visible from the train, looking from the distance like a Roman aqueduct. What remains is the central wall, which is adobe above and Inca masonry below. This was probably the largest roofed building ever built by the Incas. On either side of the high wall, great sloping roofs were supported by rows of unusual round pillars, also of masonry topped by adobe. Nearby is a complex of barracks-like buildings and round storehouses. This was the most holy shrine to the creator god Viracocha, being the site of a miracle in which he set fire to the land – hence the lava flow nearby. There are also small Inca baths in the corner of a field beyond the temple and a straight row of ruined houses by a square. The landscape is extraordinary, blighted by huge piles of black volcanic rocks."

Entrance to the site is US$1.75. There is a basic shop at the site. The school next door greatly appreciates donations of books and materials.

South from Cusco

Pacarijtambo is a good starting point for the three to four hours walk to the ruins of **Maukallaqta**, which contain good examples of Inca stonework. From there, you can walk to **Pumaorca**, a high rock carved with steps, seats and a small puma in relief on top. Below this are more Inca ruins.

From Cusco, buses and trucks to Pacarijtambo take four hours, US$2. You can find lodging for the night in Pacarijtambo at the house of the Villacorta family and leave for Cusco by truck the next morning. On the way back, you'll pass the caves of Tambo Toco, where a legend says that the four original Inca brothers emerged into the world.

West from Cusco

The Cusco-Machu Picchu train follows the road west from the city through the Anta canyon for 10 kilometres, and then, at a sharp angle, the Urubamba canyon, and descends along the river valley, flanked by high cliffs and peaks.

Cusco & the Sacred Valley

In the town of **Anta** felt trilby hats are on sale. *Restaurant Dos de Mayo* is good. Bus to Anta from Cusco is US$0.30.

76 kilometres from Cusco, beyond Anta, on the Abancay road, two kilometres before Limatambo at the ruins of **Tarahuasi**, a few hundred metres from the road, is a very well-preserved **Inca temple platform**, with 28 tall niches, and a long stretch of fine polygonal masonry. The ruins are impressive, enhanced by the orange lichen which give the walls a beautiful honey colour.

Dr Ken Heffernan of Australia, writes: "The ruins at Tarahuasi were part of of the Inca *Tanpu* called 'Limatambo' in the 16th century, along the road to the famous Apurímac bridge. The lands immediately surrounding the *tanpu* were then claimed by a son of Huayna Capac, Cristóbal Paullu Inca and his wife, Doña Catalina Tocto Usica. The extent of Inca agricultural terraces in the valley of Limatambo and Mollepata exceeds 100 hectares."

There is accommodation in Limatambo at **F** *Albergue*. There is also a nice restaurant hidden from the road by trees.

100 kilometres from Cusco along the Abancay road is the exciting descent into the Apurímac canyon, near the former Inca suspension bridge that inspired Thornton Wilder's *The Bridge of San Luis Rey* (see **Further reading**, page 83). Also, 153 kilometres along the road to Abancay from Cusco, near Curahuasi, famous for its anise herb, is the stone of **Sahuite**, carved with animals, houses, etc, which appears to be a relief map of an Indian village. Unfortunately, 'treasure hunters' have defaced the stone. There are other interesting carvings in the area around the Sahuite stone.

In Curahuasi camping is possible on the football pitch, but ask the police for permission. There is a restaurant on the main road into town.

Cusco & the Sacred Valley

Lake Titicaca

5

Lake Titicaca

200 Arequipa to Juliaca

201 Juliaca

204 Puno

213 The islands

215 Frontier with Bolivia

219 Puno to Cusco

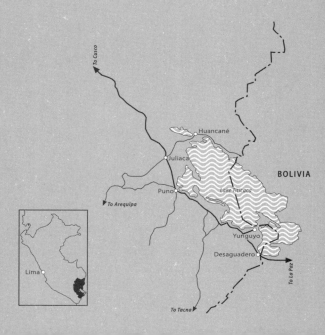

*Straddling Peru's southern border with landlocked
Bolivia are the deep, sapphire-blue waters of mystical
Lake Titicaca. This gigantic inland sea covers 8,000
square kilometres and is the highest navigable lake in
the world, at 3,856 metres above sea level. Its shores
and islands are home to one of Peru's oldest peoples
who predate the Incas by a thousand years. You can
wander through traditional villages where Spanish is
a second language and where ancient myths and
beliefs still hold true.*

Lake Titicaca

Lake Titicaca

Arequipa to Juliaca

By rail The railway from Arequipa winds its way up the valley towards Juliaca. Skirting El Misti and Chachani the train climbs steadily past Yura, Socosani and Pampa de Arrieros. After another 80 kilometres it reaches Crucero Alto, the highest point on the line, at 4,500 metres. The beautiful lakes Lagunillas and Saracocha lie on opposite sides of the railway, which flirts with their shores for nearly an hour.

As the descent continues streams become more plentiful. The scenery changes over the next few hours from desolate mountain peaks to a fertile pampa with a fairly populous agricultural community.

NB Since there is no day train, much of this stunning scenery is, unfortunately, not visible en route. The train, however, is more comfortable than travelling by bus.

By road The rough road from Arequipa to Juliaca climbs steeply for the first 50 kilometres, before reaching a plateau. Its highest point is at Alto de Toroya, 4,693 metres. The scenery is beautiful as the road passes lakes, salt flats and small villages. The road is paved for the first 30 kilometres to Chiguata. The paved road starts again at Santa Lucia (Km 218). If driving, a four-wheel drive

Lake Titicaca

vehicle is strongly recommended. Even in the dry season, there are rivers to cross and sand stretches. After heavy rain it is impassable.

This takes three days by bicycle. If heading for Puno it is better to go via Juliaca than taking the direct branch to Puno. Restaurants along the way sell mostly basic foodstuffs and drinks: at **Chiguata**, Km 30; **Salinas**, Km 82; at Km 113, south from **Pati**; **Alto de Toroya**, Km 176; **Tincopalca**, Km 176, where it is also possible to sleep; **Santa Lucía**, Km 218, also *alojamiento*; and at **Deustua**, Km 252. The route covers 282 kilometres in total.

Juliaca

289 kilometres northeast of Arequipa, Juliaca, is freezing cold at night and not a particularly attractive place.

Population: *142,576*
Altitude: *3,825 metres*
Phone code: *054*
Coloured map 6, grid B2

On the huge Plaza Melgar, several blocks from the main part of the town, is an interesting colonial church. At the large market in the plaza on Sunday, you can buy wool and alpaca goods. There is another daily market (Mercado Santa Bárbara) in the plaza outside the railway station, which is more tourist oriented. Tupac Amarú market, on Moquegua, seven blocks east of the railway line, is a cheap black market. The Galerías Artesanías on Plaza Bolognesi is a good place to find cheap alpaca sweaters. A first class hospital is run by the Seventh Day Adventists.

Lake Titicaca

Essentials

Sleeping
■ *on maps*
Price codes:
see inside front cover

A2-3 *Suites Don Carlos*, (ex-*Hotel de Turistas*), Jr M Prado 335, on the outskirts of town, T321571/327270, E dcarloslim@tci.net.pe. 30 double rooms, 14 singles/matrimonials and a presidential suite, prices include taxes, good facilities, continental breakfast US$6.50, lunch/dinner US$13. **B** *Hostal Don Carlos*, Jr 9 de Diciembre 114, Plaza Bolognesi, T323600/322120. Owned by the same group, comfortable, modern facilities, includes taxes, continental breakfast US$4.20, lunch/dinner US$8.50. **C** *Hostal Samari*, Noriega, T321870, F321852. Clean, modern, with restaurant.

D *Karlo's Hostal*, Unión 317, T322568. Clean, comfortable, hot water. **D** per person *Royal Inn*, San Román 158, T321561, F321572. Clean, with private bathroom and TV, good restaurant. Recommended. **D-E** *Yasur*, Jr M Núñez 414. With bathroom, **F** without, no hot water, basic and relatively clean, a small bar and restaurant are open in the evening. **E** per person *Hostal Perú*, San Román 409, on Plaza Bolognesi, T321510. With bathroom,

BOLIVIA

Sorata

Achacachi

San Pablo

Straits of Tiquina

Laguna Huiñaymarca

Tiahuanaco

Guaqui

LA PAZ

cheaper without, clean, comfortable, hot water sometimes, basic restaurant. Recommended. **G** *Hostal Ferrocarril*, San Martín 249. Clean, friendly, water until 1900.

NB There are water problems in town, especially in the dry season.

Eating
● *on maps*

Trujillo, on San Martín. Very good food, good selection and good value, US$3-4 for a meal. *Rico Pan*, 2 doors down from *Trujillo*. Bakery and café with a good selection of cakes and bread, opens at 0600, good coffee. There are many chicken places on M Núñez, some of which are quite upmarket. A jazz bar *Waikiki*, on the same block as *Hotel Yasur*, is dark and cosy, open late (or until the last customer leaves), good sangria and live music.

Transport

Air connections The airport is small but well-organized. There are daily flights to Lima (1 hour and 45 minutes) with *AeroPerú* and *Aero Continente*; check if the US$65 'tourist coupon' is in effect. There are also daily flights to **Arequipa** (30 minutes) and **Cusco** (35 minutes). Flights to and from Cusco have been suspended at the time of writing. A taxi to the airport costs about US$2-2.50. **Airport buses** leave from Plaza Bolognesi to the airport, US$0.70. **Tourist buses** run direct from Puno to the airport and vice versa; US$1.80 per person, 1 hour.

Juliaca

■ Sleeping	7. Yasur	2. Combis to Puno
1. Hostal Don Carlos		3. Cruz del Sur buses
2. Hostal Ferrocarril	● Eating	4. Tranpsortes Los
3. Hostal Perú	1. Trujillo	Angeles minibuses
4. Hostal Samari		to Puno
5. Karlo's Hostal	🚌 Transport	
6. Royal Inn	1. Bus to Airport	

N
0 metres 100
0 yards 109

Buses There are daily buses to **Cusco**, 344 kilometres, 12 hours, US$8. The road is now paved and in good condition. Check on the current situation regarding safety before taking a night bus to or from Cusco. To **Puno**, 44 kilometres, 45 minutes, US$0.50; buses leave from Calle Nicolás de Piérola, past the railway. Kombis to Puno leave from Plaza Bolognesi, also US$0.50. A taxi to Puno is about US$15. From Puno transport goes to the Bolivian border and on to La Paz. To **Huancané** (on the north side of Lake Titicaca), 51 kilometres, 3½ hours, US$1.75, several buses and trucks daily. It is a bumpy ride on a poor road, but the views are wonderful. It is a further 50 kilometres, US$1.75, to the Bolivian border. There are several checkpoints and the trip can take a few hours. Buses and trucks leave daily, but not very frequently, on this route.

Trains The station at Juliaca is the junction for services between **Arequipa**, **Puno** and **Cusco**. Carriages are put onto the right rails for their next destination, a process which can take several hours and can prove too much for tired passengers (though there is the opportunity to buy alpaca goods through the carriage window while you're waiting). It is advisable to get off the train and continue to Puno by bus or colectivo (US$0.50, 45 minutes), which is much quicker, safer and more comfortable. You do not have to change trains in Juliaca if you buy a through ticket from one terminus to the other using the same class all the way. Stay in your carriage at Juliaca and watch your possessions closely. See also under Arequipa (page 234), Puno (page 209) and Cusco (page 164).

The ticket office opens when the train comes in. Trains from Cusco arrive on Monday, Wednesday, Friday and Saturday at about 1730, and from Arequipa on Sunday and Wednesday at 0600-0630. Prices to Cusco and Arequipa are the same as from Puno. The train is frequently cancelled in the rainy season and you have to travel by bus.

NB Beware of pickpockets and thieves at the station, where they get on the train to join those already on board. Also beware of overcharging by taxi drivers at the railway station.

Around Juliaca

There are good thermal springs at the village of **Putina**, 84 kilometres northeast of Juliaca, five and a half hours by bus or truck, US$2.50. 71 kilometres northeast of Juliaca is the old town of **Azángaro** with a famous church, La Asunción, which is filled with *retablos* and paintings of the Cusco school.

The town of **Pucara** lies 63 kilometres to the north, with pre-Inca ruins and its famed pottery (see page 205). The people here are friendly and curious. There are some restaurants along the main road. The sheep farm of San Antonio, between Ayaviri and Chiquibambilla, owned by the Prime family, who are descendants of British emigrants, can be visited.

A highly recommended trip is 23 kilometres northwest of Juliaca to the unspoiled little colonial town of **Lampa**, known as the 'Pink City', with a splendid church, La Inmaculada, containing a copy of Michelangelo's 'Pietà'. Also of interest is the Kampac Museo, Ugarte 462, a museum with sculptures and ceramics from the Lampa and Juli areas. The owner lives next door. There is a tourist office with friendly guides for free. Nearby are three Inca fortresses. It also has a good Sunday market. There is a basic *hostal*, **G** per person. Buses leave daily from 2 de Mayo (take a tricycle to get there), one hour, US$0.70.

Lake Titicaca

Puno

Coloured map 6, grid B2 *On the northwest shore of Lake Titicaca, Puno, is Capital of its Department and Peru's folklore centre with a vast array of handicrafts, festivals and costumes and a rich tradition of music and dance.*

Puno isn't the most attractive of cities but with its surly seediness comes a certain vitality, helped by the fact that most of the population appear to be young students. The main plaza is worth a look and the lakeside quarter, largely flooded since the rise in the lake's water level, is interesting, but dirty. Being so high up, Puno gets bitterly cold at night: in June-August the temperature at night can fall to -25°C, but generally not below -5°C.

Sights

A good idea in Puno, Juliaca and other Andean towns, when moving about with heavy baggage, is to hire a 3-wheel cycle cart, 'Trici-Taxi', which costs about US$0.20 per kilometre

The impressive baroque exterior of the **Cathedral**, completed in 1657, belies an austere interior. Beside the Cathedral is the famous **Balcony of the Conde de Lemos**, on the corner of Deustua and Conde de Lemos, where Peru's Viceroy stayed when he first arrived in the city. A short walk up Independencia leads to the **Arco Deustua**, a monument honouring those killed in the battles of Junín and Ayacucho. Nearby, is a mirador giving fine views over the town, the port and the lake beyond. The walk from Jr Cornejo following the Stations of the Cross up a nearby hill, with fine views of Lake Titicaca, has been recommended, but be careful and don't go alone.

Museums The **Museo Municipal** has been combined with the private collection of precolumbian artefacts bequeathed to the city by their owner, Sr Carlos Dreyer. *Conde de Lemos 289.* ■*Open Monday to Friday 0730-1330. Entrance US$1.*

The historic ship, ***Yavari***, which is the oldest ship on Lake Titicaca, is berthed in the port of Puno and is now open to visitors as a Museum and Bar. The iron-hulled ship, painted in her original livery of black, white and red, is moored alongside the jetty from which the boats to the islands leave (see **The Islands** below). The ship was built in England in 1862 and, together with her twin, the *Yapura* (now the Peruvian Navy's Hospital ship and called the *BAP Puno*), was shipped in kit form to Arica. From Arica, the two ships went by rail to Tacna from where the 2,766 pieces were carried by mule to Lake Titicaca. The journey took six years. The *Yavari* was eventually launched on Christmas Day 1870 and on 14 June 1871 sailed on her maiden voyage. The *Yapura* followed in 1873. For those interested in steam trains, the Bolinder four-cyclinder hot bulb semi-diesel engine on view today replaced the original dried llama dung steam engine in 1913. From after the War of the Pacific until the nationalization of the Railways and Lake Fleet in 1975, the *Yavari* was operated as a passenger/cargo vessel by the London-based Peruvian Corporation. The ship was bought in 1987 and is being restored by an Anglo-Peruvian Association. Visitors are very welcome on board the *Yavari* and will be shown over the ship and its exhibition of archival documentation and memorabilia on the Lake Fleet by the Captain, Carlos Saavedra. ■*Entrance is free but donations are most welcome to help with maintenance costs.* **Project addresses**: 61 Mexfield Road, London, SW15 2RG, England, T/F44-1818740583. In Lima: c/o *Invertur*, Avda Las Magnolias 889, Oficina

A load of bulls

The village of Pucara, north of Juliaca, is famous for its distinctive pottery, a detailed style dubbed grotesque because the figures' features are wildly exaggerated. The figures are usually left unpainted and unglazed, and the earth colour and rough surface play a part in the overall effect. Among the figures produced, the best known is the Pucara bull.

The llama was a votive symbol for the Incas, often carved out of stone and used for burning incense and other sacred purposes, until the bull, introduced to the Americas by the invading Spanish, took its place as a symbol of strength and virility. In some fiestas in the surrounding area, bulls are cut on the neck and their blood offered to Pachamama, the mother earth. Flowers are then thrown at the animal and coca leaves placed on its wounds to cure the pain.

Coca leaves are even painted on the ceramic versions of the popular Pucara bull, which gained fame with the introduction of the Puno-Cusco railway. The train stops frequently and the bulls can be sold easily to passing travellers.

208, San Isidro, T00511-4423090, F00511-4424180. In Puno: c/o *Solmartours*, Jr Arequipa 140, T005154-352901, F005154-351654.

Essentials

Competition between the hotels is intense when trains and buses arrive and hotel touts besiege arriving train and bus passengers. There is often free transport to the hotel. If you're taking a room with a bathroom, check first if it has hot or cold water. Check on the early morning water supply, as some only have water after 0730, too late if you are going out by train or on an island tour. Note that Puno suffers from power and water shortages. Note also that some hotels are full of dubious street tour sellers (see below under Tour agencies).

Sleeping
■ *on maps*
Price codes:
see inside front cover

A3 *Libertador Isla Esteves*, on an island linked by a causeway 5 kilometres northeast of Puno (taxi US$3), T367780, F367879, W www.libertador.com.pe. Built on a Tiahuanaco-period site, spacious, good views, phone, bar, good restaurant, disco, good service, electricity and hot water all day. **A3** *Hostal Hacienda*, Jr Deustua 297, T/F356109. Refurbished colonial house, with bathroom, hot water, TV, includes breakfast, café, comfortable, carpeted rooms, friendly. Recommended. A new *Hotel Posada del Inca* is planned to open in 1999. It is part of the same chain which presently has hotels in Lima, Cusco and Yucay.

B *Sillustani*, Jr Lambayeque 195, T351431. Includes breakfast, good service, clean, friendly, cold rooms, ask for an electric heater, hot water. **B** *Hostal Colón Inn*, Tacna 290, T351432. Recently renovated, colonial style, good rooms with private bathroom and hot shower, clean, good service, restaurant and pizzería, the Belgian manager Christian Nonis is well known, especially for his work on behalf of the people on Taquile island. **B-C** *Hostal Italia*, Teodoro Valcarcel 122, T352521, 2 blocks from the station. With bathroom, good, safe, hot water, good food, clean, staff helpful.

Lake Titicaca

Recommended. **B-C** *El Buho*, Lambayeque 142, T351409. Clean, hot water, nice rooms, friendly, ask for a room with a radiator. Recommended.

C *Don Miguel*, Avda Torre 545, T351371. With shower, restaurant, clean. **C** *Ferrocarril*, Avda La Torre 185, opposite the station, T351752. With bathroom and hot water, **E** without bathroom and with cold water in the old part of the building, modern, good rooms, but noisy, poor service, central heating adequate, accepts many credit cards and changes Bolivian currency. **C** *Internacional*, Libertad 161, T352109. With shower, an extra bed costs US$1.50, hot water morning and evening, secure. **C** *Hostal La Rosa Lacustre*, Jr Arequipa 386, T355173. With bathroom, hot water, café.

D *Hostal Arequipa*, Arequipa 153, T352071. Clean, friendly, cold water, will change travellers' cheques at good rates, stores luggage, secure, arranges tours to the islands, OK. **D** *Hostal Imperial*, Teodoro Valcarcel 145, T352386. With bathroom, hot water before 1100 and in the evenings, friendly, helpful, stores luggage, clean, comfortable, safe. **D** *Hostal Rubi*, Jr Cajamarca 152-154, T356058, T/F353384. Friendly, safe, breakfast US$2, good. **D** *Hostal Tumi*, Cajamarca 237, T353270. Has been divided into two hotels, on first and second floors, both secure, hot water, breakfast available, a bit dark and gloomy but otherwise OK. **D-E** *Hostal Nesther*, Deustua 268, T351631. Also has triples, with bathroom, hot water, 0730-0900, clean. Recommended.

Puno

■ Sleeping	la Candelaria	12. Hostal Nesther
1. Colón Inn	7. Hostal Arequipa	13. Hostal Q'oñiwasi
2. Don Miguel	8. Hostal Europa	14. Hostal Rubi
3. El Buho	9. Hostal Italia	15. Hostal Tumi
4. Ferrocarril	10. Hostal Los Uros &	16. Internacional
5. Hospedaje Margarita	Hostal Imperial	17. Sillustani
6. Hospedaje Virgen de	11. Hostal Monterrey	

E *Europa*, Alfonso Ugarte 112, near the train station, T353023. Very popular, luggage may be stored, but don't leave your valuables in the room, shared bathrooms, hot water sometimes, garage space for motorcycles. E *Hostal Monterrey*, Lima 447A, T351691. Popular, reasonable, some rooms with bathroom, better than those without, communal bathrooms are reported dirty, hot water 0630-0900 but unreliable, restaurant poor, secure for luggage, motorcycle parking US$0.50, has colectivo service to La Paz, US$12. E *Los Uros*, Teodoro Valcarcel 135, T352141. Cheaper without bathroom, hot water 0700-1000 and 1900-2100, plenty of blankets, clean, breakfast available in cafeteria, quiet, good value, small charge to leave luggage, good value laundry service, friendly, often full, changes travellers' cheques a reasonable rate. Recommended.

F *Hostal Extra*, Moquegua 124. Hot water 24 hours, secure, popular, luggage stored, OK. F *Hostal Puno*, Jr Los Incas 208, near the train station, T356733/356746. Cheaper without bathroom, hot water, good beds, very comfortable, helpful. Recommended. F per person *Hostal Q'oñiwasi*, Avda La Torre 135, opposite the rail station, T353912. Clean, warm rooms, friendly, hot water on request, luggage store, breakfast available, safe. Recommended. F *Hostal Virreynal*, Arequipa 342. Friendly, clean, no hot water. **F-G** per person *Hospedaje Virgen de la Candelaria*, Jr Tarapacá 139 (no sign), T353828. Shared rooms, hot water, breakfast US$1.50, laundry service, luggage stored, family atmosphere, helpful, secure, cooking facilities, can arrange local tours. Recommended. **F-G** per person *Hospedaje Residencial Margarita*, Jr Tarapacá 130, T352820. Large building, clean, nice family atmosphere, hot water most of the day. Recommended. **F-G** per person *Hostal Illampu*, Avda La Torre 137, T353284. With bathroom, warm water, café, laundry, safe box, TV, exchange money, friendly, helpful with train tickets, arranges excursions (ask for Sra Olga).

G per person *Hostal Inti*, Avda La Torre, opposite the station. Noisy, basic, hot shower US$1 extra, small.

Youth Hostel: F-G per person *Albergue Juvenil Virgen de Copacabana*, Ilave 236, T354129 (no sign). Huge rooms, well-furnished, hot water, "awesome bathroom", good location, quiet, friendly and helpful owners, will wash your clothes for a reasonable fee, full breakfast for US$1.30, a real bargain. Highly recommended.

Eating
● *on maps*

Don Piero, Lima 360. Huge meals, live music, try their 'pollo coca-cola' (chicken in a sweet and sour sauce), slow service, popular, tax extra. The restaurant next door is also called *Don Piero*, where you can get decent chicken, salad, fries and a

● Eating
1. Don Piero
2. Hilda's House
3. Pascana
4. Pizzería El Buho

Buses
1. Cruz del Sur buses
2. To Juliaca
3. Yunguyo & Desaguadero

soft drink for US$1.50. *Internacional*, Libertad 161, 2 blocks from the plaza. Very popular, excellent trout, good pizzas, not cheap and service variable. *Pizzería El Buho*, Jr Libertad 386. Excellent pizza, cosy atmosphere, open 1800 onwards. *Al Paso Antojitos*, Lima 373. A recommended snack bar for cake, pies and coffee. *Pascana*, Lima 339. Specializes in *parrilladas*, vegetarian dishes also available, folk shows. *Hilda's House*, Moquegua 189. Excellent food at reasonable prices. *Samaná*, Puno 334. Inconsistent service, sometimes has live folk music from 2100, open fire and snacks and drinks. *Ricardos*, Jr Lambayeque 117. Clean, good breakfasts, serves sandwiches, friendly. Recommended. *Monterrey*, behind the hotel of the same name. Good fish, good value lunches, otherwise expensive. *Mi Perú*, on the corner of Arequipa and Jr Deza. Popular with locals, cheap, huge portions, friendly. *Goodmann*, on Pardo. A popular vegetarian restaurant. *Adventista*, Jr Deza 349. Good.

Cafés   *Rico Pan*, at Arequipa 459 and also at Lima 357. Café and bakery, great cakes, excellent capuccino, espresso and Irish coffee, good juices and pastries, good breakfasts and other dishes, reasonable prices, great place to relax, open 0600-2300, closed Sunday. *Café Delissa*, Libertad 215. Open from 0600, espresso coffee, good vegetarian food, excellent set lunch US$1.50. *Café Ayllu*, Arequipa y Puno. Very good pastries. There is an unnamed café on the corner of Libertad and Tacna, which serves good breakfasts and pastries. Also an excellent patisserie at Lima 430, for croissants, fresh bread and cakes.

Bars &   *Peña Hostería*, Lima 501. Good music. Recommended. *Pub Ekeko's*, Jr Lima 355. Live
Nightclubs   music every night, happy hour 2000-2130.

Festivals   The very colourful *Fiesta de la Virgen de* la Candelaria takes place during the first 2 weeks in **February**. Bands and dancers from all the local towns compete in this *Diablada*, or Devil Dance, with the climax coming on Sunday. The festival is famous for its elaborate and grotesque masks, which depict characters in local legends as well as caricatures of former landowners and mine bosses. The festivities are better at night on the streets than the official functions in the stadium. Check in advance on the actual date because Candelaria may be moved if pre-Lentern carnival coincides with it. This festival is great fun and shouldn't be missed if you're in the vicinity around this time.

Other festivals include a candlelight procession through darkened streets, which takes place on **Good Friday**, with bands, dignatories and statues of Jesus. On **3 May** is *Invención de la Cruz*, an exhibition of local art. On **29 June** is the colourful festival of *San Pedro*, with a procession at Zepita (see page 211). Another takes place on **20 July**. In fact, it is difficult to find a month in Puno without some sort of celebration.

Finally, remember, remember **5 November**, when there's an impressive *pageant* dedicated to the founding of Puno and the emergence of Manco Capac from the waters of Lake Titicaca. The procession from the lake winds its way to the stadium where a ceremony takes place with dancers from local towns and villages. This is not the best time to visit Taquile and Amantaní since many of their inhabitants are at the festival.

Shopping   The **Market** on the railway between Avda Los Incas and Lampa is one of the best places in Peru for llama and alpaca wool articles. Many of the jumpers, hats and gloves are hand-made. You will also be hassled on the street, and outside restaurants to buy woollen goods. In the covered part of the market mostly fruit and vegetables are sold, but there are also model reed boats, attractive carved stone amulets and Ekekos. There is also a food and clothing market next to the stadium. **NB** We have received reports of robbery in the market, so take care.

Pot luck

One of the most intriguing items for sale in Andean markets is Ekeko, the god of good fortune and plenty and one of the most enduring and endearing of the Aymara gods and folk legends.

He is a cheery, avuncular little chap, with a happy face to make children laugh, a pot belly due to his predilection for food and short legs so he can't run away. His image, usually in plaster of paris, is laden with sacks of grain, sweets, household tools, baskets, utensils, suitcases, confetti and streamers, rice, noodles and other essentials. Dangling from his lower lip is the ubiquitous lit cigarette. Believers say that these little statues only bring luck if they are received as gifts, and not purchased.

Trains The railway runs from **Puno** to **Juliaca** (44 kilometres), where it divides, to **Cusco** (281 kilometres) and **Arequipa** (279 kilometres). A train runs to **Cusco** on Monday, Wednesday, Thursday and Saturday at 0700, arriving in Juliaca at 0800 and in Cusco at about 1800 (try to sit on the right hand side for the views). Trains to **Arequipa** leave on Monday and Friday at 1945, arriving about 0600. In the wet season the services may be cut to 2-3 times a week, or even be cancelled for short periods. Always check.

Fares: Puno-Cusco: *Económico* US$9, Pullman US$19, Inca US$23. Puno-Arequipa: 2nd class, US$9; 1st class, US$11; pullman (*turismo ejecutivo*), US$19; Inca US$23. The ticket office is open from 0630-1030, 1600-1900 Monday-Saturday, and on Sunday in the afternoons only. Tickets can be bought 1 day in advance, or 1 hour before departure if there are any left. Travel agencies are sometimes the only option, but they can be unreliable; do not pay in full before receiving the tickets and always check the date and seat number. Hotels can help with getting tickets as well.

The station is well guarded by police and sealed off to those without tickets. Tourists only are allowed on Pullman and Inca class carriages. See also under Arequipa (page 234) and Juliaca (above) on safety. There is a *menú* available in the Inca and Pullman carriages (US$6.50 for lunch or dinner). It's much cheaper to buy food at the stations en route.

Buses Most companies have offices on Avda Sol, eg Cruz del Sur. Daily buses to **Arequipa**, 297 kilometres, 8-10 hours (longer in the rainy season), US$7-8 (US$5.50 with *Emes Tours*, leaving at 0700 and 1700). Colectivos charge US$12, 9 hours. The road is in poor condition and mudslides cause problems in the rain. All buses seem to go at night and it's a very cold journey. The route does not go through Juliaca. To **Lima**, 1,011 kilometres, US$18, all buses go through Arequipa, sometimes with a change of bus. See under Arequipa.

To **Juliaca**, 44 kilometres, 45 minutes, US$0.50; kombis run all day from Jr Tacna near the corner with Libertad. Taxi to Juliaca is about US$15. To **Cusco**, 388 kilometres, US$8, road now fully paved. Most buses at night, also during the day (6 hours) on Wednesday and Saturday at 0730 (with Libertad, C Melgar, opposite CIVA). **NB** Robberies have been reported on this route so check on current safety beforehand. To **Moquegua**, 262 kilometres, 10 hours, US$7, a few buses run daily on a poor, bumpy road. To **Tacna**, via Ilave (see page 211), 375 kilometres, 17 hours (in the dry season), US$7, with Gironda and Trans Ponce (better). The road is unpaved and it's a rough and cold journey which can be difficult in the rainy season. The views are spectacular. **NB** Watch out for thieves around the bus offices. There are also hotel touts posing as taxi drivers who will take you to the hotel of their choice rather than yours.

Banks *Banco de Crédito*, Lima y Grau. Changes TCs before 1300 at US$1 commission, cash advance on Visa. For cash go to the *cambios*, the travel agencies or the better hotels. The best rates are with the money changers at the market but check your Peruvian soles carefully. The rates for soles to Bolivianos is poor. It's better to wait till Yunguyo at the border.

Transport

Directory

Lake Titicaca

Communications Post Office: Jr Moquegua 267. **Telephone:** Telefónica at Arequipa y Moquegua. There's also an international phone and fax office next to the church on Parque Pino. **Internet:** *Hardtech*, Jr Arequipa 345, oficina 106, inside a small gallery, T368308, E hardtech@puno.perured.net. They have 5 terminals and are open 0900-2000.

Embassies & consulates *Bolivian Consulate*, Jr Arequipa between Parque Pino y Jr Deza. Issue a visa on the spot, US$10, open 0830-1330 Mon-Fri.

Laundry *Lavandería América*, at Jr Moquegua 169, is very expensive. *Lavandería Lava Clin*, Deustua 252, El Sol 431 and Teodorno Valcarcel 132, is also very expensive. In general, Puno laundries charge per item and are very expensive places to wash your clothes. It's better to wait until Cusco, where they charge by the kg.

Tour companies & travel agents Agencies organize trips to the Uros floating islands and the islands of Taquile and Amantaní (which is usually included in the Taquile trip), as well as to Sillustani, and other places. Make sure that you settle all details before embarking on the tour. Alternatively, you can easily go down to the lake and make your own arrangements with the boatmen. **NB** Watch out for the many unofficial street tour sellers – or 'jalagringos' – who offer hotels and tours at different rates, depending on how wealthy you look. Once you realize they have charged more than the going rate, they'll be gone. They are everywhere: train station, bus offices, airport and hotels. Ask to see their guide's ID card. The following agencies have been recommended as reliable and helpful and offer good value. *Allways Travel*, Tacna 234, Av del Puerto 362, T/F355552, E awtperu@mail.cosapidata.com.pe. Very helpful and reliable, speak German, French, English and Italian, ask for Eliana if you have any problems in general. They offer a unique cultural tour to the island of Anapia in Lake Wiñaymarka, beyond the straits of Tiquina. *Cusi Tours*, Valcarcel 103, T352591. *Edgar Adventures*, Jr Lima 328, T353444, F354811. Run by Edgar Apaza F. and Norka Florez L. who speak English, German and French. *Ecoturismo Aventura*, Jr Lima 458, T355785. *Feiser Tours*, Teodoro Valcarcel 155, T353112. *Kolla Tour*, Jr Moquegua 679, T352961, F354762. Sell airline tickets and have their own boat for tours on the lake. *Imperio Tours*, Valcarcel 191, T367690. Good for travel to La Paz. Most agencies will go and buy train tickets for you, at varying rates of commission.

Tourist offices *InfoTur*, C Lima y C Deustua. They are friendly and helpful with general information, they sell a city guide and map for US$1.20. *Ministry of Tourism*, Jr Deustua 351, T352811. Helpful with complaints. *Touring Automóvil Club del Perú*, C Arequipa 457.

Useful addresses Immigration: Libertad 403, T352801. For renewing entry stamps, etc. The process is very slow and you must fill in 2 application forms at a bank, but there's nothing else to pay.

Around Puno

Anybody interested in religious architecture should go from Puno to visit the villages along the western shore of Lake Titicaca.

Chucuíto An Inca sundial can be seen near the village of Chucuíto, which has an interesting church, La Asunción, and houses with carved stone doorways. Nearby, are cave paintings at Chichiflope. There is accommodation one kilometre north of town on the road from Puno at **C** *Las Cabañas*, includes breakfast, nice rooms, clean, new furniture but lacks atmosphere, courtyard can be used for parking bicycles, hot water, negotiable in low season, T(054)352108, leave message for Alfredo Sánchez. Also **E** *Albergue Juvenil*, T(054)351276. Great wee cottages, meals, will collect you from Puno. Highly recommended.

Juli The main road then by-passes the little town of Juli, 83 kilometres southeast, which has the best examples of religious architecture in its four churches.

San Pedro, designated as the Cathedral, has been extensively restored. It contains a series of superb screens, some in ungilded mahogany and others taken from other churches, as well as some fine paintings, and a collection of coloured objects in the sacristy.

San Juan Bautista has two sets of 17th century paintings of the lives of St John the Baptist and of St Teresa, contained in sumptuous gilded frames. San

Juan is now a state museum. It also has intricate *mestizo* carving in pink stone. ■*Open mornings only. Entrance US$1.15.*

Santa Cruz is another fine Jesuit church, partly roofless, so that it is easy to photograph the carvings of monkeys, papayas and grapes. The keys to Santa Cruz and San Juan Bautista are kept by the couple who look after San Juan Bautista.

The fourth church, **La Asunción**, now abandoned and its fine bell tower damaged by earthquake or lightning, has an archway and atrium which date from the early 17th century. A school of picture restoration is working on its mass of paintings.

Beautiful needlework can be bought at the plaza in Juli. This is also a good place for alpaca bags, blankets and *mantas*. There is a nice walk from Juli to the red rock formations known as Caballo Cansado. Near Juli is a small colony of flamingos. Many other birds can be seen from the road. A colectivo from Puno is US$0.80. There's accommodation at **G** *Alojamiento El Rosal*, Puno 128, just off the plaza, which is basic but OK; and also **G** *Hostal Municipal*, which is very basic.

The church at **Pomata**, which is being restored, is spectacular, with beautiful **Pomata** carvings, in Andean *mestizo* baroque, of vases full of tropical plants, flowers and animals in the window frames, lintels and cornices, and a frieze of dancing figures inside the dome – which is unusual in Peru – and alabaster windows (John Hemming). For accommodation, ask for Sra Rosa Pizano, on the plaza, No 30.

The church at **Zepita** is also worth visiting.

On the road to Juli is Ilave, where the road for Tacna branches off. It is typical **Ilave** of a gaunt *altiplano* town, with a good Sunday market where you can buy woven goods. Many buses and colectivos go there from Puno (US$1.40). Ilave-Tacna: (320 kilometres), US$6, 16 hours, at 1400 and 1700 with Trans Ponce (the best), and Gironda.

Sillustani

A highly recommended trip is to the *chullpas* (precolumbian funeral towers) of Sillustani in a beautiful setting on a peninsula in Lake Ayumara, 32 kilometres from Puno on an excellent road.

"Most of the towers date from the period of Inca occupation in the 15th century, but they are burial towers of the Aymara-speaking Colla tribe. The engineering involved in their construction is more complex than anything the Incas built – it is defeating archaeologists' attempts to rebuild the tallest 'lizard' *chullpa*. Two are unfinished: one with a ramp still in place to raise blocks; the other with cut stones ready to go onto a very ambitious corbelled false dome. A series of stone circles to the east of the site are now thought to be the bases of domed thatch or peat living huts, rather than having any religious meaning. The quarry near the towers is also worth seeing." (John Hemming).

There are local people at the site, in traditional costume, who sell drinks and some handicrafts. Guides are also available here. Photographers will find the afternoon light best, though this is when the wind is at its strongest and can kick up a mini-sandstorm. It's also best not to wear contact lenses. The scenery is barren desert, but nonetheless impressive. On the lake before the ruins there are flamingos and ducks. Take warm clothing, water and sun protection. The site has a restaurant (but no electricity) and a museum by the entrance gate.

There are Inca ruins at Tancatanca and Caluxo.

Lake Titicaca

☞ *The sacred lake*

Lake Titicaca has played a dominant role in Andean beliefs for over two millenia. This, the highest navigable body of water in the world, is the most sacred lake in the Andes.

From the lake's profound, icy depths emerged the Inca creator deity, Viracocha. Legend has it that the sun god had his children, Manco Capac and his sister, Mama Ocllo, spring from the its waters to found Cusco and the Inca dynasty.

The name Titicaca derives from the word 'titi', an Aymara mountain cat and the Quechua word 'caca' meaning rock. The rock refers to the Sacred Rock on the Isla del Sol (on the Bolivian side) which was worshipped by the pre-Incan people on the island. The mountain cat inhabited the shores of the lake and is said to have visited the Isla del Sol occasionally.

The link between the rock and the cat comes from the legend that the ancient indigenous people saw the eyes of a mountain cat gleaming in the Sacred Rock and so named it Titicaca, or Rock of the Mountain Cat. It was this that gave rise to the idea of the sun having its home there.

The titi has characteristics – such as its aquatic ability and the brilliance of its eyes – that conceptually link it with a mythological flying feline called ccoa. The role of the ccoa was (and in some parts still is) important throughout the Andes. It is believed to have thrown lightning from its eyes, urinated rain (hence the expression), spit hail and roared thunder. It was generally associated with the gods that coolled the weather.

Among indigenous people today the ccoa is believed to be one of the mountain god's servants and lives in the mountains. It is closely involved in their daily life and is considered the most feared of the spirits as it uses lightning and hail.

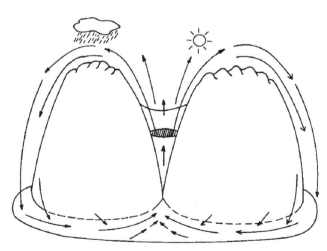

The origin and circulation of the waters of Lake Titicaca as perceived by the Incas

■Entrance US$2.25. Take an organized tour, which lasts about three to four hours and leaves at 1430. Some tours include transport and entrance fee, about US$7-8. Some offer only transport and cost US$3, meaning it is cheaper to pay the entrance fee at the site. A bus, including site entrance, leaves from C Tacna at 1430, and costs US$5. Alternatively, take a Juliaca bus to the Sillustani turnoff (US$0.35); from here a 15-kilometre paved road runs across the altiplano to the ruins. Moto-taxis and some kombis run to Atuncolla (10 kilometres away with a lovely colonial church), US$0.40, or US$0.85 to Sillustani. Go early to avoid tour groups at the site. A taxi from Puno costs about US$25.

A lasting tradition

One of the most enduring textile traditions in Peru is found among the people of Taquile. Each family possesses at least four different types of costume: for work; leisure; weddings and festivals.

For weddings, which all take place on 3 May, when the planet Venus – Hatun Chaska – is visible, the bridegroom wears a red poncho provided by the best man. As a single man he wore a half red, half white cap, but to signify his married status he wears a long red hat and a wide red wedding belt, or chumpi. His bag for coca leaves, ch'uspa, is also filled.

The bride wears a wide red hat (montera) and her hands are covered with a ritual cloth (katana-oncoma). A quincha, a small white cloth symbolizing purity, is hidden in her skirt. With her red wedding blouse, or gonna, she wears a gathered skirt or pollera, made from 20 different layers of brightly-coloured cloth. She also wears a belt (faja) and black cloak known as a chukoo.

The wool used for weaving is usually spun by the women, but on Taquile men spin wool, as well as knitting their conical hats (chullos). In fact, only the men on Taquile know how to knit. By the age of 10, a boy can knit his own Chullo Santa María, which is white-tipped to show single status. When he marries, or moves in with a woman, he adopts the red-tipped chullo, which is exclusive to the island. Today, much of the wool for knitting is bought ready-spun from factories in Arequipa.

The Islands

Coloured map 6, grid B2

The Uros 'floating islands' are made of piles of reeds. Though the Uros people on the islands have intermarried with the Aymara and no pure Uros exist, the present Puno Bay people still practise some Uro traditions. Aymara influence, however, predominates. The islanders fish, hunt birds and live off the lake plants, most important of which are the reeds they use for their boats, houses and the very foundations of their five islands.

Though tourism has eased the flow of islanders to the mainland to escape the grinding poverty, its effects have been criticised. Tourism has not only opened their simple, private lives to the glare of cameras and camcorders, but has also helped to erode much of their proud culture as the Uros people have modified their traditional ways to cater for tourists' tastes.

The islands furthest from Puno are most worth seeing but some visitors find this 'peep show' a rather uncomfortable and unsettling experience. Also many tourists report that though the people are friendly, they are very poor and consequently visitors are subjected to a hard-sell approach for handicrafts. Some have dubbed the islands the 'floating souvenir stalls'. You'll also be constantly asked for 'tips', though this is less persistent out of season. Rather than giving the children money or gifts, you could buy their little reed boats or give fruit. There is no drinking water on the floating islands and you need to be careful where you walk, as the surface can be very unsteady underfoot.

■*Motorboats charging upwards of US$3.50 per person take tourists to the islands. Prices should not be over US$5-6 (which is what agencies charge in season). Pay half before you leave and half on your return. Boats leave from the harbour in Puno about every 30 minutes from about 0630 till 1000, or whenever there are 10 or more people to fill the boat, and take three to five hours. Local boats may also be hired. The earlier you go the better, to beat the crowds of tourists. Out of season there are no regular boats, so either get a group together and pay US$10 for the boat, rent a boat at US$1-2 per person, or pay an agency US$15-20.*

Uros

Lake Titicaca

Taquile An altogether more pleasant and interesting experience is to visit the island of Taquile, some 45 kilometres from Puno, where there are numerous pre-Inca and Inca ruins, and Inca terracing. The island is quiet and hospitable, except at the height of the season, when it has been described as "touristy".

The island is only about one kilometre wide and six to seven kilometres long. On the north side of the island is the warmest part of Lake Titicaca. Ask for the (unmarked) museum of traditional costumes and also where you can see and photograph local weaving. There is a cooperative shop on the plaza that sells exceptional woollen goods which are not cheap but of very fine quality. They are cheaper in the market at Puno. Travellers report that you need to spend a night on Taquile to really appreciate its stark beauty and, therefore, it may be better to travel independently and go at your own pace.

Numerous festivals take place on the island. These include: *Semana Santa*, a festival from the 2 to 7 June, the *Fiesta de Santiago*, held over two weeks in mid-July, and on the 1 and 2 August, the principal festival days, with many dances in between.

The influx of tourists unfortunately prompts persistent requests for sweets and money which irritates many travellers. Above all, stay good-humoured. You will have to listen to at least one hastily-formed *peña* band and pay for the privilege, and don't be surprised if some familiar faces show up later under the guise of a different band. Gifts of fruit, torches (there is no electricity), moisturizer or sun block (the children suffer sore cheeks), pens, pencils or notebooks are appreciated. Buy their handicrafts instead of handing out sweets indiscriminately, eg friendship bracelets.

You are advised to take with you some food, particularly fruit, bread and vegetables, water, plenty of small-value notes, candles and a torch. Take precautions against sunburn. The same applies to Amantaní (see below).

Plentiful accommodation can be found in private houses but it is best to take warm clothes and a sleeping bag. Apparently the islanders refused to allow any hotels to be built on the island to help preserve their way of life. No previous arrangements can be made. On arrival you walk up a steep path for 30 minutes (remember you are at 3,800 metres, so don't try to break any records), are greeted by the locals, pay a US$0.10 fee, sign the guest book and, if wishing to stay, are 'assigned' a family to stay with, which costs **F-G** per person, including all meals.

There are several small restaurants on the island; eg *El Inca* on the main plaza. Fish is plentiful and the island has a trout farm, but meat is rarely available and drinks often run out. Meals are a little more expensive than on the mainland.

■*Boats leave Puno harbour daily at 0800-0900. The journey takes four hours. Boats return at 1400/1430, arriving in Puno at 1830. It costs US$4.50 one way. This doesn't leave enough time to appreciate the island fully in one day. Organized tours can be arranged for about US$10-16 per person, but only give you about two hours on the island. Boats sometimes call at Uros on the outward or return journey. Make sure you and the boatman know exactly what you are paying for.*

Amantaní Another island well worth visiting, is Amantaní. It is very beautiful and peaceful, and many say is less spoiled, more genuine and friendlier than Taquile. There are six villages and ruins on both of the island's peaks, Pacha Tata and Pacha Mama, from which there are excellent views. There are also temples and on the shore there is a throne carved out of stone.

On both hills, a fiesta is celebrated on 15 January (or thereabouts). The festivities in January have been reported as spectacular, very colourful,

Mother Earth

Pachamama, or Mother Earth, occupies a very privileged place in Aymara culture because she is the generative source of life. The Aymara believe that Man was created from the land, and thus he is fraternally tied to all the living beings that share the earth. According to them, the earth is our mother, and it is on the basis of this understanding that all of human society is organized, always maintaining the cosmic norms and laws.

Women's and men's relationship with nature is what the Aymara call ecology, harmony and equilibrium. The Aymara furthermore believe that private land ownership is a social sin because the land is for everyone. It is meant to be shared and not only used for the benefit of a few.

Vicenta Mamani Bernabé of the Andean Regional Superior Institute of Theological Studies states: "Land is life because it produces all that we need to live. Water emanates from the land as if from the veins of a human body, there is also the natural wealth of minerals, and pasture grows from it to feed the animals. Therefore, for the Aymaras, the Pachamama is sacred and since we are her children, we are also sacred. No one can replace the earth, she is not meant to be exploited, or to be converted into merchandise. Our duty is to respect and care for the earth. This is what white people today are just beginning to realize, and it is called ecology. Respect for the Pachamama is respect for ourselves as she is life. Today, she is threatened with death and must be liberated for the sake of her children's liberation."

musical and hard-drinking (so what's new!). There is also a festival on the first Sunday in March with brass bands and colourful dancers. Another fiesta is the *Aniversario del Consejo* (of the local council), which might not be as boring as it sounds.

The residents make beautiful textiles and sell them quite cheaply at the Artesanía Cooperativa. The people are Quechua speakers, but understand Spanish.

There are no hotels. You are assigned to stay with local families on a rota basis; or ask your boat owner where you can stay. Accommodation is in our **F** range. This includes three meals of remarkable similarity. If you tire of chips and rice, there is one restaurant, *Samariy*.

■*Boats from the harbour in Puno leave at 0800 daily, and return at 1430. The round trip costs US$9. The journey takes four to five hours – take water. A one day trip is not possible as the boats do not always return on the same day. Several tour operators in Puno offer two to three day excursions to Amantaní, Taquile and a visit to the floating islands. These cost US$16-30 per person, including meals, depending on the season and size of group. This gives you one night on Amantaní and three or four hours on Taquile. It may be better to visit the islands independently and go at your own pace. If you wish to visit both Taquile and Amantaní, it is better to go to Amantaní first. From there a boat goes to Taquile at around 0800, costing US$2.50 per person. There is no regular service – the boat leaves if there are enough passengers.*

Frontier with Bolivia

There are two principal routes across the border, both of which are fairly straightforward. The one listed first is by far the more popular of the two. There is a third and rarely travelled route, and, finally, it is possible to cross the border by hydrofoil or catamaran as part of a tour. All are described below.

Peruvian time is 1 hour behind Bolivian time.

Lake Titicaca

Puno to La Paz via Yunguyo and Copacabana

Leaving Peru The road is paved from Puno to Yunguyo (the border) and the scenery is interesting. The views are also good on the Bolivian side. Several agencies in Puno sell bus tickets for the direct route from Puno to La Paz, taking six to eight hours, US$13-15 (not including the Tiquina ferry crossing, US$0.20). They leave Puno at 0800 and stop at the borders and for lunch in Copacabana, arriving in La Paz at 1700. You only need to change money into Bolivianos for lunch on this route. Bus fare Puno-Copacabana is around US$4. There are local buses and colectivos all day between Puno and Yunguyo, three hours, US$2. They leave from Avda Sol in Puno. From Yunguyo to the border (Kasani), colectivos charge US$0.60 per person. From the border it is a 20-minute drive to Copacabana. Colectivos and minibuses leave from just outside Bolivian immigration, US$0.50 per person. A taxi from Yunguyo to Copacabana costs about US$1.50 per person.

At the border **Peruvian immigration** The office is five minutes' drive from **Yunguyo** (shared taxi from plaza US$0.25 per person). It is open 0700-1800. The border closes at 1900. When leaving you must get an exit stamp before crossing the border and a tourist visa on the other side. 90 days is normally given when entering Peru (30 days for Bolivia). Be aware of corruption at customs and look out for official or unofficial people trying to charge you a departure fee (say that you know it is illegal and ask why only gringos are approached to pay the 'embarkation tax').

Bolivian Consulate Near the main plaza in Yunguyo, open Monday-Friday 0830-1500, for those who need a visa. Some nationalities have to pay, eg US$12 for French, US$20 for Canadians. There is no consulate in Puno, you must get a visa here.

In **Yunguyo**: **F-G** per person *Hostal Isabel*, San Francisco 110, at Plaza de Armas, T350233, ext 19. Shared bathroom, hot water, good value, will change money and arrange transport. On the plaza are **G** *Hostal Amazonas*, with restaurant; and **G** *Hostal Yunguyo*. Both are very basic.

Exchange Good rates are available at the two *casas de cambio* in the main plaza in Yunguyo; better than at the border, and good for changing bolivianos, cash only. Travellers' cheques can be exchanged though rates are poor.

Into Bolivia The Bolivian border town of **Copacabana** is famous for its miracle-working Dark Virgin of the Lake, La Virgen de Candelaria, housed in a fine basilica. From the town, excursions can be made to Isla del Sol and Isla de la Luna on Lake Titicaca. There is a wide variety of hotels, restaurants and other services. All road transport from Copacabana to La Paz has to take the ferry across the lovely Straits of Tiquina.

Puno to La Paz via Desaguadero

Leaving Peru This is the most direct route road – 150 kilometres on a mostly paved road – passing through Chucuíto, Ilave, Juli and Pomata (see above). Desaguadero is a cold, miserable place, which straddles the border.

Colectivos and buses run frequently from Puno to Desaguadero; two and a half hours, US$2. The last bus from the border to Puno leaves at 1930. There are buses to La Paz (105 kilometres from Desaguadero), four hours, US$2-3. The last one leaves at 1700, though buses may leave later if there are enough passengers.

At the border **Immigration offices** Peruvian immigration is beside the bridge. It is open 0830-1230 and 1400-1930. Bolivian immigration is open the same hours. Both offices are usually closed for dinner around 1830-1900. 30 days is normally given on entering Bolivia, ask for more if you need it, or get an extension in La Paz. Get your exit stamp on the Peruvian side, cross the border and get an entrance stamp on the Bolivian side.

Sleeping and eating Accommodation on the Peruvian side is dubious looking to say the least: **F** *Alojamiento Internacional*. There's better accommodation on the Bolivian side at **G** per person *Hotel Bolivia*, beside the immigration office, clean, shared bathroom. There are several restaurants on both sides of the bridge.

Exchange It is better to change money (even Bolivianos) on the Peruvian side. Money changers are just before the bridge, opposite immigration.

Into Bolivia The road as far as Guaqui (22 kilometres) is in poor condition, but the rest of the road to La Paz is newly paved. This particular border crossing allows you to stop at Tiahuanaco en route.

Along the east side of Lake Titicaca

This is the most remote route, via **Huancané**, and **Moho** (the last town in Peru). The border is reached before **Puerto Acosta** (Bolivia). There is accommodation in Moho, **G**. One bus leaves on weekdays to Juliaca, seven hours, but it is often cancelled. This route is recommended only on weekends when there is more traffic. After Puerto Acosta, the road is very bad. Make sure you get an exit stamp in Puno. There is a new lodge on the island of Suasi. You can stay here en route to the border or arrange a tour from Puno. Contact: Ecotourism and Lodging Consortium, T622772/351417, F355694 (Puno), E awtperu@mail.cosapidata.com.pe.Martha Giraldo. Or book through any tour agency in Puno.

To La Paz by hydrofoil or catamaran

There are luxury services from Puno/Juli to La Paz by *Crillon Tours* hydrofoil, with connections to tours, from La Paz, to Cusco and Machu Picchu. All Puno travel agents have details, or Avda Camacho 1223, PO Box 4785, La Paz, T374566/7, F391039 (in USA: 1450 South Bayshore Drive, Suite 815, Miami, FL 33131, T(305)3585353, F3720054). The itinerary is: Puno-Copacabana by bus; Copacabana-Isla del Sol-Huatajata (Bolivia) by hydrofoil; Huatajata-La Paz by bus; 13 hours. At Huatajata *Crillon* has the **A1** *Inca Utama Hotel and Spa*, 5-star accommodation, health facilities based on natural remedies, together with the Andean Roots cultural complex (4 different museums representing 7 cultures) and an observatory. *Crillon* also has *La Posada del Inca*, a hotel in a restored colonial hacienda on the Isla del Sol. Visits to these establishments can be incorporated into *Crillon's* tours.

Similar services, by catamaran, are run by *Transturin*, whose dock is at Chúa, Bolivia; bookings through Transturin: offices in Puno at Libertad 176, ask for Esther de Quiñones, T352771; Cusco, Portal de Panes 109, oficina 1, Plaza de Armas, T222332; La Paz, Avda Mcal Santa Cruz 1295, 3rd Floor, T373881/342164.

Puno to Cusco

On the way from Puno to Cusco there is much to see from the train, which **By rail**
runs at an average altitude of 3,500 metres. At the stations on the way, people
sell food; roast lamb at Ayaviri and stuffed peppers at Sicuani. You can also
buy local specialities such as pottery bulls at Pucara (where rooms are available at the station), woollen caps, wool and rugs at Sicuani and knitted alpaca
ponchos and pullovers and miniature llamas at Santa Rosa, where rooms are
also available.

There are three hotels in **Ayaviri**, including **G** *Hostal Ayaviri*, Grau 180.
Basic and unfriendly.

The railway crosses the altiplano, climbing to **La Raya**, the highest pass
on the line; 210 kilometres from Puno, at 4,321 metres. Up on the heights
breathing may be a little difficult, but the descent along the Río Vilcanota is
rapid. To the right of **Aguas Calientes**, the next station, four kilometres from
La Raya, are steaming pools of hot water in the middle of the green grass; a
startling sight. The temperature of the springs is 40°C, and they show beautiful deposits of red ferro-oxide. The springs are not developed, but bathing is
possible to the left, where the hot spring water joins the cold creek. At
Maranganí, the river is wider and the fields greener, with groves of eucalyptus trees.

The Vilcanota plunges into a gorge, but the train winds above it and
round the side of the mountain. At **Huambutío** the railway turns left to follow
the Río Huatanay on the final stretch to Cusco. The Vilcanota here widens
into the great Urubamba canyon, flanked on both sides by high cliffs, on its
way to join the Ucayali, a tributary of the Amazon.

The road Puno-Cusco is now fully paved and in good condition. Most people **By road**
take the train but, as said above, in the wet season, trains may be cancelled.

The road climbs steadily after Juliaca, passing Pucara (see page 203) then
running through the villages of Ayaviri and Santa Rosa and on up to the pass
at La Raya.

Sicuani

38 kilometres beyond La Raya pass **Sicuani** (*Altitude*: 3,690 metres) is an
important agricultural centre and an excellent place for items of llama and
alpaca wool and skins. They are sold on the railway station and at the excellent
Sunday morning market. Around Plaza Libertad there are several hat shops
selling local hats. Sicuani lies 250 kilometres from Puno and 137 kilometres
from Cusco (bus, US$1.25). (For more information about places between
Sicuani and Cusco, see page 193.)

D *Centro Vacacional*, the best in town but some way from the centre. Recom- **Sleeping**
mended. **D** *Royal Inti*, on the west side of the old pedestrain bridge across the river.
Modern, clean and friendly. **E** *Obada*, Tacna 104, T351214. Has seen better days, large,
clean, hot showers. **E** *Tairo*, Mejía 120, T351297. Modern, noisy. **E** *Samari*, next to
Royal Inti. New, noisy. **F** *Manzanal*, Avda 28 de Julio 416. Cold shower, basic, friendly,
noisy. **G** *Quispe*, basic, no shower, friendly.

Wiphala, is a pub-restaurant on the plaza. Attractive, friendly, serves enormous por- **Eating**
tions, try the *milanesa con arroz chaufa*, but leave yourself several days to finish it.

Lake Titicaca

Recommended. Next door is *Pizzería Ban Vino*, and on the opposite side of the plaza is *Viracocha* which is OK. There are several *picanterías* such as *Mijuna Wasi*, Tacna 146, which prepares typical dishes such as *adobo* served with huge glasses of *chicha* in a delapidated but atmospheric courtyard. Recommended. In 2 de Mayo, running northeast from the plaza, there are several cafés which are good for snacks and breakfasts. *Piano Bar*, just off the first block of 2 de Mayo, is the best nightspot in town.

Alternative routes from Cusco to Arequipa

Branch roads both south and north of Sicuani lead to a road past the Tintaya mines which forms an alternative route Cusco-Arequipa. The surface is poor to the mines, but improves thereafter. It is a spectacular journey. There are several buses daily, with *Cruz del Sur* and *Chasqui*. From Sicuani, the road passes the pretty lake, Laguna Langui Layo, then climbs to a radio-transmission antenna. A few kilometres from the road is **Yauri**, isolated on a plateau by a canyon. There's accommodation at **G** *Hostal El Tigre*, nice rooms, but water shortages.

A road southwest from Yauri, requiring high clearance vehicles, leads on to Sibayo, Chivay and Arequipa. Alternatively, to the southeast, the road skirts **Laguna Condorama**, one of the highest lakes in South America (4,700 metres), past more mining operations, the Majes irrigation scheme and on to the Arequipa-Juliaca road. Sicuani to Arequipa is about 400 kilometres.

Lake Titicaca

Arequipa

Arequipa

224 Arequipa

238 Colca Canyon

241 Chivay

243 Cabanaconde

244 Trekking in the Colca Canyon

245 Toro Muerto

245 Cotahuasi Canyon

246 Cotohuasi

247 Trekking in the Cotahuasi Canyon

248 Towards the Valley of the Volcanoes

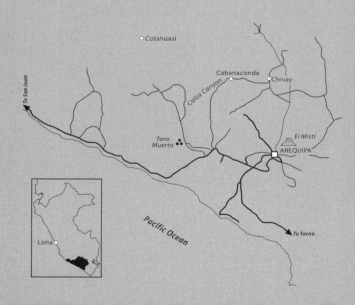

This part of southwest Peru is well-established on the tourist itinerary. The distinctive colonial architecture of the city of Arequipa is only one of the attractions in a region of smoking volcanoes, deep canyons and terraced valleys. One of these canyons, the Cotahuasi, is the deepest in the world. Another, the Colca, is home to ancient peoples whose lives, until very recently, were completely untouched by the hand of tourism. It also happens to be the best place in the whole country to get up a close up view of the majestic condor.

There's a unique feeling to this part of Peru which, in part, stems from the stubborn pride of its people who have continuously attempted to gain more independence from Lima. Fellow Peruvians will jokingly refer to this region as the "Independent Republic of Arequipa", but don't believe them when they kindly inform you of the need for a visa.

Arequipa

Population: *619,156*
Altitude: *2,380 metres*
Phone code: *054*
Coloured map 5, grid C6

The city of Arequipa (1,011 kilometres from Lima by road) stands in a beautiful valley at the foot of El Misti volcano, a snow-capped, perfect cone, 5,822 metres high, guarded on either side by the mountains Chachani (6,057 metres), and Pichu-Pichu (5,669 metres). The city has fine Spanish buildings and many old and interesting churches built of sillar, a pearly white volcanic material almost exclusively used in the construction of Arequipa.

Ins and outs

Getting there   Rodríguez Ballón airport is 7 kilometres from town. For transport to and from the airport, see page 233. The bus terminal is a 10-15 minute drive south of the centre. The train station is a 15-minute walk from the centre (see map on page 229).

Getting around   Arequipa is a nice, compact town with the main places of interest and hotels within a few blocks of the Plaza de Armas. Take a bus or taxi if you want to the visit the suburbs.

Climate   Arequipa enjoys a wonderful climate, with a mean temperature before sundown of 23°C, and after sundown of 14½°C. The sun shines on 360 days of the year. Annual rainfall is less than 150 millimetres.

Arequipa Area

○ **Places in the Colca Canyon**
1. Coporaque
2. Ichupampa
3. Lari
4. Madrigal
5. Tapay
6. Yanque
7. Achoma
8. Maca
9. Mirador Cruz del Cóndor
10. Cabanaconde

The history

The city was re-founded on 15 August 1540 by an emissary of Pizarro, but it had previously been occupied by Aymara Indians and the Incas. It has since grown into a magnificent city – arguably the most strikingly beautiful in the country – exuding an air of intellectual rigour and political passion. Among its famous sons and daughters are former President Fernando Belaunde Terry and novelist and failed presidential candidate, Mario Vargas Llosa. Now, Arequipa is the main commercial centre for the south, and its fiercely proud people resent the general tendency to believe that everything is run from Lima.

Security Theft can be a problem in the market area, especially after dark, and at the bus offices in San Juan de Dios, but the police are conspicuous, friendly, courteous and efficient. (See also below.)

Sights

The elegant **Plaza de Armas**, beautifully laid-out with palm trees, gardens and fountain, is faced on three sides by colonial arcaded buildings with many restaurants, and on the fourth by the Cathedral. Behind the cathedral there is a very attractive alley with handicraft shops.

The central **San Camilo market**, between Perú, San Camilo, Piérola and Alto de la Luna, is worth visiting, as is the **Siglo XX market**, to the east of the rail station. At **Selva Alegre** there is a shady park in front of the *Hotel Libertador*, which is within easy walking distance of all the famous churches and main plaza.

Arequipa is said to have the best-preserved colonial architecture in Peru, apart from Cusco. The oldest district is **San Lázaro**, a collection of tiny climbing streets and houses quite close to the *Hotel Libertador*, where you can find the ancient **Capilla de San Lázaro**.

A cheap tour of the city can be made in a Vallecito bus – one and a half hours for US$0.30. It is a circular tour which goes down Calles Jerusalén and San Juan de Dios.

Churches Because of the ever-present danger of earthquakes churches in the city were built low. They are usually open 0700-0900 and 1800-2000. The massive, twin-towered **Cathedral** on the Plaza de Armas was founded in 1612 and largely rebuilt in the 19th century. It is remarkable for having its façade along the whole length of the church and takes up one full side of the plaza. Inside is the fine Belgian organ and elaborately-carved wooden pulpit. The entrance to the Cathedral is on the plaza.

A visit to the church of **La Compañía**, on General Morán and Ejercicios, is recommended. The main façade (1698) and side portal (1654) are striking examples of the florid Andean *mestizo* style. Also of note is the **Capilla Real** (Royal Chapel) to the left of the sanctuary, and its San Ignacio chapel with a beautiful polychrome cupola. The stark, impressive cloister is at Morán 118 y Palacio Viejo 115. ■*Open 0900-1200, 1500-1800 daily. Entrance US$0.50.*

Also well worth seeing are the churches of **San Francisco** (Zela 103), **San Agustín** (corner of San Agustín y Sucre), the early 17th century **La Merced** (La Merced 303), and **Santo Domingo** (Santo Domingo y Piérola). Opposite San Francisco is a handicraft centre, housed in a beautiful former prison.

Arequipa

La Recoleta, a Franciscan monastery built in 1647, stands on the other side of the river, on Recoleta. It contains several cloisters, a religious art museum, a precolumbian museum, an Amazon museum, a library with many rarities, and is well worth visiting. ■*Open Monday-Friday 0900-1200, 1500-1700, Saturday 0900-1200. Entrance US$1.75. The church itself is open only 0900-1200, 1500-1800.*

The **Santa Rosa Convent** is at San Pedro y Santa Rosa. It was founded on 12 July 1747, by nuns from the much larger Santa Catalina Convent.

Santa Catalina Convent By far the most interesting visit is to the Santa Catalina Convent, opened in 1970 after four centuries of mysterious seclusion. This is the most remarkable sight in Arequipa and a complete contrast to what you would expect from nuns who had taken vows of poverty. The convent has been beautifully refurbished, with period furniture, pictures of the Arequipa and Cusco schools and fully-equipped kitchens. It is a complete miniature walled colonial town of over two hectares in the middle of the city, where about 450 nuns lived in total seclusion, except for their women servants.

The few remaining nuns have retreated to one section of the convent, allowing visitors to see a maze of cobbled streets, flower-decked cloisters and buttressed houses. These have been finely restored and painted in traditional white, browns and blues.

■*Santa Catalina 301. T229798. Open 0900-1600 daily. Entrance US$4.50. The tour they offer you at the entrance is worthwhile and lasts one and a half hours; there's no set price and many of the guides speak English. There is a small café, which sells cakes made by the nuns and a special blend of tea.*

Colonial houses Arequipa has several fine seignorial houses with large carved tympanums over the entrances. Thanks to their being one-storey structures, they have mostly withstood the earthquakes which regularly pound this city. They are distinguished by their small patios with no galleries, flat roofs and small windows, disguised by superimposed lintels or heavy grilles.

One of the best examples is the 18th century **Casa Tristan del Pozo**, better known as the **Gibbs-Ricketts house** with its fine portal and puma-head waterspouts. It is now the main office of Banco Continental, at San Francisco 108 y San José. ■*Open 1700-2000.*

Other good examples are: the **Casa del Moral**, or Williams house, which also has a museum, in the Banco Industrial, on Calle Moral 318 y Bolívar; and the **Casa Goyeneche**, La Merced 201 y Palacio Viejo, which is now an office of the Banco Central de la Reserva, ask the guards who will let you view the courtyard and fine period rooms. Also worth seeing are: **Casa de la Moneda**, at Ugarte y Villalba; **Casa de los Pastor**, at Bolívar 206, now regional administration offices; **La Casona Chávez de la Rosa**, at San Agustín 104, now part of the Universidad San Agustín (interesting art and photography exhibitions); and **Casa Irriberry** (1793), at Santa Catalina y San Agustín.

Museums Opposite the San Francisco church is the interesting **Museo Histórico Municipal** with much war memorabilia. ■*Open Monday-Friday 0800-1800. Entrance US$0.50.*

The **archaeological museum** at the Universidad de San Agustín, Avda Independencia between La Salle and Santa Rosa, has a good collection of ceramics and mummies. Apply to Dr E Linares, the Director, T229719. ■*Open Monday-Friday 0800-1400. Entrance US$1.*

The **Museo Santuarios de Altura** contains the frozen mummies recently found on Ampato volcano. The mummy known as 'Juanita' is particularly fascinating (see page 239). The museum is on block 200 of Santa Catalina on the corner with Ugarte, opposite the convent. Juanita went on tour to Japan in late 1998 and probably won't return until the end of 1999. ■*Open Monday to Saturday 0900-1830. The US$2 entry fee includes a 20 minute video of the discovery in English followed by a guided tour in English or Spanish.*

In the hillside suburb of **Cayma** is the delightful 18th century church (open only until 1600), and many old buildings associated with Bolívar and Garcilaso de la Vega. Many local buses go to Cayma. There is a new luxury *Hotel Cayma*.

Arequipa suburbs

Another suburb is **Yanahuara**, where there is a 1750 *mestizo*-style church (opens 1500), with a magnificent churrigueresque façade, all in *sillar*. Accommodation is available at **B** *Hostal Kolping*, León Velarde 406, T253748, F253744, safe. There's live music at *Peña El Moro*, on Parque Principal. A score of *picanterías* specialize in piquant foods such as *rocoto relleno* (hot stuffed peppers), *cuy chactado* (seared guinea-pig), *papas con ocopa* (boiled potatoes with a hot yellow sauce) and *adobo* (pork stew). Try them at lunchtime.

The thermal baths of Jesús are 30 minutes by car, on the slopes of Pichu-Pichu. ■*Open 0500-1230. To get there cross the Gran Puente bridge and turn right up Lima.*

Tingo, which has a very small lake and three swimming pools, should be visited on Sunday for local food such as *anticuchos* and *buñuelos*. ■*Take bus 7, US$0.20.*

Three kilometres past Tingo, beside the Sabandía river on the Huasacanche road, is **La Mansión del Fundador**. Originally owned by the founder of Arequipa, Don Garcí Manuel de Carbajal, in 1540, it has been open to the public since 1897 and restored as a museum with original furnishings and paintings. ■*Entrance US$2.50, with cafeteria and bar.* Nearby is the **Mirador Sachaca** with fine panoramic views. ■*Entrance US$0.35. Take a bus marked 'Sachaca' from C La Merced.* Four kilometres from the centre, in the district of Sachaca, is the **Palacio Goyeneche**.

Eight kilometres north of Arequipa is the **Molino de Sabandía**, the first stone mill in the area, built in 1621. There is a swimming bath and the surrounding countryside is pleasant; a worthwhile trip. ■*Entrance US$1.50. A round trip by taxi costs US$4.* Nearby is *Restaurante El Lago*, with swimming pool and horseriding. Adjoining Sabandía is **Yumina**, with many Inca terraces which are still in use.

Yura, is a pleasant town, 29 kilometres from Arequipa in a small, interesting valley on the west slopes of Chachani. It is popular with Arequipeños for its thermal baths and verdant riverside picnic spots. To reach the baths, walk down to the river from the main road by the *Yura Tourist Hotel* (see below). The first set of baths contains four small pools which are not suitable for swimming. Follow the river to the next one, which is bigger. Note that the water is not very hot. ■*Open Tuesday-Saturday, until 1500. Entrance US$1.50. To return to Arequipa, catch a colectivo on the main road by the hotel.*

There's accommodation at **D** *Yura Tourist Hotel*, with bath, meals available. Also an unsigned hotel opposite, **F**, which is good. To get there, a bus leaves every three hours from San Juan de Dios, US$0.40.

El Misti

At 5,822 metres, El Misti volcano offers a relatively straightforward opportunity to scale a high peak. Start from the hydroelectric plant, after first registering with the police there, then you need one day to the Monte Blanco shelter, at 4,800 metres. Start early for the four to six hours to the top, to get there by 1100 before the mists obscure the view. If you start back at 1200 you will reach the hydroelectric plant by 1800.

Alternatively, buses leave Arequipa for Baños Jesús, then on to Chiguata, from where you can walk to the base of El Misti. Be sure to take plenty of food and water. It takes two days to reach the crater. Guides may be available at Cachamarca. Further information is available from Carlos Zárate (see Climbing below), or some of the tour agencies.

Essentials

Sleeping
■ *on maps*
Price codes: see inside front cover

A2 *Maison d'Elise*, Avda Bolognesi 104, T256185, F271935. Attractive Mediterranean-style village with pool, large rooms, also suites and apartments, helpful staff. **A2** *Portal*, Portal de Flores 116, T215530, F234374. Excellent, wonderful views, expensive, rooftop swimming pool, *El Gaucho* restaurant. **A2** *Posada del Puente*, Avda Bolognesi 101, T253132, F253576, beside Puente Grau, alongside Río Chili. Attractive, small, friendly, good, restaurant. Recommended. **A2-3** *Libertador*, Plaza Simón Bolívar, Selva Alegre, T215110, F241933. Safe, swimming pool (cold), gardens, good meals, pub-style bar, cocktail lounge, tennis court. **A3** *El Conquistador*, Mercaderes 409, T212916, F218987. Clean, safe, lovely colonial atmosphere, owner speaks English, thin walls. **A3** *Hostal Casa Grande*, Luna Pizarro 202, Vallecito, T214000, F214021. Includes taxes, small, cosy, well-furnished, quiet, friendly, good services. Recommended. **A3** *Hostal La Gruta*, La Gruta 304, Selva Alegre, 5 minutes from the centre, T224631, E hostal_lagruta@LaRed.com.pe. Price includes breakfast, cable TV, garden, laundry, 24-hour café, fax service, parking. **A3** *Maison Plaza*, Portal San Agustín 143, T218929, F212114. With breakfast, bathroom and TV, clean, friendly, good value. **A3** *La Plazuela*, on Plaza Juan Manuel Polar 105, Vallecito (5 minutes' walk from the centre), T222624, F234625. A lovely old house next to a small park, nicely furnished, hot water 24 hours, cable TV, laundry service, cafeteria open 0600-2200, restaurant, owners speak English.

B *Crismar*, Moral 107, T215290, F239431, opposite the main Post Office. With bathroom, modern, safe, noisy, central, good restaurant. **B-C** *Casa de Mi Abuela*, Jerusalén 606, T241206, F242761. Very clean, friendly, safe, hot water, laundry, cable TV, swimming pool, rooms at the back are quieter and overlook the garden, **D** without bathroom, self-catering if desired, English spoken, tours and transport organized in own agency, which has good information (T226414), small library of European books, breakfast or evening snacks on patio or in beautiful garden, **A3-B** for apartment for 4. Highly recommended. **B-C** *Jerusalén*, C Jerusalén 601, T244441/81, F243472. Hot water, comfortable, modern, good restaurant, safe, car parking.

C *Casa de Melgar*, Melgar 108-A, T222459. Excellent rooms, with bathroom, hot water all day (solarpanel), safe, clean, friendly, nice courtyard, good breakfast. **C** *Hostal Las Mercedes*, Avda La Marina 1001, end of C Consuelo, T/F213601. Includes breakfast, they will provide sandwiches and a soft drink instead if you're going on an early morning tour, clean, safe (but its surroundings are not too secure), snacks available. Highly recommended. **C** *La Hostería*, Bolívar 405, T/F289269. Small, friendly, comfortable and attractive. Recommended. **C** *Miamaka*, San Juan de Dios 402, T241496, F227906. Excellent service, helpful, English spoken. Highly recommended. **C** *Villa Baden Baden*, Manuel Ugarte 401, Selva Alegre, T222416. Run by Sra Bluemel de Castro, 6 rooms, breakfast included, German, French and English spoken, very informative about the area and climbing, safe. Recommended.

Arequipa

12. Hostal Regis
13. Hostal Santa Catalina
14. Hostal Tumi de Oro
15. Jerusalén
16. La Bóveda Inn & Lashmivan Restaurant
17. Libertador
18. Lluvia de Oro
19. Maison D'Elise
20. Maison Plaza
21. Portal
22. Posada del Puente
23. Res Rivero
24. Tambo Viejo

● **Eating & Bars**
1. Anushka
2. Balcón Arequipa
3. Blues Bar

4. Bonanza
5. Café Manolo
6. Central Garden
7. Govinda
8. La Rueda
9. Las Quenas
10. Monza
11. Pizzería Los Leños
12. Pizzería San Antonio
13. Romie (Bar)

🚌 **Buses**
1. Cruz del Sur buses
2. Ormeño buses

○ **Other**
1. AeroPerú & Aero Continente
2. Ideal Travels

■ **Sleeping**
1. Americano
2. Casa de Melgar
3. Casa de mi Abuela
4. Crillón Serrano & Tito
5. Crismar
6. El Conquistador
7. Hostal Casa Grande
8. Hostal El Cóndor
9. Hostal La Portada del Mirador
10. Hostal La Reyna
11. Hostal Núñez

N

0   metres   100
0   yards   109

To bus station & the South

D *El Gobernador*, Rivero 303, T244433. With bathroom, **E** without, hot water, safe motorcycle parking, good beds, luggage store. Recommended. **D** per person *Hostal El Solar*, C Ayacucho 108, T/F241793. Nice colonial building, clean rooms with cable TV, private bathroom, hot water 24 hours, includes breakfast served in nice patio, very secure, quiet. Recommended. **D** *Hostal Le Foyer*, Ugarte 114 y San Francisco, T286473. Beautiful colonial house, hot water 24 hours, laundry, luggage store, safe, helpful, breakfast included (though not always ready for 0730). Recommended. **D** *Hostal Tumi de Oro*, San Agustín 311A, 2½ blocks from the Plaza de Armas, T281319, F231633. With bathroom, cheaper without, French and English spoken, hot water, roof terrace, tea/coffee facilities, safe. Recommended. **D-E** *Hostal Bolívar*, esquina Bolívar y Moral. Colonial-style, recently renovated, breakfast served in patio. Recommended. **D-E** *Posada de Sancho*, Santa Catalina 213 A, near the convent, T287797. Hot showers 24 hours (usually), clean, safe, nice patio and terrace with a view of El Misti, good breakfast, very friendly owners, English and German spoken, good travel information, offer cheap tours but rather pushy.

E *Americano*, C Alvarez Tomás 435, T211752. In an unsafe area, hot shower at any time, clean, safe hotel, friendly, doors close at 2130. **E** *Crillón Serrano*, C Perú 109, T212392. With bathroom, hot water all day, but you must pay for water to wash clothes, very friendly and welcoming, roof terrace with great views. **E** *Embajador*, Jerusalén 619, T281048. With bathroom, cheaper without, hot water, helpful, English-speaking staff. **E** *Hostal El Cóndor*, San Juan de Dios 525, T213323. Clean, good. **E** *Hostal Fernández*, Quesada 106, Yanahuara, T254152. 10 minutes from the centre, good for a longer stay, beautiful garden with parrot, views of El Misti, family affair, safe, breakfasts, hot water, clean. Recommended. **E** *Hostal La Portada del Mirador*, Portal de Flores 102, Plaza de Armas, T211539. Basic, clean, safe, friendly, will store luggage, great views from the roof. **E** *Hostal Núñez*, Jerusalén 528, T233268. With bathroom, cheaper without, hot water, laundry, safe, friendly, a bit neglected but still clean and a good place to meet other travellers, small rooms, breakfast on roof terrace overlooking the city. Recommended. **E** *Hostal Regis*, Ugarte 202, T226111. Colonial house, French-style interior, clean, hot water all day, cooking and laundry facilities, sun terrace with good views, safe, luggage store, new rooms being built. Recommended. **E** *Hostal Santa Catalina*, Santa Catalina 500, T233705. Clean, hot water, friendly, noisy, safe, luggage stored. Recommended. **E** *La Bóveda Inn*, Jerusalén 402, above *Lashmivan* restaurant, T281685. Clean, safe, good showers, friendly, nice patio. Recommended. **E** *Lluvia de Oro*, Jerusalén 308, T214252, F235730. English-speaking, breakfast US$2, good views, friendly. Recommended. **E** *Residencial Rivero*, Rivero 420, T229266. With bathroom, clean, friendly, helpful, washing facilities. Recommended but not a very safe area.

F per person *Albergue El Misti*, Salaverry 302, 3 blocks from the rail station, T/F245760. Family rooms with bathroom, singles and shared rooms in an elegant old mansion, arranges cultural tours, also Spanish classes. **F** *Colonial House Inn*, Puente Grau 114, T/F223533. Hot water, big rooms, quieter rooms at the back, good breakfast. **F** per person *Hostal La Reyna*, Zela 209, T286578. Shared bathroom, hot water 24 hours, clean, very friendly, the daughter speaks a little English, great breakfast for US$1.15, other meals available, rooftop seating, will store luggage and arrange trips to the Colca Canyon. Excellent value and very highly recommended. **F** per person *Tambo Viejo*, Avda Malecón Socabaya 107, IV Centenario, T288195, F284747, 6 blocks south of the plaza near the rail station. Family home, quiet, very friendly, nice garden, hot water 24 hours, laundry, cable TV, breakfast available (including vegetarian), book exchange, money changed, excellent. Very highly recommended. **F** per person *Tito*, C Perú 105-B, T234424. Shared bathroom, good value, friendly.

G *Hostal Moderno*, Alto de la Luna 106. Large rooms, laundry, hot water, safe. Recommended.

Central Garden, San Francisco 127. Good food. *Sol de Mayo*, Jerusalén 207, T254148. **Eating:** Excellent traditional Aruiqapeña food. Recommended. *Anushka*, Santa Catalina 204. **expensive** Open 1800-2300, or later if busy, live music, Friday and Saturday, German specialities, ● *on maps* friendly, handicrafts are sold on the same premises. *La Rueda*, Mercaderes 206. Excellent *parrilladas*. *Las Quenas*, San Catalina 215, opposite the convent. Excellent food, also a *peña* in the evening.

Tradición Arequipa, Avda Dolores 111, Paucarpata, T242385. High quality restaurant **Eating:** serving excellent food, popular with tourists and locals alike. *Monza*, Santo Domingo **mid-range** 1½ blocks from the plaza. Good set meal and breakfast. *Bacuch*, Melgar 413. Good Swiss food. *Balcón Arequipa*, Merced y Bolognesi. Good view over the plaza. Popular with the locals, good breakfasts and fruit juice, slow service. *El Fogón*, Santa Marta 112. Serves large steaks and chops, good. *Bonanza*, Jerusalén 114-116. For meat and pasta dishes, very good. *Pizzería San Antonio*, Jerusalén y Santa Marta. Popular with locals and tourists. *Pizzería Los Leños*, Jerusalén 407, near San Francisco. Excellent, good atmosphere, evenings only.

El Dólar, San Juan de Dios 106. Clean, cheap, friendly, all meals available. Recom- **Eating:** mended. *Pizza Presto*, Gen Morán 108. Good. *Mister Pollo*, Avda Estados Unidos, Urb **cheap** 13 de Enero. Good, cheap chicken and chips. On the same street is *El Good Fish*. Good set meals. There are many other cheap restaurants on Avda Estados Unidos. *André de París*, better known as *El Emperador*, Santa Catalina 207. Excellent set lunches. *Harumi*, San José 216. Snack bar and Chinese food, good value. *Café El Buho*, in Casona Chávez de la Rosa. Good set lunch for US$1.50 with a choice of dishes. Recommended. *Caffe Boveda*, Portal San Agustín 129. In an attractive renovated 'portal', serves good value breakfasts and lunches, US$2 set lunch. *La Canasta*, Jerusalén 115. Bakes excellent baguettes twice daily, also serves breakfast and delicious apple and brazil nut pastries. At Jerusalén 603, Jutta Grau and Carlos Gutierrez bake wonderful German breads. They speak English, French and German and donate all profits to the disadvantaged.

Typical Arequipeño food is available at the San Camilo market. A good local speciality is Mejía cheese. You should also try the *queso helado*, which is frozen fresh milk mixed with sugar and a sprinkling of cinnamon. The local chocolate is excellent as is the toffee and the fruit drinks called *papayada* and *tumbada*, which are local specialities in the market and restaurants. Try *Casa Tropical*, on the first block of Rivero for a huge selection.

Govinda, Jerusalén 505. Excellent set meal for US$1.25, good yoghurt and muesli **Eating:** (also called *Madre Natura*, which has a branch at Grau 310). Recommended. **vegetarian** *Lashmivan*, Jerusalén 402. Good set lunch for US$1.25, pleasant courtyard. *Come y Vive Mejor*, C Nueva 410A. Cheap and good. *Mathesis*, Jerusalén 224. A bit more expensive than the others. *La Avellana*, Santa Marta 317-B. Good, cheap lunch *menú*.

Café Manolo, Mercaderes 113. Great cakes and coffee. *Pastelería Salón de Té*, **Cafés** Mercaderes 325. Very clean, open early, good breakfasts. *Café Suri*, on the Plaza. For sandwiches and pastries. *El Café*, San Francisco 125. Popular meeting place. *Café Forum*, San Francisco 156. Smart, popular with young locals.

Bars *Romie*, Zela 202, T234465, bar with *peña*, Tuesday-Saturday. *Blues Bar*, San **Bars &** Francisco 319-A, T233796. Plays classic blues and often has live rock, US$5 cover if live **nightclubs** band is playing, includes a drink, drinks US$1.50, very popular. *Video Bar*, on Jerusalén. *El Barril*, Moral y Jerusalén. Serves snacks, good pisco sour.

Arequipa

Discos *Discoteca Casablanca*, Avda Sucre, Puente Bolognesi. Garage entrance, clean, well-run and safe, pool room downstairs. *Disco Fragavoss*, Santa Catalina 109-A, T232651. Young crowd. Recommended. There are many good discos on Avda Ejército in the suburb of Yanahuara.

Peñas *El Sillar*, Santa Catalina 215, T215468. Salón concierto. Typical folk music, open Monday-Saturday from 2000. Recommended. *Peña Waykopac*, Jerusalén 204. Good atmosphere, open Friday and Saturday. *Peña Chunenea*, Pasaje la Catedral 4. *Peña Boveda*, Portal San Agustín 129. Due to open on the first floor in 1999. Watch out for the local folk-music group Chachani, said to be one of Peru's best.

Festivals   In **January** is *El Día del Reyes* in the district of Tiabaya, traditionally celebrated by shaking the fruit from pear trees. On **10 January** *Sor Ana de Los Angeles y Monteagudo* is a festival for the patron saint of Santa Catalina monastery. On **2-3 February** the *Fiesta de la Virgen de la Candelaria* is celebrated in the churches of Cayma, Characato, Chiguata and Chapi with masses, processions of the Virgin through the streets, and fireworks.

On **3 March** the *Fiesta de La Amargura* is a movable feast in Paucarpata, during which the Passion Play is enacted in the main plaza. *Domingo de Cuaresma*, in the district of Tiabaya, is also dedicated to Jesus Christ. Residents gather in the plaza and carry the cross from there up to a nearby hilltop, crossing the Río Chili.

The **Semana Santa** celebrations in Arequipa are carried out *Sevillano* style, with the townsfolk turned out in traditional mourning dress. There are huge processions every night, culminating in the burning of an effigy of Judas on **Easter Sunday** in the main plazas of Cayma and Yanahuara, and the reading of his 'will', containing criticisms of the city authorities. Afterwards, people retire to the *picanterías* to partake of a little *Adobo a la Antaño* with some *pan de tres puntas*.

On **1 May** the *Fiesta de la Virgen de Chapi* is a great pilgrimage to the sanctuary of Chapi and one of the most important religious ceremonies in the region. May is known as the *'Month of the Crosses'*, with ceremonies on hilltops throughout the city. On **15 May** the popular fiesta of **San Isidro Labrador** takes place in Sachaca, Chuquibamba and other towns and villages in the valley, and lasts for 7 days.

On **13 June** a remembrance of San Antonio de Padua, patron of hopeless cases, is held in the churches of Tingo Grande and San Francisco, among others. On **29 June**, in the district of Yanahuara, the Fiesta de San Juan, the local patron saint, is held with a mass and fireworks.

On **6-31 August** is the *Fiesta Artesanal del fundo El Fierro*, a sale and exhibition of artesanía from all parts of Peru, taking place beside Plaza San Francisco. At the same time, **6-17 August** is the celebration of the *city's anniversary*; various events are held, including music, dancing and exhibitions. On the eve of the actual day, the 15th, there is a splendid firework display in the Plaza de Armas and a decorated float parade. There is also a mass ascent of El Misti from the Plaza de Armas. It is virtually impossible to find a hotel room during the celebrations. On **30 August** *El Día de Santa Rosa* is celebrated in the churches of Tomilla, Cayma and Huancarqui in the Majes Valley.

In Arequipa **November** is also the month of the traditional *guaguas*, which are *bizcochos* filled with *manjar*.

Shopping   Arequipa is an excellent place to buy top quality alpaca knitwear. The *Condor Tips* factory at Avda Tahuaycani, in Sachaca district, 10 minutes from the centre by taxi, and *Alpaca 111*, Jerusalén 115, Of 208, T212347, are both recommended for high-quality alpaca and wool products. *Lanificio*, La Pampilla sin número, T225305, is a factory selling high-quality alpaca cloth at better prices than Lima outlets. At *Fundo del Fierro* shop 14, on Plaza San Francisco, alpaca-wool handicrafts from Callalli in the Colca canyon are sold.

Bookshops There are good bookshops near the Post Office. For international magazines, look along C San Francisco, between Mercaderes and San José. Old books and magazines are bought and sold at *Compra y Venta de Libros y Revistas*, on C Puente Grau.

Hairdressing *Peluquería Adán y Eva*, Piérola 108, haircut for US$2.70. *Peluquería La Favorita*, Mercaderes 130.

Markets There are also markets which are good for general handicrafts. The covered market opposite the Teatro Municipal in C Mercaderes is recommended for knitted goods, bags, etc. Also worth a try is the market around Valdivia and Nicolas de Piérola. The large artesanía market behind the old prison on Plaza San Francisco is also worth a visit.

Casa Secchi, Avda Víctor Andrés Belaunde 124, in Umacollo (near the aeroplane statue), sells good arts, crafts and clothing. Also *Artesanías Peruanas*, Puente Bolognesi 147, and *Empresa Peruana de Promoción Artesanal (EPPA)*, Gen Morán 120.

Arequipa is also noted for its leather work. The main street of saddlers and leather workers is Puente Bolognesi. The handicraft shop in the old prison opposite San Francisco is particularly good for bags. *Sombrería El Triunfino*, N de Piérola 329-331, has a good selection of hats, but is expensive. *El Zaguán*, Santa Catalina 105, is good for handicrafts. There are 3 antique shops in C Santa Catalina. There are several shops in San Camilo and Mercaderes selling good fake top label jeans at low prices (no larger sizes).

Photography Sr Fernando Delange, N-10 Urbanización Adepa, T233120, repairs all kinds of electrical equipment as well as cameras. *Foto Esparza*, Mercaderes 132-2, English spoken, cameras mended. *Foto Mundo Color*, San Francisco 218-A, will develop good quality prints in 1 hour, US$3.50 for 24.

Watch repairs *Cáceres e Hijos*, San Francisco 123.

Car hire & taxis National, Bolívar 25, US$70 per day including tax, insurance and **Transport** 200 kilometres; **Avis**, Puente Bolognesi near plaza. **Car repairs**: *Automec*, Avda Tahuaycani cuadra 2, Tahuaycani. **Bicycle repairs and equipment**: *Hoz Trek Bicicletas*, Villalba 428, T223221. **Taxi**: US$4-5 from the airport to the city (can be shared) US$1 from the bus terminal or the railway station to the Plaza de Armas. *Nova Taxi*, T252511. *Fono Car*, T212121. *Telemóvil*, T221515. *Taxitur*, T422323.

Air connections Rodríguez Ballón airport is 7 kilometres from town, T443464. To and from **Lima**, several flights daily with AeroPerú and Aero Continente. A special tourist fare may be available from as low as US$65, so shop around. Also daily flights to **Tacna**, to **Cusco**, and to **Juliaca**.

A reliable means of transport to and from the airport to the hotel of your choice is with *King Tours*, T243357/283037, US$1.20 per person. You need to give 24 hours notice for the return pick-up from your hotel. The journey takes 30-40 minutes depending on the traffic. **Transport to the airport** may be arranged when buying a ticket at a travel agency, for US$1 per person, but it's not always reliable. **Local buses** go to about 500 metres from the airport.

Buses All buses leave from the main terminal at Avda Andrés A Cáceres sin número, Parque Industrial, opposite *Inca Tops* factory, south of the train station; 15 minutes from the centre by colectivo US$0.20, or taxi US$1.75 (10 minutes). A terminal tax of US$0.35 must be paid on entry. All the bus companies have their offices in the terminal, though a few also have offices on and around C San Juan de Dios (5-6 blocks from

Plaza de Armas): *Ormeño*, San Juan de Dios 657, T218885/227852; *Transportes Zevallos*, San Juan de Dios 621, T216325; *Flores Hnos*, 28 de Julio 106-108, T244988; *Cruz del Sur*, Avda Salaverry 121, T213905/238447. Tickets can be bought here in advance, saving a long hike to the terminal.

Warning Theft is a serious problem in the bus station area and the surrounding restaurants. Take a taxi to and from the bus station and do not wander around with your belongings. Be very careful on San Juan de Dios at all times.

To **Lima**, 1,011 kilometres, 16-18 hours, 'normal' service US$9, 'Imperial' US$22 (video, toilet, meals, comfortable seats, blankets) several daily; *Ormeño* (T219126, or San Juan de Dios 657, T218885) and *Cruz del Sur* (T232014, or Avda Salaverry 121, T213905) are recommended. The road is paved but drifting sand and breakdowns may prolong the trip. Buses will stop at the major cities en route, but not always Pisco. The desert scenery is spectacular.

To **Nasca**, 566 kilometres, 9 hours, US$9, several buses daily, mostly at night and most buses continue to Lima. Beware, some bus companies to Nasca charge the Lima fare. To **Moquegua**, 213 kilometres, 3 hours, US$4, several buses and colectivos daily. To **Ilo**, several buses daily, 5½ hours, US$5, also Servicio Imperial with *Cruz del Sur* (a/c, movies, hostess), 4 hours, US$7. To **Tacna**, 320 kilometres, 6-7 hours, US$5, several buses daily; also by colectivo, *Expreso Tacna* (San Juan de Dios 537, T213281), who will collect you from your hotel, US$7.

To **Cusco**, 521 kilometres, 12-15 hours (longer in the rainy season), US$10-12, several buses daily (Cruz del Sur and Chasqui at 0700) and in the evenings. It's best to travel by day for the superb scenery. The road is good as far as Espinar, reaching nearly 5,000 metres near Condorama, but poor thereafter to Sicuani. To **Juliaca**, 279 kilometres, 8-9 hours, US$5-8; colectivos charge US$12 and take 8 hours in the dry season, leaving from C Salaverry when full. Most buses and colectivos, of which a few go daily, continue to Puno, another 44 kilometres, 30 minutes. Mudslides are a problem in the rainy season and the road is in poor condition, it also gets bitterly cold at night. Direct to **Puno**, 297 kilometres, 8½-10 hours, US$10-11, buses daily at 1600 and 1700; colectivo US$12, 9 hours (all services take longer in the wet). Although the route does not go via Juliaca, the road conditions are identical. **NB** Check on the security situation before travelling Arequipa-Cusco by overnight bus.

Trains The railway system goes from Arequipa to **Juliaca**, where it divides, one line going north to **Cusco**, the other south to **Puno**. (See also under Puno, page 209 and Cusco, page 164.)

To **Juliaca-Puno**: the train leaves on Sunday and Wednesday (also Friday in the high season) at 2100. It arrives in Juliaca at 0600-0630, and in Puno at 0700-0730. The train returns from Puno on Monday and Friday at 1945, arrives in Juliaca at 2045 and then arrives in Arequipa on Monday and Friday at 0600. To **Cusco**: the train leaves at 2100 and arrives at 1800 (see also under Juliaca, page 203). Trains are subject to delays and cancellation in the rainy season, always check.

There are four different **classes**: 2nd class, no seat reservations, not recommended; 1st class, reserved seats, but anyone is allowed into the carriage (it's a good local experience if you don't mind watching your belongings all the time); Pullman (*turismo ejecutivo*) class, with closed doors, only ticket holders are allowed in the carriage, heating, blankets provided, safer and warmer than 1st or 2nd but not any more comfortable; and Inca class, with reclining seats and video, only ticket holders are allowed in the carriage. You can travel all the way through if you stay in the same class; you only need change trains in Juliaca when changing classes. **Fares**: Arequipa-Puno, 2nd class US$9, 1st class US$11, pullman US$19, Inca US$23. Arequipa-Cusco: Económico US$14, Pullman US$30.

Tickets are now sold the day before departure. If you wish to reserve a seat in advance, you must pay a deposit (if the ticket seller doesn't mention a deposit, remind them of it). It is wise to reserve tickets at least 48 hours before the day of departure, especially if you're travelling on weekends or public holidays. The ticket office is at Avda Tacna y Arica 201; for reservations T223600, information T233928/229012; open 0630-1030, 1400-1800 Monday-Friday; 0800-1200, 1500-1800 on Saturday and Sunday. You can buy tickets through travel agencies (check date and seat number). Try to board the train as early as possible as there isn't much room for luggage.

Warning Theft is a major problem on 1st and 2nd class. Thieves are very well-organized and work in groups, using all the tricks to distract you while someone else steals your bags. The best way is to lock your luggage on the rack and watch it (it is easier if you have only one bag). Pay attention at all times and do not leave the train. Sit with a group if possible to help each other. Always have a torch/flashlight to hand. The Pullman class from Arequipa to Juliaca is recommended because it is safest at night. Take a taxi to and from the train station and do not hang around the station area. Also, if you feel bad on the train ask for the oxygen mask at once.

Directory

Airline offices All airline offices are on the Plaza de Armas: *AeroPerú*, Portal San Agustín 145, T211616. *Aero Continente*, Portal San Agustín 113, T219914/219788. *Servicios Aéreos AQP*, T242030/216767. For private hire and tourist flights to the Colca Canyon. Most tour agencies sell air tickets. Prices are quoted in dollars but payment is in soles so check exchange rate carefully.

Banks *Banco Internacional*, Mercaderes 217. Exchanges Citicorp TCs. *Banco de Crédito*, Santo Domingo y Jerusalén. Accepts Visa Card and gives good rates, no commission. Recommended. *Banco Continental*, La Uruguaya Department Store, Mercaderes 133. *Banco del Sur del Perú*, C Jerusalén, close to the Post Office. Changes TCs, low rates, accepts Mastercard, has ATM for withdrawals with Visa. *Arequipa Inversiones*, Jerusalén 190-C, T238033. *Sergio A del Carpio D*, Jerusalén 126, T242987. Good rates for dollars. *Diners Club*, San Francisco 112. It is almost impossible to change TCs on Sat afternoon or Sun. Try to find a sympathetic street changer. Better rates for cash dollars in banks and *casas de cambio*. Also try some tour agencies such as *Ideal Travel*, *Lima Tours* or *Via Tours* (see below).

Climbing: *Zárate Expeditions*, Avda Alfonso Ugarte 305, Urb Jesús María, Paucarpata, T/F463624. Run by brothers Carlos and Miguel Zárate of the Mountaineering Club of Peru. They are highly recommended mountaineers and explorers, they have good information and advice and rent some equipment.

Communications The central **Post Office** is at Moral 118, opposite *Hotel Crismar*. Letters can only be posted at the Post Office during opening hours. Mon-Sat, 0800-2000, Sun 0800-1400. **Telephone and fax** at Alvarez Thomas y Palacio Viejo. **DHL:** T281365, for sending documents and money. Also Western Union representative. **Internet:** *Centro Internet UNSA*, San Agustín 115, T218781, E postmaster@cim.unsa.edu.pe. Open Mon-Sat 0900-1900, US$1 per 30 mins. *Café Internet*, at Club Internacional, Avda Bolognesi sin número, E juank@clubinter.org.pe. Open Tues-Fri 1300-2000, Sat 0900-2000, Sun 0900-1700. *Net Central*, Alvárez Thomas 219, E netcentral@netcentral.lared.net.pe. Open 0900-2300. *Varnie Benavides*, Santa Catalina 113-A. Open 0900-2300.

Cultural centres *Instituto Cultural Peruano-Norte Americano*, in the Casa de los Mendiburo, Melgar 109, T243201. Has an **English Library**. *Instituto Cultural Peruano Alemán*, Ugarte 207, T218567. *Instituto Regional de Cultura*, Gen Morán 118 (altos), T213171. *Instituto Nacional de Cultura*, Alameda San Lázaro 120, T213171. *Alianza Francesa*, Santa Catalina 208, T218406/215579.

Embassies & consulates There are only consulates in Arequipa. *British*, Mr Roberts, Tacna y Arica 145, T241340. Open Mon-Fri 0830-1230, 1430-1800, reported as very friendly and helpful. *French*, Estadio Oeste 201-A, IV Centenario, T232119 (Sun T224915). Open Mon-Fri 1530-1900. *German*, in Colegio Max Uhle, Avda Fernandini sin número, Sachaca. Mon-Fri 0900-1300, Casilla 743. *Dutch*, Mercaderes 410 (Banco Wiese), Sr Herbert Ricketts, T219567, F215437, Casilla 1. Open Mon-Fri 0900-1300, 1630-1830. *Swedish*, Avda Villa Hermosa 803, Cerro Colorado, T259847/270616. Open Mon-Fri 0830-1300, 1500-1730. *Swiss*, Avda Miguel Forga 348, Parque Industrial, T232723. *Italian*, La Salle D-5, T221444. Open 1130-1300, in the afternoon T254686 (home). *Spanish*, Ugarte 218, 2nd Flr, T214977 (home T224915). Open Mon-Fri 1100-1300, Sat 0900-1300. *Chilean*, Mercaderes 212, 4th Flr, Oficina 401-402, Galerías Gameza, T/F233556. Entrance to lift is 30m down the passageway down Mercaderes on left, open Mon-Fri 0900-1300,

Arequipa

take your passport 0900-1100 if you need a visa. *Bolivian*, Piérola 209, 3rd Flr, Oficina 321, T213391. Open Mon-Fri 0900-1400, 24 hrs for visa, go early.

Hospitals & medical services Hospitals: *Regional Honorio Delgado*, Avda A Carrión sin número, T238465/231818. *General Base Goyeneche*, Avda Goyeneche sin número, T211313. *Nacional del Sur*, Filtro y Peral sin número, T214430 in emergency. **Dentist:** *Dr José Corrales*, San Juan de Dios 216. **Doctors:** *Dr Julio Postigo*, Independencia 225. *Dr Jorge A del Carpio Alvarez*, Santo Domingo 123, oficina 303, T215483, only Spanish spoken but recommended. **Clinics:** *Clínica Arequipa SA*, esquina Puente Grau y Avda Bolognesi, T253424. Fast and efficient with English-speaking doctors and all hospital facilities, consultation costs US$18, plus US$4 for sample analysis and around US$7 for a course of antibiotics. *San Juan de Dios*, Avda Ejército 1020, Cayma, T252256/255544. *Monte Carmelo*, Gómez de la Torre 119, T231444, T/F287048. *Clínica de Urgencias Meza*, Urb Aurora J-11, cercado, T234883. **Ambulance:** T289900 (24 hours). **Pharmacy:** *Farmacia Libertad*, Piérola 108. Owner speaks English.

Language courses Silvana Cornejo, 7 de Junio 118, Cerrito Los Alvarez, Cerro Colorado, T254985. US$6 an hour, negotiable for group, she speaks German fluently and is recommended. Her sister Roxanna charges US$3 an hour. Fidelia and Charo Sánchez, T224238, are recommended, Fidelia speaks French, and Charo speaks English. Classes are also available at the Instituto Peruano-Norte Americano and Instituto Cultural Peruano Alemán (see above).

Laundry *Magic laundry*, Avda Cayma 617. Coin-operated, open daily. *Lavendería del Pueblo*, Ejercícios 558. *Don Marcelo*, T421411 (morning), T229245 (afternoon). Delivery service.

Tour companies & travel agents *Ideal Travels*, Ugarte 208 (½ block from Santa Catalina convent), T245199, F242088, E idealperu@mail.interplace.com.pe (Head office T244439). Open Mon-Fri 0800-1900, Sat 0830-1300, tours to Colca Canyon (2 days, 1 night, US$60, all meals, rafting US$33), Cotahuasi Canyon, Andagua Volcanic valley, Majes River, Cotahuasi River, Toro Muerto, Callalli alpaca and vicuña ranch, jeep and microbus rentals, also rent bikes for US$10 daily, excellent bilingual guides, international ticket reservations, accepts credit cards. Recommended.

The following agencies have also been recommended as helpful and reliable. Most run tours to the Colca Canyon (see page 240). *Amazonas Explorer*, PO Box 333, Arequipa, T212813, F220147, E info@amazonas-explorer.com, www.amazonas-explorer.com. A very experienced operator especially in rafting. *Conresa Tours*, Jerusalén 409, T285420/247186 (24 hrs T602355), E conresatours@clubinter.org.pe. *Santa Catalina Tours*, Santa Catalina 223, T/F216994. Offer unique tours of Collagua communities in the Colca Canyon. Recommended. *Colca Trading Company*, San Isidro F-3, Vallecito, T247221, F277128, E pachuco@mail.interplace.com.pe. Tours of alpaca herding and weaving communities in Colca region. Run by James Vreeland. *Colonial Tours*, Santa Catalina 205, oficina 1, T285980. *Wasi Tours*, Jerusalén 613 and Santa Catalina 207. *Illary Tours*, Jerusalén 204-B, T220844. English-speaking guides. *Expeandes*, La Merced 408, oficina 1, T212888, F228814, PO Box 1403. Owner Ricardo Córdoba Mercado runs adventure trips and rents equipment. *MediTours*, Pasaje Catedral 100, T288849. Run by Mercedes Díaz, German, English, French and Italian-speaking guides. *Holley's Unusual Excursions*, T/F258459 (home) any day 1700-0700, or all day Sat and Sun, or Mon-Fri 0800-1600 T222525/225000 and leave a message, E angoho@lared.net.pe. Expat Englishman Anthony Holley runs trips in his Land Rover

to El Misti, Toro Muerto, the desert and coast. A recommended guide for climbing, trekking, mountain biking and river rafting in the Colca Canyon is Vlado Soto, he can be contacted at La Merced 125, CC Unicentro, oficina 139, PO Box 1988, T424223, T/F226610, E jbustios@ ucsm.edu.pe. He is knowledgeable and helpful and also rents equipment. *JR Tours*, Jerusalén 410-A. Rent camping equipment and sell Blue Gaz gas canisters. *Volcanyon Travel*, C Villalba 428. T223221, F288344, E hotrekl@ucsm.edu.pe. Various mountain bike tours in the Colca Canyon. *Transcontinential Arequipa*, Puente Bolognesi 132, oficina 5, T213843/235799, F218608, E prodena@lared.net.pe. Cultural and wildlife tours in the Colca Canyon.

Many agencies on Jerusalén, Santa Catalina and around Plaza de Armas sell air, train and bus tickets and offer tours of Colca, Cotahuasi, Toro Muerto, Campiña and city. Prices vary so shop around. **NB** Don't pay for a tour in advance. Always settle the details before starting the tour and check that there are enough people for the tour to run. Quite often travel agents work together to fill buses and use lots of touts. If a travel agency puts you in touch with a guide, make sure they are official. It is not advisable to book tours to Machu Picchu here. Make these arrangements in Cusco.

Tourist offices Tourist information office is on the Plaza de Armas, opposite the Cathedral, T211021, ext 113. Open 0800-1900. They are very helpful and friendly and give free street plans. *Oficina de Protección al Turista*, T(0800)42579, 24 hrs, toll-free, or T212054 during office hours. **Tourist Police:** Jerusalén 317, T251270/239888. They are very helpful with complaints or giving directions. *Ministry of Tourism*, La Merced 117, T213116, will handle complaints. *Touring y Automóvil Club del Perú*, Avda Goyeneche 313, T215631. For mechanical assistance, T215640.

Arequipa

Camelid fibre

4,000 years before the Spanish conquistadors set oot on Peruvian soil, the indigenous peoples excelled at the textile arts. This age-old weaving tradition would not have been possible, however, without the necessary raw materials.

While cotton was cultivated for this purpose on the arid coast, up on the high Andean plain there was a ready supply of weaving fibre in the shape of the native camelids – llamas, alpacas, vicuñas and guanacos – which are distant cousins to the camel. The alpacas and llamas are thought to have been domesticated as early as 4,000 BC.

The fibres and skins of the wild camelids – guanacos and vicuñas – were used prior to domestication of their cousins. In fact, guanaco skins were used as clothing by the early hunters who roamed the bleak, high Andean plateau, or altiplano, before 4,000 BC.

By 1,500-1,000 BC there is evidence of domesticated camelids on the coast while llamas were being used for ritual burial offerings, indicating their increasing prestige. Thus, the importance of camelids to Andean man, both in practical and ideological terms, was probably a long-established tradition by this time.

Because camelid fibre is so easy to spin and dye, the ancient weavers developed extraordinarily fine spinning techniques. The precolumbian peoples prized the silky-soft fibre of the alpaca, in particular. Living at altitudes of 4,000m, where temperatures can drop to -15°C, these animals have adapted to the extreme conditions and developed a coat that not only has thermal properties but is also soft and resistant.

It is these qualities that have led to worldwide demand. Production of alpaca fibre, however, remains low owing to the fact that more than 75 percent of Peru's alpacas are in the hands of small breeders and peasant communities who still herd and manage their animals in much the same way as their ancestors.

The Colca Canyon

Coloured map 5, grid B6   *The Colca Canyon is twice as deep as the Grand Canyon and was thought to be the deepest canyon in the world – until the nearby Cotahuasi Canyon was found to be all of 163 metres deeper. This is an area of astounding scenic beauty. Giant amphitheatres of pre-Inca terracing become narrow, precipitous gorges, and in the background looms the grey, smoking mass of Sabancaya, one of the most active volcanoes in the Americas, and its more docile neighbour, Ampato. Unspoiled Andean villages lie on both sides of the canyon, inhabited by the Cabana and Collagua peoples.*

The Río Colca snakes its way through the length of this massive gorge, 3,500 metres above sea level at Chivay (the canyon's main town) falling to 2,200 metres at Cabanaconde, at the far end of the canyon. The roads on either side of the canyon are at around 4,000 metres and Nevado Ampato, a short distance to the south, rises to 6,288 metres.

The name Colca derives from the Inca practice of storing harvested crops in sealed vaults which they called *colcas*, carved into the canyon walls. Now, though, the name is synonymous with a rather large bird. Would-be David Attenboroughs flock here for a close encounter of the bird kind with the giant Andean condor at the aptly-named *Cruz del Cóndor*.

Despite its history, this part of southern Peru was practically unknown to the outside world until the late 1970s when a Polish team made the first descent by raft and canoe. The canyon appears on 19th century maps and the first aerial reconnaissance was made in 1929 by US

Appeasing the Gods

To the Incas, Nevado Ampato, in the Colca region, was a sacred god who brought life-giving water and good harvests and, as a god claimed the highest tribute, the sacrifice of one of their own.

In September 1995, anthropologist, Johan Reinhard, of Chicago's Field Museum of Natural History, accompanied by Peruvian climber, Miguel Zárate, whose brother, Carlos is a well-known Arequipa mountain guide, were climbing Ampato when they made a startling discovery, at about 6,000 metres. They found the perfectly-preserved mummified body of an Inca girl. Wrapped tightly in textiles, this girl in her early teens must have been ritually sacrificed and buried on the summit.

Mummies of Inca human sacrifices have been found before on Andean summits, but the girl from Ampato, nicknamed Juanita, is the first frozen Inca female to be unearthed and her body may be the best preserved of any found in the Americas from precolumbian times. The discovery is considered of worldwide importance, as the body is so well preserved. The intact body tissues and organs of naturally mummified, frozen bodies are a storehouse of biological information. Studies will reveal how she died, where she came from, who her living relatives are and even yield valuable insights about the Inca diet.

Juanita's clothes are no less remarkable. The richly-patterned, dazzling textiles will serve as the model for future depictions of the way noble Inca women dressed. Her lliclla – a bright red and white shawl beneath the outer wrappings – has been declared "the finest Inca woman's textile in the world".

Ampato, with its icy summit, may seem an unlikely Inca ceremonial site. However, the mountain was described as one of the principal deities in the Colca Canyon region. The Incas appeased the mountain gods, who were said to supply water to their villages and fields, with children as sacrifices. The Cabana and Collagua people even bound their children's heads to make them look like the mountains from which they believed they were descended.

A subsequent ascent of Ampato revealed a further two mummies at the summit. One is a young girl and the other, though badly charred by lightning, is believed to be a boy. If so, it may mean that these children were ritually sacrificed together in a symbolic marriage.

Nowadays, villages in the Colca continue to make offerings to the mountain gods for water and good harvests, but thankfully the gods' have modified their tastes, now preferring chicha to children.

Navy Lt George R Johnson (published as *Peru from the Air* by the American Geographical Society, 1930). In 1931 Johnson returned by land with Robert Shippee and the account of their Shippee-Johnson Peruvian Expedition was reported in the *Geographical Review* of the American Geographical Society in October 1932 ('Lost Valleys of Peru') and the *National Geographic* of January 1934.

The Colca Canyon was 're-discovered' from the air again in 1954 by Gonzalo de Reparaz. Two good studies of the region are *El Valle del Colca. Cinco Siglos de Arquitectura y Urbanismo*, by Ramón Gutiérrez (Buenos Aires, 1986) and *Discovering the Colca Valley*, by Mauricio de Romaña, with photographs by Jaume Blassi and Jordi Blassi (Barcelona, 1987). (With thanks to Daniel Buck, Washington DC.)

Festivals This is a region of wild and frequent festivals. On **2-3 February** Virgen de la Candelaria is celebrated in the towns of Chivay and Cabanaconde, with dancing in the plaza, and over 5 days in Maca and Tapay. *Semana Santa* is celebrated with particular gusto in the villages of the Colca Canyon.

27 April is the celebration of the apostle Santiago. **During April and May** many festivals are held in the Colca canyon: La Cruz de Piedra is celebrated over 5 days in **May** in the main plaza in Tuti, near Chivay. On **13 June** San Antonio is celebrated in the villages of Maca, Callalli and Yanque. On **14 June**, in Sibayo and Ichupampa, the *Fiesta de San Juan* is held over 5 days. On **21 June** is the anniversary of the district of Chivay in Cailloma.

On **14-17 July** the *Fiesta de la Virgen del Carmen* is held in Cabanaconde and Pampacolca, when folk dancing takes place in the streets. Of particular interest is the dance of *Los Turcos*, which represents the indigenous peoples' struggle against the conquistadors. This fiesta is also held in the churches of Yura, Carmen Alto, Congata, Tingo Grande and the Convent of Santa Teresa in Arequipa city (see above). On **25 July** in Coporaque and Madrigal, in the Colca canyon, is the *Fiesta de Santiago Apostol*. From **26 July to 2 August** various religious ceremonies, accompanied by dancing, are held in honour of the **Virgen Santa Ana** in Maca.

On **15 August** in Chivay is the fiesta of the Virgen de la Asunta, the town's patron saint, which lasts 8 days. In **September** in Tisco, the *Virgen de la Natividad* is held over 5 days. On **8 December** *Inmaculada Concepción* is held in Chivay and Yanque, when groups of musicians and dancers present the traditional dance, the *Witite*, lasting 5 days. On **25 December** once again in Yanque, just in case you haven't had enough, the *Witite* is held over 6 days.

Tours of the Travel agencies in Arequipa arrange a 'one-day' tour to the Cruz del Cóndor for
Colca Canyon US$18-20. They leave Arequipa at 0400, arriving at the Crus del Cóndor at 0800-0900, followed by an expensive lunch stop at Chivay and back to Arequipa by 2100. It is not recommended, especially for those with altitude problems, as it is too much to fit into one day. Two day tours cost US$20-30 per person with an overnight stop in Chivay. You should allow at least two to three days when visiting the Colca Canyon.

Arequipa to Chivay

A poor dirt road runs north from Arequipa, over the altiplano, to Chivay, the first village on the edge of the Canyon. The road affords fine views of the volcanoes Misti, Chachani, Ampato and the active Sabancaya.

About an hour out of Arequipa, on the road to Chivay, is the **Aguada Blanca National Vicuña Reserve** (see map). If you're lucky, you can see herds of these rare and timid cameloids near the road. If taking a bus to the reserve to vicuña-watch, there should be enough traffic on the road to be able to hitch a ride back to Arequipa in the evening.

Chivay is the main linking point between the two sides of the canyon. A road heads northeast to **Tuti**, where there is a small handicrafts shop, and **Sibayo**, with a *pensión* and grocery store. A long circuit back to Arequipa heads south from Sibayo, passing through **Callalli** (where Arequipa buses can be caught for Cusco), **Chullo** and **Sumbay**. This is a little-travelled road, but the views of fine landscapes with vicuña, llamas, alpacas and Andean duck are superb.

Another road from Sibayo goes northwest, following the northern side of the Colca mountain range to **Cailloma**, **Orcopampa** and **Andagua** (see page 248). Water from the Colca river has been diverted through a series of tunnels and canals to the desert between Repartición and Camaná, to irrigate the Majes pampa.

Crossing the river at Chivay going west to follow the canyon on the far side, you pass the villages of **Coporaque**, **Ichupampa** (a footbridge crosses the river between the two villages and another connects Ichupampa with Achoma), **Lari**, **Madrigal** (a footbridge connects to Maca) and **Tapay** (connected by a footbridge to Cabanaconde).

Chivay

Chivay is the gateway to the canyon and the overnight stopping point for two-day tours run by agencies in Arequipa. At 3,600 metres, the nights can be bitterly cold. The indigenous people who inhabit this part of the canyon are called Collaguas. The local women traditionally wear a white hat with a ribbon round it.

The hot springs of **La Calera** are four kilometres away. To get there take one of the regular colectivos (US$0.25) from beside the market or it's a pleasant hour long walk. There are several large hot pools and showers but only one pool is open to tourists; entry US$1.25. The hot springs are highly recommended after a hard day's trekking. A reconstructed *chulpa* on the hilltop across Puente Inca gives good views over the town. There is a very helpful tourist office in the Municipalidad on the west side of the plaza which gives away a useful map of the valley.

Sleeping **C** *Rumillacta*, 3 blocks from the plaza off the Arequipa road, T521098. Attractive cabins with hot showers and a cosy bar/dining area. Recommended. **C** *Wasi Kolping*, 10 blocks south of the town, opposite the Plaza de Toros, T521076. Comfortable cabins with hot shower, very clean and quiet, good views.

D *El Posada del Inca*, Salaverry 330, T521032. Modern, with hot showers, carpeted rooms, safe, clean and friendly. **D** *Hostal Colca*, Salaverry 307, 2 blocks from the plaza. Dormitory rooms and some with private bathrooms, good restaurant, friendly, water infrequent. **E** *Hostal Anita*, on the north side of the plaza. Clean, with bathroom, hot water, rooms look onto a small garden, friendly. Recommended. **E** *Hostal Municipal*, on the west side of the plaza. Large clean rooms, with hot showers, friendly. Recommended. **E** *Hostal Plaza*, on the north side of the plaza. Clean, friendly. **E** *Inca*, on Salaverry. Spacious rooms, good restaurant. **F** per person *Los Leños*, on Bolognesi, 1 block from the plaza and 1 block to the left. Clean, safe, very friendly, excellent breakfast and tomato soup. Recommended.

Many of the better hotels are regularly used by tour groups. There are several other hotels and family homes where you can stay; ask around.

Eating There are several good, attractively decorated restaurants in Chivay, which are both cosy and friendly. They serve good value set meals for around US$3 which offer a choice of dishes. *Casa Blanca*, next to *Hostal Plaza*, does a superb trout *ceviche*. *Fonda del Cazador*, also on the north side of the plaza, serves delicious alpaca steaks. *Calamarcito's*, 1 block from the plaza, is popular with locals for special occasions. Other good places to eat include the 2 restaurants adjoining *Hotel Posada del Inca*, also *Ricardito* and *Posada del Condor*, both in Salaverry. The latter hires out traditional local costumes at US$2 per hour, for both men and women, but only in smaller sizes.

Bars & nightclubs The popular *Witite* bar at Gálvez 210, opens at 2030, has a dance floor and plays a range of rock and Latin music. *Rolo's* bar, at Bolognesi 705, is also good, and *Latigos* disco stays open until the early hours.

Transport Most buses follow the new road via **Yura** following the railway, which is being developed as a new route to Cusco from Arequipa. *Trans Andalucia* (recommended), *Cristo Rey* and *Chasqui* have buses at 0300 and 1230, 4 hours, US$4. It is a rough route and cold in the morning, reaching 4,825 metres at the Pata Pampa pass, but the views are worth it. Buses return to Arequipa at 1100 and 2200. Buses all leave from the main terminal in Arequipa but you can get your ticket the previous day at the bus company offices in C San Juan de Dios. Some companies leave Arequipa at 0400, but go via Sibayo, which takes 7 hours and costs more.

For **Cabanaconde** and **Cruz del Cóndor** catch the *Cristo Rey* or *Chasqui* bus arriving from Arequipa at 0600-0630, which gets you to the Mirador (US$1) by 0730. If you miss the bus try hitching a lift with a tour bus. *Trans Colca* has 1 bus daily, leaving at 1230 from Arequipa, along the old route, which continues on to Madrigal via Yanque, returning from Madrigal at 2100.

Kombis leave from beside the market for **Achoma** (every half hour), **Maca** (every hour), Ichupampa (every hour) and **Puente Callalli** (every hour), to connect with Cusco buses coming from Arequipa.

Treks from Chivay

From Chivay you can hike to Coporaque and Ichupampa, cross the river by the footbridge and climb up to Achoma, a one-day hike. It's better to follow the road, which seems longer, or you'll end up lost in a maze of terraced fields. Half an hour above Coporaque there are interesting cliff tombs and just beyond the village the Huari ruins of Ullu Ullu. The footbridge to Yanque (see below) is between Coporaque and Ichupampa. If you feel too tired to walk back to Chivay, why not catch a colectivo from the plaza in Yanque for US$0.25. It takes two days to walk from Chivay to Cabanaconde (70 kilometres), you can camp along the route. You will have to walk all day in the sun – there is no shade. You'll need plenty of drinking water and sun block.

Chivay to Cabanaconde

Yanque From Chivay, the main road goes west along the Colca Canyon. The first village encountered, after eight kilometres, is Yanque – a four hour walk with excellent views. There's an interesting church and a footbridge to the villages on the other side of the canyon. Beside the renovated Inca bridge on the Yanque to Ichupampa road, a 20-minute walk from Yanque plaza, is a large, warm thermal swimming pool; US$0.75. There's accommodation at **C** *Colca Lodge*, reservations at Zela 212, Arequipa, T/F212813, E colcalodge@grupoinca.com.pe. With bathroom, hot water, swimming pool, restaurant, hiking, riding, cycling tours.

Next is **Achoma**, 30 minutes from Chivay along the Cabanaconde road. **E** *Aldea Turística de Colca*, is a luxury bungalow complex, bungalows for six are **C**, all meals are provided, it has electricity, heating and hot water. Book through Receptur in Lima or Arequipa, or *Ricketts Turismo*, Mercaderes 407, Arequipa, T225382. It is open April-November only. There is also an old settlement for road workers where you can camp.

The road continues to **Maca**, which barely survived an earthquake in November 1991. People are still living in tents that were provided at the time. Then comes the tiny village of **Pinchollo**, with a basic *hospedaje*. You can walk from here to the Sabancaya geyser in approximately seven hours. For information, ask for Eduardo, who acts as a guide. He lives next to the plaza. *El Día de San Sebastián* is celebrated over five days from 20 January in Pinchollo.

From Pinchollo the road winds its way on to the Mirador, or **Cruz del Cóndor** at the deepest point of the canyon. The view from here is wonderful but people don't come for the view. This is where the immense Andean vulture, the condor, can be seen rising on the morning thermals.

The reason this particular spot is so unique is that the condors swoop by in startling close up, so close, in fact, that you feel you can reach out and touch them. It is a breathtaking and very humbling experience. The best time to arrive in the morning is a matter of some dispute, though the consensus is around 0900. If you get there by 0730, you won't miss them, but you may be faced with a long, chilly wait. They fly off to look for carrion on the higher slopes of the surrounding peaks at 0900-1000. The condors can also be seen returning from a hard day's food searching at around 1600-1800. Just below the Mirador is a rocky outcrop, which allows a more peaceful viewing but take great care on the loose scree (or you'll end up on the menu). Binoculars are recommended. Snacks and drinks are available. It is possible to camp at the mirador. Buses from Chivay stop here very briefly.

To get to the Mirador from Cabanaconde, take one of the return buses which set off at around 0800-0830, and ask to be dropped off at the Mirador, just in time for the morning performance. Or you can walk along the road, which takes about three hours. Horses can be hired to save you the walk; arrange the night before in Cabanaconde. To walk from the Mirador to Cabanaconde, follow the road until Cabanaconde is in sight, then turn off the road 50 metres after a small reservoir down a walled track. After about one kilometre turn left on to an old Inca road and continue down to rejoin the road into Cabanaconde.

Cabanaconde

From the Mirador it is a 20-minute bus ride to this friendly, typical village at 3,287 metres, the last in the Colca Canyon. The indigenous people of this part of the canyon are Cabanas and the women wear round embroidered hats. The plaza is brimming with life. Women squat on their haunches, selling bruised fruit and a few knobbly root crops. Their distinctive flower-patterned hats, voluminous skirts and intricately embroidered blouses bring a splash of colour to the uniform brown adobe buildings. Children tend sheep, goats and llamas; old men lead burdened mules while pigs laze in the sun and chickens peck at the ground. At dusk large groups of animals wander back into the village to the corrals adjoining most houses.

The views into the canyon are excellent and condors can be seen from the hill just west of the village, a 15 minute walk from the plaza, which also gives views of the amazing terraces, arguably the most attractive in the valley, to the south of the village. The hill is surrounded by a two kilometre long Huari wall, six metres high and four metres wide in places. It also encompasses the village football field where it is possible to see condors overflying a late afternoon game.

Cruz del Cóndor

Arequipa

Cananaconde suffered badly during the earthquake in April 1998. Many buildings collapsed and many people were injured. Note that local women are very camera-shy. If you really must intrude, then at least ask permission first and be considerate if they say no.

Sleeping and Electricity in Cabanaconde lasts until 2300, so a torch/flashlight is a good idea. There
eating are several basic hotels.

F *Virgen del Carmen*, 5 blocks up from the plaza. Clean, hot showers, friendly, may even offer you a welcoming glass of *chicha*. **G** *Hostal Valle del Fuego*, 1 block from the plaza, T280367. Basic but clean, friendly. Recommended. Good meals available for around US$3 at their restaurant *Rancho del Sol*. The friendly owner, Pablo Junco, is a wealth of information, he usually meets the incoming buses but otherwise turn left facing the church on the plaza and it's 1 block along on the right. **G** *Hostal San Pedro*, 2 blocks from the plaza, and **G** *Colcamayo*, on the plaza, are both pretty basic. There are several basic restaurants around the plaza, including *Rancho del Colca*, which is mainly vegetarian.

Transport *Cristo Rey* and *Chasqui* buses at 0300 and 1230, and *Andalucia* (recommended) at 1230 from Arequipa to **Chivay** go on to **Cabanaconde**; a further 75 kilometres, 2 hours, US$1.50. The road can be very bad in the wet. The buses leave Cabanaconde for **Arequipa** at 0800-0830 and 2030. There is also a *combi* to **Chivay** at 0500-0600. *Sr de los Andes* has a bus each day and *Trans Colca* on alternate days, both at 0500, to **Arequipa** via **Huambo**, 7-8 hours, US$6.

Trekking in the Colca Canyon

There are many hiking possibilities in the area. Make sure to take enough water as it gets very hot and there is not a lot of water available. Moreover, sun protection is a must. Some treks are impossible if it rains heavily in the wet season, but most of the time the rainy season is dry. Check beforehand. Ask locals for directions as there are hundreds of confusing paths going into the canyon. Buy food for longer hikes in Arequipa. Topographical maps are available at the Instituto Geográfico Militar in Lima, and good information can be obtained at the South American Explorers Club.

Two hours below Cabanaconde is an 'oasis' of palm trees and swimming areas which is worth visiting. It's four and a half hours back up, ask for the best route.

Tapay is another two hours above the 'oasis', on a good trail with great views. It's possible to stay overnight in Tapay, or camp at the houses just before the bridge. There is running water in a supply channel in the morning and evening; ask the locals.

A longer hike from Cabanaconde goes to **Chachas** and takes four or five days. Follow a small path to the west, descending slowly into the canyon (three hours); ask locals for directions to **Choco**. Then cross the Río Colca by the Puente Colgado (an Inca bridge) and go up to Choco, 2,473 metres (five to six hours). From Choco climb high above the village up to the pass at 4,500 metres and then down to Chachas, at 3,100 metres (eight to 12 hours). Sometimes there is transport from Chachas to **Andagua** in the valley of the volcanoes. Otherwise it is a day's hike. (For more details, see page 248). This is a superb walk through untouched areas and villages. You need all camping equipment, food and plenty of water, as there is hardly any on this trek.

Toro Muerto

The world's largest field of petroglyphs at **Toro Muerto** is near **Corire**, which lies north of the Pan-American Highway between Camaná and Repartición (see page 274). You can make a return day trip from Arequipa, if you leave really early, but it's better to allow two days. Buses to Corire leave from Arequipa main terminal hourly from 0500 onwards, three to four hours.

To reach the petroglyphs, there's a turn-off on the right heading back out of Corire. It's about a one hour walk. Ask directions en route. Just before the site is a tiny settlement of very basic wattle and daub huts. There are two sign-posts on the track leading up from here into the desert valley.

The higher you go, the more interesting the petroglyphs, though many have been ruined by graffiti. The sheer scale of the site is awe-inspiring and the view back down the arid desert valley against the backdrop of the distant lush, green irrigated fields is wonderful. Allow several hours to appreciate the place fully and take plenty of water and protection against the fierce sun, including sunglasses.

You can also hire a taxi and guide to visit Toro Muerto, leaving at 0800 and taking three hours in total. Expect to pay around US$20-30 (less in the low season).

There are several restaurants around the plaza in Corire and a *Banco de Crédito*. There's accommodation at **E** *Hostal Willys*, on the Plaza de Armas, which is clean and helpful. Also *Hostal Manuelito*, three blocks from the plaza, is good and friendly. There's another *Hostal*, one block from the plaza, which is OK, has hot water but is noisy from the disco next door.

Cotahuasi Canyon

*North of Corire, on the same road that branches off the Pan-American, is **Aplao**.* *Coloured map 5, grid B5* *Beyond Aplao the road heads north through **Chuquibamba**, traversing the western slopes of Nevado Coropuna, Peru's third highest peak at 6,425 metres, before winding down into **Cotahuasi**.*

The canyon, situated in the northwest of the Department of Arequipa, has been cut by the Río Cotahuasi, whose waters are formed by the Río Huayllapaña flowing from the north, above Pampamarca, and the Río Huarcaya from the west, above Tomepampa. The river cuts its way westwards and then southwards through the deepest parts of the canyon, below Quechualla. It flows into the Pacific as the Río Ocuña, having joined with the Río Marán along the way.

At its deepest, at Ninochaca (just below the village of Quechualla), the canyon is 3,354 metres deep, 163 metres deeper than the Colca Canyon and the deepest in the world. From this point the only way down the canyon is by kayak and it is through kayakers' reports since 1994 that the area has come to the notice of tourists. It was declared a Zona de Reserva Turística in 1988.

The vertiginous gradient of the canyon walls and the aridity of its climate allow little agriculture but there are several charming citrus-growing villages downstream, among them **Chaupa**, **Velinga** and **Quechualla**.

In Inca times the road linking Puerto Inca on the Pacific coast and Cusco ran along much of the canyon's course. It was used for taking fish to the ancient Inca capital. Parts of the road are still intact and there are numerous remains of *Andenes*, or terraces, which supported settlement along the route. There are also Huari and other pre-Inca ruins.

Rafting in the canyon

It is possible to raft or kayak from a point on the Upper Cotahuasi, just past the town, almost to the Pacific (boats are usually taken out of the water at the village of Iquipi), a descent of 2,300 metres. The season is May-August; rapids class three to five; some portaging is unavoidable. (See the **Further reading** section on page 83.)

Cotahuasi

Population: 4,000
Altitude: 2,600 metres

Cotahuasi town nestles in a sheltered hanging valley beneath Cerro Huinao, several kilometres away from the erosive action of the Río Cotahuasi. Though above the citrus zone itself, it has fertile, irrigated environs. The name Cotahuasi derives from the Quechua words 'Cota' (union) and 'Huasi' (house), literally translating as united house or close-knit community.

It is a peaceful, colonial town of narrow streets and whitewashed houses with gently subsiding balconies. The main street, Jirón Arequipa becomes a part of the plaza on busy Sunday mornings. The only traffic seen is the occasional glimpse of the mayor's car, the odd tractor and the infrequent comings and goings of the two buses (see below).

Sleeping and eating **F** *Hostal Villa*, just off the plaza. **G** *Alojamiento Chávez*, Jr Cabildo 125, T210222. Has rooms around a pleasant courtyard, friendly, Sr José Chávez is helpful on places to visit, if a little vague on timings. Recommended. *Restaurant El Pionero*, Jr Centenario. Clean, good *menú*. Three small restaurants/bars on Jr Arequipa offer basic fare. There are many well-stocked *tiendas*, particularly with fruit and vegetables.

Transport Two bus companies leave daily from **Arequipa** bus terminal, 13-14 hours, US$9: *Empresa Mendoza*, at 1400, returning from Cotahuasi plaza at 1600; *Empresa Virgen del Carmen* at 1430, returning at 1500 from the plaza. On arrival in Cotahuasi you may sleep on the bus till dawn. Both companies stop for refreshments in **Chuquibamba**, about halfway.

Directory There is no place to change money. The **PNP** are on the plaza; it is advisable to register with them on arrival and before leaving. Some survey maps are available in the Municipalidad and PNP. They may let you make photocopies at the shop on the corner of the plaza and Arequipa. Sr Chávez has photocopies of the sheets covering Cotahuasi and surroundings.

Cotahuasi Town

Trekking in the Cotahuasi Canyon

One of the main treks in the region follows the Inca trade road from **Cotahuasi to Quechualla**. The path starts next to the football pitch beside the airstrip. It heads downhill to **Piro**, which is almost a satellite of Cotahuasi and the gateway to the canyon (the path heads round to the right of the village, just above it). The path then crosses the river twice as it follows its course to **Sipia** (three hours), near which are the tremendously powerful, 150 metres high **Cataratas de Sipia**. Climb to the bluff just beyond the mouth of the black hole and you'll have a superb view downriver. Take care near the falls if it is windy. Water is a problem further down the canyon, if continuing, fill up your water bottles near the falls.

The next three hour stretch to **Chaupo** is not for those of a nervous disposition as the path is barely etched into the canyon wall, 400 metres above the river in places. The towering cliffs are magnificent reds and browns and dissected by near vertical water channels.

The first opportunity to camp comes at Chaupo, which lies on the pampa, 100 metres above the river. Water is available here. Ask permission to camp in the citrus groves and do not pick the fruit – it's cultivated as a cash crop. Llamas and other camelids are herded on the pampa.

Next is **Velinga**, a village which was almost wiped out by Chagas disease. Now only six families remain. Take the path down to the river before the village and cross over the concrete bridge to the right bank. Half a kilometre further on you may need to wade for about 15 metres at the foot of a cliff to regain the path. Stay on the same side of the river.

Before Quechualla are the extensive ruins of **Huña**. They are dilapidated but the remains of terraces and houses give a good idea of the importance of this route in precolumbian times. There is an almost intact 100 metres stretch of Inca road above a bend in the river on the approach to **Quechualla**. It can be a bit scary in parts but the alternative is to wade waist deep through the river.

Quechualla is a charming village and administrative capital of the district. It sits up on a cliff above the river. The church and school overlook the wooden bridge and the short climb up to the citrus groves. Trellised vines provide some welcome shade in the street. Though the village is populated by only eight families, you may be able to sleep in the schoolhouse. Ask Sr Carmelo Velásquez Gálvez for permission. Below the village, on the opposite side of the river are the ruined terraces of **Maucullachta**.

A 16 kilometres hike continues to the ruins of **Marpa**, which are in better condition than Maucullachta. The canyon walls, however, are too steep to continue along the river. You need to climb eight kilometres, on a path at right angles to the river, to Huachuy, then descend a further eight kilometres to the ruins near the river. There is no water en route; allow four more days.

NB If it rains, Quechualla can be cut off for days as sections where the river has to be waded become too deep and treacherous (eg just past Velinga).

Other treks from Cotahuasi

It is a three hour walk to the ruins of **Pampamarca**, north of Cotahuasi. The ruins are impressive, as is the high waterfall. The village is well-known for rugmaking.

The thermal baths of **Luicho** lie between Tomepampa and Alca. Take a bus to Tomepampa; the first leaves at 0600, there are several more. A days' walk beyond Tomepampa is the spectacular rock forest of **Santo Santo**. Start the trek from Huaynacotas, near Luicho.

Towards the Valley of the Volcanoes

A road goes to the east from the Cotahuasi road to **Andagua**, a village lying at the head of the valley of the volcanoes. There are several hotels in Andagua and on the plaza *Restaurant Sarita* will cook good, cheap meals for you.

A bus leaves from Arequipa on Sunday, Wednesday and Friday at 1530, with Empresa Delgado. To Arequipa: Trans Alianza leaves at 1300 and goes the long way via Cailloma, US$9; Trans Trebol leaves at 1600 or 1700 and takes the shorter route via Aplao and Corire, nine and a half hours, US$8. Both buses arrive in Arequipa in the very early morning, but you can sleep on the bus until daybreak.

The Arequipa-Andagua bus goes on to **Orcopampa**, from which the thermal springs of Huancarama can be visited.

From Andagua there is a road to **Chachas**, a picturesque little village on the edge of a lake. A truck leaves for Andagua around 1000, usually on Saturday, Tuesday and Thursday (ask the locals, they know when it's leaving). A woman in the village will let you sleep in a spare room next to her house. She also provides an evening meal. The cost is not fixed and is left up to you – around US$2 per person should be OK.

The area is heavily cultivated and there are perfect views of the valley of the volcanoes from the top of the hill above Chachas. It is possible to hike from Chachas to Choco and on to Cabanaconde via the Río Colca in four or five days (see page 244).

South Coast

7

South Coast

252 Lima to Pisco

255 Pisco

257 Paracas Peninsula and Ballestas Islands

260 Inland from Pisco

261 Ica

264 Ica to Nasca

265 Nasca

269 Nasca Lines

272 South of Nasca

276 Moquegua

279 Ilo

281 Tacna

284 Frontier with Chile

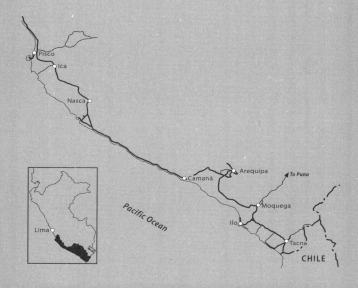

The Pan-American Highway runs all the way south from Lima to the Chilean border. This part of Peru's desert coast has its own unique attractions. The most famous, and perhaps the strangest, are the mysterious Nasca Lines, whose origin and function continue to puzzle scientists the world over. The Paracas peninsula is one of the world's great marine bird reserves and was home to one of Peru's most important ancient civilizations. Further south, the Ica valley, with its wonderful climate, is home to that equally wonderful grape brandy known as pisco.

South Coast

Lima to Pisco

El Silencio
San Bartolo
Pucusana
Chilca
Mala

The first 60 kilometres south from Lima are dotted with a series of seaside resort towns and clubs. First is **El Silencio**, at Km 30, which is good, then **Punta Hermosa** at Km 35, and **Punta Negra** at Km 40. **San Bartolo** is 43 kilometres south from Lima. Accommodation is available at *Posada del Mirador*, Malecón San Martín 105, T290388, **C** in bungalows or **A3** full board, *Handbook* users are welcome. **Santa María**, 45 kilometres from Lima, has the beautiful **A3** *Santa María Hotel*, with meals included.

Next comes the charming fishing village of Pucusana, 60 kilometres south from Lima. There are excellent views from the cliffs above the village. You can hire a boat for an hour, but fix the price beforehand and stick to it. Don't sail in the direction of the smelly factory, but to the rocks where you can see seabirds close at hand. There is a compulsory police checkpoint before the turning to Pucusana. The *Hotel Bahía* has good seafood.

Most beaches have very strong currents and can be dangerous for swimming. If you're unsure, ask locals

The small beach resort of **Chilca**, 14 kilometres south of Pucusana, is 30 minutes by colectivo from the market place. There isn't much to see, but a long, deserted beach does present camping possibilities. You can walk along the beach from Chilca to Salinas (five kilometres), which has mineral baths. There are a few restaurants and *pensiones*. In summer (December-February), these places fill up with holidaymakers from Lima.

At **Mala**, 24 kilometres south of Pucusana, two kilometres inland from Pan-American Highway, are four hotels, but it can still be difficult to find accommodation.

San Vicente de Cañete

About 150 kilometres south of Lima, on the Río Cañete, this prosperous market centre is set amid desert scenery. It is commonly called Cañete. The town hosts a festival during the last week in August. At Cerro Azul, 13 kilometres north of Cañete, is a unique Inca sea fort known as **Huarco**, which is now badly damaged.

Sleeping, eating and transport D *Hostal Casablanca*. Reasonable. **D** *Hostal San Francisco*, Santa Rosa 317, 2 blocks north of the plaza, T912409. With bathroom, **E** without, clean, friendly, quiet. Recommended. **F** *Hostal María Victoria*. With bathroom, clean. A recommended restaurant is *Cevichería Muelle 56*, Bolognesi 156. There are also several good Chinese restaurants. The main bus stop is on the highway; wait for the service you want going north or south and hope there are free seats. To Pisco, US$1.30. To Lunahuaná: unless you are on a Lima-Cañete-Imperial bus, take a combi from the highway to Imperial, then a bus to Lunahuaná.

Lunahuaná

A paved road runs inland, mostly beside the Río Cañete, through **Imperial**, which has a market on Saturday, Sunday and Monday (good for every type of household item), and **Nuevo Imperial** to the Quebrada de Lunahuaná. After the town of **Lunahuaná** (40 kilometres from Cañete), the road continues unpaved to Huancayo up in the sierra; bus US$9 (see page 425).

Lunahuaná consists of the town of the same name and several *anexos* – **Paullo**, **San Jerónimo**, **Langla**, **Jita**, **Condoray**, **Uchupampa** and **Catapalla**. The whole valley is totally dependent on the Río Cañete, for irrigation and for its chief tourist attraction of rafting and kayaking. Beyond the reach of the water, the surrounding countryside is completely barren, but

South Coast

not without its own appeal. In early morning and at dusk the hills are painted in infinite shades of grey and brown, framed by the clear blue sky, fertile green valley and rushing water.

Eight kilometres before Lunahuaná is **Incawasi**, the ruins of an Inca city. A new road cuts right through the middle of the site which dominates the valley and *quebradas* that run down into it. Incawasi is said to have been a replica of Cusco, with its divided trapezoidal plaza. The site was built outside the fertile zone of the valley and its rough walls blend in perfectly with the barren hills.

Paullo is the first of the *anexos* reached after Incawasi. Here stand the ruins of the first church of Lunahuaná. In summer, when the river is high, rafting trips start from just below the plaza. In the low river season a temporary footbridge crosses the river to **Lúcumo**.

Two kilometres further on is **San Jerónimo**, the area's white-water rafting centre; there are several agencies to choose from (see below). Other adventure tourism activities include paragliding and there is an artificial wall for climbing.

Lunahuaná town is beyond **Langla** and **Jita**. The 18th century church on the plaza has a pleasant interior. Opposite the west door, at the top of the plaza, are the Banco de la Nación and Municipalidad. There is no phone in Lunahuaná.

Beyond Lunahuaná are **Condoray** and **Uchupampa**. Past Uchupampa the road paving ends before the road crosses the Río Cañete to **Catapalla**. A little further on is a *puente colgante* (suspension bridge). Across the road bridge turn right to the village or left to the pre-Inca remains of **Cantagallo**. The site is not signposted; ask directions. Miguel Casas Sánchez in Catapalla can guide to these ruins.

South Coast

Lunahuaná

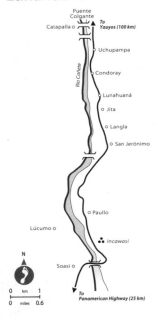

Bodegas It is interesting to visit the *bodegas* (wine cellars) in the valley and try the wine. The best-known is *Los Reyes* (T4373187/4340872), in the *anexo* of **Condoray** (see above), where you can try their pisco, wine, *manzanilla* and *arope* (a grape juice concentrate). A good time to visit is during February and March when you can see the traditional methods of treading the grapes by foot to the beat of the drum.

Other *Bodegas* in the area are: *El Olimpo*, in Uchupampa, beside the *Hotel Embassy*, T4607698 (see below); *Viña Santa María*, in Condoray, beside *Hostal Río Alto*, T4378892. Also in Condoray are *Del Valle*, by *La Laguna* restaurant, and *Viñas del Sur*, T4373187. There are also *Bodegas* in Catapalla, Socsi, Langla and Jita.

Rafting and kayaking Several places offer rafting and kayaking; eg *Camping San Jerónimo*, *Aldea*, *Aventura Perú* all in San

Jerónimo and Paullo. From November-April the river is high (highest from December) and during those months the white-water rafting is at levels four to five. May-October is the low water season when only boat trips are possible (levels one to two). Excellent kayaking is two and a half hours upriver. Rafting costs US$15 per person for one and a half hours. Annual championships are held every February. (See also page 62.)

Essentials
■ *on maps*
Price codes:
see inside front cover

Sleeping A3-B *Embassy* and *Embassy Río*, in Uchupampa, T4723525. With all facilities, restaurants, disco, gardens, rafting, large property, good, popular with families. In Condoray: B *Río Alto*, T4635490, just outside Lunahuaná. Rooms or bungalows for 7, pool, with bathroom, hot water, restaurant, disco, rafting, very nice. C *Del Valle*, T4499995. With swimming pool, restaurant and TV room. C *Las Viñas*, just before Uchupampa, T4373187. Bungalows, also camping, F per person, rafting. D *Hospedaje Juan Paulino*, T4372624. Restaurant does barbecues and *pachamanca* (stewed meat cooked underground), camping F. E per person *La Cabañita*, T4488515. E per person *La Fogata*, T4738379. E per person *Hostal San Jerónimo*, in San Jerónimo, T4971601. With restaurant and disco. E per person *Hostal El Paso*, in Jita, T4240624. Restaurant, garage. Also **camping** at *Camping Henry's*, at Langla, F per person.

In Lunuhuaná: D *Los Casuarinos*, Grau 295, T (Cañete) 034912627. D *Hostal Lunahuaná*, T4240624. With restaurant and disco. D-E *Grau*, Grau 205. Shared bathroom, clean, all meals available. **Camping** at *Camping Win Wan*, F-G per person, with restaurant and disco.

● *on maps* **Eating** In Lunahuaná: *Lester*, on block 3 of Grau. Good. *Sol y Río*, Malecón Araoz. Also arranges rafting. There are several other restaurants in town and in the surrounding *anexos*.

Festivals *Fiesta de la Vendimia*, the grape harvest festival, is held in first weekend in **March**. At the end of **September/beginning October** is the lively *Fiesta del Níspero* (medlar festival).

Chincha Alta

35 kilometres north of Pisco, near Chincha Baja, is **Tambo de Mora**, the old port, with nearby archaeological sites at Huaca de Tambo de Mora, La Centinela, Chinchaycama and Huaca Alvarado. **Chincha** itself is a fast-growing town (*Population*: 110,016) where the negro/criollo culture is still alive. For more details, see the chapters on **People** (page 517), **Food** (page 56) and **Music** (page 526).

Essentials **Sleeping** B *Hacienda San José*, is a 17th century sugar and cotton estate ranch-house, just outside town. The price is for full board, great lunch stop, the buffet is recommended, with pool, garden, small church, colonial crafts, underground from the basement runs a labyrinth of tunnels believed to link up with Tambo de Mora in order to facilitate the contraband trade in black slaves from Africa. The catacombs, where many of those slaves are interred, can be visited, US$15 per person. On the Pan-Americana is C *Palacios de los Mariscos*, which has an excellent restaurant. In the town of Chincha is F *Hostal La Rueda*, near the plaza. Breakfast is extra, hot showers, swimming pool, lounge. There are several other hotels in town.

Festivals Among other things (olives, for one) Chincha is famous for its many festivals. On **6 January** is the *Celebración del Nacimiento de la Beata Melchorita Saravia*. The *Verano Negro*, or Black Summer, is at the **end of February**. During this time the black culture of the area, repressed for so many centuries, is freely expressed in the dancing competitions, though black participation in the festival is still somewhat limited. In the **second week of March** is the *Festival de la Vendimia*. In **mid-July** is the *Virgen del Carmen* festival and the tourist week takes place during the **end of October/beginning of November**. Also in November is the *Festival de Danzas Negras*. Not enough? Well, on **4 December** there's the *Peregrinación a la Ermita de la Beata Melchorita*.

Pisco

Despite being christened as San Clemente de Macera by the Spanish in 1640, the town had already been unofficially named after the famous local brandy and always would be known as Pisco. Now the largest port between Callao and Matarani, 237 kilometres south of Lima, it serves a large agricultural hinterland.

Population: 82,250
Phone code: 034
Coloured map 5, grid B2

Ins and outs

All the bus terminals are in the centre of town. However, if arriving by bus, make sure it is going into town and will not leave you at the Cruce which is a 10-minute combi ride from the centre (US$0.30) and not a particularly safe area after dark. **Getting there**

The town is small and compact. All you want to do and see is contained within a 300 metre radius of the Plaza de Armas. Taxis can be caught here. Combis from the Cruce (see above), stop at *Hostal Comercio* by Plaza Belén. **Getting around**

South Coast

Pisco

■ **Sleeping**
1. Colonial
2. Embassy
3. Embassy Suites
4. Hostal Belén
5. Hostal Candelabro
6. Hostal Pisco

● **Eating**
1. Chifa Progreso
2. Ch'Reyes
3. Don Manuel

🚌 **Buses**
1. Bus stop from El Cruce
2. Empresa General San Martín Buses
3. Etersuma buses (to Lima)
4. Ormeño buses

Sights

Pisco lies a short distance to the west of the Pan-American Highway. The town was originally divided into two: Pisco Pueblo with its colonial-style homes with patios and gardens; and Pisco Puerto, which, apart from fisheries, has been replaced as a port by the deep-water Puerto General San Martín, beyond Paracas. The two have since expanded into one fairly unattractive town.

In Pisco Pueblo, half a block west of the quiet Plaza de Armas, with its equestrian statue of San Martín, is the **Club Social Pisco**, at Avenida San Martín 132, the HQ of San Martín after he had landed at Paracas Bay. There is an old Jesuit church on San Francisco, one block from the plaza, separated from the Municipalidad by a narrow park. The newer **Cathedral** is on the main plaza. Avenida San Martín runs from the Plaza de Armas to the sea. You may find it a pain in the neck to visit the pleasant cemetery at the end of Calle San Francisco. This was the centre of a female vampire craze in 1993, apparently connected with the grave of an English woman, Sarah Ellen, who died in 1913.

Essentials

South Coast

Sleeping
■ *on maps*
Price codes:
see inside front cover

The town is full at weekends with visitors from Lima. Mosquitoes are a problem at night in the summer.

C *Embassy Suites* on Bolognesi, 1 block from the plaza. TV, fax, restaurant. **C** *Hostal Candelabro*, Callao y Pedemonte, T532620. TV, fridge, fax service, hot water, café, bar on roof, laundry, safe, clean. **D** *Embassy*, on Jr Comercio just off the Plaza de Armas, T532809. With bathroom, clean, noisy, nice bar on roof, has disco, trips to Ballestas Islands, under the same ownership as *Embassy Suites*. **D** *Hostal Belén*, on Plaza Belén, T533046. With bathroom, clean, comfortable, electric showers. Recommended. **D** *Hostal Pisco*, on Plaza de Armas, T532018. With bathroom, **F** without, hot water, clean, rooms without windows, good tour company adjoining hotel, parking for motorcycles. **D** *Posada Hispaña*, Bolognesi 236, T536363, F4614907 (Lima). 5 rooms each with loft and bathroom, hot water, can accommodate groups, comfortable, clean, information service, English, French, Italian and Catalán spoken. Highly recommended. **E** *Hostal San Jorge*, Jr Comercio 187, T/F534200. Sometimes has hot water, friendly, very clean, good. **E-F** *Colonial*, on the pedestrianized part of Jr Comercio. Shared bathroom, large rooms with balcony overlooking plaza, very clean. **F** *Hostal Progreso*, Progreso 254. Shared bathrooms, clean, water shortages. **F-G** per person *Hostal Comercio*, on the pedestrianized part of Jr Comercio. Basic and not very clean, but friendly and with good restaurant.

At Pisco Puerto: E *Portofino*, in the slum area on the sea front. Basic, friendly, clean, good seafood at restaurant, expensive breakfast, arranges day excursion to Paracas, but avoid the nearby *peña* which is poor and can be dangerous. **F** per person *Hostal Pisco Playa* (Youth Hostel), Jr José Balta 639, Pisco Playa, T532492. Clean, kitchen and washing facilities, quite nice, breakfast US$1.50.

Eating
● *on maps*

As de Oro, San Martín 472. Good food at reasonable prices, closed on Monday. *Don Manuel*, Comercio 187. US$2-4 for a main dish. *Ch'Reyes*, Jr Comercio block 100. Good, set meal US$1. Also on pedestrianized block of Comercio: *El Boulevard*, and *Snack Pizza Catamarán*. *Chifa Progreso*, on Callao at Plaza de Armas. Good lunches.

The following seafood restaurants are all recommended and can be found along the shore between Pisco and San Andrés, and in San Andrés (buses from Plaza Belén, near *Hostal Perú*): *La Fontana*, Lima 355; *La Estrellita*; *Olimpia*, Grecia 200; and *Mendoza*.

San Pedro takes place at the end of **June**. The second week of **September** is desig- **Local festivals** nated tourist week, and on **21 November** is the grandly titled *Peregrinación a la Hermita de la Beata de Humay.*

To **Lima**, 242 kilometres, 3-4 hours, US$5 with *Ormeño* (San Francisco, 1 block from **Transport** the plaza) and *San Martín* (San Martín 199). Buses leave almost hourly 0715-1800. Also colectivos. For buses from Lima, see under Lima, Ins and outs.

To **Ayacucho**, 13 hours, US$8, the road is now completely paved but is not well-travelled, with few buses. Make sure to take warm clothing as it gets cold at night. To **Huancavelica**, 269 kilometres, 14 hours, US$8, only 1 bus a day (*Oropesa*, Conde de la Monclova 637) and a few trucks; the road condition is as for Ayacucho. There is regular transport to **Ica**, US$2 by colectivo, US$1 by bus, 40 minutes, 70 kilometres; with *Ormeño* and also *Saavedra* (Callao 181). To **Nasca**, 210 kilometres, US$1.50, 3 hours, buses go via Ica (you may have to change buses, see under Ica below). *Ormeño* have direct buses at 1230 and 1430. To **Arequipa**, US$11, 10-12 hours, 3 daily.

Banks *Banco de Crédito* on the Plaza de Armas. Gives good rates for Amex TCs and cash. Also on **Directory** Plaza is *Interbanc*. **Communications** Telephone and fax office is on the Plaza de Armas between Avda San Martín and Callao. **Hospitals & medical services** *Dr Carlos Alfonso Bonilla Flores*, at C San Francisco 219, T523373. Doesn't speak English but is very helpful and will make hotel visits.

Paracas Peninsula and Ballestas Islands

Coloured map 5, grid B2

15 *kilometres down the coast from Pisco Puerto is the bay of Paracas, sheltered by the Paracas peninsula. It is named after the Paracas winds – sandstorms that can last for three days, especially in August. The wind gets up every afternoon, peaking at around 1500.*

Paracas National Reserve

The whole peninsula, a large area of coast to the south and the Ballestas Islands are all part of a National Reserve, created in 1975, which covers a total of 335,000 hectares, on land and sea. It is one of the most important marine reserves in the world, with the highest concentration of marine birds. The regiòn is economically important as a major producer of guano. Entrance to the reserve is US$1.70 per person.

The fauna on view also includes a wide variety of sea mammals and rare and exotic birds. Condors can

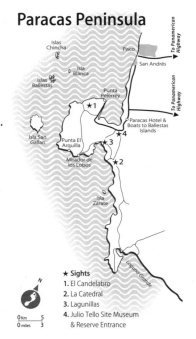

Paracas Peninsula

Islas Chincha

Pisco

San Andrés

Isla Blanca

Islas Ballestas

Punta Pejerrey

★1

To Panamerican Highway

To Panamerican Highway

Paracas Hotel & Boats to Ballestas Islands

Isla San Gallan

Punta El Arquilla

★3

★4

Mirador de los Lobos

★2

Isla Zárate

Laguna Grande

N

0 Km 5
0 miles 3

★ **Sights**
1. El Candelabro
2. La Catedral
3. Lagunillas
4. Julio Tello Site Museum & Reserve Entrance

The Paracas Necropolis Culture

The Paracas Necropolis culture inhabited this region between 1300 BC and AD 200 and is renowned for its finely woven textiles, in particular their mantos (large decorated cloth) embroidered with anthropomorphic, zoomorphic and geometric designs. These mantos were used to wrap the mummified bodies in their funerary bundles whose discovery gave anthropologists and archaeologists vital clues into this civilization. The bodies were often found to have trepanned skulls. Trepanation was a form of brain surgery performed by the Paracas people in which metal plates were inserted to replace broken sections of skull – a common injury among warring factions at that time. The Paracas culture also practised the intentional deformation of infants' skulls for aesthetic reasons.

even be seen in February and March from the rough road between Paracas and Laguna Grande. These massive vultures feed on the ready supply of sea lion carcasses.

Rather more delicate are the flamingos which feed in Paracas bay, a short walk from the museum (see below). Note that boat trips do not go to see the flamingos and that from January to March they head for the sierra. It is said that these graceful red and white birds inspired General San Martín to design Peru's red and white flag of independence.

NB The devastating effects of the 1997/98 El Niño were particularly felt along this coast and the islands offshore. The seabird, sea lion and penguin populations were decimated on the Ballestas islands (see below). It is hoped they will recover, but it may take some time.

Around the peninsula

The **Julio Tello site museum** is at the entrance to the Reserve. The exhibits are from the burial sites discovered by the Peruvian archaeologist, Julio C Tello, under the Paracas desert in 1925. The best examples of textiles and funerary bundles can be found in the Museo de la Nación and archaeological museum, Pueblo Libre, in Lima. ■ *Open daily 0900-1700, with a shop which sells guide books, film and drinks. US$1.*

The tiny fishing village of **Lagunillas** is five kilometres from the museum across the neck of the peninsula. It has clean, safe beaches free from sting rays and good eating places, eg *Rancho de la Tía Fela*. A network of good dirt roads, reasonably well signed, crosses the peninsula. For walking, details are available from the Park Office or ask for 'Hoja 28-K' map at Instituto Geográfico Nacional in Lima for US$5. Note that it is not safe to walk if alone and that it is easy to get lost in the hot, wide desert area.

Other sites on the peninsula include **Mirador de los Lobos** at **Punta El Arquillo**, six kilometres from Lagunillas, which looks down on a raucous mob of sea lions. **La Catedral** is a rock formation in the cliffs, six kilometres from Lagunillas in the opposite direction. Some guides may tell you that this was the site for the filming of *Planet of the Apes*. Unfortunately, Charlton Heston isn't around to verify this claim.

Nearby, is a monument which marks the spot where San Martín landed in Peru, on 8 September 1820, after liberating Argentina. Soon after, a ship-load of British troops, led by Lord Cochrane, arrived to help the General plan his strategy to break the Spanish stranglehold in the region.

About 14 kilometres from the entrance to the Reserve is the precolumbian **Candelabro** (or Candelabra) traced in the hillside. At least 50 metres long, it is best seen from the sea, but still impressive from the land.

South Coast

An economic mess

The islands lying off the coast of southern Peru are the breeding grounds for millions of sea birds, whose droppings have accumulated over the centuries.

Though the ancient Peruvians knew of the benefits of guano – the name given to the natural fertilizer – and used it on their crops, it wasn't until 1840 that the vast deposits of the stuff were commercially exploited. It was at this time that Peru first began to trade abroad, particularly with France and England. Almost simultaneously, guano began to replace rare metals as the country's main export.

However, with the economy heavily based on the sales of bird droppings, Peru was caught in a vicious circle of borrowing money on future sales, then having to repay loans at vastly-inflated rates. This unhealthy state of affairs was exacerbated in 1864 when Spain, in a petulant show of aggression towards her ex-colony, decided to occupy the guano islands of Chincha, to the south of Lima, thereby leaving the Peruvian government really up to its neck in it.

The main producers of guano are the Guanay Cormorant and the Peruvian Booby. They gather in colonies on the islands, attracted by the huge shoals of anchovy which feed on the plankton in the cold water of the Humboldt current.

There are differing theories as to its exact purpose. Some believe it to be linked to the Nasca lines (see page 269), 200 kilometres to the south, others that it is related to the Southern Cross constellation and was used to help guide ancient sailors. Others still contend that it represents the cactus used by the ancient high priests for its hallucinogenic powers. A few cruel cynics have even suggested – God forfend – that it was the work of some opportunistic local guides.

To reach the Candelabro, hitch along the paved road which leads to Punta Pejerrey, then get off at the left fork and you will see a trail. It is a one and a half hour walk under a blazing sun, so take water and sunscreen.

By private transport it takes about 50 minutes to Lagunillas from the entrance, 45 minutes to La Mina and 1 hour to Mirador de los Lobos. Make sure your car is in good condition, never leave it unattended, and travel in a group as robbery has been a problem in the past. The Reserve can be reached by the coast road from San Andrés, passing the fishing port and a large proportion of Peru's fishmeal industry. Alternatively, go down the Pan-American Highway to $14\frac{1}{2}$ kilometres past the Pisco turning and take the road to Paracas across the desert. After 11 kilometres turn left along the coast road and 1 kilometre further on fork right to Paracas village. Return to the main road for the entrance to the Reserve, where you can ask for a map.

Ballestas Islands

The Ballestas islands, dubbed the "poor man's Galápagos" by many, are nonetheless spectacular in their own right and well worth visiting. They are eroded into numerous arches and caves, hence their name – *ballesta* means bow, as in archery. These arches provide shelter for thousands of seabirds, some of which are very rare, and countless sea lions, though numbers have been greatly reduced by El Niño (see above). A former guano factory can be seen on one of the islands and several others have installations. The book *Las Aves del Departamento de Lima* by Maria Koepcke is useful. Trips to the Islas Ballestas leave from the jetty at El Chaco, the beach and fishing port by Paracas village.

Short trips last three hours and leave early in the morning. Tours may be cancelled if the sea is too rough. The full trip includes Isla San Gallán, where there are thousands of sea lions, and is recommended. All boats are

South Coast

speedboats with life jackets, but some are very crowded. Wear warm clothing. You will see, close up, sea lions, guano birds, pelicans, penguins and, if you're lucky, dolphins swimming in the bay. The boats pass Puerto San Martín and the Candelabra en route to the islands. Tours to the islands cost US$11 per person, and to the peninsula US$20 per person but are a lot cheaper out of season.

Tours Recommended for trips to Islas Ballestas are *Blue Sea Tours*, C Chosica 320, San Andrés, Pisco, T533469, anexo 35; also at El Chaco. Guides Jorge Espejo and Hubert Van Lomoen (speaks Dutch) are frequently recommended and there is no time limit on tours. Also recommended are *Paseo Turístico Islas Ballestas*, C San Francisco 109; *Ballestas Travel Service*, San Francisco 249, T533095; and *Paracas Tours*, San Francisco 257. *The Zarcillo Connection*, Arequipa 164, T262795, are also good for the Paracas National Reserve. The main hotels in Pisco and Paracas will also arrange tours, eg *Hotel Paracas*, US$30 in their own speed boat, 0900-1700.

Essentials

Sleeping **A3** *Paracas*, T Pisco 532220 or Lima 4723850, F4475073. Bungalows on the beach, good food, not cheap, good buffet lunch on Sunday, fine grounds facing the bay, it is a good centre for excursions to the Peninsula and flights over Nasca, it has tennis courts and an open-air swimming pool (US$2 for non-residents), it also houses the Masson ceramics collection which is worth seeing. **C** *Hostal Santa Elena*, a few kilometres from the Paracas National Park, sandwiched between 2 fishmeal factories, reservations in Lima T718222. Very clean, with restaurant 'the cook is legendary', the beach is safe for swimming as there are no sting rays, local trips can be organized. **C** *El Mirador*, at the turn-off to El Chaco, no phone, reservations in Lima, T4458496, ask for Sra Rosa. Hot water, good service, boat trips arranged, meals available, sometimes full board only. **D** *Alojamiento El Amigo*, 5 rooms, nice view from first floor, with bathroom.

Camping is possible on the beach near the *Hotel Paracas* at a spot called La Muelle. There are no facilities and the sea is polluted. Ask for permission to camp in the reserve, but note that there is no water. Do not camp alone as robberies occur.

Eating There's excellent fried fish at the open-sided restaurants at El Chaco (see below), eg *Jhonny y Jennifer*, friendly; and *El Chorito*, close to *Hotel Paracas*.

Transport A taxi from Pisco to Paracas costs about US$3-4. Combis to/from El Chaco beach (marked 'Chaco-Paracas-Museo') leave when full, US$0.30, 25 minutes. Some of them continue to the museum and Lagunillas. The last one returns at around 2200. There are also several buses which leave from the market in Pisco (last bus back at about 1600). There is no public transport on the peninsula.

Inland from Pisco

*From the Pan-American Highway near Pisco, a paved road runs 317 kilometres up to **Ayacucho** in the sierra, with a branch to **Huancavelica**. At **Castrovirreyna** it reaches 4,600 metres. The scenery on this journey is superb.*

Tambo Colorado 48 kilometres from Pisco on this road is Tambo Colorado, one of the best-preserved Inca ruins in coastal Peru. It includes buildings where the Inca and his retinue would have stayed. Many of the walls retain their original colours. On the other side of the road is the public plaza and the garrison and messengers' quarters. The caretaker will act as a guide, and he has a small collection of items found on the site. Entrance is US$1.50.

From Humay, go to Hacienda Montesarpe, and 500 metres above the hacienda is the line of holes known as 'La avenida misteriosa de las picaduras de viruelas' (the mysterious avenue of smallpox spots) which stretches along the Andes for many kilometres. Its purpose is still unknown. There's a bus from Pisco which leaves at 0800, with Oropesa; US$1.60, 3 hours. Also colectivos, US$1.20 per person. Get off 20 minutes after the stop at Humay. The road passes right through the site. Return by bus to Pisco in the afternoon. For the bus or truck back to Pisco wait at Sr Mendoza, the caretaker's house. A taxi from Pisco is US$30.

Huaytará & Incahuasí The town of Huaytará is four hours by bus from Pisco. The whole side of the church is a perfectly preserved Inca wall with niches and trapezoidal doorways. 20 minutes from town are the ruins of Incahuasí with thermal baths. On 24 June is the Fiesta of San Juan Bautista, which involves a week of processions, fireworks, bullfights and dancing day and night (and probably the occasional drink). There's accommodation at **D** *Hotel de Turistas*, which also offers food and tours; and **E** *Municipal*, which has warm water. A bus from Pisco is US$2.25 (rising to US$5.50 for the festival!). A Molina bus goes from Lima, taking 6 hours.

Guadalupe From Pisco the Pan-American Highway runs 60 kilometres south to Guadalupe, where *Restaurant Sol de Mayo*, one block north of the main plaza, does a good *menú* for US$1.50.

Ica

Population: *161,406*
Phone code: *034*
Coloured map 5, grid B2

10 kilometres further south is Ica, Peru's main wine centre, on the Río Ica. The city is also famous for its tejas, a local sweet of manjarblanco, which is sold behind the Luren church.

Ins and outs

Getting there Buses from Lima travel along the Av Municipalidad nearly into the centre of town. Most hotels though are on the far side of the Plaza de Armas. Beware of thieves at the bus stations, even in daylight. Be especially careful when transferring between buses to or from Nasca, Pisco or Lima. This is when most robberies occur. Also beware of thieves posing as hotel or tour agents.

Getting around Ica is much more spread out than Pisco. You will need a taxi to get around especially if you intend to visit the bodegas.

Sights

The San Jerónimo church at Cajamarca 262 has a fine mural behind the altar. The waters of the Choclacocha and Orococha lakes from the eastern side of the Andes are tunnelled into the Ica valley and irrigate 30,000 hectares of land. The lakes are at 4,570 metres and the tunnel is over nine kilometres long.

Bodegas The **Bodega El Carmen** is on the right-hand side when arriving from Lima. This pisco distillery has an ancient grape press made from a huge tree trunk and is worth a visit.

The **Vista Alegre** wine and pisco distillery can also be visited (though a good grasp of Spanish is essential) and its shop is recommended. ■ *Official*

South Coast

tours on Friday and Saturday 0830-1130. A local bus drops you at the entrance, or it's a 10-15 minutes' walk on the other side of the river.

10 kilometres outside Ica, in the district of Subtanjalla, is José Carrasco González, **Bodega El Catador**, a shop selling home-made wines and pisco, and traditional handicrafts associated with winemaking. In the evening it is a restaurant-bar with dancing and music. The best time to visit is during harvest – late February to early April – when wine and pisco tasting is usually possible. Try *Cachina*, a very young white wine 'with a strong yeasty taste', which is drunk about two weeks after the grape harvest. ■ *Open 0800-1800. Take a bus from the second block of Moquegua, every 30 minutes, US$0.10.*

Near Bodega El Catador is **Bodega Alvarez**. The owner, Umberto Alvarez, is very hospitable and won the gold medal for the best pisco in Peru in 1995. Ask about their *pisco de mosto verde* and the rarer, more expensive, *pisco de limón*, which will set you back US$40 per bottle.

A very good, strong *moscatel* is made by Sr Luis Chipana and sold in unlabelled bottles. He is always short of bottles so it's best to take your own. A visit is recommended, but you'll need good Spanish. Sr Chipana lives on the main plaza beside his bodega. Ask for him in the bar on the plaza.

Museums   **Museo Regional** houses mummies, ceramics, textiles and trepanned skulls from the Paracas, Nasca and Inca cultures. There's a good, well-displayed collection of Inca counting strings (*quipus*) and clothes made of feathers. Also good and informative displays with maps of all sites in the Department. Behind the building there is a scale model of the Nasca lines with an observation tower. It's a useful orientation before visiting the lines. The attendant paints copies of motifs from the ceramics and textiles in the original pigments

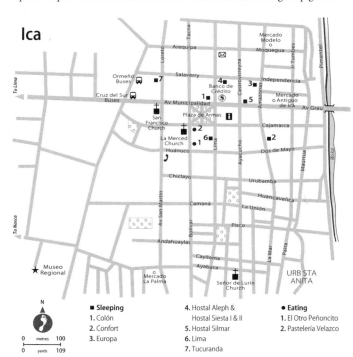

Ica

■ **Sleeping**
1. Colón
2. Confort
3. Europa
4. Hostal Aleph &
   Hostal Siesta I & II
5. Hostal Silmar
6. Lima
7. Tucuranda

● **Eating**
1. El Otro Peñoncito
2. Pastelería Velazco

0   metres   100
0   yards   109

Pisco: a history in the making

A visit to Peru would not be complete without savouring a pisco sour. Peruvians are mighty proud of their national tipple, which has turned out to be one of the few positive results of conquest.

Peru was the first conquered territory in Spanish America to produce wines and brandies. The cultivation of grapes began with the import of vinestalks from the Canary Islands. The crop spread from the outskirts of Lima and reached as far as Cusco and Ayacucho in the Andes, but it was in Ica that the enterprise really took off, owing mainly to the region's exceptional climate.

A hundred years after the conquest, the wine and pisco trade had grown considerably. Ica sent its wine to Huamanga, Cusco, Lima and Callao. And from Pisco ships left for other important ports like Guayaquil, several in Central America, as well as Valparaíso and Buenos Aires. Reports of maritime trade in the 16th and 17th centuries reveal the growing prestige of grape brandy as pisco exports eventually displaced those of wine.

Pisco trade surged in spite of royal bans to halt the vineyard explosion that endangered the Spanish wine industry. But despite the restrictions, the industry continued to expand during most of the 18th century.

Though a few firms utilize modern procedures to manufacture and market larger quantities, pisco is still mostly made by small, independent producer. The traditional method of crushing the grapes by foot can still be found and the fermented grape juice is emptied into stills, called falcas, which are crucial to the process of true pisco production. Also more conventional wineries still rely on wood from the carob tree. This slow-burning fuel is said to provide a constant source of heat that makes for a finer flavour.

Another important factor is the type of grape. The unscented quebranta grape, brought to the Americas by the Spaniards, lends its unique characteristics to the making of the renowned "pure pisco". There are also fragrant piscos from Moscatel and Albilla varieties, "creole piscos" made with prime fragrant grapes and green piscos made with partially fermented grape juice.

The Ica valley still ranks as Peru's foremost producer of pisco, followed by the nearby valleys of Pisco, Chincha and Lunahuaná and Moquegua further south. Other production centres include Vitor in Arequipa, Locumba in Tacna and Surco in Lima.

South Coast

(yours for US$1), and sells his own good maps of Nasca for US$1.65. ■ *Open 0745-1900, Monday-Saturday, Sunday 0900-1300. US$1.15, students US$0.65. To get there, take bus 17 from the Plaza de Armas (US$0.50).*

Essentials

Hotels are fully booked during the harvest festival and prices rise greatly.

A2 *Las Dunas*, Avda La Angostura 400, T231031, F231007. Prices don't include 18% tax and service, about 20% cheaper on weekdays, located in a complete resort with restaurant, swimming pool, horse riding and other activities, it has its own air-strip for flights over the Nasca Lines, 50 minutes. Highly recommended. Lima offices: Ricardo Rivera Navarrete 889, Oficina 208, San Isidro, Casilla 4410, Lima 100, T/F4424180. **C-D** *Hostal Siesta I*, Independencia 160, T233249. With bathroom, hot water, friendly owner. Also *Siesta II*, T234633, which is similar. **C** *Hostal Silmar*, Castrovirreyna 110, T235089. Hot water, TV, carpets. **E** *Tucaranda*, Lambayeque, next to the Ormeño bus terminal. With private bathrooms. **E** *Colón*, on the Plaza de Armas. With bathroom, **F** without, basic, dirty, old, noisy, restaurant. **E** *Confort*, La Mar 251, 4 blocks from the plaza. Clean, motorcycle parking. **E** *Hostal El Aleph*, Independencia 152. Good.

Sleeping
■ *on maps*
Price codes:
see inside front cover

F *Lima*, Lima 262. Basic, quiet. **F** *Europa*, Independencia 258. Clean, cold water, good. **F** *Salaverry*, Salaverry 146, T214019. Basic but clean, shared bathroom, cold water.

Eating
● *on maps*

Macondo, Jr Bolívar 300. Good for fish. Recommended. *El Otro Peñoncito*, Bolívar 255. Set lunch US$6, friendly, clean, good toilets. *El Fogón*, Municipalidad 276. Good and cheap. *El Edén, Casa Naturista*, Andahuaylas 204. Vegetarian. *Pastelería La Spiga*, Lima 243. Recommended. *Pastelería Velazco*, on Plaza de Armas. Clean, good service. Recommended. There's a good restaurant at the Ormeño bus terminal.

Festivals

The wine harvest festival (*Festival Internacional de la Vendimia*) is held in **early March** as is the *Concurso Nacional de Marinera*. On **1 May** is *Fiesta de la Cruz*. Also in **May, the 17**, is *Día Internacional del Pisco* (you don't need to be told what happens – use your imagination). In the **third week of June** is Ica Week and the **last week of September** is *Tourist Week*. In the **first 2 weeks of October** the image of *El Señor de Luren*, in a fine church in Parque Luren, draws pilgrims from all Peru, when there are all-night processions.

Transport

To **Pisco** (70 kilometres), 40 minutes, US$1 by bus, several daily; also colectivos from opposite the Ormeño terminal. *Ormeño* is at Lambayeque 180. All bus offices are on Lambayeque blocks 1 and 2 and Salaverry block 3. To **Lima** (302 kilometres), 4 hours, US$5, several daily including Soyez and Flores (see also Lima, Buses). To **Nasca** (140 kilometres), 2 hours, US$2; several buses and colectivos daily, including Ormeño, the last bus leaves at 2100. To **Arequipa** the route goes via Nasca, see under Nasca.

Directory

Banks Avoid changing TCs if possible as commission is high. If you need to, though, *Banco de Crédito* is reasonable. **Communications** Post Office: at Lima y Moquegua. **Telephone:** at Avda San Martín y Huánuco. **Tourist offices** Some information is available at travel agencies. Also try *Touring y Automóvil Club del Perú*, Manzanilla 523.

Ica to Nasca

Huacachina

Five kilometres from Ica, round a palm-fringed lake and amid impressive sand dunes, is the attractive oasis and summer resort of Huacachina. Its green sulphur waters are said to possess curative properties and attract thousands of visitors who come to swim and relax in this peaceful setting. Sleeping in the open is pleasant here, and swimming in the lake is beautiful, but watch out for soft sand (and, as elsewhere, watch your belongings). Sandboarding on the dunes has become a major pastime here, attracting fans from Europe and elsewhere. Board hire is US$0.50, from Manuel's restaurant, where you can also pitch a tent. Take a bus from the plaza in Ica to Huacachina, US$0.50, 10-15 minutes, or a taxi for US$1.50. **C** *Hotel Mossone*, is at the eastern end of the lake, T231651, F236137. A great place to relax, **A3** full board. **F** *Salvatierra*. Private bathroom, cheap but run down.

Palpa

Known as the 'Capital de la Naranja' (the Orange Capital), Palpa (*Population*: 15,000) is a hospitable town 97 kilometres south of Ica. The Plaza de Armas, on which the Municipalidad and church stand, is bordered by arches. Some colonial-style buildings survive. The climate is hot and dry (average annual temperature 21.4°C) and the main crops, besides oranges, are other fruits (eg plums, bananas) and cotton. There is also fishing for shrimp in the river. The *Fiesta de la Ciruela y Vendimia* (plum harvest) is in **March/April**. The town's tourist week is in the last week of July. The main *fiesta* is on **15 August**. **F** *San*

Francisco, 2 blocks from the plaza. Other hotels include the *Palpa*. There are also several *pensiones*, including *El Sol*, which is not recommended. Most restaurants are along the Pan-American Highway.

There are several archaeological sites, of different periods, not far from the town. The **Ciudad Perdida de Hualluri**, on the west side of the Panamericana Sur, 16 kilometres from Palpa, five kilometres from the Highway (Distrito Santa Cruz), is a ruined pre-Inca city. At the entrance to the site is a huarango tree which is over 1,000 years old. In Sector Sacramento, two kilometres from the Highway, is the **Puente Colgante del Inca**, built during the reign of Pachacútec. 15 kilometres from Palpa, on the road to Laluta, are the **Petroglifos de Chichictara**, more than 360 drawings on 65 large rocks depicting human and anthropomorphic figures, felines, llamas, dogs, condors, snakes and other creatures. They are said to date from the Chavín period. Other drawings can be found at **Llipata** and at the **Reloj Solar**, north of the city, 500 metres east of the Panamericana (the main design here is said to be a calendar marking the seasons of the year). The **Ciudadela de Santa Rosa** (five kilometres from Distrito Río Grande) and other ruins can also be visited.

Sights around Palpa

    Guides and information Seek information from the Consejo Municipal. There are no travel agencies in town. Otherwise ask for information and guides in Nasca. Recommended is César Barrios Castañeda at *Alegría Tours* (see below), who will take visitors in return for the cost of transport.

Nasca

Nasca lies 141 kilometres south of Ica by the Pan-American Highway, set in a green valley surrounded by mountains, 444 kilometres from Lima. Its altitude puts it just above any fog which may drift in from the sea. The sun blazes the year round by day and the nights are crisp. Overlooking the town is Cerro Blanco (2,078 metres), the highest sand dune in the world, which is popular for sandboarding and paragliding. The Virgen de la Guadelupe festival is held on 29 August to 10 September.

Population: 30,000
Altitude: 619 metres
Phone code: 034
Coloured map 5, grid B3

Ins and outs

The bus stations are grouped together at the western end of town on the Av Los Incas, just off the Panamerica Sur after it has crossed the Rio Tierras Blancas.

Getting there

Most of the hotels are spread out along Jr Lima and around the Plaza de Armas and are within easy walking distance of the bus station.

Getting around

Sights

Nasca would be just like any other anonymous desert town were it not for the 'discovery' of a series of strange lines etched on the desert plain to the north. Tourists in their thousands now flock to the town to fly over the famous Nasca Lines, whose precise purpose still remains a mystery.

    Nasca was badly damaged by an earthquake in 1996. Among the buildings destroyed was the municipality's museum on the main plaza. There are no plans to rebuild it, but there are plans to open another museum in late 1998, based on the studies of Professor Oreffice Italiano at the ruins of Cahuachi (see below).

Sights around Nasca

The Nasca area is dotted with over 100 cemeteries and the dry, humidity-free climate has preserved perfectly invaluable tapestries, cloth and mummies.

At the cemetery of **Chauchilla**, 30 kilometres south of Nasca, grave robbing *huaqueros* ransacked the tombs and left remains all over the place. Bones, skulls, mummies and pottery shards litter the desert. A tour is worthwhile and takes about two hours. It should cost about US$7 per person with a minimum of three people. On the Panamericana Sur, heading south from Nasca, Chauchilla is on the left, unsigned, 10 kilometres from the highway.

20 kilometres from Nasca, **Poroma** cemetery is on the right, signed (poorly). Cemetery tours usually include a visit to a gold shop. Gold mining is one of the main local industries and a tour usually includes a visit to a small family processing shop where the techniques used are still very old-fashioned.

Some tours also include a visit to a local potter's studio. That of Sr Andrés Calle Benavides, who makes Nasca reproductions, is particularly recommended. He is very friendly and takes time to explain the techniques he uses. His small gallery is a bit on the expensive side. Anyone interested in precolumbian ceramics is welcome to make an appointment to visit him independently. He is very knowledgeable on the coastal desert cultures.

The Paredones ruins, also called Cacsamarca, are Inca on a pre-Inca base. They are not well-preserved. The underground aqueducts, or *puquios*, built 1,500 years ago, still provide water for the local people. They are beautifully built and even have S-bends to slow down the flow of water, and they're

Nasca

■ **Sleeping**
1. Alegría
2. Hostal Don Agucho
3. Hostal El Sol
4. Hostal Las Líneas
5. Internacional
6. Lima
7. Nasca
8. Nasca Lines

● **Eating**
1. Chifa Nam Kug
2. Fuente de Soda Jumbory
3. La Taberna
4. Los Angeles
5. Mister Tiburón II
6. Sudamérica

🚌 **Buses**
1. Ormeño
2. Cruz del Sur
3. Tepsa
4. Comité Auto Nasca-Ica
5. Cóndor de Aymaraes
6. Señor de Lurín

very cool. 33 aqueducts irrigate 20 hectares each, and to this day local farmers have the job of cleaning the section for which their group has been responsible for as long as they can remember. By taxi it is about US$10 round trip, or go with a tour.

Cantalloc is a 30 minutes to an hour walk through Buena Fe, to see markings in the valley floor. These consist of a triangle pointing to a hill and a *tela* (cloth) with a spiral depicting the threads. Climb the mountain to see better examples. This is best done with a guide, or by car.

Cahuachi, to the west of the Nasca Lines, comprises several pyramids and a site called **El Estaquería**. The latter is thought to have been a series of astronomical sighting posts, but more recent research suggests the wooden pillars were used to dry dead bodies and therefore it may have been a place of mummification. Tours cost about US$5 per person (minimum of three).

On the Nasca-Cusco road, two hours out of Nasca (see **Ins and outs** above), is the **Reserva Nacional Pampas Galeras**, which has a vicuña reserve. There is a military base and park guard here. It's best to go early as entry is free.

Essentials

A3 *Nasca Lines*, Jr Bolognesi, T522293, F522293. With a/c, comfortable, rooms with private patio, hot water, peaceful, restaurant, good but expensive meals, safe car park, pool (US$2.50 for non-guests, or free if having lunch), they can arrange package tours which include 2-3 nights at the hotel plus a flight over the lines and a desert trip for around US$250. Recommended. **A3** *De La Borda*, an old hacienda at Majoro about 5 kilometres from town past the airstrip, T522576. Lovely gardens, pool, excellent restaurant, quiet, helpful, English-speaking manageress.

B *Maison Suisse*, opposite the airport, T/F522434. Nice, comfortable, safe car park, restaurant, pool, new rooms with jacuzzi, accepts Amex, good giftshop, shows video of Nasca Lines.

C *Hostal Don Agucho*, Paredones y San Carlos, T522048. Very clean, nice, friendly, pool, garage. **C** *Albergue Villa Verde*, Pasaje Angela sin número, T523373. A small country-style lodge in quiet gardens, pursues environmental improvements, pool, bar, parking. **C-D** *Alegría*, Jr Lima 168, T/F523775, T522444, Cellular 667381, E info@nazcaperu.com, www.nazcaperu.com. 4 new bungalows and 20 rooms with bathroom and continental breakfast, prices include tax, also rooms with shared bathroom, **E**, hot water, cafeteria, garden, manager (Efraín Alegría) speaks English and Hebrew, laundry facilities, safe luggage deposit (including for bus passengers not needing a hotel), book exchange, email facilities for US$2 per hour, free video on the lines at 2100, very popular and highly recommended. Efraín also runs a tour agency

Sleeping
■ *on maps*
*Price codes:
see inside front cover*

South Coast

with English, French and German speaking guides (see **Tours** below), flights and bus tickets arranged. Those arriving by bus should beware being told that *Alegría* is closed, or full, and no longer runs tours; if you call the hotel they will pick you up at the bus station free of charge day or night. **C-D** *Hostal Las Líneas*, Jr Arica 299, T522488. Clean, spacious, restaurant. Recommended.

D *Internacional*, Avda Maria Reiche, T522166. With bathroom, hot water, garage, café, poor reports but new bungalows may be better. **D-E** *Lima*, Avda Los Incas 117, opposite Ormeño bus terminal, T522497. **E** without bathroom, hot water, clean, their agency offers tours and flights.

E *Hostal El Sol*, Jr Tacna, on Plaza de Armas, T522064. With bathroom, basic but friendly, hot showers, small. **E** *Hostal Restaurant Via Morburg*, JM Mejía 108, near Plaza de Armas, T/F522566 (in Lima T4791467, F4620932). With bathroom, fan, hot water, small swimming pool, TV room, free pisco sour on arrival, excellent and cheap restaurant on top floor. Recommended.

F per person *Hostal El Pajonal*, Jr Callao 911, near Plaza de Armas. With bathroom, clean, friendly. Recommended. **F** *Nasca*, C Lima 438, T/F522085, hot water, noisy, clothes washing facilities, luggage store, hard sell on tours and flights, bargain hard for better price, mixed reports, safe motorcycle parking, dirty bathrooms.

Camping in the grounds of *Restaurant Nido del Cóndor* opposite the airport.

Eating
● *on maps*

Nido del Cóndor, opposite the airport. Also has shop, videos and swimming pool. *Aviance*, Arica 213. Recommended for *menú*. *Cañada*, Lima 160. Cheap, good *menú*, excellent pisco sours. Recommended. *Los Angeles*, half a block from Plaza de Armas. Good, cheap, try *sopa criolla*, and chocolate cake. *Concordia*, Lima 594. Good, also rents bikes at US$1 an hour. *Chifa Nam Kug*, on Bolognesi near the plaza. Recommended. *La Púa*, Jr Lima, next to *Hotel Alegría*. Good. *La Taberna*, Jr Lima 326. Excellent food, live music, friendly, popular with gringos, it's worth a look just for the graffiti on the walls. *Mister Tiburón II*, C San Martín. Clean, good food. *Sudamérica*, Lima 668. Good local food, especially meat. *Fuente de Soda Jumbory*, near the cinema. Good *almuerzo*. *Panadería Pin-Pan*, Lima y F de Castillo.

Shopping

There is a small market at Lima y Grau, and the Mercado Central is between Arica and Tacna.

Transport

To **Lima** (446 kilometres), US$5-8, 7 hours, several buses and colectivos daily. Recommended companies include: *Ormeño*, on Avenida Los Incas near the *Montecarlo* hotel; *Cruz del Sur*, next to *Hotel Alegría*; *Sudamericana*, in the *Hotel Alegría* and Civa. Cruz del Sur and Ormeño have an Imperial service for US$12.50, which arrives in San Isidro, a much safer area of Lima (see page 92).

To **Ica**, 2 hours, US$2, and to **Pisco** (210 kilometres), 3 hours, US$1.50; several buses and colectivos daily. Buses to **Camaná**, 390 kilometres, 6 hours, US$6, several daily. They continue to **Moquegua**, 244 kilometres, 4 hours, US$4. To **Tacna**, 793 kilometres, 12 hours, US$12, several buses daily.

To **Arequipa**, 623 kilometres, 10 hours, US$10, several buses daily; *Ormeño*, at 1900 and 2100, *Sudamericano*, 0300 and 2030, and Cruz del Sur at 2000 and 2230. *Cruz del Sur* and *Ormeño* have an Imperial service with *cochecama* for US$17.50. Delays are possible out of Nasca because of drifting sand across the road or because of mudslides in the rainy season. Travel in daylight if possible – buses that leave around 0300, 0330 do most of the journey in daylight. Book your ticket on previous day. Watch out for bus companies charging the full fare from Lima to Arequipa and for overbooking.

Buses to **Cusco**, 659 kilometres, 25 hours, US$18. The road is paved as far as the **Reserva Nacional Pampas Galeras** (see below); from there to **Puquío**, at 155 kilometres, it is in poor condition, but slowly being upgraded. From Puquío, via **Chalhuanca** (where gasoline is sold from the drum) to **Abancay** (309 kilometres), the road is poor but also being upgraded. Paving should be complete by May 1999. From Abancay to Cusco the road is paved.

There are now two bus companies which travel the **Lima-Nasca-Abancay-Cusco** route – *Cóndor de Aymaraes* and *Wari Tours*. Their offices are at the exit from Nasca on the road to Puquío. Check on safety before travelling on this route.

Directory

Banks *Banco de Crédito*, Lima y Grau. Changes cash and TCs at decent rates, also cash advance on visa. *Banco de la Nación*, offers poor rates. *Interbanc*, on the Plaza de Armas. Changes cash and will advance on Visa. Some street changers will change TCs, but at a poor rate. **Communications** Post **Office:** at Lima 816. Also at *Hotel Alegría*. **Telephone:** *Telefónica del Perú* for international calls with coins on Plaza Bolognesi. Also on Plaza de Armas and at Lima 359 where you can send or receive fax messages and make international collect calls. **Internet:** facilities at *Hotel Alegría*. **Tour companies & travel agents** *Algería Tours*, run by Efraín Alegría at *Hotel Alegría* offer inclusive tours (see **Sleeping** above) which have been repeatedly recommended. Guides with radio contact and maps can be provided for hikes to nearby sites. Juan Valdivia is very knowledgeable on the Nasca and Paracas cultures and speaks English. They are planning to run a specialized tour to the San Fernando Reserve to see the marine wildlife, as well as tours to Puerto Inca and the Inca ruins at Atiquipa. The Fernández family, who run the *Hotel Nasca*, also run local tours. Ask for the hotel owners and speak to them direct. Also ask Efraín Alegría or the Fernández family to arrange a taxi for you to one of the sites outside Nasca (eg US$50 to Sacaco, 30 minutes at site). It is not recommended to take just any taxi on the plaza as they are unreliable and can lead to robbery. It is not dangerous to visit the sites if you go with a trustworthy person. Also recommended is Juan Tohalino Vera of *Nasca Trails*, at Ignacio Morsesky 122, T522858, he speaks English, French, German and Italian. Taxi drivers usually act as guides, but most speak only Spanish. **NB** All guides must be approved by the Ministry of Tourism: ask to see an identity card. Tour and hotel touts try to overcharge or mislead those who arrive by bus: do not conduct any business at the bus station. **Useful addresses** Police: at Avda Los Incas.

Nasca Lines

About 22 kilometres north of Nasca, in the Ingenio valley, along the Pan-American Highway, are the famous Nasca Lines. Cut into the stony desert are large numbers of lines, not only parallels and geometrical figures, but also designs such as a killer whale, a monkey, birds (one with a wing span of over 100 metres), a spider and a tree. The lines, which can best be appreciated from the air, were etched on the Pampa sands by the Nasca people. It's estimated that they were begun around 400 BC and continued to be made for perhaps another thousand years.

Coloured map 5, grid B3

South Coast

The mystery of the lines   Since the Nasca Lines were first spotted from the air 70 years ago, their meaning, function and origin have tormented scientists around the world.

Dr Paul Kosok, a North American scientist, gave the first scientific explanation in 1941, when he observed a line pointing towards the place where the sun would have risen on the midwinter solstice in ancient Nasca times. So impressed was he, that he described the Nasca pampa as "the biggest astronomy book in the world".

By the 1950s Maria Reiche (see below), inspired by Kosok, was mapping the area and discovered giant animals too vast to be appreciated from the ground. Her many years of research led her to the conclusion that they were a huge astronomical calendar.

There are those who disagree with the German mathematician's hypothesis. The International Explorers Society, for example, were convinced that the desert artists would not have drawn something they themselves could not see. They set out to prove that the ancient Peruvians could fly, based on the fact that the lines are best seen from the air, and that there are pieces of ancient local pottery and tapestry showing balloonists as well as local legends of flying men. In 1975, they made a hot-air balloon of cloth and reed, called it *Condor I* and attempted to fly it for 15 minutes over the pampa. Unfortunately for them, the flight lasted only 60 seconds, thereby leaving the issue unresolved.

Some of the competing theories as to the function of the Nasca lines are rather far-fetched. Erich Von Daniken, in his book *Chariots of the Gods*, posited that the pampa was an extraterrestrial landing strip. This idea, however, only succeeded in drawing to the site thousands of visitors who tore across the lines on motorbikes, four-wheel drives, horses and whatever else they could get their hands on, leaving an indelible mark. It is now an offence to walk or drive on the pampa, punishable by heavy fine or imprisonment.

In 1980, George A Von Breunig claimed that the lines were part of a giant running track – presumably designed for an ancient Peruvian version of the Olympic Games. A similar theory was proposed by the English astronomer Alan Sawyer.

Other theories are that the Nasca designs represent weaving patterns and yarns (Henri Stirlin) and that the plain is a map demonstrating the Tiahuanaco Empire (Zsoltan Zelko). Dr Johan Reinhard brings together ethnographic, historical and archaeological data, including the current use of straight lines in Chile and Bolivia, to suggest that the Lines conform to fertility practices throughout the Andes.

Recent research   The most recent research, carried out by the BBC series 'Ancient Voices', points to yet another theory. The clues to the function of the lines are found in the highly advanced pottery and textiles of the ancient Nascans, which relate directly to the subject matter of the lines. Some pots and tapestries show a flying being emitting discharge from its nose and mouth. This is believed to portray the flight of the shaman (or religious practitioner). The shaman consumes certain psycho-active drugs that convince him he can fly and so enter the real world of spirits in order to rid sick people of evil spirits.

In this way, the lines were not designed to be seen physically from above, but from the mind's eye of the flying shaman. This also explains the presence of incongruous creatures such as a monkey or killer whale. They were chosen because they possess the qualities admired and needed by the shaman in his spirit journeys.

But this does not explain the spectacular geometric figures. These straight lines seem to be a feature of ancient Peruvian ritual behaviour and are perhaps like ley lines in Europe – invisible paths of perceived energy. The

Maria Reiche – Guardian of the lines

The greatest contribution to our awareness of the lines is that of Maria Reiche, who lived and worked on the Pampa for over 50 years. The young German mathematician arrived in Peru in the early 1930s and would dedicate the rest of her life to removing centuries of windswept debris and painstaking survey work.

Maria Reiche's years of meticulous measurement and study of the lines led her to conclude that they represented a huge astronomical calendar. She also used her mathematical knowledge to determine how the many drawings and symbols could have been created with such precise symmetry. She suggested that those responsible for the lines used long cords attached to stakes in the ground. The figures were drawn by means of a series of circular arcs of different radius. Reiche also contended that they used a standard unit of measurement of 1.30m, or the distance between the fingertips of a person's extended arms.

As well as the anthropomorphic and zoomorphic drawings, there are a great many geometric figures. Reiche believed these to be a symbolic form of writing associated with the movements of the stars. In this way, the lines could have been used as a kind of calendar that not only recorded celestial events but also had a practical function indicating the times for harvest, fishing and festivals.

Whatever the real purpose of the Nasca lines, one fact remains indisputable: that their status as one of the country's major tourist attractions is largely due to the selfless work of Maria Reiche, the unofficial guardian of the lines. Maria Reiche died in June 1998.

Pampa's most remarkable features are the trapezoids, which are thought to have been ritual spaces where offerings were made to the gods, in the hope of favours in return.

Scientists have discovered evidence of a terrible 40-year drought around AD 550 or 600. This coincides not only with the abandonment of the nearby Cahuachi temples but also with a period of increased bloody warfare and increased line-making in the desert sands. This would seem to indicate that the Nascans grew increasingly desperate in the face of continued drought, abandoned traditional religious practices, and instead made more and more sacrificial offerings to the gods.

In 1976 Maria Reiche had a platform called the mirador put up at her own expense, from which three of the huge designs can be seen – the Hands, the Lizard and the Tree. Her book, *Mystery on the Desert*, is on sale for US$10 (proceeds to conservation work) at the hotel. In January 1994 Maria Reiche opened a small museum (entry US$0.50), five kilometres from town at the Km 416 marker. Lectures on the Nasca Lines are held at Calle Michaela Bastides 218.

Further reading *Pathways to the Gods: The Mystery of the Andes Lines*, by Tony Morrison (Michael Russell, 1978), obtainable in Lima. *The Mystery of the Nasca Lines*, also by Tony Morrison (Nonesuch Expeditions, 1987). *Lines to the Mountain Gods: Nasca and the Mysteries of Peru* by E Hadingham (Random House, 1987). An account of the balloon flight is in *Nasca, the flight of Condor 1*, by Jim Woodman, Murray, 1980 (Pocket Books, NY 1977). *The Nasca Lines – a new perspective on their origin and meaning* (Editorial Los Pinos, Lima 18), by Dr Johan Reinhard.

Tours of the Nasca Lines

By land Taxi-guides to the mirador, 0800-1200, cost US$7 per person, or you can hitch, but there is not always much traffic. Travellers suggest the view from the hill 500 metres back to Nasca is better. An *Ormeño* bus leaves for the lines at 0900 (US$1.75); hitch

South Coast

back, but have patience. Go by an early bus as the site gets very hot. Better still, take a taxi and arrive at 0745 before the buses.

By air Small planes take 3-5 passengers to see the Nasca Lines. Reservations can be made at the airport for flights with **Aerocóndor** – their office is opposite *Hotel Nasca Lines*. Flights can also be booked at *Hotel Alegría* with **Alas Peruanas** (experienced pilots fluent in English), *Hotel Nasca*, **Aero Montecarlo**, **AeroParacas** (T667231, F522688) or **Aero Ica in Jr Lima** and at the airport. These companies are well-established and recommended. There are others. The price for a flight is US$35-50 per person, plus US$2 airport tax. It is best to organize a flight direct with the airlines. Flights should last from 30 to 45 minutes, but are sometimes cut to 20, and are bumpy with many tight turns – many people are airsick. Best times to fly are 0800-1000 and 1500-1630 when there is less turbulence and better light.

Aerocóndor in Lima (T4425663, or at the *Sheraton Hotel*, T4333320) and **Aero Ica** (T4418614/8608) both offer flights over the lines from Lima in a 1-day tour (lunch in Nasca) for US$260 per person; or flights from Ica for US$130 per person. Aero Ica also offers a night in *Maison Suisse* plus flight for US$65, but book 48 hours in advance. A taxi to the airport costs US$1.35; bus, US$0.10. Make sure you clarify everything before getting on the plane and ask for a receipt. Also let them know in advance if you have any special requests.

South of Nasca

Sacaco 30 kilometres south of Nasca is Sacaco, which has a museum built over the fossilized remains of a whale excavated in the desert. The keeper lives in a house nearby and is helpful. Take a bus from Nasca, C Bolognesi, in the morning (check times in advance) towards Puerto de Lomas. Ask the driver where to get off and be ready for a 30 minute-walk in the sun. Return to the Pan-American Highway no later than 1800 for a bus back. Do not go two to three days after a new moon as a vicious wind blows at this time.

Puerto de Lomas Lying seven kilometres off the Pan-American Highway, on the coast, is Puerto de Lomas, a fishing village with safe beaches which are popular in February and March. It is one and a half hours by bus from Nasca, US$1.75 (one hour by car). **C** *Hostal Capricho de Verano*, T210282. Beautifully-situated on the cliffs, bungalows with bathroom, clean, same owner as *Hostal Don Agucho* in Nasca, run by very friendly elderly couple, special rates for young travellers. Recommended. 100 metres beyond is *Restaurant Alojamiento Melchorita*. There are also several fish restaurants.

San Juan Before Puerto de Lomas a branch road leads off the Pan-American to the ports of San Juan and San Nicolás, built to ship iron ore from the Marcona field, 29 kilometres inland, and Acarí, 53 kilometres east again, where a copper deposit is also being worked. San Juan has a beautiful deep-water bay. There is accommodation in **E** *Hotel Pacífico*, clean. Recommended.

From Puerto de Lomas the highway heads south through Yauca to Chala. The Yauca valley is almost entirely devoted to olive trees, so have a few soles ready to buy some when the bus stops.

Chala 173 kilometres from Nasca, Chala is a friendly fishing village with nice beaches but it is only safe to swim near the harbour. The town has expanded greatly in recent years on the back of gold-mining in the nearby hills. It now consists of 'old' Chala and Chala Norte, spread out along three kilometres of

Footprint Handbooks

Travel guides for free spirits

Footprint Handbooks
6 Riverside Court
Lower Bristol Road
Bath
BA2 3DZ
England

RCS99

the Panamericana. Good fresh fish is available in the morning and it may be possible to go fishing with the local fishermen. All the better hotels are in old Chala. **C** *Turistas*, in a renovated building, with bathroom. **D** without, large rooms, good beds, friendly, hot water, restaurant, great sea view. **F** *Hostal Grau* and next door is *Hostal Evertyh*. Both are very clean, comfortable and friendly with rooms facing the ocean. Restaurants *Chimona* and *Pulpo Real* serve big plates of delicious seafood. Try *chicharrones de pulpo* (octopus) and *lenguado* (fried fish).

Colectivos leave daily from Nasca in the morning, US$4 per person, 2 hours. Buses stop in Chala Norte, a 10-minute walk from the hotels. If heading south, the night buses from Lima arrive at 0600-0700, and there are others in the early evening. Buses heading north come through nearer 0500, or in the early afternoon.

10 kilometres north of Chala are the large precolumbian ruins of Puerto Inca   **Puerto Inca** on the coast in a beautiful bay. On their discovery in the 1950s, the ruins were misunderstood and thus neglected. It is now recognized that this was the port for Cusco. The site is in excellent condition. The drying and store houses can be seen as holes in the ground (be careful where you walk). On the right side of the bay is a cemetery, on the hill is a temple of reincarnation, and the Inca road from the coast to Cusco is clearly visible. The road was 240 kilometres long, with a staging post every seven kilometres so that, with a change of runner at every post, messages could be sent in 24 hours.

There is a good two hour walk from Puerto Inca to Chala. Take one of the paths going up behind the ruins on the south side of the bay and swing slightly inland to cross a deep *quebrada*. The path then continues through spectacular rock formations with dramatic views of the coast towards the road. A Chala colectivo can be picked up just north of the town. **C** *Puerto Inka*, at Km 603 on the Panamericana Sur (for reservations T691494, or Avda Ejército 506, oficina 202, Arequipa, T/F258798). A great place to relax, with a superb beach, excellent beach, boats and diving equipment for hire, disco, hammocks, highly recommended but used by tour groups and busy in the summer months. Also camping for US$2 per person. A taxi from Chala costs US$5, or take a Yauca colectivo to Km 603 (US$0.50 per person) and walk down the track to the bay (30 minutes). South of Chala the Pan-American passes **Atico** (**F** *Hostal La Unión*, basic) and **Ocoña** before reaching **Camaná** (392 kilometres from Nasca). The stretch of road between Atico and Ocoña is one of the loveliest on the entire south coast. It is also one of the most dangerous if you happen to be cycling.

Camaná

This picturesque little coastal town lies 222 kilometres south from Chala. It has a good food market and there is a small swimming pool on Avenida Mcal Castilla (new Pan-American Highway), US$1.

Five kilometres away is **La Punta**, the most popular of Camaná's beaches, especially during summer weekends when it is packed with young Arequipeños who come to party in the many bars and discos lining the beach road. One of these is *El Cangrejo*, one of the most popular discos in southern Peru. It's very busy and exclusive with an US$8 cover charge. There are many cheap restaurants lining the beach road, though most don't look too clean.

The beach is pleasant but has little shade and is dangerous for swimming owing to the strong undertow. Parasols can be hired for US$1.50. Colectivos leave frequently day and night from Camaná, US$0.25.

South Coast

32 kilometres south of Camaná is the tiny, pleasant village of **Quilca** on the Río Quilca. Camaná sends its products to the small port nearby. In colonial times it was the unloading point for goods imported via Arequipa to Potosí. It is now a seedy harbour. The village of Quilca is further along, perched on a cliff overlooking the Río Siguas.

A bus leaves daily at 0900 and returns from Quilca at 1330; US$1.40, two hours. The journey is spectacular and offers the chance of seeing large birds of prey and desert foxes. There is nothing much at the port so it's better to stay on until the village itself. The bus stops outside the only restaurant in town (which has a good set lunch), then continues to the fertile valley below before turning round for the return trip.

The coastal village of **Chira**, 12 kilometres north of Camaná is worth a visit for its impressive sea cliffs, sea birds and quiet beaches. Catch a colectivo to **Atico** and ask to get off at Chira; US$0.70, 30 minutes.

Sleeping **NB** Hotels tend to be full in January, February and March. **B** *San Diego*, on the plaza, T572854. "Lives up to its name in terms of its facilities and appearance". **C** *Plaza*, on the plaza, T571051. **C-D** *Turistas*, Avda Lima 138, T571113. Old colonial building, with bathroom and breakfast, big rooms, helpful, safe, restaurant downstairs. Recommended. **D** *Camaná*, 9 de Septiembre, 1 block from the plaza. With bathroom and hot water. **D** *Lider 2*, Avda Mcal Castilla 678 (new Pan-American Highway), T571365. With bathroom, hot water, clean, comfortable, front rooms noisy. **D** *Residencial Selva*, Prolongación 2 de Mayo 225, Urb Granada, T572063. With bathroom, cold water, modern, spacious, clean, very friendly, laundry facilities, cafeteria, patios and gardens, not very central but the owner will collect you if you call him on arrival in Camaná, discount for longer stays. Highly recommended. **E** *Lider 1*, Avda Lima 268 (old Pan-American Highway), T571474. With bathroom, clean, good restaurant, safe motorcycle parking for US$3. **F** *Hostal Lugapra*, Jr Piérola 220. Clean, with bathroom, friendly.

Eating *Chifa Hong Kong*, on the Plaza de Armas. Excellent food at reasonable prices, popular. *Turístico Trujillana*, Avda Pizarro 304, T571252. Seafood, including delicious local shrimps, and *peña*. Recommended. *Snack Barucci*, Jr 28 de Julio, on the corner of the Plaza. Modern and classy but overpriced, popular. *Willy Pollería*, Avda Lima 137. Good, cheap chicken and chips. *Savory Club*, Jr 28 de Julio 218. Good food but overpriced and not too friendly. The best place for breakfast is the food market, where you can enjoy excellent, cheap fruit juices, spinach pies and *empanadas*. The freshwater shrimps are delicious.

Bars & *La Barra*, Avda Mcal Castilla 600. Good, loud music, popular. *Barucci*, Jr 28 de Julio, on **nightclubs** the corner of the Plaza, beneath the snack bar of the same name. Impressive sound and light system, US$2.50 cover charge. *Encuentros Video Pub*, Avda Mcal Castilla. Good videos, cheap beer, poor sound.

Transport Many buses leave daily to **Lima**, (eg *Ormeño*), US$12, 12 hours; also to **Arequipa**, many daily (eg *Transportes Turismo*), US$4, $3\frac{1}{2}$ hours. To **Pisco** with *Flores Hnos* and *Sudamericano*, US$7, 8 hours. Many companies have their offices on Avenida Lima.

Inland to Arequipa

The Pan-American Highway swings inland from Camaná to **El Alto** where a road branches left off the Pan-American Highway and leads to **Corire**, Aplao and the valley of the Río Majes (see page 245). The Pan-American then runs along the top of a plateau with strange ash-grey sand dunes . These are unique in appearance and formation. All are crescent shaped and of varying sizes, from six to 30 metres across and from two to five metres high, with the points of the crescent on the leeward side. The sand is slowly blown up the convex side, drifts down into the concave side, and the dunes move about 15 metres a year.

The road suddenly descends into the canyons of the Siguas and Vitór rivers. There is an *hostal* (**F**) and restaurants five kilometres south of **Siguas** and an *hostal* in the village of **Vitór**.

At Repartición, 42 kilometres southwest of Arequipa, 134 kilometres from Camaná, a branch of the Panamericana Sur leads south through Moquegua to Tacna and Arica on the Chilean border. Cyclists warn that the road to Moquegua is very hilly. From this latter road a branch leads off from **La Joya** west to Mollendo and Matarani.

Repartición

Mollendo

130 kilometres south of Arequipa, Mollendo (*Population*: approximately 30,000. *Phone code*: 054) has now been replaced as a port by Matarani (see below), though port workers still live mostly in Mollendo, where the main customs agencies are. The town now depends partly upon the summer attraction of its beaches, despite the presence of a smelly oil refinery. During the high season (January to April) hotels can be full. Out of season, Mollendo has the appearance of an abandoned wild west town, with its ramshackle wooden houses, some painted in gaudy colours.

Three sandy beaches stretch down the coast. The small beach nearest town is the safest for swimming. The swimming pool on the beach is open January-March. Out of season the beaches are littered with rubbish. On 6 January the town celebrates the anniversary of the district and start of the summer season.

On the coast, a few kilometres southeast by road (US$0.40 by colectivo), is the summer resort of **Mejía**. The small national reserve at the lagoons has 72 resident species of birds and 62 visiting species.

South Coast

B-C *El Hostalito*, Blondell 169, T533674. Very spacious rooms with TV, breakfast served, "the best in town". **C** *Hostal Cabaña*, Comercio 240, on the plaza. A wooden building with huge balconies, with bathroom, **F** per person with shared bathroom, clean, good, but just a bit on the expensive side. **D** *Hostal Willy*, Deán Valdivia 437-443. With bathroom, hot water, TV, modern, clean and spacious, though some rooms may be noisy because of the nearby disco. Recommended. **E** *El Muelle*, on Arica. Without bathroom, basic and not very clean. **E-F** *Hostal San Martín*, on Melgar opposite the market. Cold water only but very clean, great value, good views from top rooms. Recommended. **F** *Hostal California*, Blondell 541, T535160. Best rooms at the top, restaurant. Recommended. There are several cheap places on Arequipa, also on Arica and Tacna. Note that many hotels increase their rates over the weekend in the summer season.

Sleeping

La Cabaña, Comercio 208. Excellent, cheap set meals. *Tambo*, on Comercio. Excellent food at moderate prices. *La Pizzería*, Comercio 301. Good. Also on Comercio is *Marco Antonio*, which is expensive but serves great coffee. *Chifa San Wha*, Comercio 412, T532712. Owned by the mayor, good food but not cheap. *Pollería La Granja*, Deán Valdivia 595, T533097. Very friendly, clean, cheap. *Juguería Zanahorias*, on Arequipa. Good fruit juices.

Eating

Video Bar, on Comercio. Good music and videos, and big jugs of beer for US$2.50. *El Observatorio*, Comercio y Deán Valdivia. A massive, booming, semi-open-air disco, "has to be seen to be believed", no cover charge.

Bars & nightclubs

Transport   Buses to **Arequipa**, 129 kilometres, buses and colectivos daily, 2 hours, US$3, many companies on Comercio opposite the church. To **Moquegua**, 156 kilometres, 2 hours, US$2-3, several buses and colectivos daily. To **Tacna**, 315 kilometres, direct transport on Thursday only, otherwise take a colectivo early in the morning to El Fiscal (restaurant), about 100 kilometres before Moquegua, where you can connect with Arequipa-Tacna buses. To **Lima**, 3 times a week with *TEPSA*, or take an Arequipa bus to Km 48 on the Pan-American Highway where you can catch an Arequipa-Lima bus.

Matarani

14½ kilometres to the northwest of Mollendo is the port of Matarani. The town is small, pleasant and quiet. There is a good tourist restaurant near the main plaza. It can be reached by colectivo on a good road, US$0.50. Stay on the colectivo until you reach the port gates, where the port captain will be happy to show you around (take your passport). You can walk back to the town, which is recommended for the views, or catch a colectivo from the gates.

Moquegua

Population: 110,000
Altitude: 1,412 metres
Coloured map 6, grid C1

Moquegua (213 kilometres from Arequipa), is a peaceful town in the narrow valley of the Moquegua River and enjoys a sub-tropical climate. The town was formerly known as Santa Catalina de Guadalcazar, but thankfully reverted to its original name, which means 'silent place' in Quechua. This could be due to the rather taciturn nature of its inhabitants.

Ins and outs

Getting there   The bus station is out of town off the Pan-american Highway. The road into town runs along Av La Paz. It joins the main street (Avda Balta) at the large roundabout.

Getting around   A nicely compact town, the main street is Avda Balta running two blocks north of Plaza de Armas. On Saturday nights Jr Moquegue west from the plaza to Jr Piura, becomes the centre of activity.

Moquegua is not a pretty sight from the Pan-American Highway, but the old centre, a few blocks above the road, is well worth a look for its quiet, winding, cobbled streets and 19th century buildings. The Plaza de Armas, with its mix of ruined and well-maintained churches, colonial and republican façades and llama-shaped hedges, is one of the most interesting small-town plazas in the country. The fountain is said to have been designed by Eiffel, though there is some debate on the matter. The decadent statuary of the fountain in front of the Santo Domingo church is seen by some as a challenge to the traditional Catholic religious iconography within the church. The roofs of many of the old houses are built with sugar-cane thatch and clay and their sculpted door surrounds are particularly notable.

The Inca Emperor, Mayta Capac, sent his captains to carry out a pacifying occupation of the fertile valleys around Moquegua. They founded two settlements, Moquegua and Cuchuna, which is thought to be the site of present-day Torata. Today, most of the valley below the city grows grapes and the upper part grows avocados (*paltas*), wheat, maize, potatoes, some cotton, and fruits. 23 kilometres northeast from Moquegua is Cuajone, one of the most important copper mines in Peru.

Sights

There are several interesting colonial houses which make a good, short walking tour. **Casa de Regidor Perpetuo de La Ciudad** or **Casa Conde de Alastaya**, is an 18th century house at Jr Moquegua 404-414. **Casa de Fernández de Córdova** is at Jr Ayacucho 540, on the plaza. At Jr Lima 849 is **Casa de Samuel Ordóñez**, which is now the PNP radio control HQ. **Casa de Doctor Martínez**, at Jr Ayacucho 828, has a collapsed interior but baroque elements can be seen in the ornate façade. **Casa de Jiménez de la Flor**, at Ayacucho 550-570, on the Plaza de Armas, is notable for its high-relief carved retablo figures.

Also worth seeing are: **Casa de Don Pacífico Barrios**, Jr Moquegua 818-822; **Casa de Diez Canseco**, esquina Tarapacá y Ayacucho. Some of these houses are private, but the owners may allow entry.

Near *Hotel El Mirador* (see below) are some interesting *bodegas*.

Museums **Museo Contisuyo** on the Plaza de Armas, is within the ruins of the Iglesia Matriz, which was rebuilt after many earthquakes over the centuries, but finally left as a ruin in 1868. It covers the Pucara, Huari, Tiahuanaco, Colla, Lupaca and Inca cultures and displays artefacts from around the area. ■ *Open Tuesday 1700-2000, Wednesday-Sunday 1000-1300, 1500-1700.*

Essentials

The main street is Avda Balta. On Saturday nights Jr Moquegua, from the Plaza de Armas to Jr Piura, becomes the centre of activity.

Sleeping **C** *El Mirador*, 1 kilometre from town on the road to the airport. With pool, clean, friendly, hot water, disco. **C** *Limoneros*, Jr Lima 441, T761649. With bathroom, hot water, **D** without bath, car park, discount for groups of more than 10, pool (usually

■ *on maps*
Price codes:
see inside front cover

Moquegua

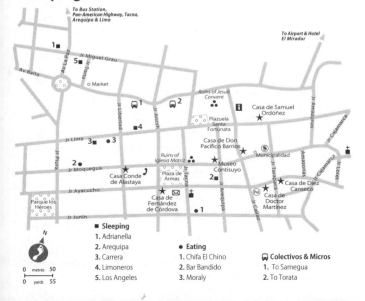

■ **Sleeping**
1. Adrianella
2. Arequipa
3. Carrera
4. Limoneros
5. Los Angeles

● **Eating**
1. Chifa El Chino
2. Bar Bandido
3. Moraly

🚐 **Colectivos & Micros**
1. To Samegua
2. To Torata

South Coast

empty), old house with basic rooms, nice garden. **D** *Hostal Adrianella*, Miguel Grau 239, T763469. All rooms with bathroom, clean, modern, hot water, TV. **D** *Los Angeles*, Jr Torata 100-A, T762629. Hot water, TV, friendly, may be able to negotiate discount for groups, special rates for children. Recommended. **E** *Arequipa*, Jr Arequipa. Clean, hot water sometimes. **F** *Hostal Carrera*, Jr Lima 320, T762113. Clean, friendly. Recommended.

Eating *Moraly*, Lima y Libertad. Good sized portions, moderate prices, "best in town". Rec-
● *on maps* ommended. *Chifa El Chino*, Jr Tacna, just off the plaza, beside Santo Domingo church. *Bar Bandido*, Jr Moquegua 333. European-style bar, serves pizzas.

Festivals In mid-**October** is *Santa Fortunata*. The main celebration is *Día de Santa Catalina* on 25 **November**, which is the anniversary of the founding of the colonial city.

Transport Bus from **Lima**, US$16. **Moquegua-Ilo**, 95 kilometres, 1½ hours, US$1, a few buses daily. To **Tacna**, 159 kilometres, 2 hours, US$2, several buses and colectivos daily. To **Puno**, 262 kilometres, 10 hours, daily with San Martín and others, US$7. To **Arequipa**, 3½ hours, US$4, several buses daily.

Directory **Banks** *Banco de Crédito*, esquina Moquegua y Tarapacá. The only bank that changes TCs, will also advance money on Visa, open 0915-1315, 1630-1830. **Communications** Post Office: on the Plaza de Armas in a colonial house. **Telefónica del Perú**: is at Jr Moquegua 434. **Tourist offices** Jr Callao 121, is more administrative than service oriented, closes 1600.

Around Moquegua

Torata 24 kilometres northeast from Moquegua is Torata, a quiet, small town with a nice, shaded plaza. Above the town, on a hill above the right of the two crosses which overlook the town, are the Huari ruins of Torata Alta, a 30-minute walk away. The ruins are in a poor state but you can still get a good idea of their extent and the shape and size of the houses from the low surviving walls. The site enjoys good views over to Cerro Baúl. To get there take a micro or colectivo from Avenida Balta, between Jr Ancash y Tacna. From the cross on the Moquegua-Cuajone road the last few kilometres to Torata is not paved.

Cerro Baúl A highly recommended trip is to Cerro Baúl, 2,590 metres. This can be com-bined with the ruins at Torata to make a full day's excursion. The mountain is like a *tepuy*, with sheer sides and flat top, hence its name, which means trunk. There are excellent views for miles around from the summit. The mountain became famous in legend as the place of refuge for the Chuchunas, who resisted the peaceful invasion of the Incas. Eventually the Chuchunas were starved off the mountain, but the refuge had lasted for a considerable time as their children regularly made nocturnal food raids into the Inca camps below.

To get to Cerro Baúl, take a micro for Torata, or for Cuajone, and get off at the crossroads for Torata, at the top of the pass beneath the northern end of the mountain. The path leads up the gradual slope from the road. There is a steep section for the last 200 metres with some scrambling involved, but it's not too difficult or steep. It takes 45 minutes from the road to the top. The path leads to a Christian shrine (two crosses), where offerings are made for good crops and to allay sickness. At the near end are extensive Huari ruins. Covering the entire flat summit, which is 1½ kilometres long and 200 metres wide, are hundreds of modern arrangements of stones and miniature shrines, a mixture of pagan and Christian.

Four and a half kilometres from Moquegua is Samegua, known as avocado **Samegua**
town, with many restaurants. To get there take a micro from Avenida Balta,
between Libertad and Ancash. It takes 10 minutes.

Omate (*Altitude*: 2,160 metres. *Population*: 3,000), is a small town, 146 kilo- **Omate**
metres to the north of Moquegua on an unpaved road, and 129 kilometres to
the south of Arequipa (five hours). The town is important for its famed
Semana Santa processions. Nearby are the thermal baths at **Ulucán**.

Ilo

Moquegua's exports – avocados and wine – go by an excellent 96 kilometre road Population: 95,000
to the fast developing industrial city and important port of Ilo. Its main indus- Phone code: 054
tries are copper refining, fishing, fish oil products and, more recently, tourism. In Coloured map 5, grid C6
1992, Bolivia was given part of the beach south of Ilo, now called Bolivia Mar,
and Bolivia also got half of the Zona Franca, a tax free industrial zone, for the
import and export of Bolivia's goods.

There are three Ilos: Ilo Viejo; Ilo Nuevo; and the present town. Ilo Viejo was
founded by the French as a port for their ships. In precolumbian times,
between 900 and 1300 AD, it was the centre of the Chiribaya culture. The old
part has pleasant seafront gardens, an amphitheatre for theatre productions, a
gazebo (La Glorieta) at the end of a short pier (not recommended for long
walks), an old fishing pier (Muelle Fiscal), old port buildings and a sheltered
fishing harbour.

The present town is pretty ugly, with a fishmeal factory, oil tanks, and
dusty cobbled streets and 'half-door' saloons. Uglier still is Ilo Nuevo, a
breezeblock town built by the Southern Peru Copper Corporation for its
engineers and their families on a plateau out of sight of Ilo Viejo. The *Festival
del Olivo* takes place in September.

Sights

Plaza Grau is the smallest and the most attractive of the three main plazas and
has a ship and mast in its centre. **Templo San Jerónimo**, on Plaza de Armas,
was constructed in 1871 – its clock tower was made in Germany. **La Glorieta**,
the Mirador at the end of the pier, was built in 1915. It is a symbol of the prosperity of the old fishing port. Beside it is the old fishing quay, the Muelle Fiscal, which dates from 1870.

One of the more notable older civic buildings is known as the **Casa
Antigua** and is opposite the Capitanía del Puerto. It now houses the Ilo Social
Club. The **Casa de Cultura**, on Avenida Grau sin número on the seafront,
doubles up as a source of tourist information, with leaflets on precolumbian
culture. It is a very distinctive, red and white building, with very friendly and
helpful staff.

Museo Eduardo Jiménez Lazo, on the Plaza de Armas, shows Chiribaya
and more recent exhibits. **Museo Naval** is in the Capitanía building at the
harbour, it is good on local nautical history and has navigational relics, diving
gear, some of Admiral Grau's manuscripts and a good explanation of the War
of the Pacific.

Valle de los Olivares, also known as Valle Ilo, lies 15 kilometres to the
north. The main attraction is the **Museo de Sitio El Algarrobal** which is

dedicated to the local Chiribaya culture and displays mummies, ceramics and some textiles. There are petroglyphs in the garden. Ask for the director Gerardo Carpio to show you around; he speaks slowly and clearly in Spanish.

Open Tuesday to Friday 0730-1400 and Saturday 0900-1300, closed Monday. US$0.80. There are two buses daily from the main plaza. A taxi costs US$6 return including one hour at the museum.

Six kilometres south of Ilo lies **Punta Coles**, a Nature Reserve similar to the Ballestas Islands, further north near Pisco, where sea lions and guano birds can be seen. You need permission from the Capitanía del Puerto, which may or may not be given, then need to charter a boat.

There are many beaches nearby. **Playa de Lizas**, six kilometres to the south of Ilo. It becomes very crowded with Peruvian tourists during the summer. One kilometre southwest of town is **Puerto Ingles**, a beautiful rocky cove.

Essentials

Sleeping

■ *on maps*
Price codes:
see inside front cover

C *Gran Hotel*, Avda Boca del Río sin número, a long way from the centre, T782411. With bathroom, restaurant. **C** *Karina*, Abtao 780 y Mcal Nieto, T781531. Breakfast included, hot water, all rooms with bath, modern and very clean, very friendly, telephone, TV US$2 extra, car parking US$2 extra per day. **C** *Romicor*, Moquegua y Ayacucho, T781195. With

Ilo Viejo

■ Sleeping
1. El Paraíso
2. Karina
3. Romicor
4. San Martín

● Eating
1. Criss
2. Los Corales
3. Marcelo's

0 metres 50
0 yards 55

bathroom, hot water. **D** *El Paraíso*, Zepita 751 y Mcal Nieto, T781432. All rooms with bathroom, hot water, dig the groovy 70s psychedelic interior. **D** *San Martín*, C Matará 325. With bathroom, cheaper without, hot water, car parking US$1.50 per night.

There are many other hotels in town, some of which are almost certainly cheaper than those above, especially around the bus station.

Marcelo's, Moquegua y 28 de Julio 335, on the corner of the Plaza de Armas. Good, basic, cheap *menú*. *Criss*, Ayacucho 416. Good value *menú*. *Los Corales*, Jr Abtao 412. Good but expensive. *El Peñon*, at the bottom of 28 de Julio, off Plaza Grau. Very good food, especially fish, US$3.50 average, balcony overlooks seaport. **Eating** ● *on maps*

Buses to **Moquegua**, US$1.50 with *Flores Hnos*. Micros and colectivos to Moquegua and Tacna leave from Alto Ilo. Many of the large bus companies which run buses between Moquegua and Lima start in Ilo, but they are not very full when they arrive in Moquegua. A new bus terminal is being built on the main road into town from Moquegua. *Flores Hnos* and *Cruz del Sur* don't leave from the bus terminal but from the parallel street nearer the sea. **Transport**

Banks *Banco de Crédito*, Zepita y 28 de Julio. **Communications** *Telefónica del Perú*, Moquegua y 2 de Mayo, on the corner of the plaza. **Directory**

Toquepala

70 kilometres south of Moquegua a sign points to the **Minas de Toquepala**, which are 64 kilometres further on a good road. A bus service runs from Tacna. There is a good view of the valley which is full of cacti. Toquepala village, lying in a hollow, has a guest house with swimming pool, a church, clubhouse and an American School, and is a pleasant place. However, it is a private mining community and permission from the management must be obtained in advance to visit the village.

A nearby cave contains paintings believed to date from 8,000 BC, but it is very hard to find. Helio Courier planes reach it from Moquegua in 12 minutes and from Ilo in 26 minutes. You can also take a taxi from Tacna.

The Southern Peru Copper Corporation is exploiting its copper property at Toquepala, east of Moquegua, at an altitude of 3,050 metres. All exports are through Ilo, along the 183 kilometres railway and road from Toquepala. The SPCC smelter is on the coast, 18 kilometres from the port of Ilo.

Tacna

Backed by the snow-capped peak of Tacora, Tacna is 156 kilometres south of Moquegua by the Pan-American Highway, 42 kilometres from the Chilean frontier, and 64 kilometres from the international port of Arica, to which there is a railway. It is 1,292 kilometres from Lima by road.

Population: 174,366
Altitude: 550 metres
Phone code: 054
Coloured map 6, grid C2

Tacna was in Chilean hands from 1880 to 1929, when its people voted by plebiscite to return to Peru. There are good schools, housing estates, a stadium to seat 10,000 people, an airport, many military posts and one of the best hospitals in Peru.

Around the city the desert is gradually being irrigated. The local economy includes olive groves, vineyards and fishing. The waters of Laguna Aricota, 80 kilometres north, are now being tapped for further irrigation and hydroelectric power for industry.

Ins and outs

Getting there As this is the nearest town to Chile, transport links are good with the rest of the country. The airport is some way out of town to the southwest and there is no transport direct to the border from here. The bus station is on Hipólito Unánue, 1 kilometre from the plaza (colectivo US$0.25). It is well-organized, local tax US$0.40, baggage store, easy to make connections to the border, Arequipa or Lima. Tickets can be purchased several days before departure and buses fill up quickly. **NB** Beware of touts selling bus tickets at inflated prices. The railway station is closer into town in the west on Crnl Albarracin. It is still a taxi drive into the centre though.

Getting around The town is quite spread out although there are several hotels around the Plaza de Armas. You will need to catch a bus or taxi to see much.

Sights

Everything closes
1300-1600 in Tacna

Above the city, on the heights, is the **Campo de la Alianza**, scene of a battle between Peru and Chile in 1880. The cathedral, designed by Eiffel, faces the main square, Plaza de Armas, which contains huge bronze statues of Admiral Grau and Colonel Bolognesi. The interior is austere but the round stained glass windows, each with a different motif, accentuate the fine, clean lines. The bronze fountain is said to be the duplicate of the one in the Place de la Concorde (Paris) and was also designed by Eiffel.

The **Parque de la Locomotora**, near the city centre, has a British-built locomotive, which was used in the War of the Pacific. There is a very good railway museum at the station. *Open 0800-1300. US$0.45.* The museum in the **Casa de la Cultura** has precolumbian pottery and war relics, it is very good and entry is free.

Essentials

Sleeping
■ *on maps*
Price codes:
see inside front cover

Accommodation is hard to find in the centre, especially at Christmas-time, because of Chileans on shopping sprees.

A2 *Gran Hotel Tacna*, Avda Bolognesi 300, T724193, F722015. Gardens, 2 swimming pools, safe car park, good breakfast for US$4, English spoken, disco, casino, gym, friendly. **A3** *Holiday Suites*, Alto de Lima, T715371, F711764. 10 minutes' walk from the centre, follow Avda Bolognesi to the University, from where it's 1 block to the left. With pool and car park. **B** *Gran Hotel Central*, San Martín 561, T712281, F726031. Central, friendly, secure, English spoken. Recommended. **B-C** *El Mesón*, Unánue 175, T725841, F721832. Modern, nice, phone and TV, friendly. **D** *Lima*, San Martín 442, T711912, on Plaza de Armas. Sporadic hot water, with bathroom, bar, good restaurant, friendly, stores luggage, smelly. **D** *San Diego*, Ayacucho 86-A, T712398. Shared bathroom, clean, friendly, basic. **E** *Hostal HC*, Zela 734, T712391. Hot water, discounts available, cafeteria next door, laundry service, videos, very friendly. Recommended. **E** *Lido*, C San Martín 876, near the Plaza de Armas. With hot showers. Recommended. **F** *Hostal Buen Amigo*, 2 de Mayo 445. Clean, secure, no water at night. **F** *Hostal Arica*, Pasaje Bacigalupo, Avda Leguía, T715818. Good value, friendly, hot water.

Eating
● *on maps*

Sur Perú, Ayacucho 80. Recommended. *Los Tenedores*, San Martín 888. Good, clean, expensive. *Hostal Lido*, San Martín 876 A. Good value. *Pizzeria Puco*, Libertad pedestrianized street, half a block from San Martin. Good. *El Sameño*, Arias Aráguez, entre Zarumilla y Olga Grooman. Good value fish restaurant. *Margarita's Café*, Unánue 141. Excellent French pastry and desserts, nice ambience, cheap. Highly recommended. *Delfín Azul*, Zela 747. Good. *Helados Piamonte*, 1 block from *Hotel Tacna*. Good ice cream. You can get hot food from the supermarket *Caneda y Cía*, at San Martín 770.

Transport

There are daily flights to **Lima** with *AeroPerú* and *Aero Continente*. Also to **Arequipa** with a connecting flight to **Juliaca**. A taxi to town and the bus terminal costs US$5. There is no transport direct to the border. The cheapest way is to take a taxi to town first, then take a colectivo.

Buses To **Moquegua**, 159 kilometres, 2 hours, US$2, several buses and colectivos daily. There are no direct buses to **Mollendo**, so catch one of the frequent buses to El Fiscal (US$4, 4 hours), then a colectivo to Mollendo for US$1.50.

To **Arequipa**, 7 hours, US$4, several buses daily, 0800-1000, 1900-2200 (eg *Ormeño*, Aráguez 698 y Grooman). To **Nasca**, 793 kilometres, 12 hours, US$9, several buses daily, most en route for Lima. Several buses daily to **Lima**, 1,239 kilometres, 21-26 hours, US$27 with *Cruz del Sur* and *Ormeño*. Recommended.

At the Tacna/Moquegua departmental border there are checkpoints at which all buses stop for inspection of imported goods from Chile (there are loads!). This can take time as negotiation with the officials is required and they can be impossible. Do not carry anything for a Peruvian, only your own belongings.

Buses leave from the Zona Franca near the airport and market area, **not** the bus terminal, to **Ilave** on the Puno-La Paz highway, 320 kilometres, 16 hours (can be longer in the rainy season), US$6; with *Gironda*, *Río Blanco* and *Ponce* companies. The road, via **Tarata** (where Inca terraces are still in use) and **Challapalca**, is in fair condition, but it is a bumpy and cold journey and can be hard in the wet, though the views are spectacular. Luggage packed on the roof racks has been known to disappear. It might be better to fly to Juliaca and then take a bus. Plenty of local buses and colectivos leave all day from Ilave to **Puno**, a further 55 kilometres, 1 hour, US$1. To **La Paz** there is a direct *Litoral* bus, T724761, on Wednesday at 0700, US$17.50, 13-16 hours (but it can be much longer in the rainy season).

South Coast

Tacna

To Bus station, Panamericana Norte & Alto de la Alianza

To Panamericana Norte & Stadium

Olga Grooman

Cnrl Albarracín

Chilean Consulate

Presbítero Andía

Zarumilla

Coronel Mendoza

Railway Museum

Julio Mac Lean

Augusto Leguía

2 de Mayo

Coronel Mendoza

1 4

Hipólito Unanue

28 de Julio

Grl Deustua

Arias Aráguez

Grl Vizcarra

Grl Varela

To Holiday Suites Hotel (200m)

Fco Lazo

Cnrl Inclán

Teatro Municipal

Modesto Basadre

Fco de Zela

3

de la Barca

6

General Blondel

1

Banco de la Nación

San Martín

Callao

Cathedral

2

Casa de la Cultura Museum

4

Simón Bolívar

To Panamericana Sur, Airport, Arica (Chile)

3

Ayacucho

Av Bolognesi

5

Pallardelli

Av Restauración

N

0 metres 400

0 yards 436

■ **Sleeping**
1. El Mesón
2. Hostal Buen Amigo
3. Hostal HC
4. Gran Central
5. Gran Tacna

6. Lido
7. Lima

○ **Other**
1. Aduana
2. Plaza de Armas
3. Plaza de la Locomotora
4. Touring y Automóvil Club

Directory **Airline offices** *Aero Continente*, Apurímac 265. *AeroPerú*, Ayacucho 96. **Banks** *Banco de Crédito*, San Martín 574. No commission for TCs (Amex, Citicorp, City Bank) into soles. Also at *Banco Wiese*, San Martín 476. *Banco de Perú*, C Gral Blondel, between Gral Deustua y Arias Aráguez. Changes TCs into soles at reasonable rate, open Sat 0930-1200. Best rates are at the *cambio* on Junín, between *Hotel Junín* and Avda Bolognesi. **Communications** *Telefónica del Perú*, Zela 727. **Tourist offices** Some travel agencies will provide information (not very reliable, though). *Secretaría de Estado de Turismo*, Avda Bolognesi 2088, T3778. *Touring y Automóvil Club del Perú*, Avda 2 de Mayo 55.

Frontier with Chile

Leaving Peru **Road** It is 46 kilometres to Arica, 1-2 hours, depending on waiting time at the frontier. Buses to Arica charge about US$2 and colectivo taxis about US$4 per person. All leave from the bus terminal in Tacna throughout the day. If you're in a hurry, make sure that the colectivo you choose is full (most of the time 6 passengers) because it will not leave before. You can change your remaining soles at the bus terminal. A Chilean driver is perhaps more likely to take you to any address in Arica. 'Agents' operate on behalf of taxi drivers at the bus terminal. You may not see the colectivo until you have negotiated the price and filled in the paperwork.

Trains Monday, Wednesday and Friday at 0530 and 0700 (check times) from Tacna to Arica, US$1.25, 2 hours. The station opens 1 hour before departure to prevent smugglers from entering as the trains are normally used by smugglers. There are customs, but no immigration facilities for those arriving by train from Chile.

NB Between October and March Peruvian time is 1 hour earlier than Chilean time, and 2 hours earlier from October to February or March; it varies annually.

At the border **Peruvian immigration** There is a checkpoint before the border, which is open 0900-2200. Peruvian immigration is closed on public holidays. You need to obtain a Peruvian exit stamp (quick) and then a Chilean entrance stamp, which can take a while, but formalities are straightforward. Drivers will help, or do it all for you. If you need a Chilean visa, you have to get it in Tacna. The Chilean Consulate is on Clnl Albarracín (see map); it is open only during office hours, closed weekends and holidays. Note that no fruit or vegetables are allowed into Chile.

Crossing by private vehicle For those leaving Peru by car buy *relaciones de pasajeros* (official forms, US$0.45) from the kiosk at the border or from a bookshop; you will need 4 copies. Next, return your tourist card, visit the PNP office, return the vehicle permit and finally depart through the checkpoints.

Exchange Coming into Peru from Chile, you can only change pesos into soles with street money changers in Tacna at a poor rate (look out for forged notes). Banco de la Nación will not change money. Money changers line Avenida Bolognesi, they are also at one end of the new bus terminal where the rates are described as 'not too bad' (see also **Banks** above).

Into Chile **Arica**, Chile's most northerly city, is 19 kilometres south of the border (*Population*: 174,064). It has road and rail links with La Paz, Bolivia, road links with the rest of Chile and is a good starting place for visits to Andean national parks, such as Lauca. It has a wide selection of hotels, restaurants and services. The bus terminal has an information centre with maps and a list of hotels. It is in the corner, near the entrance.

Cordillera Blanca

8

Cordillera Blanca

289 Trekking and climbing in the
Cordillera Blanca

293 Huaraz

301 North from Huaraz

302 Carhuaz

304 Yungay

307 Caraz

312 South of Huaraz

315 Chavín

316 Chavín de Huantar

317 Callejón de Conchucos

321 Cordillera Huayhuash and Raura

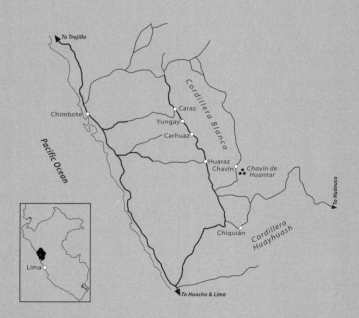

The Cordillera Blanca is one of Peru's most popular tourist destinations. This region of jewelled lakes and sparkling white mountain peaks attracts mountaineers, hikers, cyclists and rafters in their thousands. Even the archaeologist is catered for in the shape of the pre-Inca ruins of Chavín de Huantar.

Amongst the highest mountains in South America, the Cordillera Blanca offers some of the finest scenery, as well as the best climbing and trekking in the country. The region's main centre is Huaraz. Here you can see nearly two dozen snow-crested peaks of over 5,000 metres including Huascarán, the highest mountain in Peru at 6,768 metres.

This area contains the largest concentration of glaciers found in the world's tropical zone: a source of both beauty and danger. The turquoise-coloured lakes (cochas) which form in the terminal moraines are the jewels of the Andes and visitors should hike up to at least one during their stay. At the same time these glacial lakes have caused much death and destruction when dykes have broken, sending tons of water hurtling down the canyons wiping out everything in their path. The levels of some have been artificially lowered for flood control and to feed the huge Cañón del Pato dam. The result has improved safety but has also marred some of the area's great scenic beauty.

Cordillera Blanca

The area

Coloured map 3, grid B3 *The snow-capped Cordillera Blanca runs north to south for almost 200 kilometres. Alongside it to the west lies its alter ego, the bare and dry **Cordillera Negra**, which rises to 4,600 metres. The valley of the Río Santa, known as the **Callejón de Huaylas**, separates the two ranges. The Santa arises in Laguna Conococha, at the south end of the two mountain chains and flows due north between them, before turning west to enter the spectacular Cañón del Pato and making it's way to the Pacific.*

*To the east of the Cordillera Blanca lies another set of valleys, the **Callejón de Conchucos**, containing the archaeological treasures of Chavín de Huantar (see page 315). Both the Callejones de Huaylas and Conchucos are well-populated. There are picturesque villages with narrow cobblestone streets and odd-angled house roofs. This is an agricultural centre, with potatoes and barley grown at the higher altitudes and maize, alfalfa, fruits and flowers lower down.*

*These valleys also provide road access to the region's wonders. Many excellent trekking routes and approaches to climbers' base camps cross from one callejón to the other, over the high passes of the Cordillera Blanca. Further south lie the **Cordilleras Huayhuash and Raura**, offering more spectacular climbing and hiking in a less visited area (see page 321).*

Ins and outs

When to go The dry season (May to September) is the best time to visit the region, and the only time for climbing most summits. Trekking is also possible at other times of the year, but conditions are less amenable and the views are less rewarding.

Getting there There are three main routes to reach the Cordillera Blanca. Probably the easiest is the paved road which branches east off the Pan-American Highway north of Pativilca, 187 kilometres from Lima (see page 330).

A second route is via the Callán pass from Casma to Huaraz (see page 332), a rough but beautiful trip through the heart of the Cordillera Negra.

The third alternative is from Chimbote to Caraz via the Cañón del Pato (see page 336), also a very scenic journey, with magnificent views of this spectacular canyon.

Huascarán National Park

Established in July 1975, the park includes the entire Cordillera Blanca above 4,000 metres. It covers a total area of 3,400 square kilometres and is 180 kilometres from north to south and 20 kilometres from east to west. It is a UNESCO World Biosphere Reserve and part of the World Heritage Trust. The park's objectives are to protect the unique flora, fauna, geology, archaeological sites and extraordinary scenic beauty of the Cordillera. Please make every attempt to help by taking all your rubbish away with you when camping. The park office is in the Ministry of Agriculture, at the east end of Avda Raymondi in Huaraz (T722086). It is open only in the mornings. It provides limited general information but is useful for those planning specific research activities. ■ *US$1.80 for a day visit, or US$22 for trekking and climbing trips involving overnight stays of any duration. In 1998 these fees were only being collected at Llanganuco (see page 305).*

A blooming century

The giant Puya Raimondi, named after Antonio Raimondi, the Italian scholar who discovered it, is a rare species, considered to be one of the oldest plants in the world.

Often mistakenly referred to as a cactus, it is actually the largest member of the Bromeliad family and is found in only a few isolated areas of the Andes. One of these areas is the Huascarán National Park, particularly the Ingenio and Queshque gorges, the high plateaus of Cajamarquilla, along the route leading to Pastoruri in the Pachacoto gorge and by the road from Caraz to Pamparomas.

At its base, the Puya forms a rosette of long, spiked, waxy leaves, two metres in diameter. The distinctive phallic spike of the plant can reach a height of 12 metres during the flowering process. This takes its entire lifespan – an incredible 100 years – after which time the plant withers and dies.

As the final flowering begins, usually during May for mature plants, the spike is covered in flowers. As many as 20,000 blooms can decorate a single plant. During this season, groups of Puya Raimondi will bloom together, creating a spectacular picture against the dramatic backdrop of the Cordillera Blanca.

Trekking and climbing in the Cordillera Blanca

The Cordillera Blanca offers the most popular backpacking and trekking in Peru, with a network of trails used by the local people and some less well defined mountaineers' routes. There are numerous possibilities for day-hikes, trekking and climbing. Of these only a very few routes are currently used by most visitors, hence they accumulate trash and other signs of impact. While these favourite treks (notably Santa Cruz-Llanganuco and Olleros-Chavín) are undeniably interesting, prospective trekkers should consider the various excellent alternatives in order to enjoy a less crowded experience and help conserve the area's great natural beauty.

The many other options include: **Laguna Parón**, with its impressive cirque of surrounding summits (access from Caraz, see page 307); **Hualcayán to Pomabamba**, traversing the northern end of the Cordillera Blanca with fine views of Alpamayo and many other peaks (access from Caraz); Laguna 69 at the end of Llanganuco valley (access from Yungay); the **Ulta Valley** and **Laguna Auquiscocha**, between the massifs of Huascarán, Ulta and Hualcán (access from Carhuaz, see page 302); to name but a few. There remains a good deal to be discovered in the area and your creativity in choosing a route is certain to be rewarded. See also under **Adventure sports** (page 60).

Advice to climbers and hikers

The height of the mountains in the Cordillera Blanca and nearby ranges and their location in the tropics create conditions different from the Alps or even the Himalayas. Fierce sun makes the mountain snow porous and the glaciers move more rapidly. The British Embassy advises climbers to take at least six days for acclimatization, to move in groups of four or more, reporting to the **Casa de Guías** (see page 291) or the office of the guide before departing,

Cordillera Blanca

giving the date at which a search should begin, and leaving the telephone number of your Embassy with money. Rescue operations are very limited. Insurance is essential (cannot be purchased locally), since a guide costs US$50-70 a day and a search US$2,000-2,500. A search by helicopter costs US$10,000 (up to 4,500 metres only).

Be well prepared before setting out on a climb. Wait or cancel your trip when weather conditions are bad. Every year climbers are killed through failing to take weather conditions seriously. Climb only when and where you have sufficient experience.

Callejón de Huaylas

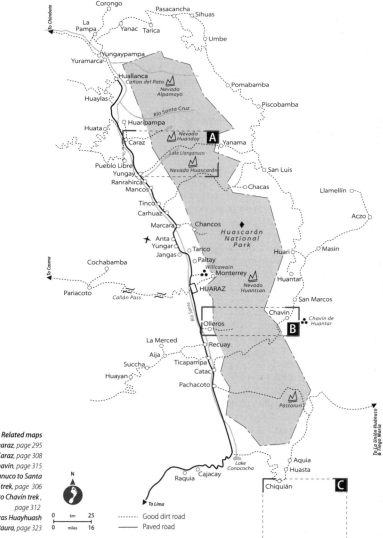

Related maps
Huaraz, page 295
Caraz, page 308
Chavín, page 315
A Llanganuco to Santa
Cruz trek, page 306
B Olleros to Chavín trek ,
page 312
C Cordilleras Huayhuash
& Raura, page 323

Cordillera Blanca

To Chimbote
Corongo
Pasacancha
Sihuas
La Pampa
Yanac
Tarica
Umbe
Yungaypampa
Yuramarca
Huallanca
Cañon del Pato
Nevado Alpamayo
Pomabamba
Huaylas
Piscobamba
Río Santa Cruz
Huata
Huaripampa
Caraz
Nevado Huandoy
Yanama
Pueblo Libre
Lake Llanganuco
Yungay
Nevado Huascarán
Ranrahirca
Mancos
San Luis
Chacas
Llamellín
Tinco
Carhuaz
Aczo
Marcara
Chancos
Huascarán National Park
To Casma
Anta
Yungar
Tarico
Huari
Masin
Jangas
Paltay
Cochabamba
Willcawain
Monterrey
Huantar
Pariacoto
Callán Pass
HUARAZ
Nevado Huantsan
Río Santa
San Marcos
Olleros
Chavin
Chavín de Huantar
La Merced
Recuay
Aija
Succha
Ticapampa
Catac
Huayan
Pachacoto
Pastoruri
To La Unión Huánuco & Tingo María
Lake Conococha
Aquia
Huasta
Raquia
Cajacay
Chiquián
To Lima

N

0 km 25
0 miles 16

······· Good dirt road
——— Paved road

A

B

C

Most circuits can be hiked in five days. Although the trails are easily followed, they are rugged and the passes very high – between 4,000 and nearly 5,000 metres – so backpackers wishing to go it alone should be fit and properly acclimatized to the altitude, and carry all necessary equipment. Essential items are a tent, warm sleeping bag, stove, and protection against wind and rain (climatic conditions are quite unreliable here and you cannot rule out rain and hail storms even in the dry season). Trekking demands less stamina since equipment can be carried by donkeys.

NB Check locally on public safety conditions. A few robberies of hikers have taken place. Do not camp near a town or village, never leave a campsite unattended and always hike with others when heading into the remote mountain districts.

On all treks in this area, respect the locals' property, leave no rubbish behind, do not give sweets or money to children who beg and remember your cooking utensils, tent, etc, would be very expensive for a campesino, so be sensitive and responsible.

Hiring guides and muleteers

The Dirección de Turismo issues qualified guides and *arrieros* (muleteers) with a photo ID. Always check for this when making arrangements; note down the name and card number in case you should have any complaints. Prices for specific services are set so enquire before hiring someone. Prices in 1998: *arriero*, US$10 per day; donkey or mule, US$4 per day; trekking guides US$30-50 per day; climbing guides US$50-70 per day, depending on the difficulty of the peak. In the low season guides' prices are about 20-30% less. You are required to provide or pay for food for all porters and guides. **NB** Some guides speak English and are friendly but lack technical expertise; others have expertise but lack communicative ability. You may have to choose between the former and the latter.

Casa de Guías, Plaza Ginebra 28-g in Huaraz, T721811, F722306. This is the climbers' and hikers' meeting place. It is useful with information, books, maps, arrangements for guides, *arrieros*, mules, etc. They provide rescue facilities (may be very expensive) and you can register here free of charge before heading out on your climb or trek. Be sure to advise of your return or any delay.

Recommended mountain guides

Hugo Cifuentes Maguiña and his brother César (speaks English and a little French), at Avda Centenario 537 or in the *Casa de Guías*. Augusto Ortega, Jr San Martín 1004, T724888, is the only Peruvian to have climbed Everest.

Climbing courses

Several of the agencies and *Casa de Guías* run rock climbing courses at Monterrey (behind *Hotel Baños Termales Monterrey*, see page 300) and Huanchac (30 minutes walk from Huaraz). Ask for details from the *Casa de Guías* and tour agencies in Huaraz. They charge US$7.50-10 per person per day, including guide and transport.

Recommended trekking guides

Tjen Verheye, Jr Carlos Valenzuela 911, T722569, is Belgian and speaks Dutch, French, German, and reasonable English, runs trekking and conventional tours and is knowledgeable about the Chavín culture. Irma Angeles, T722205, speaks some English, knows the Huayhuash well. Genaro Yanac Olivera, T722825, speaks good English and some German, also a climbing guide. Vladimiro Hinostrosa, at Hostal Sol Andino (see below), is a trekking guide with knowledge of the entire region. See also under **Tour agencies** in Huaraz for organized trips.

Hiring camping gear

Several trekking agencies sell camping gaz cartridges. White gas (called *bencina blanca*) is available from *ferreterías*, but shop around to avoid overcharging. For trekking provisions see **Shopping**, page 298.

Cordillera Blanca

Mining the mountains

The department of Ancash contains important mineral deposits including zinc, silver, gold and perhaps uranium (the latter is not discussed openly). 12,000 different sites have been prospected in the Cordillera Negra alone. An open pit mine and smelter were due to open in late 1998, 12 kilometres north of Huaraz.

Even before the first ingot was produced, the project brought changes to the Callejón de Huaylas. A number of hotels are permanently booked for mine staff, while the cost of accommodation and other services has begun to rise. Unemployed from all over Peru have come to the area in search of jobs, but few work opportunities materialized for the local population. The US/Canadian consortium operating the mine has promised to minimize environmental impact, but there can be little doubt that this large-scale project will leave its mark on the economic and social environment, as well as the natural environment of the Callejón de Huaylas.

Similar developments are taking place east of San Marcos, near Chavín in the Callejón de Conchucos, where a large underground mine and concentrator are under construction, due to begin production in the year 2000. This previously remote and isolated area is undergoing rapid change.

In the Cordillera Huayhuash, a Japanese corporation began a major mining project in 1997, in the vicinity of Pocpa and Laguna Jahuacocha, the jewel of the entire region. Other mines are under consideration and some local residents have proposed the creation of a Huayhuash National Park to protect the region's unique natural beauty, as well as its economically important tourist potential.

The following agencies are recommended for hiring gear: *Andean Sport Tours*; *Monttrek*; *Chavín Tours*; *Pablo Tours*. See under **Tour agencies** in Huaraz for their addresses. *Casa de Guías* rents equipment and sells dried food. Also *Lobo*, Luzuriaga 557, T724646. On the 2nd floor of the *Hotel Residencial Cataluña*, Avda Raymondi, T72117, José Valle Espinosa, 'Pepe', hires out equipment, organizes treks and pack animals, sells dried food, and is generally helpful and informative.

Check all camping and climbing equipment very carefully before taking it. Gear is usually of poor quality and mostly second hand, left behind by others. Also note that some items may not be available, so it's best to bring your own. All prices are standard, but not cheap, throughout town. All require payment in advance, passport or air ticket as deposit and will only give 50% of your money back if you return gear early.

Maps and books An excellent map of the Callejón de Huaylas and Cordillera Huayhuash, by Felipe Díaz, is available in many shops in the region and at Casa de Guias in Huaraz. Maps of the area are available from the IGN in Lima. **Hidrandina**, the state hydroelectric company, at 27 de Noviembre 773, has dye-line maps of the Cordillera Blanca; open in the morning only. Several guides and agencies have their own sketch maps of the most popular routes. Maps are also available by international mail-order from **Latin American Travel Consultants**, PO Box 17-17-908, Quito, Ecuador, F(593-2) 562566, E LATC@pi.pro.ec.

The South American Explorers' Club publishes a good map with additional notes on the popular Llanganuco to Santa Cruz loop, and the **Instituto Geográfico Nacional** has mapped the area with its 1:100,000 topographical series. These are more useful to the mountaineer than hiker, however, since the trails marked are confusing and inaccurate.

Apart from the book by Hilary Bradt (see **Tourist information**, page 35), a useful guide to the area currently in print is *Peruvian Andes* by Philipe Beaud; it costs US$24 and is available through Cordee in the UK, some shops in Huaraz and the South

American Explorers' Club. *Callejón de Huaylas y Cordillera Blanca*, by Felipe Díaz (Spanish, English and German editions), is a useful guide to the area and is available locally. *La Cordillera Blanca de Los Andes*, by Antonio Gómez and Juan José Tomé (1998, Spanish only) is principally a climbing guide, but contains some trekking and general information, available locally. Another climbing guide is *Climbs of the Cordillera Blanca of Peru*, by David Sharman (1995), available locally, as well as from Cordee in the UK and Alpenbooks in the USA. *Parque Nacional Huascarán*, by Jim Bartle, is a beautiful soft-cover photo collection with English and Spanish text.

Huaraz

The main town in the valley is Huaraz, capital of the Department of Ancash, 420 kilometres by road from Lima. The city was half destroyed in the earthquake of May 1970 so don't expect red-tiled roofs or overhanging eaves. The Plaza de Armas has been rebuilt, except for the Cathedral, which is being resited elsewhere. What the reconstructed city lacks in colonial charm, however, it more than makes up for by its spectacular setting at the foot of the Cordillera Blanca. The peaks of Huascarán, Huandoy, and San Cristóbal loom so close as to seem almost a part of the architecture.

Population: 80,000
Altitude: 3,091 metres
Phone code: 044
Coloured map 3, grid B3

Ins and outs

The bus stations are in the centre of town and are conveniently close to many of the hotels and hostals.

Getting there

Small enough to get around by foot providing sensible precautions are taken especially at night (see below). The walk to the mirador in the southeast of the town takes about an hour. The standard fare for a taxi in town is about US$0.70-90. Radio taxis T721482 or 722512.

Getting around

On first impressions Huaraz may seem a bit of a one-horse town, but it is a major tourist centre as well as a busy commercial hub, especially on market days (Monday and Thursday). The region is both a prime destination for hikers and international climbers, as well as a vacation haven for Peruvian urbanites seeking clean mountain air and a glimpse of the glaciers. School groups flock to the city from September to December.

Huaraz is brim full of hotels of all categories and the main thoroughfare, Avda Luzuriaga, is bursting at the seams with travel agencies, climbing equipment hire shops, *pizzerías*, cafés and bars. For those seeking a quieter ambience, there are many other options a block or two away from the main drag. A small cluster of cafés and restaurants offers a pleasant, tranquil, atmosphere on Jirón Julián de Morales, one block east of Luzuriaga.

NB Huaraz has its share of crime, especially since the arrival of mining in the area (see above) and during the high tourist season. Muggings have been reported on the way to the Mirador Rataquenua and Pukaventana (see below). A minimum groups size of three is recommended for this walk; on no account should women go alone. Also avoid the area by the river and deserted streets at night, be careful near the market and keep a close eye on your luggage at the bus stations.

Sights

For good panoramic views go to the *Mirador Rataquenua* at the cross (visible from Huaraz). It's a one hour walk from the town – turn left past the cemetery and head uphill through a small forest. To get a truly amazing view of the whole valley, continue past the *Mirador* up to *Pukaventana*. (See above regarding safety for both these excursions.)

Museo Regional de Ancash, Instituto Nacional de Cultura, on Plaza de Armas, contains stone monoliths and *huacos* from the Recuay culture. The exhibits are well labelled and laid out. ■ *Open Tuesday-Saturday 0800-1900, Sunday and Monday 0800-1500. US$1.80 and includes entry to Willkawain ruins on the same day (see page 300).*

The **Museo de Miniaturas del Perú** is at the Gran Hotel Huascarán. It has models of Huaraz and Yungay before the earthquake, plus an interesting (honest!) collection of Barbie dolls in Peruvian dress. ■ *Open Monday-Friday, 0800-1300, 1500-1800. US$0.85.*

Essentials

Sleeping
■ *on maps*
Price codes:
see inside front cover

Hotels are plentiful (there are many more than those listed below) but fill up rapidly during the high season (May-September), especially during public holidays and special events (such as the *Semana de Andinismo*) when prices rise. Lodging in private homes is common during these periods. Since 1997, some hotels are fully booked for mine staff (see above).

A1-2 *Hostal Andino*, Pedro Cochachín 357, some way southeast from the centre (not a safe area after dark), T721949, T/F722830, E andino@mail.cosapidata.com.pe. The best in town, restaurant (fondue expensive), breakfast is US$7 extra, safe parking, Swiss run, friendly but check exactly what you're being charged for, 2nd floor rooms with balconies and views of Huascarán are more expensive, climbing and hiking gear for hire. Recommended. **A2-3** *Gran Hotel Huascarán*, Avda Centenario block 10, at the north end of town, T721640, F722821. An uninspiring ex-state hotel, large rooms, poor restaurant, **C** for camping in courtyard with use of facilities.

B *El Tumi I*, San Martín 1121, T721784. Good restaurant (serves huge steaks), fairly good, advance reservations advised. **B** *Grand Huaraz*, Larrea y Loredo 721, T722227, F726536. Modern (new in 1998), with cafeteria. **B** *Hostal Montañero*, Plaza Ginebra 30-B (ask at Casa de Guias), T/F722306. Hot water, very clean, modern, comfortable, friendly, good value, climbing equipment rental and sales. Recommended. **B** *Las Retamas*, Cascapampa 250, 1 block from the *Gran Hotel Huascarán*, T/F721722. Pleasant with garden, parking.

C *Hostal Colomba*, Francisco de Zela 278, on Centenario across the river, T721501/727106, F722273. Lovely old hacienda, bungalow, family-run (German), garden, friendly, safe car parking. **C** *Hostal Los Portales*, Raymondi 903, T721402, F721247. With bathroom, hot water, parking, a pleasant place to stay, closed for renovations in 1998. **C** *Edward's Inn*, Bolognesi 121, T/F722692. Cheaper without bathroom, clean, not always hot water, laundry, friendly, food available, insist on proper rates in low season, popular, Edward speaks English and knows a lot about trekking and rents gear (not all guides share Edward's experience). Highly recommended.

D *Casablanca*, Tarapacá 138, near the market, T722602, F721578. Clean, pleasant, modern. **D** *El Pacífico*, Luzuriaga 630, T721683, F724416. With bathroom, hot water, good restaurant. **D** *El Tumi II*, San Martín 1089, T721784. With bathroom, reasonable value, beds not too comfortable. **D** *Hostal Copa*, Jr Bolívar 615, T/F722619, E copa@telematic.com.pe. Cheaper without bathroom, limited hot water, laundry facilities, clean, owner's son Walter Melgarejo is a well-known guide, popular with trekkers, restaurant. **D** per person *Hostal Mi Casa*, Tarapacá 773, T723375. Includes breakfast, very friendly, owner Sr Ames is an expert on glaciers, his son is a climbing and rafting guide. **D** *Hostal Oscar*, La Mar 624, T722720. With bathroom, hot water, cheap breakfast next door, good beds, **E** in low season. Recommended. **D** *Hostal*

Raymondi, Raymondi 820, T721082. With bathroom, cheaper without, hot water only in the mornings in the ground floor shower, comfortable, charges for left luggage, café serves good breakfast. **D** *Hostal Rinconcito Huaracino*, Fitzcarrald 226, T725865. Cheaper without bathroom, modern, clean, front rooms are noisy. **D** *Hostal Tany*,

Huaraz

■ Sleeping	11. Hostal Estoico	4. Las Cuyas	○ **Others**
1. Alojamiento	12. Hostal Galaxia	5. Monte Rosa	1. Ames River Runners
Soledad	13. Hostal Los Andes	6. Taberna Tambo (bar)	& Familia Alcides
2. Casa de Jaime	14. Hostal Los Portales		Ames
3. Casablanca	15. Hostal Maguiña	**🚌 Buses**	2. Casa de Guías
4. Edward's Inn & Hostal	16. Hostal Montañero	1. Buses to Caraz	3. Chavín Tours
López	17. Hostal Oscar	2. Chavín Express	4. Huascarán National
5. El Tumi I	18. Hostal Quintana	3. Civa Cial	Park office & Ministry
6. El Tumi II	19. Hostal Raymondi	4. Combis to Caraz	of Agriculture
7. Hostal Andino	20. Hostal Tany	5. Cruz del Sur	5. Monttrek
8. Hostal Colomba	21. Hostal Yanett	6. Empresa 14	6. Mountain Bike
9. Hostal Continental	22. Residencial Cataluña	7. Expreso Ancash	Adventures
10. Hostal Copa		8. Movil Tours	7. Pablo Tours
	● **Eating & Bars**	9. Transportes Huandoy	8. Pyramid Tours
	1. Amadeus (bar)	10. Transportes Moreno	
	2. Créperie Patrick	11. Transportes	
	3. Huaraz Querido	Rodríguez	

0 metres 100
0 yards 109

Cordillera Blanca

Lúcar y Torre 468, T722534, with bathroom, cheaper without, hot water at night, spotlessly clean. **D** *Hostal Yanett*, Avda Centenario 164, at the north end of town across the river, T721466. Friendly, hot water, clean, large rooms, restaurant for breakfast. Recommended. **D** *Samuel's*, Bolívar 504, T/F726370. Cheaper without bathroom, clean, modern, small rooms. **D** *Schatzi*, Bolívar near Raimondi. Clean, nice courtyard.

E *Alojamiento Belenita*, D Antúnez 772, 1 block from Plaza Belén, T721896. Price includes breakfast, shared bathroom, hot water, courtyard, cooking and laundry facilities, friendly. **E** *Alojamiento María Gloria*, Pasaje Valenzuela 854 near Plaza Belén, T722112, cheaper without bathroom, hot water, meals available. **E** *Alojamiento Norma*, Pasaje Valenzuela 837, near Plaza Belén, T721831. Includes breakfast, cheaper without bathroom, hot water. Recommended. **E-F** *Casa Jansy's*, Jr Sucre 948. Hot water, meals, laundry, owner Jesús Rivera Lúcar is a mountain guide. Recommended. **E** *Hostal Chong Roca*, J de Morales 687, T721154. With bathroom, very clean, friendly, hot water 24 hours, huge rooms. Recommended. **E** *Hostal Continental*, 28 de Julio 586 near Plaza de Armas, T724171. Clean, hot water, friendly, cafeteria. Recommended but avoid the rooms overlooking the street as there are 2 noisy *peñas* nearby. **E** *Hostal Estoico*, San Martín 635, T722371. Cheaper without bathroom, friendly, clean, safe, hot water, laundry facilities, good value. Recommended. **E** *Hostal Galaxia*, Jr de la Cruz Romero 638, T722230. Cheaper without bathroom, hot water, laundry facilities, basic, friendly. Recommended. **E** *Hostal Los Andes*, Tarapacá 316, T721346. Cheaper without bathroom, warm water, clean, laundry facilities, noisy, not very comfortable but friendly. **E** *Hostal Quintana*, Mcal Cáceres 411, T726060. Cheaper without bathroom, hot shower, laundry facilities, clean, basic, stores luggage, friendly, popular with trekkers, some beds are new and comfortable but others are not. **E** *Hostal Virgen del Carmen*, Jr de la Cruz Romero 664, T721729 (or Lima, 481-5311). Cheaper without bathroom, hot water, run by a lovely, friendly and helpful old couple from Lima, homely atmosphere, nice clean rooms, cheap laundry service. Highly recommended. **E** *Residencial Cataluña*, Avda Raymondi 822, T722761. With bathroom, basic, restaurant open only in the high season, clean, safe, noisy, tepid water. **E** *Alojamiento El Rey*, Pasaje Olivera 919 near Plaza Belén, T721917. With bathroom, **G** per person with shared bathroom, basic but clean, cooking and laundry facilities, family run, friendly and charming people, meals available. **E** *Hostal Gyula*, Parque Ginebra 632, opposite the Casa de Guías, T721567, E hotelperu@infoweb.com.pe. With bathroom, hot water, clean, very friendly and helpful, has good information on local tours, stores luggage. Noisy at weekends but recommended.

F-G per person *Albergue Churup*, Jr Pedro Campos 735, La Soledad, T722584. 4 rooms for up to 6 people, 3 bathrooms, lounge, very clean, laundry facilities, kitchen, luggage store, English spoken, excellent breakfast for US$1. Highly recommended. **F-G** per person *Alojamiento El Farolito*, Avda Tarapacá 1466, T725792. With bathroom, hot water, laundry service, cafeteria. **F** *Albergue El Tambo*, Confraternidad Internacional Interior 122-B. Clean, laundry and cooking facilities, 3 rooms with 12 beds, friendly. **F-G** per person *Alojamiento Nemys*, Jr Figueroa 1135, T722949. Secure, hot shower, breakfast US$2.40, good for climbers, luggage store. Recommended. **F** *Alojamiento San Martín de Porres*, Pasaje San Martín de las Porres off Las Américas 300 block, T721061. Clean, friendly. Recommended. **F** per person *Alojamiento Soledad*, Jr Amadeo Figueroa 1267, T721196 (in Lima 423-3181), E ghsoledad@hotmail.com. Including free laundry service, hot water, family-run, cafeteria, secure. Recommended. **F** per person *Hostal López*, behind *Edward's Inn*, ask near the Estadio just off Avda Bolognesi at Santa the river end. Lukewarm showers, washing facilities for clothes, beautiful garden and restaurant, good views, luggage stored, very friendly. **F-G** per person *Hostal Maguiña*, Avda Tarapacá 643, opposite Rodríguez bus terminal. Noisy in the morning, hot water, laundry facilities, breakfast available, luggage stored, clean, English and French spoken, helpful in arranging trekking and equipment hire. Recommended. **F** *Sol Andino*, Yungay 265, Independencia,

T725681. With bathroom, hot water, kitchen and laundry facilities, trekking information.

G per person *Casa de Familia Gómez Díaz*, Jr Eulogio del Río 1983, T723224. Hot water, very clean and quiet, family atmosphere, good beds. **G** per person *Casa de Jaimes*, C Alberto Gridilla 267, T722281, 2 blocks from the main plaza. Clean dormitory with hot showers, washing facilities, has maps and books of the region, use of kitchen, popular. Noisy but recommended. **G** *Familia Sánchez*, Jr Caraz 849. Clean, basic, warm water, helpful, cheap breakfast.

There are usually people waiting at the bus terminals offering cheap accommodation in their own homes.

Youth Hostels **E** per person *Alojamiento Alpes Andes*, at Casa de Guías, Plaza Ginebra 28-g, T721811, F722306. Member of the Peruvian Youth Hostel Association, 1 dormitory with 14 beds and another with 6 beds, with very good restaurant, laundry, free luggage store, the owner Sr López speaks English, French and German and is very helpful, he is the mountain guides administrator. **F** per person *Hostal la Montañesa*, Avda Leguía 290, Centenario, T711217. Member of the Peruvian Youth Hostel Association. **F** per person *Nilo's Camp*, J de Morales 757, T/F725974. Kitchen and laundry facilities.

Out of town **C** *Complejo Turístico Eccame*, in Yungar near the airport, at Km 18 on the road to Caraz, T721933. Country setting, horse riding. A 4-star hotel was under construction in 1998 in Vichay, 5 minutes from Huaraz.

Note that middle and high-class restaurants charge a 28% tax on top of the bill. *Monte Rosa*, J de la Mar Cuadra 6. Good pizzería, open 1830-2300, Swiss owner is Victorinox representative, offering knives for sale and repair service, also has climbing and trekking books to read. *Pizza Bruno*, Luzuriaga 834. "By far the best pizza", excellent crepes and pastries, good service, open from 1830, French owner Bruno Reviron also organizes treks. *Huaraz Querido*, Bolívar 981. Excellent cevichería. Recommended. *Créperie Patrick*, Luzuriaga 424 y Raymondi. Excellent crepes, fish, quiche, spaghetti and good wine. *Euskalerria*, Luzuriaga 406. Basque cuisine, good food and service, trekking information. *Siam de Los Andes*, Gamarra corner J de Morales. Authentic Thai cuisine.

Eating: expensive
● *on maps*

La Familia at Luzuriaga 431. Popular with gringos, vegetarian dishes, good for regional food such as cuy. *Chez Pepe*, Luzuriaga 570, good pizza, chicken, meat, warm atmosphere, run by Pepe from Residencial Cataluña. *Alpes Andes*, Plaza Ginebra in Casa de Guias. Muesli, yoghurt etc in the morning, pastas and pizzas in the evening. *Monttrek Pizza Pub*, Luzuriaga 646 (upstairs from the agency). Good pizzas and pastas, indoor climbing wall, shows videos. *Warmi Juicio*, Pasaje Octavio Hinostroza 522, 2 blocks from Plaza de Armas. Good fish and ceviche. *Sihuasino*, Parque Cuba near San Francisco church. Good for regional specialities such as pachamanca and chicha. *Tejas*, Francisco de Zela. A good example of a Recreo, a restaurant that specializes in typical local dishes, the cuy is especially recommended, open only at weekends. *Manos Norteñas*, J de Morales 747, northern coastal cooking. *Rinconcito Minero*, J de Morales 757. Swiss-run, breakfast, lunch, coffee and snacks. *Fuentes de Salud*, on J de la Mar. Vegetarian, recommended. *Bistro de los Andes*, J de Morales 823, T/F726249. Great food, owner speaks English, French and German. Recommended.

Eating: mid-range

A Fuego Lento, San Martín 643. Popular with locals, good set meals. Recommended. *La Estación*, Plazuela Belén. Video pub which serves a good lunch for only US$1, also good steaks, nice atmosphere, very friendly owner. Recommended. *Las Cuyas*, Morales 535. Good meals and breakfasts, popular with gringos. *Faby Star*, on Sucre. Serves good local dishes, try their 'huge' milaneza. *Piccolo*, de la Mar, 1 block off

Eating: cheap

Cordillera Blanca

Luzuriaga. Pizzería, very popular with gringos. *La Fontana*, Avda Tarapacá 561. Excellent pancakes and juices. *Chifa Jim Hua*, Luzuriaga 645, large, tasty portions. *Querubín*, J de Morales 767. Clean, friendly, good breakfast and set meals, also vegetarian, snacks and à la carte. Recommended. *Café Central*, Luzuriaga 808. Good breakfast for US$1.30, great chocolate cake and apple pie.

Cafés   *Café Andino*, J de Morales 753, 1 block from the Plaza de Armas. American run café and book exchange, a nice place to relax and write postcards. *Café de Paris*, San Martín 686. French-run, excellent pastries.

Bars & nightclubs   **Bars** *People's*, San Martín y 28 de Julio. *Oro Viejo*, Bolívar 653. *Las Kenas*, Jr Gabino Uribe near Luzuriaga. Live Andean music, happy hour 2000-2200, good pisco sours. Next door, upstairs, is *Aquelarre*, popular with *gringos*, soft music, nice atmosphere.

Discos and peñas *Imantata*, Luzuriaga 424, disco and folk music. *La Cueva del Oso*, Luzuriaga 674, taverna-style, good peña. *Taberna Tambo*, José de la Mar, folk music daily, disco, open 1000-1600, 2000-0200, knock on door to get in. *Amadeus*, Parque Ginebra, bar-disco. *Monttrek Disco*, Sucre just off Plaza de Armas, in converted cinema, reasonable prices. *La Cascada*, on Luzuriaga, disco tavern. *Neo*, Lúcar y Torre 460, disco.

Festivals   *Semana Santa*, or Holy Week, is widely celebrated and always colourful and lively. The town's Patron saints' day is *El Señor de la Soledad*, during the week starting **3 May**, with parades, dancing, music, fireworks and much drinking. The *Semana del Andinismo* is an international climbing and skiing week, held in **June**. The festivals of *San Juan* and *San Pedro* are celebrated throughout the region during the last week of **June**. On the eve of *San Juan* fires are lit throughout the valley to burn the chaff from the harvest. The following day the entire valley is thick with smoke.

Sports   **Mountain biking**   Contact Julio Olaza at *Mountain Bike Adventures*, Lúcar y Torre 530, T724259, F724888, E olaza@mail.cosapidata.com.pe. US$20 for 5 hours, various routes (see page 67). Julio speaks excellent English and also runs a book exchange, sells topo maps and climbing books. He also rents comfortable rooms, **F** per person, luggage stored, discount for bikers. See also tour agencies below.

River rafting and canoeing   Contact Carlos Ames *River Runners*, Avda Tarapacá 773 y La Mar 661, T723375, F724888 (see page 62). See also tour agencies below.

Shopping   **Handicrafts**   Local sweaters, hats, gloves, ceramics, and wall hangings can be bought from the stalls on Pasaje Mcal Cáceres just off Luzuriaga, also on Bolívar cuadra 6 and elsewhere. *Andean Expressions*, Jr J Arguedas 1246, near La Soledad church, T722951, is run by Lucho, Mauro and Beto Olaza, and is recommended for hand-printed T-shirts and sweatshirts with unusual motifs.

Groceries and trekking provisions   Two well stocked supermarkets are *Ortíz*, Luzuriaga 401 corner Raymondi (good selection) and *Militos*, Sucre 775. Other shops include *Bodega Chong Roca*, Jr J de Morales 661 and *Comercial Anita*, Jr San Cristóbal 369. The central market offers a wide variety of canned and dry goods, including nuts and dried fruit, as well as fresh fruit and vegetables. Be sure to check expiry dates. *Panadería Robles*, Bolívar 479, has good bread that keeps well on treks.

Photography   *Foto Galería Andes*, at Pasaje Cayetano Requena, near the market, is good for camera repairs and sells professional photos of the Cordillera Blanca.

Transport   **Air connections**   There is no regular air service. There are private charters from Lima with AeroCóndor.

Buses to/from Lima   420 kilometres, 7 hours, US$7-9. The road is in good condition. There is a large selection of buses to Lima, both ordinary service and luxury coaches, with departures throughout the day. Many of the companies have their offices along Fitzcarrald and on Avda Raymondi. Some recommended companies are: *Cruz del Sur*, Lúcar y Torre 573, T723532; *Transportes Rodríguez*, Tarapacá 622, T721353; *Expreso Ancash* (Ormeño), Raymondi 845; *Civa Cial*, San Martín 508, T721947; *Movil Tours*, Raymondi 616, T722555.

Other long distance buses To **Casma** and **Chimbote** via the Callán pass (150 kilometres) 6-7 hours, US$6 (sit on the left for best views): *Transportes Moreno*, Raymondi 892, T721344, daily at 2000; *Transportes Huandoy*, Fitzcarrald 261, T722502, daily at 0800. To **Chimbote**, 185 kilometres: *Transportes Moreno*, daily at 0700, US$6, 8-9 hours via Caraz and the Cañón del Pato (sit on the right for the most exciting views; see page 336). Other companies go to Chimbote via Pativilca; *Turismo Chimbote*, Raymondi 815, T721984, US$7, 6 hours. To **Pativilca**, 160 kilometres, 4 hours, US$3.50. To **Trujillo**, all buses go at night, 8-9 hours, US$7: *Chichaysuyo* (Fitzcarrald 369), *Turismo Chimbote*, *Empresa de Transportes* 14 (Fitzcarrald 216, T721282).

Within the Cordillera Blanca area Several buses and frequent minivans run daily, 0500-2000, between Huaraz and **Caraz**, 1½ hours, US$1.10. They stop at all the places in between. They depart from the parking area under the bridge on Fitzcarrald (beware of theives here). To **Chavín**, 110 kilometres, 4 hours, US$3, and on to Huari, 150 kilometres, 6 hours, US$4.50 from Huaraz: *Chavín Express*, Mcal Cáceres 338, T724652, daily at 0830, 1030, 1300 and 1400; *Lanzón de Chavín*, Tarapacá 602, Tuesday, Thursday and Saturday at 1030 to Huari. To **Chacas** (US$7) and **San Luis** (US$7.60), with *Trans Huandoy*, 7 hours (also to Llamellín). To **Huallanca**, via Pachacoto (see page 312), US$3.50. Some trucks and buses run this route, continuing to **La Unión** and **Huánuco**. Colectivos to **Recuay**, **Ticapampa** and **Catac** leave daily at 0500-2000, US$0.65, from Mcal Cáceres y Tarapacá. To **Chiquián** for the Cordillera Huayhuash, see page 324.

Banks *Banco de Crédito*, on the Plaza de Armas. Closed 1300-1630, changes cash, no **Directory** commission on TCs into soles, good rates, 5% commission charged on TCs into dollars, cash advance on Visa, very long line-ups. *Interbanc*, on Plaza de Armas. Cash and TCs, cash advance on Visa. *Banco Wiese*, Sucre 766. Changes cash and cheques. *Casa de Cambio Oh Na Nay*, next to Interbanc. Gives good rates for cash dollars, but poor rates for other currencies. There are several other casas de cambio and many street changers (be careful) on Luzuriaga.

Laundry *B & B*, La Mar 674. US$1.20 per kg, special machine for down garments and sleeping bags, French run. Recommended. *Fitzcarrald*, Fitzcarrald. Close to the bridge. *Lavandería Liz*, Bolívar 711. US$2 per kg. Also at the Casa de Guías (see page 291).

Communications Post: Serpost is on Luzuriaga opposite the Plaza de Armas. Open 0800-2000 daily. **Telecommunications:** Telefónica del Perú, Sucre 409 y Luzuriaga. National and international phone and fax, open 0700-2300 daily. There are many other private calling centres along Luzuriaga, plus coin phones everywhere. **Internet:** *Univesidad Nacional (UNSAM)*, Avda Centenario 200. Posted hours 0800-2200 daily, but sometimes closes on weekends, US$2 per hour, minimum 30 mins. *Avance SRL*, Luzuriaga 672. 0700-2300 daily, US$3 per hour, US$1.75 per email message, US$1.75 to read or write a diskette, good equipment but expensive. Also on the 2nd floor of the Telefónica del Perú office, US$3.30 per hour, open till 2300.

Tour companies & travel agents Huaraz is overflowing with agencies and quality varies. Try to get a recommendation from someone who has recently returned from a tour, climb or trek. All agencies run conventional tours to Llanganuco, Pastoruri (both US$9 per person) and Chavín (US$10 per person). Many hire equipment (see **Trekking and climbing in the Cordillera Blanca,** page 289) and also offer rafting on Río Santa (US$15 for half a day), climbing and trekking tours and ski instruction. Most agencies provide transport, food, mules and guides. Prices are generally 20% lower during the low season, which is from Oct to Apr. **NB** Tour agencies shouldn't recommend Pastoruri as a first trip. It's best to go to Llanganuco first to acclimatize. The following are recommended: *Pablo Tours*, Luzuriaga 501, T721145. *Chavín Tours*, Luzuriaga 502, T721578 (Willy Gordillo can also be found at *Hostal Casablanca*, address above, T722602); *Jirishanka Sport*, Sucre cuadra 7, T722562. Climbing, trekking, horse riding, 4WD hire, they also rent rooms, **E** per person, with bath, hot water, breakfast. *Baloo Tours*, J de Morales 605, T/F725994.

Cordillera Blanca

Organizes tours and rents gear. *Monttrek*, Luzuriaga 646, upstairs, T721124. Good trekking and climbing information, advice and maps, run ice and rock climbing courses (at Monterrey), tours to Lago Churup and the 'spectacular' *Luna Llena* tour; they also hire out mountain bikes, run ski instruction and trips, and river rafting. Next door in the Pizzería is a climbing wall, good maps, videos and slide shows. For new routes and maps contact Porfirio Cacha Macedo, 'Pocho', at *Monttrek* or at Jr Corongo 307, T723930. *Andean Sport Tours*, Luzuriaga 571, T721612. Have a basic practice wall behind the office. They also organize mountain bike tours, ski instruction and river rafting. *Explorandes*, Avda Centenario 489, T721960, F722850, E postmast@ exploran.com.pe.

Tourist office Basic tourist information is available from the *Policía de Turismo* off Luzuriaga by Plaza de Armas. Open Mon-Fri 0900-1300, 1600-1900, Sat 0900-1300.

Around Huaraz

Willkawain About eight kilometres to the northeast is the Willkawain archaeological site. The ruins date from AD 700 to 1000, which was the second and imperial phase of the Huari empire. During this period, the Huari influence spread north from the city of the same name near Ayacucho. The Huari empire was remarkable for the strong Tiahuanacu influence in its architecture and ceramics. The Huari introduced a new concept in urban life, the great walled urban centre.

The site consists of three large two-storey structures with intact stone slab roofs and several small structures. The windowless inner chambers can be explored with the help of a flashlight, though most of the rooms are inaccessible. A few, however, have been opened up to reveal a sophisticated ventilation system and skilful stone craftsmanship. Entrance to the site is US$1.40.

Even if you're not an archaeology buff, the trip is worth it for a fascinating insight into rural life in the valley. A good grasp of Spanish will greatly enhance the pleasure of this experience as the locals are very welcoming. A recommended trip is to take a colectivo up to the ruins and walk back down to Huaraz. It's about a two-hour walk.

Take a bus from the corner of Raymondi & Luzuriaga (or walk) past the *Hotel Huascarán*. After crossing a small bridge take a second right (well signposted), from where it's about a 2 hour uphill walk. Ask frequently as there are many criss-crossing paths. Beware of dogs en route (and begging children). Alternatively, the purple city bus (line 2B) will take you to Marian, a 15 minute walk from the ruins. About 500 metres past Willkawain is Ichiwillkawain with several similar but smaller structures.

Monterrey

North of Huaraz, six kilometres along the road to Caraz, are the thermal baths at Monterrey (*Altitude*: 2,780 metres). It's a good place for a day trip to soak in the thermal baths and an alternative place to stay for those seeking peace and quiet. The baths are run by the *Hotel Baños Termales Monterrey* and, owing to the high iron content, the water is dark brown but not dirty.

There are two pools: the lower pool is US$0.90; the upper pool, which is nicer is US$1.35. There are also individual and family tubs which cost US$1.35 per person for 20 minutes. The upper pool is closed on Mondays for cleaning. It gets crowded at weekends and holidays.

Sleeping **B** *Baños Termales Monterrey*, Avda Monterrey, at the top of the hill, T/F721717. Slightly run down but classic old spa, price includes breakfast and use of pools, restaurant, bar, good location for walking, there is a rock face behind the hotel which is used for climbing practice. **B** *El Patio*, Avda Monterrey, 250 metres downhill from the baths, T/F01-437-6567 (Lima). Includes breakfast, meals on request, bar, friendly, colonial-style. Recommended. **C** *El Nogal*, on a side street off Avda Monterrey across from El Patio. Modern.

There are several country style restaurants in Monterrey which are popular with locals and busy at weekends, serving trout, *pachamanca* and other regional specialities. Along the Huaraz-Caraz road at Km 7 is *Las Terrazas*. At Km 6.5 is *El Cortijo*. At Km 5.5 *El Viejo Molino*, T721268, along the Río Santa. There are several cheaper restaurants and stands along Avda Monterrey. **Eating**

City buses along Avda Luzuriaga go as far as Monterrey (US$0.22), until 1900. A taxi costs US$2-3. **Transport**

To the east of Huaraz, off the road to Unchus and Pitec, are the ruins of **Huahullac**.

North from Huaraz

Huaraz to Carhuaz

The main road north from Huaraz through the **Callejón de Huaylas** goes to **Taricá** (not to be confused with Tarica at the north end of the Cordillera Blanca), where there is a home pottery industry. Good value purchases can be made from Francisco Zargosa Cordero. There's accommodation at: **F** *Hostal Sterling*, no hot water, meals, friendly.

The next town is **Marcará**, 26 kilometres from Huaraz (one hour, US$0.50). There's accommodation at: **D** *La Lomita*, Malecón Sur s/n, Familia García; and **E** *Alojamiento Restaurant Suárez*, Leguia 144, basic, shared bathroom. There are also basic restaurants and shops.

Pick-ups and colectivos go east from Marcará along a branch road three kilometres to **Chancos**, a little settlement with hot baths. There is accommodation in the shape of two very basic *alojamientos*, including *Bonilla*, half a kilometre west of town, and several basic restaurants and food stalls.

There is an uninviting lukewarm pool (US$0.45), as well as some none too clean private tubs (US$0.90) and very popular natural steam baths in caves (US$1.35 per person). The caves are interesting and worth a try, with locked changing rooms (cave 5 is the smallest and hottest). Buy eucalyptus leaves and other aromatic herbs from the local children to add some fragrance to your steam bath.

From Chancos the road and transport continue to **Vicos**, three kilometres further up the Huandoy valley. Vicos is seven kilometres from Marcará (one and a half hours, US$1.50). Vicos is in superb surroundings with views of Nevados Tocllaraju and Ranrapalca. To hike from Chancos to Vicos takes about two hours up the valley through farmland. A trail leads from Vicos to Laguna Lejíacocha, taking four hours.

There are archaeological sites at **Copa**, **Kekepampa** and **Joncopampa**. The latter is considered to be second only to Chavín in the region. From Vicos, cross the river on a footbridge, and it's about one hour further to Joncopampa.

From Vicos, you can walk through the Quebrada Honda, over the Portachuelo de Honda pass at 4,750 metres, to **Chacas**, an excellent, not difficult hike, which takes about four days.

Cordillera Blanca

Carhuaz

Coloured map 3, grid B2 Seven kilometres further on from Marcará is Carhuaz, a friendly, quiet mountain town with a pleasant plaza with tall palm trees and lovely rose bushes.

There is very good walking in the neighbourhood (see below). Market days are Wednesday and Sunday. The latter is much larger, and *campesinos* bring their produce to town. Good peaches are grown locally, among other crops. The local fiesta in honour of the *Vírgen de las Mercedes* is celebrated from 14 to 24 September and rated as the best in the region. The locals are renowned for their lively celebrations, hence the town's nickname, *Carhuaz alegría*.

Essentials

Sleeping **B** *El Abuelo*, Jr 9 de Diciembre y Tumbes, T794149. New in 1998, modern, comfortable, cafeteria, parking, ask at Heladería El Abuelo on main plaza. **D** per person *Casa de Pocha*, 1 kilometre out of town towards Hualcán, at foot of Nevado Hualcán, ask directions in town, T cellular 613-058 (Lima 462-1970). Nice country setting, price includes all meals, entirely solar and wind energy powered, hot water, sauna, home-produced food (vegetarian available), horses for hire, camping possible. **E** *Hostal Residencial Carhuaz*, Avda Progreso 586, T794139, just off the plaza. Cheaper without bathroom, varying standards of rooms (check first), basic but pleasant, hot water, nice courtyard and garden. **F** *Hostal La Merced*, Ucayali 600, T794241. Excellent, clean, friendly, hot water, some rooms with private bathroom. Recommended.

Several **casas de alojamiento** have been set up as part of a pilot project of family run guest houses, all with private bathrooms and hot water. Prices are in the **D** range, ask at Heladería El Abuelo on main the plaza, T794149. These include: *Río Santa*, Avda Santa Rosa 351, T794128, Familia Vinatea, comfortable, friendly, parking; *Las Torrecitas*, Amazonas 412, Familia Torres; *Las Bromelias*, Jr Brasil 208, Familia Henostroza; *El Tejado*, Amazonas 642, Barrio El Trimfo, Familia Bustos.

3 kilometres south of town, in Acopampa, in a country setting, is the Australian run *La Abeja*.

Eating *Los Pinos*, Avda Amazonas 645. Good typical food and set meals. Recommended. *El Palmero*, Avda Progreso 490. Good value and friendly. There are several other restaurants on the plaza. *Café Heladería El Abuelo*, on the Plaza de Armas, sells local ice-cream, sweets and snacks, is clean and friendly, and also sells regional maps and guides.

Transport All transport leaves from the main plaza. There are one or two trucks daily and one minivan (0800) going up the **Ulta valley** to **Chacas** (see page 319), 87 kilometres, 4-5 hours, US$4.50. The road works its way up the Ulta valley to the pass at Punta Olímpica from where there are excellent views. The dirt road is not in a very good condition owing to landslides every year (in the wet season it can be closed). The trucks continue to **San Luis** (see page 319), a further 10 kilometres, 1½ hours. Each Thursday, a bus (*Trans Huandoy*) does the trip from Carhuaz to **Chacas** and returns; US$6 one way, 5 hours. To **Huaraz**, colectivos and buses leave 0500-2000, US$0.65, 1 hour. To **Caraz**, 0500-2000, US$0.90, 1 hour.

Cordillera Blanca

Treks from Carhuaz

Trek 1 to Yanama The trek up to the **Ulta valley** over the Punta Yanayacu pass to Yanama is little used but offers impressive views of Huascarán and other peaks. It takes three days. If you catch a truck up the valley to where the road begins to zig-zag up to the pass, it will shorten the trek by one day. If not, start hiking from Shilla, 13 kilometres east of Carhuaz, or Huaypan. There is a daily bus to Shilla, US$0.30, and several combis to Huaypan on Wednesday and Sunday only, US$0.50, one hour.

Trek 2 to Laguna Auquiscocha A shorter trek in the same direction is to Laguna Auquiscocha at 4,319 metres. It is a hard three hours' walk from where the trail begins by the road, to some beautiful waterfalls below Aquiscocha. You can camp or make a day trip.

Trek 3 to hot springs Baños de La Merced, seven kilometres east of Carhuaz, near the village of Hualcán, were badly damaged by a landslide in 1993. The hot springs can be seen bubbling between the rocks by the river's edge and there are some small rock pools in which the enthusiastic can bathe.

From the plaza in Carhuaz follow Comercio to the top of the hill, turn right as far as *cinco esquinas* (five corners), turn left and follow the road uphill. When you reach the bridge, cross it left to Hualcán and ask directions from there. There is transport to Hualcán leaving from the plaza in Carhuaz on Wednesday and Sunday.

Trek 4 to Laguna 513 Half an hour beyond Baños de Pariacaca (see Trek 3 above) is the village of **Pariacaca** (no facilities) from where a trail continues into the mountains. In three hours you can reach **Laguna Rajupaquinan** and, 45 minutes beyond, the imaginatively named **Laguna 513**, with beautiful views of the surrounding peaks. If you continue, you will see the Auquiscocha lakes which you can reach in another three hours. Laguna 513 can also be reached directly from Hualcán in about four hours, along the north side of the river. This latter trail has fewer rocks to negotiate. Make sure to take adequate gear and a map if you plan to go beyond Pariacaca.

Mancos

From Carhuaz it is a further 14 kilometres to Mancos, at the foot of Huascarán. There's accommodation at *La Casita de mi Abuela*, Barrio Huascarán (a nice dormitory), *Pukio*, Jr Comercio 110, and *La Plazza*, on the Plaza de Armas, can provide meals. *Los Cactos*, at Km 49 in Ranrahica, is nice. There are also some basic shops and restaurants.

Climbers of Huascarán can go to **Musho** to reach the base camp. You can do a strenuous 30 kilometres, one-day walk which gives great views of Huascarán. From Mancos follow the road east and take the branch for Tumpa, about 13 kilometres away. Ask directions as the road branches several times. Continue north to Musho for about one kilometre. You can descend via Arhuay to Ranrahica, which is between Mancos and Yungay on the main road. There are daily colectivos from Mancos to Musho. Transport to Ranrahica and Arhuay is on Wednesday and Sunday only.

Cueva Guitarreros is a cave in the Cordillera Negra which contains rock paintings dating back some 12,000 years. Access is either through Mancos, from where it is about 30 minutes walking along an overgrown trail (with many spines!), or through Tingua and Shupluy further south, from where it takes about one hour.

The **Chirpas thermal springs**, which have a high lithium content, are near the caves. There are good views of Huascarán from around this area.

Yungay

Coloured map 3, grid A2   *Eight kilometres north of Mancos the main road passes through Yungay. The original town was completely buried during the 1970 earthquake by a massive mudslide caused when a piece of Huascarán's glacier was pried loose by the quake and came hurtling towards the town. It was a hideous tragedy in which 20,000 people lost their lives. The earthquake and its aftermath are remembered by many residents of the Callejón de Huaylas and the scars remain part of the local psyche.*

The original site of Yungay, known as Yungay Viejo, has been consecrated as a *camposanto* (cemetery). It is a desolate, haunting place, utterly barren save for four palm trees from the old Plaza de Armas. Nearby, atop a hill, is the old cemetery with a large statue of Christ, where a handful of residents managed to escape the disaster. There are a few monuments marking the site of former homes.

The new settlement is on a hillside just north of the old town, and is growing gradually. It has a pleasant modern plaza and a concrete market, good on Thursday and Sunday, which is good for stocking up on supplies for hiking.

Excursions from Yungay   A day walk from Yungay to **Mirador de Atma** gives beautiful views of Huascarán, Huandoy and the Santa valley. From town, follow a new dirt road east for three kilometres (about one hour). You can return via the Quebrada Ancash road which runs further north, between the Río Ancash and Cerro Pan de Azucar. This will bring you to the Yungay-Caraz road about one kilometre north of Yungay. It is about a three hours round trip.

Matacoto, six kilometres from Yungay, is in the Cordillera Negra at 3,000 metres, with excellent views of Huascarán, Huandoy and other major peaks. The turn-off is at Huarazcucho (Km 251), three kilometres south of new Yungay. It is another three kilometres from here, across the bridge over the Río Santa to Matacoto. Trucks go daily 0700-1300, US$0.50. On other days transport costs US$8. Matacoto can also be reached in three hours from Mancos (see above).

Essentials

Sleeping   **E** per person *COMTURY*, Complejo Turístico Yungay, Prolongación 2 de Mayo 1019, 2.5 kilometres south of the new town, 700 metres east of the main road in Aura, the only neighbourhood of old Yungay that survived, T722578. Nice bungalows with space for up to 10, in a pleasant country setting, hot water, fireplace, friendly, restaurant with regional specialities, camping possible. **E** *Hostal Gledel*, Avda Arias Grazziani, north past the plaza, T793048. A few cheaper rooms are available, owned by Sra Gamboa, who is hospitable and a good cook, very clean, shared bathroom, hot water, excellent meals prepared on request, nice courtyard. Highly recommended. **E** *Hostal Yungay*, Jr Santo Domingo on the plaza, T793053. Clean, basic, shared bathroom. **F** *Hostal Blanco*, follow the hospital street at north end of plaza and continue up hill, there are signs, T793115. Shared bathroom, basic, nice views.

The following **casas de alojamiento** have been set up as part of a pilot project of family run guest houses. Prices are in the **E** range: *Manantial*, Carretera Antigua, Barrio Aura, Familia Infantes; *La Suiza Peruana*, Avda Arias Grazziani s/n, Familia Sullca; *San José*, Avda Arias Grazziani, Familia Infantes.

Eating

Alpamayo, Avda Arias Grazziani s/n, at the northern entrance to town. Good. *El Portal*, by the market. Okay. There are several small *comedores* in and around the market and by the plaza.

Festivals

On **October 17** is *Virgen del Rosario*. On **October 28** is the *anniversary of the founding of the town*, celebrated with parades, fireworks and dances.

Transport

Buses, colectivos and trucks run all day to **Caraz** (12 kilometres, US$0.45), and **Huaraz** (54 kilometres, 1½ hours, US$1.10). To **Yanama**, via the Portachuelo de Llanganuco pass at 4,767 metres, 58 kilometres, 4-5 hours, US$4.50. Buses and trucks leave Yungay daily from in front of the Policía Nacional, 1 block south of the plaza, at around 0800 but you may have to wait until they are full. Some buses and trucks continue to **San Luis**, a further 61 kilometres (3 hours, US$2.50), **Huari** (61 kilometres) and **Chavín** (38 kilometres, 6 hours, US$3.50). On Tuesday and Saturday the bus continues north to **Piscobamba** and **Pomabamba** (US$11 Yungay-Pomabamba). Buses or colectivos will do the route to the Llanganuco lakes when there are enough people, and only in the dry season, 1½ hours; colectivo US$4.50, bus US$2.50. Huaraz travel agencies organize trips to Llanganuco for about US$8 (see page 299).

Llanganuco to Santa Cruz trek

For trekkers this is one of the finest and most heavily used walks in the Cordillera Blanca. It usually takes four to five days. It is considered somewhat easier in the opposite direction (Santa Cruz to Llanganuco), requiring three to four days (see **Treks from Caraz**, page 310 for details). **Please take all your rubbish with you**. Note that the following numbers correspond to the numbers on the map.

1   Arrive in Yungay early for transport to Yanama (see above).

2   Entry point to the **Huascarán National Park**. The park office is situated here below the lakes at 3,200 metres, 17 kilometres from Yungay. Accommodation is provided for trekkers who want to start from here, US$2 per person. The entrance fee to the park for trekkers and climbers is US$22. Although you can start hiking up the Llanganuco valley from the park office, most hikers continue by bus or truck to **María Huayta** (see below), where the Llanganuco-Santa Cruz trail starts. From the park office to the lakes takes about five hours (a steep climb). There is a *refugio* at the lakes. From the lakes to the pass will take a further two to three hours, with perfect views of the surrounding peaks. Just before the zig-zag climb up to the pass, there is a trail, very difficult to find, heading north, up to the Pisco base camp and the Demanda valley where, to the left, Laguna 69 is situated and, to the right, the Broggi glacier. There is a doorless *refugio* by the Broggi glacier, so you can spend the night after hiking up from the lakes, continue next day to Laguna 69 and return in time to catch a truck to Yanama.

3   This is the military control point. About 50 metres before the control is a morraine which is the short-cut to the Portachuelo pass.

Cordillera Blanca

4 From the Portachuelo de Llanganuco down to **Vaquería** at 3,700 metres, is about nine kilometres. However, get off here, at **María Huayta** (Km 66). From this point you will find a trail beside the house that takes you down to the trail to Colcabamba (four kilometres, three hours. If you don't get off here, the truck or bus will leave you in Vaquería, which is three kilometres up in the valley.

5 **Colcabamba** is a small village with basic lodging and food, should you decide to stay there. Familia Calonge is recommended, friendly, good meals. You can arrange an *arriero* and mule for about US$9 per day.

6 From Colcabamba the trail goes up the **Huaripampa valley**. As you enter the valley, you cross a bridge. There is a trail to the left which you should not follow. As you climb up to a curve you'll see another trail leading off to the right; do not follow this.

7 Push open the gates and continue through.

8 The trail starts again but it is best to keep close to the river to avoid the swamps. There are good camping spots from here to Punta Pucaraju.

Llanganuco to Santa Cruz Trek

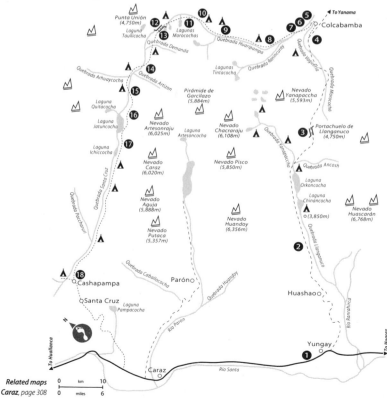

Related maps
Caraz, page 308

9 Quebrada Paría: here you'll see a signpost. The trail continues up to the right.

10 From **Paría** you'll find a forest of quenoales. The trail crosses the river here; look for a wide spot which has rocks to use as stepping stones.

11 After 15 minutes you'll reach some large boulders on your right. Here you'll find the trail on your left. Start climbing and look for markers (piles of stones) on the way.

12 Once you reach the wall of the morraine begin the climb to the highest point at **Punta Unión**, 4,750 metres. The views from here are wonderful. Look for the markers.

13 Go through the pass and a few metres ahead you'll see a marker to the right. Follow the track down to the pampa. From here it is downhill through the Santa Cruz valley to Cashapampa. You can camp anywhere on the way.

14 Cross the pampa and you'll reach a swamp from where you can see a signpost across the river. Follow the river; on the right you'll see a quenoal forest. In the middle of the river is a large rock. Five metres before the rock is a natural bridge to cross the river. A bit further on is a good side trek up to the Alpamayo base camp.

15 Recrossing the river, you'll see a signpost. Follow the trail until you reach a large boulder. On the left is a cave; head towards it to get back on the right trail, otherwise you'll end up in the middle of the swamp.

16 Once you reach **Jatuncocha**, the trail goes up to the left through the rock avalanche.

17 About 45 minutes further on you reach another swamp. The trail continues on the left.

18 At the end of the Santa Cruz valley you reach a eucalyptus forest. Don't cross the bridge but follow the trail and in 15 minutes you'll be in **Cashapampa**. Trucks from Cashapampa to Caraz leave at 0600, 1200, 1300 and 1400; two hours, US$1.35. Alternatively, hike via the little village of Santa Cruz to Caraz, in about five hours. You can stay overnight in a private house in Cashapampa for US$1.

Caraz

12 kilometres north of Yungay is the pleasant town of Caraz, a good centre for walking and the access point for many excellent treks and climbs. It is increasingly popular with visitors as a more tranquil alternative to Huaraz.

Population:
approximately 14,000
Altitude: 2,250 metres
Phone code: 044
Coloured map 3, grid A2

In July and August Caraz enjoys splendid views of Huandoy, Huascarán from its lovely plaza filled with rose bushes. In other months, the mountains are often shrouded in cloud. Caraz has a milder climate than Huaraz and is more suited to day trips. The sweet-toothed will enjoy the excellent locally-produced *manjar blanco*, a sort of toffee, from which it derives its nickname, *Caraz dulzura*.

Cordillera Blanca

Sights

The ruins of **Tunshukaiko** are in the suburb of Cruz Viva, to the north before the turn-off for Parón. This is a poor area so be discreet with cameras etc.

There are seven platforms from the Huaraz culture, dating from around BC 500. Minimal excavations have taken place and only the tops of a couple of the structures are accessible, some of which are estimated to have been up to 50 metres in height.

To get there, from the plaza in Caraz follow San Martín uphill, turn left on 28 de Julio, continue past the bridge over the Río Llullán. At the level of the turn-off for Parón ask the way as the ruins are behind some houses to the left. There isn't much to see at this time, but walking around will give you some idea of just how large these structures are.

Museo Arqueológico de Caraz has a small but interesting collection of ceramics and artefacts from the region. It's also a good place to ask about the ruins. ■ *1 de Mayo y Mcal Cáceres. Open 0800-1400. Free.*

Essentials

Sleeping   **D** *Hotel Restaurant Chamanna*, Avda Nueva Victoria 185, 25 minutes walk from the centre of town, from the plaza follow San Martín uphill, turn left at 28 de Julio, continue past the turnoff to Lago Parón. Run by Germans Ute Baitinger and Reiner Urban, clean cabañas set in beautiful gardens, hot water, secure, excellent French and international cuisine, will lend out tents for the Llanganuco-Santa Cruz trek. Highly recommended.

E *Caraz Dulzura*, Saenz Peña 212, about 10 blocks from the city centre, follow San Martín uphill north from the plaza, T791523 (Lima 287-1253). 6 double rooms, hot water, with bathroom and TV, cheaper without, very comfortable, great service, clean and airy rooms. Highly recommended. **E** *Chavín*, San Martín 1135 just off the plaza, T791171. With bathroom, sometimes hot water, owner can arrange transport to Lago Parón. **E** *Hostal La Casona*, Raymondi 319, 1 block east from the plaza, T791334. **F** without bathroom, cold water, clean, lovely little patio. **E** *La Suiza Peruana*, San Martín 1133 by the plaza. With bathroom, cheaper without, not clean. **E** *Moroví*, Luzuriaga 3a cuadra, at the south end of town, T791409. **F** without bathroom, clean, friendly, helpful, hot water. **E** *Regina*, Los Olivos s/n y Gálvez, at the south end of town, 1 block west of road to Yungay, T791520. Modern, with bathroom, hot water, clean, good value.

Caraz

To Hotel Restaurant Chamanna & Caraz Dulzura
To Cañon del Pato Laguna Parón & Tunshukaiko ruins

Santa Cruz
La Mar
Jr Córdova
San Martín
Sucre
Grau
Jr Bolognesi
Market
Market
Jr Alfonso Ugarte
Av Santa Rosa
Manco Capac
Cathedral
Municipalidad
Plaza de Armas
Transportes Moreno
Jr Daniel Villar
Antonio
Pony's Expeditions & Café de Rat
L Prado
José Gálvez
To Pueblo Libre, Alojaminto Caballero & Los Pinos Hostel
To Yungay

N

Archaeology Museum

0 metres 50
0 yards 55

■ **Sleeping**
1. Chavín
2. Hostal La Casona
3. Suiza Peruana

Cordillera Blanca

F *Alojamiento Caballero*, D Villar 485, T791637, or ask at *Pony's Expeditions* on the plaza. Shared bathroom, hot water, washing facilities, stores luggage, basic, family run and friendly. **F** *Ramírez*, D Villar 407, T791368. Basic, shared bathroom, cold water, helpful. **F** *Familia Aguilar*, San Martín 1143, T791161. Basic, shared bathroom, friendly, Prof Bernardino Aguilar Prieto has good information on the Cordillera Negra.

Youth Hostel E *Los Pinos*, Parque San Martín 103, T791130. With bathroom, hot water, a member of the Peruvian Youth Hostel Assoc, discount for IYHF members, camping on the premises costs US$1.75 per person.

Jeny, Daniel Villar on the plaza. Good food at reasonable prices. *El Mirador*, Sucre 1202 **Eating** on the plaza. Nice view from terrace, good set lunch and BBQ chicken at night, popular. Recommended. *Esmeralda*, Avda Alfonso Ugarte 404. Good set meal, friendly, recommended. *La Roca*, San Martín 1029. Cheap set meal. *La Olla de Barro*, Sucre 1004. Good set meal, English spoken. *La Punta Grande*, D Villar 595. Cheap local dishes. *Los Eucaliptos*, Sucre 1107. Set lunch, popular with locals. *Caraz Dulzura*, D Villar on the plaza. Excellent home made ice cream. *Establo Alameda*, D Villar 420. Excellent manjar blanco and sweets. *Burger Wasi*, D Villar 425. Burgers and snacks. *El Portal*, on San Martín. Good snacks and sweets. *Café de Rat*, Sucre 1266, above *Pony's Expeditions*. Serves breakfast, drinks and snacks, darts, travel books, nice atmosphere, recommended.

3 kilometres from town along the road to Cañon del Pato is *La Capullana*, in a pleasant garden setting, good food, expensive, poor service. *Palmira*, 500 metres south of town, east of the main road. Serves excellent trout, open 1200-1800, pleasant outdoor setting with small zoo.

Taberna Discoteca Alpamayu Inn, on Bolognesi. Moderate prices, a bit impersonal, **Bars &** popular with local kids. *Taberna Disco Huandy*, Mcal Cáceres 119. Reasonable prices, **nightclubs** good atmosphere.

Virgen de Chiquinquirá is held on **20 January**. *Holy Week* features processions and **Festivals** streets carpeted with flower petals. *Semana Turística* takes place during the last week in **July**, with sports festivals, canoeing, parasailing and folkloric events.

The best shop for camping supplies is Kike, at Sucre 918. Some camping food is avail- **Shopping** able from *Pony's Expeditions*, who also sell camping gaz canisters and white gas (see below).

Parasailing Parasailing is practiced at Km 259 on the road to Huaraz but you must **Sports** supply all your own equipment.

Swimming There is a cold water pool at the southern entrance to town. Adults US$0.45, children US$0.20.

Long distance buses From Caraz to **Lima**, 470 kilometres; several buses (6 compa- **Transport** nies, all along D Villar) leave daily, fares ranging from US$6 (eg *Chinchaysuyo*) to US$10 (*Expreso Ancash*), 11 hours. All buses go via Huaraz and Pativilca. Most buses on the Lima-Huaraz route continue to Caraz. To **Chimbote**, with *Trans Moreno* (D Villar 318), via Huaraz and Casma at 1700 daily, US$7, 10 hours; via Huallanca and Cañón del Pato 0900 every second day, US$7, 8 hours. To **Trujillo**, via Pativilca, with *Chinchaysuyo* (D Villar 230), at 1800 daily, US$9, 11-12 hours.

Regional buses From Caraz to **Huaraz**, several buses and frequent minivans leave daily, 0500-2000, 1½ hours, US$1, the road is in good condition. A taxi costs US$10. To **Yungay**, 12 kilometres, 15 minutes, US$0.45. To the village of **Parón** (for

Cordillera Blanca

trekking in Laguna Parón area) pickups leave from the corner Santa Cruz and Grau by the market, from Monday to Saturday 0500 and 1300, and Sunday 0300 and 1300, 1 hour. They return from Parón at 0600 and 1400. To **Cashapampa** (Quebrada Santa Cruz) buses leave from Santa Cruz between Grau and Sucre by the market, hourly from 0830 to 1530, 2 hours, US$1.25. To **Huallanca** (for the Cañón del Pato, see page 336), several buses leave daily from Manco Capac corner Grau, near the market.

Directory **Banks** *Banco de Crédito*, D Villar 217. Cash and TCs at good rates, no commission. *Comercial Fournier*, Sucre 907. Cash only, daily 0800-1330, 1600-2000. *Pony's Expeditions* (see below) cash only, good rates. *Importaciones América*, Sucre 721, T791479 (Esteban). Good rates and service, open weekends and evenings. **Communications** Post **Office:** at San Martín 909. **Telecommunications:** national and international phone and fax service at Raymondi y Sucre. Also several others. **Internet:** *Enter*, Santa Cruz 215, 2nd Flr, by the market, T791851. US$3 per hour, not always reliable. **Tour companies & travel agents** *Pony's Expeditions*, Sucre 1266, near the Plaza de Armas, T/F791642. Open daily 0900-1300 and 1600-2100, English, French and Quechua spoken, excellent and reliable information about the area. Owners Alberto and Haydée Cafferata are very knowledgeable about treks and climbs. Local tours and trekking are arranged, maps and books for sale, also equipment for hire, highly recommended. Another trekking guide is Mariano Araya, who is also keen on photography and archaeology. Ask at the municipality. **Tourist office** At Plaza de Armas, in the municipality, T791029. Limited information.

Treks from Caraz

To Pueblo Libre

A good day hike with nice views of the Cordillera Blanca is to Pueblo Libre. Follow Jr D Villar east across the Río Santa bridge and turn south to Tunaspampa, an interesting desert area with cacti and hummingbirds. Continue through the villages of Shingal, Tocash and Rinconada on to Pueblo Libre. It is about a four hour round trip, or you can take a colectivo back to Caraz.

A longer day walk – about seven hours in total – with excellent views of Huandoy and Huascarán follows the foothills of the Cordillera Blanca, south from Caraz. To leave town, follow Bolognesi up to 28 de Julio, turn right, go past the 2 de Mayo (Markham) High School and climb Cerro San Juan; about 45 minutes. Continue south towards the eucalyptus forest (one hour 20 minutes). After climbing a steep hill, where you get to a small house, take the smaller branch to the left. This leads to the main local summit in an area known as Ticrapa (two hours). Head down to Punyan on the Caraz-Yungay road (three hours), where you can take transport back to Caraz.

To Lago Parón

From Caraz a narrow, rough road goes east 32 kilometres to Lago Parón, in a cirque surrounded by several, massive snow-capped peaks, including Huandoy, Pirámide Garcilazo and Caraz. The water level has been lowered to protect Caraz, and the water from the lake is used for the Cañón del Pato hydroelectric scheme. The gorge leading to it is spectacular.

It is about a two-day trek (25 kilometres) up to the lake at 4,150 metres, or a five to six hour walk from the village of Parón. Where possible follow the walking trail which is much shorter than the road. By climbing up the slippery moraine to the south of the lake towards Huandoy, you get a fine view of Artesonraju. If there is room, you might (at the discretion of the guard) be able to stay at the refuge run by EGENOR (has kitchen and bathroom).

A trail follows the north shore of the lake to a base camp on the north side of the inflow, about two hours past the refuge. Beyond this point, the trail divides, one branch goes towards Pirámide Garcilazo (5,885 metres) and Pisco (5,752 metres), another to Laguna Artesoncocha at the base of an enormous glacier, and a third towards Artesonraju (6,025 metres).

There are camping possibilities along these trails. Try to find shelter in the quenoal stands or behind a ridge, as the wind can be very strong and the nights are cold. The views are magnificent as you are always surrounded by many beautiful peaks. When you ford a river, remember that the flow increases significantly in the afternoon with the meltdown, so make sure you can get back to your camp early. On the route to Artesonraju there is a morraine camp, just before reaching the glacier. You will need a map if you are going past Laguna Parón.

A taxi from Caraz costs US$30, or from Huaraz, US$50 return.

Santa Cruz Valley

The famous Llanganuco-Santa Cruz hike is done most easily starting in the Santa Cruz valley. Take a vehicle from Caraz in the morning up to Cashapampa (see **Caraz regional buses** above). It takes about four days, up the Santa Cruz Valley, over the pass of Punta Unión, to Colcabamba or Vaquería (see Llanganuco to Santa Cruz trek on page 305 for details). In this direction the climb is gentler, giving more time to acclimatize, and the pass is easier to find.

Three kilometres north of Cashapampa, or a one to two hour hike, are the hot-baths of **Huancarhuas**.

It is almost impossible to hitch from the end of the trail back to Yungay (described by travellers as exhilarating and terrifying). Be on the road by 0800 to catch the daily truck or buses coming from Yanama.

Alpamayo valley

This offers a beautiful, but difficult, 10 day trek from Cashapampa to Pomabamba, which is for the experienced only. From Cashapampa head up to the Cullicocha lake, passing the first pass at Los Cedros (4,850 metres), down the Mayobamba valley and up the third pass at 4,500 metres. Then into the Tayapampa valley, on to the village of Huillca, up the fourth pass at 4,280 metres and down to Collota, Yanacollpa and Pomabamba. **NB** Please carry out *all* your rubbish.

Cordillera Negra

For hikes in the Cordillera Negra, a truck leaves from Caraz market at 1000 to Huata at 2,700 metres, where there is a religious sanctuary and a dirty hotel (**F**). From here you can climb to the Quebrada de Cochacocha (3,500 metres) at the top of which is the Inca ruin of Cantu (excellent views), and on to the Inca lookout, **Torreón Andino** (5,006 metres).

Take water, food and tent with you. Allow three days for the hike, as there are lagoons near the peak. Six kilometres down a track off the Caraz-Huata road are the Inca ruins of Chonta. Seek advice from Prof Bernardino Aguilar Prieto in Caraz, San Martín 1143, T791161. Also refer to his Torreón Andino Information book before climbing it.

A large stand of **Puya Raimondi**, can be seen in the Cordillera Negra west of Caraz, along the road to Pamparomas. Take a truck or bus for

Pamparomas from the market as far as the Yuashtacruz pass at 4,300 metres (also known as *La Punta*). From the pass it is a short walk to the plants.

There is usually transport five days a week from around 0700 to 0900 (US$2, two and a half hours), ask beforehand. There are regular buses returning to Caraz, only on some days. If there is no bus, you can walk back to Caraz in six to eight hours, but it is easy to get lost and there are not many people to ask directions along the way. Take warm clothing, food and water. You can also camp near the puyas and return the following day. To hire a pickup costs US$25-35.

South of Huaraz

Recuay &
Olleros

South of Huaraz on the main road (27 kilometres, 30 minutes) is **Recuay**, one of the few provincial capitals which survived the 1970 earthquake and conserves its colonial features. On 11-16 September is the *Festividad Señor de Burgos de Recuay*.

The road passes the turn-off for **Olleros** at 3,450 metres, the starting point for the spectacular three-day hike to Chavín, along a precolumbian trail (see below). Some basic meals and food supplies are available here, but no accommodation.

An alternative trek from Olleros is to **Quebrada Rurec** via **Huaripampa**, a small village with a few *bodegas* which will sell or prepare food. Public transport is available to Huaripampa. There are granite walls of up to 600 metres at

Olleros to Chavín Trek

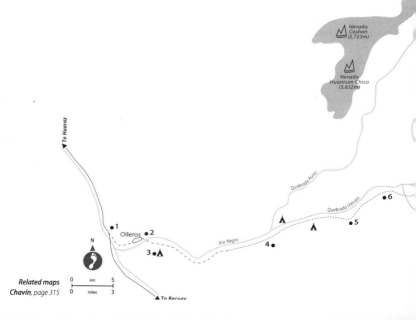

Nevado
Cashan
(5,723m)

Nevado
Huantsan Chico
(5,632m)

To Huaraz

Quebrada Rurec

Quebrada Uquian

6

Olleros
1
2
5
N
Río Negro
4
3

Related maps
Chavín, page 315

| 0 | km | 5 |
| 0 | miles | 3 |

To Recuay

Rurec, the highest in the Cordillera Blanca, which are recommended for rock climbing. The trek itself is also worthwhile.

Olleros to Chavín trek

Getting there You can get off at the main road and walk the 2 kilometres to Olleros, or catch a truck or minibus from Huaraz (at Tarapacá y Jr Cáceres, near *Edward's Inn*) to the village, 29 kilometres, US$0.30.

1 If you take a Huaraz-Catac minibus, get off at the cross before the Bedoya bridge. As you start uphill take the shortcut to Olleros to avoid the main road.

Note that the numbers in the text relate to the numbers on the map

2 About 50 metres past the main plaza in Olleros take the street on the right heading towards the bridge.

3 When you reach Canray Chico, turn right to keep on the road which follows the Río Negro. Keep the river on the left. The track is not always clear but it's difficult to get lost.

4 At this point a track branches off to the left into the Quebrada Rurec (see above); continue straight ahead.

5 Here you'll see a corral and, on the right, two small hills with houses. Head for the houses; don't follow the road with the bridge.

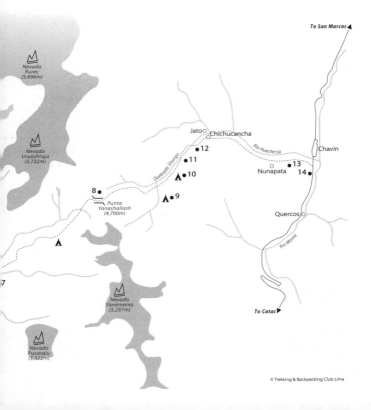

Cordillera Blanca

6 Once you pass the swamps and the corrals you'll climb up to some houses. A big stick would be useful here to fend off the resident canines.

7 Head towards the trees, at which point you start the climb towards the pampas that will lead to the **Punta Yanashallash**. This is a good spot to camp for the night. At the top of the valley, it divides into four valleys. The path swings right to avoid the marsh then heads up the second valley on the left, often with a ridge between the path and the river, to the highest point. It is quite easy to lose the track here, but keep heading in the direction of the pass and you'll pick it up eventually. It's a slow, gradual climb to the pass.

8 Here you reach the **Punta Yanashallash**, which is marked by great piles of rocks. From here you start going downhill.

9 Here you'll find a collection of houses or huts and a good camping spot.

10 Cross the swampy area and river before the trail starts again.

11 Follow the narrow trail which takes you down to another swampy area. Stay on the right side of the swamp and cross a small wooden bridge with some houses at the other end.

12 Follow the river until a large wooden bridge; cross it to continue the trail, which leads to the village of **Chichucancha**. Note that the valley leading down to Chavín is much more cultivated and populated. It may be better to camp near the foot of the descent from the pass in order to avoid beggars.

13 Head down into the Quebrada Huachecsa till you reach Punta Huancayo where you can see the ruins of **Chavín de Huantar**.

14 Go through the village of Nueva Florida to reach the road. The town of Chavín is on the left and the archaeological ruins are straight ahead (see below).

Recuay to Chavín

The main road continues 11 kilometres south from Recuay to **Catac**, where a good dirt road branches east for Chavín. There's accommodation in Catac at *Hostal Central* and one other place, both are basic. *Restaurant La Familia* is good.

From Catac to Chavín is a magnificent, scenic journey, if frightening at times. There's currently a lot of road building in progress between Catac and Laguna Querococha. Beyond Laguna Querococha, there are good views of the Yanamarey peaks and, at the top of the route, the road is cut through a huge rock face, entering the Cauish tunnel at 4,550 metres. On the other side it descends the Tambillo valley, then the Río Mosna gorge before Chavín.

South from Catac

Several kilometres south of Catac on the main road is **Pachacoto** from where a road goes to **Huallanca** on the other side of the Cordillera Blanca (133 kilometres, six to seven hours), not to be confused with the town of the same name by the Cañón del Pato. There is not a lot of local transport on this route.

In this southern part of the Cordillera there are few high, snow-covered peaks, but the glacier of **Pastoruri** is used as the only skiing area in Peru. It is nothing compared to other skiing areas in South America, there aren't even ski lifts, but it is a place to get in a little practice. Tours and private transport can be arranged in Huaraz. Expect to pay around US$80 for a van for up to 10 people.

NB Pastoruri receives many large groups, and trash is a serious problem here. The glacier is receding rapidly, and in 1998 there were suggestions that the area be closed to visitors in order to allow it to recover.

A good place to see the impressive Puya Raimondi plants is the Pumapampa valley. Hike up the trail from Pachacoto to the park entrance – two and a half hours – where there is a park office. You can spend the night here. Walking up the road from this point, you will see the gigantic plants. Another good spot, and less visited, is the **Queshque Gorge**. Follow the Río Queshque from Catac (see above); it's easy to find.

Chavín

The town of Chavín, just north of the famous ruins (see below), is the commercial centre for the nearby potato and corn growing area. Carved stone replicas are produced for the tourist trade.

Altitude: 3,160 metres
Coloured map 3, grid B3

Chavín has a pleasant plaza with palm and pine trees. The shops are well stocked with basic supplies and there is a small, basic market. There is nowhere to change money in town. Gasoline is available at north end of town. The local *fiesta* takes place on July 13-20.

There are hot sulphur baths (Baños Termales de Chavín) about two kilometres south of Chavín at Km 68 in the village of **Quercos**. They consist of one small pool and four individual baths in a pleasant setting by the Río Mosna. Camping is possible here. Buy detergent in the shop above baths and scrub your tub before bathing. ■ *Entry is US$0.45.*

Chavín

Chavín ruins ⚒

To Thermal baths (1.5 km)

Río Huachecsa

17 de Enero

● 3

2 ●

1 ●

3 ■

✝

⌂ Market
(PO)

■ 2

Transportes
Cóndor de
Chavín

■ 1

N

Sketch map

■ Sleeping
1. Gantu
2. Inca
3. Montecarlo

● Eating
1. Chavín Turístico
2. La Ramada
3. Las Chositas

Essentials

Sleeping

D *Rikai*, on 17 de Enero (north). New in 1997, modern, best in town, with private bathroom, hot water. **D** *La Casona*, Wiracocha 130, Plaza de Armas, T754020. With private bathroom, **E** with shared bath, hot water. **E** *Inca*, Wiracocha 160. With bathroom, **F** without, good beds, hot water on request, nice garden, friendly, undergoing renovations in 1998. **F** per person *Montecarlo*, 17 de Enero 101S (south), T754014. Shared bathroom, cold water, cold at night, member of the Peruvian Youth Hostel Association. **F** *Gantu*, Huayna Capac 135. Very basic, shared bathroom, cold water.

Cordillera Blanca

Eating   From north to south along the main street, 17 de Enero, are: *Las Chositas*, with garden setting, serves trout. *La Ramada*, regional dishes, also trout and set lunch. *Sr de Murhuay*, basic set meal. *Chavín Turístico*, the best in town, good *menú* and à la carte, clean, nice courtyard, friendly. *Mi Ranchito*, on the Plaza de Armas, regional dishes, OK. *El Lanzón de Chavín*, regional dishes, set lunch, friendly.

Transport   For buses to **Huaraz**, see under Huaraz; 110 kilometres, 4 hours, US$3. Buses to Huaraz from Huari pass through Chavín between 0400-0600 daily but are often full. Trucks go in the afternoon. There is plenty transport to **Catac**, 2½ hours, US$2. Many buses or trucks from there to Huaraz; 1 hour, US$0.50. Huaraz travel agencies organize daily tours to the ruins and sometimes you can hitch a ride back with them. A taxi to Huaraz takes 4 hours and costs US$20.

To **Lima**, 438 kilometres, 14 hours, US$9, with *Cóndor de Chavín* twice a week. Most buses from Lima go on to **Huari** and **Pomabamba**. *Perú Andino* and *Solitario* pass through Chavín, daily except Thursday, en route to Lima. There's a more frequent service on Wednesday and Sunday.

From Chavín to **Huari**, 38 kilometres, 2 hours, buses leave in the afternoon. To **San Luis** (a further 61 kilometres, 3 hours), and **Piscobamba** (62 kilometres, 3 hours): several buses and trucks serve this route as far as Huari on quite a good dirt road. The scenery is very different from the other side of the Cordillera Blanca, very dry and hot.

Directory   **Communications** Post office and telephone service at 17 de Enero 365N (north). Open 0630-2200.

Chavín de Huantar

Coloured map 3, grid B3   *Chavín de Huantar, a fortress temple, was built about 600 BC. It is the only large structure remaining of the Chavín culture which, in its heyday, is thought to have held influence in a region between Cajamarca and Chiclayo in the north to Ayacucho and Ica in the south. In 1985, UNESCO designated Chavín a World Heritage Trust site.*

The site is in good condition despite the effects of time and nature. The easternmost building was damaged in 1993 when the Mosna river burst its banks, while in 1945 a major landslide along the Huachecsa river completely covered the site with mud. It took many years to remove the rubble and some structures remain hidden.

The main attractions are the marvellous carved stone heads and designs in relief of symbolic figures and the many tunnels and culverts which form an extensive labyrinth throughout the interior of the structures. The carvings are in excellent condition, though many of the best sculptures are in Huaraz and Lima. The famous Lanzón dagger-shaped stone monolith of 800 BC is found inside one of the temple tunnels.

In order to protect the site some areas are closed to visitors. Although some of the halls have electric lights, take a torch. The guard is also a guide and gives excellent explanations of the ruins. Marino González is another knowledgeable guide. There is a small museum at the entrance, with carvings and some Chavín pottery. ■ *Open 0800-1600 Monday-Saturday, 1000-1600 Sunday and holidays. US$2.25, students US$1.35. Camping is possible with permission from the guard.*

You will receive an information leaflet in Spanish at the entrance. The guard also sells other reference material including *Chavín de Huantar* by Willhelm and Nancy Hoogendoorn, an English/Spanish guide to the ruins which includes a description of each building and an historical overview.

The stone gods of Chavín

Archaeologists have been able to learn very little about the Chavín culture, whose architecture and sculpture had a strong impact on the artistic and cultural development of a large part of the coast and central highlands of Peru. Based on physical evidence from the study of this 17-acre site, the temple of Chavín de Huantar is thought to have been a major ceremonial centre.

What first strikes visitors upon arrival at Chavín is the quality of the stonework found in the temple walls and plaza stairways. The sculptures have three functions: architectural, ornamental and the third is purely cultist and includes the Lanzón, the Tello obelisk and the Raimondi stela. The latter two currently grace the Museum of Anthropology and Archaeology in Lima.

At 5 metres high, the Lanzón is the crowning glory of the Chavín religion and stands at the heart of the underground complex. Its Spanish name comes from the lance, or dagger-like shape of the monolith which appears to be stuck in the ground. Carved into the top of the head are thin, grooved channels and some speculate that animals, or even humans, may have been sacrificed to this god. Others, however, suggest that the Lanzón was merely the dominant figure for worship.

Named after the Peruvian scientist, Julius C Tello, the Tello obelisk belongs to the earliest period of occupation of Chavín (ca 100 BC). It represents a complex deity – perhaps a caiman-alligator – connected with the earth, water and all the living elements of nature. Carved on the body are people, birds, serpents and felines which the divine beast has consumed.

The Raimondi stela was named after the Italian naturalist, who also gave his name to the famous plant, not to mention a fair percentage of the streets in the region. It shows a feline anthropomorphic divinity standing with open arms and holding some sort of staff in each hand.

Together, the figures carved on the stones at Chavín indicate that the resident cult was based principally on the feline, or jaguar, and secondarily on serpents and birds.

The Raimondi Stela

Cordillera Blanca

Callejón de Conchucos

Along the east side of the Cordillera Blanca, which is known as the Callejón de Conchucos, runs a good, but narrow, dirt road, subject to rapid deterioration when it rains. Public transport is less frequent and less reliable here than in the Callejón de Huaylas, with some towns getting only two buses per week, direct from Lima. Private vehicles, usually large trucks, are few and far between. The region has also seen less foreign tourists and some discretion, as well as responsible behaviour, is called for. If you plan to travel in this area, allow plenty of time, especially in the rainy season.

From Chavín you can return to Huaraz by road, via Huari, San Luis, Yanama and Yungay (see page 304) but travel along this route can be very slow as the bus service is infrequent.

The road north from Chavín descends into the dry Mosna river canyon. After eight kilometres it reaches **San Marcos**, a small, friendly town with a nice plaza. There are a few basic restaurants and *hostales*, including **F** *Familia Luis Alfaro*, across from the church. Gasoline is available 24 hours.

20 kilometres beyond San Marcos, at the junction of the Huari and Mosna rivers, is the village of **Pomachaca** (Las Tunas), where a road branches northeast to **Llamellín**. The main road continues north and climbs, criss-crossing the Huari river amid dry hills, to reach Huari 12 kilometres further on.

Huari

The town, perched on a hillside at 3,150 metres, has steep streets and enjoys good views of the surrounding mountains. The Plaza de Armas and cathedral are modern, having been rebuilt after the 1970 earthquake. It has a small fruit and vegetable market, which is quite busy on Sunday, and well-stocked shops. The water supply can be intermittent. The local *fiesta* of *Nuestra Señora del Rosario* is held during the first two weeks of October.

Sleeping **F** *El Dorado*, Bolívar 341. Basic, comfortable, sunny patio, shared bathroom, hot water. **F** *Añaños*, Alvarez 437, next to the market. Very basic but clean. There are a few others which are very basic, all **F**.

Eating *Los Angeles*, Ancash 669, off the main plaza. Mainly chicken, popular. *Rinconcito Huaracino*, Bolívar 530. Good *menú*, open till 2100. *Centro Virgen del Rosario*, San Martín by Parque Vigíl. Serves coffee, sweets and snacks, very clean and friendly, open evenings and Sunday, run by an Italian nun and her students.

Transport Bus companies have their offices around Parque Vigil. To **Huaraz**, 5-6 hours, US$4.50; all companies depart daily 0200-0400, also on Friday at 1500. To **San Luis**, buses leave on Tuesday and Saturday: with *El Solitario* at 0600, *Perú Andino* at 0830. Buses heading north pass through Huari between 2200 and 2400. To **Lima**, 13 hours, US$10: with *Turismo Huari* on Sunday, Wednesday and Friday at 0630, *Perú Andino* on Sunday and Wednesday at 0800. On the other days, except Thursday, buses bound for Lima originating further north pass Huari between 1000 and 1200.

Directory **Communications** The **post office** is at Luzuriaga 324 by Parque Vigíl. The **telephone office** is at Libertad 940. Open 0700-2200 daily.

Huari to Chacas trek

There is a spectacular two to three days walk from Huari to Chacas via Laguna Purhuay, as described by John Myerscough from Derbyshire in England: "The route is clearly shown on the IGM map, sheet 19. The walking is very easy, over a 4,500 metres pass and through two of the best valleys I've ever been in. Plenty of streams and lots of good places for camping. Amazing rock strata."

To get to **Laguna Purhuay**, climb the stairs at the end of Jr Luzuriaga, in Huari, to the main road, turn right, or north, and walk for about three kilometres to the village of Acopalca, which has a fish farm where you can buy trout. Turn left after crossing the bridge in town (ask directions). It is a one and a half hour walk up to the lake. The path to Chacas forks left just before the lake. Another good trail crosses the outflow and climbs above the eastern shore to a good lookout, then divides: the left fork descends to the inflow, which is a narrow gorge called *La Cola* (the tail); the right fork climbs to the village of Cachitzin (no facilities). There are no good trails along the shore of the lake.

Alberto Cafferata of *Pony's Expeditions*, Caraz (see page 310), writes: "The Purhuay area is beautiful. It has splendid campsites, trout, exotic birds and, at its north end, a 'quenoal' forest. This is a microclimate at 3,500 metres, where the animals, insects and flowers are more like a tropical jungle, fantastic for ecologists and photographers." A day walk to Laguna Purhuay is recommended for those who don't want the longer walk to Chacas.

Chacas to Pomabamba

10 kilometres south of San Luis, off the main road, is Chacas, with its fine church. The local *fiesta patronal* is in mid-August, with bullfights, a famous *carrera de cintas* and fireworks. Seek out the Taller Don Bosco, a woodcarving workshop run by an Italian priest. **Chacas**

There are a few basic shops, restaurants, a small market and two or three basic hostals, including *Hostal de Pilar.*

It is a two-day hike from Chacas to **Marcará** (see page 301) via the Quebradas Juytush and Honda (lots of condors to be seen). The **Quebrada Honda** is known as the Paraíso de las Cascadas because it contains at least seven waterfalls.

From Huari the road climbs to the Huachacocha pass at 4,350 metres and descends to San Luis at 3,130 metres. There is accommodation at **G** *Hostal Rotta*, also a few basic restaurants, shops and a market. Buses run to Chavín on Wednesday and Sunday, 5 hours, US$6. To Huaraz, 8 hours, via Yanama and the pass at 4,730 metres under Huascarán, and Pomabamba. Trucks also provide transport in this area. **San Luis**

A large sanctuary to **Nuestro Señor de Pumayukay**, built by Italian priests, is a 15-minute ride from San Luis towards Pomabamba and then a turn-off to the east.

28 kilometres north of San Luis, a road branches left to Yanama, 50 kilometres from San Luis, at 3,400 metres. It has one marked hotel outside and one unmarked hotel, **G**, on the plaza; ask at the pharmacy. Food is available, but no electricity in the village, which is beautifully surrounded by snow-capped peaks. A day's hike to the ruins above the town affords superb views. There's a daily bus between Yungay and Yanama (US$4.50, 5 hours), continuing to Pomabamba, on Tuesday and Saturday. It returns twice a week, US$11. Trucks also go along this route. **Yanama**

The road continues from Yanama to **Yungay** and is particularly spectacular. Eckhart Harm of Germany writes: "The 70 kilometres stretch from Yanama to Yungay is the most exciting of roads. If you leave early in the morning, you will always have the sun in the right place for taking photos. Between snow-capped peaks you ascend to the Portachuelo de Llanganuco pass from

Cordillera Blanca

where you have an overwhelming view of Huascarán, Huandoy, Laguna de Llanganuco and other mountains, and the endless serpentines of the road winding down to the lake."

The main road through the Callejón de Conchucos continues north from San Luis for 62 kilometres to **Piscobamba**. There is a basic, but clean and friendly hotel, and one other, both **F**. There are also a few shops and small restaurants. 22 kilometres beyond Piscobamba is Pomabamba.

Pomabamba Known as "City of the Cedars", though none can be seen, Pomabamba is worth a visit on several counts. There are very hot natural springs there, the furthest are the hottest. There is a small museum opposite the restaurant on the corner of the main plaza, which the people in the courtyard offices will open free on request.

Sleeping and eating F *Estrada*, C Lima. Good. F *Hostal Pomabamba*, on the main plaza. Basic, safe for luggage. **G** *No nos Ganan*, ½ block from the plaza. Basic but OK. Also: *Alpamayo*, on the plaza, and *San Martín de Porres*, off the smaller plaza, both are basic. Family lodging, **F**, at the house of Sr Alejandro Via, on Jr Primavera s/n. There are rooms for rent above the Marino agency. The restaurant on the corner of the main plaza is friendly and good (cold though). *Canela* is recommended for food.

Tour companies & travel agents *One Pyramid Travel*, Huaraz 209, T721283. Run by Victor Escudero, who speaks English, and specializes in archaeological tours, including some little known, unspoilt places. Recommended.

Occasional buses run from San Luis. There's a bus to Lima twice a week via San Luis and Chavín. Also to Chimbote twice a week via Sihuas.

Treks from Pomabamba

Several good walks into the Cordillera Blanca start from near Pomabamba. You can go via Palo Seco or Laurel to the Lagunas Safuna, from where you can go on, if you're fit enough, to **Nevado Alpamayo**, dubbed 'the most beautiful mountain in the world'. The glacier of Alpamayo is an incredible sight. From there, continue down to Santa Cruz and Caraz for several days' hard walking in total.

For the less energetic, it is a good four and a half to five hours' walk up to the quite large and extensive, though sadly dilapidated, ruins of **Yaino**, on top of a very steep mountain and visible from the main plaza of Pomabamba.

Ask directions in the village and on the way, too. The walls are beautifully built and there are two very large buildings, a square one and a circular one. The site commands excellent views of the many peaks of the Cordillera. The walk to Yaino and back to Pomabamba can be done in a day if you start early. Take food and lots of water; you can get very dehydrated climbing and per-spiring in the thin dry air. It's also very cold high up if the sun goes in, so go with warm, waterproof clothes.

Pomabamba to Yuramarca

From Pomabamba the road goes north through cold, wild mountains and valleys, passing in 23 kilometres Palo Seco and Andeymayo. The mining town of **Pasacancha** (hotel and restaurant), 56 kilometres beyond Palo Seco, is the junction for a road north to **Sihuas** (basic but expensive accommodation). Buses leave twice a week from Pomabamba via Sihuas to Chimbote, 16 hours.

Daytime trucks run from Pasacancha, through Tarica (not to be confused with Taricá, 16 kilometres north of Huaraz) and Yanac, past pre-Inca *chullpas* to Tres Cruces (basic friendly restaurant, no accommodation). Trans Moreno buses from Tres Cruces go to Yuramarca, north of the Cañón del Pato, and on to Caraz (and from there to Yungay and Huaraz).

A detour from Yuramarca is along a frightening road to **Corongo**. There is a bus from Caraz once a week with Empresa Callejón de Huaylas from the main plaza, but only travel in the summer or you may be stuck for a considerable time.

Places like San Luis, Piscobamba, Pomabamba and Sihuas were on the royal Inca Road, that ran from Cusco to Quito.

Cordilleras Huayhuash and Raura

Lying south of the Cordillera Blanca, the Cordillera Huayhuash has been dubbed the "Himalayas of America" and is perhaps the most spectacular in Peru for its massive ice faces which seem to rise sheer out of the contrasting green of the Puna. Azure trout-filled lakes are interwoven with deep quebradas and high pastures around the hem of the range. You may see tropical parakeets in the bottom of the gorges and condors circling the peaks.   *Coloured map 3, grid B3/4*

Although the area may well have been inhabited for thousands of years, the Huayhuash only became known to the outside world following a plane crash at Jahuacocha in 1953. Since then the number of visitors has grown steadily, with a hiatus during the era of insurgency in the 1980s (see Safety and conduct, below). Although less touristy that the Cordillera Blanca, it nonetheless receives significant numbers of trekkers and climbers every year.

Trekking in the Cordillera Huayhuash is generally considered difficult, and certainly requires stamina (12 to 14 days for the complete loop, see below) but the trails are good and most gradients are relatively gentle. There are up to eight passes over 4,600 metres, depending on the route.

There are two traditional trekking routes in the Huayhuash, described below: a complete loop around the range, starting and ending in Chiquián; and a half-circuit, starting in Chiquián and ending in Cajatambo. These are but two of very many excellent options however, and hikers are urged to be creative in choosing their routes and camp sites, both to enjoy more pristine surroundings and to allow over-used areas to recover. A mini-trekking route to Jahuacocha and back (approximately four days) has become popular with some trekkers.

Both the Huayhuash and Raura ranges are approached from **Chiquián** in the north, **Churín** in the south or **Cajatambo** to the southwest. The area is remote and isolated but not entirely uninhabited. The local villagers are generally herdsmen, tending flocks of cattle, sheep and alpacas.

Remember that you must be entirely self-sufficient and that evacuation in the event of illness or accident may require several days.   **Safety & conduct**

The residents of the region are poor and the presence of visitors has had its impact. Children beg for sweets, pencils or money and adults may also ask for handouts; be polite but firm in your refusal. Do not leave your gear unattended at any time and stow everything in your tent overnight.

Fortunately armed robberies are rare; no incidents have been reported since a trekker was murdered at Paso Carnicero in 1996. The entire region

Cordillera Blanca

was under the control of *Sendero Luminoso guerrillas* during the 1980s and early 90s. While this threat has passed, the arms distributed at the time remain in circulation. The eastern side of the range, in the Department of Huánuco, has a reputation for more aggressive behaviour, be especially cautious in this area (see Central Highlands, page 451).

You will encounter many cattle and dogs guarding them throughout the trek. It's best to give both a wide berth. Carrying a walking stick or crouching to pick up a stone will usually discourage the canines. Throwing stones has been known to provoke an attack.

Trash is an important problem at the usual camp sites and you should personally pack out everything you bring in; you cannot trust muleteers in this regard. Much of the area is above tree-line, the remainder has been badly deforested. Make sure you have a reliable stove and enough fuel for cooking and resist the temptation to use what little firewood remains.

Provisions Huaraz is the region's supply centre, all but the most specialized items may be obtained here. If you require freeze-dried meals however, these should be brought from abroad. Chiquián's shops are usually well stocked with basic supplies, including locally produced butter and cheese, although prices may be a bit higher here. Almost nothing is available in the hamlets along the route, but fresh trout may be purchased by some of the lakes and a very few items (mostly beer, soft drinks and potatoes) might be purchased in Llamac, Carhuacocha, Huayllapa and Pacllón. Take coins and small bills as there is seldom any change. Bring a fishing line and lure to supplement your diet.

Mule hire It is sometimes a problem in the high climbing/trekking season to hire mules straightaway. This is because all the ones from Chiquián are kept at Llamac and Pocpa. It may take a day to bring the mules to Chiquián. For prices for donkeys and muleteers see page 291. You can bargain but be reasonable.

The muleteers themselves are a quite mixed bunch, ranging from excellent to entirely irresponsible. Best to get a recommendation from someone who has recently returned from a trek, otherwise call ahead to *Hostal San Miguel* or ask at *Restaurant Yerupajá* or *Panadería Santa Rosa* (see Chiquián below). Do not hire muleteers who approach you on the street, there have been a number of rip-offs. Always ask to see a valid *carnet* from the *Dirección de Turismo*. You should also make your priorities clear to the muleteer in advance of the trek (pace, choice of route, camp sites, etc.) or else you will be led around with the line, "all the *gringos* do this".

A guide for the Huayhuash is Sr Delao Callupe. Ask for him in Chiquián.

The Huayhuash Circuit

The traditional trek starts in **Chiquián**. From there, descend to the **Río Pativilca** and down the dry canyon to the confluence of the **Río Llamac**. Head eastwards up river to **Llamac**.

A must is a side trip to **Laguna Jahuacocha**, which lies beneath **Yerupajá** (Peru's second highest peak at 6,634 metres) and Nevados **Jirishanca** and **Rondoy**. The lake offers the most idyllic campsite in the Cordillera. It is reached over the Punta Llamac pass at 4,300 metres, southeast of Llamac. First head southwest along a path just beneath the cemetery and zig-zag up above the town.

The main circuit trail is regained over a 4,800 metres pass beneath Rondoy. From there, descend to Matacancha and climb again to the **Punta Cacanan** pass (the continental divide at 4,700 metres). This northernmost point on the trek gives access to the village of **Janca**, **Laguna Mitúcocha** and the eastern flank of the Cordillera.

A very steep short cut on scree is through the gap in the northern spur of the range above Matacancha and Janca village on the other side. This could save two or three hours.

The eastern side of the Cordillera is a chain of passes, lakes and stunning views of **Jirishanca Chico**, **Yerupajá Chico, Yerupajá** and **Siulá Grande**. From Janca, a small side valley leads off **Quebrada Mitucocha** to **Punta Carhuac** (4,650 metres) and beyond to **Laguna Carhuacocha**, with magnificent camping and views. Following on from there are **Punta Carnicero** (4,600 metres, a section of Inca road and petroglyphs are found nearby), the twin lakes of **Azulcocha** and **Atoqshaico** (just beyond the pass) and **Huayhuash village** (one house).

The next pass, **Portachuelo Huayhuash** (4,750 metres, the continental divide) overlooks the superb southward line of pyramidal peaks and rounded ice caps of the **Cordillera Raura**. A path leads from **Laguna Viconga** below (near the dam), over a pass and hugs the western flank of the Raura all the way to **Oyón**.

Four hours away from Oyón is **Churín**, which boasts the "best thermal baths in Peru". There is also a small thermal pool one kilometre past the outflow of Viconga, along the trail to Cajatambo. Note that water is released from the Viconga dam daily 0500-1100, and you cannot ford the outflow during this time.

If you are bailing out at **Cajatambo**, it is downhill all the way from Laguna Viconga, apart from a short sting in the tail at the end. Those continuing the circuit must cross the **Punto Cuyoc** (5,000 metres), sometimes snowbound, with outstanding 360° views. The highpoint of the circuit in every sense of the word.

Cordilleras Huayhuash and Raura

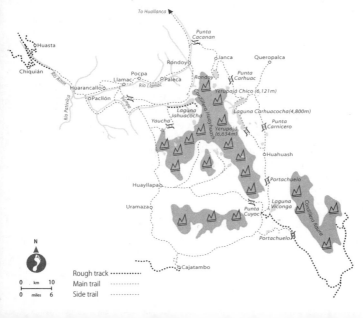

Cordillera Blanca

There follows a long, gentle descent into the **Quebrada Guanacpatay** and an optional one day side trip up the valley of the **Río Huayllapa** to **Laguna Jurao** and **Laguna Sarapcocha**, both beautiful glacial lakes.

The route continues downhill to the village of **Huayllapa**, just before town it turns north to begin climbing to the **Tapush Pass** (4,800 metres) below the summit of **Diablo Mudo**.

The direct trail from Tapush to Pacllón was badly damaged in 1998, requiring an extra day's travel via the **Yaucha Pass** (4,800 metres) back to Jahuacocha by way of the **Quebrada Huacrish**. It offers outstanding views.

Following the **Río Pacllón** all the way to the town of the same name, brings you to within a day's walk back to Chiquián.

Chiquián

Population: approximately 5,000.
Altitude: 3,400 metres
Phone code: 044

Chiquián is usually the starting point for the Huayhuash circuit. It is a town of narrow streets and overhanging eaves. An interesting feature is a public television mounted in a box on a pedestal which sits proudly in the Plaza de Armas, around which folks gather every evening. There is a *Semana Turística* during the first week of July and the local *fiesta* is celebrated on 30 August in honour of Santa Rosa.

Sleeping *El Rápido*, Figueredo esquina 28 de Julio. private bathroom, hot water, due to open early 1999. **E** *Hostal San Miguel*, Jr Comercio 233, T747001. Nice courtyard and garden, clean, many rooms, popular, poor water supply, overpriced. **F** *Hostal Inca*, 1 block from plaza. *Yerupajá*, on Grau, 3 blocks from the Plaza. Small and basic.

Eating *Yerupajá*, Jr Tarapacá 351; and *El Refugio de Bolognesi*, Tarapacá 471. Both offer basic set meals. There are several others. *Panificadora Santa Rosa*, Comercio 900, on the plaza. For good bread and sweets.

Transport Three bus companies run from Huaraz to Chiquián, 120 kilometres, 3 hours: *El Rápido*, at Huascarán 117, on the corner with Raymondi, at 0600, 1400, 1800, US$2.40; *Virgen del Cármen*, around the corner on Raymondi; and Chiquián Tours, on Tarapacá behind the market. From Chiquián to Huaraz: several buses leave the plaza from 0530 to 0600 daily, and *El Rápido*, Jr Figueredo 216, at 1730. Direct buses also go from Chiquián to Lima, 353 kilometres, 8 hours, US$5.25, with *Tubsa*, *Firesa* and *Cavassa* overnight. There is also a connection from Chiquián to Huallanca, with some trucks and buses doing this route, though not daily. From Huallanca trucks and buses go on to La Unión and Huánuco.

Cajatambo

The southern approach to the Cordillera Huayhuash is a small, developing market town, with a beautiful 18th century church and a lovely plaza. **F** *Hostal Miranda*, Jr Tacna 141. Homely, friendly, small rooms. Recommended. **G** *Hostal Cajatambo*, on the plaza. Basic, cheap, not for the squeamish as the courtyard is a chicken slaughterhouse. **G** *Hostal Trinidad*, Jr Raimondi 141. Basic. *Restaurant Andreita*, is at Avda Grau 440. Buses to Lima leave daily at 0600, US$8.80, with Empresa Andina (office on plaza next to *Hostal Cajatambo*). The only way back to Huaraz is via Pativilca on the coast, a long detour.

North coast

9

North coast

328 Lima to Chimbote

333 Sechín

334 Chimbote

336 Trujillo

345 Chan Chán

348 Huanchaco

350 Chiclayo

357 Sipán

359 Túcume

362 Piura

370 North to Ecuador

375 Tumbes

379 Frontier with Ecuador

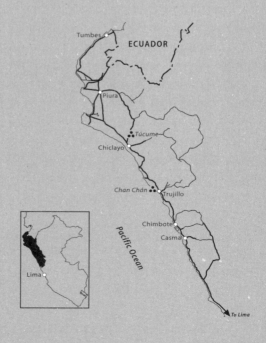

This part of Peru is well known to those heading overland to or from Ecuador, but compared to the likes of Cusco, Arequipa or Lake Titicaca in the south, it receives relatively few short-term visitors. Yet the thin belt of coastal desert that runs north from Lima to the Ecuadorean border is home to some of the country's greatest treasures.

Peru's north coast could well be described as the Egypt of South America. This is a region of numerous monumental ruins, built by the many highly-skilled pre-Inca cultures that once thrived here. Among the best known are **Chan Chán**, **Túcume**, **Sipán** and **Batán Grande**.

But it's not all pyramids and royal tombs. The elegant city of **Trujillo** is one of the finest examples of colonial architecture in the country. There are charming villages such as **Huanchaco**, with its bizarre-looking reed fishing rafts, as well as great seafood and unrivalled hospitality. In addition, the north coast enjoys a rain free climate all year, and sports Peru's finest beaches for bathing and surfing.

El Niño caused road damage from Chiclayo north to Tumbes in 1998, especially around Piura. Travel times in this region in June 1998 were up to twice as long as the normal times shown below. Check on road conditions beforehand.

North Coast

Lima to Chimbote

Between Lima and Pativilca there is a narrow belt of coastal land deposited at the mouths of the rivers and, from Pativilca to the mouth of the Río Santa, north of Chimbote, the Andes come down to the sea. Between Lima and Pativilca cotton and sugar-cane are grown, though the yield of sugar is less than it is further north where the sunshine is not interrupted by cloud. Much irrigated land grows vegetables and crops to supply Lima and Callao. Between June and October, cattle are driven down from the Highlands to graze the lomas (fog meadows) on the mountain sides when the mists come.

The Pan-American Highway parallels the coast all the way to the far north, and feeder roads branch from it up the various valleys. Just north of Ancón (see page 140), the Pasamayo sand dune, stretching for 20 kilometres, comes right down to the seashore. The old road which snakes along the base beside the sea is spectacular, but is now closed except to commercial traffic and buses. The new toll road (US$0.85), which goes right over the top, is much safer and you get spectacular views over the nearby coast and valleys.

Chancay Lying on the coast, at Km 87, Chancay suffers from severe water shortages, but there is a fresh water source on the beach. The sea here can be dangerous and heavily polluted, and if that doesn't put you off, then the awful smell from the fish processing factories certainly will. There is no bus terminal but it's easy to catch long distance buses on the Pan-American Highway.

Sleeping and eating **C** *Hostal Villa de Arnedo*. Clean and friendly, pool open in summer, restaurant. Recommended. **E** *Hostal Chancay*. Safe, good beds, can wash clothes. The 'castle' at Chancay, a pseudo-medieval summer house (built 1922-42) on the beach, is planned to be converted to a 220-bed hotel. It's currently open to visitors; entry US$1, café, playground. *Pizzería Donatello* on the plaza. Expensive but good. *Costa Azul*, with gardens, overlooking sea. Also good.

Chancay Valley Just inland from Chancay is **Huaral** (**C** *El Parque II*, good facilities), which gives access to the Chancay Valley, up which are the extraordinary, little-visited ruins of **Chiprac**, **Rupac** and **Añay**.

Chiprac is a two and a half hour climb from Huascoy (see below). The Salvador family have accommodation and Carlos is a recommended guide for the ruins, though a guide is not strictly necessary. It is a good day's walk there and back with time to take photographs and eat. Huascoy celebrates the *Fiesta de San Cristóbal* in the week before Independence (28 July), with a procession, masses, dancing, fireworks and football matches.

Rupac is best reached from La Florida. Its ruins are the best preserved of the group, though less extensive than Chiprac. All the ruins have complete roofs, which is unique in Peru.

For Añay, go to Huaral as for the other ruins, then get transport to Huayopampa (basic accommodation) or La Perla from where the ruins can easily be reached. Get a guide to take you there from either village.

Transport Take a bus to Haural from Plaza de Acho, by the bullring, in Lima (beware of thieves). Then take the Juan Batista bus, on Tuesday and Friday, to Huascoy (US$2), 2 kilometres beyond San Juan, which is up beyond Acos. This is described as "a hair-raising, breath-taking and bone-shaking ride, up to 3,500 metres above sea-level."

North Coast

At Km 101 is Huacho, where you can turn off the Pan-American and head **Huacho**
west to Puerto Huacho (*Population*: 35,900), which is the outlet for cotton
and sugar grown in the rich Huaura valley. There are cotton-seed oil and
other factories. The port and sea are sometimes alive with huge jellyfish.

Sleeping and transport C *Hostal Villa Sol*. Clean, pleasant, restaurant,
pool, playground. E *Hostal Maury*. Basic but friendly. E *Italia*. Shared bathrooms, clean. F *El Pacífico*. Safe but dirty, water problems, inadequate
clothes-washing facilities. *Hostal de Milagritos*, comfortable. Camping is possible at El Paraíso beach. Bus, 2½ hours, US$2, or Comité 18, daily colectivos,
US$2.50. Buses north usually arrive full. They can be caught at the round-
about on the Pan-American. There are regular combis to Sayán (see below).

Huacho to Churín

The journey inland from Huacho, up the Huaura valley, is spectacular. 60
kilometres inland is **Sayán**, an attractive agricultural town at the base of the
Andean foothills. It is a nicer place to stay en route to Churín than the coastal
towns. There are several hotels and restaurants. Regular combis go to Huacho
from Avda Balta. Buses from Lima for Churín stop at the bridge.

Churín

Beyond **Sayán** are terrific rock formations, then the road passes through sub-   *Population: 2,000*
tropical vegetation around **Churín**, one of Peru's best-known spas, with hot,   *Altitude: 2,080 metres*
sulphurous springs which are used to cure a number of ailments. The climate
is dry, temperatures ranging from 10° to 32°C. The area is covered in trees and
famous for cheese. Churín is very popular with Limeños. Accommodation
and buses are fully booked at holiday times. The valley was cut off during the
El Niño floods, but a rough road was re-opened in July 1998.

A highly recommended excursion can be made up a side valley, five kilo-   **Excursions**
metres below Churín. Combis leave from beside the church (0800-0900,
US$3 round trip fare, returning 1500-1700), for the two hours trip to
Huancahuasi (**G** *Hostal Turistas*). The new Huancahuasi baths include a
pool that President Fujimori has swum in (hot, US$0.70 per person), while on
the opposite side of the river the new **Picoy** baths include excellent private
pools carved out of the rock (hot, US$0.30 per person). Snacks such as
'pachamanca' are available at riverside stalls. The trip also includes a stop-off
at Picoy, which has a remarkable colonial church with a highly carved façade,
and at **Chiuchin** (**E** *Hostal Doña Hermina*, set in attractive grounds). The
Chiuchin baths (hot, US$30 per person for pool; US$0.50 per person for private baths) are now rather neglected and run down.

Sleeping All hotels are within a couple of blocks of each other. Prices double at peak   **Essentials**
holiday periods, otherwise they are a bargain. **B** *Santa Rosa*, T373014, international
T373015. Modern with the usual facilities. **C** *Las Termas*, T373005. Has rooms with a
pool in the town centre and others up at the La Meseta baths. **D** *Hostals Beatriz and
Danubio*, T373028. Modern, clean, quiet, friendly. **E** *Hostal La Cabana*. Clean, with
attractive courtyard.

Eating Churín is full of restaurants and cafés offering healthy portions and a wide
range of 'dulces' (desserts). Local delicacies include honey, alfajores, flavoured manjar
blanca, cheeses and calabaza (a delicious pudding made from squash).

North Coast

Transport Trans Estrella Polar, Espadín and **Beteta** each have several buses a day to Lima, 6-7 hours, US$5. Some buses from Lima continue to Oyón, 1 hour. From Oyón it is possible to continue over the sierras to Cerro de Pasco by truck on a very rough high altitude road.

Loma de Lachay National Reserve One kilometre north of the turn-off to Sayán (see above) is a sandy track which leads to the **Loma de Lachay National Reserve**, three kilometres further on. A four-wheel drive vehicle is recommended to get there.

This small reserve is a typical example of '*loma' habitat, and it holds several important species. Loma* vegetation is formed during the winter months, when fog caused by the Humboldt Current drives inland, rises and condenses, and forms a dew on the surrounding landscape. This dew is sufficient to sustain the seasonal *loma* or 'fog vegetation' that is the home of birds such as the endemic Raimondi's Yellow-finch and Thick-billed miner.

In September-October the plants are in bloom and very beautiful. There is a visitors' centre, trails, camping and picnic areas. The reserve is very popular with Lima residents at the weekend.

Huacho to Barranca Just across the river from Huacho, is **Huaura** where the balcony is still preserved from which San Martín declared the country's independence from Spain. Try *guinda*, the local cherry brandy.

The road passes from the wide valley of Mazo through the irrigated valley of San Felipe. Midway between Huaura and Supe, on the coast road, is **Medio Mundo**, with a lake between the village and the sea. It is a good camping spot, with tents for rent, which is guarded at weekends. Bring food and water – there is none for bathrooms or drinking. The turn-off is outside the village on the Pan-American Highway, to the left; look for the sign, 'Albufera de Medio Mundo'. It is hot and busy in summer.

There is more desert and then the cotton-fields of San Nicolás lead to **Supe** (F *Hostal Grau*) at Km 187, a small busy port shipping fishmeal, cotton, sugar and minerals. At **Aspero**, near Supe, is one of the earliest prehistoric sites in Peru (see History section, page 498).

Barranca At Barranca (Km 195. *Phone code*: 034) the beach is long and not too dirty, but windy. *Banco de la Nación*, accepts TCs but at poor rates

Sleeping and eating D *Chavín*. With bathroom, warm water, clean, good value and recommended, though the front rooms are noisy, it also has a restaurant on the 1st floor for lunch and dinner (try *arroz con conchas*), breakfast bar and café opens onto the street by the main entrance. E *Hostal Casablanca*, on the beach front. F *Casanova*, on the main street. With bathroom, clean but unwelcoming, safe motorcycle parking. F *Jefferson*, Lima 946. Clean, friendly. F *Pacífico*. With bathroom, clean, good value. G *Colón*, Jr Gálvez 407. Friendly, basic. There are many other hotels on the main street, and plenty of bars and restaurants. *Cevichería Fujino*, Arica 210. Good for fish. Try the *tamales*.

Transport Buses stop opposite the service station (*el grifo*) at the end of town. From Lima to Barranca, takes 3½ hours, US$3. As bus companies have their offices in Barranca, buses will stop there rather than at Pativilca or Paramonga (see below). Several buses leave daily from Barranca to Casma, 155 kilometres, 3 hours, US$3. Also daily buses and trucks to Huaraz; 4 hours, US$6.

The straggling town of **Pativilca** (Km 203), has a small museum and a good, cheap restaurant, *Cornejo*.

Pativilca to Huaraz

Just beyond Pativilca, a good paved road turns east for Huaraz in the Cordillera Blanca (see page 293).

The road at first climbs gradually from the coast. At Km 48, just west of the town of **Chasquitambo** (*Restaurante Delicias*) it reaches *Rumi Siki* (Rump Rock), with unusual rock formations, including the one that gives the site its name. Beyond this point, the grade is steeper and at Km 120 the chilly pass at 4,080 metres is reached. Shortly after, **Laguna Conococha** comes into view, where the Río Santa arises. Delicious trout is available in Conococha village. A dirt road branches off from Conococha to **Chiquián** (see page 324) and the Cordilleras Huayhuash and Raura to the southeast.

After crossing a high plateau the main road descends gradually for 47 kilometres until **Catac** (see page 314), where another road branches east to Chavín and on to the Callejón de Conchucos (see page 317). Huaraz is 36 kilometres further on and the road then continues north through the Callejón de Huaylas.

Four kilometres beyond the turn-off to Huaraz, beside the highway, are the **Paramonga** well preserved ruins of the Chimú temple of Paramonga. Set on high ground with a view of the ocean, the fortress-like mound is reinforced by eight quadrangular walls rising in tiers to the top of the hill. It is well worth visiting. ■ *US$1.20. No buses run to the ruins, only to the port (about 15 minutes from Barranca). A taxi from Paramonga and return after waiting costs US$4.50, otherwise take a Barranca-Paramonga port bus, then it's a 3 kilometre walk.*

The town of Paramonga is a small port, three kilometres off the Pan-American Highway, four kilometres from the ruins and 205 kilometres from Lima.

Between Pativilca and Chimbote the mountains come down to the sea. The road passes by a few very small protected harbours in tiny rock-encircled bays – **Puerto Huarmey**, **Puerto Casma** and **Vesique**. Between Paramonga and Huarmey there are restaurants at Km 223 and 248. In Huarmey, on the Pan-American Highway is: **C-D** *Hotel de Turistas*. Small, clean, good service, restaurant, noisy from road traffic. **D** *Hostal Santa Rosa*, on the plaza.

Casma

The town, largely destroyed by the 1970 earthquake, has since been rebuilt, partly with Chilean help. It has a pleasant Plaza de Armas, several parks and two markets including a good food market. The weather is usually sunny, hence its title *Ciudad del Sol Eterno* (City of Eternal Sun).

Sleeping D *Hostal El Farol*, Tupac Amaru 450, T/F619732. Best in town, ask for the **Essentials** cheaper rate in the low season, with bathroom, includes continental breakfast, hot water in most rooms, good restaurant, pleasant garden setting, parking. Recommended. **D** *Hostal Ernesto's*, Garcilaso de la Vega y Gamarra, T711475. Modern, clean, with bathroom, hot water, bakery downstairs. **D** *Indoamerica*, Avda Huarmey 130, T711395. Cheaper without bathroom, hot water, clean, good but front rooms are noisy, changes cash dollars. **E** *Gregori*, Luis Ormeño 579, T711073. Cheaper without bathroom, clean but noisy, restaurant downstairs. **F** *Hostal Central*, Plaza de Armas 140. Dirty, cold water, very basic but friendly and helpful.

Eating *Sechín*, Nepeña esquina Mejía, near the plaza. Friendly, good set meal and chicken. *Tío Sam*, Huarmey 138. Chinese and *criollo* food. *El Farol*, at the hotel, good set meal and à la carte. There are several *cevicherías* on Avda Ormeño 600 block and cheap restaurants on Huarmey. *Heladería El Pibe*, Gamarra 466. Good for ice-cream.

Bars and nightclubs *Discoteca Las Terrazas*, Avda Lima, near the plaza. *Discoteca Flamenco*, Avda Nepeña.

Transport There are several buses daily from **Lima**, 370 kilometres, 6 hours, US$5. Buses to **Lima** leave at 1000 and 2400, with Turismo Chimbote, Ormeño 544; and at 0100 with Chinchaysuyo, Ormeño 526. To **Chimbote**, 55 kilometes, several buses and colectivos leave daily, 1 hour, US$1. To **Trujillo**, 175 kilometres, daily buses, 3 hours, US$2.50.

Most buses heading north from Lima pass Casma between 0400-0600, and buses heading south pass through between 0900-1200. Wait by the gas station at the east end of Avda Ormeño. At other times, take a bus to Chimbote.

Bus to **Huaraz** (150 kilometres), at 0800 and 2100 daily via Pariacoto, 6-7 hours, US$6, with Transportes Moreno (for a description of the route see below). Buses also go via Pativilca, US$6.60, with Turismo Chimbote at 2200 and Chinchaysuyo at 2330. (For a route description see above.)

Directory Banks Good rates for cash and TCs, no commission, at *Banco de Crédito*, Bolívar 181. *Hotel Indoamericano* for cash only. **Communications Post Office:** at Fernando Loparte, 1 block from the Plaza de Armas. National and International **phone** and **fax** at *Sonia's*, Huarmey 302, and *Luz*, Avda Ormeño 118.

Casma to Huaraz

From Casma a road runs inland over the **Callán pass** (4,224 metres) 150 kilometres to Huaraz. It's a difficult but beautiful trip, and worth taking in daylight. Not all buses take this route, so check before leaving.

From Casma the first 30 kilometres are paved, then a good dirt road follows for 30 kilometres to **Pariacoto**. From here to the pass the road is rough, with landslides in rainy season, but once the Cordillera Negra has been crossed, the wide, gravel road is better with spectacular views of the Cordillera Blanca. **Sleeping and eating In Pariacoto:** F *Hostal Eddier*, on the plaza. Basic but nice. G *Alojamiento Saenz Peña*, Gonzalo Salazar, cuadra 5. Basic. *Restaurant Iris* is good.

Casma

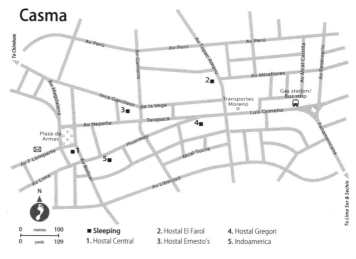

■ **Sleeping**	2. Hostal El Farol	4. Hostal Gregori
1. Hostal Central	3. Hostal Ernesto's	5. Indoamerica

North Coast

Sechín

This is one of the most important ruins on the Peruvian coast. It consists of a *Coloured map 3, grid B2* large square temple completely faced with carved stone monoliths – probably over 500 of them – representing two lines of warriors marching towards the principal entrance from opposite sides. Between each warrior are carvings of men being eviscerated, heads with blood gushing from eyes or mouths, dismembered legs, arms, torsos, ears, eyes and vertebrae.

The mural is thought to narrate the results of a battle, with the fates of the conquerors and the conquered graphically depicted. The style is unique in Peru for its naturalistic vigour. The importance of the site lies in the fact that it is one of the oldest centres in the country to demonstrate the development of warlike activity and the extent to which extreme violence was a part of life.

Within the stone temple is an earlier, pre-ceramic mud temple with painted walls. The complex as a whole forms a temple-palace associated with the development of the local pre-Chavín Sechín culture, dating from about 1500 BC. Three sides of the large stone temple have been excavated and restored. You cannot see the adobe buildings inside the stone walls, which belong to an earlier period. They were later covered up and used as a base for a second storey which unfortunately has been completely destroyed.

Some experts think the temple and surroundings were buried on purpose. Others believe it was engulfed by natural disaster. The latter theory is supported by finds of human skeletons. Tombs have been found in front and at the same level as the temple. A wall of a large adobe building under excavation can be seen and runs round the sides and back of the temple.

There is an attractive, shady picnic garden. Photography is best around midday. The Max Uhle Museum by the ruins has an interesting display of Sechín artefacts and a replica of the façade of the inner adobe temple. If you need a guide ask in advance for Wilder León or Carlos Cuy, who speaks English and French. Outside the museum is an orientation map showing the location of the different archaeological sites in the Casma area.

■ *Open to tourists, 0830-1830 daily. US$2.25, children half price; the ticket is also valid for the museum and Pañamarca (see page 336). It is quite easy to walk to the ruins from Casma. Follow Avda Ormeño east and at the circle turn right and follow the Pan-American Highway. Walk about 3 kilometres south to a well posted sign showing a left turn for Huaraz (this is at Km 370), then simply follow the road for 2 kilometres to the ruins. Frequent colectivos leave from in front of the market in Casma for US$0.30 per person, but leave early in the morning; or take a moto-taxi for US$0.50 per person.*

Two kilometres further along is Sechín Alto, two pyramids of the late Chavín period, but these have not yet been excavated.

Located two kilometres east of the Pan-American Highway at Km 391, 18 **Playa Tortugas** kilometres north of Casma, Playa Tortugas is a fishing village on a nice bay with calm water and a rocky beach. From the north end of the bay the road continues to **Playa Huayuna**, a windy, closed bay with a sandy beach and a scallop farm. From the south end of Tortugas a road goes to **Rincón de Piños**, a beach with wild surf. To the south of Casma, at Km 345, are the sandy beaches of **La Gramita** and **Las Aldas**.

Chimbote

Population: 296,600
Phone code: 044
Coloured map 3, grid A2

In one of Peru's few natural harbours, a port has been built to serve the national steel industry. Chimbote is also Peru's largest fishing port; fishmeal is exported and the smell of the fishmeal plants is very strong. There are no tourist attractions as such, but the city has become increasingly important as an access to the Cordillera Blanca.

Ins and outs

Warning Chimbote is a thoroughly unsafe (and unpleasant) city, and many travellers are attacked and robbed here. All visitors should take extensive precautions, always use taxis from bus stations to their hotel, and preferably not venture out at night. Also note that water shortages can be a problem, so make sure your hotel has a tank before taking a room.

Getting there The airport is at the south end of town. The bus stations are on Avda Victor Raul Haya de la Torre more or less in the middle of town. Hotels are close to them.

Getting around Although Chimbote is small enough to walk around, don't: take a taxi instead. Radio taxis from T334433, T327777 and T322005.

Sights

Chimbote carries the dubious honour of being the spot where Cholera first landed in South America in 1991. The city was damaged by the 1970

Chimbote

To Trujillo & Transportes Moreno

Pacific Ocean

■ **Sleeping**
1. Gran Hotel Chimú
2. Hostal Antonio's
3. Ivansino Inn
4. Presidente

🚌 **Buses**
1. Cruz del Sur
2. Turismo Chimbote
3. Ormeño-Continental

0 metres 50
0 yards 31

earthquake. Today, it has a spacious Plaza de Armas, the cathedral and several public buildings have since been rebuilt, and the modern Municipal building has a small art gallery downstairs (open 0900-2000). Bathing is forbidden on the bay, though there is a public swimming pool at Vivero Forestal. Flocks of brown pelicans and masked boobies can be seen from the beach.

Note that the main street, Avda Victor Raul Haya de la Torre is more commonly known as José Pardo.

Essentials

A1 *Gran Hotel Chimú*, José Gálvez 109, T/F321741. Price includes breakfast, minibar, safe parking. **B** *Hostal Antonio's*, Bolognesi 745, T/F33026. Clean, hot water, minibar. **B** *Ivansino Inn*, Haya de la Torre 738, T331395, F321927. Includes breakfast, comfortable, clean, modern, cable TV, minibar. **B** *Presidente*, L Prado 536, T322411, F321988. With bathroom, clean, friendly, hot showers, safe parking (extra), poor snack bar. Recommended. **C** *Hostal Karol Inn*, Manuel Ruiz 277, T/F321216. Clean, with bathroom, hot water, a good place to stay, family run, laundry service, cafeteria. **C-D** *Residencial El Parque*, E Palacios 309, on the main plaza, T323963. A converted old home, with bathroom, hot water, clean, nice, friendly. **D** *Augusto*, Aguirre 265, T324431. With bathroom, clean, front rooms noisy, water intermittent as elsewhere in town, overpriced. **D** *Felic*, Haya de la Torre 552, T325901. **E** without bathroom, clean, quiet. Recommended. **D** *San Felipe*, Haya de la Torre 514, T323401. With bathroom, hot water, clean, friendly, comfortable, restaurant. **D** *Venus*, Haya de la Torre 675, T321339. With bathroom, dirty but friendly, near bus stations, useful if you arrive at night. **E** *Hostal Playa*, Malecón Miguel Grau 185, T321788. OK, safe, clean. **E** *Hostal Paraíso*, Haya de la Torre 1015, T323718. Cheaper without bathroom, basic, clean, near the Ormeño bus station. **E** *Sagitario*, José Gálvez 1174, next door to Transportes Moreno, T333676. New in 1998, clean, simple, good value, convenient for those travelling to and from Huaraz. **F** *Hostal El Santa*, Espinar 671. Basic.

Sleeping
■ *on maps*
Price codes:
see inside front cover

Pollo Gordo, Prado y Aguirre. Good chicken and cold beer. *Buenos Aires*, Aguirre near the beach. A popular lunch place. *Marisquito*, Bolognesi near Palacios. Good local food, disco at night. *Chifa Cantón*, Bolognesi. Good Chinese food. *La Fogata Inn*, Villavicencio. Good grilled food. *Aquarius*, Haya de la Torre 360. Vegetarian. There are several cheap restaurants on Haya de la Torre by the plaza. An excellent bakery is *Delca*, at Haya de la Torre 568.

Eating
● *on maps*

Air connections Flights to and from **Lima**, daily with *Aerocóndor*. Check schedules in advance as they change frequently. **Buses** From **Lima**, to Chimbote, 420 kilometres, 6 hours, US$7-9. Several buses daily including: *Turismo Chimbote*, VR Haya de la Torre 670, T321400, recommended; *Cruz del Sur*, Bolognesi 716, T331021; *Continental* (Ormeño), J Balta 289, esquina Haya de la Torre.

To **Trujillo**, 130 kilometres, 2½ hours, US$2.50. Buses leave every half an hour from the corner of Galvez y Pardo (Hoya de la Torre). To **Tumbes**, 889 kilometres, 13 hours, US$11; *Continental* at 1630, and Cruz del Sur at 2200.

Buses to **Huaraz**: *Transportes Moreno*, José Gálvez 1178, T321235, honours reservations by phone, friendly, helpful, recommended; *Trans San Pedro*, Haya de la Torre 670, T342016. They travel via the Santa Valley and Cañón del Pato, leaving at 0800 every second day, US$6, 10 hours; and via Casma and Pariacoto at 2000 daily, 10 hours, US$6. (For a description of the Cañón del Pato route, see below.)

Transport

Banks *Banco de Crédito* and *Interbanc*, both on Bolognesi and M Ruiz. For TCs and cash. *Casa Arroyo*, M Ruiz 292. For cash only. There are other *casas* and street changers along M Ruiz between Bolognesi and VR Haya de la Torre. **Communications** Post: *Serpost*, Jr Tumbes behind

Directory

North Coast

market. **Telecommunications:** *Telefónica* main office, Tumbes 356. National and international fax and phone. Also at Haya de la Torre 420 and M Ruiz 253. **Tour companies & travel agents** *Chimbote Tours*, Bolognesi 801, T325341, F324792. Helpful and friendly, English spoken.

Around Chimbote

About 25 kilometres south of Chimbote, at Km 405 on the Pan-American Highway, a paved road leads east to the Nepeña valley, where several precolumbian ruins including Cerro Blanco, Pañamarca and Paredones can be found.

The village of Capellanía is 11 kilometres from the crossroads. Just beyond are the ruins of **Pañamarca**. The site includes a two-storey stone structure, built on a hill, dating from the formative period (2000 BC-100 AD) and many adobe structures from the Moche period, including three pyramids. Remains of polychromatic murals and animal sculptures can also be seen.

20 kilometres from Pañamarca, via the villages of San Jacinto and Moro, is the site of **Paredones**, a large stone structure, with four metre high granite walls and a very impressive gateway known as 'Portada de Paredones' or 'Puerta del Sol'. It is believed to have been a Chavín palace.

Chimbote to Huaraz

The route from Chimbote to Huaraz passes through the Santa Valley and the spectacular Cañón del Pato, one of the most thrilling, or terrifying bus trips in all of Peru.

Just north of Chimbote, a road branches northeast off the Pan-American Highway and, joining another road from the town of Santa, goes up the Santa valley following the route, including tunnels, of the old Santa Corporation Railway. This used to run as far as **Huallanca** (not to be confused with the town of the same name southeast of Huaraz), 140 kilometres up the valley, but the track was largely destroyed by the 1970 earthquake.

At Huallanca is an impressive hydroelectric plant, built into a mountain, which cannot be visited. Everything closes early. There is accommodation at the *Hotel Huascarán*, which is good and friendly.

At the top of the valley the road goes through the very narrow and spectacular **Cañón del Pato** before reaching the Callejón de Huaylas and going on south to Caraz and Huaraz.

An alternative road for cyclists is the private road known as the 'Brasileños', used by a Brazilian company which is building a water channel from the Río Santa to the coast. The turn-off is 15 kilometres south of the bridge in Chao, on the Pan-American Highway.

North of Chimbote the highway crosses the valleys of Chao and Virú, and after 137 kilometres reach the first great city of Northern Peru, Trujillo. The Virú valley contains the largest single sand dune in South America. Between Virú and Trujillo the desert is being turned 'green' with asparagus, thanks to the huge Chavimochi irrigation project.

Trujillo

Population: 750,000
Phone code: 044
Coloured map 3, grid A1

Trujillo, capital of the Department of La Libertad, disputes the title of second city of Peru with Arequipa. Founded by Diego de Almagro in 1534 as an express assignment ordered by Francisco Pizarro, the city was named after the latter's native town in Spain.

There is enough here to hold the attention for several days. The area abounds in precolumbian sites, there are beaches and good surfing within easy reach and the city itself still has many old churches and graceful colonial homes built during the reigns of the viceroys. Besides the Cathedral it has 10 colonial churches as well as convents and monasteries.

Ins and outs

Trujillo has confusing double street names: the smaller printed name is that generally **Street names** shown on maps, in guide books and in general use. **NB** Tourists may be approached by vendors selling *huacos* and necklaces from the Chimú period. The export of these items is strictly illegal if they are genuine, but they almost certainly aren't.

Not surprisingly communications with the rest of the country are good. The airport is **Getting there** a little way out of town to the west - you will come into town along Av Mansiche. There is no central bus terminal and none of the bus stations are in the centre. They are in the northern half of the city beyond the inner ring road, Avda España. There is little in the way of accommodation near them but there are lots of colectivos to get you to your hotel. Further transport details are on page 342.

With its compact colonial centre and mild, spring-like climate, Trujillo is best explored **Getting around** on foot. The city is generally safe but be especially careful at bus stations when arriving or leaving; guard your luggage very carefully. Also take care beyond the inner ring road, Avda España, towards the hill and in the Sánchez Carrión district at night. Bus and colectivos, on all routes, cost US$0.20-0.35; colectivos are safer as there are fewer people and fewer pick-pockets. Taxis around town costs US$1. To Chan Chán or the airport is US$5; to Huanchaco, US$6.50. Beware of overcharging, check fares with locals. A taxi can be hired from *Hotel Libertador* for US$7 an hour, or contact the Tourist Police (see below). A reliable taxi driver is Félix Espino, T232428. Always use official taxis, which are mainly yellow with a large white sticker on the windscreen with Trujillo's coat of arms and serial number.

The area

La Libertad was once the foremost producer of sugar in Peru but is still struggling to recover from an economic crisis brought on by social changes in the 1970s and 80s. Other agricultural products are asparagus, rice, fruit, potatoes and cereals. Mining is also important to the region's economy. 18 kilometres by road from Trujillo is the area's port, Salaverry.

Sights

The focal point is the pleasant and spacious **Plaza de Armas**. The prominent sculpture represents agriculture, commerce, education, art, slavery, action and liberation, crowned by a young man holding a torch depicting liberty. Fronting it is the **Cathedral**, dating from 1666, with its museum of religious paintings and sculptures next door. Also on the plaza are the *Hotel Libertador*, the colonial style Sociedad de Beneficencia Pública de Trujillo and the Municipalidad.

The **Universidad de La Libertad**, second only to that of San Marcos at Lima, was founded in 1824. Near the Plaza de Armas, at Jr Pizarro 688, is the spacious 18th century **Palacio Iturregui**, now occupied by the **Club Central**, an exclusive and social centre of Trujillo. Exhibitions of local ceramics are often held. ■ Open *1100-1300 and 1600-2000. US$2.*

Las Delicias is a clean beach with good surf, about 20 minutes by bus (US$0.35) and 15 minutes by taxi from Trujillo. Buses leave from Las Incas around Huayna Capac.

Colonial houses Two other beautiful colonial mansions on the plaza have been taken over. The Banco Central de Reserva is in the Colonial-style **Casa Urquiaga (or Calonge)**, Pizarro 446, which contains valuable precolumbian ceramics. ■ Open *0900-1600. Monday-Saturday. Free.* The other is **Casa Bracamonte (or Lizarzaburu)**, at Independencia 441, with occasional exhibits. Opposite the Cathedral, is the **Lynch House**, boasting the oldest façade in the city.

Other mansions, still in private hands, include **Casa del Mayorazgo de Facalá**, Pizarro 314, which is now the Banco Wiese. Its former owner was Don Pedro de Tinoco whose wife embroidered the first Peruvian flag to be hoisted following Trujillo's independence from Spanish rule in 1820. ■ *Free when the bank is open.* The **Casa de la Emancipación**, Jr Pizarro 610 (Banco Continental), is where independence from Spain was planned. ■ *Open daily 0900-1300 and 1700-2000.*

The **Casa del Mariscal de Orbegoso**, Orbegoso 553, named after the ex-President, General Luis José de Orbegoso, is a museum, owned by Banco Internacional. ■ *Open daily 0900-1300 and 1600-1900. Free.* **Casa Ganoza Chopitea**, Independencia 630 opposite San Francisco church, is architecturally the most representative house in the city and considered the most outstanding of the viceroyalty. It combines Baroque and Rococo styles.

Churches Many churches were damaged in the 1970 earthquake. One of the best, the 17th century **La Merced** at Pizarro 550, with picturesque moulded figures below the dome, has been restored, but part of the dome has collapsed because of building work next door. The US$2 entry includes **El Carmen** church and monastery at Colón y Bolívar, which has been described as the 'most valuable jewel of colonial art in Trujillo'. Next door is the Pinacoteca Carmelita. **La Compañía**, near Plaza de Armas, is now an auditorium for cultural events.

In **San Francisco**, on the corner of Gamarra and Independencia, is the still-preserved renaissance pulpit which survived the earthquake of Saint Valentine's Day that destroyed the city in 1619. Other old churches include: **Belén** on the 6th block of Almagro; **Santa Clara** on the 4th block of Junín; **San Agustín** on the 6th block of Mcal Orbegoso; **Santa Ana** on the 2nd block of the same street; and **Santo Domingo** on the 4th block of Bolognesi.

Plazuela El Recreo, at the north end of Pizarro, was known as El Estanque during the colonial period as it housed a pool from which the city's water was distributed. A marble fountain by Eiffel now stands in the square, transferred from the Plaza de Armas in 1929, fronted by several open-air restaurants. There are two markets, one on Gamarra, the Mercado Central, and the Mercado Mayorista on Calle Sinchi Roca.

Museums **Museo de Arqueología**, houses a large and interesting collection of thematic exhibits. ■ *Casa Risco, Junín 662 y Ayacucho. Open 0830-1400. US$1.*

The basement of the **Cassinelli** garage on the fork of the Pan-American and Huanchaco roads contains a superb private collection of Mochica and Chimú pottery and is highly recommended. The caretaker gives a thorough explanation including demonstrations of the whistling *huacos* and is knowledgeable on any subject you care to discuss (in Spanish). ■ *Open 0830-1130, 1530-1730. US$2.50.*

North Coast

Museo de Zoología de Juan Ormea, Jr San Martín 349, has interesting displays of Peruvian animals. ■ *Open 0800-1400. Free, but donations are welcome, and needed.*

For old car freaks, look for the funeral director's premises, just off the main plaza, where there are hearses as old as a 1910 Chevrolet with wooden coachwork and wheelspokes. The proprietor is happy to show you around.

Essentials

L3 *Libertador*, Independencia 485 on Plaza de Armas, T232741, F235641. Price includes tax, pool (can be used by non-guests if they buy a drink), cafeteria and restaurant, continental breakfast US$5, excellent buffet lunch on Sunday. Recommended. **A2** *El Gran Marqués*, Díaz de Cienfuegos 145-147, Urb La Merced, T/F249582. Price includes tax and breakfast, modern, pool, sauna, jacuzzi, restaurant. Recommended. **A3** *Cassino Real*, Pizarro 651, T206651, F257416. Includes tax and American breakfast, car rental provided. **A3** *Los Conquistadores*, Diego de Almagro 586, T203350, F235917. Price includes tax and American breakfast, bar, restaurant, very comfortable. **A3-B** *Pullman*, Jr Pizarro 879, T/F205448. Includes breakfast, discounts in low season. Recommended.

C *Continental*, Gamarra 663, T241607, F249881. Opposite the market, includes tax, clean, good, safe. Restaurant recommended. **C** *Hostal Residencial Las Terrazas*, Avda Manuel Vera Enríquez 874, Urb Primavera, behind Hotel Primavera, T232437. With bathroom, hot water, TV, phone, garage, cafeteria, garden, pool, good value, friendly. **C** *Opt Gar*, Grau 595, T242192. With bathroom and TV, good, friendly, excellent restaurant (lunch only for non-guests) and snack bar. Recommended. **C** *Residencial Los Escudos*, Orbegoso 676, T255961. With bathroom, make sure you ask for the hot water to be switched on, small garden, expensive laundry service, friendly, door locked at night, secure, manager speaks English. Recommended. **C** *San Martín*, San Martín 743-749, T234011. **D** without bathroom, good value, small restaurant, good for breakfast, clean but noisy. Recommended. **C** *Vogi*, Ayacucho 663, T243574. Includes tax, with bath, TV, clean, safe, quiet. Recommended.

D *Colonial*, Independencia 644. Clean, attractive, friendly. Recommended. **D** *Hostal Recreo*, Estete 647, T246991. With bathroom, TV, clean, friendly, safe, restaurant. Recommended. **D-E** *Hostal Chan Chán*, Huayna Cápac 201 esquina Sinchi Roca 304, T242964/251301. With bathroom, hot water, TV, cafeteria. **D-E** *Hostal Residencial Las Flores*, Atahualpa 282-284, T242527. Clean, big rooms, good value. **D-E** *Primavera*, Avda N de Piérola 872, Urb Primavera, near Empresa Díaz bus terminal, T231915, F257399. With bathroom, hot water, restaurant, bar, pool. **D-E** *Roma*, Nicaragua 238, next to El Aguila bus station, T259064. Clean, secure, friendly, helpful, luggage stored. Recommended. **D** *Sudamericano*, Grau 515, T243751. With bathroom, hot water, phone, laundry service, parking, bar-restaurant, clean, reasonable value. **D-E** *Trujillo*, Grau 581, T243921. With bathroom, clean, good value. Recommended.

E *Grau*, Grau 631, T242332. With bathroom, clean, good value. **E** *Hostal Americano*, Pizarro 792, T241361. A vast, rambling old building, next to the cinema, rooms without bathrooms are noisy and very basic, most rooms don't have window (Nos 134 and 137, and those either side of 303, have windows, balconies and good views), safe, a good meeting place as all backpackers seem to end up here. **E** *Hostal Royers*, Avda Los Incas 687, T257095. With bathroom, friendly but dirty, basic, hot water 1200-1400, the 3rd floor is the best for water. **E** *Hostal Central*, Ayacucho 728, T246236. Basic but clean, friendly, bargaining possible.

F *Hostal Lima*, Ayacucho 718, T244751. Popular with gringos, dirty, terrible bathrooms. **F** *Hostal Internacional*, Bolívar 646, T245392, cheaper without bathroom, very basic.

Sleeping
■ *on maps*
Price codes:
see inside front cover

North Coast

Also: **E** *Familia Moreno*, Huáscar 247. Near the centre, clean, cold water, quiet and safe. **F** *Catrina Castillo*, Pedro Muñiz 792 (10 blocks from the Plaza de Armas). Friendly.

Clara Bravo (see **Guides** below) can recommend local families for accommodation from **F** per person.

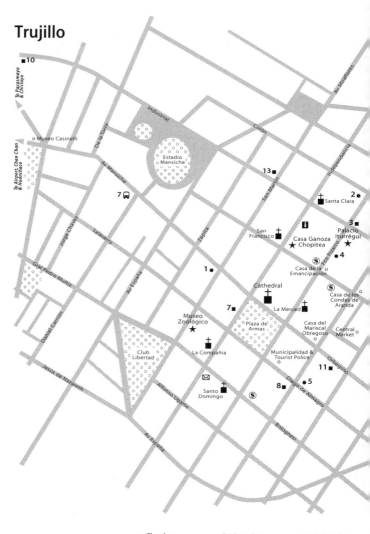

Trujillo

Related maps
Around Trujillo,
page 340

■ **Sleeping**	**7.** Libertador	**14.** Sudamericano
1. Continental	**8.** Los Conquistadores	**15.** Trujillo
2. Grau	**9.** Opt Gar	
3. Hostal Americano	**10.** Primavera	● **Eating**
4. Hostal Chan Chán	**11.** Residencial Los	**1.** ABC
5. Hostal Recreo	Escudos	**2.** Café Romano
6. Hostals Royers &	**12.** Roma	& De Marco
Lima	**13.** San Martín	**3.** Chifa Oriental

North Coast

La Mochica, Bolívar 462. A typical restaurant with a good reputation. *Chifa Oriental*, Gamarra 735. Recommended. *El Pesquero*, Junín 118. Good fish. *Romano*, Pizarro 747. Good *menú*, breakfasts, coffee and cakes, but slow service.

Eating
● *on maps*

De Marco, Pizarro 725. Good, especially the ice creams and coffee, set menu US$2.50, desserts and cakes, good source of information for passing cyclists. Next door is *Asturias*, a nice café with good juices and snacks. *Pollería El Bolívar*, Pizarro 501 y Plaza de Armas. Good chicken and salad for US$2.50. *El Sol*, Pizarro 660. Good, cheap set meals, including vegetarian dishes. *Juguería San Agustín*, Pizarro 691. Good juices, good *menú*, popular, excellent value. *La Selecta*, Pizarro 870. Set lunch for US$1.75, good value. *La Pizza Nostra*, Pizarro 568. Italian dishes, cheap chicken and fries. *ABC*, Orbegoso y San Martín. Good for chicken. *Rincón de Vallejo*, Orbegoso 303. Good menú for US$1. *Pizzería Valentino*, Orbegoso block 2. Very good. *Reyno del Sol*, Bolívar 438. Good breakfasts and vegetarian meals, friendly, nice rooftop setting, open at 0800. *La Naturaleza*, Gamarra 455. Wide range of Vegetarian dishes.

Eating: cheaper

It's difficult to find a meal before 0800. A Monday speciality is shambar, a thick minestrone made with gammon

There are several good, cheap seafood restaurants at Plazuela El Recreo, at the end of Pizarro, with outdoor seating and a pleasant atmosphere. For really cheap meals try the market at Grau y Gamarra. Wholewheat bread can be bought at *Panadería Chalet Suizo*, Avda España e Independencia. For excellent ice cream try *Tartufo*, at the corner of Gamarra y Bolívar, a huge helping costs US$0.70.

Taverna Chelsea, Estete 675. Bar, restaurant, live Salsa at weekends (US$4 entry), lively. Highly recommended. *Las Tinajas*, Pizarro y Almagro, on Plaza de Armas. A pub-disco with live rock music and *peña* on Saturday. *Luna Rota*, América Sur 2119, at the end of Huayna Capac. Very popular with locals. *La Taberna*, Avda Húsares de Junín 350, Urb La Merced. Good for Andean folk music. *Canana*, San Martín 791. Bars and restaurant, live music at weekends, video screens. Recommended.

Bars & nightclubs

Sports There's an outdoor **swimming pool** next to Mansiche stadium, where buses leave for Chan Chán and Huanchaco. It's open 0900-1300 and 1600-1800, entry US$0.50.

Entertainment

North Coast

5

■**5**

El Carmen

■**6**
★

3 ■**2**
9■

Market

3 🚌

4 🚌
9■

🚌**1**

■**4**

Clara Luz Bravo

To Chimbote & Lima

. El Sol
. La Mochica

🚌 **Buses**
. Chinchaysuyo buses
2. Cruz del Sur buses
3. Huaca del Sol y de la Luna buses

4. Huanchaco, Chan Chán, Arco Iris & Huaco Esmeralda buses
5. Olana buses
6. Ormeño buses
7. Transportes Dorado

Festivals The two most important festivals are the *National Marinera Contest* and the *Festival Internacional de La Primavera*. The former is held in the last week of **January** and consists of hundreds of couples competing in six categories, from children to seniors (see Música criolla, page 528). This event is organized by the Club Libertad and has taken place since 1960.

The *Festival de la Primavera* is held in the last week in **September**. Organized by the Club de Leones, it is a celebration of the arrival of Spring and has grown over the years to become one of Peru's most important tourist events. The festival is not for the politically sensitive as it is basically a massive beauty pageant with beauty queens from South and North America participating. Also featured are Trujillo's famous *Caballos de Paso*, a fine breed of horses with a tripping gait that has made them renowned worldwide. These horses, a Spanish legacy, have been immortalized in Peruvian waltzes. Riders still compete in their own form of the Marinera dance and buyers from around the world congregate to see them shown at the Spring Festival.

Other major festivals include the *Feria de San José* held in Las Delicias (see Sights above) on **19-22 March**. *Festival de la Música* takes place on **18 June**.

Shopping **Camera repairs** *Laboratorios de Investigación Científica*, San Martín 745, over the Fuji shop opposite *Hotel San Martín*, good. Hugo Guevara, *G&M Color*, Ayacucho 825, T255387, and España 2787, T/F259483. 1 hour developing service and electrical repairs.

Transport **Air connections** There are daily flights to and from **Lima** with *AeroPerú* and *Aero Continente*; also with *Aerocondor*, continuing to Arequipa and Tacna. To **Piura** with *AeroPerú*. To **Tarapoto** with *Aero Continente*. To **Pucallpa** and **Iquitos** with *AeroPerú*. Check flight times as they change frequently. A taxi to the airport costs US$5; or take a bus or colectivo to Huanchaco and get out at airport turn-off then walk 2 kilometres (US$0.25).

Buses To and from **Lima**, 548 kilometres, 8-9 hours on a good road. There are many bus companies doing this route, among those recommended are: *Ormeño*, Avda Ejército 233, T259782, normal service 4 daily, US$10, super especial (meal, drinks included), US$15; *Cruz del Sur*, near Avda Ejército (see map), T261801, US$8.70; *Empresa Díaz*, Nicolás de Piérola 1079 on Panamericana Norte, T232476, US$6.50, leaves at 2130. Also *Trans Piura* (de la Torre 259) and *Trans Chiclayo* (de la Torre 271). *Trans Olana* (Oltursa), Avda Ejército 342, T2603055, offer a *bus cama* service to Lima, with full reclining seats, a/c, heating, meals and drinks, US$22.50, depart at 2300, with connection at Lima for Arequipa. **NB** Cheaper buses tend to arrive at night and do not have terminals, dropping passengers in the street.

Combis leave regularly from the first block of Avda Mansiche to: **Pacasmayo**, 120 kilometres, 2 hours, US$1.50; on to **Chiclayo**, 209 kilometres, 3 hours, US$3-3.50; then to **Piura**, 278 kilometres, 6 hours, US$6.50; and **Tumbes**, 282 kilometres, US$9-12, 9-12 hours (depending on whether it's direct or not). Companies include: *Transportes Dorado*, Daniel Carrión y Avda Mansiche, T242880, leave at 1830, 1930; *Chinchaysuyo*, González Prada 337, US$5.30, leave at 1215, 2220; and *Cruz del Sur* at 2000.

Direct buses to **Huaraz**, 319 kilometres, via Chimbote and Casma (169 kilometres), US$5, at 2000 with *Emp de Trans* 14 (Moche 544, T261008); also *Trans San Pedro* (Moche 435, T245546). There are several buses and colectivos to **Chimbote**, with *El Sol/LitPerú/América Express* from Tupac Yupanqui 300, 135 kilometres, 2 hours, US$2.50; then change at Chimbote (see above). Also daily buses to Huaraz via Pativilca, with Chan-Chán, Avda La Marina, at 2100, and Chinchaysuyo, González Prada 337, at 2030; US$7, 10 hours.

To **Cajamarca**, 300 kilometres, 7-8 hours, US$6.50: with *Trans Vulkano*, Carrion 140, T235847, at 1030 and 2130 (also to Chiclayo); *Trans Mercurio*, Avda Mansiche 403, at 2230; and *Empresa Díaz* at 1300, 2200.

Transportes Guadalupe, Avda Mansiche 331, has buses to **Tarapoto**, via Jaén, Chachapoyas and Moyobamba, departing at 1000 daily, 24 hours, US$20. To **Tayabamba** (see page 385) with *Trans Agreda* and *Garrincha*, one bus each per week, US$25, 30 plus hours on a very rough road.

Airline offices *AeroPerú*, Pizarro 470, T234241/242727. *Aero Continente*, Orbegoso 582, T248174, T/F244592.

Directory

Banks *Banco de Crédito*, Gamarra 562. No commission on cash or Amex TCs into soles only, good rates, also Visa cash advance. *Interbanc*, Pizarro y Gamarra. Good rates for cash, no commission on TCs, reasonable rate, Visa cash advance, quick service. *Banco Wiese*, Pizarro 314, *Casa de Mayorazgo de Facalá*. Good rates for cheques, no commission into soles, cash advance on MasterCard. Note that banks close 1300-1615. They give the same rate for cash dollars as street changers, *casas de cambio* and travel agencies. There's a Unicard cashpoint at *Extebandes*, which works for Royal Bank of Canada cardholders.

Communications Post Office: Independencia y Bolognesi. **Telecommunications:** Telefónica del Perú, Bolívar 658, national and international phone calls and faxes. There's Internet access at Centro Comercial Zar Zar, Jr Bolívar 634.

Embassies & consulates *British*, Honorary Consul, Mr Winston Barber, Jesús de Nazareth 312, T235548. *Finnish*, Bolívar 200, T276122. *German*, Honorary Consul, Dr Guillermo Guerra Cruz, C Estados Unidos 105-107, Urb El Recreo, T245903, F261922.

Hospitals & medical services Hospital: *Clínica Peruano Americana*, Avda Mansiche 702, T231261. English spoken, good.

Laundry *Lavandería y Tintorería Luxor*, Grau 633. Open 0800-2000, cheap, next day service. *Miriam Ganoja*, Grau 6th block. Laundry and dry cleaning.

Tour companies & travel agents *Chacón Tours*, Avda España 106-112, T255212. Recommended. *Trujillo Tours*, San Martín y Almagro 301, T233091, F257518. Work with Lima Tours. *Cóndor Travel*, Independencia 5, T/F244658. *Sigma Tours*, Pizarro 570, T201335, F201337. Recommended. Prices vary and competition is fierce so shop around for the best deal. Few agencies run tours on Sun and often only at fixed times on other days. To **Chan Chán**, **El Dragón** and **Huanchaco**, 3 hrs for US$15 per person. To **Huacas del Sol** and **de la Luna**, 2 hrs for US$13 per person. To **El Brujo**, US$20-25 per person. City tours cost US$6.50 per person (minimum of 2 people; discounts for 4 or more). **Guides:** many hotels work on a commission basis with taxi drivers and travel agencies. If you decide on a guide, make your own direct approach. *Clara Bravo*, Huayna Capac 542, T243347, T/F255043, E microbewhite@yahoo.com, cellular (044)662710, is an experienced official tourist guide with her own transport. She speaks Spanish, German and understands Italian. She takes tourists on extended circuits of the region and is good for information (archaeological tour US$16 for 6 hrs, city tour US$7 per person, US$53 per car to El Brujo, with extension to Sipán, Brüning Museum and Túcume possible). Clara works with English chartered accountant *Michael White* (speaks German and some French), who provides transport, plus translation and business services. He is very knowledgeable about tourist sites, including the Priestesses of San José de Moro. He also produces and sells T-shirts with local motifs; E microbewhite@yahoo.com.

North Coast

☞ *The Moche culture*

One of the most remarkable pre-Inca civilizations was the Moche people, who evolved during the first century AD and lasted until around AD 750. Though these early Peruvians had no written language, they left a vivid artistic record of their life and culture in beautifully modelled and painted ceramics.

Compared with the empires of their successors, the Chimú and Inca, the realm of the Moche was very small, covering less than 250 miles of coast from the valleys of Lambayeque to Nepeña, south of present-day Chimbote. Though a seemingly inhospitable stretch of coast, the Moche harnessed rivers spilling from the Andean cordillera, channelling them into a network of irrigation canals that watered the arid coastal valleys. The resultant lush fields produced plentiful crops, which, along with the sea's bountiful harvest of fish and seafood, gave the Moche a rich and varied diet. With the leisure allowed by such abundant food, Moche craftsmen invented new techniques to produce their artistic masterpieces. It is these ancient pottery vessels that have made the greatest contribution to our understanding of this great civilization.

These masters of sculpture used clay to bring to life animals, plants and anthropomorphic deities and demons. They recreated hunting and fishing scenes, combat rituals and elaborate ceremonies. They depicted the power of their rulers as well as the plight of their sick and invalid.

The violence and death of war is a common theme in their work; prisoners of war are apparently brought before tribunals where their throats are cut and their blood consumed by those present. Decapitation and dismemberment are also shown.

Moche potters were amazingly skilled at reproducing facial features, specializing in the subtle nuances of individual personality. In addition to these three-dimensional sculptures, the Moche potter was skilled at decorating vessels with low-relief designs. Among the most popular scenes are skeletal death figures holding hands while dancing in long processions to the accompaniment of musicians. The potters also developed a technique of painting scenes on ceramic vessels. Over a period of several centuries the painters became increasingly skillful at depicting complex and lively scenes with multiple figures. Because of their complexity and detail, these scenes are of vital importance in reconstructing Moche life.

The early introduction of moulds and stamps brought efficiency to the production of Moche ceramics. By pressing moist clay into the halves of a mould, it was possible to produce an object much more rapidly than modelling it by hand. Similarly, the use of stamps facilitated the decoration of ceramic vessels with elaborate low-relief designs. Mould-making technology thus resulted in many duplications of individual pieces. Since there were almost no unique ceramic objects, elaborate ceramics became more widely available and less effective as a sign of power, wealth and social status of the elite.

Although among the most sophisticated potters in Spanish America, the Moche did not use ceramics for ordinary tableware. Neither do their ceramics show many everyday activities, such as farming, cooking and pottery making. This is because Moche art expresses the religious and supernatural aspects of their culture and nothing of everyday life is illustrated for its own sake. See also under History, on page 496.

Drawing of the decoration of a Moche pot, depicting a warrior holding a naked prisoner

The Chimú culture

Chimú was a despotic state which based its power on wars of conquest. Rigid social stratification existed and power rested in the hands of the great lords. These lords were followed in the social scale by a group of urban courtiers who enjoyed a certain amount of economic power. At the bottom were the peasants and slaves. The Chimú economy was based on agriculture supplemented by fishing, hunting and craft production; they were renowned metalsmiths, working mainly with gold. Chan Chán was not looted. The Spaniards, however, despoiled its burial mounds of all the gold and silver statuettes and ornaments buried with the Chimú nobles.

Another guide is *José Soto Ríos*, who can be contacted at the Tourist Police office on Independencia (see below) or at Atahualpa 514, T251489, he speaks English. *Pedro Puertas*, English speaking, is not an official guide but very knowledgeable. He can be contacted through *Hostal Americano*. Other experienced guides are *Oscar and Gustavo Prada Marga*, Miguel Grau 169, Villa del Mar. The tourist office has a list of official guides; average cost is US$7 per hour.

Tourist offices Tourist office, Independencia 623, T/F258216, private organization, helpful, free information. Maps available from *Touring and Automobile Club*, Argentina 278, Urb El Recreo, T242101. Also from *Librería Ayacucho*, Ayacucho 570. **Tourist Police:** have an office at Pizarro 402, on the corner of Plaza de Armas, open daily 0800-2000. Also at Independencia 630, Casa Ganoza Chopitea. They are very helpful, provide useful information, and some of the staff speak English. They will negotiate a good price for taxis to visit sites; expect to pay around US$24 per car for 3-4 hrs. Any complaints about tourist services should be addressed to the *Ministerio de Industria y Turismo*, Avda España 1801, T245345/245794.

Useful addresses Immigration: Avda Larco 1220, Urb Los Pinos. Gives 30-day visa extensions, US$20 (proof of funds and onward ticket required), plus US$0.80 for *formulario* in Banco de la Nación (fixers on the street will charge more).

Chan Chán

Perhaps Trujillo's greatest attraction are the impressive ruins of Chan Chán. This crumbling imperial city of the Chimú is the largest adobe city in the world and lies about five kilometres from the city.

Coloured map 3, grid A1

North Coast

The ruins consist of nine great compounds built by Chimú kings. The nine metre high perimeter walls surrounded sacred enclosures with usually only one narrow entrance. Inside, rows of storerooms contained the agricultural wealth of the kingdom, which stretched 1,000 kilometres along the coast from near Guayaquil, in Ecuador, to Paramonga.

Most of the compounds contain a huge walk-in well which tapped the ground water, raised to a high level by irrigation higher up the valley. Each compound also included a platform mound which was the burial place of the king, with his women and his treasure, presumably maintained as a memorial. The Incas almost certainly copied this system and transported it to Cusco where the last Incas continued building huge enclosures. The Chimú surrendered to the Incas around 1471 after 11 years of siege and threats to cut the irrigation canals.

The dilapidated city walls enclose an area of 28 square kilometres containing the remains of palaces, temples, workshops, streets, houses, gardens and a canal. What is left of the adobe walls bears well-preserved moulded decorations showing small figures of fish, birds and various geometric motifs. Painted designs have been found on pottery unearthed from the debris of a city ravaged by floods, earthquakes, and *huaqeros*.

Heavy rain and flooding in 1983 damaged much of the ruins and although they are still standing, many of the interesting mouldings are closed to visitors. Thankfully, the 1998 *El Niño* had little effect.

The **Ciudadela of Tschudi** has been reconstructed. It is a 15-minute walk from the main road. It is open 0900 to 1700 (but it may be covered up if rain is expected). A ticket which covers the entrance fees for Chan Chán and the site museum on the main road, 100 metres before the turn-off, as well as Huaca El Dragón and Huaca La Esmeralda (for 2 days) costs US$3.50. A guide at the site costs US$7 per hour. Try to go in a group as the price is the same. A map and leaflet in English is on sale for US$0.75.

It is relatively safe to walk on the dirt track from turn-off to the site, but go in a group and don't stray from the road as robberies have occurred. If alone, contact the Tourist Police in Trujillo to arrange for a policeman to accompany you. On no account walk the 4 kilometres to, or on Buenos Aires beach near Chan Chán as there is serious danger of robbery, and of being attacked by dogs.

Transport from Trujillo Buses and combis leave from Zela, on the corner of Los Incas, near the market, or from the corner of España and Industrial; nos 114A or B and 6B, US$0.35, 20 minutes; US$0.25 to Chan Chán entrance. A taxi is US$5.

Other archaeological sites near Trujillo The restored temple, **Huaca El Dragón**, dating from Huari to Chimú times (1000-1470 AD), is also known as **Huaca Arco Iris** (rainbow), after the shape of friezes which decorate it. It is on the west side of the Pan-American Highway in the district of La Esperanza. ■ *Open 0800-1700. Take a combi from C España y Industrial marked 'La Esperanza'; a taxi costs US$2.*

The poorly restored **Huaca La Esmeralda** is at Mansiche, between Trujillo and Chan Chán, behind the church (not a safe area). Buses to Chan Chán and Huanchaco pass the church at Mansiche. The tour to Chan Chán includes a visit to these ruins, but tickets are not sold here.

Huacas del Sol and de la Luna A few kilometres south of Trujillo are the huge Moche pyramids, the **Huaca del Sol** (free access) and **Huaca de la Luna** (open 0900-1600, entry US$1.50, good toilets and café). The Huaca del Sol was once, before the Spanish diverted the nearby river and washed half of it away in a vain search for treasure, the largest man-made structure in the western hemisphere, reaching a height of 45 metres. The ceremonial platforms, which you can freely scramble

North Coast

Around Trujillo

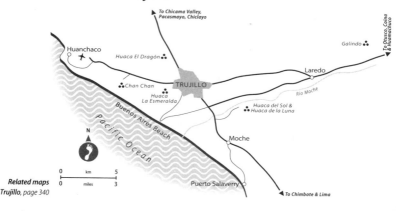

To Chicama Valley, Pacasmayo, Chiclayo

To Otusco, Caina & Huamachuco

Galindo

Huanchaco

Huaca El Dragón

Laredo

Chan Chan

TRUJILLO

Río Moche

Huaca La Esmeralda

Huaca del Sol & Huaca de la Luna

Buenos Aires Beach

N

Pacific Ocean

Moche

0   km   5
0   miles   3

*Related maps
Trujillo, page 340*

Puerto Salaverry

To Chimbote & Lima

up, have been further eroded by the weather and visitors but afford a good view over the valley.

The Huaca de la Luna, 500 metres away, received relatively little attention compared to its larger neighbour until some remarkable finds were made in the early 1990s. In fact, this is the only site where the fascinating brightly coloured moulded decorations found on the interior walls of huacas can be easily viewed. The yellow, white, red and black paint has faded little over the centuries and many metres of the intricate geometric patterns and fearsome feline deities depicted are virtually complete.

A taxi costs about US$10 return, including a one hour wait. Colectivos (golden in colour) about half hourly for Suárez y Los Incas, US$0.30, run to the base of Huaca del Sol. If you want a walk take any Moche colectivo or bus and ask to get off at the track to the Huacas. It's about an hour's interesting walk through farmland beside irrigation canals, however, it is inadvisable to walk it on your own.

North of Trujillo is the sugar estate of **Hacienda Cartavio**, in the Chicama valley (43 kilometres). The plant includes a distillery and rum factory. Visits are possible by appointment only. One of the biggest sugar estates in the world, also in the Chicama valley, is the Casa Grande cooperative. It covers over 6,000 hectares and employs 4,000 members. Visits (guided) are only possible before 1200; many buses and combis go there, US$0.75.

60 kilometres north of Trujillo, is considered one of the most important archaeological sites on the entire north coast. The complex, covering two square kilometres, consists of Huacas Prieta, Cortada and Cao Viejo. This complex is collectively known as **El Brujo** and was an important Moche ceremonial centre.   **El Brujo**

Huaca Cortada (or El Brujo) has a wall decorated with high relief stylized figures. Huaca Prieta is, in effect, a giant rubbish tip dating back 5,000 years, which once housed the very first settlers to this area. Huaca Cao Viejo has extensive friezes, polychrome relieves up to 90 metres long, four metres high and on five different levels, representing warriors, prisoners, sacrificer gods, combat and more complex scenes, with a total of seven colours in relieves. In front of Cao Viejo are the remains of one of the oldest Spanish churches in the region. It was common practice for the Spaniards to build their churches near these ancient sites in order to counteract their religious importance.

The excavations at the site will last many more years and in the next few years it is not envisaged that it will be opened to the public. Road access is poor, there are no public transport services to it, there are no tourist facilities and photography is not permitted, Superb exhibitions, including reconstructions of part of the site can be seen at **Museo de la Nación** and the **Banco Wiese Museum** in Lima and at **Banco Wiese**, Pizarro 314, Trujillo.

NB Several tour companies in Trujillo advertise tours to El Brujo but many tours have been disappointed when turned away by the Director of Excavations. For those who can prove a direct interest in visiting the site, permission can be obtained from the **Instituto Nacional de Cultura**, Independencia Block 5, Trujillo.

The complex can be reached by taking one of the regular buses from Trujillo to **Chocope** and then a colectivo (every half hour) to **Magdalena de Cao** from where it is a 8 kilometre walk to the site.

North Coast

Huanchaco

A cheaper alternative to staying in Trujillo is the fishing and surfing village of Huanchaco, which is full of hotels, guest houses and restaurants. The village is famous for its narrow pointed fishing rafts, known as *caballitos* (little horses), made of totora reeds and depicted on Mochica, Chimú, Salinar, Gallinazo, Virú and Lambayeque pottery. These are still a familiar sight in places along the northern Peruvian coast. Unlike those used on Lake Titicaca, they are flat, not hollow, and ride the breakers rather like surfboards. You can rent one on the beach, but beware of rocks in the surf. You can see fishermen set off in their reed rafts at around 0500, returning to shore about 0800 and 1600 when they stack the boats upright to dry in the fierce sun.

The village, now developed with the beach houses of the wealthy of Trujillo, is overlooked by a huge church from the belfry of which are extensive views. Entry to the pier costs US$0.10.

NB The strength of the sun is deceptive. A cool breeze off the sea reduces the temperature, but you can still be badly sunburned.

Essentials

Sleeping C *Caballito de Totora*, Avda La Rivera 219, T/F461004, E caballito@trujillovirtual.com. Includes taxes, **D** in low season, pool, friendly, English spoken, nice garden, clean, restaurant, parking, good value. Recommended. Owners Elvira and Walter also run a tourist agency, *Promter*, which is promoting the community's cultural identity through ancient fishing techniques, festivals, archaeological visits, local cuisine and mysticism. **C** *Hostal Bracamonte*, Los Olivos 503, T461162. Comfortable, good, chalets with private bathroom, or converted caravans, you can camp on the grass, pool, has its own water supply, emergency generator, rents bicycles, secure, good restaurant, English spoken. Highly recommended.

D *Hostal Sol y Mar*, Los Ficus 570. With pool, restaurant, friendly owner, garden. Recommended. **D** *Hostal Huanchaco*, Larco 287 on the plaza, T461272. Shared bathroom, cold water, clean and friendly, pool, expensive cafeteria with home-made cakes and other good meals, video, pool table. Recommended. **D** *Hostal Los Esteros*, Avda Larco 618, T461300. With bathroom, hot water, restaurant, friendly, safe motorcycle parking. **D** *Las Brisas*, Raymondi 146, T461186, F244605, E serveme@ots.com.pe. 20 rooms with bathroom, hot water, cafeteria, cable TV, comfortable.

E *Casa de los Amigos*, Las Gardineras 373, near *Hotel Bracamonte*. German-owned, basic, intermittent cold water supply, kitchen facilities, sun terrace, **F** to camp in garden.

F per person *Golden Club*, Avda La Rivera 217, T241189. 8 rooms, gym, pool, restaurant, use of kitchen, popular with surfers, very laid back atmosphere, excellent value, rooms on 1st floor cheaper. Recommended. **F** per person *La Casa Suiza*, Los Pinos 451, T461285, E c-suiza@mail.cosapidita.com.pe. 3 blocks from the beach, run by Heidi and Oscar Stacher, speak German and English, **F-G** with shared bathroom, 9 rooms, 4 with private bathrooms, hot water, nice roof balcony, excellent breakfast for US$1.50, friendly, highly recommended, good juices at the shop next door. **F** per person *Naylamp*, Prolongación Victor Larco 3, on the seafront just up from *El Peñon* restaurant, T461022. Run by Hugo and Jaqui Mendoza-Kempff, 6 rooms set around a courtyard, hammocks, nice garden, kitchen, very clean, good big beds, with bathroom, cold water 24 hours, laundry facilities, English, German, French and Italian spoken. Highly recommended. **F-G** *Hostal Solange*, Los Ficus 484, 1 block from the beach. With bathroom, hot water, good food, laundry facilities, use of kitchen. Highly recommended.

Accommodation with families is easy to find for around US$2-3 a day, including meals. For example: the friendly English-speaking *Sra Mabel Díaz de Aguilar*, near the football ground. Also basic accommodation at the house of the very friendly *Señora Lola*, Manco Capac 136, though it can be noisy at weekends. Opposite is *Sr Carlos Sánchez Leyton*, good, safe, cold water. The very friendly *Señora Nelly Neyra de Facundo* offers accommodation at Las Palmeras 425, and is recommended.

Eating *Club Colonial*, on the plaza. Reputedly the best restaurant, though expensive, run by Belgians, serving fish, chicken or meat. There are many good fish restaurants on the sea front. *El Tramboyo*, near the pier, is good, helpful and friendly. *Lucho del Mar*, serves excellent sea food. Next door is *Estrella Marina*, which is great value. Good fish also at *Pisagua*, just past the pier, and *La Esquina*, C Unión 299, opposite the pier. *Mamma Mia*, on the seafront. Good value Italian food and delicious home-made ice-cream.

    Cheaper: *Piccolo*, 5 blocks from the plaza. Cheap, friendly, live folk music weekend evenings, excellent. *Violetta*, a private house – 4 blocks directly inland from the pier. Good meals provided for US$1. *Arroyitos Chickens*, C Atahualpa 135. Excellent roast chicken, fries and salad for US$2. Try *picarones*, people come from Trujillo at weekends especially to eat them. Do not eat fish in the hut-like restaurants on the way into town from Trujillo as they aren't hygienic.

Festivals In the first week of **May** is the *Festival del Mar*, a celebration of the disembarkation of Taycanamo, the leader of the Chimú period. A procession is made in Totora boats. Also the annual *Olímpiadas Playeral* and *El Festival Internacional de la Primavera* (see Trujillo above). There are also surf competitions.

Shopping *Artesanías del Norte*, opposite *Hotel Bracamonte* on Olivos, sells local pottery, hats, T-shirts with local motifs and balsa wood products. Children sell imitation precolumbian *objets d'art* and beads. Food in the shops is no more expensive than Trujillo. There is a small fresh food market. A small market selling a wide range of artesanía is on the seafront beside the pier.

Transport Combis between Trujillo and Huanchaco are 114A or B. They both do a clockwise circuit of Huanchaco and run to the Cassinelli museum, then A goes round the west side of Trujillo onto Avda 28 de Julio and Avda Vallejo/Los Incas as far as Zela, while B goes round the east side on Avda Industrial, España and Vallejo/Los Incas also to Zela. At night they go only to España y Grau; both run till 2300 (later at weekends). Fare is US$0.25 for the 20 minute journey. 'Micros' follow similar routes to Los Incas, but in daylight only. Colectivos and some radio taxis run at night; US$4-6.

Directory **Post Office** at Manco Kapac 306. Open 0900-1445.

North of Trujillo

70 kilometres north of Trujillo this is a real surfers' hang-out, as it's the best surf beach in Peru, claiming that it has the longest left-hand point-break in the world. There are a few basic places to stay and eat.   **Puerto Chicama (Malabrigo)**

Pacasmayo (*Population*: 12,300), port for the next oasis north, is 102 kilometres north of Trujillo, and is the main road connection from the coast to Cajamarca. The paved 180 kilometres road to Cajamarca branches off the Pan-American Highway soon after it crosses the Río Jequetepeque.   **Pacasmayo**

A few kilometres north on the other side of Río Jequetepeque are the ruins of Pacatnamú, comparable in size to Chan Chán. It consists of pyramids, cemetery and living quarters of nobles and fishermen, possibly built in the Chavín   **Pacatnamú & Farfan** period. There is evidence also of Moche tribes. To get there, take a micro bus to Guadelupe, 10 kilometres from the ruins, and a taxi is possible from there for US$20. Try the Ortíz family at Unión 6, T3166.

Where the Pan-American Highway crosses the Jequetepeque are the well-signed ruins of **Farfán**, separate from those of Pacatnamú, but probably of the same period.

Sleeping and eating E *Ferrocarril*, 1½ blocks from Pacasmayo seafront on a small plaza. Quiet and clean, no hot water (ask for water anyway). F *Panamericano*, Leoncio Prado 18. With private cold shower, good value, friendly, clean, safe, reasonable restaurant downstairs. F *San Francisco*, opposite the *Panamericano*. Basic, OK. There are several cheap restaurants on the main street.

Chiclayo

Population: 411,536
Phone code: 074
Coloured map 1, grid C2

*Chiclayo, founded in the 1560s as a rural Indian village by Spanish priests, has long since outgrown other towns of the Lambayeque Department. Sandwiched between the Pacific Ocean and the Andes, Lambayeque is one of Peru's principal agricultural regions, and its chief producer of rice and sugar cane. Chiclayo is the major commercial hub, but also boasts distinctive cuisine and musical tradition (Marinera, Tondero and Afro-indian rhythms), and an unparalleled archaeological and ethnographic heritage (see **Archaeological sites** below). Chiclayo is dubbed 'The Capital of Friendship', and while that tag could equally apply to most of the north coast of Peru, there is an earthiness and vivacity about its citizens that definitely sets it apart. It can be a difficult place to leave.*

Ins and outs

Getting there José Abelardo Quiñones González airport is 1 kilometre from the town centre; taxi from centre costs US$1. There is no *terminal terrestre*; most buses stop outside their offices on Bolognesi which is south of the centre. Confusingly many of the buses leaving for the surrounding area are to the north of the centre. It is difficult to find decent cheap accommodation in Chiclayo. Also note that hotels in Chiclayo are often full.

Getting around Calle Balta is the main street but the markets and most of the hotels and restaurants are spread out over about 5 or 6 blocks from the Plaza de Armas. Mototaxis are a cheap way to get around. They cost US$0.50 anywhere in city.

Sights

On the Plaza de Armas is the 19th century neoclassical **Cathedral**, designed by the English architect Andrew Townsend, whose descendants can still be identified among the town's principals. The **Palacio Municipal** and private **Club de la Unión** are on Calle Balta, the main street.

Essentials

Sleeping
■ *on maps*
Price codes:
see inside front cover

A1 *Costa de Oro*, Balta 399, T/F209342. Includes continental breakfast, parking nearby, good services but a bit pricey, good restaurant, casino, TV in room, cable TV in lobby.

A1-2 *Gran Hotel Chiclayo*, Villareal 115, T234911/224031. Recently refurbished to a high standard, price includes taxes and breakfast, pool, safe car park, changes dollars. Still undergoing improvements but recommended. **A2-3** *Garza*, Bolognesi 756, near Balta, T228172, F228171. Excellent bar and restaurant, pool, car park, tourist office in lobby provides maps, information in English, Land Rovers, jeeps and mini-buses for hire. Highly recommended.

B-C *América*, L González 943, T229305, F241627. Includes continental breakfast, comfortable, friendly, restaurant, good value, has Travel Agency in reception. Recommended. **B-C** *Inca*, Avda L González 622, T235931. With TV and fan, restaurant, garage, comfortable and helpful.

C *Tambo Real*, Avda Luis González 532, T245641. With café-bar and laundry. **C** *Aristi*, Francisco Cabrera 102, T231074, F228673. With TV, fan, parking costs US$1 per day extra, clean, comfortable, reasonable value. **C-D** *El Sol*, Elías Aguirre 119, T/F231070. Price includes taxes, with bathroom, hot water, restaurant, pool, TV lounge, clean, comfortable, free parking, good value. **C** *Hostal Santa Victoria*, La Florida 586, Urb Santa Victoria, T/F241944. With bathroom and TV, hot water, restaurant, free parking, cash dollars exchanged, quiet, 15-20 minutes walk from the centre. **C-D** *Paracas*, Pedro Ruíz 1046, T221611, T/F236433. With bathroom, TV, good value. Recommended.

D-E *Europa*, Elías Aguirre 466, T237919. With bathroom, cheaper without, some hot water, restaurant, a bit dingy and rundown but otherwise OK. **D** *Paraíso*, Pedro Ruíz 1064, T228161, T/F240190. Near the market, with bathroom, hot water, cafetería,

Chiclayo

North Coast

	8. Hostal Adriático	2. Le París	5. Buses to Pimentel
	9. Hostal Santa Rosa	3. Mi Tía	6. Buses to Puerto Etén
	10. Inca	4. Romana	7. Chiclayo Express
■ **Sleeping**	11. Lido		8. Cruz del Sur & Civa Bus Offices
1. América	12. Paracas	🚌 **Buses**	9. Expreso Sudamericano
2. Aristi	13. Royal	1. Buses to Chongoyape	10. TEPSA
3. Costa de Oro	14. Sol Radiante	2. Buses to Lambayeque	11. Transportes Chiclayo
4. El Sol	15. Tumi de Oro	3. Buses to Monsefú	12. Vulkano
5. Europa		4. Buses to Motupe	
6. Garza	● **Eating**		*Related maps*
7. Gran Chiclayo	1. Kafé D'Kaly		*Around Chiclayo, page 355*

TV US$2 extra, good value. **D** *Royal*, San José 787, T233421. With bathroom, a big, rambling old building, a bit seedy and rundown, the rooms on the street have a balcony but are noisy. **D-E** per person *Hostal Santa Rosa*, L González 925, T224411, F236242. With bathroom, clean, friendly, laundry service, international phone service, good breakfast downstairs in snack bar. Recommended.

E-F *Aries II*, Avda Pedro Ruíz 937, T235235. Shared bath, cheap, cold water. **E** *Hostal Colonial*, Lora y Cordero 344, T237871. With bathroom, hot water, basic but clean, noisy, convenient for buses. **E** *Hostal San Ramón*, Héroes Cíviles 169, T233931. With bathroom, cold water, friendly, clean, noisy, restaurant, reasonable value. **E** *Lido*, Elías Aguirre 412A, T237642. With bathroom, fairly clean, safe, rooms near reception are noisy. **E** *Sol Radiante*, Izaga 392, T237858, hot water, comfortable, the friendly owner will provide breakfast. **E** *Tumi de Oro*, L Prado 1145, T227108. Shared bathroom, **D** with private bathroom, hot water, simple but clean, good value.

F *Hostal San José*, on Juan Cuglievan, 1 block from the Mercado Modelo. Basic, clean, acceptable, cold water.

There are several cheap hotels on Avda Balta, near the bus offices, which range from basic to hygienically-challenged. Most have only cold water: **F** per person *Adriático*, No 1009. The best of a bad bunch, fairly clean.

Eating:
Expensive
● *on maps*

Fiesta, Avda Salaverry 180 in 3 de Octubre suburb, T201970. Local specialities, first class. *Le París*, MM Izaga 716, T235485. Excellent international and creole food. *Men Wha*, Pedro Ruíz 1059. Chinese, delicious, huge portions.

Eating:
mid-range

Romana, Balta 512, T238601. First-class food, usually good breakfast, popular with locals. *The Atrium*, M Izaga 220. Good, friendly. *Che Claudio*, Bolognesi 334, T237426. *Parrillada* with reasonable *empanadas* and house wine. *Las Tinajas*, Elías Aguirre 957. Excellent seafood. *Kafé D'Kaly*, San José 728. Good *menú*, friendly. *Las Américas*, Aguirre 824. Open 0700-0200, good service. Recommended.

Eating:
cheap

Mi Tía, Aguirre 650, just off the plaza. Huge portions, great value *menú*, very popular at lunchtime. Recommended. *Govinda*, Balta 1029. Good vegetarian, open daily 0800-2000. *24 Horas*, E Aguirre 884. Good food, open 24 hours, as the name suggests. *El Algorrobo*, Avda Sáenz Peña 1220, good set lunch for US$1.10. *Flippy*, San José 710. Good fried chicken and salad for US$1.50, also juices, sandwiches etc. There are many cheap *pollerías* on Balta and Pedro Ruíz near the market; eg *Carbón Dorado*, Avda Balta 1212. *Lo Más Natural*, Arica 755, near the market. Sells good natural/organic yoghurt, also dried fruits and granola. *La Panadería*, Aguirre 610. Good bread, *pan integral*, etc, small cafetería. For great ice cream try *D'Onofrio*, on Balta, 2 blocks from the Plaza de Armas, or the *heladería* at Aguirre 600.

Local food &
drink

Local specialities include *Ceviche* and *chinguirito* (a *ceviche* of strips of dried guitar fish, which is chewy but good). *Cabrito* is a spiced stew of kid goat. *Arroz con pato* is a paella-like duck casserole. *Humitas* are *tamale*-like fritters of green corn. *King Kong* is a baked pastry layered with candied fruit and milk caramel (and truly disgusting). *Chicha* is the fermented maize drink with delicious fruit variations.

Bars &
nightclubs

Los Hermanos Balcázar, Lora y Cordero 1150, T227922. *El Embrujo*, Vicente de la Vega, T233984. *Recreo Parrillada El Gaucho*, Fco Cabrera 1291, T234441. On Dall'Orso is *Oasis* peña, *Casona* disco and pub, and *Baku's* karaoke disco. All are popular at weekends. Also good at weekends is *Crocos*, opposite the Aristi Hotel on Grau.

Festivals

This is an area rich in traditional customs and beliefs. Among the many festivals held in and around the city is *Reyes Magos* in Mórrope, Illimo and other towns on **6 January**.

This is a recreation of a medieval pageant in which precolumbian deities become the Wise Men. On **4 February** are the Túcume devil dances (see below). On **14 March** in Monsefú is *Festividad Señor Cautivo*. During **Holy Week** are traditional Easter celebrations and processions in many villages. *Fiesta de la Cruz* is held in Pimentel from **1 May**, and in the last week of **June** is *Festividad de San Pedro* in Morrope. In the first week of **June** is the Divine Child of the Miracle, in Villa de Etén. Also in Monsefú, on **27-31 July**, is Fexticum, with traditional foods, drink, handicrafts, music and dance. On **5 August** is the pilgrimage from the mountain shrine of Chalpón to Motupe, 90 kilometres north of Chiclayo. The cross is brought down from a cave and carried in procession through the village. On **24 September** is *Virgen de las Mercedes* in Incahuasi, 12 hours by truck east of Chiclayo. Indians still sing in the ancient Mochica language in this post-harvest festival. At **Christmas** and **New Year**, processions and children dancers (*pastorcitos* and *seranitas*) can be seen in many villages, eg Ferreñafe, Mochumi, Mórrope.

Shopping

Five blocks north of the main plaza on Balta is the *Mercado Modelo*, one of northern Peru's liveliest and largest daily markets. Don't miss the colourful fruits, handicrafts stalls (see *Monsefú*) and the well-organized section of ritual paraphernalia used by traditional curers and diviners (*curanderos*), which is just off Calle Arica on the south side.

James Vreeland, a North American anthropologist, considers the Chiclayo *mercado de brujos* (witch doctors' market) to be one of the most comprehensive in South America, filled with herbal medicines, folk charms, curing potions, and exotic objects used by *curanderos* and *brujos* to cure all manner of real and imagined illnesses. The stallholders are generally very friendly and will explain the uses of such items as monkey claws, dried foetuses and dragon's blood! Sra Carmen Quispe Bios of Casa La Cabalonga, stand 44, near the corner of Avda Arica and Héroes Cíviles, has been recommended as particularly helpful and informative. **NB** As in all markets, take good care of your belongings.

Paseo de Artesanías, at 18 de Abril near Balta, stalls sell woodwork, basketwork and other handicrafts in a quiet, peaceful, custom-built open-air arcade. *Mercado Moshoqueque*, Ricardo Palma y Calle Ancha, is a busy street teeming with people and good for buying food in bulk from merchants.

Transport

Air connections Daily flights to and from **Lima** with all major airlines. Also daily flights to **Piura** and **Tumbes**. *AeroPerú* flies to **Iquitos** 4 times a week. Check flight schedules in advance as they change frequently.

Buses To **Lima**, 770 kilometres, US$8-9: *Chiclayo Express*, Mcal Nieto 199, T237356; *Civa*, Avda Bolognesi 757, T242488; *Cruz del Sur*, Bolognesi 888, T225508; *Ormeño*, Bolognesi 954A; *Turismo Las Dunas*, L González 291, T229328, luxury service with a/c, toilet, meals, leaves at 2000, US$17.50; *Oltursa*, Vicente de la Vega 101, T236310, *cama* service; *Transportes Chiclayo*, Avda L Ortíz 010, T237984; *El Combe*, Quiñones 425, T231454. Most companies leave from 1600 onwards.

To **Trujillo**, 209 kilometres, with *Emtrafesa*, Avda Balta 110, T234291, and *Vulkano*, Avda Bolognesi 638, T234291. Leave hourly 0530-2000, US$3.50, 3-4 hours. Bus to **Piura**, US$3.50, leaves hourly 0630-1930. To **Sullana**, US$4.35. To **Tumbes**, US$6.50, 9-10 hours; with *Transportes Chiclayo* (see above); *Oltursa* has a overnight service which leaves at 2015 and arrives at 0530 (this is a good bus to take for crossing to Ecuador the next day), seats can be reserved, unlike other companies which tend to arrive full from Lima late at night.

Many buses go on to the **Ecuadorean border** at **Aguas Verdes**. Go to the *Salida* on Elías Aguirre, mototaxi drivers know where it is, be there by 1900. All buses stop here after leaving their terminals to try and fill empty seats, so it's possible to get a substantial discount on the fare to the border. **NB** Bear in mind that the cheapest buses may not be the most secure.

North Coast

Direct bus to **Cajamarca**, 260 kilometres; with *Vulkano*, El Cumbre (see above), *Sud Americano* (Colón 272, T238566) and *Turismo Arberia* (Avda Bolognesi 638, T236981), US$6, 7 hours, leave daily at 0700, 1300, 2130 and 2200. To **Chachapoyas**, 230 kilometres: with *Civa* at 1630 daily, 13 hours, US$7; *Turismo Kuelap*, in Tepsa station, Bolognesi 536, 1600 daily, US$9. To **Jaén**: *Civa* at 1100 and 2100, 8 hours, US$5; *Transportes Huamantanga*, in Tepsa station, 1000, 1330 and 2200 daily, US$5; *Jaén Express*, in Tepsa station, 0900, 1300 and 2145 daily, US$5. To **Tarapoto**, 18 hours, US$15.50, and **Yurimaguas**, 25 hours, US$25, with *Paredes Estrella*, in Cruz de Chalpón station, Balta corner of Bolognesi. To **Huancabamba**, with *Etipthsa*, on Monday, Wednesday and Friday from the Tepsa terminal at Avda Bolognesi 536, T229217; at 1700, 12 hours, US$9. Trucks going in all directions leave from C Pedro Ruíz 948 and from the market.

Directory **Airline offices** *AeroPerú*, San José 783, T237151/233503. *Aero Continente*, Elías Aguirre 712, T209916/17.

Banks *Banco de Crédito*, Balta 630, no commission on TCs for US$100 or more (US$11 commission if less), cash on Visa. *Interbanc*, on the Plaza de Armas, no commission on TCs, OK rate, good rates for cash, Visa cash advance. *Banco Wiese*, on the plaza, cash on MasterCard. You may have to wait for a while in the banks. It's much quicker and easier to use the ATMs. Beware of counterfeit bills, especially among street changers on the 6th block of Balta, on Plaza de Armas and the 7th block of MM Izaga.

Communications Post Office: on the first block of Aguirre, 6 blocks from the Plaza. **Telecommunications:** Telefónica del Perú on 7 de Enero 724, open 0700-2300, international phone and fax. Also on the 8th block of Aguirre. **Internet:** Biblioteca Municipal, Grau y Elías Aguirre. Mon-Fri 0800-2000, Sat 0800-1400, US$1.75 per hour. *Red del Norte*, Jr San José 165, 3rd Flr, T274785. US$1.40 per hour.

Cultural centres *Instituto Peruano Británico*, Avda 7 de Enero 296. *Instituto Nacional de la Cultura*, Avda L González 375. Has occasional poetry readings, information on local archaeological sites, lectures, etc. *Instituto de Cultura Peruano-Norteamericana*, Avda Izaga 807.

Hospitals & medical services Doctors: *Dr Hector Portila*, Clínica Pacífico, L Ortíz 420, T236378. *José Gálvez Jaime*, eye specialist, English spoken, Elías Aguirre 011, T238234.

Tour companies & travel agents *Indiana Tours*, Manual María Izaga 585, T242287, F240833, E indiana@kipu.rednorte.com.pe. Daily tours to Sipán (US$15), Thor Heyerdahl's Kon Tiki museum, archaeological excavations in Túcume, Brüning Museum in Lambayeque, Batán Grande and a variety of other daily and extended excursions with 4WD vehicles. English and Italian spoken and Handbook users welcome. *InkaNatura Travel*, San Martín 120, Oficina 301, T/F209948, E inkanatur@chavin.rep.net.pe, W www.inkanatura.com. Runs a unique series of tours aimed specifically at senior citizens, with profits directed to local education (also book through Lima offices: Manuel Bañon 461, T4402022, F4229225). *Sipán Tours*, Avda Luis González 741, T/F237413. Good for tours locally, English-speaking manager, helpful, can arrange tailor-made tours. *Lambayeque Travel Service*, Avda Santa Victoria 300, T244327, F274452. *Kaly Tours*, San José 728, T238830. Friendly, helpful, English spoken. The Brüning Museum, Sipán and Túcume can easily be done by public transport. Expect to pay US$18-25 per person for a 3-hr tour to Sipán, and US$25-35 per person for Túcume and the Brüning Museum (5 hrs). Batán Grande is US$45-55 per person for a full-day tour including Ferreñafe and Pomac. To Saña and the coastal towns is US$35-55 per person. These prices are based on 2 people; there are discounts for larger groups.

Tourist offices San José 733 y Plaza de Armas. They are very helpful and may store luggage and take you to the sites themselves. The regional tourist board plans to open an office in the same building, T233132. Their current office is at Sáenz Peña 838. The brochure *Guía de Lambayeque 1996* is available for US$5.

Sights around Chiclayo

Lambayeque 12 kilometres northwest from Chiclayo is the quiet town of Lambayeque (*Population*: 20,700). Its narrow streets are lined by colonial and republican houses, many retaining their distinctive wooden balconies and wrought iron grill-work over the windows. For some fine examples, head along Calle 8 de

Octubre: at No 410 is the opulent **Casona Itürregui Aguilarte** and, at No 328, **Casona Cuneo** is the only decorated façade in the town. Opposite is **Casona Descalzi**, perhaps the best preserved of all Lambayeque's colonial houses. Calle 2 de Mayo is also a good source of colonial and republican architecture, especially **Casa de la Logia o Montjoy,** whose 64 metre long balcony is said to be the longest in the colonial Americas.

Also of interest is the 16th century **Complejo Religioso Monumental de San Pedro** and the baroque church of the same name which stands on the **Plaza de Armas 27 de Diciembre**. The French neo-baroque **Palacio Municipal** is also on the plaza.

The town's most interesting feature, and the reason most people come to visit, is the well-known and highly recommended **Brüning Archaeological Museum**, located in an impressive modern building. It specializes in Mochica, Lambayeque, Sicán and Chimú cultures, and has a fine collection of Sipán and Lambayeque gold. The magnificent treasure from the tomb of a Moche warrior priest, found at Sipán in 1987, has also been displayed here (see Archaeological sites below). The museum is open 0830-1830 daily; entry US$1, a guided tour costs an extra US$2.

Eating and transport There are no hotels in the town but several good restaurants. *El Cántaro*, on the 1st block of 2 de Mayo, serves excellent traditional local dishes cooked by Juanita. *La Huaca*, on the 3rd block of Calle Junín, and *La Cabaña*, on the 4th block of Calle Libertad, are both good for

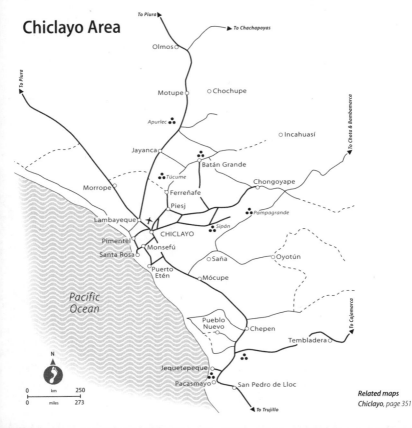

Chiclayo Area

Related maps
Chiclayo, page 351

cebiche. **Colectivos** from Chiclayo; US$0.50, 20 minutes. They leave from Elías Aguirre near Plazuela Aguirre. Also Brüning Express from Vicente de la Vega y San Martín, every 15 minutes, US$0.20.

Colonial and traditional towns The colonial town of **Ferreñafe**, northeast of Chiclayo, is worth a visit, as is the traditional town of **Monsefú**, to the southwest. It is also known for handicrafts and has a good market, four blocks from the plaza. It's open 0930-1700 but don't rush to get there early as most stallholders don't arrive until around 1000 or 1100 (see also **Local festivals** above).

Mórrope, on the Pan-American Highway north of Chiclayo, is worth a visit. The craftsmen of Mórrope still produce pottery for the towns of northern Peru using prehispanic techniques. Step inside the beautifully-restored 16th century **Capilla de la Ramada** on the plaza and you'll know how Jonah felt inside the whale. The pillars and rafters were hewed from the local *algarrobo* tree, giving the church interior the appearance of the skeleton of some enormous beast.

The ruined Spanish town of **Saña**, lies 51 kilometres south of Chiclayo. Saña was destroyed by floods in 1726, and sacked by English pirates on more than one occasion. The ruins of five colonial churches and the convents of San Agustín, La Merced and San Francisco bear witness to the former splendour of this town which, at one time, was destined to become the country's capital.

Further south, on the Pan-American Highway to Trujillo, lies **Chepén**. The town itself is not particularly fascinating but **Cerro Chepén**, towering over it, is the site of an ancient fortress, 1,000 years older than Machu Picchu. The Moche fortress contains the ruins of what may be a palace, surrounded by other buildings. The as yet unexcavated site could have been the main station in a chain of lookout posts along the north coast. Take any Trujillo bus, US$1.10.

Coastal towns There are three ports serving the Chiclayo area. The more southerly is **Puerto Etén**, a quaint port 24 kilometres by road from Chiclayo. In the adjacent roadstead, **Villa de Etén**, panama hats are the local industry.

Pimentel, north of Etén, is a chic and expensive beach resort which gets very crowded on Sundays. Holiday apartments of the Chiclayo wealthy line the seafront. The surfing between Pimentel and the Bayovar Peninsula is excellent, reached from Chiclayo (14½ kilometres) by road branching off from the Pan-American Highway. Sea-going reed boats (*caballitos de totora*) are used by fishermen and can be seen returning in the late afternoon.

A more traditional and authentic fishing village is nearby **Santa Rosa**, where fishermen use two groups of boats *caballitos* and *bolicheros* – pastel-painted craft which line the shore after the day's fishing. Santa Rosa is a pleasant, one hour walk from Pimentel, though it's a better idea to walk from Santa Rosa to Pimentel to have the wind at your back.

Sleeping, eating and transport In Pimentel: *Hostal Garnda*, Avda Lima 3. Also ask at *Restaurant Angustino* on the seafront, which serves good food. **In Santa Rosa**: There is a small hostal, *Puerto Magnolia*, which is basic, and a restaurant *Bello Horizonte*. The seafood is superb. Two specialities are *tortilla de rayo* (manta ray) and *chingurito*. **Getting there** The 3 ports can all be visited on a pleasant half day trip from Chiclayo. Aspcarpi combis leave from Vicente de la Vega 400 to Pimentel; 20 minutes, US$0.25. Colectivos run frequently to Pimentel, then to Santa Rosa, on to Etén and back to Chiclayo. They leave from Avda Ugarte, near the corner with Pedro Ruíz; US$0.30.

North Coast

The legend of Naymlap

Like much else along this stretch of the Peruvian coast, the exact origin of the people's forebears is something of a mystery. The Spaniard, Cabello de Balboa, in 1578, is said to be the first outsider to hear of a local folk legend referring to a person named Naymlap who arrived on the coast of Lambayeque along with his court, his servants and his many concubines in numerous balsa rafts.

He then built residential buildings near the coast and a temple called Chota, where he placed an idol called Yampallec, from which Lambayeque is supposed to derive its name.

The name Naymlap came to occupy an important place in the religious imagery of later civilizations through the designs of tumis, or ceremonial knives, funerary masks and countless other objects. In the ancient Muchik language spoken by the Moche, ñam means bird and lá means water, and the figures on Moche ceramics, jewellery and temple walls often have bird-like features.

Naymlap had many children but only three are known of: Cium, Nor and Cala, who founded the present site of Túcume. This dynasty is said to have ended with the death of the last governor as a result of his illicit relationship with a demon in the shape of a beautiful woman.

Sipán

At this imposing twin pyramid complex a short distance east of Chiclayo, excavations since 1987 have brought to light a cache of funerary objects considered to rank among the finest examples of precolumbian art.

Coloured map 2, grid C2

The Peruvian archaeologist Walter Alva, leader of the dig, continues to probe the immense mound that has revealed no less than five royal tombs filled with 1,800-year-old offerings worked in precious metals, stone, pottery and textiles of the Moche culture (ca AD 1-750). In the most extravagant Moche tomb discovered, **El Señor de Sipán**, a priest was found clad in gold (ear ornaments, breast plate, etc), with turquoise and other valuables. A fine site museum was opened in 1992 featuring photos and maps of excavations, technical displays and replicas of some finds.

Following the four-year restoration of the principle treasures in Germany, the Lord of Sipán's physical remains and extraordinary funerary paraphernalia were recently returned to the Brüning Museum in Lambayeque, which was remodelled in 1994 to accommodate over 600 new objects. In another tomb were found the remnants of what is thought to have been a priest, sacrificed llama and a dog, together with copper decorations. They are now on display in Lima (see Lima museums). In 1989 another richly-appointed, unlooted tomb contained even older metal and ceramic artefacts associated with what was probably a high-ranking shaman or spiritual leader, called '**The Old Lord of Sipán**'.

Tomb contents are being restored in the Brüning Museum by specialists trained in Europe. At the time of writing, yet another unlooted tomb is currently being excavated, which will take several years. You can wander around the previously excavated areas to get an idea of the construction of the burial mound and adjacent pyramids. For a good view, climb the large pyramid across from the Sipán excavation.

■ *The site museum is open 0800-1800. Entrance for the tombs and museum is US$1. A guide at the site costs US$2. Allow about three to four*

North Coast

The old Lord of Sipán

The excavations at Sipán by the archaeologist Walter Alva have already revealed a huge amount of riches in the shape of El Señor de Sipán'. This well-documented discovery was followed by an equally astounding find dating from AD 100. The tomb of the 'Old Lord of Sipán', as it has come to be known, predates the original Lord of Sipán by some 200 years, and could well be an ancestor of his.

Some of the finest examples of Moche craftsmanship have been found in the tomb of the Old Lord. One object in particular is remarkable; a crab deity with a human head and legs and the carapace, legs and claws of a crab. The gilded piece is over half a metre tall – unprecedented for a Moche figurine. This crab-like figure has been called Ulluchu Man, because the banner on which it was mounted yielded some of the first

samples yet found of this ancient fruit.

The ulluchu fruit usually appears in scenes relating to war and the ritual drinking of a prisoner's blood. One theory is that the ulluchu is part of the papaya family and has anticoagulant properties which are useful to prevent clotting before a man's blood is consumed.

hours in total to visit the site. Colectivos leave Chiclayo from 7 de Enero y Juan Fanning (this can be a dangerous area, so take a taxi there for US$1); US$0.40, 40 minutes. You can sleep at nearby Huaca Rajada is a **F** Parador Turística. 2 rooms available, meals possible, camping and use of facilities for US$1 per person.

Pampagrande 25 kilometres from Sipán is Pampagrande, a Mochica settlement interpreted by Canadian archaeologists in the 1970s as the first true northern coast city, circa AD 550.

This was the largest Moche complex 1,400 years ago, at which time as many as 10,000 people may have lived here. Pampagrande existed to enact ceremonies and rituals such as the drinking of prisoners' blood. These were presided over by a lord who also directed the production and distribution of precious materials to the artisans. Some experts believe that a prolonged drought around AD 550 displaced large groups of Moche people living to the south who moved to Pampagrande, which become the centre of a state holding sway over the Lambayeque and Jequetepeque valleys.

The precise reason for the downfall of this once-powerful city remains a mystery. The structures associated with the rich and powerful ruling class appear to have been selectively burned and then abandoned leading some to conclude that a peasant revolution may have been the cause.

Chongoyape A minor road runs to Chongoyape, a pleasant old town 60 kilometres to the east (3 kilometres west are the Chavín petroglyphs of Cerro Mulato). Nearby are the vast Taymi precolumbian and modern irrigation systems. Also near Chongoyape are the aqueduct of Racarrumi, the hill fort of Mal Paso and the ruins of Maguín.

Sleeping, eating and transport There is one hotel, **F**, near the Plaza de Armas. *Restaurant Cascada*, on the main street has a limited menu. Buses

North Coast

*f*rom Chiclayo leave from the corner of Leoncio Prado and Sáenz Peña; US$1, 1½ hours.

This site, 50 kilometres from Chiclayo, has revealed several sumptuous tombs dating to the middle Sicán period, AD 900-1100. The ruins comprise some fifty adobe pyramids, where some of the best examples of precolumbian gold artefacts, notably the 915-gram Tumi, were found.

In the ancient Muchik language, Sicán means 'house or temple of the moon' and Batán Grande, or Poma, as it was also known, was the centre of the mid-Sicán culture which shares many stylistic similarities with the later Chimú culture.

Professor Izumi Shimada has worked here for more than 15 years researching a culture which has, to a large extent, been forgotten. He has excavated **Huaca Loro**, one of five monument temples that make up the vast rectangle known as the Great Plaza. Research points to the existence of a well-structured theocracy led by a small class of priest-lords. Political, economic and religious dominance of the Sicán theocracy stretched over most of the north coast, from Sullana in the north to Trujillo in the south. Their dominion ended in the 14th century with the Chimú conquest.

The site, in 300 hectares of desert-thorn forest of mezquite (*Prosopis pallida*), known locally as Pomac forest, is now a national sanctuary and is protected by police.

Getting there Colectivos (US$1.20) leave Chiclayo from 7 de Enero block 15 and J Fanning to the main square of the sugar cane cooperative (in which the ruins are set). You must get permission to visit the site from the cooperative and go with site archaeologist. You need to speak Spanish and to pay to visit the site, which is open Monday-Friday only. A private car (taxi) from the cooperative to the site costs US$7-9 (bargain hard). You'll need a full day to visit. This is impossible in the wet season, from January to March. Seek sound advice before you go.

Túcume

About 35 kilometres north of Chiclayo, beside the old Panamericana to Piura, lie the ruins of this vast city built over a thousand years ago. This mysterious and evocative site is worth visiting around sundown, not only to avoid the fierce sun, but to add to the eerie thrill that it induces. It may be difficult to persuade anyone to accompany you, though, as local people are very superstitious.

Coloured map 1, grid C2

A short climb to the *mirador* atop **Cerro La Raya**, or **El Purgatorio**, as it is also known, offers an unparallelled panoramic vista of 26 major pyramids, platform mounds, walled citadels and residential compounds flanking a ceremonial centre and ancient cemeteries.

The entire complex covers 240 hectares and measures 1.7 kilometres from east to west and two kilometres from north to south. One of the pyramids, Huaca Larga, where excavations are currently going on, is the largest adobe structure in the world, measuring 700 metres long, 280 metres wide and over 30 metres high.

There is no evidence of occupation of Túcume previous to the Lambayeque people who developed the site between AD 1000 and 1400 until the Chimú came, saw and conquered the region, establishing a short reign until the arrival of the Incas around 1470. The Incas built on top of the existing

A tale of demons and fish

Just one of the many legends that abound in this part of Northern Peru pertains to the hill which dominates the pyramids at Túcume and the precise origin of its name. The hill is known locally as 'El Purgatorio' (purgatory), or more commonly, Cerro La Raya.

The former name derives from the conquering Spaniards' attempts to convert the indigenous people to the Christian faith. The Spanish invaders encountered fierce local resistance to their new religion and came up with the idea of convincing the people of Túcume that the hill was, in fact, purgatory. They told the locals that there lived on the hill a demon who would punish anyone not accepting the Roman Catholic faith.

In order to lend some credence to this tale, a group of Spaniards set out one dark, moonless night and built a huge bonfire at the foot of 'El Purgatorio', giving it the appearance of an erupting volcano and frightening the townsfolk half to death. Thus they came to accept the Spaniards' assertion that any unbelievers or sinners would be thrown alive into the

flames of this diabolical fire.

As if that wasn't enough to terrify the local populace, the Spanish also concocted the fiendish tale of 'El Carretón', or waggon. This was an enormous waggon pulled by four great horses which supposedly would speed forth from the bowels of 'El Purgatorio' on the darkest of nights. Driven by a dandily-dressed demon boss, and carrying his equally dandy demon buddies, this hellish vehicle careered round the town of Túcume making a fearsome racket. Any poor unbelievers or sinners unfortunate enough to be found wandering the streets would immediately be carted off and thrown into the flames of purgatory.

The alternative name of Cerro La Raya refers to the local legend of a Manta Ray that lived in a nearby lake. The local children constantly tormented the fish by throwing stones at it, so, to escape this torment, the poor creature decided to move to the hill and become part of it. The lake then disappeared and ever since, the hill has been enchanted.

structure of **Huaca Larga** using stone from Cerro La Raya. Among the tombs excavated so far is one dating from the Inca period. It is thought to be that of a warrior, judging by the many battle scars. The body is heavily adorned and was interred along with two male compatriots and no less than 19 females aged between 10 and 30.

Among the other pyramids which make up this huge complex are: **Huaca El Mirador, Huaca Las Estacas, Huaca Pintada** and **Huaca de las Balsas** which is thought to have housed people of elevated status such as priests.

Excavations at the site, led by Norwegian explorer-archaeologist, Thor Heyerdahl of *Kon-Tiki* fame, are quickly challenging many conventional views of ancient Peruvian culture. Some suspect that it will prove to be a civilization centre greater than Chan Chán. There is also evidence, including art and remains of navigation gear, that the people of Túcume were intrepid seafarers. A 10-year excavation project led by Thor Heyerdahl is under way.

The site museum is built from adobe and mezquite logs in prehispanic style. The collections show architectural reconstructions, photographs and drawings, highlighting recent finds, which include weaving paraphernalia, a ceremonial oar and a fabulous bas relief and mural depicting maritime scenes suggesting former sea trade and interregional contact. Meals and drinks are available on request. ■ *Entrance is US$1. Fatima Huaman Vera is a good English-speaking guide; she charges US$2.50.*

This typical north coast town is a 10-15 minutes' walk from the site. On the plaza is the interesting **San Pedro Church**, a mixture of baroque, churrigueresque and neo-classical styles. There are no hotels in town. The surrounding countryside is pleasant for walks and swimming in the river.

The town of Túcume

The present site of the town is not the original one but dates from 1720. Local legend has it that the town was moved following an apparition of the Virgin. The icon of the Virgin mysteriously disappeared but was later seen on top of Cerro Cueto, having her long hair combed by a native girl while gazing over pasture lands below. This was taken as a sign to relocate the church and the rest of the town with it.

Túcume celebrates the *Fiesta de la Purísima Concepción*, the town's Patron Saint, eight days prior to Carnival in February, and also in September. This is the most important festival, with music, dancing, fireworks, cockfights, sports events and, of course, much eating and drinking. During the Dance of the Devils, the participants wear horned masks, forked tails and long capes and are said to represent the diabolical drunken Spanish priests from colonial times. It also features a song and dance dedicated to the native girl who was seen combing the Virgin's hair.

Getting there Combis go from Chiclayo, Manuel Pardo block 6, US$1.50, 1 hour. A combi from Túcume to the village of Come passes the ruins hourly. A combi from Túcume to the Brüning Museum is US$0.50 and takes 30 minutes.

North on the Old Pan-American Highway

60 kilometres north of Chiclayo is the site of Apurlec beside the old Panamericana. It comprises a stone wall surrounding a hill and pyramids dating from the Tiahuanaco period, as well as irrigation canals and reservoirs. The system was enlarged during Mochica, Chimú and Inca occupation of the site. To get there from Chiclayo, take a bus from Pedro Ruíz block 5. The bus continues to Motupe.

Apurlec

Further north on the old Pan-American Highway 885 kilometres from Lima, is the peaceful town of Olmos. During the last week of June the Festival de Limón is celebrated here. **G** *Hospedaje San Martín*, very dirty, bargain hard. *Hotel Remanso*, is in a restored farmstead, good food, friendly, but not cheap.

Olmos

At Olmos, a poor road (being improved) runs east over the Porculla Pass for Jaén and Bagua (see pages 416 and 415). The old Pan-American Highway continues from Olmos to Cruz de Caña and on to Piura.

North on the New Pan-American Highway

At Lambayeque the new Pan-American Highway, which is in good condition, branches off the old road and drives 190 kilometres straight across the Sechura Desert to Piura. There is also a coast road, narrow and scenic, between Lambayeque and Piura, via Bayovar and the town of Sechura (see page 366). There is a restaurant at the junction to Bayovar, where you can sleep.

A large area of shifting sands separates the cities of Chiclayo and Piura. Water for irrigation comes from the Chira and Piura rivers, and from the Olmos and Tinajones irrigation projects which bring water from the Amazon watershed by means of tunnels (one over 16 kilometres long) through the Andes to the Pacific coast. They will eventually water some 400,000 hectares of desert land.

Sechura Desert

North Coast

The northern river – the Chira – has usually a superabundance of water. Along its irrigated banks large crops of Tangüis cotton are grown. A dam has been built at Poechos on the Chira to divert water to the Piura valley. In its upper course the Piura – whose flow is far less dependable – is mostly used to grow subsistence food crops, but around Piura, when there is enough water, the hardy long-staple Pima cotton is planted.

Cotton has been grown mainly on medium-sized properties, which have changed hands frequently in recent years and which now form communal or co-operative farms, sponsored by the agrarian reform programme. Worth seeing as an example of a fine old plantation is the former Hacienda Sojo (near Sullana) in the lower Chira valley.

The devastating 1997/98 *El Niño* has turned the Sechura Desert into an inland sea (La Niña) almost 300 kilometres long and 40 kilometres wide. The damage to crops and infrastructure has been considerable and the water may take years to subside.

NB Solo cyclists should not cross the Sechura Desert as muggings have been known to occur. Take the safer, inland route. There are several restaurants between Km 845 and 848, and another midway between Mórrope and Piura, but there are no hotels. Do not camp out if possible. Heading south, strong headwinds may make camping unavoidable. Do not attempt this alone.

Piura

Population: 324,500
Phone code: 074
Coloured map 1, grid B1

A proud and historic city, 264 kilometres from Chiclayo, Piura was founded in 1532, three years before Lima, by the conquistadores *left behind by Pizarro. There are two well kept parks, Cortés and Pizarro (with a statue of the* conquistador*), and public gardens. Old buildings are kept in repair and new buildings blend with the Spanish style of the old city.*

NB There was severe damage here in 1997-98 due to *El Niño* and three of the city's four bridges have been damaged. Only the new Panamerican Highway bridge could be used by vehicles in June 1998.

Ins and outs

Climate The winter climate, May-September, is very pleasant although nights can be cold and the wind piercing, while December to March is very hot. It is extremely difficult to find a room in the last week of July because of Independence festivities. The city suffers from water shortages.

Getting there A taxi to the airport costs US$1.60. Most bus companies are on Avda Sánchez Cerro, blocks 11 and 12 in the northwest of the town. There are no hotels in this area. It is too far to walk so take a taxi: Radio Taxis, T324509/324630.

Getting around Apart from around the Plaza de Armas, the sights and hotels are too spread out to making walking a practical proposition. Four bridges cross the Río Piura to Castilla, the oldest from C Huancavelica, for pedestrians, others from C Sánchez Cerro, from C Bolognesi, and the newest from Avda Panamericana Norte, at the north end of town.

Sights

Standing on the **Plaza de Armas** is the **cathedral**, with gold covered altar and paintings by Ignacio Merino. A few blocks away is the **San Francisco** church, where the city's independence from Spain was declared on 4 January 1821, nearly eight months before Lima.

The colonial church of **Las Mercedes** has ornately carved balconies, three-tiered archway, hand-hewn supports and massive furnishings. **San Sebastián**, on Tacna y Moquegua, is also worth seeing. The birthplace of Admiral Miguel Grau, hero of the War of the Pacific with Chile, is **Casa Museo Grau**, on Jr Tacna 662, opposite the Centro Cívico. It has been opened as a museum and contains a model of the *Huáscar*, the largest Peruvian warship in the War of the Pacific, which was built in Britain.

Interesting local craftwork is sold at the **Mercado Modelo**. **Museo Complejo Cultural**, with archaeological and art sections, is open on Sullana, near Huánuco, and though small it is very interesting.

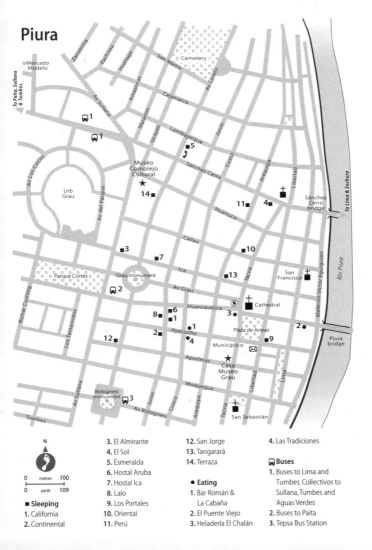

Piura

North Coast

N

| 0 | metres | 100 |
| 0 | yards | 109 |

■ Sleeping
1. California
2. Continental
3. El Almirante
4. El Sol
5. Esmeralda
6. Hostal Aruba
7. Hostal Ica
8. Lalo
9. Los Portales
10. Oriental
11. Perú
12. San Jorge
13. Tangarará
14. Terraza

● Eating
1. Bar Román & La Cabaña
2. El Puente Viejo
3. Heladería El Chalán
4. Las Tradiciones

🚍 Buses
1. Buses to Lima and Tumbes. Collectivos to Sullana, Tumbes and Aguas Verdes
2. Buses to Paita
3. Tepsa Bus Station

Essentials

Sleeping
■ *on maps*
Price codes:
see inside front cover

A1 *Los Portales*, Libertad 875, Plaza de Armas, T322952, F325920. This ex-government hotel is being refurbished and is the city's social centre, a/c, some rooms with hot water, pleasant terrace and patio, nice pool. **A3** *El Angolo*, Fortunato Chirichigno 661, Urb San Eduardo, T/F326461. Suites and bungalows, hot water, a/c, pool, cable TV, restaurant, airport pickup service.

B *Perú*, Arequipa 476, T333421, F331530. With bathroom and a/c, **C** with fan, clean, safe, friendly, laundry service, cold water, modern small rooms, restaurant.

C *El Sol*, Sánchez Cerro 411, T324461, F326307. With bathroom, hot water, small pool, snack bar, parking, accepts dollars cash or travellers' cheques but won't change them. **C** *Esmeralda*, Loreto 235, T/F327109. With bathroom, hot water, fan, clean, comfortable, good, restaurant. **C** *Miraflores*, Cayetano Heredia 503 y Avda Guardia Civil, Castilla, T327236. A/c, hot water, **E** with fan, comfortable, family run. **C-D** *San Jorge*, Jr Loreto 960, T327514, F322928. With bathroom and fan, hot water, clean. **C** *Tangarará*, Arequipa 691, esquina Ica, T326450, F328322. Central location, with bathroom, hot water, fan, clean but expensive. **C** *Vicus*, Avda Guardia Civil B-3, in Castilla across the river on the Sánchez Cerro bridge, T343186, F343249. With bathroom, hot water, fan, clean, quiet, parking.

D *Bolognesi*, Bolognesi 427, T324072. With bathroom, no fan, OK but ageing. **D** *Cocos Inn*, José Olaya 197, Castilla, T329004. Converted colonial home in quiet residential area, includes breakfast, with bathroom, cheaper with cold water, terrace, clean, friendly. **D** *El Almirante*, Ica 860, T/F335239. With bathroom, fan, clean, modern, owner is knowledgeable about the Ayabaca area (see page 368). **D** *Turismo*, Huánuco 526, T325950. With bathroom, fan, pleasant, front rooms noisy.

E *Hostal Aruba*, on Junín esquina Huancavelica, opposite *Hotel Lalo*, small rooms but clean and comfortable, fan on request, very friendly. Recommended. **E** *California*, Jr Junín 835, T328789. Shared bath, own water-tank, mosquito netting on windows, roof terrace, clean, the owner is "super, just like you wished your mother would have been when you were small!" Recommended for those lacking parental love. **E** *Continental*, Jr Junín 924, T334531. Some rooms with bathroom, clean, comfortable. **E** *Lalo*, Junín 838, T325798. Shared bathroom, cold water, very basic, **F** with double bed, washing facilities, friendly. **E** *Oriental*, Callao 446, T328891. Cheaper without bathroom and fan, clean, good value but very noisy, TV in reception. **E** *Terraza*, Avda Loreto 530, 2 blocks from the Grau monument, T325043. With bathroom, cheaper without, small rooms, basic, shabby, poor beds. **F** *Hostal Ica*, Ica cuadra 7. Dirty, very basic, cheap.

Eating:
expensive
● *on maps*

Carburmer, Apurimac 343 in Centro Comercial. Very good. *La Cabaña*, Ayacucho 598, esquina Cusco. Pizzas and other good Italian food. *Café Concierto*, Cusco 933. Pleasant and popular. *El Puente Viejo*, Huancavelica 167, ½ block from the rebuilt bridge. Very good seafood (from owners' private beds offshore at Paita). Recommended. *Las Tradiciones*, Ayacucho 579. Regional specialities, nice atmosphere, also an art gallery.

Eating:
mid-range

Gran Prix, Loreto 395. Good food, reasonable prices. *Chispita*, Sánchez Cerro 210, near the bridge. Good set meal, à la carte, fruit juices. *Ferny's*, on Ayacucho next to *Hotel San Jorge*, good food, clean.

Eating:
cheap

Chifa Canton, Libertad 377. Excellent, especially won ton soup and special rice, US$2.50 per dish, always busy. *Chifa Oriental*, on Huancavelica, 1 block west of the Plaza. Good. *Bar Román*, Ayacucho 580. Excellent set meal for US$1.75. Highly recommended. *Snack Bar*, Callao 536. Good fruit juices. There are good little cheap restaurants on Jr Junín: *Chalán del Norte* at 722, *Bianca* at 732, *El Capri* at 715. *Ganímedes*, Sánchez

Cerro y Lima. A good vegetarian restaurant, very popular set lunch, à la carte is slow but well worth it, try the excellent yoghurt and fruit. Two good places for sweets and ice-cream are: *El Chalán*, Tacna 520 on Plaza de Armas; and *D'Pauli*, Lima 541.

Piura's special dishes include *Majado de Yuca*, manioc root with pork; *Seco de Chavelo*, beef and plantain stew; and *Carne Seca*, sun-dried meat. Its best- known sweet is the delicious *natilla*, made mostly of goats' milk and molasses. Its local drink is *pipa fría*, chilled coconut juice drunk from the nut with a straw. **Local specialities**

Many of the nightspots are concentrated on Ayacucho, and some of them are also restaurants (see above). In addition are: *Bohemio's*, at 588; *Bloom Moon*, at 522; and *Café R & B Zelada*, at 562. *Discoteca La Cascada* is at *Hotel El Angolo*. **Bar & nightclubs**

26-28 July *Festival Internacional de Tunas*. **27 August** to **2 September** *Semana Turística de Piura*. **7 October** *Festival Nacional de Marinera y Tondera*. **Festivals**

There are good delicatessens around Plaza de Armas, selling local sweets. The *natilla* factory on Sánchez Cerro, Miraflores, 4 blocks from the bridge, sells *natilla* and *algarrobina* syrup. The market on *Sánchez Cerro* is good for fruit. **Chulucanas pottery** (see page 367) can be bought at two shops on Libertad and from *Milagros García de Linares*, who lives in Urbanización Santa Inés, T327322. **Photography** You can find Fuji film at Grau 202, and Kodak at Huancavélica 199 and 258. **Shopping**

Car rental Daily rates range between US$40 for a small car and US$75 for a 4WD vehicle; book ahead as availability is limited. *Piura Rent-a-car*, Sánchez Cerro 425, T325510, F324658. *Sun Rent-a-car*, Arequipa 504, T/F325456. *S y S Rent-a-car*, Libertad 777, T/F326773. **Transport**

Air connections There are daily flights to and from **Lima** with *AeroPerú* and *Aero Continente*. Also daily flights to and from **Chiclayo** with *Aero Continente*; to/from **Trujillo** with *AeroPerú*. *AeroPerú* has international flights to **Guayaquil** twice a week. Check all flight details in advance. For **local private flights**, contact pilot *Félix Pérez*, Corpac 212, Castilla Piura, T324979, or through Aerotour SA, Lima, T4415884.

Bus Most companies are on Avda Sánchez Cerro, blocks 11 and 12 (unless stated otherwise those listed below are found here). To **Lima**, 1,038 kilometres, 14-16 hours, US$13, on the Panamericana Norte. Most buses stop at the major cities on route; *Civa* is at Bolognesi y Avda Sullana, T328093. To **Chiclayo**, 190 kilometres, 3 hours, US$3, several buses daily. Also several daily buses to **Trujillo**, 7 hours, 487 kilometres, US$6. To **Tumbes**, 282 kilometres, 5 hours, US$5.25, several buses daily, eg *Cruz del Sur* (on Bolognesi) and El Dorado; also colectivos, US$8. To **Talara**, US$1.75, 2 hours, with *Talara Express* and *EPPO*. To **Paita**, depart from Avda Sullana (east side) near Ica. To **Máncora**, US$3.50, 3 hours, with *EPPO* and *El Dorado*. There are no direct buses to Bagua, Jaén or Chachapoyas from Piura, they only leave from Chiclayo.

  Crossing to Ecuador: a bus to **Aguas Verdes** leaves at 2300 and arrives at 0500, US$5.50. There are frequent buses to **Sullana**, 38 kilometres, 30 minutes (US$0.50), and colectivos (US$1); they leave from Roma y Sánchez Cerro and Loreto y Sánchez Cerro. To **La Tina** on the Ecuadorean frontier, is a further 122 kilometres, 2-3 hours, US$3. It's best to take an early bus to Sullana (start at 0630, every 20 minutes), then a colectivo.

Airline offices *Aero Continente*, Grau 140, T328223. *Aeroperú*, Libertad 951, T328297. **Banks** *Banco de Crédito*, Grau y Tacna. Cash and TCs (no commission), cheques changed in the mornings only. *Banco Continental*, Plaza de Armas. Changes TCs with commission. *Banco Latino*, changes cash only. *Casa de cambio* at Edificio Plaza Fuerte, Arequipa cuadra 6. Street **Directory**

North Coast

changers can be found on Grau and Arequipa. **Communications** Post Office: on the corner of Libertad and Ayacucho on Plaza de Armas is not too helpful. Perhaps it's better going to *Hotel Los Portales*. **Telecommunications:** Loreto 259, national and international phone and fax. Also at Ovalo Grau 483. **Embassies & consulates** *Honorary British Consul*, Casilla 193, T325693, Mr Henry Stewart. *Honorary German Consul*, Jutta Moritz de Irazola, Las Amapolas K6, Urb Miraflores, Casilla 76, T332920, F320310. **Hospitals & medical services** Dentist: *Susana Raygada Huaman*, Avda Grau 185, T326794. Speaks English. **Laundry** *Lavandería Liz-to*, Tacna 785. Charges by weight. **Tour companies & travel agents** There are several travel agents around the plaza. Particularly helpful is *Piura Tours*, C Ayacucho 585, T328873. The manager Mario speaks very good English. He will arrange transport to Tumbes with the driver delivering *El Tiempo* newspapers who picks you up from your hotel around 0300 and drops you off where the colectivos leave for the border. This costs only slightly more than the bus (US$9 instead of US$5) but is safe and easy. Also helpful is *Amauta Tours*, Apurimac 580, T322976, F322277. **Tourist offices** Information at the *Ministerio de Industria y Turismo*, Gobierno Regional, Urb San Eduardo, at the north end of town, helpful when there are problems. *Touring y Automóvil Club del Perú*, Sánchez Cerro 1237, have only outdated maps.

Around Piura

Catacaos 12 kilometres to the southwest of Piura, the village is famous for its *chicha* (maize beer) – though be careful as the quality is not always reliable – and *picanterías*, which are local restaurants, some with music. *La Casa de Tales* is recommended. The village is also noted for its *artesanía* such as tooled leather, gold and silver filigree jewellery, wooden articles and straw hats, though prices are relatively high. the village is also renowned for its celebrations in Holy Week. Colectivos leave Piura from Plaza Pizarro, US$0.50; also buses, US$0.35.

Narihualá Two kilometres south of Catacaos is the Narihualá archaeological site. It includes a large adobe pyramid, 40 metres high, from the Tallán culture which populated the Chira and Piura valleys before it was conquered by the Chimús.

Sechura On the coast near Piura is the town of Sechura. The fine 17th-century cathedral has a lovely west front which has been under renovation for a long time and is normally closed to the public. *Hospedaje de Dios* is usually full of workmen from the oil terminal at Bayovar, which is forbidden to visitors.

San Pedro San Pedro has a huge lagoon with edible crabs, flamingoes and a superb beach and a fierce sun. It's best visited in the week. There are no hotels or facilities whatsoever. Take a bus or colectivo to the right fork past Vice, about 10 kilometres from Sechura, then hitch.

Yacila Yacila is a picturesque fishing village with a few fish restaurants and a church on the beach. Nearby are La Tortuga, Parachique, Matacaballo (which is the best beach of these four places), Chullachay (the nearest beach to Sechura), Los Puertos and Angostura. Balsa boats are common on this part of the coast.

At Los Cangrejos beach nearby you can rent an apartment from Sr Belcázar, but there is little food available. A motel opens in summer, but no facilities in winter. Yacila can be reached from Piura by taking a bus or colectivo for Paita.

Paita

The port for the area, 50 kilometres from Piura, Paita (*Population*: 51,500) exports cotton, cotton seed, wool and flax. Built on a small beach, flanked on three sides by a towering, sandy bluff, it is connected with Piura and Sullana by paved highways.

It is a very old fishing port. Several colonial buildings survive, but they are in poor condition. Bolívar's mistress, Manuela Sáenz, lived the last 24 years of her life in Paita, after being exiled from Quito. She supported herself until her death in 1856 by weaving and embroidering and making candy after refusing the fortune left her by her husband. The house can be visited if you ask the people living in it, but there's not much to see. Fishing, fishmeal and whaling (at Tierra Colorada, 6½ kilometres south of Paita) are prosperous industries.

On a bluff looming over Paita is a small colonial fortress built to repel pirates. **Sights** Paita was a port of call for Spanish shipping en route from Lima to Panama and Mexico. It was a frequent target for attack, from Drake (1579) to Anson (1741).

25 kilometres up the coast is **Colán**, reached by driving down a large, sandy bluff (no public transport). Near the base is a striking and lonely church over 300 years old, but in very poor condition. There is a good beach, but Colán is rather derelict since the agrarian reform. It used to be the favourite resort of the estate-owners.

Sleeping D *Miramar*, Malecón J Chávez 418, opposite Credicoop Paita, T611083. A **Essentials** filthy old wooden mansion on seafront. E *Las Brisas*, Avda Ugarte. The best, with bathroom but little cold water, safe. *El Mundo*, on 300 block of Bolívar. Not bad but short-stay. *Pacífico*, Plaza de Armas 140, T611013. There are others but none is recommendable and mostly full anyway.

Eating The restaurant on 2nd floor of Club Liberal building, Jorge Chávez 161, serves good fish, seafood and crêpes, and is good value. *El Mundo*, Jr Junín. Quite good. There are others on the Plaza de Armas.

Transport There are colectivos and buses from Piura. TUPPSA, Sullana 527, Parque Cortéz, leaves every hour; 45 minutes, US$0.90.

Directory Banks *Credicoop Paita*, Jr Junín 380. Changes dollars cash, the guard is helpful.

East from Piura

50 kilometres northeast of Piura and 10 kilometres off the old Pan-American **Chulucanas** Highway is the small town of Chulucanas, centre of the lemon and orange growing area and, more famously, of local pottery production.

An ancient pottery technique has been discovered and revived here in the last 30 years. The local potters formerly produced only large, utilitarian terracotta pots, until the 1960s when graverobbers brought to light examples of pottery from the Vicus and Tallane cultures dating from the second half of the first millennium BC.

A group of Quechua pottery specialists researched and experimented with forms and techniques based on the precolumbian finds. These produce a very subtle and unusual effect. At first, the potters imitated the forms of the Vicus pieces but gradually they began to develop their own stylized figures. The most popular form is now the *Chichera*, a fat lady who makes and sells chicha.

The most creative potters now produce unique and highly-prized pieces, which are signed and then sold in galleries and shops in Lima and abroad. Excellent ceramics can also be bought in the town, at a shop on the plaza and

North Coast

three others are within one block. A pottery school is five kilometres away, but inaccessible in the rainy season.

Sleeping, eating and transport F *Hotel Ica*, Ica 636. *Restaurant Cajamarquino*, at Ayacucho 530. Good. **Combis** leave from Piura; US$1.50.

Canchaque The paved road continues from Chulucanas southeast to Morropán from where a dirt road goes to Canchaque, a delightfully-situated small centre for coffee, sugar-cane and fruit production.

Sleeping and transport F *Hostal Don Félix*, on the main plaza, is just tolerable. Otherwise there's basic clean accommodation for about US$2 on the right hand side of church. **Buses** leave from Piura on Sánchez Cerro at 1200; 6 hours, US$3. They are often cancelled during the rainy season.

Huancabamba

The difficult and tiring road, impossible for ordinary vehicles in the wet season, continues over a pass in the Andes of more than 3,000 metres for 69 kilometres to Huancabamba.

This very pretty town in a wonderful setting has three claims to fame. First, the predominance of European features, due to the fact that it was an important Spanish settlement in colonial times. Second, it is called 'the walking town, *la ciudad que camina*', as it is built on irregularly slipping strata which cause much subsidence. Evidence for this includes the fall of the bridge over the Río Huancabamba.

The third, and by far the most remarkable claim to fame, is that Huancabamba is the base for reaching **Las Guaringas**, a series of lakes at about 4,000 metres. Around here live the most famous witchdoctors of Peru, to whom sick people flock from all over the country and abroad.

Buses to the lakes leave at 0400 from the main plaza. Horses to the lakes can be hired for US$5. There are also trips to the village of San Antonio below Lago Carmen, and the village of Salalá below Lago Shumbe, where there is accommodation at **G** *Hotel San José* (very basic, take your own food). Ignacio León, who owns a *bodega* opposite *El Dorado* (see below) runs an early pick-up service to the outlying villages and takes trips at negotiable prices.

Local specialities include *rompope*, a rich and strong drink made of egg, spices and *cañazo* (sugar-cane spirit), roast *cuy* (guinea-pig) and local cheeses. The town hosts a tourist week in early July and the *Virgen del Carmen* festival in mid-July.

Sleeping and transport F *Hotel El Dorado*, on the main plaza. Good, clean, informative owner, with restaurant. There are also a couple of others on the plaza. A **bus** from Piura to Canchaque and Huancabamba leaves daily at 0900 and 1000 (at least 10 hours, US$9), from the Civa office at Avda Ramón Castilla 196. Buy your ticket early on the day before travelling. It returns from Huancabamba at 0700 and 1000. A truck costs US$11.50. If driving, take the Pan-American Highway south of Piura for 66 kilometres where there is a signpost to Huancabamba.

Warning In late 1995 Huancabamba remained a focus of terrorist activity. Make local enquiries before travelling to the area.

Ayabaca 225 kilometres northeast of Piura in the highlands is the pleasant town of Ayabaca (2,850 metres). This is the access point for the **Aypate** archaeological site and the **Samanga** hieroglyphics. It is also the home of **El Señor Cautivo de**

Aybaca. Many devotees make pilgrimages to his shrine, especially on 12 October. There are several *hostales* in town. Buses leave from Piura in the morning, starting at 0800, from the Mercado Modelo; 6 hours, US$7.

Sullana

Sullana (*Population*: 147,361), 39 kilometres north of Piura, is built on a bluff over the fertile Chira valley and is a busy, modern place. Avda José de Lama, once a dusty, linear market, has a green, shady park with benches along the centre. Many of the bus companies have their offices along this avenue. San Martín is the main commercial street. Parks and monuments were added in 1994/5, which have greatly improved the city's appearance. At the entrance, on the Pan-American Highway is an interesting mosaic statue of an iguana. There are lookouts over the Chira valley at Plaza Bolognesi and by the arches near the Plaza de Armas. The local fiesta and agricultural fair is *Reyes*, held on 5-29 January.

   NB Although the city is safer than it once was, you should still take great care by the market and where colectivos leave for the Ecuadorean border.

Sleeping **A3** *Hostal La Siesta*, Avda Panamericana 400, T/F502264, at the entrance to town. Hot water, fan, cable TV, **B** with cold water, pool, restaurant, laundry. **D** *Hostal Aypate*, Avda José de Lama 112, T502013. With bathroom, hot water, fan, clean, comfortable. **D** *Hostal Turicarami*, San Martín 814, T502899. With bathroom, fan, some rooms have hot water, clean, **E** without bathroom or fan. **E** *Hostal Fernando*, Grau 703, T500727. With bathroom, fan, TV, clean, friendly. **E** *Hostal Lion's*

Essentials
■ *on maps*
Price codes:
see inside front cover

Sullana

Río Chira

To Tumbes

To Piura

North Coast

Transport to Ecuadorean border

Malecón Huaman de los

Córdova
Bolivar
La Mar
Sta Rosa
Plaza de Armas
San Martín   ■5
Sucre
Leoncio Prado
Callao
Lima
Tarapacá
E-Palacios
Dos de Mayo
Tacna
Piura
■3
Grau
2■
Ugarte
⛺1
✉
4■   ■1
Espinar
Pesary Tours○
♪
Av José de Lama
La Quebrada
Piérola
⛺2   Canal
Balta

0 metres 100
0 yards 110

■ Sleeping	3. Hostal Lions Palace	⛺ Bus Stations
1. Hostal Aypate	4. Hostal San Miguel	1. Cruz del Sur
2. Hostal Fernando	5. Hostal Turicarami	2. Ormeño-Continental

Palace, Grau 1030, T502587. With bathroom, fan, patio, pleasant, quiet. **E** *Hostal San Miguel*, C J Farfán 204, T500679. Cheaper without bathroom, basic, helpful, good showers, staff will spray rooms against mosquitoes, cafeteria. **F** *Hostal Príncipe*, Espinal 588. Clean and friendly. **G** per person *Buenos Aires*, Avda Buenos Aires, 15 minutes southeast from the city centre in an unsafe neighbourhood. Friendly, dirty bathrooms.

● *on maps* **Eating** *El Parque*, E Palacios 173, corner of San Martín. Good value set meal, expensive à la carte, good quality and service, recommended. *Chifa Canton*, Farfán 248. Good cheap food, open evenings only. *Due Torri*, E Palacios 122. Italian and regional, popular with locals. *Pollería Ibañez*, J de Lama 350. Grilled meats and chicken. There are several other restaurants nearby.

Transport Taxis Radio Taxis, T502210/504354. There are several daily buses to and from **Tumbes**, 244 kilometres, 4-5 hours US$5. To **Piura**, 38 kilometres, 30 minutes, US$0.50, there are frequent buses and colectivos, US$1, taxi US$2. If you have time, it is worth continuing to Piura rather than staying in Sullana, but note that the bus from the border leaves you in an unsafe part of town (see above). To **Chiclayo** and **Trujillo** see under Piura. To **Lima**, 1,076 kilometres, 14-16 hours, US$9-18, several buses daily, most coming from Tumbes or Talara. A luxury overnight bus is US$18: with Cruz del Sur, at Ugarte 1019; and Continental (Ormeño), Tarapacá 1007. Colectivos to Paita, Colán and Esmeralda leave from the main road parallel to the market. Buses to Máncora and Talara (Empresa EPPO) leave from the market area.

Directory Banks *Banco de Crédito*, San Martín 685. Will change cash and TCs. There are also *casas de cambio* and street changers on San Martín by Tarapacá. **Communications** Post Office: at Farfán 326. **Telecommunications:** telephone and fax at Miró Quesada 213. **Tour companies & travel agents** *Pesa Tours*, Espinar 301 y Tarapacá, T/F502237. For airline tickets (flights from Piura) and information, helpful and friendly. **Useful addresses** Immigration: Grau 939.

North to Ecuador

Talara

135 kilometres from Piura and 1,177 kilometres from Lima, is Talara (*Population*: 44,500. *Phone code*: 074), the main centre of the coastal oil area, with a state-owned 60,000 barrel-a-day oil refinery and a fertilizer plant. Set in a desert oasis, the city is a triumph over formidable natural difficulties, but was badly damaged in both the 1983 and 1997/98 floods and has many shanty districts. Water is piped 40 kilometres from the Río Chira. Talara is reached via a five kilometre side road east off the Pan-American Highway. La Peña beach, two kilometres away, is still unspoilt.

Paved highways connect the town with the Negritos, Lagunitos, La Brea and other oilfields. Of historical interest are the old tarpits at La Brea, 21 kilometres inland from Punta Pariñas, south of Talara, and near the foot of the Amotape mountains. Here the Spaniards boiled the tar to get pitch for caulking their ships. Punta Pariñas itself is the westernmost point of South America.

Essentials **Sleeping NB** All hotels in Talara have problems with the water supply. **A3** *Pacífico*, Avda Aviación y Arica, T/F381719. The most luxurious in town, suites, hot water, pool, restaurant, bar, parking, pay in dollars. Other top grade hotels are: *Suites Punta Esmeralda*, Avda Aviación sin número, bungalows, swimming pool. *Hostal Charito*, Avda B 143, T381600. **D** *Hostal César*, Avda Salaverry 9, T382364, T/F381591. With bathroom, clean, rather shabby carpets, fan, safe, snack bar. **D** *Residencial Grau*, Avda Grau

The old man and the marlin

Though Ernest Hemingway's famous novel, The Old Man and the Sea, was set in a Cuban fishing village, the people of Cabo Blanco, on the north coast of Peru, claim that the great writer was inspired by their own fishing waters.

The protagonist of the book, the old fisherman, Santiago, was perhaps the product of Hemingway's own obsession with the idea of catching a marlin weighing more than 1,500 pounds. One of the very few places where such a feat is possible is off the coast of Cabo Blanco. Here, in the 1950s, the marlin were abundant and reached extraordinary sizes. Indeed, during that decade Cabo Blanco became a sort of world sport fishing capital and fishermen the world over congregated there to chase the great black marlin, the largest and the most difficult to catch owing to its tremendous strength.

So it was that when Hollywood producers decided to make a film based on Hemingway's novel they realized that the only place they could find a suitably large fish was in the waters off Cabo Blanco. In April 1955, the shooting team arrived with the writer, who was there to help them locate the fish that would appear in the movie.

Hemingway wasn't too interested in the movie, he was along for the fishing and quickly struck up a rapport with the down-to-earth local fisherfolk. In one particularly poignant anecdote they made him a gift of a bottle of pisco, a popular grape brandy, with a note saying "As long as the grapevines cry, I will drink their tears." The following morning, before going out to fish, the writer met those who had given him the pisco, smiled and said to them in Spanish, "I have drunk the tears."

Hemingway did not realize his dream of the 1,500 pound marlin during almost 2 months on the Peruvian coast, though he did manage to catch one weighing a little over 900 pounds. It was one of the largest black marlin he had ever caught and probably the last one of that size he would catch during the few remaining years of his life.

77, T382841, near the main plaza. Clean, friendly, possible to park one motor bike, owner changes dollars. **E** *Hostal Talara*, Avda del Ejército 217, T382186. Clean and comfortable. Other cheap hotels include: *Hostal El Sol*, Avda G 89, T380823; *Hostal Modelo*, Centro Comercial La Florida, T381934; *Hostal JJ*, El Parque 33, T382784.

Eating The better restaurants can be found in the main hotels. There are many cheap restaurants on the main plaza: *Bar Peña Cinthia*, Parque 14-10. *Rinconcito Chimbotano*, Parque 78-12. *Pierre*, Parque 5-17. *La Paquita*, Avda B 89. *Pichicho's*, Centro Cívico 131. *Centro Bar*, at the market. *Snack Larco*, Esplanada Cine Grau 3.

Transport Buses to and from **Tumbes**, 171 kilometres, 3 hours, US$3.50, several daily. Most come from Piura and most stop at major towns going north. To **El Alto** (Cabo Blanco), 32 kilometres, 30 minutes, US$0.75, continuing to Máncora, 28 kilometres, 30 minutes, US$0.75. To **Piura**, 111 kilometres, 2 hours, US$1.75. To **Lima**, US$15.

Beaches north of Talara

32 kilometres north of Talara, is the small port of Cabo Blanco, famous for **Cabo Blanco** its excellent sea-fishing and surfing. The scenery has, unfortunately, been spoilt by numerous oil installations. The turn-off from the Pan-American Highway is at the town of **El Alto**, where many oil workers are housed. There are several basic hotels here. Camping is permitted free of charge at Cabo Blanco, on the beach or by the Fishing Club overlooking the sea, at least in the off-season, June-December. The film of Hemingway's *The Old Man and the Sea* was shot here.

North Coast

Marlin grew scarce in the late 1960s due to commercial fishing and to climatologic and maritime factors but in the last few years the Marlin have returned. The old Fishing Club, built in the 1950s, has been remodelled in the shape of the *Fishing Club Lodge Hotel*. A launch also provides all the necessary facilities for deep-sea fishing. Now, would-be Ernest Hemingways can return to Cabo Blanco in search of their dream catch.

Sleeping B *Fishing Club Lodge*, clean, attractive, restaurant, pool, watersports, likely to be full in the New Year period. Recommended. **D** per person *El Merlín*, situated right on the beach, good value, huge rooms, good restaurant.

Los Organos Los Organos, another oil workers' town, is 15 kilometres north of El Alto, at Km 1,152 on the Pan-American Highway. There is accommodation at the *Hotel Club Náutilus*, at the north end of town.

Past **Las Arenas** resort, four kilometres south of Máncora, the road is impassable due to the damage wreaked by the 1997/98 floods. The beach is completely unspoiled, with armies of small crabs and abundant bird life, including frigates and masked and brown pelicans.

Máncora

13 kilometres north of Los Organos is Máncora, a small, attractive resort with good beaches. The water here is warm enough for bathing. This stretch of coast is famous for surfing (best November-March) and for its excellent *mero* (grouper).

The Pan-American Highway runs through the centre of town and is the main street, called Avenida Piura. At the north end of town the beach is inaccessible and dirty, and this is not a safe area. South of Máncora along the coastal road (old Pan-American Highway) are some excellent beaches which are being developed. There are several hotels (see below) and many beach homes of well-to-do Limeños.

Fresh water is piped into the area, producing the incongruous but welcome sight of green lawns and lush gardens between the sea and desert cliffs. There is a line of rocks parallel to the beach, which form interesting bathing pools at low tide, though these can be dangerous at high tide.

Essentials **Sleeping** Prices can increase by up to 100% in high season (December-March). Accommodation is listed heading from south to north. **D** *Punta Ballenas*, south of Cabo Blanco bridge at the southern entrance to town, T4470437 (Lima). **B** in the high season, with bathroom, clean, lovely setting on beach, friendly, garden with small pool, expensive restaurant. Recommended. **D** *La Posada*, by Cabo Blanco bridge, follow the dry river bed away from the beach. **C** in the high season, in a private home, nice garden, hammocks, rooms for larger groups, meals on request, parking, camping possible, good local knowledge, friendly, owner sometimes does tours in the hinterland. **E** *Sol y Mar*, Piura cuadra 2, on the beach. With bathroom, basic, clean, restaurant, popular with surfers. Recommended. **E** per person *El Angolo*, Piura 262, on the beach. With bathroom, basic, nice terrace, friendly, restaurant, camping permitted in garden. Recommended. **E** *Hostal Samara*, Piura 336. Includes breakfast, shared bathroom, 3 rooms in a private house. **E/F** *Bambú*, Piura 636. Basic, shared bathroom, clean, friendly. **E/F** *Hospedaje Crillon/Tía Yola*, Paita 168, 1 block east of Piura, behind the Tepsa office. Shared bathroom, plenty of water, clean, friendly. Recommended. **F** *Máncora*, Piura 641. Shared bathroom, very basic, the cheapest in town.

The following places are along the old Pan-American Highway south of town are: **A2** *Las Pocitas*, 2 kilometres south of Máncora, T/F4722065 (Lima). 13 rooms, attractive, nice pool and garden by the beach, very comfortable, friendly, arrange fishing and harpooning trips, balsa rafts, excellent food at US$9 for main meal, **A2** per person full board, during high season only full board available at **A1** per person, the pocitas (rock pools at low tide) are just south of the hotel. **L3** *Las Arenas*, 3.5 kilometres south of Máncora, T/F4411542 (Lima). Full board, 8 luxury bungalows, pool, lush gardens, trampoline, playground, kayaks for use, free transport from Tumbes airport, **L2** with full board during high season.

Eating You can find excellent seafood, including lobster and grouper, on Avda Piura by the centre of town. *César*, is recommended and also hires out bicycles for US$2.50 per day. *El Arpón*, good value. Recommended. *Kiosko Betty*, close to *Sol y Mar*. Friendly, good value meals. *Regina's*, for fruit salad. Also good are *San Pedro* and *Espada*.

Sport **Horse riding** German Heidi Ritter hires horses at her ranch. US$4.50 per person for a great 2 hour guided tour through beautiful countryside. Take a moto-taxi or bicycle to El Angolo, then take the main road north and turn right after the bridge. After about 1 kilometre, just before the corrals on the right, turn right and you'll see a doorway which leads to Heidi's corrals.

Transport To **Piura** with *EPPO*, US$3.50, 3 hours. To **Tumbes** (and points in between), minivans leave when full, US$1.55, 2 hours.

Directory Banks *Tienda Marlón*, Piura 613. Changes US$ cash at poor rates. **Communications** **Telephone**: at Piura 509, opposite the church. National and international calls, also collect. This is the only telephone in town. For hotel reservations leave a message at T(074)320212.

Five kilometres east of Máncora are hot mud baths (*baños del barro*), reported to be medicinal. The access is north of town, at Km 1,168, from where it is about two kilometres to the baths. Continuing along this road to Quebrada Fernández you can reach the **El Angolo game reserve**, which extends as far south as the Río Chira. Ask at *Hostal La Posada* for tours to this area.

Playa Punta Sal

16 kilometres north of Máncora is the *Carpitas* customs checkpoint, a large modern complex, where southbound vehicles are checked. Six kilometres further north, at Km 1,187, is the turn-off for **Punta Sal Grande**, a resort town at the southern end of beautiful Playa Punta Sal, a three kilometres long sandy beach, with calm surf. A few restaurants are open in the high season only and the town is very quiet in the low season. Water is trucked in so it is important to conserve it. Camping is reported to be safe along the beach between Talara and Punta Sal (Punta Negra is recommended).

Sleeping For reservations in any of the hotels in the area, leave a message at Cancas **Essentials** public telephone, T/F(074)320251. The hotels in town are listed running from north to south. **C** *Los Delfines*, near the beach. Shared bathroom, clean, nice rooms, restaurant open in high season, meals on request in low season, vegetarian available, Canadian-run, very friendly, full board **A2**, during high season **A1** full board, **A3** for a room only in high season. **C** *Hua*, on the beach, T4485667 (Lima). With bathroom, pleasant terrace overlooking ocean, discount for IYHF card holders, meals available (US$15 for 3 meals), **B** in the high season.

D *Estancia*, Calle Carrosable, set back from the beach. 4 rooms, 1 with bathroom, ask José Devescovi at first house at the entrance to town, **B** in the high season. **D** *Las Terrazas*, at the southern end of the bay, T/F4337711 (Lima). Set on a terraced hill overlooking the ocean, has a few cheaper rooms without bathroom, nice views, pleasant, comfortable, friendly, meals available, British-run, **A1** full board in high season. **D** *Caballito de Mar*, at the southern end of the bay, T4426229 (Lima). Some rooms with bathroom, nice location overlooking the ocean, comfortable, friendly, **B** full board, **A2** full board in high season.

The north end of the beach is known as **Punta Sal Chica**: **A3** *Puerto Azul Beach Resort*, access road from Panamericana Km 1,190, T/F4444131 (Lima). Nice spacious bungalows on the beach, pool, tours to mangroves and Tumbes, Tumbes airport pick-up US$20, **A2** full board, **L3** full board in high season.

L3 *Punta Sal Club Hotel*, access road at Km 1,192, T(074)521386 (radio-phone via Tumbes), T/F442-5961 (Lima). 18 bungalows, 12 rooms, solar heated water, attractive, comfortable, relaxing, good beach, watersports, pool, horse riding, deep-sea fishing, transport to Tumbes airport US$10 per person, **L2** with full board in high season, recommended.

Punta Sal to Los Pinos

The fishing village of **Cancas** is just north of Punta Sal Chica (Km 1,193). It has a few shops, restaurants, a gas station and a police checkpoint where vehicles must stop and southbound foreigners may be required to register. From Punta Mero (Km 1,204) north, the beach is used by *larveros*, extracting shrimp larvae from the ocean for use in the shrimp industry, and is no longer considered safe for camping.

Essentials Several new resorts are being built between Punta Mero and Tumbes. **A1** *Hotel Playa Florida*, at Km 1,222, resort/casino/condominium complex, T/F(074)320251, T4289110 (Lima). *Hotel Punta Camarón*, at Km 1,236. With swimming pool. **E** per person *Casa Grillo Centro Ecoturistico Naturista*, Los Pinos 563, between Bocapán and Los Pinos, 30 kilometres from Tumbes, T/F(074)525207, T/F4462233 (Lima). To get there take a colectivo from Tumbes market to Los Pinos, or get off bus on Pan-American Highway at Km 1,236.5. Youth Hostel with excellent restaurant including vegetarian meals, very friendly, great place to relax, variety of rooms, shared bath, hot water, laundry, also surfing, scuba diving, fishing, cycling, trekking, camping available, recommended.

Zorritos Zorritos, 27 kilometres south of Tumbes, is an important fishing centre. It was heavily damaged by the 1997/98 flooding but has a good beach (the water is not oily). The first South American oil well was sunk here in 1863. **D** *Hostal Turístico Zorritos*, former Hotel de Turistas. Several new hotels and resorts have recently been built, such as *Punta Sal Chica* and *Puerto Loco Beach*. The better of the 2 restaurants is *Arriba Perú*.

Caleta La Cruz This is the only part of the Peruvian coast where the sea is warm all year. There are two good beaches near Tumbes, one is at Caleta La Cruz 16 kilometres southwest, where Pizarro landed in 1532. The original Cruz de Conquista was taken to Lima. Regular colectivos run back and forth from Tumbes, US$0.80 each way. There is accommodation at **E** *Motel*.

Puerto Pizarro Puerto Pizarro is a small fishing beach 13 kilometres northeast of Tumbes. Take a motor or sailing boat to visit the mangroves from Puerto Pizarro pier (fixed tariffs), or across the lagoon to reach a good clean sandy beach. It's about a 10 minute journey. The Festival of San Pedro y San Pablo takes place on 29-30 June. There's plenty of fishing and swimming and the beach is ideal for windsurfing and water-skiing but there are few facilities. To get there, take colectivo No 6 from Tumbes; US$0.50. **Sleeping and eating** *Puerto Pizarro Motel*, bungalows 10 kilometres from the beach. No hot water, restaurant is expensive and slow but serves good food, swimming pool (which is usually empty), watersports. *Restaurant Venecia*, cheap seafood, but beware shellfish which may cause stomach upsets.

Tumbes

Tumbes, about 141 kilometres north of Talara, and 265 kilometres north of Piura, is the most northerly of Peruvian towns. It is a garrison town, so don't photograph the military or their installations – they will destroy your film and probably you as well.

Population: 34,000
Phone code: 074
Coloured map 1, grid A1

Ins and outs

A taxi to the airport costs US$4, 20 minutes. Minivans charge US$1.50. Taxis meet flights to take passengers to the border for US$7-9. There are no minivans from the airport to the border. Beware of overcharging. All bus companies have offices on Avda Tumbes. **NB** Travellers who hold a Tumbes-Huaquillas-Guayaquil ticket with Panamericana Internacional (bought outside Peru as an onward ticket) should note that Panamericana does not have an office in Tumbes. However, this ticket can be used for a colectivo (but not a taxi) to the border, caught at the corner of Piura and Bolívar. If the colectivo is full, you will be transferred to another company. Then make a connection with a bus at the border.

Getting there

Everything is fairly conveniently located close to the Plaza de Armas, although transport to the Ecuadorean border is a little bit farther out. Hotels are mostly central to the north of the river either side of Avda Tumbes and Bolívar. There is a long promenade, the Malecón Benavides, decorated with arches, beside the high banks of the Río Tumbes, views of the river are good from here.

Getting around

North Coast

Sights

There are some old houses in **Calle Grau**, and a colonial public library in the **Plaza de Armas** with a small museum. The **cathedral** is 17th century but was restored in 1985. There are two pedestrian malls, arranged with benches and plants, Paseo de Los Libertadores on Bolívar and Paseo de la Concordia on San Martín, both leading north from the Plaza de Armas. There is a sports stadium and cockfights in the Coliseo de Gallos, Avda Mcal Castilla, 9th block, on Sunday at 1500. Special fights take place on 28 July and 8 December.

Essentials

NB Avda Tumbes is still sometimes referred to by its old name of Teniente Vásquez. The water supply is poor.

A3 *Sol de la Costa*, San Martín 275, Plazuela Bolognesi, T523991, F523298. Clean, hot water, minibar, fan, restaurant, good food and service, parking extra, has nice garden with swimming pool, racketball court, provides some tourist information.
    D *Asturias*, Mcal Castilla 305, T522569. With bathroom, fan, cafeteria, clean,

Sleeping
■ *on maps*
Price codes:
see inside front cover

comfortable, friendly, recommended. **D** *César*, Huáscar 333, T/F522883. With bathroom, fan, TV. **D** *Chicho*, Tumbes 327, T/F422282. With bathroom, fan, mosquito net, TV, clean. **D** *Continental*, Huáscar 111, T523510. With bathroom, fan, pool. **D** *Florián*, Piura 400 near El Dorado bus company, T522464, F524725, clean, private bath, fan. Recommended. **D** *Kikos*, Bolívar 462, T523777. With bathroom, basic. **D** *Lourdes*, Mayor Bodero 118, 1 block from the main plaza, T/F522758. With bathroom, fan, clean, friendly, roof restaurant, slow service. Recommended. **D** *Roma*, Bolognesi 425 Plaza de Armas, T524137. With bathroom, fan, basic.

E *Amazonas*, Avda Tumbes 317, T520629. With bathroom, fan, clean, friendly, water supply in the mornings is unreliable. **E** *Córdova*, J R Abad Puell 777. With bathroom, no hot water, safe, friendly, safe for motorcycle parking. **E** *Elica*, Tacna 319, T523870. With bathroom, clean, fan, quiet, good. **E** *El Estoril*, Huáscar 361, 2 blocks from the main plaza, T524906. With bathroom, good, clean, friendly, discount for long stay. **E** *Franco*, San Martín, Paseo de la Concordia, T525295. With bathroom, fan. **E** *Gandolfo*, Bolognesi 420, T522868. With bathroom, **F** without, fan, OK. **E** *Hostal Premier*, Tumbes 227, T523077. With bathroom, basic, dirty. **E** *Hostal Tumbes*, Grau 614, T522203. With bathroom, cold water, fan, friendly, clean, good value. Recommended. **E** *Internacional*, Feijoó, T525976. With bathroom, basic, dirty. **E** *Italia*, Grau 733, T520677. Cold showers, friendly, noisy but good. **E** *Joalsy*, Mcal Castilla 539, T522199, by the market and where minivans leave for border. Basic, with bathroom,

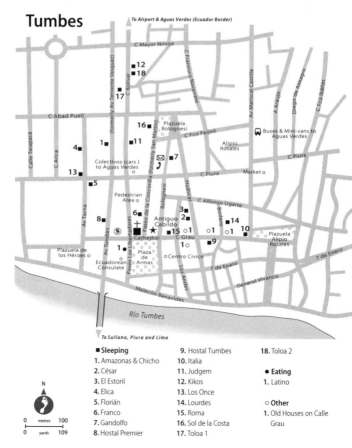

Tumbes

■ **Sleeping**	9. Hostal Tumbes	18. Toloa 2
1. Amazonas & Chicho	10. Italia	
2. César	11. Judgem	● **Eating**
3. El Estoril	12. Kikos	1. Latino
4. Elica	13. Los Once	
5. Florián	14. Lourdes	○ **Other**
6. Franco	15. Roma	1. Old Houses on Calle
7. Gandolfo	16. Sol de la Costa	Grau
8. Hostal Premier	17. Toloa 1	

F without. **E** *Judgem*, Bolívar 344, T523530. With bathroom, basic, OK. **E** *Kalulo*, Piura 1035, T524995. With bathroom, **F** without, basic, OK, poor water supply. **E** *Los Once*, Piura 417, next to the El Dorado bus office, T523717. With bathroom, basic. **E** *Toloa 1*, Avda Tumbes 430, T523771. With bathroom, fan, clean, safe, helpful. **E** *Toloa 2*, Bolívar 458, T524135. With bathroom, fan, OK.

F *Cristina*, Mcal Castilla 758, near the market, T521617. With bathroom, basic, cheap. **F** *Sudamericano*, San Martín 110, Paseo de la Concordia. Shared bathroom, very basic. There are many other cheap hotels by the market. At holiday times it can be very difficult to find a vacant room.

Europa, off the Plaza de Armas. Recommended, particularly for omelettes. *Latino*, Bolívar 163, on Plaza de Armas. Good set meals and à la carte, also *peña* most evenings. *Chifa Wakay*, Huáscar 417. Smart, good, recommended. *Río Tumbes*, Malecón Benavides sin número, at the east end of the seafront. Excellent views of the river, pleasant atmosphere, seafood specialities.

Eating: expensive
● *on maps*

Hawaii, Avda Bolívar 235, near the Plaza de Armas. Good, big portions. *Juliban*, Grau 704. Good, generous set meal. *El Algarrobo*, Huáscar across from Club Social. Good. *El Cautivo*, on the road to the airport. Their speciality on Sunday is *Kupus*, a meat and vegetable dish cooked underground. There are other inexpensive restaurants on the Plaza de Armas and near the markets.

Eating: mid-range

Heladería La Suprema, Paseo Libertadores 298. Good ice cream, sweets and cold drinks. Next door at 296 is *Bam Bam*, for breakfast and snacks.

Try *bolas de plátano*, soup with banana balls, meat, olives and raisins, and *sudado*, a local stew.

There's a well-stocked supermarket **Anilu**, on Bolívar.

Shopping

Air connections Daily flights to and from Lima with *Aero Continente*. It is essential to reconfirm flights 24 hours before departure. It is better to buy tickets in Tumbes rather than at the airport.

Transport

Bus Note that *El Niño* caused important road damage from Tumbes south to Chiclayo in 1998. This will gradually be repaired, however travel times in this region in June 1998 were up to twice as long as the normal times shown below.

Daily buses to and from **Lima**, 1,320 kilometres, normally 12-16 hours (but up to 24 hours in June 1998), US$15 (normal service), US$20 (luxury service).

Several buses travel this route daily. All bus companies have offices on Avda Tumbes: *Expreso Continental* (Ormeño group), 314; *Cruz del Sur*, 319 (T522627); *Oltursa*, 324 and 359, daily 1330, recommended; *Trans Chiclayo*, 446 (T525260); *Tepsa*, 199, old buses, unsafe, often full, not recommended. For other companies, ask around. Cheaper ones usually leave 1600-2100, and more expensive ones 1200-1400. Except for luxury service, most buses to Lima stop at major cities en route, although you may be told otherwise. You can get tickets to anywhere between Tumbes and Lima quite easily, although buses are often booked well in advance, so if arriving from Ecuador you may have to stay overnight. Piura is a good place for connections.

To **Talara**, 171 kilometres, US$3.50, 3 hours. To **Sullana**, 244 kilometres, 3-4 hours, US$4.50, several buses daily. To **Piura**, 4-5 hours, 282 kilometres, US$5.25; with *Trans Chiclayo, Cruz del Sur, El Dorado* (Piura 459) 6 a day, *Dorado Express* (Tumbes 297). *Colectivo* (Tumbes 302) costs US$7. To **Chiclayo**, 552 kilometres, 6 hours, US$7, several each day with *Cruz del Sur, El Dorado, Dorado Express, Oltursa*. To **Trujillo**, 769 kilometres, 10-11 hours, US$9, *Continental, Cruz del Sur, El Dorado, Dorado Express*. To **Chimbote**, 889 kilometres, 13-14 hours, US$10. For transport to the border, see **Frontier with Ecuador**, below.

North Coast

Directory **Banks** *Banco de Crédito*, Paseo de los Libertadores 261, for cash only, poor rates. *Banco de Comercio*, charges 5% commission. *Interbanc*, Bolívar 129, Plaza de Armas, cash and TCs at a reasonable rate, cash advance on Visa. *Banco Continental*, Bolívar 121, changes cash and Amex TCs only, US$5 commission. *Cambios Internacionales*, Avda Bolívar 161, Plaza de Armas. Cash only, good rates. Money changers on the street (on Bolívar, left of the Cathedral), some of whom are unscrupulous, give a much better rate than the banks or *cambios*, but don't accept the first offer you are given. Street changers don't change cheques. All banks close for lunch. Rates offered at the airport are bad. In general you'll get better rates at Trujillo and Piura. If you are travelling on to Ecuador, it is better to change your Soles at the border as the rate is higher. **Communications** Post Office: San Martín 208. **Entel Telephone office**, San Martín 210. Both on Paseo de la Concordia. **Embassies & consulates** Ecuadorean Consulate, Bolívar 155, Plaza de Armas, T523022, 0900-1300 and 1400-1630. Open Mon-Fri. **Laundry** *Lavandería* at Piura 1002. Pay by weight. **Tour companies & travel agents** *Rosillo Tours,* Tumbes 293, T/F523892. Information, tickets, Western Union agents. *Tumbes Tours*, Tumbes 351-A, tickets and information. **Tourist offices** *Centro Cívico*, Bolognesi 194, 2nd Flr. Helpful, provides map and leaflets. *Federación Peruana para la Conservación de la Naturaleza (FPCN)*, Avda Tarapacá 4-16, Urb Fonavi, T523412.

Around Tumbes

The Río Tumbes is navigable by small boat to the mouth of the river. It's an interesting two hour trip with fantastic birdlife and mangrove swamps.

Santuario Nacional los Manglares de Tumbes

Mosquito repellent is a must for the Tumbes area

The Santuario Nacional los Manglares de Tumbes is a national reserve, created to protect the mangrove ecosystem in the northernmost part of the Peruvian coast. It extends between the border with Ecuador in the north and Puerto Pizarro in the south.

The mangrove swamps are full of pelicans; best to visit them at high tide. A few tame birds beg for fish on the beaches. Three islands, Isla Hueso de Ballena, Isla del Amor and Isla de los Pájaros can be visited by boat (bargain hard), and are good for swimming and picnics. Take food and water.

The remains of the Cabeza de Vaca cult centre of the Tumpis Indians can be found at Corrales, five kilomteres south of Tumbes, but were heavily damaged by the 1983 and 1997/98 rains. There's a Museo de Sitio nearby.

Another access to the mangrove reserve is via the Pan-American Highway north as far as Zarumilla. Take the turn-off east, then it's nine kilometres to El Algarrobo ranger station.

Parque Nacional Cerros de Amotape

The Parque Nacional Cerros de Amotape was created to protect an area representative of the equatorial forest. It extends southeast from the south bank of the Tumbes river, towards the El Angolo game preserve northeast of Máncora. Some of the endemic species are the Tumbes crocodile, the river otter and white-winged turkeys.

Access is via the road which goes southeast from the Pan-American Highway at Bocapán (Km 1,233) to Casitas and Huásimo, it takes about two hours by car from Tumbes, and is best done in the dry season (July-November). Also access via Quebrada Fernández from Máncora and via Querecotilo and Los Encuentros from Sullana.

Zona Reservada de Tumbes

The Zona Reservada de Tumbes, formerly Bosque Nacional de Tumbes (75,000 hectares), lies to the northeast of Tumbes, between the Ecuadorean border and Cerros de Amotape National Park. It was created to protect dry equatorial forest and tropical rainforest. The wildlife includes monkeys, otters, wild boars, small cats and crocodiles.

North Coast

Access from Tumbes is via Cabuyal, Pampas de Hospital and El Caucho to the Quebrada Faical research station or via Zarumilla and Matapalo.

Frontier with Ecuador

Frontier at Aguas Verdes

Peruvian Immigration The main Peruvian immigration and customs complex is **At the border** outside Zarumilla, about 3 kilometres before the international bridge. It is open 0800-1300 and 1400-1800, Monday-Saturday, and closes at 1600 on Sunday. However there is also a small immigration office at the south end of the international bridge, which was closed in June 1998 but may be re-opened. These procedures are frequently changing so enquire locally.

Police officers on the Peruvian side of the international bridge sometimes ask for bribes. Try to avoid them if possible but if approached be courteous but firm. Porters on either side of the border charge exorbitant prices, but don't be bullied. Also note that relations between Peru and Ecuador have not always been good, but should improve following the signing of the peace treaty in October 1998.

Entering Ecuador Having obtained your exit stamp, proceed across the bridge into Huaquillas. Passports are stamped 3 kilometres north of town along the road to Machala. There's no urban transport; inter-city buses charge US$0.20 from Huaquillas; taxis US$1.50. Ecuadorean immigration is open 0800-1200 and 1400-1800, Monday-Saturday, and closes at 1600 on Sunday. The international bridge is officially open 0800-1800 daily. It is always best to cross before 1700. Allow up to 1-2 hours to complete formalities, although it can sometimes be much quicker.

With a pass from the authorities at the border you can spend the day in Huaquillas, as long as you are back by 1800. There is nothing much to see there, but Peruvians go to hunt for bargains.

Peruvian Customs There are virtually no customs formalities at the border for passengers crossing on foot, but spot-checks sometimes take place. There is a large, modern and well-organized customs checkpoint south on the Pan-American Highway between Cancas and Máncora (see above).

Crossing by Private Vehicle When driving into Peru vehicle fumigation is not required, but there is one outfit who will attempt to fumigate your vehicle with water and charge US$10. Beware of officials claiming that you need a carnet to obtain your 90-day transit permit. This is not so; cite Decreto Supremo 015-87-ICTI/TUR (but check that rules have not changed). There are frequent road tolls between Tumbes and Lima, approximately US$1, but the toll stations were closed in June 1998.

Sleeping If stuck overnight in the border area there is a hotel in **Aguas Verdes**: **E** *Hostal El Bosque*, at the south end of town on Av República de Perú 402. Shared bathroom, clean, friendly, basic, mosquito nets. There are four hotels in **Zarumilla**, at Km 1,290 on the Pan-American Highway, 5 kilometres south of Aguas Verdes. There is a signpost on the highway and the main plaza is only a few blocks away from the turn-off: **E** *Imperio*, on the plaza, T565178. Small, modern, very basic, cold water turned off at night, very clean, mosquito nets, very friendly. Recommended. **D/E** *El Rosedal*; *Caribbean*; and *Yovica*, Arica 336, T565049.

Directory Banks The money changers on the Ecuadorean side sometimes give a better rate. Beware sharp practices by money changers using fixed calculators. If you are going to change TCs into Ecuadorean sucres in Huaquillas, make sure you cross border in morning because the bank is closed after lunch. Do not change money on the minibus in Aguas Verdes, very poor rates.

Transport From Tumbes to border: colectivos leave from Calle Piura near the corner of Bolívar. US$1 per person or US$6 to hire a car, but overcharging of gringos is very common, especially from the border to Tumbes. **Make sure the driver takes you all the way to the border and not just as far as the complex 3 kilometres south of the bridge.** Minivans leave from the market area along Mcal Castilla across the Calle Alipio Rosales, US$0.50 (luggage on the roof). Run down city buses ply the same route as minivans, US$0.40, but are slower. All vehicles only leave when full, 30-45 minutes to Aguas Verdes on the Peruvian side of international bridge. They pass the turn-off for the airport from which it is a 500-metre walk to the terminal. Colectivos to the airport charge US$1.50 per person, but often ask for much more. From the border to Zarumilla by moto-taxi costs US$0.50 per person.

Into Ecuador **Huaquillas** is a small city with a reasonable selection of hotels and other services. Transport links to other parts of Ecuador (Quito, Guayaquil, Cuenca, Loja) are good. Transit Police, Customs and the Military have checkpoints on the road north so keep your passport to hand.

Frontier at La Tina-Macará

Leaving Peru At Sullana the Pan-American Highway forks. To the east it crosses the Peru-Ecuador frontier at La Tina and continues via Macará to Loja and Cuenca. The road is very scenic and is paved for 120 kilometres as far as Suyo. Work on the remaining 16 kilometres to the border was expected to be finished in 1996. The more frequently used route to the border is the coastal road which goes from Sullana northwest towards the Talara oilfields and then follows the coastline to Máncora and Tumbes (see below).

    Transport to the border Minivans leave from Sullana to the international bridge from Mercadillo Bellavista, Avda Buenos Aires y Calle 4, which is a crowded market area. They leave between 0400 and 1300 when full, US$3 per person, 2 hours. The Buenos Aires area is not safe, so it's best to take a taxi or moto-taxi to and from here. To get to Macará, walk over the bridge and take one of the pick-ups which run from the border. A bus leaves the Ecuadorean side at 1300 for Loja, so you can go from Sullana to Loja in 1 day.

At the border **Peruvian immigration** The border crossing is described as problem-free and officials are helpful. The Peruvian immigration officer can be found at the nearby *cevichería* if not at his desk. The border is reported open 0800-1800 but it may close for lunch, so it is better to cross in the morning. **Accommodation** There is one basic hotel in Suyo and two in Las Lomas (75 kilometres from Sullana).

Into Ecuador It is a 2½ kilometres taxi ride or walk from the border to **Macará**, a dusty town in a rice-growing area (*Population*: 14,296. *Altitude*: 600 metres). There are hotels and restaurants in town and money can be changed on the street or in the market (not at the bank). The fare in a pick-up from the bridge to the market in Macará is US$0.25, but beware of overcharging. From Macará there are frequent buses to Loja, 6-8 hours, US$3.50.

Northern Highlands

10

Northern Highlands

384 From the coast to Cajamarca

386 Cajamarca

394 Chachapoyas Region

396 Chachapoyas

399 Around Chachapoyas

401 South of Chachapoyas

402 Kuelap

404 Gran Vilaya

409 East of Chachapoyas

411 North of Chachapoyas

412 East to the Amazon

415 To the coast

416 Jaén

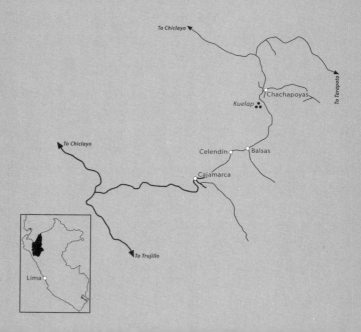

This vast area stretches from the western foothills of the Andes right across the mountains and down to the fringes of the Amazon jungle. It contains Peru's most spectacular precolumbian ruins, some of them built on a massive scale unequalled anywhere in the Americas. From the city of Cajamarca, where the Inca Atahualpa was captured by the Spanish, a tortuous road winds its way east to Chachapoyas, which lies at the centre of a region full of fantastic archaeological treasures.

From the coast to Cajamarca

Cajamarca can be reached from the coast, either directly northeast from Trujillo on a very rough road, or via Pacasmayo on a much faster paved road (see below).

The old road northeast to Cajamarca is terrible and lonely – especially for cyclists. It takes 12-15 hours by bus, as opposed to eight hours via Pacasmayo, but it is more interesting, passing over the bare puna before dropping to the Huamachuco valley.

After **Simbal** the road passes **Otusco**, an attractive Andean town with narrow cobbled streets. The town hosts a big religious festival, *Virgen de la Puerta*, on 15 December. In **Agallpampa** there is one, unsigned *hostal*. Further on, at the mining town of **Shorey**, a road branches off to **Santiago de Chuco**, birthplace of the poet César Vallejo (see **Literature**, page 530), where there is the annual festival of Santiago El Mayor in the second half of July. The main procession is on 25 July, when the image is carried through the streets. Close to **Yancabamba** is *Hostería El Viajero* and in **Quiruvilca** there is one hotel.

Huamachuco The road runs on to this colonial town, 181 kilometres from Trujillo, formerly on the royal Inca Road. It has a huge main plaza and a controversial modern cathedral. There is a colourful Sunday market.

A three hour walk takes you to the extensive ruins of hilltop pre-Inca fortifications, **Marcahuamachuco**. The ruins are some of the most dramatic and interesting in Peru. To get there, take the track which goes off to the right just after crossing the bridge on the road to Trujillo. A taxi costs US$10 per person.

Nearby, beyond the local radio station (a one hour walk), are the pre-Inca ruins of **Wiracochapampa**.

Worth seeing in the Huamachuco area are **Laguna Sausacocha** (with Inca ruins nearby) and *haciendas* Yanazara and Cochabamba, deep down in the valley of the Río Chusgón. **Yanazara**, one hour by taxi from Huamachuco, has some good thermal pools (US$0.50 per person) and basic accommodation run by priests. Yanazara is noted for its fighting bulls and is still in the hands of its long-term owner, Francisco Pinillos Montoya. There is a guest house at Cochabamba (two hours by taxi), which used to be the Andean retreat of the owners of the Laredo sugar plantation, near Trujillo. The climate, at about 2,300 metres, is mild.

Sleeping **E** *Hostal Noche Buena*, on the main plaza. New, clean, with hot showers and TV. **F** *Hostal Huamachuco*, on the plaza. Clean with hot showers. **F** *Hostal San Francisco*, Sánchez Carrión 380. Clean, hot shower. **G** *Fernando*, Bolívar 361. Good value, clean.

Eating *El Cairo*, Sánchez Carrión 754. Good food and service. Recommended. *Café Venezia*, San Martín 315, 2 blocks from the main plaza. Serves excellent cakes and pies. *Café Noche Buena*, good food, open late. *El Caribe*, on the plaza. Local dishes.

Fiestivals On the **second Sunday in August** is *Waman Raymi*, a major festival held in the ruins of Wiracochapampa (see above), a northern version of *Inti Raymi* in Cusco. A week of festivities begins on **15 August** to mark the founding of Huamacucho and features the remarkable *Turcos* – menfolk from a nearby village who wear at least 10 layered skirts when dancing.

Transport From **Trujillo**: *Trans Sánchez López* (Avda Vallejo 1390, T251270), *Trans Palacios* (España 1005, T233902), *Agreda* (Avda Tupac Amaru) and *Garrincha* each have an early morning and evening bus to **Huamachuco**, 10 hours, US$8 (US$7 return). *Sánchez López* is the most likely to have buses at other times. Take warm clothing at night. There are also colectivos from Trujillo. To **Cajamarca**, there are regular combis, 2-3 hours, US$2.

From Huamachuco buses (Trans Agreda and Garrincha which start in Trujillo and may be full by Huamachuco) run once a week to Tayabamba, on the far bank of the Marañón, passing through the old gold-mining centres of Pataz province, such as Parcoy and Buldibuyo. This journey takes a good 18 hours in 'normal' conditions. **Tayabamba**

Pataz itself is a friendly gold-mining town, about 100 kilometres from Huamachuco. From here you can reach the World Heritage Site of **El Gran Pajatén**, with its unique circular pre-Inca ruins. Ask at the Tourist Office in Cajamarca for details. A national park, Río Abiseo, incorporating Gran Pajatén and four other sites – La Playa, Las Papayas, Los Pinchudos and Cerro Central – is planned. Only archaeologists and researchers are allowed there. There are flights from Trujillo to Chagual (40 minutes) and from there it's one hour by road to Pataz. **Pataz & El Gran Pajatén**

From Huamachuco the road runs on 48 kilometres through impressive eucalyptus groves to Cajabamba, which lies in the high part of the sugar-producing Condebamba valley. It has an attractive Plaza de Armas. **F** *Flores*, on the Plaza de Armas. Friendly and clean. There are other hotels, and restaurants. Regular combis, 2-3 hours, US$2, run to Huamachuco. To Cajamarca, via San Marcos (below) Trans Palacios has morning and evening buses, 6 hours, US$5, also with Empresa Atahualpa. Expreso Cajambamba has buses to and from Trujillo (at Avenida America Sur in Trujillo). **Cajabamba**

Cajabamba can also be reached in a strenuous but marvellous three to four days' hike from **Coina**, 132 kilometres east of Trujillo at 1,500 metres in the Sierra Alto Chicama. The first day's walk brings you to *Hacienda Santa Rosa* where you stay overnight. Then you cross the mountains at about 4,000 metres, coming through Arequeda to Cajabamba. The ruins at Huacamochal may be seen en route. The scenery is spectacular. It is advisable to hire a guide, and a donkey to carry the luggage. A map of the route is available from the Post Office in Coina.

There is accommodation in Coina at **D** *Hostería El Sol* (full board or bed only), built by the late Dr Kaufmann, who opened a hospital for local people here. Details from *Hostería El Sol*, Los Brillantes 224, Santa Inés, Trujillo, T231933, Apdo 775.

The road continues from Cajabamba through **San Marcos** to Cajamarca. San Marcos is important for its Sunday cattle market. Both it and Cajabamba are on the Inca Road. There are three hotels including **G** per person *Nuevo*, with bath, water shortages, but clean and quiet. There's a bus to Cajamarca (124 kilometres), with Trans Palacios; three hours, US$2.50.

To Cajamarca via Pacasmayo

The port of Pacasmayo is the main road connection from the coast to Cajamarca (see page 349). The paved 180 kilometres road branches off the Pan-American Highway soon after it crosses the Río Jequetepeque.

Northern Highlands

Chilete 103 kilometres east of Pacasmayo (226 kilometres from Trujillo) is the mining town of Chilete. 21 kilometres from Chilete, on the road north to San Pablo, are the stone monoliths of **Kuntur Wasi**. The site is undergoing new development under a Japanese archaeological team. It now has an on-site museum, making a visit worthwhile. There's accommodation in Chilete at *Hotels Amazonas* and *San Pedro*, both **G**, both with filthy bathrooms. Rooms are hard to find on Tuesday because of the Wednesday market.

Contumazá & 40 kilometres south of Chilete is the attractive town of Contumazá on an alter-
Yonán native route from Trujillo to Cajamarca. This passes through the cane fields and rice plantations of the Chicama valley before branching off to climb over the watershed of the Jequetepeque. Further along the road to Cajamarca is Yonán, where there are petroglyphs.

Cajamarca

Population: 117,500 *Cajamarca, is a beautiful colonial town and the most important in the northern*
Altitude: 2,750 metres *highlands. This was one of the biggest cities in the Inca Empire and was where*
Phone code: 044 *the Incas and Spanish had their first showdown. Here Pizarro ambushed and*
Coloured map 1, grid C3 *captured Atahualpa, the Inca emperor. Despite their huge numerical inferiority,*
the heavily-armed Spaniards took advantage of an already divided Inca King-
dom to launch their audacious attack. The Incas attempted to save their leader
by collecting the outrageous ransom demanded by Pizarro for Atahualpa's
release. This proved futile as the Spanish, of course, executed the Inca leader
once the treasure had been collected.

Ins and outs

Getting there The airport is 3 kilometres from town; taxi US$3. It is to the northeast: take the Cerrillo road. The bus offices on the other hand are to the southeast of the centre, on the Baños del Inca road past La Recoleta church; a 20-minute walk from the Plaza de Armas.

Getting around All the main sights are clustered around the Plaza de Armas. With its many old colonial buildings it is an interesting town to wander around although the climb up Santa Apollonia hill is quite demanding.

Sights

The city's violent past is belied by today's provincial calm. Cajamarca is now better known as a producer of delicious cheese, of intricately worked mirrors (see Shopping below) and as the home of artist Andrés Zavallos, one of the founding fathers of the city's community of poets, writers, painters and musicians. Most notable of these was Mario Urteaga, the only Peruvian artist to have his work in the permanent collection at New York's Metropolitan Museum of Art.

The **Cuarto de Rescate** is not the actual ransom chamber but in fact the room where Atahualpa was held prisoner. A red line on the wall is said to indicate where Atahualpa reached up and drew a mark, agreeing to have his subjects fill the room to the line with gold and silver treasures. The room was closed to the public for centuries and used by the nuns of Belén hospital. The chamber also has two interesting murals. ■ *The entrance is on Amalia Puga beside San Francisco church. Open 0900-1300, 1500-1745 Monday-Friday,*

0900-1245 Saturday and Sunday, closed Tuesday. US$1.35. *A ticket is also valid for Belén church and nearby museums.*

The plaza where Atahualpa was ambushed and the stone altar set high on **Santa Apollonia hill** where he is said to have reviewed his subjects can also be visited (small entrance fee). There is a road to the top, or the physically fit can walk up from Calle 2 de Mayo, using the steep stairway. The view from the top, over red-tiled roofs and green fields, is worth the exertion, especially very early in the morning for the beautiful sunrises.

The **Plaza de Armas**, where Atahualpa was executed, has a 350-year-old fountain, topiary and gardens. The impressive **Cathedral**, opened in 1776, is still missing its belfry. Many belfries were left half-finished in protest against a Spanish tax levied on the completion of a church.

On the opposite side of the plaza is the 17th century **San Francisco Church**, older and more ornate than the Cathedral and home to the **Colonial Art Museum** which is filled with typically gruesome colonial paintings and icons. A guided tour of the museum includes entry to the church's spooky catacombs.

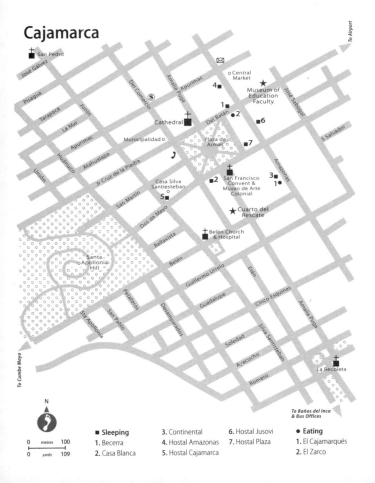

Cajamarca

Northern Highlands

■ Sleeping	3. Continental	6. Hostal Jusovi	● Eating
1. Becerra	4. Hostal Amazonas	7. Hostal Plaza	1. El Cajamarqués
2. Casa Blanca	5. Hostal Cajamarca		2. El Zarco

0 metres 100
0 yards 109

The **Complejo Belén** comprises the Institute of Culture, a museum, art gallery and a beautifully ornate church, considered the city's finest. Connected to the church is the **Pinacoteca**, a gallery of local artists' work, which was once the kitchen of an 18th century hospital for men. Across the street is a maternity hospital from the same era, now the **Archaeological Museum** (see **Museums** below). The **Cultural Institute** sells Spanish language books and good postcards and handicrafts are for sale in the cloisters of the church.

Other churches well worth seeing are **San Pedro** (Gálvez y Junín), **San José** (C M Iglesias y Angamos), **La Recoleta** (Maestro y Casanova) and **Capilla de La Dolorosa**, close to San Francisco.

The city has many old colonial houses with garden patios, and 104 elaborate carved doorways: see the **Bishop's Palace**, next to the Cathedral; the **palace of the Condes de Uceda**, now occupied by the Banco de Crédito on Jr Apurímac 719; the house of **Toribio Casanova**, Jr José Gálvez 938; the house of the **Silva Santiesteban family**, Jr Junín 1123; and the houses of the **Guerrero** and **Castañeda** families.

Museums

The **Education Faculty of the University** has a museum at Del Batán 283 with objects of the pre-Inca Cajamarca culture, not seen in Lima. The attendant knows much about Cajamarca and the surrounding area. ■ *Open 0800-1200, 1500-1700 in winter, and 0800-1200 in summer. US$0.20 (guided tour)*. The University maintains an experimental **arboretum** and agricultural station. The **Museo de Arte Colonial**, at the Convento de San Francisco, is also worth a visit (see above). The **Archaeological Museum**, one block from the Belén church at Junín y Belén, has a wide range of ceramics from all regions and civilizations of Peru, samples of local handicrafts, costumes used during the annual carnival celebrations and an informative curator. ■ *All museums are closed on Tuesday but open at weekends.*

Essentials

Sleeping
■ *on maps*
Price codes:
see inside front cover

During October there are numerous school trips to this area, so most of the budget hotels are full at this time. Hotels are also booked up during Carnival.

A2 *Laguna Seca*, Avda Manco Capac 1098, Baños del Inca, T823149, F823915, E lagseca@info.infotex. com. pe. In pleasant surroundings, private hot thermal baths in rooms, swimming pool with thermal water, restaurant, bar, disco, horses for hire. Recommended. **A3** *El Ingenio*, Avda Via de Evitamiento 1611-1709, T/F827121/828733. With bathroom, solar-powered hot water, spacious, very relaxed, fax service, helpful. Highly recommended. **A3-B** *Albergue San Vicente*, outside the town at Santa Apollonia, T822644. In an old hacienda, totally remodelled in the style of Gaudi.

B *Continental*, Jr Amazonas 760, T822758. Very clean, hot water, good restaurant, noisy. Recommended. **B-C** *Hostal Cajamarca*, in a colonial house at Dos de Mayo 311, T822532, F828813. Same owners as *Albergue San Vicente*, clean, hot water, TV, phone, food excellent, good local music, travel agency next door. Recommended. **B-C** *Hostal Los Pinos*, Jr La Mar 521, T/F825992. Lovely colonial-style house, price includes breakfast, rooms with TV.

C *Turistas*, on the Plaza de Armas, T822470/71, 822472. With bathroom, laundry service, two restaurants, bar, parking extra. **C** *Casa Blanca*, Dos de Mayo 446 on Plaza de Armas, T/F822141. Room service, clean, safe, nice old building with garden, good restaurant.

D *Hostal Amazonas*, Amazonas 528, T822620. Modern, clean, no hot water, friendly. **D** *Hostal Atahualpa*, Pasaje Atahualpa 686, T822157. Hot water in the

Northern Highlands

mornings only, clean, good value. **D** *Hostal Becerra*, Del Batán 195 (unsigned), T823496. Intermittent tepid water, modern, clean, friendly, they'll let you leave your luggage until late buses depart. **D** *Hostal Jusovi*, Amazonas 637, T822920. With bathroom, comfortable, hot water only in the morning, safe. **D** *Hostal José Gálvez*, Avda Manco Capac 552, at Baños del Inca, T821396. With private thermal bath, good value. **D** *Hostal Prado*, Jr La Mar 582, T823288, F824388. Shared bathroom, no heating. **D** *Hostal San Lorenzo*, Amazonas 1070, T/F826433. With bathroom, hot water, clean, friendly, helpful. **D** *Hostal Turismo*, Dos de Mayo 817, T823427. Clean, can be noisy at weekends but recommended.

   E *Hostal Delfort*, Apurímac 851, near the market. With bathroom, clean, spacious, good value. **E** *Hostal Dos de Mayo*, Dos de Mayo 585, T822527. Shared bathroom, hot water in the morning and evening, good value *menú* in the restaurant. Recommended. **E** *Hostal Plaza*, Plaza de Armas 669, T822058. An old building with handmade wood furnishings, mainly large rooms with many beds, private bathroom and balcony, **F** with shared bath, hot water but poor water supply, quiet, recommended (especially rooms 4 and 12), it has a new annex which is dirty but is open at 0200. **E** *Hostal Sucre*, Amalia Puga 815, T822596. With toilet and wash basin in each room, water in the morning only, good value, sometimes noisy, not very safe, poor restaurant upstairs.

   F *Hostal San José*, Angamos 358, T822002. Shared bathroom, basic, clean, cheap, hot water. **F** per person *Stilo Nuevo*, Jr Huánuco 2231, T824018/827918. Hot water, cheaper without bathroom, laundry, roof terrace, very noisy.

   There are rooms to rent at *Restaurant Encuentro Tupanakuy*, Huánuco 1279, **G** per person, very friendly. Also at *Restaurant Carimbó*, Dos de Mayo 712, **E** per person including meals.

El Cajamarqués, Amazonas 770. Excellent, elegant colonial building with garden full of exotic birds. *Los Faroles*, Jr Dos de Mayo 311, in *Hostal Cajamarca*. Local specialities, friendly, informal, *peña* in the evening. Recommended. *El Batán Gran Bufet*, Del Batán 369. Great food, US$15-20 for two including wine, local and international dishes, good wine list, some of the staff speak English, live music at the weekend, art gallery on the 2nd floor, Dutch owner. Recommended.

Eating: expensive
● *on maps*

El Zarco, Jr Del Batán 170. Very popular with local residents, also has short *chifa* menu, good vegetarian dishes, excellent fish. *Om-Gri*, San Martín, near the Plaza de Armas. Good Italian dishes. *El Real Plaza*, Jr Dos de Mayo 569. Good food, excellent hot chocolate. *La Namorina*, on the edge of town on the road to Baños del Inca, opposite Ché service station. Renowned for its speciality, *cuy frito*. The restaurant at *Hotel Continental* serves an excellent *cuy frito* with rice, salad and potatoes for US$5. *Los Maderos*, Amazonas 807. Local specialities and *peña*, open 2100-0300 Monday-Sunday. *Cascanuez Café Bar*, Amalia Puga 554, near the Cathedral. Great cakes, extensive menu. *Salas*, on the main laza. Fast service, good local food (try their *cuy frito*), best *tamales* in town.

Eating: mid-range

Las Rocas, Dos de Mayo 797. Excellent sandwiches. *Rocco's Pizza Bar*, Jr Cruz de Piedra 653. Open 1500-0030, good pizza, popular with local kids. *Christian*, Del Comercio 719. Snacks, juices, set lunch for $1.10. *Michelangelo*, on the corner of Del Batán y Amazonas. Fast food, pizza, chifa. *Bananas*, Dos de Mayo on the plaza. Good juices, fruit salads, yoghurt, sandwiches, pizza, good music. For early breakfasts go to the market.

Eating: cheap

Cajamarca is known as the Carnival capital of Peru. It hosts a messy, raucous **carnival week** with many processions and dances. But note that the level of water and paint-throwing would put Laurel and Hardy to shame. This is not for the faint-hearted. You have been warned! Also note that accommodation is virtually impossible to find at this time.

Festivals

Northern Highlands

In Porcón, 16 kilometres to the northwest, the *Domingo de Ramos* (**Palm Sunday**) processions are worth seeing. *Corpus Christi* is held in **May or June** and is a solemn religious affair. Also in the **first week of May** is *Florecer en Cajamarca*. On **24 June** is *San Juan* in Cajamarca, Chota, Llacanora, San Juan and Cutervo. An agricultural fair is held in **July** at Baños del Inca. In the **first week of September** is *Festi Danas*. On the **first Sunday in October** is the *Festival Folklórico* in Cajamarca. Also in **October**, in the second week, is the city's *'Tourist Week'*. From **24 December to 6 January** is yet another celebration, *Canta y Baila*, which is worth making a song and dance about.

Shopping Cajamarca is an excellent place to buy handicrafts. They're cheap and the quality is good. Specialities include cotton and wool saddlebags (*alforjas*). You can buy beautiful handwoven wool materials by the metre. Items can also be made to order. The market on Amazonas is good for *artesanía*.

Cajamarca is famous for its gilded mirrors. The *Cajamarquiña* frames are not carved but decorated with patterns transferred onto pieces of glass using the silkscreen process. This tradition lapsed during the post-colonial period and present production goes back less than 20 years.

The area is renowned for its dairy produce. Many shops sell cheese, butter, honey, etc. Try *La Pauca* at Amazonas 713, or *Manos Cajamarquiñas* at Tarapacá 628. Try the *Queso mantecoso*, which is full-cream cheese, or sweet *manjar blanco*, or *humitas*, which are ground maize with cheese. Eucalyptus honey is sold in the market on Calle Amazonas and is said to be a cure for rheumatism. Also try the flaky pastries filled with apple or *manjar blanco* from the street sellers.

Transport **Air** *Aero Continente* flies daily except Tuesday to and from Lima. Also with Aero Cóndor. There are also daily flights to Trujillo. **NB** Check schedules as they change frequently.

Buses To **Lima**, 856 kilometres, 17-19 hours, US$9-11, several buses daily (see below). The road is paved. To **Pacasmayo**, 189 kilometres, 5-6 hours, US$8, several buses and colectivos daily. To **Trujillo**, 296 kilometres, $7\frac{1}{2}$ hours, US$5-7, regular buses daily 1200-2230, also at 1030 with Trans Vulkano; most continue to Lima. To **Chiclayo**, 260 kilometres, 7 hours, US$6, several buses daily, most continuing to Piura (US$11.15) and Tumbes. To **Celendín**, 112 kilometres, 5 hours, US$4.35, at 0630 and 1300. The route follows a fairly good dirt road through beautiful countryside. Also to **Cajabamba**, 75 kilometres, US$4.35, 5 hours, several daily. Some buses and trucks go to **Hualgayoc, Bambamarca, Chota, Cochabamba, Cutervo** and on to **Batán Grande**, but it's not a well-travelled route.

Among the bus companies are: *Expreso Sudamericano*, Atahualpa 300, T823270 (to Lima, Chiclayo, Piura, Sullana and Trujillo); *Trans Palacios*, Atahualpa 322, T825855 (Lima, Trujillo, Celendín, Cajabamba and Bambamarca); *Trans Vulkano*, Atahualpa 315, T821090 (Chiclayo and Chepen); *Nor Peru*, Atahualpa 302, T824550 (Lima, Trujillo, Celendín, Cajabamba); *Empresa Díaz*, Ayacucho 753, T823449 (to Trujillo); *Empresa Trans Mercurio*, Juan XXIII sin número, T825630 (to Trujillo and Chiclayo); *Atahualpa*, Jr Atahualpa 299, T823060 (Lima, Celendín, Cajabamba, Chota, Trujillo and Chiclayo); *Turismo Civa*, Independencia 321, T822377 (to Lima, luxury service including meals, toilet, US$13.50); *Expreso Cajamarca*, Independencia 319, T823337; *Turismo Arberia*, Atahualpa 315, T826812 (to Chiclayo).

Directory **Banks** *Banco de Crédito*, Jr del Comercio y Apurímac. Changes TCs without commission, cash advance on Visa. *Banco Continental*, Tarapacá 721. Changes TCs at US$5 commission minimum. Dollars can be changed in most banks, travel agencies and the bigger hotels. You'll get better rates from **street changers** on Jr Del Batán and on the Plaza de Armas. **Hospitals & medical services** Hospital: Avda Mario Urteaga. **Laundry** Jr Amalia Puga 545. US$1.50 per kg. **Communications** Post Office: Serpost is at the corner of Apurimac and Amazonas. Open

0800-2045. **Telecommunications:** Telefónica del Perú main office is on the Plaza de Armas, Jr Del Comercio sin número. Also at Amalia Puga 1022, and Amazonas 518, for national and international calls. **Tour companies & travel agents** A group of local guides has formed *Cumbemayo Tours*, Amalia Puga 635 on the plaza, T/F822938. They are highly recommended, with tours to Ventanillas de Otusco (US$5 per person), Cumbe Mayo (US$6.50 per person), Kuelap and Gran Vilaya (US$30 per person per day for a 7-day tour). Others include: *Cajamarca Tours*, Dos de Mayo 323, T822813. *Inca Atahualpa Tours*, Amazonas 770, T822495. *Aventuras Cajamarca*, is in the office next to *Hotel Casa Blanca*, T/F823610. Run by Jorge Caballero. Recommended. *Inca Baths Tours*, Amalia Puga 807. Recommended for Cumbe Mayo (US$7 per person). Several travel agencies around the Plaza de Armas offer trips to local sites and further afield (eg Kuelap, normally a 5-day trip, US$200 per person). A recommended tour guide is Edwin Vásquez, ask for him in the *Cuarto de Rescate* or *Hostal Dos de Mayo*. **Tourist offices** At Belén 650, T922834. Helpful. Also tourist information at the Museum at Del Batán 283.

Around Cajamarca

The surrounding countryside is worth exploring. You can either do this on your own or choose from the many tours on offer in town.

Aylambo is a village which specializes in ceramics. These are produced in workshops which are run on ecologically sound principles. Money from the sales of products pays those working in the studios. The village is three and a half kilometres (one and a half hours' walk) from Avenida Independencia. You can visit the *Escuela/Taller* where children learn pottery. ■ *Open Monday-Friday 0730-1200, 1300-1700, Saturday 0730-1230.* **Aylambo**

Six kilometres away are the warm sulphurous thermal springs known as Los Baños del Inca, where there are baths whose temperature you can control. Atahualpa tried the effect of these waters on a festering war wound, but don't worry, the baths are cleaned after each user. ■ *Open 0500-2000 daily. The public bath costs US$0.65, private bath US$0.90 and swimming pool US$0.45 (take your own towel). Buses and combis marked Baños del Inca leave every few minutes from Amazonas, US$0.25, 15 minutes.* **Los Baños del Inca**

Northern Highlands

Around Cajamarca

Related maps
Cajamarca, page 387

Llacanora & La Colpa Other excursions include Llacanora, a typical Andean village in beautiful scenery. La Colpa, a *hacienda* which is now a cooperative farm of the Ministry of Agriculture, breeds bulls and has a lake and gardens. The cows are handmilked at 1400, not a particularly inspiring spectacle in itself, but the difference here is that the cows are called by name and respond accordingly.

Ventanillas de Otusco Ventanillas de Otusco, part of an old pre-Inca cemetery, has a gallery of secondary burial niches. Entry is US$0.75. A one-day round trip can be made: take a bus from Del Batán to Ventanillas de Otusco (30 minutes) or a colectivo leaving hourly from Revilla 170, US$0.15, then walk to Baños del Inca (one and a half hours, six kilometres), from there walk to Llacanora (one hour, seven kilometres) and then a further hour to La Colpa.

Ventanillas de Combayo A road goes to Ventanillas de Combayo, some 20 kilometres past the burial niches of Otusco. These are more numerous and more spectacular, being located in a rather isolated, mountainous area, and are distributed over the face of a steep 200 metres high hillside.

Cumbe Mayo Cumbe Mayo, a *pampa* on a mountain range, is 20 kilometres southwest of Cajamarca. It is famous for its extraordinary, well-engineered pre-Inca channels, running for several kilometres across the mountain tops. It is said to be the oldest man-made construction in South America. The sheer scale of the scene is impressive and the huge rock formations are strange indeed, but do take with a pinch of salt your guide's explanations, which can range from the humorous to the positively psychedelic. It is worth taking a guided tour since the area offers a lot of petroglyphs, altars and sacrificial stones from pre-Inca cultures. On the way to Cumbe Mayo is the Layzón ceremonial centre.

There is no bus service. A guided tour costs about US$7 per person, and a taxi US$15. There's an *hostal* at the site, **F** per person. A milk truck goes daily to Cumbe Mayo leaving at 0400 from C Revilla 170; ask Sr Segundo Malca, Jr Pisagua 482. There's a small charge, and dress warmly. To walk up takes 4 hours. The trail starts from the hill of Santa Apollonia (Silla del Inca), and goes to Cumbe Mayo straight through the village and up the hill. At the top of the mountain, leave the trail and take the road to the right to the canal. The walk is not difficult and you do not need hiking boots. Take a good torch/flashlight. The locals use the trail to bring their goods to market.

Celendín

Population: approximately 15,000
Altitude: 2,625 metres
Phone code: 044
Coloured map 1, grid C4

East from Cajamarca, the first town of note is Celendín, whose residents are known as Shilicos. It is a clean and tranquil town, with warm friendly people but a decidedly chilly climate.

The plaza and cathedral are both appealing. There is also an interesting local market on Sunday. Walk up the hill to the chapel of San Isidro Labrador for views of town and surroundings. Note the huge hats worn by the townsfolk. These are woven from fine straw and can be bought, along with other straw handicrafts, at *Artesanías San José de Pilco*, 2 de Mayo 319.

Essentials

Sleeping
■ *on maps*
Price codes:
see inside front cover

E *Celendín*, Jr Unión 305, Plaza de Armas, T855041. With bathroom, limited hot water, nice patio, clean, friendly, good restaurant. **E** *Loyer's*, José Gálvez 410, T855210. New in 1997, with bathroom, cheaper without, patio, nice.

F *Amazonas*, Dos de Mayo 316. With bathroom, cheaper without, cold water, basic, helpful. **F** *Maxmar*, Dos de Mayo 349. With bathroom, cheaper without, hot shower extra, basic, clean, parking, good value. **F** *José Gálvez*, Dos de Mayo 344. With bathroom, cheaper without, cold water, basic, friendly.

Eating
● *on maps*

La Reserve, José Gálvez 313. Good quality and value. Recommended. *El Ñato*, Salaverry 491 y José Gálvez. Good set meal and à la carte. *Pizzería El Che*, Pardo 358. Meals plus pizza in the evening. *Santa Isabel*, Jr José Gálvez 512. Clean and OK. *Bella Aurora*, Grau y José Gálvez. Good. *Jalisco*, Jr Unión, Plaza de Armas. A la carte only. There are several other places to eat. *Panadería El Carmen*, Dos de Mayo 332. Good bakery.

Festivals

The town hosts its *Virgen del Carmen* festival on **16 July**. Bullfights with *matadores* from Spain and cock fighting are all part of the well attended celebrations.

Transport

To **Cajamarca**, 107 kilometres, 4-5 hours: with *Atahualpa*, 2 de Mayo y Prado, Plaza de Armas, at 0700 daily, US$3.50; *Palacios*, Jr Unión 333, Plaza de Armas, at 0500 and 1300 daily, US$3.50; *Turismo Dias*, Pardo 456, Plaza de Armas, at 0500 daily, US$3.50. To **Chachapoyas** via Balsas and Leymebamba, 12-14 hours (may be much longer in the rainy season, take warm clothing, food and water): *Virgen del Carmen*, Cáceres 117, on Sunday at 1100 and 1230 and Thursday at 1100, US$7; *San José de Pilco*, 2 de Mayo 331, on Thursday and Sunday at 1030, US$7. Other local transport leaves from the market area.

Directory

Banks There are no banks or *casas de cambio*, but try the local shops. **Communications Post office:** Jr Unión 415. **Phone office:** José Gálvez 600 y Pardo, Plaza de Armas.

Celendín

2. El Ñato
3. La Reserve
4. Pizzería El Che

🚌Buses
1. Atahualpa
   (to Cajamarca)
2. Dias (to Cajamarca)
3. Palacios
   (to Cajamarca)
4. San José de Pilco
   (to Chachapoyas)
5. Virgen del Carmen
   (to Chachapoyas)

■ **Sleeping**
1. Amazonas
2. Celendín
3. José Gálvez
4. Loyer's
5. Maxmar

● **Eating**
1. Bella Aurora

Around Celendín

Oxamarca & La Chocta

Three hours southeast from Celendín by bus (US$2.25) is the village of Oxamarca. From here it is 10 kilometres, or a two and a half hours' walk, to the ruins of La Chocta. Strategically placed atop a steep ridge, the most notable feature of the fortress is the collection of small, square stone burial houses, known as *Chullpas*, many of which have been torn down by farmers and looted by *huaqueros*.

Morgan Davis (see Recommended Reading, page 395) writes that the *Chullpas* are thought to date from the Cajamarca II period, beginning after AD 100. There is also evidence of Inca occupation. There are no hotels or restaurants in Oxamarca. Ask Gregorio Sánchez Junio in Celendín. He has a private

Northern Highlands

museum at Jr San Martín 423 and is very helpful with maps and information about local ruins.

Llanguat One hour north by road from Celendín are the thermal baths of Llanguat, in their natural state. Check for early morning trucks to Pizón from the market area. To return, a bus passes by the baths en route to Celendín at approximately 1000. A round trip by taxi costs US$20.

To Chachapoyas

The rough narrow road from Celendín to Chachapoyas (226 kilometres) follows a winding course, crossing the wide and deep canyon of the Río Marañón at Balsas (*Altitude*: 950 metres). It then climbs steeply, over countless hair-raising hairpin bends, with superb views of the mountains and the valleys below, to reach the Barro Negro pass at 3,680 metres, before descending to Leymebamba in the upper Utcubamba valley (see page 405). The journey takes 12 to 14 hours in the dry season. It can be much longer and more dangerous when it rains. Take warm clothing, food and water.

The Chachapoyas Region

The Chachapoyas region contains the almost embarrassing archaeological riches of the Chachapoyans, also known as 'The Cloud People'. Here lie the great pre-Incan cities of Gran Vilaya, Cerro Olán and the immense fortress of Kuelap, among countless others.

The area

Theories about the Chachapoyan Empire show that their cities, highways, terracing, irrigation, massive stonework and metalcraft were all fully developed. Mark Babington and Morgan Davis write: "This is surely a region which overwhelms even Machu-Picchu in grandeur and mystery. It contains no less than five lost, and uncharted cities, the most impressive of which is Pueblo Alto, near the village of Pueblo Nuevo (25 kilometres from Kuelap). By far the majority of these cities, fortresses and villages were never discovered by the Spanish. In fact many had already returned to the jungle by the time they arrived in 1532 ... On a recent map of the area, no less than 38 sites can be counted". (See Further reading below.)

This region is called *La Ceja*, or eyebrow, of the Amazon, and offers spectacular scenery, including a good deal of virgin cloud-forest (although other sections are sadly deforested), as well as endless deep dry canyons traversed by hair-raising roads. The temperature is always in the 70s during the day but the nights are cool up around 3,000 metres. Many ruins are overgrown with ferns, bromeliads and orchids and easily missed.

The central geographic feature of the department, and its boundary with neighbouring Cajamarca, is the great Río Marañón, one of the major tributaries of the Amazon. Its turbulent course carves a gargantuan cleft among the high mountains.

Running roughly parallel to the mighty Marañón, one range to the east, is the gentler valley of the Utcubamba, home to much of the area's ancient and present population. Over yet another cordillera to the east, lie the isolated subtropical valleys of the province of Rodríguez de Mendoza, the origin of whose Caucasian inhabitants remains a mystery to this day (see page 409).

In 1998 Amazonas was one of the friendliest and most peaceful regions in all of Peru, untouched by mass tourism. Please do your share as responsible visitors to keep it that way. See also Responsible Tourism, page 39.

Ins and outs

The city of Chachapoyas is the best base for visiting this region. There is irregular air **Getting there** transport from Lima, and Chachapoyas can be reached overland from either Chiclayo, Cajamarca or Tarapoto. Unfortunately, bus schedules from Chiclayo all involve an over-night journey, missing the fine scenery along the way. A good alternative is to go by bus from Chiclayo to Jaén, continuing the next day to Chachapoyas, via Bagua Grande and Pedro Ruíz, using combis (see the corresponding sections for details). From Cajamarca, you can go first to Celendín (see above) and then on to Chachapoyas, crossing the Marañón at Balsas between descents and climbs of thousands of vertical metres. The journey is an entirely unforgettable experience in its own right.

The dry season (May to September) is infinitely preferable. During the rains, roads may **When to go** become impassable due to landslides and access to the more remote areas may be impossible, or involve weeks of delay. Likewise, trekking in the area can be very pleas-ant in the dry season, but may involve too much wading through waist-deep mud during the rainy season. Good hiking gear is essential; also a sleeping bag, tent and canned goods.

Further reading

The whole area is full of largely unexplored ruins and some of them have been studied by the Swiss archaeologists Henri and Paula Reichlen. They surveyed 39 sites in 1948 – see *Récherches archaeologiques dans les Andes du haut Utcubamba*, in *Journal des Américanistes*, which includes an accurate map. The American archaeologist Gene Savoy went further than the Reichlens; see his book *Antisuyo*. Kaufmann Doig's *Arqueología Peruana* includes a map showing the location of the '12 Cities of the Condors'. In 1992 he started a new project in the area. Ask if he is in Chachapoyas as he is worth contacting. Also worth looking at is Morgan Davis' book, *The Cloud People, an Anthropologi-cal Survey* (see under **Kuelap**, page 402).

Other sources of information on the archaeology of the region include the very informative booklet on Kuelap, available in Chachapoyas; ask Carlos Torres Mas (see below). Dr Peter Lerche, who has lived in Chachapoyas since 1983, is the author of *Los Chachapoyas y los Símbolos de su Historia* and *Chachapoyas: Guía de Viajeros*, a useful trekking guide. These may be avail-able from the author himself (see below).

Guides and contacts

Robert Dover is a British guide to sites throughout the Chachapoyas region and is recommended. Contact him through the *Gran Hotel Vilaya* in Chacha (see below). Carlos Burga, proprietor of *Hostal Revash* (see below), organizes and sometimes guides groups. He is knowledgeable, helpful and friendly, and also recommended. Martín Chumbe guides trips for about US$25 per day. He speaks some English, at a push, and can store luggage. You'll find him at Jr Piura 909 or through *Gran Hotel Vilaya*.

The German ethnologist, Dr Peter Lerche (T/F758438), is the resident expert regarding Chachapoyan cultures and trekking. He is very knowledge-able, speaks English, sometimes guides groups and has written a couple of good books on the region (see above). Dr Carlos Torres Mas, T757044, is an anthropologist who can also advise about walks in the area. Gumercindo 'Gumer' Zegarra is the proprietor of the *Gran Hotel Vilaya* and knowledgeable about happenings in and around Chachapoyas.

Charles Motley, 1805 Swann Avenue, Orlando, FL 32809, USA, E kuelap@magicnet.net, is directing a long-term private project, called *Los Tambos Chachapoyanos*, to build hostels near the region's archaeological sites. As of July 1998, one lodge had almost been completed at Choctámal near Kuelap (see page 402) and construction had begun on a second hostel in Levanto. Morgan Davis (see above), a Canadian, has written about Chachapoyan archaeology and collaborated with Motley. He visits the area regularly and is well known among the locals. Routes to Kuelap Cajamarca San Martín - Amazonas is a new partnership of four local operators to promote tourism in this region. They run a tour of the area which covers the thermal baths in Cajamarca, the Lake of Condors (see below), Kuelap and Tarapoto (see below). For more information, contact Sonia Guillén in Leymebamba (see page 405); *Laguna Seca Hotel* in Cajamarca (see page 388); *Kuelap Tourism*, Marcello Castillo, E lumen@ibm.net; *Amazonian Tourism Corp*, Carlos González Henríquez, E ctareps@protelsa.com.pe.

Chachapoyas

Population: approximately 30,000
Altitude: 2,335 metres
Phone code: 074
Coloured map 1, grid C4

Chachapoyas, or Chacha as it is known among locals, is the capital of the Department of Amazonas. It was founded on 5 September 1538, but retains only some of its colonial character, in the form of large old homes with their typical patios and wooden balconies.

Sights

The city's importance as a crossroads between the coast and jungle began to decline in the late 1940s, with the building of the road through Pedro Ruiz. However, archaeological and ecological tourism have grown gradually in the 1990s and there are hopes these will bring increasing economic benefits to the region.

The modern **Cathedral** faces a spacious plaza which fills with locals for the evening *paseo*. Other interesting churches are the **Capilla de la Virgen Asunta**, the city's patroness, at Asunción y Puno, and **Señor de Burgos**, at Amazonas y Santa Lucía. The **Instituto Nacional de Cultura (INC)** has a small museum at Ayacucho 675, with a few mummies and artefacts.

The **Mirador Guayamil** offers fine views of the city. Nearby is the **Pozo de Yana Yacu**, also known as the *fuente del amor*, at the west end of Avenida Salamanca. Legend has it that those who visit this well will fall in love and remain in Chachapoyas (though it obviously doesn't work every time). A decisive battle for independence from Spain took place at the **Pampas de Higos Urco**, at the east end of town, a 20-minute walk. **Santa Isabel**, with interesting orchid nurseries, is a 30-minute walk southeast of Chachapoyas. A hotel and restaurant were being built here in 1998.

Tour to Kuelap

Most hotels will organize tours to Kuelap and other archaeological sites when there are sufficient people. Those run by *Gran Hotel Vilaya* and *Hostal Revash* are recommended. Expect to pay around US$12 per person for a full-day trip to Kuelap including lunch.

Essentials

B *Gran Vilaya*, Ayacucho 755, T757664, F758154. E vilaya@wayna.rcp.net.pe. The best in town, parking, English spoken, all services. **D** *Revash*, Grau 517, Plaza de Armas, T757391. With private bathroom, plenty hot water, 8 rooms, clean, patio, friendly, helpful, sells Dr Lerche's guidebook. Recommended. **E** *Hostal Amazonas*, Grau 565, Plaza de Armas, T757199. Hot water, with private bathroom, cheaper with shared bathroom, large rooms, nice patio, friendly. Recommended. **E** *Hostal El Danubio*, Tres Esquinas 193, Plazuela Belén, T757337. With private bathroom, hot water, cheaper with cold, clean, friendly. **E** per person *El Dorado*, Ayacucho 1062, T757047. With bathroom, hot water, clean, helpful. **E** *Hostal Johumaji*, Ayacucho 711, T750712, F757101. With bathroom, hot water, cheaper with cold, restaurant. **E** *Hostal Kuelap*, Amazonas 1057, T757136. With private bathroom, hot water, cheaper with shared bathroom and cold water, parking. Recommended. **F** *Continental*, Jr Ortiz Arrieta 441, T751705. Hot water, not great. **F** *Laguna de los Cóndores*, Salamanca 941, T757492. Very basic, shared bathroom, cold water. Due to open in late 1998 is **D** *El Tejado*, Grau 534, Plaza de Armas.

Sleeping
■ *on maps*
Price codes:
see inside front cover

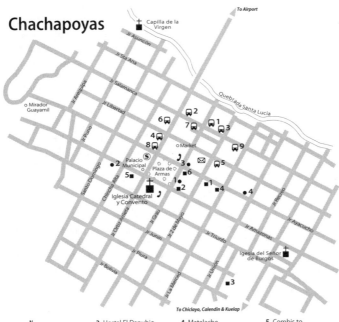

Chachapoyas

Related maps
Around chachapoyas,
page 400

Northern Highlands

0 metres 150
0 yards 164

■ **Sleeping**
1. Gran Vilaya
2. Hostal Amazonas
3. Hostal El Danubio
4. Hostal Johumaji
5. Hostal Kuelap
6. Revash

● **Eating**
1. Chacha & El Tejado
2. El Carbón
3. Kuelap

4. Matalache

🚍**Transport**
1. Cars to Pedro Ruíz
2. Civa buses & Combis to Huancas
3. Combis to Jalca Grande
4. Combis to Lamud

5. Combis to Leymebamba
6. Combis to Mendoza
7. Combis to Tingo (for Kuelap)
8. Turismo Kuelap buses
9. Virgen del Carmen buses to Celendín

Eating
on maps

There are many good, simple and cheap restaurants. Slightly upscale is *El Tejado*, upstairs at Grau 534, Plaza de Armas. Good quality, nice view and atmosphere. Recommended. *Chacha*, Grau 541, Plaza de Armas. Especially popular with locals, clean, serves good, huge portions, friendly. Recommended. *Matalache*, Ayacucho 616. Also good and very popular. *El Carbón*, Amazonas 1121. Grill and pub, nice atmosphere. *La Estancia*, Amazonas 861. Grill and video pub. *Kuelap*, Ayacucho 832. Good, friendly. Recommended. *Las Chozas de Marlissa*, Ayacucho 1133. Friendly, good for typical food, pub-type place at night, serves the strangest *pisco sour* you'll ever taste. *Chifa El Turista*, Amazonas 575. Reasonable, friendly and helpful. *Oh Qué Bueno*, Ayacucho 1033. Limited menu. *Mas Burguer*, Ortiz Arrieta, Plaza de Armas. Excellent juices, cakes, fruit salads. *Patisserie*, Jr 2 de Mayo 558. Good pastries. *Cuyería, Pollería y Panadería Virgen Asunta*, Puno 401. Order *cuy* in advance. The bakery at Ayacucho 816 does good breakfasts. Try *Dulcería Santa Elena*, at Amazonas 800, for sweets.

Festivals Among the town's festivals are *Semana Turística de Amazonas*, held in the first week of **June**. *Virgen Asunta* takes place during the first two weeks of **August**.

Shopping Many shops are well stocked with local goods. *Comercial Tito*, Libertad 860, is a good place to get supplies.

Transport **Air** As of July 1998 there was only a limited and irregular service to Lima, with flights often cancelled. It's best to enquire early and often. *TAA*, chartered by Chirimoto Tours, Ayacucho 936, T757203, F757989 (in Lima Avenida Elmer Fawcett 169, oficina 313, T4511186), flies on Saturday. *Grupo Ocho* flies every second Tuesday, US$45. You can find them in the *Hostal Revash*, Grau 517. *Servicios Aereos Colibrí* has a charter service and are in the *Gran Hotel Vilaya*. The airport is 20 minutes from town. A truck from the Plaza de Armas goes up to 2 hours before flights leave; US$1. A taxi costs US$3.

Buses To **Chiclayo** with *Civa* (Ortiz Arrieta y Salamanca), at 1600 daily, 12 hours (may be longer in the rainy season), US$7, some buses continue on to Lima; *Turismo Kuelap* (Ortiz Arrieta 412), at 1500 daily, also daily except Monday and Friday at 1600, US$9. To **Celendín**, from which there are connections on to Cajamarca: with Virgen del Carmen (Avenida Salamanca 665), on Tuesday at 0600 and 0900 and Friday at 0900, 12-14 hours (may be much longer in the rainy season, an unforgettable journey, take warm clothing, food and water), US$7; also with *San José de Pilco*, Avenida Salamanca 688, on Tuesday and Friday at 0800, US$7. To **Pedro Ruíz**, for connections to Chiclayo or Tarapoto, combis (US$2) and cars (US$2.75) leave from Grau y Salamanca, 3 hours. To **Mendoza** (86 kilometres), small buses leave from Ortiz Arrieta y Libertad, at 1000 and 1200 daily, 4-5 hours, US$3.

For **Kuelap**: several combis leave daily in the morning to **Tingo** from Grau between Libertad and Salamanca, 2 hours, US$1.50; or to **Choctámal** from Salamanca y Grau, at around 0600 and 1100 daily, 3½ hours, US$2. To **Leymebamba**, mini-buses leave from 2 de Mayo y Salamanca, at 1200 daily, 4 hours, US$1.75. combis for other regional destinations all leave from the market area. Note that these may be crowded and all departure times are approximate. *Sr. Victor Torres*, T757688, rents a double cabin pickup truck with driver for all regional destinations.

NB If driving your own vehicle, Chacha is the last petrol for a long way (84 octane only), though small amounts can be bought in Leymebamba (see below).

Directory **Banks** *Banco de Crédito*, Ortiz Arrieta 576, Plaza de Armas. Gives cash on Visa card, changes cash, and charges commission for TCs. *Hostal Revash* changes cash only, as does *Restaurant Las Rocas*, Ayacucho 932, Plaza de Armas. **Laundry** Ayacucho 826. Expensive. **Communications** Post Office: Dos de Mayo 438. **Telephone offices:** Ayacucho 926, Plaza de Armas. Also at Grau 608.

Northern Highlands

Around Chachapoyas

Huancas Huancas, a picturesque village which produces rustic pottery, stands on a hilltop north of Chacha. It's a two-hour walk starting on the airport road. combis for Huancas leave from Jr Ortiz Arrieta y Salamanca, by the CIVA bus station; 30 minutes, US$0.35. Walk uphill from Huancas for a magnificent view into the deep canyon of the Río Sonche. There is good walking in the area which also has Inca and pre-Inca ruins. A large prison complex was being built nearby in 1998.

Levanto The Spaniards built this, their first capital of the area, directly on top of the previous Chachapoyan structures. Although the capital was moved to Chachapoyas a few years later, Levanto, or Llauntu as it was originally named, still retained its importance, at least for a while, as it had been one of the seven great cities of the Chachapoyans as described by Cieza de León and Garcilaso de la Vega. It was one of the largest and most important *curacazgos*.

The Kuelap east-west Highway starts at Levanto and links with the Inca military highway at Jalca Grande (see page 404). Levanto was about mid-way on the north-south route from Colombia to the Huari, then Inca hub, at Huánuco. This stone road crosses the modern vehicle road at La Molina, about five kilometres from Chachapoyas. A 10 kilometre walk on this ancient road from Levanto is worthwhile. Nowadays Levanto is a small, unspoilt, and very beautiful colonial village set on flat ground overlooking the massive canyon of the Utcubamba River. Kuelap can, on a clear day, be seen on the other side of the rift. The town is a good centre for exploring the many ruins around, being the centre of a network of ancient ruins, fortifications, residential areas and many others. There are also many beautiful and interesting walks which can be done in the area.

A pleasant 30-minute walk uphill from Levanto are the partly cleared ruins of **Yalape**. The local people are helpful and will guide you to the ruins. Yalape seems to have been a massive residential complex extending over many hectares and including many well-preserved examples of typical Chachapoyan architecture and masonry with quite elaborate and beautiful friezes.

Morgan Davis has reconstructed an Inca building at **Colla Cruz**. On a classic Inca stone terrace, a regional-style round building has been constructed, with a three-storey high thatched roof. This garrison guarded the road which ran past Colcamar, over the Cordillera Oriental on a one and a half kilometre staircase, through Gran Vilaya, to Cajamarca's central north-south road and on to the coastal highway.

Sleeping and eating As yet there is no official accommodation in Levanto, although a hostel was being built here in July 1998, in the original Chachapoyan roundhouse style, as part of the *Tambos Chachapoyanos* project. Small groups of travellers are very welcome and beds and bedding are provided in the mayor's office and village meeting hall. There is one small shop and bar in the village (selling coffee and cola, but little food).

Transport Levanto is 2 hours by truck or a 6-hour walk from Chachapoyas by a very rough road (barely passable in the rainy season). Trucks leave from the market in Chachapoyas most days at 0600, US$0.90, and there are trucks and combis (2 hours, US$1) from outside *Bodega El Amigo* on Jr Hermosura at 1400. It takes $1\frac{1}{2}$-2 hours depending on the number of stops, or $3\frac{1}{2}$ hours by mule track. Ask in Chachapoyas market if anyone returning to Levanto will guide you for a small fee. A taxi from Chachapoyas

Sites around Chachapoyas

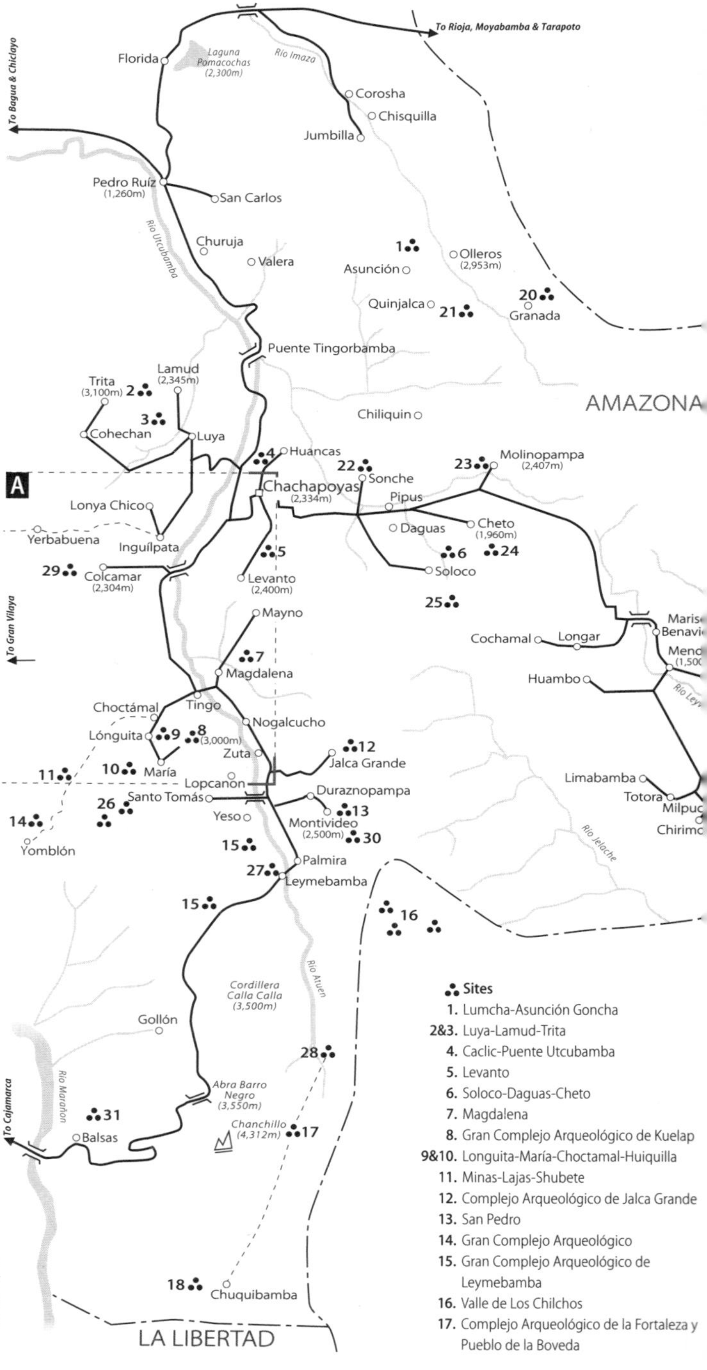

Related maps
Chachapoyas, page 397
Kuelap, page 402
A Gran Vilaya, page 407

∴ Sites

1. Lumcha-Asunción Goncha
2&3. Luya-Lamud-Trita
4. Caclic-Puente Utcubamba
5. Levanto
6. Soloco-Daguas-Cheto
7. Magdalena
8. Gran Complejo Arqueológico de Kuelap
9&10. Longuita-María-Choctamal-Huiquilla
11. Minas-Lajas-Shubete
12. Complejo Arqueológico de Jalca Grande
13. San Pedro
14. Gran Complejo Arqueológico
15. Gran Complejo Arqueológico de Leymebamba
16. Valle de Los Chilchos
17. Complejo Arqueológico de la Fortaleza y Pueblo de la Boveda

to Levanto and back, including driver waiting while you look around, is US$25.

South of Chachapoyas

Tingo (*Altitude*: 1,800 metres) is about 37 kilometres south of Chachapoyas, in the Utcubamba valley. Much of the village was washed away in the floods of 1993. In the hills above Tingo, three and a half kilometres away, is Tingo Nuevo. There is no running water or electricity. Note that the police may ask to see documents.

You can walk from Tingo to Levanto. Head up to Magdalena (30 minutes). From here it is about 30 minutes by a short cut (uphill then downhill) to the bridge at Cundechaca. From the stone bridge walk 30 minutes on the main road to Maino until you reach a wooden bridge. Near here, 100 metres before a bend in the road, look for the path which leads down into a small gorge, crosses the river (after 30 minutes) and passes the little farm which is visible from the main road. From there it's a steep, one-hour walk to a waterfall, from where you continue on the well-defined Inca road on a ridge between two gorges into Levanto. You can add two to three hours to this walk by starting at Kuelap downhill to Tingo.

Sleeping F per person *Albergue León*, no sign, walk 50 metres from the police checkpoint to the corner and turn left, it's the third house on the left (righthand door). Basic, shared bathroom, cold water, friendly, run by Lucho León, who is very knowledgeable.
Eating *Miss Tony*, is by the police

Vista Alegre
(1,900m)

SAN MARTÍN

Omia

N

0   km   10
0   miles   6

18. Gran Complejo Arqueológico de Chuquibamba
19. Unidades Arqueológicas de Milpuc y Omia
20. Pirka Pirka
21. Quinjalca
22. Sonche
23. Molinopampa
24&25. Gran Complejo Arqueológico Purum Llacta o Monte Peruvian
26. Complejo Arqueológico Santo Tomás
27. Yeso-Leimebamba
28. Complejo Arqueológico Lluy
29. Colcamar
30. Grupo Arqueológico Montevideo
31. Balsas

Northern Highlands

station, good food but a bit expensive. *Kuelap*, almost opposite, is clean and OK. Also reasonable is *El Edén*.

Local guides Oscar Arce Cáceres based at 'El Chillo' near the Río Utcubamba, 4½ kilometres outside Tingo. He owns a farm and knows the area very well. He is a very reliable guide but now charges as much as US$100 a day for his services. He also has accommodation with bath, provides good meals and stores luggage. The trek into this area, like the walk up to Kuelap, starts from Tingo – the way is all mule track. The walk from El Chillo to Kuelap is shorter than from Tingo. The return to El Chillo can be made via the village of Nogalcucho (ask for directions).

In Magdalena (a 30 minutes' walk from Tingo), Abram Torres will be happy to provide his guiding services, and his mule, for the first leg of the journey as far as Choctámal, about 4 hours away.

Transport combis from Chachapoyas to Leymebamba pass through Tingo, where they stop for lunch between 1330 and 1500 daily, but there's no guarantee of space. Tingo to Leymebamba takes 2 hours, US$1.75. There are several buses (from 0500) and pick-ups daily to Chachapoyas; 2 hours, US$1.50.

Kuelap

Kuelap (3,000 metres) is a spectacular pre-Inca walled city which was rediscovered in 1843 by Juan Crisótomo Nieto. Morgan Davis writes that though successive explorers have attempted to do justice to the sheer scale of this site even their most exaggerated descriptions have fallen short. Kuelap was built over a period of 200 years, from AD 1100 to 1300 and contained three times more stone than the Great Pyramid at Giza in Egypt.

The site lies sprawled along the summit of a mountain crest, more than a kilometre in length. It is divided into three parts: at the northwest end is a small outpost; at the southeast end of the ridge is a spread out village in total ruin; and the cigar-shaped fortress lies between the two, 700 metres long by 175 metres wide at its widest. The walls are as formidable as those of any precolumbian city. They vary in height between eight and 17 metres and were constructed in 40 courses of stone block, each one weighing between 100 and 200 kg. It has been estimated that 100,000 such blocks went into the completion of this massive structure.

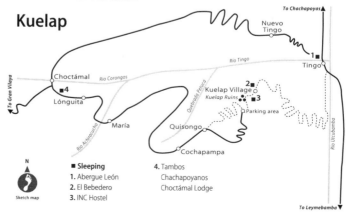

Kuelap

■ **Sleeping**
1. Abergue León
2. El Bebedero
3. INC Hostel
4. Tambos
   Chachapoyanos
   Choctámal Lodge

Sketch map

Some reconstruction has taken place, mostly of small houses and walls, but the majority of the main walls on both levels are original, as is the cone-shaped dungeon, known as *el tintero* (the inkwell). There are a number of defensive walls and passageways as well as very many houses. Although there are virtually no carvings, some structures are adorned with simple geometric friezes. An interesting feature is that almost all the buildings are circular. ■ *Open hours 0800-1700. US$4.50 (including US$1 for use of camera). The ruins are locked. The guardian, Gabriel Portocarrero, has the keys and accompanies visitors. He's very informative and friendly.*

Sleeping

When walking up from Tingo, the last house to the right of the track (*El Bebedero*, just above a small spring) offers accommodation: bed, breakfast and evening meal for US$6; good meals, friendly and helpful).

A bit further, on the left, 100 metres below the ruins, is the *Instituto Nacional de Cultura (INC)* hostel. It's a clean dormitory with room for about 12 people, in a lovely setting, US$1.75 per person, no running water (please conserve the rainwater in the buckets), simple meals may be available from the caretaker for US$1. There is free camping outside the hostel.

Outside Choctámal (see above) the *Tambos Chachapoyanos* project operates a lodge with space for 35 people in rooms with private bath, US$5 per person if you have a sleeping bag, US$7 per person if you want sheets and towels. It's in a lovely setting with great views, but cold at night. The facilities had not been completed in July 1998 and were not always open. Check beforehand at the *Gran Hotel Vilaya* in Chachapoyas.

Getting there

In 1998 there were four options for visiting Kuelap:

1) Take a tour from Chachapoyas (see page 396). These allow you to visit the ruins by vehicle in a single day, starting at 0600, returning to Chachapoyas at night, with about 3½ hours at the site.

2) Hire your own vehicle with driver in Chachapoyas. Check at Salamanca on the corner with Grau. Also Sr Victor Torres, T757688.

3) Take a combi from Chachapoyas to Choctámal. They leave from Salamanca y Grau at around 0600 and 1100 daily; 3½ hours, US$2. You can spend the night in Choctámal village (no hotels, accommodation may be available in local homes) or at the *Tambos Chachapoyanos* Choctámal Lodge, known locally as *"el hotel"*, 3 kilometres past the town (see sleeping below). The next day, it is a relatively gentle 19 kilometres, 4-5 hour, walk along the vehicle road to Kuelap. It's best to visit the site at your leisure and spend the night here (see sleeping below), then walk down the steep path (3-4 hours) to Tingo the next day.

4) Take a combi from Chachapoyas to Tingo. Several leave daily in the morning from Grau between Libertad and Salamanca; 2 hours, US$1.50. You should consider spending the night in Tingo to start climbing at dawn the next day. The strenuous 6-7 hour hike (with a 1,200 metre vertical gain) to Kuelap begins on the right hand side of the bridge, past the police station. At first the track follows the west bank of the Utcubamba, before turning right and climbing steeply into the mountains. The route is intermittently marked with red arrows painted on the rocks. It can get very hot and there is no water whatsoever until the top, but the trail may be muddy in the rainy season. Take water, food, adequate clothing and footwear, etc. The small village of **Kuelap** is reached first, the walls of the fortress become visible only at the very end of the climb.

Northern Highlands

Gran Vilaya

The name Gran Vilaya was created by US explorer, Gene Savoy, the original 'Indiana Jones', who discovered this extensive set of ruined complexes in 1985.

The region was divided into three *curacazgos* - politically independent ethnic groups that made up the Chachapoyas confederation: **Pausamarca**, **Rongia** and **Sesuya**. These names can be traced back to late Incaic sources and old colonial records. There are about 30 sites spread over this vast area, 15 of which are considered important by Morgan Davis. Among the sites are Pueblo Alto, Pueblo Nuevo, Paxamarca and Machu Llacta. It is recommended to take a letter of introduction from the Instituto Nacional de Cultura in Chachapoyas. Ask the alcalde for accommodation, meals and assistance in finding a guide, which is essential.

Getting there The whole area stretches west from the Río Utcubamba to the Río Marañon. Head north from Tingo or south from Chachapoyas as far as the Huinchuco bridge across the Río Utcubamba. On the west bank of the river a road leads to the left, if heading north, to the town of Colcamar, which is the starting point for exploring this area. A new road was being built in 1998, from Choctámal through the Yumal pass into the Gran Vilaya region, facilitating access but also placing the area's cloud-forests at considerable risk of destruction. The Choctámal Lodge (see above) is therefore a good starting point for treks into the Gran Vilaya.

Jalca Grande The town of Jalca Grande (or La Jalca as it is known locally), at 2,600 metres, lies between Montevideo and Tingo, up on the east side of the main valley. There is a market on Saturday. In the town itself, one block west of the Plaza de Armas, is the **Choza Redonda**, the remains of a Chachapoyan roundhouse which was inhabited until 1964.

Half an hour west of the town are the ruins of **Ollape**, a series of platforms with intricate fretwork designs and wide balconies. A much larger site, though more primitive, is **Moyuk Viejo**, a two and a half hours' walk to the North.

A strenuous but rewarding three to four day trek can be made from La Jalca to Huambo or Limabamba (see page 409), over the cordillera and through cloud forests to the subtropical valleys. Part of the route follows an ancient road and there are undeveloped ruins along the way. Trekking experience and self-sufficiency are indispensable.

Sleeping and transport There are no hotels but you can find a room through the Alcaldía. Don't expect too much privacy, however, as it is used until 2200, after which time there is no electricity. So bring a torch (and a pack of cards; there isn't much in the way of nightlife). combis from Chachapoyas depart from Salamanca 707 at 1400 daily; $3\frac{1}{2}$ hours, US$2. They return from La Jalca to Chachapoyas at 0500 daily.

Ubilón Jalca Grande can also be reached from Ubilón, on the main road north to Tingo, but transport is scarce (one combi daily). Otherwise it's a strenuous three hour walk uphill. There is not much in Ubilón itself, save for a few shops selling next to nothing. Cheap, basic accommodation is available at *Bodega Irmita*, which has several rooms with cold water.

Further south are the towns of **Yerbabuena** and **Puente Santo Tomás**, which
is at the turn-off for the burial *Chullpas* of **Revash**, belonging to the Revash
culture (AD 1350-1538). In Yerbabuena there is one unnamed basic
hospedaje, **G**, with running water but no electricity. There is also *Restaurant
Karina*, which is cheap, and a large Sunday market.

Revash

The ruins of Revash are roughly three hours' walk from Puente Santo
Tomás. Follow the dirt road towards **Santo Tomás**, then cross the wooden
bridge on the right and take the dirt track towards the mountains; it is a steep
climb up. Eventually small adobe houses can be seen in the cliff face, covered
by an overhang. The houses are buff coloured with red roofs and resemble
tiny Swiss cottages with crosses in the form of bricked-up windows. They are,
in fact, small tombs. There are lots of human bones lying around and cave
paintings. The tombs have long since been looted. To get close, climb up a
small goat track and walk along a ledge. It is about an hour's walk back downhill from Santo Tomás to Puente Santo Tomás, from where there is transport
north towards Chachapoyas.

Beyond Puente Santo Tomás there is a turn-off which heads east beyond
Duraznopampa to the small town of **Montevideo**. An hour's walk southeast
of Montevideo is the ruined complex of **Rumichaco/Monja**, spread along a
ridge above the town. The upper Rumichaco sector consists of massive
undecorated platforms while the lower Monja sector is better preserved with
some intricate fretwork on the platforms. Local guides can be hired; ask for
Tito Rojas Calla in Montevideo. There are no hotels in the town but ask the
owner of the only restaurant if you can sleep there.

Rumichaco/
Monja

Another Chachapoyan site is Cerro Olán, reached by colectivo to **San Pedro
de Utac**, a small village beyond Montevideo, then a 30 minutes' walk. From
the plaza a clear trail rises directly into the hills east of town to the ruins, which
can be seen from the village. Here are the remains of towers which some
archaeologists claim had roofs like mediaeval European castles.

Cerro Olán

According to Morgan Davis this was essentially a military installation and
once a small city of considerable luxury, similar in construction to La Congona
(see below) but on a grander scale. Morgan Davis considers the latter and Cerro
Olán the most impressive archaeological sites in the Chachapoyas region, after
Kuelap (see above). Ask the alcalde for accommodation.

The road south from Chachapoyas crosses the Utcubamba River then
passes through **Palmira** and heads to Leymebamba.

Leymebamba

This pleasant town derives its name from a visit in June 1480, by the Inca
Túpac Yupanqui, who stayed to celebrate the Fiesta de Inti-Raymi. From that
moment, the town came to be known as the Field of the Festival of The Sun, or
Raymi-Pampa, which in turn became Leymebamba. The city was moved
from its original location, four kilometres south, following an epidemic in the
1600s. The local fiesta is held in honour of the Virgen del Carmen on the week
preceeding July 16.

Leymebamba has electricity from 1830 to 0100 only and water is sporadic
(and should be boiled to within an inch of its life). The town's market is very
limited; try the one at Yerbabuena on Sunday morning (see above). The
young Spanish priest, Padre Diego, is very helpful, especially to Europeans.
He is involved in the new museum project (see below). The Centro de Salud is
helpful and will even visit your hotel if you're too ill to move.

Northern Highlands

Gran Vilaya Region

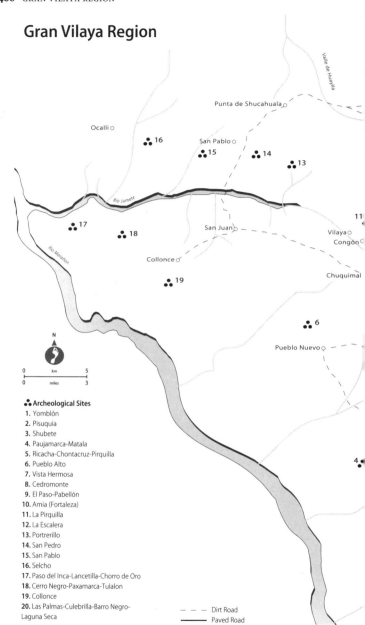

∴ Archeological Sites
1. Yomblón
2. Pisuquia
3. Shubete
4. Paujamarca-Matala
5. Ricacha-Chontacruz-Pirquilla
6. Pueblo Alto
7. Vista Hermosa
8. Cedromonte
9. El Paso-Pabellón
10. Amia (Fortaleza)
11. La Pirquilla
12. La Escalera
13. Portrerillo
14. San Pedro
15. San Pablo
16. Selcho
17. Paso del Inca-Lancetilla-Chorro de Oro
18. Cerro Negro-Paxamarca-Tulalon
19. Collonce
20. Las Palmas-Culebrilla-Barro Negro-
Laguna Seca

- - - Dirt Road
──── Paved Road

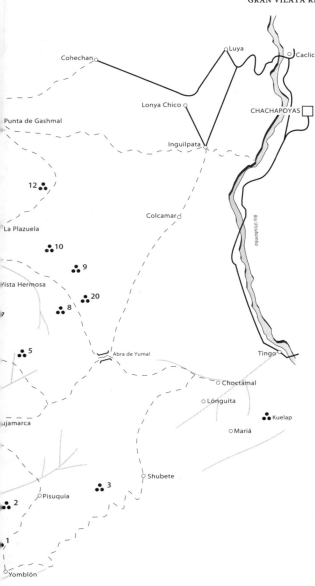

Luya
Caclic
Cohechan
Lonya Chico
CHACHAPOYAS
Punta de Gashmal
Inguilpata
12
Colcamar
Río Utcubamba
La Plazuela
10
9
Vista Hermosa
20
8
Tingo
5
Abra de Yumal
Choctámal
Lónguita
ujamarca
Kuelap
Mariá
Shubete
3
Pisuquia
2
1
Yomblón

Related maps
Chachapoyas, page 397
Kuelap, page 402

Essentials   **Sleeping** F *Didogre*, 16 de Julio 320. Basic, cold water, shared bathroom, friendly. **F** *Escobedo*, 16 de Julio 518. Cold water, very basic, doors locked at 2130. *Laguna de los Cóndores*, Jr Amazonas, half a block from the plaza. Due to open in late 1998, will have hot water and some rooms with private bathroom.

Eating *Celi*, Amazonas, Plaza de Armas. Good value, 2-course set meals for US$2.50, will cook vegetarian meals at 24 hours notice (also excellent pizzas), very clean, has fridge for cold beer, friendly. Recommended. *El Sabor Tropical*, 16 de Julio. Good chicken and chips, friendly. Try breakfast at the restaurant a few doors down. *El Caribe* on the plaza. Basic meals.

Transport Buses from Chachapoyas to Celendín (see page 398) pass through Leymebamba about 4 hours after departure, and make a lunch stop here. There's no guarantee of a seat, but you might have a better chance if you purchase your ticket in advance in Chachapoyas, advising that you will get on in Leymebamba. combis to Chachapoyas leave the plaza 0200-0400 daily, except Sunday, when they depart 0500-0600 to Yerbabuena only, where you can get other vehicles on to Chachapoyas. Inquire locally.

Laguna de los Cóndores   In 1996 a spectacular site consisting of six burial *Chullpas*, containing 219 mummies and vast quantities of ceramics, textiles, *quipus* and other artifacts from the late Inca period, was discovered at Laguna de los Cóndores, a beautiful lake in a jungle setting, south of Leymebamba.

In order to protect this material from *huaqueros*, who had already done considerable damage, all the material was moved to town. It is a major new discovery which in 1998 had only begun to be studied by scientists. A small museum has been set up on the Plaza de Armas (if closed see Denis Tafur, local director of the Instituto Nacional de Cultura, Amazonas 420, also on the plaza) and a larger one is being built with Austrian financial assistance, at the site of the original Leymebamba town, due to open in 1999. For further information contact Dr Sonia Guillén, Director, Centro Mallqui Bioanthropology Foundation, Avenida A. Márquez 2014, Jesús María, Lima 11, T2610095, F4637875, E mallqui@amautá.rcp.net.pe.

The trip to Laguna de los Cóndores takes 10-15 hours on horseback in each direction from Leymebamba. Fran Cole (Surrey) writes: "It is not for the fainthearted. Everyone who makes the trip agrees that it is the trip of a lifetime. Funnily enough, very few people want to do it twice!" Note that the route climbs to 4,800 metres before descending to the laguna. Make sure your horse is in good condition as the track is often knee deep in mud. Also take food and warm clothes. It is best done during the dry season (May to September); hire a local guide and horses. Denis Tafur (see above) may be of assistance in making arrangements. Another guide is Luis; ask for him in Leymebamba.

La Congona   There are many ruins around Leymebamba, many of which are covered in vegetation. The most spectacular is the Chachapoyan site of La Congona.

The site is a brisk three hours' walk along a clear trail which starts at the lower end of 16 de Julio. The path climbs steeply from the town, then levels off before descending to a large flat pasture. Turn left at the end of the pasture, then bear right where the trail divides, to reach the middle of three peaks, identified by a white limestone cliff. The ruins are clustered in a small area, impossible to see until you are right among them. The views are stupendous and the ruins worth the effort. This is the best preserved of three sites, with 30 decorated round stone houses (some with evidence of three

Northern Highlands

storeys) and a watch tower. "It is supposed to be the only site displaying all three Chacha friezes – zigzag, rhomboid and Greek stepped." (Richard Robinson, Newbury, England.)

There are two other sites, El Molinete and Pumahuanyuna, nearby. All three can be visited in a day but a guide is essential to explain the area and show the way to the ruins as it is easy to get lost. Sr César Jaúregui, 16 de Julio on the corner of Ayacucho, has horses and knows this area. Also ask at the INC in Leymebamba.

East of Chachapoyas

Monte Peruvia 40 kilometres east from Chachapoyas, on the road to Mendoza, are the pre-Inca ruins of Monte Peruvia (known locally as **Purunllacta**). They consist of hundreds of white stone houses with staircases, temples and palaces. The ruins have been cleared by local farmers and some houses have been destroyed. A guide is not necessary.

If you're stuck in **Pipus**, ask to sleep at restaurant *Huaracina* or at the police station next door. There are no hotels in Cheto but a house high up on the hill above the town with a balcony has cheap bed and board. The same family also has a house on the plaza. There are two small shops selling very little and a small house with one room serves basic but good meals.

There is no direct transport from Chachapoyas. Take a combi at 0930 and 1500 from Jr Salamanca, fourth block down from the market, to Pipus, which stands at the turn-off to Cheto; 1½ hours, US$1.35. You may have a long wait in Pipus for transport to Cheto; a camioneta leaves early in the morning, US$0.90. Or it's a 2-hour walk on a rough road.

Molinopampa The road east from Chachapoyas continues through Pipus to Molinopampa, two hours' drive from Chachapoyas. The town is the starting point for an adventurous five-day hike to Rioja (see page 412).

Katrina Farrar and Andy Thornton write: "Only experienced hikers should attempt this journey, which is very difficult. Food supplies for the whole journey should be purchased at Chachapoyas and a guide, absolutely essential, hired at Molinopampa. The steep trail leads through waist-high unbridged rivers, over the cold, high sierra and then for three days one follows the muddy trail down to the dense and humid jungle. We were accompanied by exotic butterflies, and never a quiet moment with the chattering of birds and monkeys. The whole magic of the jungle – trees, birds, animals and insects – can be seen untouched in their natural surroundings."

Mendoza The road carries on to Mendoza (*Altitude*: 1,500 metres), capital and supply centre of the subtropical province of the same name (Rodríguez de Mendoza), which reportedly produces the best coffee in Peru. Organically grown coffee from the area is exported directly to Europe.

Mendoza is also the starting point for an ethnologically interesting area in the Guayabamba Valley where there is an unexplained high incidence of very fair-skinned people. There are roads and public transport to the small towns of Huambo, Santa Rosa, Totora, Limabamba, Chirimoto Viejo and Milpuc; and horse trails to other more remote villages. Visitors going beyond Mendoza should be self sufficient. Padre Juan Castelli, an English priest who has been living in the area since the First World War, is very knowledgeable. In July 1998 he was based in Campo Redondo.

Northern Highlands

The Valley of the Whites

The tiny villages in the Guayabamba valley, could be any other sleepy, sub-tropical settlements. A collection of wooden houses on a fertile plain where oranges, bananas, guava and yucca grow, where colourful butterflies and mesmerizing birdsong fills the warm, humid air. But the people of this remote region are very different from your average jungle dweller. They are blond-haired, blue-eyed and fair-skinned and could easily have just stepped off the 1700 flight from Stockholm.

The population of the Guayabamba valley themselves don't know where they came from and opinions among experts vary. Some posit the theory that they originate from warring conquistador factions in the early 16th century. However, this doesn't explain the rarity of this phenomenon or the fact that the Spanish chronicler Garcilaso de la Vega describes them resisting the Incas before the conquest.

Professor Kaufmann-Doig of Lima and Dr Jacques de Mahieu of Buenos Aires believe them to be descendants of the Vikings, who came to Peru in the 11th century. Such a theory is supported by the discovery on Easter Island, west of Chile, of drawings showing Viking longships, as well as linguistic parallels between the Quechua language and Scandinavian tongues.

Whatever the explanation, the incongruous presence of these fair-skinned people in such a remote part of the country will continue to attract the attention of ethnologists and the more curious and hardier of travellers.

Sleeping and eating F *Altiplano*, Rodríguez de Mendoza 321. With bathroom, cheaper without, cold water, very basic. F *Grandez*, Pje Hilario López 110. With bathroom, cheaper without, cold water, very basic. There are several simple restaurants on Rodríguez de Mendoza.

Transport Air *Chirimoto Tours*, office on Rodríguez de Mendoza, flies to Lima every Saturday, US$55; *Grupo Ocho* to **Lima**, Pje Hilario López, every second Tuesday, US$45. These schedules vary and flights may be cancelled. **Buses** To **Chachapoyas**, from Jr Toribio Rodríguez de Mendoza, at 0200 and 1000 daily, 5 hours, US$3.50; cars leave at 0500 or when full, US$5. To **Limabamba**, three daily between 1300 and 1500, 2 hours, US$1.20.

Directory Post and telephone offices are on Rodríguez de Mendoza.

West of Chachapoyas

Lamud 37 kilometres northwest of Chachapoyas, on a turn-off from the road north to Pedro Ruíz (see below), is Lamud, which is a convenient base for several interesting archaeological sites. The local fiesta of *Señor de Gualamita* on 14 September is well attended.

At **San Antonio**, half an hour from Lamud, is a sandstone cliff face with several groups of burial tombs high on a ledge. They are difficult to see unless you know what you're looking for (they are basically small piles of stones). The ruins, set on the hill above, are a residential complex, thought to form part of a group of people belonging to the Chipuric. The main nucleus is almost completely ruined. A guide is not necessary, but ask for directions.

Three hours from Lamud (10 kilometres on a very poor mule track), are the ruins of **Pueblo de los Muertos**, circular stone houses overlooking the valley. The view is spectacular but it is easy to lose your way and the ruins are very difficult to find as they are overgrown. Since being brought to public attention by Gene Savoy in the mid 1960s, the site has been largely destroyed by local grave robbers. Ask directions before setting out and be patient.

Sleeping and eating In Lamud: **D** *Hostal Kuelap*, Garcilaso de la Vega 452, on the plaza. Clean, basic, friendly, hot water, **E** with cold water and shared bathroom. A few doors down is Restaurant *María*, which is cheap, friendly and obliging, steak and chips is recommended, ask for *pension* which is 3 meals for US$1.80, excellent value, popular, the owner's son is a good local guide and charges around US$10 per day.

Transport Buses and combis from Chachapoyas to Lamud, and Luya (see below), leave between 1000 and 1230 when full from Libertad y Ortiz Arrieta, near the market; US$1.50, 1½ hours. The road is unpaved but in reasonable condition.

A 20-minute drive south of Lamud, on the same road, is the village of Luya. There is basic accommodation at **G** *Hostal Jucusbamba*.

Trekking around Luya

Three kilometres or one and a half hours' walk from Luya is **Chipuric**, a residential complex belonging to the Chachapoyas culture. The site consists of burial tombs set in a cliff face on a high ledge with circular stone buildings on the hill above. The tombs, which are one metre high and look like beehives, have all been looted. Continue along the dirt road from Luya until it forks; take the higher road with the irrigation canal. At **Pueblo Molino** (a small cluster of houses and one shop), the cliff face and the burial tombs are visible. On the lower road which passes below the cliff on the other side of the river, is Chipuric town. The cliff is steep but it's possible to climb up to the tombs with some difficulty and quite a few scratches from the thorn bushes. There are great views from the top, though.

Carajía, also known as Solmol, is two and a half hours' walk from Luya but more accessible from **Trita**. A short walk from Trita, in the valley behind the village, are the stone burial figures set into an impressive cliff face. Just below the tombs are plenty of human bones, if you look carefully. Ask for directions in Luya. It's best to take a local guide. Expect to pay around US$3.50-5 a day.

A good way to get to know the local people and to fully appreciate the magnificent scenery of this region is a three to four day trek starting from Luya. Walk two to two and a half hours to **Shipata** and from there to the 'Sarcófagos' (30-40 minutes). Ask around for directions. You cannot get to the Sarcófagos, but can view them from the other side of the valley, with binoculars preferably. At Shipata you can stay with Sra Rosa Zota, who will cook you dinner and breakfast. A better option, however, is to continue one to one and a half hours to **Cohechan**. To get there from the Sarcófagos, you have to go back to Shipata.

Continue from Cohechan to **Belén** (four to five hours) and **Vista Hermosa** (two and a half to three hours). In this area there are several Chachapoyan ruins. You can lodge with Sr Cruz. From Vista Hermosa to **Youmal** involves a tough climb of 1600-1700 metres but from there to **Choctámal** the trail thankfully descends. It is possible to stay with Wilson Jiménez in Choctámal (see also page 403). It is a further two and a half to three hours to **Tingo**.

North of Chachapoyas

The road north from Chachapoyas heads through the beautiful Utcubamba River canyon to Pedro Ruíz, at a crossroads where you can either head west to

Pedro Ruíz

Chiclayo on the coast or east to Tarapoto, Yurimaguas and the jungle. This is a small but important junction town, situated at 1,370 metres, at the confluence of the Río Ingenio and the Utucubamba.

Sleeping & eating D *Casablanca*. New in 1998, private bathroom, comfortable. **E** *Amazonense*. Cheaper with shared bathroom, basic, clean, friendly, helpful. Recommended. **F** *Marginal*. Shared bathroom, basic. There are several restaurants. *Shilico* is recommended.

Transport Many buses to and from **Chiclayo**, **Tarapoto** (9-10 hours) and **Chachapoyas** all pass through town, mostly at night from 2000-2400. There is no way to reserve a seat and buses are usually full. combis (US$1.75) and cars (US$2.75) go to **Bagua Grande**, 2 hours. combis (US$1.75) and cars (US$2.75) also go to Chachapoyas, 3 hours.

Directory Banks *Banco de la Nación* changes cash only. As does Comercial Argón.

Around Pedro Ruíz There are many interesting options for walking in the surrounding hills, covered with patches of cloud-forest and a good deal of undeveloped archaeology.

Catarata Chinata is a lovely 150 metres waterfall which can be reached by walking along the trail to the village of San Carlos, about two hours uphill. Continue uphill past San Carlos then turn left along a smaller track to the waterfall, a further two hours. Ask the locals for directions. It's a very nice full-day hike through sections of cloud-forest.

To get to the **Cocachimbo valley**, take a combi to Cocahuayco along the road to Chachapoyas (30 minutes, US$1.50), then follow the track uphill to the left. It's a two-hour climb to Cocachimbo. The surrounding valley has many beautiful waterfalls. It is not always easy to get transport back to Pedro Ruíz.

Pomacocha lake, at 2,150 metres above sea level, is one of the largest lakes in Peru. The blue-green water is surrounded by *totora* reeds. Take a combi to Florida or Balsapata along the road to Rioja (one hour, US$1.75); the lake is near the road.

An easy downhill walk four kilometres along the main road to Bagua Grande brings you to the pretty **Corontachaca waterfall** by the roadside. A spring of sulphurous lukewarm water is found at the base of the cascade.

East to the Amazon

The eastern branch of the road at Pedro Ruíz runs all the way to Yurimaguas. The road has been improved as far as Tarapoto and is now partly paved but is still prone to landslides in the wet season.

Nueva Cajamarca 152 kilometres east of Pedro Ruíz is the new town of Nueva Cajamarca, with a few thousand inhabitants. There is a large market for local produce. There's an hourly colectivo to Rioja (US$1.30, 45 minutes) and a colectivo to Chachapoyas; US$12, 11-12 hours. There's accommodation at **F** *Puerto Rico*, on the main road, and **F** *Perú*, off to the right towards Rioja.

Rioja Just beyond Nueva Cajamarca is Rioja. There is a road from here to Naranjillo and Aguas Verdes, with a five-hour walk to Venceremos. It's a pleasant way to see the jungle in good weather, but don't attempt it otherwise.

An easy excursion can be made to the Cueva de los Huácharos, which are unexplored caves (take a torch). Take a truck to La Unión (45 minutes), walk 40 minutes to Palestina then 50 minutes more to the caves. Ask locals for directions.

Sleeping and eating *Hostal San Martín*, Grau 540; *San Ramón*, Jr Faustino Maldonado 840; and *Carranza*, Jr Huallanga. All are basic. *Restaurante Los Olivos* is recommended.

Transport There are flights to **Lima** from Rioja, 2 hours, with *Aero Continente*, who also fly to **Yurimaguas** and **Iquitos**. Check schedules in advance. There are regular combis to **Moyobamba** (30 minutes) and on to **Tarapoto** (US$5).

Moyobamba

Moyobamba, a pleasant town, in an attractive valley, is the capital of San Martín district. It was hit by an earthquake in April 1991. Mosquito nets can be bought cheaply. This area has to cope with lots of rain in the wet season and in some years the whole area is flooded. The ruins of **Pueblo de los Muertos** are nearby. In the last week of June the town celebrates its annual tourist week festival, in the last week of July is the *Fiesta de Santiago* and the third week of November is the *Semana de la Orquídea*.

Population: 14,000
Altitude: 915 metres
Phone code: 094
Coloured map 1, grid B5

NB There have been guerrilla and drug activities in this region so take good care. Tourists must register with the PNP.

Sights **Puerto Tahuiso** is the town's harbour, where locals sell their produce at weekends. From **Morro de Calzada**, there is a good view of the area. Take a truck to Calzada (30 minutes), then walk up for 20 minutes. There are Baños Termales, four kilometres from Moyobamba on the Rioja road, which are worth a visit.

The more adventurous can hike to the **Gera waterfalls**, 21 kilometres from Moyobamba in the jungle. Take a micro to Jepelacio. From there, take a good path through a well-populated valley, crossing two bridges on the way, then head along the river through dense jungle. There are three more river crossings but no bridges, so it's potentially dangerous.

Sleeping **A3** *Turistas*, Puerto Mirador, Jr Sucre, 1 kilometre from the centre T562594/848, F562050 (in Lima T4423090, F4424180, Avda R Rivera Navarrete 889, of 208, San Isidro). Includes breakfast, nice location, pool, good restaurant. **E** *Hostal Atlanta*, Alonso De Alborado 865, T562063. With bathroom, clean, good but noisy. **F** *Hostal Country Club*. Clean, comfortable, friendly, nice garden. Recommended. **F** *Hostal Cobos*, with bathroom, good. **F** *Hostal Los Andes*, clean. Also *Monterrey* and *Mesía*, which are both basic and cheap.

Eating *La Olla de Barro*, on Pedro Canga. Typical food, expensive. Also on Pedro Canga is *Chifa Kike Ku*.

Transport **Flights** to **Lima** once a week with *Expreso Aéreo*. Also to **Huánuco**, **Juanjui**, **Tarapoto** and **Tingo María**. **Cars** to **Tarapoto** (3 hours, US$6) and **Rioja** (30 minutes, US$1.30) leave when full from Jr Pedro Canga. There are also **pickups**, which are slower and cheaper. **Bus** to Yurimaguas with Guadalupe (Jr Callao block 5), US$8.75.

Directory **Banks** *Banco de Crédito*, Jr San Martín y Alonso de Alborado. *Viajes Turismo Río Mayo*, Jr San Martin 401. **Tourist offices** *Dirección Regional de Turismo*, is at Jr San Martín 301, on the plaza,

Northern Highlands

T562043. Information on excursions and hikes is available from the *Instituto Nacional de Cultura*, Jr Benavides, 3rd block. *Emigdio Soto* is an expert on trips to native communities in the Alto Mayo area, contact him at the Proyecto Especial Alto Mayo. For jungle trips contact *Orlando Peigot Daza* (Spanish only) at Yurayacu village.

Tarapoto

The road is paved for a short way out of Moyobamba, then deteriorates to Tarapoto (*Phone code*: 094), a busy town with several hotels. There's a good local market one and a half blocks from the Plaza de Armas on Avenida Raimondi. Rioja, Moyobamba and Tarapoto are growing centres of population, with much small-scale forest clearance beside the road after Balsapata. The road is heavily used by trucks, with fuel and meals available. Food and accommodation are relatively expensive in this remote region. Tourists must register with the police on arrival. In the second week of July is the town's tourist week festival.

Sleeping **A3** *Río Shilcayo*, Pasaje Las Flores 224, 1 kilometre out of town, T522225, F524236 (in Lima T4479359). With bathroom, excellent meals, non-residents can use the swimming pool for a fee. **D** *Edinson*, Avda Raimondi, 1 block from Plaza de Armas, T522723. With bathroom, cheaper without, cold water, clean and comfortable. **D** *Hostal San Antonio*, Jr Jiménez Pimentel 126, T522226. With private bathroom and TV, courtyard. Noisy but recommended. **E** *Tarapoto*, T522150. With fan, clean. **F** *Hostal Americano*. Fan and private bathroom with each room. **F** *Juan Alfonso*, Jr Pedro de Urzúa. With shower, noisy. **F** *Las Palmeras*, just off the plaza. Small and dingy, lacks water. Not recommended. **G** *Los Angeles*, near the plaza. Good value, laundry facilities, restaurant.

Eating The best are *Real* and *El Camarón*, though both are expensive. *Las Terrazas*, serves typical food and is recommended. There are many others, such as *El Mesón*.

Transport **Air** Flights to **Lima** with *Aero Continente*, who also fly to **Yurimaguas** and on to **Iquitos**. To **Pucallpa**, *Aero Continente* fly twice a week, and daily to **Juanjui, Tocache** and **Tingo María**. *Expreso Aéreo* has flights to/from **Tarapoto**. Book in advance, particularly in the rainy season. Many smaller airlines operate flights to **Yurimaguas**, eg *Aerotaxi Ibérico*. Turn up at airport at 0700-0800, wait for it to open, wait for people to turn up, wait for a list for your destination to be drawn up and you should get away later in the morning. A taxi to the airport is US$1.75. There's no bus service, but it's no problem to walk.

Buses To/from **Rioja**, US$7. To/from **Moyobamba**, 116 kilometres, several buses daily, US$3.50, 5 hours; 3½ hours, US$7 by colectivo. There are daily buses from Tarapoto to **Chiclayo**, via Moyobamba, Rioja, Bagua and Olmos, 690 kilometres, 22 hours, US$17, and to **Trujillo**, 25 hours, US$19; with *Paredes Estrella* at 1300 and 1400, *Turismo Ejecutivo* at 0830 and 1130 and *Trans Guadalupe*. To **Yurimaguas**, US$5-10, 4-5 hours, trucks and pick-ups daily (see below for road conditions). Truck/pick-up leaves for Yurimaguas (usually 0800-0900, and in the afternoon) from Jorge Chávez 175, down Avenida Raimondi two blocks, then left five blocks along Avenida Pedro de Uruaz. Pick-ups also leave from this street to other destinations.

Directory **Banks** *Banco de Crédito*, Maynas 134. Efficient, no commission on TCs. *Interbanc*, near the plaza. Charges no commission on changing TCs for soles. There are many street changers around the Plaza de Armas.

Around Tarapoto

La Mina de Sal is a salt mine outside the city. **Laguna Azul** (or Laguna Sauce as it is also known) is a big lake 10 kilometres from Tarapoto, with *cabañas* for rent on the shore. They cost US$80 per night for four beds and a shower. They are very basic and no fresh water or food is available. A colectivo takes two and a half hours and costs US$2.50. You can go river rafting on the Río Mayo for US$10 per person.

35 kilometres from Tarapoto, on the road to Moyobamba, a road leads off to **Lamas** where there is a small but highly recommended museum, with exhibits on local Indian community (Lamistas). Ask at the café opposite if the museum is shut. There's also a market in the early morning. Colectivo from Tarapoto; 30 minutes, US$0.70. From Lamas you can visit the waterfalls at **Shapawanca** (taxi US$7, 15 minutes).

About 14 kilometres from Tarapoto on the spectacular road to Yurimaguas are the 50 metre falls of **Ahuashiyacu**, which can be visited by tour from Tarapoto (US$18 including lunch) or by hiring a motorcycle from *Grand Prix* (Shapajo y Raimondi, US$3.50 an hour). A restaurant nearby serves reasonable food and has two rooms to rent (**G** per person, basic but OK). The road continues for 10 kilometres through lush vegetation to a small village (with restaurant).

Tarapoto to Yurimaguas

The journey from Tarapoto to Tingo María (see page 458) is not advisable. In the rainy season the roads are impossible and it is a drugs-growing area. From Tarapoto it is 136 kilometres to Yurimaguas on the Río Huallaga (see page 460). The spectacular road can be very bad in the wet season, taking six to eight hours for trucks (schedules above). Once the plains are reached, the road improves and there is more habitation. **Shapaja** is the port for Tarapoto, 14 kilometres from town, served by colectivos. At Shapaja cargo boats can be caught to Yurimaguas. There's plenty of birdlife and river traffic to be seen. From Yurimaguas on the Río Huallaga, launches go to Iquitos.

To the Coast

*The road from Pedro Ruíz (see page 411) goes west for 65 kilometres to Bagua Grande, at first through a narrow gorge, the ridges covered with lush cloud-forest, then along the broad and fertile lower Utcubamba valley. It then crosses the Marañón at Corral Quemado. From the confluence of the Marañón with the Río Chamaya, the road follows the latter, past bare cliffs covered by dry scrub, towering over the deep river canyons. It reaches the **Abra de Porculla** (at 2,150 metres, the lowest pass through the Peruvian Andes) in 60 kilometres, before descending to join the old Pan-American Highway at **Olmos** (see page 361). From here you can go southwest to Chiclayo, or northwest to Piura. The road from Pedro Ruíz west to Olmos was being paved in 1998, but remains prone to landslides during the rainy season.*

Bagua Grande This is the first town of note heading west from Pedro Ruíz. It's a hot and dusty place, sprawled along its main street, Avenida Chachapoyas. Bagua Grande is not very safe. If arriving late, ask to sleep on the bus until daybreak. Police may ask to see travellers' documents here. The town celebrates the *Fiesta de Santiago* over the last week in July and in September holds its tourist week festivities. Banco de Crédito, Avda Chachapoyas 1978. Cash only.

Northern Highlands

Sleeping All the hotels are on Avda Chachapoyas. **E** *Montecristo*, No 2274, T754191. With private bathroom, basic but clean. **E** *Francys*, No 2280, T754038. Cheaper without bathroom, basic. **E** *Iris*, No 2390, T754115. Basic. There are several others.

Eating *Pollería La Famosa*, Avda Chachapoyas. Cheap and good. *Restaurant Central*, at Avda Chachapoyas 1553, is also good.

Transport Many buses pass through Bagua Grande en route from Chiclayo to Tarapoto and Chachapoyas and *vice-versa*, mostly at night. Cars (US$2) and combis (US$1) to Jaén leave from the west end of Avenida Chachapoyas, 1 hour. From the east end Avenida Chachapoyas, cars (US$2.75) and combis (US$1.75) leave to Pedro Ruíz, 2 hours. Taking a mototaxi (US$0.35) between the two stops is a good alternative to walking in the heat.

NB Near Bagua Grande, along a side road is **Bagua Chica**, also referred to as just **Bagua**, a garrison town which has gained importance since the 1995 border skirmish with Ecuador. Pay careful attention to the names when arranging transport, so you are not taken to the wrong Bagua.

Northeast to Sameriza

From Bagua Grande the road continues northwest, then forks: southwest to **Chamaya**, for Jaén and the coast, and northeast to **Sameriza**, the first port on the Marañón. The northeast branch passes through **Aramango** and **Nazareth** and continues to another fork, north to **Oracuza** and northeast to Sameriza and **Puerto Delfus**, both on the Río Marañon.

To reach Sameriza, pick-ups run twice daily from Bagua Grande to Imasa. Get out at Campamento Mesones Muro, 15 minutes before Imasa (US$4, seven hours), where you must register with the police. This can be a time-consuming procedure. For the 150 kilometres from Mesones Muro to Sameriza, you have to wait for a pick-up – which can take anything up to six days – and then be prepared for a two to three day journey because of poor roads and missing bridges.

The *m/n Fernández* makes the journey from Sameriza to Iquitos every second week. It takes four days downriver, and six days upriver. Take a hammock as there are only a few cabins available. **NB** We have received reports of violent attacks on tourists by local Aguarana Indians on this route.

Jaén

Population: approximately 25,000
Altitude: 740 metres
Phone code: 074
Coloured map 1, grid B3

Seven kilometres west of Bagua Grande, a road branches northwest at Chamaya (one basic hostel, El Volante) to Jaén. This is the best place to break the journey from Chachapoyas or the jungle to Chiclayo and vice-versa.

Although it was founded in 1536, the city retains little of its colonial character. Rather, it is the modern and prosperous centre of a rich agricultural region producing rice, coffee, and cocoa. From 1563 to 1789 it was governed by the *Real Audiencia de Quito* and it remains close to territory disputed by the two countries, hence Peruvian patriotism runs high here and

Jaén has been dubbed *"Corazón de la Peruandidad"*. The local festival of *Señor de Huamantanga* on 14 September is widely attended.

Sights

A colourful modern cathedral dominates the large plaza around which most services of interest to the visitor are clustered. A museum at the Instituto 4 de Junio, Hermógenes Mejía sin número, displays pre-colombian artifacts from the Pakamuros culture.

Essentials

C *El Bosque*, Mesones Muro 632, T/F731184. With fridge, pool, parking, gardens, best in town.

   D *Prim's*, Diego Palomino 1353, T731039. With fridge, small pool. **D** *Hostal Cancún*, Diego Palomino 1413, T730589. Clean and pleasant. Recommended.

Sleeping
■ *on maps*
Price codes:
see inside front cover

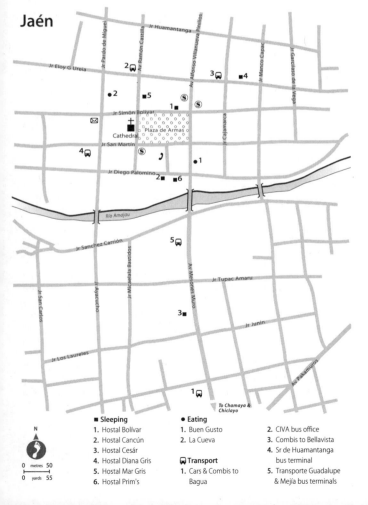

Jaén

Northern Highlands

■ **Sleeping**
1. Hostal Bolívar
2. Hostal Cancún
3. Hostal Cesár
4. Hostal Diana Gris
5. Hostal Mar Gris
6. Hostal Prim's

● **Eating**
1. Buen Gusto
2. La Cueva

🚍 **Transport**
1. Cars & Combis to Bagua

2. CIVA bus office
3. Combis to Bellavista
4. Sr de Huamantanga bus terminal
5. Transporte Guadalupe & Mejía bus terminals

N

0 metres 50
0 yards 55

D *Hostal César*, Mesones Muro 168, T/F731491. Parking, all services, nice. **D** *Hostal Bolívar*, Bolívar 1312, Plaza de Armas, T731080. Clean. **D** *Hostal Mar Gris*, Mariscal Castilla 342, T733220. **D** *Hostal Diana Gris*, Urreta 1132, T731119. Family run and friendly.

E *Santa Elena*, San Martín 1528, T731223. With private bathroom, basic. **F** *San Martín*, San Martín 1642. With private bathroom, basic. **F** *Requejo*, Mariscal Castilla 345. Shared bathroom, clean, basic.

| Eating | *La Cueva*, Pardo Miguel 304. Recommended. *El Buen Gusto*, Villanueva Pinillos 150. |
| ● *on maps* | Good set meal. There are many others around the plaza. |

Transport **Bus** to **Chiclayo** with *CIVA*, Mariscal Ureta 1300 y V Pinillos, at 1030 and 2100 daily, 8 hours, US$5. It continues to **Lima** (US$17) on Monday, Wednesday and Friday. Also to **Chiclayo**: *Señor de Huamantanga*, Pardo Miguel y San Martín, at 0830, 1245, 2200, 2300 daily, US$5; *Paredes Estrella*, Mesones Muro 211, at 1000, 2100, US$5. To **Tarapoto** via Perdo Ruíz (the crossroads for Chachapoyas, 4 hours, US$5): *Paredes Estrella* at 1600, 12 hours, US$12; *Transportes Mejía*, Mesones Muro 100, at 1300, 1600, US$12; *Jaén Express*, Tupac Amaru 109, at 1200, 1700, US$12. combis (US$1) and cars (US$2) run in the early morning and when full from Avenida Mesones Muro y Los Laureles to Bagua Grande (1 hour), where connections can be made for Pedro Ruíz.

Directory **Banks** *Banco de Crédito*, Bolívar y V Pinillos. Cash only. *Banco Continental*, Ramon Castilla y San Martín. Cash, US$5 commission for TCs. *Cambios Coronel*, V Pinillos 360 (Coronel 2 across the street at 339). Cash only, good rates. *El Pionero*, V Pinillos 325. Cash only. **Communications** Post Office: Pardo Miguel y Bolívar. **Telephone office**: Pasaje Bracamoros 1161, off the plaza. **Internet**: *Computron*, Mesones Muro 132, T732155. US$0.70 per email message or US$3.50 per hour.

Around Jaén

Jaén lies in a bowl ringed by hills and the surrounding countryside offers off-the-beaten-track hiking, caves and undeveloped archaeology. There is no organized tourism here, but plenty of opportunities for the adventurous to strike out on their own.

To bathe in the Marañon, take a combi from the corner of Cajamarca and Eloy Ureta to Bellavista (40 minutes, US$0.50). From here it is a 45 minute walk alongside rice paddies to the river, ask for directions. Swimming is possible but mind the strong current. Many locals go there on Sundays.

El Almendral thermal baths are eight kilometres east of Chamaya on the road to Bagua. **Agua Azul Stella**, a stone monolith from the Chavín culture found in the district of Chontalí, is 72 kilometres from Jaén. There is a small museum at the site. The **Ayahuaca Temple**, a necropolis located in the Pucará disrict (48 kilometres, three and a half hours) is reputedly associated with metaphysical phenomena.

A road runs north from Jaén to **San Ignacio** (114 kilometres), near the frontier with Ecuador. There is no official border crossing here. It passes the valley of the Chinchipe, renowned for its lost Inca gold. San Ignacio has a *fiesta* on 31 August. combis from Jaén take four hours, US$2.75.

Central Highlands

11

Central Highlands

422 Lima to Huancayo

424 Jauja

425 Huancayo

432 Huancavelica

434 Ayacucho

442 Ayacucho to Cusco

444 East of La Oroya

448 North of La Oroya

449 Cerro de Pasco

451 Huallaga Valley

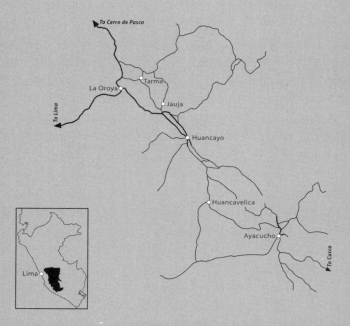

This vast, unexplored area of stunning mountain scenery and timeless Andean towns and villages is a must for those who appreciate traditional, good quality textiles and ceramics, or who enjoy the occasional lively festival. The main highlights include the cities of Huancayo, Ayacucho and the surrounding villages – the main production centres of textiles and ceramics. Ayacucho also hosts one of the largest and most impressive Holy Week celebrations in Latin America.

Ayacucho was the home of the Maoist terrorist movement, Shining Path (see page 506), and was particularly affected by the troubles. As a result, large parts of the central highlands are only just opening up to tourism once more. People in these parts are relieved to see tourists return to their towns and cities and treat them with great friendship and hospitality. There are still many military checkpoints and it is advisable to travel only during the day. Knowledge of Spanish is essential, as is informing yourself regularly of the current political situation.

Travellers should note that the northern part of the central Andes, north from Tingo María, in the Huallaga valley, is the main cocaine producing region and largely under the control of narco-traffickers. If travelling in this area, travel only by day and do not, under any circumstances, stray from the main routes.

Lima to Huancayo

The Central Highway between Lima and Huancayo more or less parallels the course of the railway (see page 429). The road is paved from Lima to Huancayo, but all the other roads in this region are in poor condition, especially when wet.

At La Oroya (see below), the central highway divides. Its southern branch follows the valley of the Río Mantaro, to Huancayo, and on to Huancavelica or Ayacucho. The northern branch runs to Cerro de Pasco and on to Huánuco, Tingo María and Pucallpa. 25 kilometres north along the road to Cerro de Pasco is the turning east for Tarma and La Merced (see page 444).

There are several places to stay on the Central Highway between Lima and Chosica (see page 116). There are others in the residential district of **Chaclacayo**, just before Chosica.

Chosica

Population: 31,200
Altitude: 860 metres
Coloured map 3, grid C3

Chosica is 40 kilometres from Lima and the real starting place for the mountains. It is a popular winter resort because it is above the cloudbank covering Lima in winter. Beyond the town looms a precipitous range of hills almost overhanging the streets. There are 4 basic *hostales* in Chosica, 2 are off the main road near the market, and the other 2 up the hill on the left. All have water problems. **E** *Hostería La Villa del Sol*, on the pedestrian street perpendicular to 28 de Julio. This is the best in town and is a big old building. **E** *Hostal Chosica*, 28 de Julio. Not too good and unwelcoming. Colectivos for Chosica leave from the first block of Montevideo (around the corner from the Ormeño terminal), when full, between 0600 and 2100, and cost US$0.60.

San Pedro de Casta

40 kilometres beyond Chosica, up the picturesque Santa Eulalia valley, is the village of San Pedro de Casta, which has some interesting sights nearby. **Marcahuasi** is a table mountain about three kilometres squared, at 4,200 metres, nearby. The *meseta* has been investigated by the late Daniel Ruzo. There are three lakes, a 40 metres high 'monumento a la humanidad', and other mysterious lines, gigantic figures, sculptures, astrological signs and megaliths which display non-American symbolism. Ruzo describes this pre-Incaic culture in his book, *La Culture Masma*, Extrait de l'Ethnographie, Paris, 1956. Others say that the formations are not man-made, but the result of wind erosion. The trail starts behind the village of San Pedro, and bends to the left. It's about two hours to the *meseta*. Guides cost about US$3 a day, and are advisable in misty weather. Tours can be arranged with travel agencies in Lima.

Beyond San Pedro is **San Juan de Iris**, a tiny village, outside which impressive ruins have been discovered. A bus or truck leaves from *Restaurant 41* in Chosica at 0900, if you're lucky, and takes seven hours.

There are the ancient ruins of a small town on the hill of San Pedro de Casta, which date from 1500 BC. On the hills of **Loma de los Papas** are the ruins of **Tambo Inca**, and an ancient cemetery lies to the south. To get there take a daily bus from Chosica at 0800.

Sleeping and transport The only accommodation in San Pedro is in a cold shelter, for less than US$1. Take all necessary camping equipment and buy food in Chosica as there is nothing beyond that point. The bus to San Pedro de Casta leaves Chosica from Parque Echerique, opposite the market, daily except Sunday, at about 0800 (when full); it takes 3 hours and costs US$2. The road is in a reasonable condition until the Callahuanca hydroelectric station.

Central Highlands

Chosica to La Oroya

Beyond Chosica each successive valley looks greener and lusher, with a greater variety of trees and flowers.

San Bartolomé, Km 57, at 1,513 metres, can be reached by a Sunday train from Lima (see page 130), in the dry season only.

Matucana, Km 84, at 2,390 metres, is set in wild scenery, where there are beautiful walks. There is basic accommodation available.

The road continues to climb to **San Mateo** (Km 95, 3,215 metres), where the San Mateo mineral water originates. There is basic accommodation in: **E** *Hotel Andino* (with restaurant); and **F** *Hotel La Posada*, which is dirty. From San Mateo a spectacular side-road branches off to the Germania mine.

Beyond San Mateo is **Infiernillo** (Little Hell) Canyon, at Km 100. Car excursions can be made from Lima.

Between Río Blanco and **Chicla** (Km 107, 3,733 metres), Inca contour-terraces can be seen quite clearly. After climbing up from **Casapalca** (Km 117, 4,154 metres, accommodation), there are glorious views of the highest peaks, and more mines, at the foot of a deep gorge.

The road climbs to the Ticlio Pass, before the descent to **Morococha** (Km 169. *Altitude*: 4,600 metres) and **La Oroya**. A large metal flag of Peru can be seen at the top of Mount Meiggs, not by any means the highest in the area, but through it runs Galera Tunnel, 1,175 metres long, in which the Central Railway reaches its greatest altitude, 4,782 metres (see below under Huancayo).

Ticlio, at Km 132, is the highest passenger station in the world, at 4,758 metres. It lies at the mouth of the tunnel, on one side of a crater in which lies a dark, still lake. There are still higher points on the railway on the branch of the line that goes through Morococha – 4,818 metres at La Cima, and 4,829 metres on a siding. At Morococha is the Centromín golf course, which welcomes playing visitors. It stands at 4,400 metres and disputes the title of the world's highest with Mallasilla, near La Paz, in Bolivia.

La Oroya (*Population*: 36,000. *Altitude*: 3,755 metres) is the main smelting **La Oroya** centre for the region's mining industry. It can seem a dreary place with its slag heaps, but is nevertheless full of vitality. It stands at the fork of the Yauli and Mantaro rivers, 196 kilometres from Lima by a road (For places to the east and north of La Oroya, see page 444 and 448 respectively.)

Sleeping **F** *Hostal Regional*, Lima 112, T391017. With bathroom, basic, hot water in the morning. **F** *Hostal Inti*, Arequipa 117, T391098. Shared bathroom, hot water, clean. **F** *Hostal Chavín*, Tarma 281. Shared bathroom, good, cheap restaurant. **F** *Mister*, Arequipa 113, T391149. Basic, the front rooms are better, others are dingy.

Eating *El Tambo*, 2 kilometres outside town on the road to Lima. Good trout and frogs. Recommended as the best restaurant. *La Caracocha*, Lima 168. Cheap, good menú. *Punta Arenas*, Zeballos 323. Good seafood, chifa. There are lots of *pollerías* in front of the train station in C Lima.

Transport For buses to the Central Highlands see under Lima, Buses (page 128). To **Lima** from La Oroya takes 4½ hours and costs US$5.20. To **Jauja** (80 kilometres), takes 1½ hours and costs US$1. **Jauja to Huancayo**, 44 kilometres, takes 1 hour and costs US$1. To **Tarma**, 1½ hours, US$1.35. To **Cerro de Pasco**, 131 kilometres, 3 hours, US$2.20. To **Huánuco**, 236 kilometres, 6 hours, US$4.35. **Huánuco to Tingo María**, 118 kilometres, 3-4 hours, US$1.75. **Tingo María to Pucallpa**, 284 kilometres, 7-9

Central Highlands

hours, US$7.85. Buses leave from C Zeballos, adjacent to the train station. Colectivos also run on all routes (see under Lima). They are quicker but only leave when full and prices are double that of the bus fares.

Jauja

Altitude: 3,330 metres
Phone code: 064
Coloured map 3, grid C5

80 kilometres southeast of La Oroya is the old town of Jauja, Pizarro's provisional capital until the founding of Lima. It has a very colourful Wednesday and Sunday market. Jauja is a friendly, unspoilt town, in the middle of a good area for walking.

Sights

There is a good **archaeological museum**, with artefacts from the Huari culture. A modernized church retains three fine 17th-century altars. The **Cristo Pobre** church is claimed to have been modelled after Notre Dame and is something of a curiosity.

On a hill above Jauja there is a fine line of Inca storehouses, and on hills nearby the ruins of hundreds of circular stone buildings from the Huanca culture (John Hemming). There are also ruins near the **Laguna de Paca** three and a half kilometres away. A mototaxi to Laguna de Paca costs US$0.90 minimum for 2 people, plus US$0.45 per additional person. Combis to Laguna de Paca, Paca, Acolla, etc, leave from Jr Tarma several times daily and cost US$0.45.

Essentials

Sleeping **E** *Cabezon's Hostal*, Ayacucho 1027, T362206. The best in town with bathroom and hot water. **E** *Ganso de Oro*, R Palma 249, T362165. Shared bathroom, hot water, good restaurant, US$2-4 per meal. **E** *Hostal Los Algarrobes*, Huancayo 264, T362633. Shared bathroom, hot water in the morning. **E** *Hostal Francisco Pizarro*, Bolognesi 334 (opposite the market), T362082. Shared bathroom, hot water.

Eating *Marychris*, Jr Bolívar 1166, T362386. For lunch only, *menú* US$1.55, excellent food. *Hatun Xauxa*, Jr Ricardo Palma 165. Good, cheap food and hot rums. *Centro Naturista*, Huarancayo 138. Serves fruit salad, yoghurt, granola, etc. *Fuente de Soda "Rossy's"*, Jr Bolognesi 561. Great cakes, OK pizza and snacks.

Festivals *Festival 'La Tunantada'* is held on **22 July**. See also under Mantaro Valley (page 431) for festivals held throughout the region.

Transport **Buses** To **Lima**: direct with *Mcal Cáceres*, from the Plaza de Armas, daily at 1100 and 2230, cost US$5.35-6.65 (service from Huancayo). Highly recommended. *Sudamericano* also leave from the Plaza de Armas; *Costa Sierra* leave from R Palma 145 and are recommended.

To **Cerro de Pasco**, *Oriental* leave from 28 de Julio 156, and *Turismo Central* from 28 de Julio 150, 5 hours, US$3.55. *Oriental* and *Turismo Central* also go to **Huánuco**, 7 hours, US$5.35. Buses to **Tingo María**, 12 hours, US$6.65; and **Pucallpa**, 24 hours, US$12. To **Tarma**, US$2.25, hourly with *ET San Juan* from Jr Tarma; continues to **Chanchamayo**, US$4.50. To **Satipo**, with *Turismo Central*, 12 hours, US$6.25.

Directory **Banks** No TCs are accepted at the *Banco de Crédito*. *Dollar Exchange Huarancayo*, on Jr Huarancayo, gives a much better rate than *Banco de Crédito*. **Communications** Telefónica: at

Bolognesi 546, T(064)362020, T/F361111. Also at Ricardo Palma, opposite the *Hotel Ganso de Oro*, T/F362395, gives better service and prices. **Correo Central:** Jr Bolívar.

18 kilometres to the south of Jauja, on the road to Huancayo, is Concepción **Concepción** (*Altitude*: 3,251 metres), with a market on Sunday as well as a colourful bull-fight later in the day during the season.

From Concepción a branch road leads for six kilometres to the **Convent of Santa Rosa de Ocopa**, a Franciscan monastery set in beautiful surroundings. It was established in 1725 for training missionaries for the jungle. It contains a fine library with over 20,000 volumes and a biological museum with animals and insects from the jungle. ■ *Open 0900-1200 and 1500-1800, and closed Tuesday.*

The road to **Satipo** branches off near the Convento de Santa Rosa de Ocopa. The scenery is spectacular, with snow-capped mountains in the Paso de la Tortuga, followed by a rapid drop to the Caja de Silva in Satipo (see page 447).

Eight kilometres from Concepción is **Ingenio**, with a fish farm in lovely countryside and restaurants in which to try the trout.

Huancayo

The city is in the beautiful Mantaro Valley. It is the capital of Junín Department and the main commercial centre for inland Peru. All the villages in the valley produce their own original crafts and celebrate festivals the year round (see below). At the important festivals in Huancayo, people flock in from far and wide with an incredible range of food, crafts, dancing and music (also see below).

Population: 258,209
Altitude: 3,271 metres
Phone code: 064
Coloured map 3, grid C5

Ins and outs

The railway station for Lima is relatively central in the east of the city. The other station **Getting there** (for trains to Huancavelica) is in the suburb of Chilca to the southwest of the city (15 minutes by taxi). Most of the bus offices are some way out of the centre as well to the south of the Río Florída, the middle of the city's three rivers.

Note that the Plaza de Armas is called Plaza Constitución. Huancayo is quite spread **Getting around** out with all the main sights as well as the Sunday market quite a way from the centre. Take the bus or a taxi.

Sights

The Sunday market gets going after 0900 (giving a little taste of Huancayo at festival time) every week even though it has been described as expensive and offering little choice. It is better to go to the villages for local handicrafts. The stalls on Jirón Huancavelica, three kilometres long, still sell typical clothes, fruit, vegetables, hardware, handicrafts and, especially, traditional medicines and goods for witchcraft. There is also an impressive daily market behind the railway station.

The museum at the Salesian school has over 5,000 pieces, including jungle birds, animals and butterflies, insects, reptiles and fossils.

For a rare insight into the world of Andean mysticism and magic, you can visit *Wali Wasi* ('sacred house' in Quechua), run by mystic, Pedro Marticorena Oroña Laya. He has paintings of Andean visions, masks made of

Central Highlands

cow dung and roots turned into gods and animals, and also offers Quechua lessons and cheap accommodation. A visit is described as "a truly memorable experience". Take a *micro* marked 'Umuto' and get off one block before the cemetery; the house is at Hualahoyo 2174.

On the outskirts of town is **Torre-Torre**, impressive, eroded sandstone towers on the hillside. Take a bus to Cerrito de la Libertad and walk up. Not far from here is a large park with a depressing zoo, but with a good swimming pool. ■ *Entry costs US$0.25.*

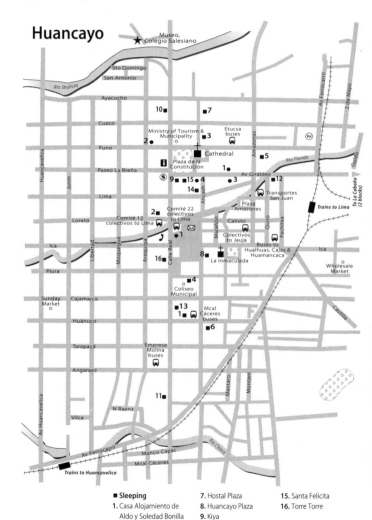

Huancayo

■ **Sleeping**
1. Casa Alojamiento de Aldo y Soledad Bonilla
2. Central
3. Confort
4. El Dorado
5. Hostal Baldeón
6. Hostal Palace
7. Hostal Plaza
8. Huancayo Plaza
9. Kiya
10. Los Angeles
11. Percy's
12. Pussy
13. Presidente
14. Roger
15. Santa Felicita
16. Torre Torre

● **Eating**
1. Chifa El Centro
2. El Inca
3. Marco Antonio
4. Olímpico

Essentials

B *Huancayo Plaza*, Ancash 729, T231072, 235211. In an old building, with bathroom, some rooms are small, quiet, restaurant serves good meals for US$3.50. **B** *Presidente*, C Real 1138, T231736, 231275. With bathroom, clean, friendly, helpful, safe, breakfast only. Recommended.

   C *Hostal Alpaca*, Giráldez 494, T223136. With bathroom, hot water, TV, carpets, friendly, snack bar downstairs. **C** *Kiya*, Giráldez 107, Plaza Constitución, T231431, 235619. With bathroom, hot water, restaurant does not serve breakfast, phone, avoid the noisy rooms on Avda Real. **C** *Santa Felicita*, Plaza Constitución, T235476, 235285. With bathroom, hot water, good.

   D *El Dorado*, Piura 428, T223947. With bathroom, hot water, friendly, clean, some rooms with TV are in the **C** category. **D** *Hostal La Breña*, Arequipa 510, T223490. With bathroom, hot water all day, clean, carpets. **D** *Hostal Plaza*, Ancash 171, T210509. Clean, hot water, ask for a room at the front. **D** *Percy's*, Real 1399, T231208, shared bathroom, hot water in morning, basic but clean. **D** *Roger*, Ancash 460, T233488. With bathroom, hot water, basic, clean. **D** *Rey*, Jr Angaráes 327, T226324. With bathroom, hot water in the morning, OK.

   E per person *Casa Alojamiento de Aldo y Soledad Bonilla*, Huánuco 332, ½ block from Mcal Cáceres bus station, T232103 (Lima 463-1141). Price includes breakfast, or **D** per person full board, beautiful colonial house, hot water all day, heaters, owners speak English, laundry, secure, relaxing, nice courtyard, they can arrange local tours, book ahead to guarantee a reservation. Highly recommended. **E** *Confort*, Ancash 231, 1 block from the main plaza, T233601. All rooms with bathroom, those with hot water are nicer, but more expensive, very clean, ask for a room not facing the street for peace and quiet, car parking costs US$1. **E** *Hostal Palace*, Ancash 1127, T238501. With bathroom, clean, hot water, restaurant. **E** *Pussy*, Giráldez 359, T231565. Not what the name might suggest, **F** with shared bathroom, hot water all day, safe, friendly, luggage stored, comfortable beds.

   F per person *Hostal Baldeón*, Amazonas 543, T231634. Friendly, kitchen and laundry facilities, hot shower. **F** per person *La Casa de Mi Abuela*, Avda Giráldez 693. Hot shower, price includes breakfast, good value, clean, friendly, laundry facilities, meals available, run by Lucho Hurtado's mother. **F** per person *Peru Andino Lodging & Excursions*, Pasaje San Antonio 113-115, 3 blocks from Avda Centenario, 10-15 minutes' walk from the centre, T223956. Price includes breakfast, clean rooms with hot showers, several with private bathroom, safe area, cosy atmosphere, run by Sra Juana, her daughter speaks some English, friendly, they also organize trekking and mountain bike tours, cooking and laundry facilities. Highly recommended.

   The following places are all in the **F** price category, with shared bathrooms and cold water, unless stated otherwise: *Central*, Loreto 452, T211948. Large place, basic, hot water in the morning. *Hostal San Martín*, Ferrocarril 362, near the rail station. Clean, charming place. *Los Angeles*, Real 245, T231753. Hot water, basic, restaurant. *Prince*, Calixto 578, T232331. Large and basic, hot water in the morning. *Torre-Torre*, Real 873, T231118. Hot water.

   There is a **Youth Hostel**, *Albergue Los Andenes del Inti*, at Jr Lima 354, 9th floor, edificio Murukami, T234143/223785, 231636.

The following restaurants serve typical dishes for about US$4-5, plus 18% tax. *El Inca*, Puno 530. Good salads. *Inti Palacio*, Lima 354. *Olímpico*, Avda Giráldez 199. Recommended as the best in town.

The following places serve typical food for about US$2-3 a dish, or with a fixed price *menú*. *Lalo's*, Giráldez 365. *El Pino*, Real 539. *Pinkys*, Giráldez 147. *Los Tres Sillares*, Lima 170. Serves typical Arequipeña food. *Chifa El Centro*, Giráldez 238. Chinese food,

Sleeping
Prices may be raised in Holy Week

■ *on maps*
Price codes: see inside front cover

Eating: expensive
● *on maps*

Eating: cheaper

Central Highlands

good service. *La Cabaña*, Avda Giraldez 652. Great pizzas, ice-cream, *calentitos*, and other dishes, folk music at weekends. Great atmosphere and repeatedly recommended, owned by Beverly Stuart and Lucho Hurtado (also speaks English), they also have 2 rooms, **G** including breakfast, with hot water, washing and cooking facilities. They organize Spanish courses for beginners for US$200 per week, including accommodation with local families, as well as weaving, playing traditional music, Peruvian cooking and lots of other things. They also have maps and a book exchange. Lucho also works as a guide and runs trips in the mountains or jungle, and hires bikes for tours of rural communities. Contact him in Huancayo (E incas&lucho@hys.com.pe), or through the South American Explorers Club in Lima. *Marco Antonio*, Avda Giráldez 255. Cheap, excellent set lunch, friendly. Recommended. *Los Maduros*, Puno 599, near the main plaza. Good pizzas. *Nuevo Horizonte*, Jr Ica 578. Excellent set meal for only US$1. *Chez Viena*, Puno 125. Good cakes.

There is an excellent **vegetarian** restaurant on Arequipa 700 block, between Loreto and Ica. Also lots of cheap restaurants along Avda Giráldez serving set *menú*. Breakfast is served in the Mercado Modelo from 0700.

Bars & nightclubs **Bars** *Café Billar*, Paseo de Breña 133. Open 0900-2400, serves beer and snacks, pool tables.

Discotheques *El Molino*, Huancas, by the river. *A1A*, Bolognesi 299. Most discos open around 2000 and close at 0200. Some charge an entrance fee of US$3-4.

Peñas All the *peñas* have folklore shows with dancing, open normally Friday, Saturday and Sunday from 1300 to 2200. Entrance fee is about US$2 per person. *Taki Wasi*, Huancavelica y 13 de Noviembre. *Ollantaytambo*, Puno, block 2.

Entertainment **Cinemas** *Ciné Pacífico*, Real, block 6, and *Ciné Mantaro*, Real 950, El Tambo. Tickets cost US$2.

Festivals *Festividad del Tayta Niño* is held on **19-31 of January**. *Festividad de la Virgen de Cocharcas* is held on **8 September** (see also Mantaro Valley below). *Festividad de San Jerónimo de Tunan* takes place on **30 September**. The *Semana Turística de Huancayo* begins on **16 November**.

Shopping All handicrafts are made outside Huancayo in the many villages of the Mantaro Valley (see below), or in Huancavelica. The villages are worth a visit to learn how the items are made. *Casa de Artesano*, on the corner of Real and Paseo La Breña, at Plaza Constitución, has a wide selection of good quality crafts. There is a large cooperative, *Kamaq Maki*, at Santa Isabel 1856, which exports alpaca goods. Open Monday-Friday 0900-1400. It is well-organized and employs many artesans; its aim is to control the market and prices. It is very helpful and will be happy to take you to meet the manufacturers of the goods. The workshop has a small shop; contact Arturo Durán, T231206/233183. *Artesanía Sumaq Ruray*, Jr Brasilia 132, San Carlos 5th Block, T237018. Produces fine weaving, but it's not cheap.

Transport **Road** There are regular buses to **Lima**, 6-7 hours on a good paved road, costing US$9-10. Travelling by day is recommended for the fantastic views and, of course, for safety. If you must travel by night, take warm clothing. Recommended companies: *Mcal Cáceres*, Jr Huánuco 350, T231232; *Cruz del Sur*, Ayacucho 287; Etucsa, Puno 220, several a day (*bus cama*, US$11). Many other companies ply this route, many are cheaper but also less comfortable and less safe. Small buses for Lima congregate 15 blocks north of Plaza Constitución on C Real; there is much competition for passengers. *Comités 12 and 22*, both on C Loreto, and *Comité 30*, C Giráldez, run to Lima in 6 hours, when the car is full, which can mean waiting all day; they cost US$12 per person.

To **Ayacucho**, 319 kilometres, 11 hours, US$7. *Empresa Molina*, C Angaraes 287, leave at 0700, 1700 and 1800 and *TransFano* at 1830, both are recommended. Also *Antezana*, Arequipa 1301, leave at 2100. The road has improved but is still very difficult in the wet. Take warm clothing. The military seem to have established control over this route after years of terrorist disruption. Check the situation in advance, travel by day, and keep abreast of what is going on. After Izcuchaca, on the railway to Huancavelica, there is a good road to the Kichuas hydroelectric scheme, but thereafter it is narrow with hair-raising bends and spectacular bridges. The scenery is staggering, but sit on the right or you'll have 11 hours of staring at a solid rock wall. From Huanta the road descends into Ayacucho.

To **Huancavelica**, 147 kilometres, 5 hours, US$3. Several buses leave daily, including *Empresa Hidalgo*, *Loreto 350*, *San Pablo*, *Ancash 1248*, at 1400. The road is in poor condition but being improved, and takes much longer in the wet. The scenery is spectacular. Most travellers use the train.

To **Cerro de Pasco**, 255 kilometres, 5-6 hours, US$3-4. *Transporte Salazar*, Giráldez 245, leave on Sunday and Monday at 2100. From there to **Huánuco**, 105 kilometres, 3 hours, US$2. From Huánuco to **Tingo María**, 118 kilometres, 5 hours, and on to **Pucallpa** takes 11 hours. *Comité 12* does this route for US$15 per person, leaving when full. There is quite a good paved road to **La Oroya**, but from there to Cerro de Pasco parts are still under construction (mid 1998).

To **Satipo**, 229 kilometres, 12 hours, on a very difficult road, which is impossible in the wet; *San Juan*, Quito 136, is a recommended company. The bus goes via Jauja, Tarma and La Merced (5 hours, US$4.50). *San Juan* and *Los Canarios* (Puno 725) go to **Oxapampa**, taking 12 hours. Some trucks and a few buses travel to **Cañete**, 289 kilometres, 10 hours, US$4. It is a poor road, with beautiful mountain landscapes before dropping to the valley of Cañete.

To **Jauja**, 44 kilometres, 1 hour. Colectivos leave from Huamaumarca y Amazonas; ones via San Jerónimo and Concepción have 'Izquierda' on the front. Most buses to the Mantaro Valley leave from several places around the market area. Buses to **Hualhuas**, **Cajas** and **Huamancaca** leave from block 3 of Pachitea. Buses to **Cochas** leave from Amazonas y Giráldez.

Train There are two unconnected railway stations. The Central station serves Lima, via La Oroya (298 kilometres). The Lima-Huancayo railway is now in operation once more, which is fortunate, for it is one of the great engineering feats of the 19th century. For details of the train service, see Lima, Ins and outs, page 92.

From the small station in Chilca suburb (15 minutes by taxi, US$1), trains run 142 kilometres to **Huancavelica**, on a narrow gauge track (3 feet). There are 2 trains: the *autovagón* (*expreso*) leaves at 0630 Monday-Saturday and at 1400 on Sunday. It costs US$2.20 normal, US$3.75 buffet class. The journey takes 4½ hours, and is a spectacular one with fine views, passing through typical mountain villages. Meals, drinks and snacks are served on the train, and at the village stations vendors sell food and crafts.

The local train leaves at 1230 Monday-Saturday, and takes 6½ hours. It costs US$1.75 2nd class, US$2 1st class and US$3.50 buffet class. You can buy tickets 1 day in advance, or an hour before departure. Services can be suspended in the rainy season.

Banks *Banco de Crédito*, Real 1039. Changes TCs with no commission, cash advance on Visa. **Directory**
Western Union Money Transfer, Ancash 540, oficina 302, T224816/235655. Open Mon-Fri 0900-1300 and 1600-2000, Sat 0900-1300. There are several *casas de cambio* on the 4th and 5th Blocks of Real. Street changers hang out there as well. Also travel agencies and banks will change dollars. **Cultural centres** Peruvian-North American Cultural Institute: Jr Guido 740. **Andes Spanish Institute:** offers Spanish classes for US$5 an hour, lodging for US$4-5 per person, tourist information and a restaurant. Contact Eva Diaz: evaedu@hotmail.com or Veronica Rodríguez:

👉 *Lima-Huancayo railway*

This masterpiece was the project of the great American railway engineer, Henry Meiggs, who supervised the construction from 1870 until his death in 1877. It was built by the Pole Ernesto Malinowski, with imported Chinese labour, between 1870 and 1893.

The ruling grade of the Central Railway is about $4\frac{1}{2}°$. Along the whole of its length (335 kilometres to Huancayo) it traverses 66 tunnels, 59 bridges, and 22 zig-zags where the steep mountainside permits no other way of negotiating it. During its years of operation, this was a tough journey, with altitude sickness an ever-present problem. This discomfort was more than compensated, though, by the spectacular views during the ascent which are beyond compare. Railway buffs may like to know that the last Andes type 2-8-0 steam locomotive, No 206, is still in working order, although usually locked in a shed at Huancayo. It was built specifically for this route in 1953 by Beyer Peacock of Manchester.

VERONICARE@yahoo.com. **Tourist offices** *Ministry of Tourism*, is now housed in the *Casa de Artesano* (see **Shopping** above). It has information about the area and is helpful; open 0730-1330 Mon-Fri. *Turismo Huancayo*, C Real 517 oficina 6, T233351, organizes local tours and is recommended. A recommended guide book is *Guia Turística del Hermoso Valle del Mantaro* (Spanish), costing US$4 from the bookshop at Jr Ancash 435.

The Mantaro Valley

The main attraction in the area is the Mantaro Valley, which is rich in culture, music, typical food, dances and handicrafts and plays host to numerous festivals (see below).

To the west of the Río Mantaro, 19 kilometres from Huancayo, is **Viques**, which is known for the production of belts and blankets. Seven kilometres away, **Huayucachi** organizes festivals with dancing and impressive costumes in January and February and also makes embroidery. At **Tres de Diciembre** is a fish farm, with some good restaurants and swimming pool. To get there, walk from Huamancaca.

The ruins of **Warivilca**, 15 kilometres from Huancayo, are near **Huari**, with the remains of a pre-Inca temple of the Huanca tribe. There is a museum in the plaza, with deformed skulls, and modelled and painted pottery of successive Huanca and Inca occupations of the shrine. The ruins and museum are under the supervision of a local archaeologist and are slowly being restored. ■ *Open 1000-1200, 1500-1700. US$0.15. The museum is open in the morning only. To get there, take one of the micros for Chilca, which leave from Calle Real.*

Between Pilcomayo and Huayo (15 kilometres) is the **Geophysical Institute of Huayo**, on the 'Magnetic Equator' – $12\frac{1}{2}°$ south of the geographical equator. Here meteorological, seismic and cosmic-ray observations are made. A visit is recommended and the best time is in the morning, or when the sun is shining.

Chupaca is a picturesque village with a good Saturday market. A colectivo leaves from the fruit and vegetable market. On the way to Chupaca is the village of **Ahuac**. One block down from the Plaza de Armas, in the Colegio Amauta, is a museum with items found at the nearby Huanca ruins of **Arwaturo**. Opposite the school is a shop where you can buy excellent chicha from the señora. There is a small restaurant on the plaza in Ahuac, which serves a set lunch for US$1.

Also west of the river, 17 kilometres from Huancayo, is **Laguna Nahuinpuquio**, a nice lake with pleasant surrounding countryside. **Sicaya,** eight kilometres away, holds festivals in August and has an 18th century church. The ruins of **Guaqui-Guaqui** are just outside the village of **Matahulo**. **Muquiyauyo** is famous for its Semana Santa celebrations.

The villages of **Cochas Chico** and **Cochas Grande**, 11 kilometres away on the east side of the river, are both well worth visiting. This is where the famous *mate burilado*, or gourd carving, is done (see page 526). You can buy them cheaply direct from the manufacturers, but ask around. You can also enjoy beautiful views of the Valle de Mantaro and Huancayo. *Micros* leave from the corner of Amazonas y Giráldez, US$0.25.

Hualahoyo (11 kilometres from Huancayo) has a little chapel with 21 colonial canvases. **San Agustín de Cajas** (eight kilometres) makes fine hats, and **San Pedro** (10 kilometres) makes wooden chairs. In the village of **Hualhuas** (12 kilometres) you can find fine alpaca weavings. One particularly recommended place to buy them is *Tahuantisuyo*, run by Familia Faustino Maldonado y Agripina, on a side road on the way to the San Jerónimo junction.

The village of **San Jerónimo** is renowned for the making of silver filigree jewellery, on sale at the Wednesday market. The village holds its fiesta in August. There are ruins two to three hours' walk above San Jerónimo, but seek advice before hiking to them.

Festivals

There are so many festivals in the Mantaro Valley that it is impossible to list them all. Practically every day of the year there is a celebration of some sort in one of the villages. We list a selection below.

La Huaconada de Mito takes place in Mito on **1-3 January**. *Festividad del Tayta Niño* on **19-31 January** in Huayucachi. As in the rest of the country, there are carnival celebrations for the whole of **February**, with highlights on **2**, *Virgen de la Candelaria*, and **17-19** *Concurso de Carnaval*.

Semana Santa is impressive throughout the valley, especially the **Good Friday** processions. *Fiesta de la Cruz* also takes place throughout the valley on **1 May**, as does *Fiesta de Santiago* on **24-30 July**. On **8 September** is *La Virgen de Cocharcas*, held in Concepción, Jauja and more famously in Sapallanga, 8 kilometres south from Huancayo. Held on different dates in **September** is the *Semana Turística del Valle del Mantaro*.

Izcuchaca

Between Huancayo and Huancavelica, Izcuchaca is the site of a bridge over the Río Mantaro. The name in Quechua means 'stone bridge'. The bridge was partly rebuilt in the 18th century. On the edge of town is a fascinating pottery workshop whose machinery is driven by a water turbine. There is also a small shop. The town celebrates the *Fiesta de la Virgen de Cocharcas* on 5-10 October. A nice hike is to the chapel on a hill overlooking the valley. It's one to one and a half hours each way.

There are two hotels. One is on the plaza, **G**, with no bathroom, you have to use the public bath by the river. The other is just off the plaza, a yellow 3-storey house, **G**, no shower, toilet suitable for men only, chamber pot supplied, only blankets on bed, and cold. The 0630 train from Huancavelica arrives at 0800, then continues to Huancayo. The trip costs US$1.15. The train tends to be very crowded. Sit on the left for the best views. The train from Huancayo passes at around 1700. A daily colectivo leaves to Ayacucho at 1000-1100, and takes 8 hours.

Central Highlands

Huancavelica

Population: 37,500
Altitude: 3,680 metres
Coloured map 3, grid C5

Capital of its Department, Huancavelica is a friendly and attractive town, surrounded by huge, rocky mountains. It was founded in the 16th century by the Spanish to exploit rich deposits of mercury and silver. Very few of the mines remain open, and those that do are a few hours from town. It is predominantly an indigenous town, and people still wear traditional costume. There are beautiful mountain walks in the neighbourhood.

Ins and outs

Getting there All bus companies have their offices on and leave from C Muñoz at the east end of town. Just a little beyond them and about half a kilometre from the Plaza de Armas is the train station.

Getting around The department of Huancavelica saw much terrorist activity in the past, but since 1992 the military has regained control and it is safer to visit. Always carry your documentation, travel by day and find out about latest conditions before travelling.

Sights

The cathedral, located on the Plaza de Armas, has an altar considered to be one of the finest examples of colonial art in Peru. Also very impressive are the five other churches in town. The church of San Francisco, for example, has no less than 11 altars. Sadly, though, most of the churches are closed to visitors.

Bisecting the town is the Río Huancavelica. South of the river is the main commercial centre. North of the river, on the hillside, are the thermal baths. There are also hot showers, but take a lock for the doors. ■ *Open 0600-1500. It costs US$0.15 for private rooms, but the water is not very hot, and US$0.10 for the hot public pool.*

There is a colourful daily market, which is smaller than in the past, and most handicrafts are transported directly to Lima, but you can still visit craftsmen in neighbouring villages. There is a daily food market at Muñoz y

Huancavelica

■ Sleeping	● Eating	🚌 Buses
1. Hostal Tahuantinsuyo	1. Las Magnolias	1. Hidalgo
2. Mercurio	2. Mochica Sachún	2. Expreso Huancavelica
3. Presidente	3. Olímpico	3. Oropesa
4. Santo Domingo	4. Paquirri	4. San Pablo
5. Savoy	5. Pollería Joy	
6. Virrey		

Barranca. The Potaqchiz hill, just outside the town, gives a fine view. It's about an hour's walk up from San Cristóbal.

Essentials

C *Presidente*, Plaza de Armas, T952760. Lovely colonial building, cheaper without bathroom, overpriced. **E** *Mercurio*, Jr Torre Tagle 455, T952773. Unfriendly, basic, cold water. **F** *Camacho*, Jr Carabaya 481. Best of the cheap hotels, hot shower in the morning only, clean and well maintained, excellent value. **F** *Hostal Tahuantinsuyo*, Carabaya 399, T952968. With bathroom, hot water in mornings, dirty and dingy. **F** *Santo Domingo*, Avda Barranca 366, T953086. **F** *Savoy*, Avda Muñoz 294. Both are cheap, very basic, with shared bathroom and cold water. **F** *Virrey*, Avda Barranca 317. Basic, cold water.

Sleeping
■ *on maps*
Price codes:
see inside front cover

Paquirri, Jr Arequipa 137. Good but expensive. *Mochica Sachún*, Avda Virrey Toledo 303. Great *menú* for US$1.50, otherwise expensive, popular. *Pollería Joy*, Toledo y Arequipa. Good for chicken. *La Casona*, Jr Virrey Toledo 230. Good value *menú* and *peña*. *Las Magnolias*, Manuel Muñoz 1 block from the plaza. OK.

Eating:
expensive
● *on maps*

There are lots of cheap, basic restaurants on C Muñoz and Jr Virrey Toledo. All serve typical food, mostly with a set *menú* for around US$1.50. Also cheap are: *La Estrellita*, Avda Sebastián Barranca 255. *Olímpico*, Jr JM Chávez 124. *Super Gordo*, Avda Celestino Muñoz 488. *Yananaco*, Avda Cáceres 533.

Eating:
cheap

Fiesta del Niño Perdido is held on **9-14 January**. *Fiesta de la Cruz* on **1 May**. *Fiesta de Santiago* is on **24-30 July**. In **September** there is a tourist week with a huge crafts market, music and dancing.

Festivals

Road To **Huancayo**, 147 kilometres, 5 hours, US$3.50, it's a rough road but is being improved. There are several buses a day, eg *Expreso Huancavelica* and *Empresa Hidalgo*.

Transport

To **Lima** there are two routes: one is via Huancayo, 445 kilometres, 13 hours minimum, US$8. Most buses to Huancayo go on to Lima, there are several a day. The other route is via **Pisco**, 269 kilometres, 12 hours, US$9. There's only 1 bus a day at 0600, with *Oropesa*. Buy your ticket 1 day in advance. Some trucks also travel this route. The road is in very poor condition, but the views are spectacular and worth the effort. Be prepared for sub-zero temperatures in the early morning as the bus passes snowfields, then for temperatures of 25-30°C as the bus descends to the coast in the afternoon.

Train See under Huancayo. The *autovagón/expreso* leaves for Huancayo daily at 0630, the local train leaves at 1230, Monday-Saturday.

Banks *Banco de Crédito*, Virrey Toledo 300 block. **Communications** Post Office: on Toledo, 1 block from the Plaza de Armas. **Telephones:** Carabaya y Virrey Toledo. **Tourist offices** *Ministerio de Industria y Comercio, Turismo y Artesanías*, Jr Nicolás de Piérola 180, open Mon-Fri 0730-1400, very helpful. *Instituto Nacional de la Cultura*, Plaza San Juan de Dios. Open Mon-Sat 1000-1300, 1500-1900, director Alfonso Zuasnabar, a good source of information on festivals, archaeological sites, history, etc. Gives courses on music and dancing, and lectures some evenings. There is also an interesting but small archaeology and anthropology museum.

Directory

Huancavelica-Ayacucho

Getting to Ayacucho (247 kilometres) is a problem, as there are no buses. Either take the train to Izcuchaca, stay the night and take the colectivo (see above), or take the morning train to La Mejorada where you can catch the 1000 Expreso Molino bus from Huancayo to Ayacucho.

Alternatively take a bus to Santa Inés, then a truck to **Rumichaca**, the junction where buses and trucks on the Lima-Ayacucho route pass. Buses go through Rumichaca at 0300-0400 only, but there are many trucks and police at the checkpoint who may help with lifts. Take an Oropesa bus from Huancavelica to Santa Inés at 0600, which allows plenty of time for a truck to Rumichaca and then another to Ayacucho. Rumichaca-Ayacucho is seven hours by truck and four hours by bus. The road is in an appalling condition. The journey is a cold one but spectacular as it is the highest continuous road in the world, rarely dropping below 4,000 metres for 150 kilometres.

Out of Huancavelica the road climbs steeply with switchbacks between herds of llamas and alpacas grazing on rocky perches. Around Pucapampa (Km 43) is one of the highest habitable *altiplanos* (4,500 metres), where the rare and highly prized ash-grey alpaca can be seen.

Santa Inés, 78 kilometres, has one very friendly restaurant where you can sleep and several others. Nearby are two lakes (Laguna Choclacocha) which can be reached in two and a half hours. 50 kilometres beyond Santa Inés at the **Abra de Apacheta** (4,750 metres), 98 kilometres from Ayacucho, the rocks are all colours of the rainbow, and running through this fabulous scenery is a violet river. These incredible colours are all caused by oxides. 11 kilometres later is the Paso Chonta and the turnoff to **Huachocolpa**. By taking the turnoff and continuing for three kilometres you'll reach the highest drivable pass in the world, at 5,059 metres.

Alternative route to Ayacucho

There is another route to Ayacucho from Huancayo, little used by buses, but which involves not so much climbing for cyclists. Cross the pass into the Mantaro valley on a reopened road to **Quichuas**, which has no hotel, but there is a basic place to sleep, three kilometres away by a dam. Then on to **Anco**, where there are two very basic places to sleep with no running water, and to **Mayocc** (lodging). At Mayocc a bridge is being repaired. From Mayocc go to **Huanta**, where there are several hotels, crossing a bridge after 10 kilometres (20 kilometres from Huanta). Then it's a paved road to Ayacucho.

Ayacucho

Population 105,918
Altitude: 2,740 metres
Phone code: 064
Coloured map 5, grid A4

The city is built round Parque Sucre, the main plaza, with the Cathedral, Municipalidad and Palacio de Gobierno facing on to it. It is famous for its hugely impressive Semana Santa celebrations, its splendid market and, not least, a plethora of churches – 33 of them no less – giving the city its alternative name La Ciudad de las Iglesias. A week can easily be spent enjoying Ayacucho and its hinterland. The climate is lovely, with warm, sunny days and pleasant balmy evenings. It is a warm, hospitable, tranquil place, where the inhabitants are eager to promote tourism. It also boasts a large, active student population. The University, founded in 1677, and closed in 1886, was reopened in 1958.

Ins and outs

Getting there The airport is to the east of the city along Av Castilla. A taxi to the centre costs US$1;

Central Highlands

buses or colectivos leave for the Plaza de Armas. At the airport walk ½ block down the street for a bus to the centre. The bus offices are much nearer the centre of town, in the northeast.

Since 1992 the area has been under military control and even though there are lots of **Getting around** checkpoints, few travellers have encountered problems visiting the region. Tourist services have been re-established, and many new hotels have opened. Make sure you get the latest information before going, and travel by day. Ayacucho suffers from water shortages. There is usually no water between 0900 and 1500, but many hotels have their own water tanks. This is a large city but the interesting chuches and colonial houses are all fairly close to the Plaza de Armas. Barrio Santa Ana is further away to the south and you will probaly want to take a micro or taxi to get to it.

Background

Ayacucho is the capital of its Department. The city was founded by the invading Spanish on 9 January 1539, who named it San Juan de la Frontera. This was changed to San Juan de la Victoria after the Battle of Chupas, when the king's forces finally defeated the rival Almagrist power.

Despite these Spanish titles, the city always kept its original name of Huamanga. It became an important base for the army of the Liberator Simón Bolívar in his triumphant sweep south from the Battle of Junín. It was here, on the Pampa de Quinua, on 9 December 1824, that the decisive Battle of Ayacucho was fought, bringing Spanish rule in Peru to an end. Huamanga was, therefore, the first city on the continent to celebrate its liberty. In the midst of the massive festivities, the Liberator decreed that the city be named Ayacucho – meaning 'City of Blood'.

For much of the 1980s and early 1990s, this title seemed appropriate as the Shining Path terrorized the local populace, severely punishing anyone they suspected of siding with the military. Now, though, peace has returned to this beautiful colonial Andean city.

Sights

For a fascinating insight into Quechua art and culture, a visit to **Barrio Santa Ana** is a must. The district is full of *artesanía* shops, galleries and workshops. *Galería Latina*, at Plazuela de Santa Ana 605, has been recommended. The owner, Alejandro Gallardo Llacctahuamán, is very friendly and has lots of information on weaving techniques.

Also recommended is the *Wari Art Gallery*, run by Gregorio Sulca and his family, at Jr Mcal Cáceres 302, Santa Ana, T912529. Gregorio, like his father before him, is one of the foremost Quechuan artisans and artists in all Peru and the gallery displays a selection of their works. He will gladly explain the Quechua legends, weaving and painting techniques, and anything else you care to know, including the problems the city encountered at the hands of Shining Path. A recurring theme in his work is the desire for peace during the years of terrorism. The technique he uses, learned from his father, is unique, and considering the quality and length of time involved, his textiles are reasonably priced. Gregorio also keeps a garden of Andean plants and will explain their various uses. A good grasp of Spanish is essential to appreciate fully this unique experience. Visitors to the gallery should climb to the roof of the Instituto de Cultura Quechua next door, which affords wonderful views of the city and surrounding hills.

Also worth a visit is the **Mirador Turístico**, on Cerro Acuchimay, which

An officer and a not-so-gentle nun

One of the most bizarre tales knocking around in the annals of Ayacucho's history relates to the mysterious case of the missing nun and the gender-bending soldier.

At the beginning of the 17th century, the courageous and audacious Army officer, Antonio de Erauzo, was finally captured and brought to justice, after putting several of his adversaries to the sword up and down the length and breadth of the country. He was condemned to death and duly asked a priest to hear his last confession and give him communion.

However, seconds before the priest could administer it, the soldier took the host in his hands and fled. No one dared stop him for fear of committing an act of sacrilege. He took refuge in a nearby church (not difficult given the profusion of them in this city) where he asked for Bishop Fray Agustín de Carbajal to hear his confession.

The townsfolk, who had been eagerly watching events unfold, soon learned the astonishing truth. The officer was, in fact, a woman called Catalina, who, on being chosen by her parents for the service of God, fled from a Spanish convent, assuming the disguise of a male person.

On putting an end to the mystery of her identity, Catalina mysteriously escaped once more, assumed a new identity and spent her last days in Mexico, dressed as a man and working as an arriero, or mule-herd. To the people of Ayacucho, however, Catalina would always be known as La Monja Alferez, the officer nun.

offers great views over the city. Take a *micro* from the corner of 28 de Julio and Plaza de Armas to Carmen Alto, then walk two blocks.

Churches The construction of Ayacucho's many colonial religious buildings is said to have been financed by wealthy Spanish mine-owners and governors. Unfortunately many have fallen into disrepair and are closed to the public. Visitors are advised to see the 17th century **Cathedral**, built in 1612. Its three strong, solid naves are of simple architecture, in contrast to the elegant decoration of the interior, particularly the superb gold leaf altars. ■ *The Cathedral is open daily 1730-1845; it also has a Museo de Arte Religioso, but it is closed indefinitely.*

San Cristóbal was the first church to be founded in the city, and is possibly the oldest in South America. Buried beneath its floor are the remains of some of the combatants from the Battle of Chupas. Another old church is **La Merced**, whose high choir is a good example of the simplicity of the churches of the early period of the Viceroyalty. In 1886 a flagstone was discovered with the sculpted image of a sleeping warrior, known popularly as the 'Chejo-Pacheco'. **La Compañía de Jesús** (1605), has one of the most important façades of Viceregal architecture. It is of baroque style and guarded by two impressive 18th century towers. The church also has an adjacent chapel. ■ *Open Sunday 1200-1230 and 1730-1800.*

Also of note are the churches of **San Francisco de Asís** (■ *Open daily 1000-1200 and 1500-1700),* and **Santa Teresa** (1683, ■ *Open daily 0600-0700)* with its monastery. Both have magnificent gold-leafed altars heavily brocaded and carved in the churrigueresque style. **Santa Clara** is renowned for its beautifully delicate coffered ceiling, and as the place where La Monja Alferez took refuge to avoid execution. ■ *Open Wednesday-Sunday 0630-1600.* One of the city's most notable churches is **Santo Domingo** (1548). Its fine façade has triple Roman arches and Byzantine towers. ■ *Open daily 0700-0800.*

Central Highlands

Ayacucho is well-endowed with fine colonial houses. To the north of the **Colonial houses**
Parque Sucre, on the corner of Portal de la Unión and Asamblea, are the
Casonas de los Marqueses de Mozobamba y del Pozo, also called
Velarde-Alvárez. On the same Portal is the house of Canon Manuel Frías,
where the writer and caricaturist, Abraham Valdelomar (who also used the
pseudonym El Conde de Lemos after 1915), tragically died. In the Portals to
the west, where the family seats of Astete and Guevara were once found, is the

Ayacucho

■ Sleeping
1. Central
2. Colmena
3. Grau
4. Hostal Ayacucho
5. Hostal El Sol
6. Hostal San Blas
7. Hostal 3 Máscaras
8. Hostelería
   Santa Rosa
9. Plaza
10. Residencial La
    Crillonesa
11. Samary
12. San Francisco
13. Valdelirios

● Eating
1. Del Morochucos
2. La Buena Salud
3. La Casona
4. Tradición

🚌 Buses
1. Buses & Trucks to
   Abancay & Cusco
2. Fano
3. Trans Mar
4. Trans Molina

Central Highlands

Casona where the chief magistrate, Nicolás de Boza y Solís, lived and which served as a prison cell for the Independence heroine, María Parado de Bellido.

Casa Jaúregui is situated opposite the church of La Merced, and **Casa Olano** is in Calle de la Compañía. On the 5th block of Jr Grau, before San Blas, is the house where Simón Bolívar and José Antonio de Sucre stayed. In 1824 the house was occupied by the Flores family and is perhaps the finest example of a typical Castillian house. On the 5th block of 28 de Julio is **Casona Vivanco** (see below).

Museums **Museo Histórico Natural**, in the University. ■ *Jr Arequipa 175. Open daily 0900-1300. US$0.35.* **Museo Arqueológico Hipólito Unanue** has many Huari artefacts ■ *Opposite the University Residences, on Avda Independencia, at the northern end of town. Open 0800-1300, 1500-1700, Monday-Friday, 0900-1300 Saturday. US$1.30.* **Museo Andrés A Cáceres**, is housed in the late 16th century Casona Vivanco. The museum displays prehispanic, colonial, republican and contemporary art. ■ *Jr 28 de Julio 508. Open 0900-1230, 1400-1700, Monday-Saturday. US$0.45.*

Essentials

Sleeping
■ *on maps*
Price codes:
see inside front cover

A3 *Plaza*, 9 de Diciembre 184, T912202, 912314. Beautiful colonial building but the rooms don't match up to the palatial splendour of the reception. It's comfortable, has TV, and some rooms overlook the plaza.

B *Valdelirios*, Bolognesi 520, T913908, 914014. Lovely colonial-style mansion, beautifully-furnished, pick-up from the airport for US$1.30, restaurant, bar, disco at weekends, reserve at least 24 hours in advance. Recommended. **B-C** *Yañez*, Mcal Cáceres 1210, T912464. A bit pricey, with bathroom, clean, cable TV, well furnished rooms, it's a former hospital so the decor is slightly clinical.

C *Hostal 3 Máscaras*, Jr 3 Máscaras 194, T914107. **D** with shared bathroom, nice colonial building with patio, clean, basic rooms, hot water 0600-1100, overpriced. **C** *Hostelería Santa Rosa*, Jr Lima 166, T/F912083. Lovely colonial courtyard, hot water mornings and evenings, friendly, car park, restaurant. Recommended. **C** *San Francisco*, Jr Callao 290, T912959, 914501. Price includes breakfast, friendly, comfortable, nice patio. Recommended.

D *Colmena*, Jr Cusco 140, T912146. With bathroom, hot water 0700-0900, clean, small rooms, secure, pleasant courtyard. **D** *Hostal El Mirador*, Jr Bellido 112, T912338. Clean, large rooms, washing facilities, great view from the roof terrace. **D** *Hostal Las Orquídeas*, Jr Arequipa 287, T914435. With bath, intermittent hot water, clean, basic, very noisy from disco next door at weekends. **D** *Hostal Plateros*, Jr Lima 206. With bathroom, hot water, clean and comfortable. **D** *Residencial La Crillonesa*, Nazareno 165, T912350. With bathroom, clean, friendly, hot water, washing facilities, discount for longer stay, great views from roof terrace. **D** *Samary*, Jr Callao 335, T/F912442. Discount for non-Peruvians, clean, safe, hot water in mornings. Friendly and recommended. **D** *Hostal San Blas*, Jr Chorro 167, T910552. With bathroom, hot water all day, clean, friendly, washing facilities, nice rooms, cheap meals available, discount for longer stay, Carlos will act as a local tour guide and knows everyone. Recommended.

E *Central*, Jr Arequipa 188, T912144. Shared bathroom, clean, large rooms, good value, **F** in the low season. **E** *Grau*, Jr San Juan de Dios 192, T912695. With bathroom, hot water, clean, washing facilities, good value. **E** per person *Hostal El Sol*, Avda Mcal Castilla 132, T913069. Hot water all day, clean, well-furnished large rooms. Recommended. **E** *Hostal Luz Imperial*, Jr Libertad 591 (altos). Cheaper without private bathroom, hot water in mornings, basic, clean, friendly. **E** *Hostal Wari*, Mcal Cáceres 836, T913065. Shared bathroom, hot water in the morning, clean, basic, large rooms. **E** *Huamanga*, Jr Bellido 535, T912725. Basic, clean, hot water costs US$1.30 extra.

E *Magdalena*, Mcal Cáceres 810, T912910. Cheaper without private bathroom, basic but good.

F *Hostal Ayacucho*, Jr Lima 165, T912759. Shared bathroom, cold water, basic.
F *Santiago*, Nazareno 177, T912132. Shared bathroom, hot water in mornings, clean and OK.

Tradición, San Martín 406. Popular, good cheap *menú*. *San Agustín Café Turístico*, Jr Cusco 101. Good food and lemon meringue pie. Recommended for snacks. *La Casona*, Jr Bellido 463. Regional specialities, try their *puca picante*, beef in a thick spicy sauce, rather like Indian curry. Recommended. *Del Morochucos*, Jr 9 de Diciembre 205, opposite Santo Domingo church. Large selection, pizzas, *parrillada* etc, very popular, live music, nice colonial-style building. *Portales*, on plaza, Portal Unión. Popular. *Urpicha*, Jr Londres 272. Recommended for typical food. *Restaurant Nino*, Jr Salvador Cavero 124. Recommended for local dishes.

Eating: expensive
● *on maps*

La Buena Salud, Jr Asamblea 206. Vegetarian, cheap *menú*. *Pollería Nino*, Jr Garcilaso de la Vega 240. Friendly and recommended for chicken (US$2.25). Also good for chicken is *Tivole*, Jr Bellido 492. *Fuente de Soda La Compañía*, 28 de Julio 151. Good for juices, cakes and snacks. Try *mondongo*, a soup made from meat, maize and mint, at the market near Santa Clara on Jr Carlos Vivanco. Sra Gallardo has been recommended. Those wishing to try *cuy* should do so in Ayacucho as it's a lot cheaper than Cusco.

Eating: cheaper

Taberna Liverpool, Mcal Cáceres 620. Good for blues and rock music, owner Edwin is a great Beatles fan, he also plays Quechua rock music, also videos and pizzas. *Punto Caliente Video Pub*, Asamblea 131. Open Tuesday-Sunday, very popular, good atmosphere. *Crema Rica*, on the main plaza. Restaurant and video pub, very popular. *Peña Machi*, on Jr Grau. *Peña* on Friday and Saturday, the rest of the week it's a disco.

Bars & nightclubs

Cinema On 9 de Diciembre, opposite the *Hotel Plaza*.

Entertainment

This area is well-known for its festivals throughout the year. Almost every day there is a celebration in one of the surrounding villages. Check with the Ministry of Tourism.
Festival Internacional de la Tuna y Cochinilla is held on **31 January to 1 February**, for real 'dye' hards. Carnival in **February** is reported as a wild affair. Ayacucho is famous for its *Semana Santa* which begins on the Friday before **Holy Week**. There follows one of the world's finest Holy Week celebrations, with candle-lit nightly processions, floral 'paintings' on the streets, daily fairs (the biggest on Easter Saturday), horse races and contests among peoples from all central Peru. All accommodation is fully booked for months in advance of Holy Week. Many people offer beds in their homes during the week. Look out for notices on the doors, especially on Jr Libertad.
On **25 April** is the anniversary of the founding of Huamanga province. *Virgen de las Nieves* is held on **5 August** in Cora-Cora and Parinacochas. On **20-26 August** is *Semana Turística Andamarca*, in Andamarca of all places. Also in **August** is the *Semana Turística de Ayacucho*. On **8 September** the *Festividad de La Virgen de Cocharcas* takes place in Quinua (see below), as does the *Semana de la Libertad Americana*, on **3-10 December**, to honour the Battle of Ayacucho.

Festivals

Ayacucho is a good place to buy local crafts including filigree silver, which often uses *mudejar* patterns. Also look out for little painted altars which show the manger scene, carvings in local alabaster, harps, or the pre-Inca tradition of carving dried gourds. The most famous goods are carpets and *retablos*. In both weaving and *retablos*, scenes of recent political strife have been added to more traditional motifs.
Owing to the dramatic decline in tourism in recent years, many craftsmen left Ayacucho, but are now returning and re-establishing their businesses. For carpets, go

Shopping

Central Highlands

to Barrio Santa Ana, *Familia Sulca*, Jr Mcal Cáceres 302 (see under Sights above); or *Familia Fernández*. In Barrio Belén, *Familia Pizarro*, Jr San Cristóbal 215, works in textiles and *piedra huamanga* (local alabaster) and produces good quality. (See also Arts and crafts, on page 521).

Transport   **Air connections**   To **Lima**, daily flights with *Aero Continente* and *AeroPerú*. To Cusco, daily with *Aero Continente*.

Bus   To **Pisco**, 332 kilometres, 10-12 hours in the dry season, US$7-10; buses leave between 1500 and 1700. It is a poor road but with good views. Most buses go on to Lima (14-15 hours, US$9-11). Companies include: *Fano*, Pasaje Cáceres 150, T912813; *TransMar*, Avda Mcal Cáceres 896; *Trans Molina*, Tres Máscaras 551.

To **Huancayo**, 319 kilometres, 8-10 hours, US$6-7. Daily at 1800-1900 with *Trans Molina, Fano, Yazala* (Avda Mcal Cáceres 879, T914422) and *Antezana* (Avda Manco Cápac 467). The road is paved as far as Huanta, thereafter it is rough, especially in the wet season, but the views are breathtaking.

For **Huancavelica**, take a Pisco bus to Pámpano, via the Abra de Apacheta (Apacheta-Pámpano, 5 hours). In Pámpano wait in a restaurant till the next day as there are no hotels. A bus runs to Santa Inés at 1100 or 1200, arriving at 1900. From Santa Inés take a truck to Huancavelica, or there is a bus between 1600-1700. It is 3 hours from Santa Inés to Huancavelica (see above).

To **Andahuaylas**, 252 kilometres, takes 12 hours (more in the rainy season), US$8-9. *Trans Fano* leave on Monday, Wednesday, Friday and Saturday at 0600; *Ayacucho Tours* (Avda Mcal Cáceres 880), leave daily at 0630. These buses continue to **Abancay**, 135 kilometres, 5½ hours, US$5, and on to **Cusco**, a further 195 kilometres, 7 hours (in the dry season), US$7. It takes 2 days to Cusco, with an overnight stop in Andahuaylas. There are no direct buses. *Trucks* to Abancay and Cusco leave from opposite *Hostal El Sol*, 0500-0600. Road conditions are terrible, and landslides a common occurrence in the wet season. The scenery, though, is stunning and makes up for it.

NB Terrorist activity has declined in recent years, but robberies are a problem and there are numerous military checkpoints. Buses sometimes even travel in convoy with a police escort. Check on current conditions.

Directory   **Airline offices**   *Aero Continente*, Jr 9 de Diciembre 160, T912816. **Banks**   *Banco de Crédito*, 28 de Julio y San Martín. No commission on cheques, cash advance on Visa. Many street changers can be found at Portal Constitución on the plaza, they offer a good rate for cash. *Casa de Cambio DMJ*, at Portal Constitución 4. Good rates for cash, cheques at 1% commission, open Mon-Sat 0800-1900. To change cash or cheques on a Sun, contact Andrés Harhuay Macoto or Carito Acevedo Vallejo at Portal Constitución, or T913547. **Communications**   Post Office and Telefónica: Asamblea 293. **Tour companies & travel agents**   *Morochucos Travel Service*, Portal Constitución 14, T/F912261. City tours, tours to Huari, Quinua, Huanta and Inca ruins at Vilcashuamán, also agent for AeroPerú. Also local tours with *Wari Tours*, Portal Independencia 70, T913115. *Quinua Tours*, Jr Asamblea 195, T912191. Manager Zumilda Canales de Pérez is very helpful. **Tourist offices**   *Ministerio de Turismo (MICTI)*, Asamblea block 4, T912548/913162. Open Mon-Fri 0800-1300, friendly and helpful. **Useful addresses**   Tourist Police: at Dos de Mayo y Arequipa. For information on the recent and current political situation, journalist Ylpidio Enrique Vargas Palomino, at Jr 3 Máscaras 171-A, T912987, has been recommended as friendly and helpful.

Sights around Ayacucho

Vilcashuamán   These impressive Inca ruins are to the south of Ayacucho, beyond Cangallo. John Hemming writes: "There is a five-tiered, stepped *usnu* platform faced in fine Inca masonry and topped by a monolithic two-seat throne. The parish church is built in part of the Inca sun temple and rests on stretches of Inca terracing. Vilcashuamán was an important provincial capital, the crossroads

The Huari influence

The city of Huari had a population of 50,000 and reached its apogee in AD 900. Its influence spread throughout much of Peru: north to Cajamarca; along the north coast to Lambayeque; south along the coast to Moquegua; and south across the sierra to Cusco. Before the Inca invasion the Huari formed a chanca – a confederation of ethnic groups – and populated the Pampas river and an area west of the Apurímac. This political agreement between the peoples of Ayacucho, Andahuaylas, Junín and Huancavelica was seen by the Incas in Cusco as a threat. The Incas fought back around 1440 with a bloody attack on the Huari on the Pampa de Ayacucho, and so began a period of Inca domination. The scene of this massacre is still known as Rincón de los Muertos.

where the road from Cusco to the Pacific met the empire's north-south highway." There are 3 hotels in the village of Vilcashuamán, all **F**, and all basic but clean. Tours can be arranged with Travel Agencies in Ayacucho. A full day tour includes Intihuatana. Alternatively stay overnight. Market day is Wednesday. Buses and colectivos run from Avda M Castilla, on Tuesday, Thursday and Saturday at 0600, returning Wednesday, Friday and Sunday at 0600, taking 5-6 hours, and costing US$4.50.

Vischongo Near Vilcashuamán is the village of Vischongo. About an hour's walk uphill from the village are the Inca baths of **Intihuatana**, which are worth seeing as much for their superb location on a beautiful lake as for the ruins themselves. From Vilcashuamán to Vischongo takes one hour and costs US$0.45. Vischongo to Ayacucho takes five hours, and costs US$2.70. It is possible to see both ruins in a day, though it's more relaxing to spend the night in Vilcashuamán, or better still, camp at the lake near Vischongo.

Huari A good road going north from Ayacucho leads to Huari, dating from the 'Middle Horizon', when the Huari culture spread across most of Peru. This was the first urban walled centre in the Andes and was used for political, administrative, ceremonial, residential and productive purposes. The huge irregular stone walls are up to 12 metres high and rectangular houses and streets can be made out. There are large areas of flat stone which may have been for religious purposes and there are subterranean canals and tunnels.

The most important activity here was artistic productivity. High temperature ovens were used to mass produce ceramics of many different colours. The Huari also worked with gold, silver, metal and alloys such as bronze, which was used for weapons and for decorative objects. Examples of pottery finds at the site can be seen in the archaeological museum in Ayacucho.

Buses leave from the Ovalo in Barrio Magdalena. There are no specific times; they leave when full from 0700 onwards. Buses go on to La Quinua (US$1), and Huanta (US$1.35, see below). Trips can be arranged to Huari, La Quinua village and the battlefield with travel agencies in Ayacucho.

La Quinua This village, 37 kilometres northeast of Ayacucho, has a charming cobbled main plaza and many of the buildings have been restored. There is a small market on Sunday. Nearby, on the Pampa de Quinua, a huge obelisk commemorates the battle of Ayacucho. The obelisk is 44 metres high, representing 44 years of struggle for independence. There is also a small and poorly displayed museum. ■ *Entry US$1.40.*

The village's handicrafts are recommended, especially ceramics. Pottery has been produced here for many centuries, but over the past decade conflict

Central Highlands

between the Peruvian military and the Shining Path guerrillas has left Quinua almost deserted, as many of the artisans fled to the relative safety of Lima, where they had to adapt to different clay and working conditions. Today, the area is more peaceful and it is hoped they will return.

The pieces made in Quinua range from model churches and nativity figures to humorous groups of musicians and gossiping women. The rich red local clay is modelled mainly by hand and decorated with local mineral earth colours. Traditionally, the churches are set on the roofs of newly-occupied houses to ward off evil spirits. Virtually every roof in the village has a church on it – including the church itself. San Pedro Ceramics, at the foot of the hill leading to the monument, and Mamerto Sánchez, Jr Sucre, are good places to find typical local ceramics.

The village's festival, *Fiesta de la Virgen de Cocharcas* (see Fiestas & festivals above) consists of three days of processions, dancing and bullfighting.

It is a beautiful 18 kilometres' walk downhill from La Quinua to Huari, where trucks leave for Ayacucho until about 1700. Tombs of the Huari nobles are being excavated along the road from Ayacucho to Quinua.

The Huanta valley This picturesque region, 48 kilometres northeast of Ayacucho, consists of the districts of Huanta, Luricocha, Santillana, Ayahuanco, Huamanaguilla and Iguaín. The town of Huanta is one hour from Ayacucho, on the road to Huancayo. It was here that the Pokras and Chancas warriors put up their last, brave fight against the Inca invasion.

From Huanta, the lakes of Qarqarcocha, San Antonio, Chakacocha, Yanacocha and Pampacocha can be visited, also the valley of Luricocha, five kilometres away, with its lovely, warm climate. Huanta celebrates the *Fiesta de la Cruz* during the first week of May, with much music and dancing (and possibly the occasional drink). Its Sunday market is large and interesting.

The area is notable as the site of perhaps the oldest known culture in South America, 20,000 years old, evidence of which was found in the cave of **Pikimachay**. The remains are now in Lima's museums. The cave is 24 kilometres from Ayacucho, on the road to Huanta. It is a 30-minute walk from the road.

North to the Río Apurimac A road runs northeast from Ayacucho to **San Francisco**, lying in the tropical lowland forests of the Apurímac valley. There are three basic hotels: E *Suria*, is the best but still dirty. The town can be reached by *micros* from Ayacucho, which leave from the Ovalo in Barrio Magdalena on Saturday (returning on Monday). It takes 10-12 hours on a very bad road, often impassable in the wet season and very cold at night. Check on the political situation before travelling.

From San Francisco you can take a morning canoe to **Luisiana**, about two hours upstream. There is an airstrip at Luisiana with daily connections to Ayacucho (if there are over five passengers). Details are available in the Ayacucho Tourist Office. From San Francisco you can make excursions to nearby villages on cargo canoes, but it is very difficult to find transport all the way to Pucallpa unless you have a large group of people and are willing to pay handsomely.

Ayacucho to Cusco

Chincheros The road towards Cusco goes through Chincheros, 158 kilometres from Ayacucho and three hours from Andahuaylas. It's not the most picturesque town in Peru, but the townsfolk are very friendly. Ask for the bakery with its outdoor oven (if you don't smell it first). 15 minutes before Chincheros, on the road from Andahuaylas, is Uripa with a good Sunday market. *Micros* regularly run between the two towns.

About three hours to the north of Chincheros is the town of Huaccana. There are four little lakes on the way and a larger one near the town which can easily be visited. The valley is beautiful and practically free from other tourists. There is a very basic dormitory on the plaza in Huaccana, and a basic, unmarked restaurant. A bus leaves for Ayacucho at 0400 and 1300. You may be able to hitch a lift with one of the trucks, if you're up before daybreak. **G** per person *Hostal Don José*, clean, friendly, pleasant courtyard, warm. **G** per person *Hostal Municipal*, on the plaza, clean, very quiet. **Huaccana**

Andahuaylas

80 kilometres further on from Chincheros, in a fertile, temperate valley of lush meadows, cornfields and groves of eucalyptus, alder and willow, stands Andahuaylas (*Phone code* 084). The town offers few exotic crafts, no lighting except in the plaza, poor transport, but beautiful scenery. There is a good market on Sunday.

C-D *Turístico Andahuaylas*, Avda Lazaro Carrillo 620, T721224. **E-F** per person *Las Américas*, near *Delicias*. Hot water in the morning and evening, clean, friendly. Recommended. **F** *Cusco*, Casafranca 520. Hot shower. **F** *Delicias*, Ramos 525. Hot showers, ask for extra blankets, cold at night. Basic but recommended. **F** *Wari*, Ramos 427. Hot shower. **G** *Bienvenidos*, Andahuaylas 364. Cheap, noisy, dirty toilets. **G** per person *Hostal Waliman*, Avda Andahuaylas 266, near where the buses leave for Cusco. Basic. **Sleeping**

Good, cheap food can be found at *Corazón Ayacuchano*, Avda Andahuaylas 145. *Las Floridas*, serves a good set meal for US$0.80. A recommended *chifa* is at Jr Juan A Trellas 279. **Eating**

Air connections There are daily flights to Lima with Transporte Andahuaylas, and every Wednesday with Grupo Ocho. **Transport**

Bus Daily buses to **Ayacucho**, a minimum of 12 hours, US$8-9; *Ayacucho Tours* and *Fano* leave between 1300 and 1500. There are no direct buses early in the morning, so you will miss most of the stunning scenery. To **Abancay** with *Señor de Huanca* at 0600 and 1300 daily, 5½ hours, US$5. To **Cusco**, same company at 0600, and *Empresa Andahuaylas* at 1300, 12 hours, US$9.

Around Andahuaylas

The scenery is pleasant on the old road by the river to **Talavera**. **San Jerónimo** is another picturesque town nearby.

Most worth seeing is Pacucha (*Population*: 2,000), the largest of six villages on the shores of a large lake, with a view of the mountains to the northwest. In the plaza, where the trucks stop, women sell bread, coffee and hot lunches, the only food for 16 kilometres. There are dirt roads around the lake. Allow at least three hours to walk right round – more if you want to take it easy and have a chat with the locals, who are courteous and friendly – but be back in Pacucha before dark to ensure transport back to Andahuaylas. The wildlife **Pacucha** includes many types of wild duck and other birds, sometimes including flocks of green parrots.

Opposite Pacucha, two kilometres past the lake, are the ruins of a Chanka fortress called **Sóndor**. Except for Andahuaylas itself, this is a mainly Quechua-speaking region. It is also one of the poorest parts of Peru. Mini-vans leave daily when full to Pacucha from the centre of Andahuaylas, about every 30 minutes. It's a 40-minute ride (US$0.65). Sunday is market day.

Abancay

Nestled between mountains in the upper reaches of a glacial valley, this friendly town is first glimpsed when you are 62 kilometres away. There is a petrol station. The town celebrates the *Yawar Fiesta* in July, and for lovers of blood sports there's the *Campeonata Nacional de Gallos de Navaja* on the 1-3 November. *Phone code*: 084.

Sleeping **B** *Hotel de Turismo Abancay*, Avda Díaz Barcenas 500, T321017 (Cusco, 223339). With bathroom, good food for US$3, comfortable, old-fashioned house, safe car park, camping for US$3. **E** *Leonard I* and **F** *Leonard II*. Both clean and safe. **F** *Hostal Sawite*, on Nuñez. Hot water 24 hours, clean, friendly, ask them to turn off the TV in the main passage if you want to sleep. **G** *El Misti*, okay. **G** *Gran*. With bathroom.

Eating *Elena*, on the same street as the bus companies. Good.

Transport Several bus companies leave from Abancay to **Cusco** on Avda Arenas near the market, daily at 0600 and 1300, US$7, 6-7 hours (in the dry season); *colectivos* also leave from here. The scenery en route is dramatic, especially as it descends into the Apurímac valley and climbs out again. There is a checkpoint at the Apurímac border. The road is paved and in good condition from Curahausi to Cusco. Coming from Cusco, after the pass it takes an hour to zig-zag down to Abancay. The 2000 bus from Cusco arrives around 0300, but there is no guarantee of a seat to Andahuaylas, even with a through ticket. See page 196 for sites of interest between Abancay and Cusco.

To **Andahuaylas**, US$4, 6 hours, departures at 0300, 0500, 0600, 1300 and 2000 daily; change there for Ayacucho. Landslides are common on this route, as well as lots of checkpoints, which involve getting off the bus.

To **Nasca** on the Panamericana Sur, 464 kilometres, via Chalhuanca and Puquío, daily buses or trucks, 20 hours, US$14.

East of La Oroya

A paved road heads north towards Cerro de Pasco and Huánuco. 25 kilometres north of La Oroya, a turn-off branches east and drops 600 metres before it reaches Tarma. Beyond Tarma the road continues its steep descent. In the 80 kilometres between Tarma and La Merced the road, passing by great overhanging cliffs, drops 2,450 metres and the vegetation changes dramatically from temperate to tropical. This is a really beautiful run.

Tarma

Population: 105,200
Altitude: 3,050 metres
Phone code: 064
Coloured map 3, grid C4

This nice little flat-roofed town, founded in 1545, with plenty of trees, is now growing, with garish modern buildings. It still has a lot of charm, however. The Semana Santa celebrations are spectacular, with a very colourful Easter Sunday morning procession in the main plaza. Accommodation is hard to find at this time but you can apply to the Municipalidad for rooms with local families. The town is also notable for its locally-made fine flower-carpets (see Festivals below). The cathedral is dedicated to Santa Ana. The surrounding countryside is beautiful.

NB The immediate area is now free from terrorist activity but it's best to travel by day for safety and to enjoy the scenery.

Sleeping
■ *on maps*
Price codes:
see inside front cover

B *Los Portales*, Avda Castilla 512, T321411. Out of town, with bathroom, hot water. **B-C** *La Florida*, 6 kilometres from Tarma (for reservations T Lima 4246969, 4324361). 18th century hacienda, 6 rooms with bathroom, hot water, price includes breakfast, owned by German-Peruvian couple Inge and Pepe who arrange excursions. Highly recommended. Also camping for US$3.

D *Hostal Galaxia*, on Plaza de Armas, T321449. With bathroom, hot water, car parking for US$1. **D** *Hostal Internacional*, Dos de Mayo 307, T321830. With bathroom, hot water 1800-0800, clean.

E *Hostal Bolívar*, Huaraz 389, T321060. With bathroom, hot water, reasonable. **E** *Hostal Central*, Huánuco 614. Shared bathroom, hot water, has an observatory which opens Friday at 2000. **E** *Hostal El Dorado*, Huánuco 488, T321598. Hot water, reasonable. **E** *Hostal Tuchu*, Dos de Mayo 561. Shared bathroom, hot water in the morning. **E** *Vargas*, Dos de Mayo 627, T321460. With bath, hot water in morning, OK.

F *Hostal Ideal*, Moquegua 389. Basic.

Tarma

■ **Sleeping**	4. Hostal Internacional	● **Eating**	🚍 **Buses**
1. Hostal Central	5. Hostal Tuchu	1. Señorial	1. To Acobamba & Palca
2. Hostal El Dorado	6. Vargas		2. To Chanchamayo
3. Hostal Galaxia			3. To Huancayo
			4. To Lima

0 metres 100
0 yards 109

Central Highlands

Eating
● *on maps*

Señorial, Huánuco 138. The 'best in town', good *menú*. **Chavín Café**, beneath *Hostal Galaxia*, on Plaza de Armas. Recommended for trout. **Don Lucho**, Lima 175. Good. **El Rosal**, on Callao near Transportes Chanchamayo. Reasonable and clean. There are also several places on Lima, including a vegetarian. The *manjarblanco* of Tarma is famous, as well as *pachamanca, mondongo* and *picante de cuyes*.

Festivals

Aside from *Semana Santa*, Tarma hosts many other festivals. *Carnaval Tarmeño* is held on **20-25 February**. Also taking place during *Semana Santa* is the *Concurso de Alfombras de Flores* (flower carpet competition). Taking place throughout **May** is *Festividad Señor de Muruhuay*. On **23-24 May** is the *Circuito Turístico de Ciclismo de Montaña*. The *Festival de la Papa* (potato, not father) is held on **23-27 June**. **23-29 July** is the *Semana Turística*. The *Fiesta de la Siembra del Maíz* is on **28-30 September**, in Tarma as well as Acobamba (see below). *Festival del Pan Tarmeño "La Wawa"* is held on **1-2 November** (the same time as All Saints).

Transport

Direct buses leave daily to **Lima**, 231 kilometres, 6 hours, US$5.25. *Transportes Chanchamayo*, Callao 1002, T321882, is recommended as the best; also *Expreso Satipo*, Ucuyali 384. There is a good lunch stop at El Tambo before La Oroya, with superb fried trout. The road is paved throughout.

To **Jauja**, US$1.80. To **Huancayo**, 3 hours, US$2.50. Daily *colectivos* from Jr Huánuco 439 run almost hourly to Huancayo; they cost US$4, and take 2½ hours. Bus to **La Oroya**, US$2.40, colectivo, US$3. Bus to **La Merced**, US$2.65. Colectivos often leave for La Merced and San Ramón (collectively known as Chanchamayo – see below), from Dos de Mayo blocks 2 and 3, US$3.45.

Directory

Banks *Banco de Crédito*, Lima 407. Changes Amex TCs. **Communications** Telefónica del Perú: is on the Plaza de Armas. **Tourist offices** *Club de Turismo de Tarma*, Moquegua 653, offer tours of the local area which cost around US$4.50-9, depending on the length of the tour: eg to San Pedro de Cajas, Grutas de Guagapo, Acobamba and El Señor de Muruhuay (see below). They go on weekends and need a minimum of 15 people, which is easy during the dry season but can be difficult during the rainy season, except at peak holiday times. Alfonso Tapía E at *Hostal Central* will show people around. He is very friendly and likes to practise his English and German.

Around Tarma

Acobamba

Eight kilometres from Tarma, the small hillside town of Acobamba has the futuristic **Santuario de Muruhuay**, with a venerated picture painted on the rock behind the altar. It also has fine *tapices* made in San Pedro de Cajas which depict the Crucifixion. There are festivities during May (see above). Daily buses leave Acobamba to Tarma (US$0.20, or a pleasant two hours' walk), La Oroya (US$0.60) and Huancayo. Three buses a week go direct to Lima (Coop San Pedro). There are two *alojamientos*, both **G**: Doña Norma's, near the plaza, is basic but clean and friendly.

Palcamayo

The **Grutas de Guagapo**, also known as *La gruta que llora* (the cave that weeps), is four kilometres from the town of Palcamayo. The caves can be entered for about 300 metres. Even without a guide you can penetrate the cave for some way with a torch. A bus leaves twice daily from Tarma; US$1, two hours.

San Pedro de Cajas

Beyond Palcamayo, the road continues to San Pedro de Cajas, a large village which used to produce most of the coloured sheep-wool weavings for sale in Lima. Most of the weaving families have now moved to Lima. There are no buses, but you can walk it in three hours. This road joins the one from La Oroya to Cerro de Pasco below Junín. The town holds the *Festival de La Pukcha (Hilado)* on 28-30 June. There is accommodation in the village at **G** *Hotel Comercio*, in Calle Chanchamayo; also two restaurants, but no shops.

Chanchamayo

East from Tarma are the towns of San Ramón and La Merced, collectively known as Chanchamayo. Regular colectivos run between the two towns for US$0.25.

San Ramón (*Population*: 7,000) is 11 kilometres before La Merced. **C-D** *El Refugio*, 5-10 minutes' walk from town. Set in beautiful tropical gardens, with bathroom, cheaper without breakfast or hot water. **E** *Conquistador*, on the main street. Shower and parking. *La Estancia*, Tarma 592. Serves local specialities. There are other places on the main street. Flights leave from San Ramón. There is an 'air-colectivo' service to **Puerto Bermúdez**, which continues to **Atalaya**, **Satipo**, **Puerto Inca** (see page 467) and **Pucallpa**. Air-colectivos go to Lima and to most places in the jungle region where there is an airstrip. Flights are cheap but irregular, and depend on technical factors, weather and goodwill. Aero-taxis can be chartered (*viaje especial*) to anywhere for a higher price, with a maximum of five people, but you have to pay for the pilot's return to base.

La Merced (*Population*: 10,000), lies in the fertile Chanchamayo valley. Sometimes Campa Indians come to town selling bows and arrows. There is a festival in the last week of September. **E** *Cosmos*, opposite the police station. The best value, with bathroom. **F** *Romero*, Plaza de Armas. Good but noisy and water in evenings only. The best restaurant is *Shambari-Campa*, on the Plaza de Armas. Many buses go here from Lima: *Transportes Chanchamayo*, Avda Luna Pizarro 453, La Victoria, Lima, is the best, also *Expreso Satipo*. It takes 9 hours and costs US$6.40. There are many buses from Tarma, US$2.65, 3 hours. A bus goes to **Puerto Bermúdez** at 1000 with *Túpac Amaru*; 8 hours, US$6.40. To get to **Pucallpa**, take a launch from Puerto Bermúdez to Laurencia (which takes 8 hours or more, be prepared for wet luggage), then a truck to Constitución (20 minutes), and from there a colectivo to Zungaro, 1½ hours. From **Zungaro**, colectivos take 4½ hours to Pucallpa. Alternatively, you can take a truck from La Merced to Pucallpa. The journey takes 3 days, and between 0830 and 1400 each day expect to be drenched by rain.

East of Chanchamayo

About 22 kilometres north from Chanchamayo is **San Luis de Shuaro**, three kilometres before which a road runs east up the valley of the Perené river. There are large coffee plantations at an altitude of only 700 metres. Saturday and Sunday are market days.

Warning Latest reports suggest that Oxapampa, the Perené region and Satipo are still dangerous due to narco-terrorist activity. Check on the situation before travelling into these areas.

The jungle town of Satipo is the main centre of this region. **D** *Hostal Majestic*. With bathroom, electricity 1900-2300 only. **F** *La Residencial*. 4 rooms, clean, garden, swimming pool. Recommended. There are many smaller hotels, all

Satipo

Central Highlands

very basic, the best being **E** *Palmero*, with bathroom, not very clean. For good food try *Dany's Restaurant*. To get to Satipo take a Lobato or Los Andes bus from La Merced at 0800, US$7.20. Daily buses run direct from Satipo to Huancayo and Lima at night, a very cold journey, US$9.50, 12 hours, with Los Andes and Lobato. Check whether the tunnels are open before travelling.

North of Chanchamayo

The road has been extended from San Luis de Shuaro over an intervening mountain range. A turn-off east leads to **Puerto Bermúdez** on the Río Neguachi. There is clean accommodation in **F** *Hostal Tania*, opposite the dock where motorized canoes tie up, and an eating house opposite the airstrip. Boat passages are possible from passing traders.

Oxapampa 56 kilometres from La Merced is Oxapampa (*Population*: 5,140. *Altitude*: 1,794 metres), 390 kilometres from Lima, in a fertile plain on the Río Huancabamba, a tributary of the Ucayali. A third of the inhabitants are descendants of a German-Austrian community of 70 families which settled in 1859 at **Pozuzo**, 80 kilometres downstream, and spread later to Oxapampa. There is much livestock farming and coffee is planted on land cleared by the timber trade. On 5 August the town hosts a festival, the *Virgen de Las Nieves*.

Sleeping and eating **E** *Rey*, with bathroom, clean, cold water, small beds. **F** *Arias*, cheaper without bathroom, clean, best value. **F** *José*, without bathroom, hot water, clean, pleasant. **F** *Hostal Jiménez*, Grau 421. Refurbished, clean, cold water, shared bathroom. **F** *Hostal Liz*, Avda Oxapampa 104. Clean, small rooms, cold water. **F** *Santo Domingo*, old but clean, no hot water. **G** *Hostal Santa Isolina*, Jr M Castilla 177. With bathroom, cold water. **G** *La Cabaña*, on the plaza. A smelly dump, cold water. **G** *San Martín*, even worse, tiny rooms, smelly bathroom. *Oasis*, is a highly recommended restaurant.

Transport Colectivos run from La Merced. Also taxis at 0600, US$2, 4 hours.

North of Oxapampa 25 kilometres from Oxapampa is **Huancabamba**, from where it is 55 kilometres to Pozuzo. The whole road between La Merced and Pozuzo is very rough, depending on the season. There are no less than 30 rivers to be crossed. Downstream 40 kilometres from Pozuzo is Nuevo Pozuzo. There is no transport, it's a two-day walk. There is an interesting museum opposite the church in the town centre. The town celebrates the *Semana Turística de Pozuzo* during the last week in July.

Sleeping In Pozuzo: **E** *Hostal Tirol*, includes meals. Clean. Recommended. **F** *Hostal Prusia*, clean. **F-G** *Hostal Maldonado*. Clean. Recommended.

Transport Buses leave from Lima to Pozuzo with La Victoria (28 de Julio 2405, Lima) on Monday, Thursday and Saturday at 0800, US$12, about 16 hours.

North of La Oroya

A paved road runs 130 kilometres north from La Oroya to Cerro de Pasco. It runs up the Mantaro valley through narrow canyons to the wet and mournful Junín pampa at over 4,250 metres, one of the world's largest high-altitude plains. An obelisk marks the battlefield where the Peruvians under Bolívar *defeated the Spaniards in 1824. Blue peaks line the pampa in a distant wall. This windswept sheet of yellow grass is bitterly cold and the only signs of life are the young herders with their sheep and llamas. The rail line follows the eastern shores of the Lago de Junín. The town of **Junín**, with its picturesque red-tiled roofs, stands beside the lake.*

13 kilometres east of the village of **Shelby**, served by the railway from La Oroya to Cerro de Pasco, a good section of Inca road can be seen. Its course is marked by the lonely ruins of Bonbón, an Inca community centre only recently identified, which in turn lies close to the modern dam holding back the Río Mantaro as it flows out of the northern end of Lago de Junín.

NB The central highlands have suffered from terrorist activity in recent years, but since 1992 the area seems to be under military control. Travellers have started to visit the region again, with good reports. Before going, though, check on the situation, only travel by day, and stay in contact with the locals.

Lima to Cerro de Pasco

An alternative to the La Oroya route from Lima to Cerro de Pasco is the road via Canta. From Canta you can visit the pre-Inca ruins of **Cantamarca** – many of the buildings still have roofs, supported by pillars. It is a two to three hours' walk up to the ruins, from where there are extensive views. Accommodation in Canta is limited, but *Hostal Kalapacho* is friendly and good value. There is one good restaurant in town. There are 3 buses daily to and from Lima, US$3.60, with El Canteño company, San Román 151-153, Lima.

Canta

Continuing through the beautiful high pass of La Viuda (4,748 metres), the road goes to the mines of **Alpamarca**. A truck leaves from Canta at 0200, take warm clothes, a blanket, camping gear and food. From Alpamarca there are two or three buses per week to **Huallay**, near where are the Inca ruins of **Bon Bón Marca** and the thermal baths at **Calera**.

Cerro de Pasco

This long-established mining centre is 130 kilometres from La Oroya by road. The town is famous as the site of one of the battles of the War of Independence, on 6 December 1820, when local hero, Antonio Alvarez de Arenales, defeated Diego de O'Reilly's royalist troops. The actual battlefield is one kilometre away, on Cerro Uliachin.

Population:29,810
Altitude: 4,330 metres
Phone code: 064
Coloured map 3, grid B4

Cerro de Pasco is not an attractive place but is nevertheless very friendly. For a long time, it was known as the first settlement in South America, when the Italian explorer, Antonio Raimondi, discovered 10,000-year-old remains here. It is also interesting as Peru's major mining community. Copper, zinc, lead, gold and silver are mined here, and coal comes from the deep canyon of Goyllarisquisga, the 'place where a star fell', the highest coal mine in the world, 42 kilometres north of Cerro de Pasco.

The town seems to defy gravity as its buildings and streets cling precariously to the edge of a huge abyss. Not surprisingly for a place that claims to be the highest city in the world, nights are bitterly cold. Travellers should also note that the streets don't conform to the usual grid pattern, so it can be quite easy to get lost.

Central Highlands

A new town, **San Juan de Pampa**, has been built one and a half kilometres away. There is accommodation in the *Gran Hotel* (noisy, no hot water, poor service).

Essentials

Sleeping   **E** *Hostal Arenales*, Jr Arenales 162, near the bus station. Clean, friendly, hot water. **F** *El Viajero*, on the plaza. Clean but no hot water. **F** *Santa Rosa*, also on the plaza. Basic and very cold.

Eating   *Los Angeles*, Jr Libertad, near the market. Recommended. *El Espignol I*, Jr Libertad 195. *El Espignol II*, Jr Arenales 164. Fish, chicken, *menú* and other dishes. Local specialities are trout and fried frog.

Festivals   *Festival de La Chonguinada Cerreña* takes place during the first week in **May**. On the **22-24 May** is *Semana Turística de Huarica*. On **5 August** is the *Virgen de Las Nieves*. In the last week of **November** is the *Semana Turística de Pasco*.

Transport   Buses to **Lima** leave at 0830 and 2000, 9 hours, US$7, with *Empresa de Transportes Carhuamayo*; their office is near the Avda Montevideo entrance to the market (in Lima: Avda Grau 525, T4330785, 4278605). To **La Oroya**, buses leave from Plaza Arenales at 0900 and later, 3 hours, US$2.20. Cars also travel this route, leaving when there are enough passengers, US$9.50. To **Huancayo**, 5-6 hours, US$3-4. Colectivos to **Huánuco** leave from the Plaza de Armas, US$6.20; there are also buses between 0800 and 0900, 5 hours, US$2. Cerro de Pasco has a central bus station, which is unusual in Peru.

Directory   **Banks** *Banco de Crédito* is on Jr Bolognesi.

Around Cerro de Pasco

Huayllay   40 kilometres southwest of Cerro de Pasco, on the way to Lima, is Huayllay. Nearby is the **Santuario Bosque de Piedras**, with unique weathered limestone formations in the shape of a tortoise, elephant, alpaca, etc. There is a small *campesino* settlement nearby. Take a bus from Cerro de Pasco and get off at the crossroads near Villa de Pasco. It is about 15 minutes out of town, on the road to Lima. Camionetas pass by bound for Huayllay, which is about 1 hour away.

Valle de Huachón   80 kilometres southeast of Cerro de Pasco is the Valle de Huachón. There are excellent hiking opportunities in the valley and around the *nevados* of Incatama (5,130 metres), Jancahuay (5,180 metres), Ranrajanca (5,182 metres) and Carhuarajo (5,160 metres). The valley also gives access to Nevado Huaguruncho (5,730

Cerro de Pasco

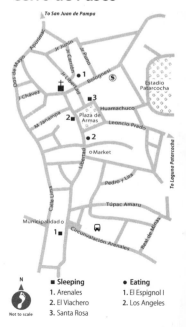

To San Juan de Pampa

Estadio Patarcocha

Plaza de Armas

Market

To Laguna Patarcocha

Municipalidad

N

Not to scale

■ **Sleeping**
1. Arenales
2. El Viachero
3. Santa Rosa

● **Eating**
1. El Espignol I
2. Los Angeles

metres), which is the snowy peak visible from the road on the way to Huánuco. To reach the valley, take a bus to **Tambo del Sol**, on the road to Lima.

Another recommended excursion is to the precolumbian funeral towers at **Cantamasia**, reached on muleback. West of Cerro de Pasco, off the Huayllay road, is the **Laguna de Pun Rún**.

The Yanahuanca Valley

65 kilometres northwest of Cerro de Pasco is **Yanahuanca**, in the beautiful valley of the same name. From the village you can reach one of the longest surviving stretches of Inca road. Two kilometres up the Yanahuanca Valley a lesser valley cuts northwards between the towering crags.

The road, its paving uneven and disturbed by countless horse and donkey convoys, leads up the smaller valley, its course sometimes shared by a stream, to the village of **Huarautambo**, about four kilometres away. This village is surrounded by many pre-Inca remains. For more than 150 kilometres the *Camino Incaico* is not only in almost continuous existence from the Yanahuanca Valley but is actually shown on the map issued by the Instituto Geográfico Militar. The clearest stretch ends at Huari in Ancash, having passed by such places as **La Unión** (see page 454) and **San Marcos**. After Huari its route can be followed, less distinctly, through **Llamellín** and in the hills behind **San Luis**, **Piscobamba** and **Pomabamba** (see page 320).

The Huallaga Valley

The Central Highway from Cerro de Pasco continues northeast another 528 kilometres to Pucallpa, the limit of navigation for large Amazon river boats. The western part of this road (Cerro de Pasco-Huánuco) has been rebuilt into an excellent paved highway.

Population: 118,814
Altitude: 1,894 metres
Phone code: 064
Coloured map 5, grid A5

The descent along the **Río Huallaga** is dramatic. The road drops 2,436 metres in the 100 kilometres from Cerro de Pasco to Huánuco, and most of it is in the first 32 kilometres. From the bleak vistas of the high ranges the road plunges below the tree line into another world of tropical beauty. The only town of any size before Huánuco is **Ambo**.

NB The Huallaga valley is the country's main coca-growing area, with both drug-trafficking and guerrilla activity. The main centre of activity is between Tingo María and Tarapoto, so it is best to avoid the region at present. It does appear to be safe to visit Huánuco, Tingo María and Pucallpa, but as the area is under military control there are many checkpoints. Travelling during the day is strongly advised and seek full information before going.

Huánuco

Huánuco is an attractive Andean town with an interesting market on the Upper Huallaga.

Sights

The two churches of **San Cristóbal** and **San Francisco** have both been much restored. The latter has some 16th century paintings. There is a small but interesting natural history museum at Gen Prado 495, called **Museo de Ciencias**. Many of the displays have multiple language signs. ■ *Entry is US$0.50.*

Essentials

Sleeping
■ *on maps*
Price codes:
see inside front cover

Hotels are often fully booked, so you should arrive early. **B** *Gran Hotel Huánuco*, Jr D Beraun 775. Restaurant, pool, sauna, gym, parking. Recommended. **D** *Cusco*, Huánuco 616, 2 blocks from the Plaza de Armas. With bathroom, cafeteria, OK. **F** *Hostal Residencial Huánuco*, Jr Huánuco, near the Plaza de Armas. With bathroom, hot water, garden, use of kitchen, washing facilities, it's more expensive than the others in this range but excellent value. Highly recommended. **F** *Imperial*, Huánuco 581. With cold shower (intermittent water), reasonable value, clean and quiet. *Las Vegas*, on Plaza de Armas. Recommended. **F** *Lima*, Plaza de Armas, 28 de Julio 9222. With bathroom.

Camping: it is possible to camp by the river, near the stadium. A good area for camping outside town is the **Five lakes of Pichgacocha**. Take a *camioneta* to La Libertad – 31 kilometres from Huánuco; turn-off the main road to Lima near Santa Rosa – then walk 20 kilometres.

Eating
● *on maps*

La Casona de Gladys, Gen Prado 908. Good, cheap local food. *Vegeteriano*, Dos de Mayo 751. Also try the *chifas* on Damaso Beraun, 1 block west of the Plaza de Armas.

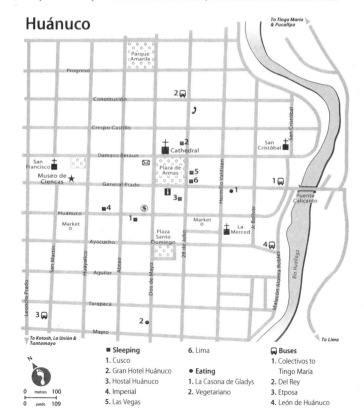

Huánuco

	■ Sleeping	6. Lima	**🚌 Buses**
	1. Cusco		1. Colectivos to
	2. Gran Hotel Huánuco	**● Eating**	Tingo María
	3. Hostal Huánuco	1. La Casona de Gladys	2. Del Rey
	4. Imperial	2. Vegetariano	3. Etposa
	5. Las Vegas		4. León de Huánuco

0 metres 100
0 yards 109

On the **20-25 January** is the *Carnaval Huanuqueño*. On **21 March** is the *Festival de las*   **Festivals**
Cataratas. In San Rafael, in the province of Ambo, is the festival of *El Señor de Chacos*
on **1 May**. On **3 May** is *La Cruz de Mayo*, in Huánuco. On **16 July**, the *Fiesta de la Virgen*
del Carmen. The *Festival de la Perricholi* is held during the last week of **July**. **12-18**
August is Tourist Week in Huánuco. **25-27 September** is the *Festival del Cóndor Pasa*.
28-29 October is *Fiesta del Rey y del Señor de Burgos*, the patron of Huánuco. **25**
December, *Fiesta de los Negritos*.

Air connections There are connecting flights to Tingo María, Tocache, Juanjui,   **Transport**
Pucallpa, Saposoa, Tarapoto, Yurimaguas, Moyobamba, Rioja, Trujillo and Chiclayo.
Check all flight details in advance. Flights may be cancelled in the rains or if not full.

Bus Buses to **Lima**: US$9, 9 hours, with *León de Huánuco*, Malecón Alomía Robles
821 (28 de Julio 1520, La Victoria, Lima); 3 a day leave in the early evening. A colectivo
to Lima, costing US$20, leaves at 0400, arriving at 1400; book the night before at Gen
Prado 607, 1 block from the plaza. Recommended. *Transportes del Rey*, 28 de Julio
1201 (28 de Julio 1192, La Victoria, Lima), also have buses to Lima.

Daily buses go to **Cerro de Pasco**, 5 hours, US$2. 'Mixto' Huánuco-Cerro de Pasco,
half bus, half truck, departs at 0400, 3 hours, US$3.60. There's also a colectivo, No 1 or
12, at 0500, US$6.20. To **Huancayo**, 8-9 hours, US$5-6. Buses to **Tingo María**, 3-4
hours, US$1.75. Also colectivos, US$4.35, 2 hours; many start from near the river
bridge, 2 blocks from the main plaza.

Bus to **Pucallpa**, US$11, with La Perla del Oriente (Etposa), 0800 and 1600, 10-12
hours. Recommended. Buses make stops for meals but some of them are few and far
between, so it's a good idea to take your own food, especially given the frequency of
breakdowns. This route has many checkpoints and robberies can occur. You are
advised to travel by day and check on the current situation regarding safety.

Banks *Banco de Crédito*, at Dos de Mayo 1005. **Communications** Telefónica del Perú: at 28   **Directory**
de Julio 1157. **Tourist offices** Gen Prado 716, on the Plaza de Armas. A good contact for
adventure tours is *César Antezana*, Jr Pedro Puelles 261, T513622.

West of Huánuco

The road to La Unión and Tantamayo passes the 'Crown of the Inca', also
known as Lacsahuarina, meaning 'Two Princesses' in Quechua. This distinctive rock formation is at the pass before the descent into the upper canyon of
the Río Marañon.

Five kilometres away on the road west to La Unión is Kotosh (*Altitude*: 1,812   **Kotosh**
metres), the Temple of Crossed Hands, the earliest evidence of a complex
society and of pottery in Peru, dating from 2000 BC. You must ford a stream
to get there, and beware of the vicious black flies. The ruin has been sadly
neglected since the original excavation in 1963.

Tantamayo (3,600 metres) is a farming village surrounded by precolumbian   **Tantamayo**
ruins from the **Yarowillca** culture.

Japallan is perhaps the most scenically sited, guarding the entrance to
the valley leading from the spectacular Marañon canyon. To get there, cross
the river from Tantamayo and walk west to San Pedro de Pariarca. At the start
of the village take the path to the right to Pariash (Upper Pariarca), and head
for the ruins silhouetted on a ridge.

The ruins of **Selinin** are just above Pariash. The most elaborate ruins are
Piruru and **Susupillu**. Piruru was occupied continuously for 1,700 years,

from 3000 BC as a ceremonial, and later ceramics, centre. Both sites have high-rise stone dwellings. To reach Susupillu head northeast through the tiny village of La Florida. There are other ruins further afield.

All the above mentioned ruins are visible from Tantamayo and can be reached on foot in about three to four hours; guides are available to visit the sites. The walks to the ruins are arduous; take warm clothing, a hat and suntan lotion. The scenery is stunning. Pictures and information on the sites are available from Huánaco Post Office. In Tantamayo there are 4 basic hotels and 1 restaurant, *Ortega*, on the corner of the plaza. Buses leave from Huánuco at 0730 and 0800, returning at 1800 and 0100, with Transportes Balla, San Martín 575; US\$6.50, 10 hours.

La Unión From Huánuco, a poor dirt road leads all the way to La Unión, capital of Dos de Mayo district. It's a friendly town, but electricity can be a problem and it gets very cold at night.

On the pampa above La Unión are the Inca ruins of **Huánuco Viejo**, a two and a half hour walk from the town, a great temple-fortress with residential quarters. To get there, take the path starting behind the market and climb towards the cross, which is at the edge of a plateau. Continue straight through the village on the wide path. Note that, though the locals are friendly, some of their dogs are not always well disposed to strangers. The views of the pampa, surrounded on all sides by mountains, are beautiful. Seemingly at the foot of a mountain, in front and to your right, is a silvery metallic roof of a little chapel, behind which are the ruins – about a 20-minute walk through herds of cattle. You should take warm clothing and be prepared for some violent thunderstorms. (Karen Kubitsch, Germany.)

Sleeping and eating G *Hostal Turista* and G *Hostal Dos de Mayo*. Neither are safe for left luggage. *Restaurant El Danubio*, near the market. Good home cooking.

Transport From Huánuco two buses leave daily at 0745 from Tarapacá, returning at 0600 and 0700; US\$4.35, 8 hours. A truck leaves in the late morning, 10½ hours. La Unión-Tingo Chico, US\$2.70. There is a daily bus to Lima which gets crowded.

It is possible to get to the Callejón de Huaylas from here. La Unión-Huaraz direct is very difficult because most transport does the route La Unión-Chiquián-Lima. Change buses in **Chiquián** (see page 293) or at the Conococha crossroads, but check times if you can to avoid being stranded in the dark. Alternatively ask for trucks going to **Huallanca** and from there to Pachacoto, one hour south of Huáraz. Check local political conditions before taking this route and only travel by day.

NB There are vigilante forces made up of local people in this area. If you're camping wild they will come to check that you are not a threat. This can be nerve-wracking at night, but if you're friendly you'll have no problems. (Alycea Lamb-Horth.)

You can, if you're so inclined, hike to the Cordillera Raura (see page 323) from **Laguna Lauricocha**. To reach the lake from La Unión take a camioneta to **Baños**, then take another camioneta from there to **Antacolpa**. It's half a day's walk to the lake from here. In 1959, caves were discovered by the lake with 9,500 year-old human remains and some paintings. This is where the Río Marañon rises, eventually becoming the Ucayali and then Amazon rivers, before spilling into the Atlantic Ocean, 5,800 kilometres away to the east.

The Amazon Basin

12

The Amazon Basin

458 Northern Jungle

463 Pucallpa

467 Iquitos

477 Southern Jungle

478 Manu Biosphere Reserve

483 Puerto Maldonado

487 Tambopata-Candamo Reserved Zone

Iquitos

Río Marañón

BRAZIL

Río Ucayali

Pucallpa

Río Ucayali

To Cerro de Pasco

Río Inuya

Río Urubamba

Río de las Piedras

Lima

Río Apurímac

MANU
NATIONAL PARK

Manú
Puerto Maldonado

TAMBOPATA CANDAMO
RESERVE ZONE

To Cusco

The immense Amazon Basin covers a staggering four million square kilometres, an area roughly equivalent to three quarters the size of the United States. But despite the fact that 60 percent of Peru is covered by this green carpet of jungle, less than six percent of its population lives there. This lack of integration with the rest of the country makes it difficult to get around easily but does mean that much of Peru's rainforest is still intact. The Peruvian jungles are home to a diversity of life unequalled anywhere on Earth.

It is this great diversity which makes the Amazon basin a paradise for nature lovers, be they scientists or simply curious amateurs. This part of Peru contains some 10 million living species, including 2,000 species of fish and 300 mammals. It also contains over 10 percent of the world's 8,600 bird species and, together with the adjacent Andean foothills, 4,000 butterfly species.

This incredible biological diversity, however, brings with it an acute ecological fragility. Ecologists consider the Amazon rainforest as the lungs of the earth – the Amazon Basin produces 20 percent of the Earth's oxygen – and any fundamental change in its constitution, or indeed its disappearance, could have disastrous effects for our future on this planet.

The mighty Amazon

The principal means of communication in the jungle is by its many rivers, the most important of which is the Amazon, the longest river in the world. The Amazon rises high up in the Andes as the Marañon, then joins the Ucayali and winds it way east to finally disgorge into the Atlantic, over 6,000 kilometres from its source. At its mouth, the Amazon is 300 kilometres wide. This mighty waterway was so named by the Spaniard Francisco de Orellana, during his epic voyage in 1542, owing to an encounter with a hostile, long-haired indigenous group which he took to be the fearsome women warriors of Greek legend.

The Northern Jungle

Standing on its banks, in the northeastern corner of the country, is the city of Iquitos, made famous during the rubber boom of the late 19th century and now the main tourist attraction in this part of the Peruvian jungle. Iquitos stands in splendid isolation, accessible only by air or river, and still retains something of its frontier feel. Further south, the region's second city, Pucallpa, can be reached by road from the Central Andes.

The overland route from the Central Andes to Pucallpa runs from **Huánuco** east to **Tingo María**, and gives the first views of the vast green carpet of jungle. 25 kilometres beyond Huánuco the road begins a sharp climb to the heights of Carpish (3,023 metres). A descent of 58 kilometres brings it to the Huallaga river again; it then continues along the river to Tingo María. The road is paved from Huánuco to Tingo María, including a tunnel through the Carpish hills. Landslides along this section are frequent and construction work causes delays.

NB Although this route is reported to be relatively free from terrorism, robberies do occur and it is advisable to travel only by day. There are three police/army checkpoints where soldiers may demand money to pass through; it is not necessary to pay.

Tingo María

Population: 20,560
Altitude: 655 metres
Phone code: 064
Coloured map 3, grid A4

Tingo María is on the middle Huallaga, in the *Ceja de Montaña*, or edge of the mountains. The climate here is tropical, with an annual rainfall of 2,642 millimetres. The town can be isolated for days in the rainy season. The altitude, however, prevents the climate from being oppressive. The Cordillera Azul, the front range of the Andes, covered with jungle-like vegetation to its top, separates it from the jungle lowlands to the east. The mountain which can be seen from all over the town is called *La Bella Durmiente*, the Sleeping Beauty.

The meeting here of Sierra and Selva makes the landscape extremely striking. Bananas, sugar cane, cocoa, rubber, tea and coffee are grown. The main crop of the area, though, is coca, grown on the *chacras* (smallholdings) in the countryside, and sold legitimately and otherwise in Tingo María.

NB Watch out for gangs of thieves around the buses and do not leave luggage on the bus if you get off. Note that this is a main narco-trafficking centre and although the town itself is generally safe, it is not safe to leave it at night. Also do not stray from the main routes, as some of the local population are suspicious of foreign visitors.

Amazon Basin

Sights

Six and a half kilometres from Tingo, on a rough road, is a fascinating cave, the **Cueva de las Lechuzas**. There are many oilbirds in the cave and many small parakeets near the entrance. Take a motorcycle-taxi from town, US$1.75. It's US$0.45 for the ferry to cross the Río Monzón just before the cave and entry to the cave is US$0.90. Take a torch, and do not wear open shoes. The cave can be reached by boat when the river is high.

13 kilometres from Tingo is the small gorge known as **Cueva de las Pavas**, which is good for swimming. **El Velo de las Ninfas** is a magnificent waterfall set in beautiful jungle, with lagoons where you can swim. 10 kilometres away, on the Huánuco road, are the **Cuevas de Tambillo**, with beautiful waterfalls and pools for swimming.

A small university outside the town, beyond the *Hotel Turistas*, has a little museum-cum-zoo, with animals native to the area, and botanical gardens in the town. Entrance is free but a small tip would help to keep things in order.

Essentials

A3 *Madre Verde*, some way out of town on the road to Huánuco, near the University, T/F561608/562047. Several chalets set in beautiful surroundings, with and without bathroom, restaurant, swimming pool. **E** *Hostal Marco Antonio*, Jr Monzón 364, T562201. Quiet, restaurant of the same name next door. **F** *Hostal Aro*, Avda Ucayali

Sleeping
■ *on maps*
Price codes:
see inside front cover

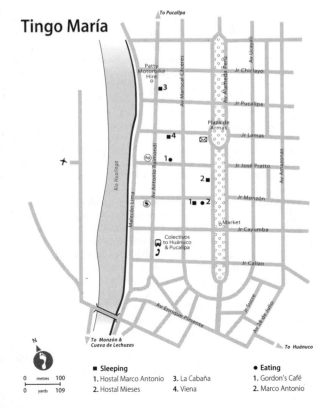

Tingo María

To Pucallpa

Patty Motorbike Hire

Av Mariscal Cáceres
Av Alameda Perú
Av Ucayali

Jr Chiclayo

Jr Pucalipa

Plaza de Armas

■4   ☒   Jr Lamas

Av Antonio Raimondi
Av Amazonas

1●   Jr José Pratto

2■   Jr Monzón

Malecón Lima

Río Huallaga

1■ ●2

Market
Jr Cayumba

Colectivos to Huánuco & Pucallpa

Jr Callao

Av Enrique Pimente
Jr Sucre
Av 28 de Julio

To Monzón & Cueva de Lechuzas

To Huánuco

0   metres   100
0   yards   109

■ **Sleeping**
1. Hostal Marco Antonio   3. La Cabaña
2. Hostal Mieses   4. Viena

● **Eating**
1. Gordon's Café
2. Marco Antonio

Amazon Basin

553, secure. **F** *Hostal Mieses*, Avda Alameda Perú 365, near the plaza. **F** *La Cabaña*, Raimondi 600 block. Fairly clean, good restaurant. **F** *Viena*, Jr Lamas. With bathroom, good value, clean. **NB** Hotels are often fully-booked.

Eating
● *on maps*
Gordon's Café, Jr José Pratto 229. Clean, friendly, good food and service, cheap pisco sours. *El Antojito 2*, Jr Chiclayo 458. Good local food.

Transport
Air Flights to **Lima**, **Huánuco**, **Juanjui** and **Tarapoto**; check the times. Services are unreliable. There are cancellations in the rainy season or if the planes are not full.
Buses To **Huánuco**, 118 kilometres, 3-4 hours, US$1.75; several micros daily and colectivos, US$4.35, 2 hours. Direct buses continue to Lima. To **Pucallpa**, 284 kilometres, 12 hours, US$5.50. Many of the big bus companies (eg: *Leon de Huánuco*, *Transmar* and *Transportes del Rey*) pass through Tingo María on their way to **Pucallpa**, from Lima, in the middle of the night. *Ucayali Express* colectivos leave from the corner of Raimondi and Callao. There are other colectivos and taxis, which all leave in the early morning in convoy. There is daily transport to **Juanjui**, 340 kilometres, 15-20 hours, US$9. This is not a recommended journey because of narco-terrorist activity. **Tarapoto** is a further 145 kilometres; 4 hours, US$2.

Directory
Tour companies & travel agents *Tingo María Travel Tours*, Avda Raimondi 460, T562501. For local excursions.

North to Yurimaguas

The Río Huallaga winds northwards for 930 kilometres from its source to the confluence with the Marañon. The Upper Huallaga flows fast and furiously, but by the time it becomes the Lower Huallaga it moves slowly through a flat landscape. The main port of the Lower Huallaga, Yurimaguas, is below the last rapids and only 150 metres above the Atlantic Ocean, yet distant from that ocean by over a month's voyage. Between the Upper and Lower lies the Middle Huallaga: that third of the river which is downstream from Tingo María and upstream from Yurimaguas.

The valleys, ridges and plateaux have been compared with Kenya, but the area is so isolated that less than 100,000 people now live where a million might flourish. The southern part of the Middle Huallaga centres upon Tingo María. Down-river, beyond Bellavista, the orientation is towards **Yurimaguas**, which is connected by road with the Pacific coast, via Tarapoto and Moyobamba (see page 414).

At **Tulumayo**, soon after leaving Tingo María, a road runs north down the Huallaga past **La Morada**, successfully colonized by people from Lima's slums, to **Aucayacu** and **Tocache**, which has an airport. The road has been pushed north from Tocache to join another built south from Tarapoto and has now been joined at Tarapoto to the Olmos-Bagua-Yurimaguas Transandean Highway to the coast at Chiclayo. The road is paved to 20 kilometres past Aucayacu, thereafter it is gravel.

Sleeping
In Aucayacu: **E** *Hotel Monte Carlo*, with bathroom, and one other hotel. Both are poor. **In Tocache**: **F** *Hostal San Martín*; and **F** *Hostal Sucre*.

Transport
Air A small plane flies between Tocache and Juanjui.
Bus Colectivos run from Tingo María to **Tocache** US$13, 4½ hours; or bus US$9.50, 6 hours. Tarapoto-Tocache, US$7.50 by colectivo. Colectivos and taxis run from Tocache to **Yurimaguas**. A daily camioneta runs from Tarapoto to **Yurimaguas**, US$7-9, 6-8 hours. The Juanjui-Tocache road has 5 bridges, but the last one across the

Amazon Basin

Lope de Aguirre

One of the most famous expeditions into the mysterious, inhospitable world of the Amazon jungle in search of El Dorado was made by a Spanish noble from Navarra, Ursúa, along with his wife, Doña Inés and the adolescent daughter of his second-in-command, Lope de Aguirre. The rest of the party comprised over 300 Spaniards and 500 Indians.

Leaving Lima in 1560, his party crossed the Andean cordillera before penetrating the dense rainforest and navigating the Huallaga river. The journey, however, was cut short for Ursúa one night when he was murdered by the mutinous Lope de Aguirre, whose loyalty to the Spanish Crown was weakening as he felt that he had not been adequately compensated

for his heroic exploits and hardship.

Lope de Aguirre took command of the group and resolved to punish any signs of loyalty to the Spanish Crown by death. He kept true to his threat, killing Doña Inés, on the pretext that her bed could no longer be supported by the deteriorating ship. He even killed his own daughter to prevent her falling into the hands of an Amazon tribe.

Despite the decimation of the expedition group, Lope de Aguirre's lust for gold drove him on down the Amazon, turning off down the Río Negro and Orinoco, before reaching the Atlantic. It is an exciting, if infamous tale, well dramatized by German director, Werner Herzog, in the film, "Aguirre, Wrath of God".

Huallaga, just before **Juanjui**, was washed away in 1983 to be replaced by an efficient ferry; it costs US$9.20 per vehicle. Juanjui-Tarapoto by colectivo US$12.50.

River For the river journey, start early if you do not wish to spend a night at the river village of Sión. There are no facilities, but the nights are not cold. The river runs through marvellous jungle with high cliffs. Boats sometimes run aground in the river near Sión. Take food and water purifier. Balsa wood rafts also ply this stretch of river.

Yurimaguas

The town (*Population*: 25,700) has a fine church of the Passionist Fathers, based on the Cathedral of Burgos, in Spain. A colourful market is held from 0600-0800, full of fruit and animals. Tourist information is available from the Consejo Regional building on the main plaza. There's a branch of Interbanc, which changes cash at poor rates, or try the travel agents.

There are some interesting excursions in the area, including to the gorge of Shanusi and the lakes of Mushuyacu and Sanango. Mopeds can be hired for US$2.35 per hour, including fuel.

Warning There has been guerrilla activity in the Yurimaguas region and visitors can expect attention from the police. It is also a centre for anti-narcotics operations. A good contact is Luis Dalman. The South American Explorer's Club in Lima has his address and telephone number.

Sleeping **E** *Leo's Palace*, Plaza de Armas 104-6. Good, friendly, reasonably-priced, restaurant. **F** *Camus*, Manco Capac 201. No sign, but it does exist. **F** per person *Yurimaguas*, in the centre of town. With fan, helpful, noisy, laundry facilities.

Transport **Air** To **Lima** (2 hours), 3 flights weekly with *Aero Continente*, who also fly 3 times weekly to **Tarapoto** and **Iquitos**. Flights are cancelled in the wet season or if they're not full.

Bus To **Moyobamba**, with *Guadalupe* (Raymondi y Levean, T3990), at 0630, US$8.75.

River By ferry to **Iquitos** takes 2 days and 2 nights (upstream takes longer), take a hammock, mosquito net, water-purification, fruit and drinks. There are police

Amazon Basin

inspections at each end of the trip. Fares usually include meals, US$18, cabins cost more. To buy a hammock costs US$20-30 in Yurimaguas, mosquito nets are poor quality. Ask at the harbour for smaller boats, which can take up to 10 days.

Lagunas

The river journey to Iquitos can be broken at Lagunas, 12 hours from Yurimaguas. You can ask the local people to take you on a canoe trip into the jungle where there's a good chance of seeing caiman (alligators), monkeys and a variety of birds, but only on trips of four days or so.

Sleeping G *Hostal La Sombra*, Jr Vásquez 1121. Shared bathroom, basic, friendly, good food. *Montalbán*, Plaza de Armas (no sign). 2 clean rooms, friendly owner, Sr Inga. There's also accommodation at the Farmacia.

Transport **Boat** The *Constante* sails from Yurimaguas to Lagunas 2-3 times a week (US$4.50). From there connections are difficult to Iquitos. Times of boats to Iquitos and Pucallpa are very vague; you should confirm departures the day before by radio. The boats pass by the villages of Castilla and Nauta, where the Huallaga joins the Ucayali and becomes the Amazon.

Jungle trips

Pacaya-Samiria Reserve There are good jungle trips from Lagunas to the Pacaya-Samiria Reserve. When arranging a guide and boat from Lagunas, make sure you take enough fuel for the boat. Before entering the Reserve you pass through a village where you must pay US$4.50. Officially, you need a permit from INRENA in Lima. Trips are mostly on the river, sleeping in hammocks, and include fishing. The typical cost is around US$70 per person for 6 days, with guide and boats. Take water purifier and mosquito repellent on excursions that involve living off the land.

Edinson and Klever Saldaña Gutiérrez, Sgto Flores 718, are good guides. As are Job and Genaro (ask at *Hostal La Sombra*), who include basic food, with fishing and hunting. Juan Huaycama, at Jáuregui 689, is highly recommended.

Tingo María to Pucallpa

From Tingo María to the end of the road at Pucallpa is 288 kilometres, with a climb over the watershed – the Cordillera Azul – between the Huallaga and Ucayali rivers. The road is good for 60-70 kilometres after Tingo María and 70 kilometres before Pucallpa. In between it is affected by mud and landslides in the rainy season. There are eight army checkpoints.

When the road was being surveyed it was thought that the lowest pass over the Cordillera Azul was over 3,650 metres high, but an old document stating that a Father Abad had found a pass through these mountains in 1757 was rediscovered, and the road now goes through the pass of Father Abad, a gigantic gap four kilometres long and 2,000 metres deep. At the top of the pass is a Peruvian Customs house; the jungle land to the east is a free zone. Coming down from the pass the road bed is along the floor of a magnificent canyon, the Boquerón Abad. It is a beautiful trip through luxuriant jungle and ferns and sheer walls of bare rock punctuated by occasional waterfalls plunging into the roaring torrent below.

East of the foot of the pass the all-weather road goes over the flat pampa, with few bends, to the village of **Aguaytía**. Here you'll find a narcotics police

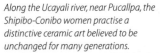

A symbolic art form

Along the Ucayali river, near Pucallpa, the Shipibo-Conibo women practise a distinctive ceramic art believed to be unchanged for many generations.

Their pieces are unique in the Americas for their geometric decoration, but no one knows their true significance. One theory is that the lines represent a primitive map of the waterways of the region; others that they represent the constellations.

The same designs are stamped on cloth and were formerly painted on people's bodies during certain tribal rituals. Mud from the banks of local rivers is used to dye their ceramics and textiles. The mysterious geometric lines are painted on white cotton fabrics woven on their backstrap looms. When the mud dries and the fabric is washed, the design remains.

The Shipibo vessels are made with a specific purpose in mind and each one is regarded as imbued with deep spiritual meaning. Today, the Shipibo have organized themselves to market their products, though the forms and techniques of production remain unchanged.

checkpoint, gasoline, accommodation in the *Hostal San Antonio* (**F**, clean), and two restaurants. From Aguaytía the road continues for 160 kilometres to Pucallpa – five hours by bus, US$4.35. There are no gas stations on the last half of the journey.

Pucallpa

The capital of the Department of Ucayali is a rapidly expanding jungle town on the Río Ucayali, navigable by vessels of 3,000 tons from Iquitos, 533 nautical miles away. The town's newer sections have paved streets, sewers and lights, but much of the frontier atmosphere still exists. Pucallpa is notable for defying the rules of Spanish pronunciation – the double 'l' is pronounced as one.

Population: approximately 400,000.
Phone code: 064
Coloured map 3, grid B5

Ins and outs

The airport is to the northwest of the town. Bus from the airport to town, US$0.25; *motos* US$1; taxi US$2-3. The foating dock at La Hoyada is about five kilometres northeast of the town. Buses and colectivos go to there. In the dry season boats dock 3 kilometres from the bus stop, from where it's a dusty walk, or take a taxi for US$3.

Getting there

Most of the accommodation is not far from the Plaza de Armas. The office of *Ucayalli Express* as well as the depot for buses to Yarinacocha are also in this quarter. You will probably want to take a taxi to visit the Museo Regional.

Getting around

The area

The floating port of **La Hoyada** and **Puerto Italia** are about five kilometres away and worth a visit to see the canoe traffic and open-air markets. Both are reached by dirt roads. The economy of the area includes sawmills, plywood factories, a paper mill, oil refinery, fishing and boat building; timber is trucked out to the Highlands and the coast. Large discoveries of oil and gas are being explored, and gold mining is underway nearby. The Ganso Azul oilfield has a 75-kilometre pipeline to the Pucallpa refinery.

The climate is tropical. The dry season is during July and August and the rainy seasons are October-November and February-March. The town is hot and dusty between June and November and muddy from December to May.

Amazon Basin

NB There is much military control because of narcotics activity, which is expanding. The city itself is safe enough to visit, but don't travel at night.

Sights

Parque Natural Pucallpa is a zoo on the left on the road to the airport. You can see many jungle animals and most of the cages are OK, though some are inadequate. The zoo is set in parkland with a small lake; ■ *US$0.90.*

Museo Regional has some good examples of Shibipo ceramics, as well as some delightful pickled snakes and other reptiles. ■ *Jr Inmaculada 999. Open 0800-1200 and 1600-1800. US$0.90.*

Pucallpa

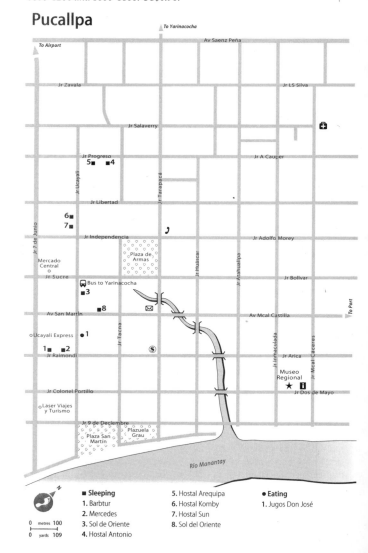

■ Sleeping
1. Barbtur
2. Mercedes
3. Sol de Oriente
4. Hostal Antonio

5. Hostal Arequipa
6. Hostal Komby
7. Hostal Sun
8. Sol del Oriente

● Eating
1. Jugos Don José

0 metres 100
0 yards 109

Amazon Basin

Essentials

A3 *Sol del Oriente*, Avda San Martín 552, T575154, T/F575510. With bathroom, pool and
good restaurant. **A2** *Divina Montaña*, 14 kilometres outside Pucallpa on the road to
Tingo María, T571276. Bungalows for rent, restaurant, swimming pool, sports facilities.
B *Hostal Antonio*, Jr Progreso 547, T573122, F573128. With gym. **D** *Hostal Arequipa*, Jr
Progreso 573. With bathroom, good, clean. **D** *Mercedes*, Raimondi, good, but noisy with
good bar and restaurant attached, swimming pool. **E** *Barbtur*, Raimondi 670 (opposite
the bus stop), T572532. With bathroom, **F** without, friendly, clean, good beds. **E** *Hostal
Komby*, Ucayali 300 block. Comfortable, swimming pool, excellent value. **E** *Hostal Sun*,
Ucayali 380, next to *Komby*. With bathroom, cheaper without, clean, good value.
E *Tariri*, on Raimondi. Clean, good food. **F** *Marinhor*, Raimondi 699. Grubby but economical, helpful. **F** *Hostal Mori*, Jr Independencia 1114. Basic.

Sleeping
■ *on maps*
Price codes:
see inside front cover

El Alamo, Carretera Yarinacocha 2650. Good typical food. *El Sanguchón*, Jr Tarapacá
829, near Banco de Crédito. Clean, good sandwiches and coffee. *El Golf*, Jr Huáscar
545. **Cevichería**. *Jugos Don José*, Jr Ucayali y Raimondi. One of the oldest in town.
Cafetería Antonio, Cnel Portillo 307, 2 blocks from the *Museo Regional*. Good coffee.
    Typical dishes: *patarashca* is barbecued fish wrapped in *bijao* leaves. *Zarapatera*,
a spicy soup made with turtle meat served in its shell, but consider the ecological
implications of this dish. *Chonta salad* is made with palm shoots, and *juanes*, is rice
with chicken or fish served during the San Juan festival. *Tacutacu* is banana and
sauces. The local beer 'San Juan' is good.

Eating
● *on maps*

The city hosts its *Fiesta de San Juan* on **24 June**, and during **5-20 October** is Pucallpa's
Aniversario Political and the Ucayali regional fair.

Festivals

Many Shibipo women carry and sell their products around Pucallpa and Yarinacocha.
Artesanías La Selva, Jr Tarapacá 868, has a reasonable selection of indigenous
craftwork. For local wood carvings visit the workshop of sculptor, Agustín Rivas, at Jr
Tarapacá 861.

Shopping

Air Daily flights to **Lima** (1 hour), with *Aero Continente*, and with *Grupo Ocho* every
Friday. Daily to **Iquitos** with *AeroPerú* and *Aero Continente*. To **Huánuco** and **Tingo
María.**
    Bus There are regular bus services to **Lima**, 812 kilometres, 18-20 hours (longer in
the rainy season, November-March), US$11. To **Tingo María**, 284 kilometres, 7-9
hours, US$7.80, combis leave at 0600, 0700 and 0800 with *Ucayali Express* (7 de Junio
y San Martín). All buses have police guard and go in convoy. For road conditions see
above. Take blankets as the crossing of the Cordillera at night is bitterly cold. It's recommended to cross the mountains by day as the views are wonderful.
    River To **Iquitos** there are only 3 boats with cabins, but don't count on getting
one. Hammocks are cooler in any case. These are: *Florico*, *Carolina* and *Manuel*. The
trip takes 3-4 days, and costs US$22 per person, or US$27 including food.
    You can go to Puerto La Hoyada and Puerto Italia to find a smaller boat going to
Iquitos. The Capitanía on the waterfront may give you information about sailings, but
this is seldom reliable. Do not pay for your trip before you board the vessel, and only
pay the captain. Some boat captains may allow you to live on board a couple of days
before sailing. Boats going upstream on the Amazon and its tributaries stay closer to
the bank than boats going down, which stay in mid-stream.
    The smaller boats call often at jungle villages, but otherwise the shores can only be
seen at a distance. Boats leave very irregularly. When conditions are bad they leave in
convoy and none may leave afterwards for 4 to 6 weeks. Avoid boats that will be loading en route, this can take up to 6 days. Further down the Río Ucayali are **Contamaná**,

Transport

Amazon Basin

with a frontier-town atmosphere, and **Requena**, from which launches sail to Iquitos, taking 12 hours. Unlike most other villages, which are *mestizo*, **Roroboya**, about 12 hours downstream from Pucallpa, is Shipibo Indian.

NB Travellers to Iquitos may need confirmation from the PNP that their documents are in order, this must then be signed by the Capitanía otherwise no passenger can be accepted on a trip leaving Pucallpa. No such clearance is necessary when returning to Pucallpa. Passenger services are in decline owing to competition by air and priority for cargo traffic. It may be better to make journeys in short stages rather than Pucallpa-Iquitos direct. There's a risk of illness as the river water is used for cooking and drinking. Tinned food, mosquito netting, hammock and fresh water are necessary purchases, and fishing line and hooks are advisable. Vegetarians must take their own supplies. Bottled drinking water is reportedly impossible to find in Pucallpa. 2 litre bottles of carbonated water are readily available but expensive at US$4-6 a bottle. Also take lots of insect repellent, water purifier and tummy pills.

Directory **Banks** It is easy to change dollars cash at the banks, travel agencies, the better hotels and bigger stores. There are also lots of street changers (watch them carefully). *Banco de Crédito* is the only place to change TCs. Cash advances can be made on Visa at *Banco de Crédito* and *Interbanco del Perú*. **Cultural centres** Art school: *Usko Ayar Amazonian School of Painting*, in the house of artist Pablo Amaringo, a former *vegetalista* (healer), is at Jr LM Sánchez, Cerro 465-467. The school provides art classes for local people, and is financially dependent upon selling their art. The internationally-renowned school welcomes overseas visitors for short or long stays to study painting and learn Spanish and/or teach English with Peruvian students. The painting is oriented around the Amazonian cultures, in particular the healing and hallucinogenic effects of *ayahuasca*. For more information see the book, *Wizard of the Upper Amazon*. **Tour companies & travel agents** *Laser Viajes y Turismo*, Jr 7 de Junio 1043, T571120, T/F573776. Recommended as helpful for planning a jungle trip. **NB** Pucallpa is recovering from years of terrorist disruption and jungle tours are still in a disorganized state. It's best to negotiate a price for a group with the boatmen on the waterfront. Expect to pay around US$30 per day per person and use only accredited guides. **Tourist offices** *Ministerio de Industria y Turismo* (MICTI), is at Jr Dos de Mayo 999, T571303, T/F575110. They are helpful with tourist information. Ask for advice about visiting the Río Piski area, which has authentic Shibipo culture. There is no passenger traffic, so the trip may be expensive.

Lake Yarinacocha

The main tourist attraction of the area, especially with Peruvians, is the picturesque Lake Yarinacocha, where you can see river dolphins. The lake is also home to the Indian market of Moroti-Shobo ('The House of Selling and Buying'), a cooperative organized by Shipibo-Conibo craftsmen. Fine handicrafts are sold in their shop and you can visit them in Yarinacocha (T571551). Also on the lake are the Hospital Amazónico Albert Schweitzer, which serves the local Indians, and Summer School of Linguistics for the study of Indian languages (callers by appointment only).

A good place to swim is at **San José**. Take the road out behind the power station round the lake beyond the Summer School of Linguistics.

Certain sections of Lake Yarinacocha have been designated as a reserve. The beautifully-located **Jardín Botánico Chullachaqui** can be reached by boat from Puerto Callao to Pueblo Nueva Luz de Fátima. It's a 45-minute trip, then an hour's walk to the garden, entry is free. For information about traditional medicine contact Mateo Arevalomayna, San Francisco de Yarinacocha, president of the group Ametra, an organization which is working to reestablish the use of traditional remedies; T573152, or ask at Moroti-Shobo.

B *La Cabaña Lodge*, T616679, F579242. Prices include all meals and transport to and | **Sleeping**
from Yarinacocha harbour, run by Ruth and Leroy from the USA, great food, jungle
trips from US$50 per day including boat, guide and food. Next door is **B-C** per person
La Perla, includes all meals, German-Peruvian owned, English and German spoken,
no electricity after 2100, good, jungle tours organized. **D-E** *Los Delfines*, T571129.
New rooms with bathroom, fan, fridge, some with TV, clean. **F** *El Pescador*, in Puerto
Callao. The cheapest place in town, friendly, restaurant, 20 new rooms and an extension have been added. There are also some small houses for rent on a weekly basis.

There are many restaurants and bars on the waterfront and near the plaza, and also | **Eating**
stalls which barbecue fresh fish and local dishes. Among the recommended restaurants are: *El Cucharón*; *Grande Paraíso* (good view, also has a *peña* at night, popular
with young people); and *Orlando's*, Jr Aguaytía.

Yarinacocha is 20 minutes by colectivo or bus from the market in Pucallpa, US$0.30, or | **Transport**
15 minutes by taxi, US$2.

San Francisco and Santa Clara can be visited at the far end of the lake on its | **San Francisco &**
western arm. Both are Shibipo villages still practising traditional ceramic and | **Santa Clara**
textile crafts. A canal near Santa Clara links Lake Yarinacocha with the Río
Ucayali. There are a few other villages nearby, such as Nuevo Destino and
Santa Marta, which are within an hour's walk. The Shibipo people are very
kind and friendly and a visit is recommended.

To reach these villages take one of the motorized canoes, *peke-pekes*,
which leave from Puerto Callao when full, US$0.90. In San Francisco a nice
place to spend the night is in the house of Alberto Sánchez Ríos, *Casa
Artesanal Shibipo*, which is very friendly and warmly recommended.

Another recommended excursion in the Pucallpa area is six to seven hours by | **Laguna Imitia &**
boat south to Laguna Imitia and Laguna Chauya. There are many indigenous | **Laguna Chauya**
villages on the shores and boats sometimes glide through the dense, overhanging vegetation around the lakes. To get there take a colectivo (US$9 per
person), *peke-peke* or a hired boat from the port in Pucallpa.

You can take a colectivo from Pucallpa south to **Zungaro** (US$4.50), where a | **Puerto Inca**
30-minute boat ride can be taken to Puerto Inca on the Río Pachitea, about
120 kilometres north by air from Puerto Bermúdez (see page 447) and close to
the Carretera Marginal (under construction). It is a gold-rush town, expanding quickly, with two hotels: *Don José's Alojamiento*, **G**, clean, safe, laundry,
big rooms. Recommended.

Iquitos

Capital of the Department of Loreto and chief town of Peru's jungle region, | *Population: 350,000*
Iquitos stands on the west bank of the Amazon. Some 800 kilometres down- | *Phone code: 094*
stream from Pucallpa and 3,646 kilometres from the mouth of the Amazon, the | *Coloured map 2, grid B4*
city is completely isolated except by air and river.

Ins and outs

Francisco Secada Vigneta airport, in the southwest, handles national and interna- | **Getting there**
tional flights (to/from Miami), T231501/233094. A taxi to the airport costs US$2.50 per
person. A *motocarro* (motorcycle with 2 seats) is US$2.20. A bus from the airport

Amazon Basin

(US$0.20) goes as far as the market area, about 12 blocks from the Plaza de Armas, a taxi from there is US$1.30. The port is in the north of the town. **NB** From May to July the river rises and the port in Iquitos moves. Boats leave from Puerto Nanay at Bellavista or from Puerto de Morona-cocha.

Getting around Iquitos is well spread out and it is several blocks from the bus station into town. Hotels are dotted about all over the place. The best way to get around is by motorcycle. **Motorcycle hire:** *Rider*, Pevas 219; *Park Motors*, Tacna 579, T/F231688. Expect to pay: mopeds, US$2.60 per hour, US$35 for 24 hours; Honda 125, US$4.50 per hour, US$44 for 24 hours; Honda 125, US$4.50 per hour; Yamaha DT175, US$5.20 per hour, US$65 for 24 hours.

History

Founded in 1757 as San Pablo de los Napeanos by the Jesuits, this was the first port of note on the great river. Rapid growth followed the Rubber Boom of the late 19th century, though the city's new-found wealth was short lived. By the second decade of this century the rubber industry had packed its bags and left for the more competitive Oriental suppliers. Remnants of the extravagant opulence of the boom period can still be seen in the fine, two-storey houses decorated with Portuguese tiles which lend an air of faded beauty to the river embankment.

Iquitos has recently taken on a new lease of life as the centre for oil exploration in Peruvian Amazonia. It is also the main starting point for tourists wishing to explore Peru's northern jungle, with direct flights to and from Miami. Though it may seem at times that the city is attempting a new world record for the highest concentration of motorcycles in a built-up area, it is nevertheless a friendly, relaxed place with an almost languorous pace of life.

Sights

The incongruous **Iron House** stands on the Plaza de Armas, designed by Eiffel for the Paris exhibition of 1889. It is said that the house was transported from Paris by a local rubber baron and is constructed entirely of iron trusses and sheets, bolted together and painted silver. It now houses a restaurant upstairs and cafeteria downstairs.

Belén, the picturesque, friendly waterfront district, is lively, but not safe at night. Most of its huts were built on rafts to cope with the river's 10-metre change of level during floods, which are most likely between November and April. Now, they're built on wooden or concrete stilts. The main plaza has a bandstand made by Eiffel. In the high water season canoes can be hired on the waterfront to visit Belén for US$3 an hour. The market at the end of the Malecón is well worth visiting, though you should get there before 0900 to see it in full swing. On Pasaje Paquito, one of its side streets, there are bars that serve the local sugar cane rum.

Also worth seeing is the old **Hotel Palace**, now the army barracks, on the corner of Malecón Tarapacá and Putumayo. Of special interest are the older buildings, faced with *azulejos* (glazed tiles). They date from the rubber boom of 1890 to 1912, when the rubber barons imported the tiles from Portugal and Italy and ironwork from England to embellish their homes. There are other buildings left over from the rubber boom, such as the *Seminario San Agustín*, at Nauta 197.

Werner Herzog's film *Fitzcarraldo* is a *cause célèbre* in the town and Fitzcarrald's house still stands on the Plaza de Armas.

The **Museo Amazónico** is housed in the renovated Prefetura palace on

The rubber boom

The conquest and colonization of the vast Amazon basin was consolidated by the end of the 19th century with the invention of the process of vulcanizing rubber. Many and varied uses were found for this new product and demand was such that the jungle began to be populated by numerous European and North American immigrants who came to invest their money in rubber.

The rubber tree grew wild in the Amazon but the indigenous peoples were the only ones who knew the forests and could find this coveted tree. The exporting companies set up business in the rapidly-expanding cities along the Amazon, such as Iquitos. They sent their 'slave-hunters' out into the surrounding jungle to find the native labour needed to collect the valuable rubber resin. These natives were completely enslaved, their living conditions were intolerable and they perished in their thousands. This led to the extinction of many indigenous groups.

One particularly notable figure from the rubber boom was Fitzcarrald, son of an immigrant Englishman who lived on the Peruvian coast. He was accused of spying during the 1879 war between Peru and Chile and fled to the Amazon where he lived for many years among the natives.

Thanks to Fitzcarrald, the isthmus between the basin of the Ucayali river and that of the Madre de Dios river was discovered. Before this, no natural form of communication was known between the two rivers. The first steamships to go up the Madre de Dios were carried by thousands of natives across the eight kilometre stretch of land which separated the two basins. Fitzcarrald died at the age of 36, one of the region's richest men, when the ship on which he was travelling sank.

The Rubber Barons lived in the new Amazonian cities and travelled around in luxurious boats which plied the great river. Every imaginable luxury was imported for their use: latest Parisian fashions for the women; finest foreign liqueurs for the men; even the best musical shows were brought over from the Old World. But this period of economic boom came to a sudden end in 1912 when rubber grown in the French and British colonies in Asia and Africa began to compete on the world market.

the corner of Malecón Tarapacá and Calle Morona. It has displays of Amazon native art.

Essentials

If possible, avoid visiting Iquitos around Peruvian Independence Day (27 and 28 July) and Easter as it is very expensive and crowded and excursion facilities are overloaded. Hotels are generally more expensive than the rest of the country, but discounts of 20% or more can be negotiated in the low season (January-April).

A1 *Real Hotel Iquitos*, Malecón Tarapacá, 1 block from Plaza de Armas, T231011, F236222. Includes tax and breakfast, good a/c rooms. **A2** *El Dorado*, Napo 362, T237326, F232203. Pool (open to restaurant users), cable TV, bar and restaurant. Highly recommended. **A2-3** *Victoria Regia*, Ricardo Palma 252, T231983, F232499. A/c, fridge, cable TV, free map of city, safe deposit boxes in rooms, good restaurant and pool. Recommended. **A3** *Hostal Acosta*, Calvo de Araujo y Huallaga, T235974. Similar to *Victoria Regia* minus the swimming pool. **A3** *Jhuliana*, Putumayo 521, T/F233154. Includes tax and breakfast, friendly, nice pool, restaurant. Recommended.

B *Amazonas*, Plaza de Armas, Arica 108, T232015. Modern, a/c, phone, fridge bar, TV. **B** *Hostal Ambassador*, Pevas 260, T233110. Includes tax, a/c, transport to and from airport, member of Peruvian Youth Hostel Association, cafeteria, owns *Sinchicuy Lodge* (see below). Recommended. **B** *Europa*, Brasil 222, T231123, F235483. A/c, cable TV,

Sleeping
■ *on maps*
Price codes:
see inside front cover

Amazon Basin

phone and fridge in every room, pleasant café/bar, good views from 5th floor.

C *Internacional*, Próspero 835, T/F234684. A/c, with bathroom, cable TV, fridge, phone, friendly, secure, medium-priced restaurant, good value. Recommended.

D *El Sitio*, Ricardo Palma 541, T239878. With bathroom, very clean, fan, cafeteria. Highly recommended. **D** *Hostal Bon Bini*, Pevas 386, T238422. With bathroom, very clean, fridge, good value. Recommended. **D** *Hostal La Pascana*, Pevas 133, T231418.

Iquitos

■ **Sleeping**
1. Acosta
2. Amazonas
3. El Dorado
4. El Sitio
5. Europa
6. Hostal Ambassador
7. Hostal Anita
8. Hostal Bon Bini
9. Hostal Don José Inn
10. Hostal Karina
11. Hostal La Pascana
12. Hostal Rolando's Amazon River
13. Hostal Tacna
14. Internacional
15. Isabel
16. Jhuliana
17. Loreto
18. Real Iquitos
19. Victoria Regia

● **Eating**
1. Ari's Burger
2. Chifa Wai Ming
3. El Mesón
4. La Casa de Jaime
5. La Pascana
6. Olla de Oro

0 metres 100
0 yards 109

With cold shower, basic, fan, clean, breakfast available, luggage store, TV lounge, luxuriant garden, relaxed, popular, book exchange, ask for Coby, a Dutch lady who will
take tours on her houseboat, the *Miron Lenta*. Highly recommended.

E *Hostal Don José Inn*, Fitzcarrald 456, T234257. With bathroom, fan, TV, clean,
good, breakfast and evening meal on request for US$2.25. **E** *Hostal Rolando's Ama-
zon River*, Esquina Fitzcarrald y Nauta 307, T233979. With bathroom and fan, restaurant, they also own *Albergue Supay* (see Jungle tours below). **E** *Hostal Vargas*, Avda
Quiñones, outside town on the road to the airport. Clean, good value. Recommended.
E *Hostal Karina*, Putumayo 467, T235367. Water all day, fan. **E** *Hostal Libertad*, Arica
361, T235763. With bathroom, basic but good value. **E** *Isabel*, Brasil 164, T234901.
With bathroom, very good, clean, but plug the holes in the walls, secure, often full.
E *Loreto*, Próspero 311, T234191. With bathroom, clean, basic, fan. **E** *Pensión
Económico*, Moore 1164, T265616. Clean, large rooms, water all day, quiet, not cen-
tral, no sign outside, friendly, breakfast on request. Recommended.

F per person *Hostal Aeropuerto*, Avda Corpac block 100 y Malvinas, near the air-
port, clean, OK, fan in room, friendly, other 'services' available. **F** *Hostal Anita*, Ramírez
Hurtado 742, T235354. With bathroom, no fan, basic. **F** *Hostal Tacna*, Tacna 516,
T230714. With fan, basic but clean, good value, rooms at front with balcony are noisy.

Eating
● *on maps*

El Dorado Inn, C Huallaga 630. Good value and good menu. *La Gran Maloca*,
Sargento Lores block 100, opposite Banco Continental. A/c, high class. *El Mesón*, Jr
Napo 116. Local specialities include wild boar, alligator, turtle, tapir and other endangered species. *La Casa de Jaime*, Malecón Maldonado, on the waterfront. Excellent
steaks, also vegetarian meals, owner Jaime Acevedo is charming, speaks perfect English, also German, and will give excellent advice about jungle trips, the wonderful
mozzarella cheese is not to be missed, it comes from water buffaloes brought from
Africa by Cubans and produced locally in a factory built by Italians, also book
exchange, frequented by tour operators, consuls and ex-pats, interesting ambience,
book exchange. Very highly recommended. *La Pascana*, Ramírez Hurtado 735. Good
fish and *ceviche*, friendly, popular, try the *vientequatro raices*, 20% discount for *Handbook* users, open at lunchtimes only. *Wai Ming*, San Martín at Plaza 28 de Julio. Good
Chinese if a little expensive. *Casa de Hierro*, Plaza de Armas, Próspero y Putumayo,
2nd floor. Nice location but the food is not great. On the first floor is *El Copoasu*, a cafeteria which serves malt beer with egg and fresh milk, a good pick-me-up. *Ari's Burger*, Plaza de Armas, Próspero 127. Medium-priced fast food, popular with tourists.
Olla de Oro, Calvo de Araujo 579. Near the main indoor market, excellent food,
friendly service. Recommended. *Hueng Teng*, esquina Pucallpa y Nauta, Chinese,
cheap. Recommended. The cheapest restaurants are to be found on and around Plaza
28 de Julio.

Heladería La Favorita, Próspero 415. Good ice-cream (try local flavour *aguaje* – see
below). *Juguería Paladar*, Próspero 245. Excellent juices.

Try the local drink *chuchuhuasi*, made from the bark of a tree, which is supposed to
have aphrodisiac properties but tastes like fortified cough tincture (for sale at Arica
1046), and *jugo de cocona*, and the alcoholic *cola de mono* and *siete raices*
(aguardiente mixed with the bark of 7 trees and wild honey), sold at *Exquisita
Amazónica*, Abtao 590. You can eat cheaply, especially fish and *ceviche*, at the 3 markets. Palm heart salad (*chonta*), or *a la Loretana* dish on menus is excellent; also try
inchicapi (chicken, corn and peanut soup), *cecina* (fried dried pork), *tacacho* (fried
green banana and pork, mashed into balls and eaten for breakfast or tea), *juanes*
(chicken, rice, olive and egg, seasoned and wrapped in bijao leaves and sold in restaurants). *Camu-camu* is an interesting but acquired taste, said to have one of the highest
vitamin C concentrations in the world.

Amazon Basin

Bars & nightclubs	**Bars** *La Ribereña*, Raymondi 453. With terraced seats on a newly-built plaza. *Snack Bar Arandú*, good views of the Amazon river. *Teatro Café Amauta*, Nauta 248. Live music, open 2200-2400, good atmosphere, popular, small exhibition hall.

Discotheques *Bamboleo*, Malecón Tarapacá 328. Very popular, open 2300 till late. *La Pantera Rosa*, Moore 434. Free entrance, open Monday-Saturday until 0300. *La Estancia*, Napo 100 block. Restaurant by day, dancing at night, popular. *Yutopia Karaoke*, Napo 168. *Dreams*, Tacna block 100. *Noa Noa*, esquina Pevas y Fitzcarrald.

Cinemas	*Bolognesi*, San Martín 390, on Plaza 28 de Julio. Poor sound.

Festivals	On **5 January** is the anniversary of the founding of Iquitos. During *Carnival* you can see the local dance *La Pandilla*. The **third week in June** is *Tourist week*, with regional music, held in the *Mercado Artesanal de San Juan*. On **24 June** is the *Festival of San Juan*, patron saint of Loreto. On **28-30 August** is *Santa Rosa de Lima*, celebrated in Rumococha (see below). On **22-25 September** is *Santo Tomás*, in the village of the same name (also see below). On **8 December** is *Inmaculada Concepción*, celebrated in Punchana, near the docks.

Shopping	Places where you can buy handicrafts are: *Amazon Arts and Crafts*, Napo block 100; *Mercado Artesanal de Productores*, 4 kilometres from the centre in the San Juan district, on the road to the airport (take a colectivo); and *Artesanías de la Selva*, R Palma 190. For camera accessories try *Aspinwall*, Raimondi 138. There are pharmacies at Tacna 156 and at Próspero 361-3. Records and tapes at *Discotiendas Hikari*, San Martín 324. Cheap haircuts at *Barbería Jupiter*, Napo 323. A good local newspaper is *La Región*.

NB Locals sell necklaces made with red and black rosary peas (Abrus pecatorius), which are extremely poisonous. Do not give them to children. They are illegal in Canada, but not in the USA.

Transport	**Air** To **Lima**, daily with *Aero Continente* and *AeroPerú*. *Aero Continente* fly via Pucallpa. To **Yurimaguas**, **Cajamarca** and **Tarapoto** with *Aero Continente*. *Grupo Ocho*, the Peruvian airforce, flies to various frontier towns. *AeroPerú* flies to and from **Miami**. When entering Peru on this flight, a 90-day tourist visa is given on arrival.

Iquitos flights are frequently delayed; be sure to reconfirm your flight in Iquitos, as they are often overbooked, especially over the Christmas period. Check times in advance as itineraries frequently change.

Aircraft for hire: Expertour, Putumayo 124, T238162; they have a Cessna with bilingual US pilot, minimum 3-4 people.

River River boats to **Pucallpa**, leave every second day, usually at 1700. The journey takes 6/7 days when river is high, and 3/4 days when it's low. The price depends on demand, eg US$22 per person in a hammock, or US$26 per person with bed and cabin. To **Yurimaguas** takes 4/5 days, longer if cargo is being carried, which is usually the case; it costs US$13-18 per person, and boats leave more or less daily.

You can find information on boats and tickets at *Bellavista*, Malecón Tarapacá 596; or in the Puerto Masusa district of Puchana, at Avda La Marina with *Masusa* (take a bus from the centre, 10 minutes). Cabins are 4 berth and you have to buy both a first class ticket, which entitles you to food (whether you want it or not) and deck space to sling your hammock, and a cabin ticket if you want the 'luxury' of a berth. There are adequate washing and toilet facilities, but the food is rice, meat and beans (and whatever can be picked up en route) cooked in river water. There is a good cheap bar on board.

A weekly luxury 54-passenger boat, Río Amazonas, sails down-river from Iquitos and **Tabatinga (Brazil)**, operated by *Amazon Tours and Cruises* (see Jungle tours below). It leaves on Sunday, and costs US$525 per person (US$445 for groups of 10

General hints for river travel

A hammock is essential, but they are expensive in Iquitos. A double, of material (not string), provides one person with a blanket. Board the boat many hours in advance to guarantee hammock space. If going on the top deck, try to be first down the front; take rope for hanging your hammock, plus string and sarongs for privacy. On all boats, hang your hammock away from lightbulbs (they aren't switched off at night and attract all sorts of strange insects) and away from the engines, which usually emit noxious fumes. Another useful tip is not to sling your hammock near the bottom of the stairwell on double decked river boats, as this is where the cook slaughters the livestock every morning.

Guard your belongings from the moment you board. There is very little privacy; women travellers can expect a lot of attention. Stock up on drinking water,

fruit and tinned food in Iquitos. Take plenty of prophylactic enteritis tablets; many contract dysentery on the trip. Also take insect repellent.

If you plan to stop off along the way at small villages on the river in Peru, you can usually get a passing boat to make an unscheduled stop and pick you up. The best way to do this is to flag it down with a white sheet. This is what the villagers do if they want a passing boat to stop at their village. Note that this method doesn't work on the Brazilian part of the river, where boats don't make unscheduled stops. The only way to board a Brazilian boat between stops is to hire a canoe to take you out to meet it in mid-river then flag it down.

Public river transport can be extremely uncomfortable, but with patience, perseverance and a strong stomach it is still far from impossible.

plus). The return journey to Iquitos is on Wednesday. Another boat making this trip is **M/V Arca** (US$495 per person – US$420 for groups of 10 plus). It returns Wednesday-Saturday.

There are no boats direct to Manaus. Take a boat to **Islandia**, opposite Tabatinga (Brazil). The journey costs US$25-30 per person with a cabin and meals (cheaper with a hammock). It takes around 12-24 hours to Islandia; 4/5 boats leave each week on Thursday and Saturday, usually at 1700-1800. From Islandia take a small boat to **Benjamín Constant** and from there boats leave for **Manaus**. It is roughly 8 days from Islandia to Manaus. Boats for Manaus also leave from a little way down-river from **Marco**, the port for **Tabatinga**. Speedboats run between Iquitos and Islandia with **Amazon Tours and Cruises** (US$75), on Tuesday, Friday and Sunday, book ahead. It takes 2 days upstream and 11 hours downstream. The *Ruiz* is highly recommended for river journeys to the frontier or to Pucallpa; US$20 with your own hammock, no food. *Ecograss* is also recommended; US$25-30 per person including food.

Crossing the Frontier

Details on exit and entry formalities seem to change frequently, so when leaving Peru, check in Iquitos first at Immigration (see below) or with the Capitanía at the port. Latest reports are that the boat to Islandia stops in Santa Rosa for Peruvian exit/Brazilian entry formalities.

Note that the Brazilian immigration office in Tabatinga is open during the weekend and late into the night. Do not listen to any taxi drivers who may tell you otherwise. Immigration officials are reported as relaxed and extremely helpful. They may even help you find a berth for your onward journey to Manaus.

Directory

Airline offices *Aero Continente*, Próspero 231, T233162, F233990. *AeroPerú*, Próspero 248, T232513. **Banks** *Banco de Crédito*, Plaza de Armas. For Visa, also cash and TCs at good rates. *Banco Continental*, Sgto Lores 171. For Visa, 1% commission on TCs. *Banco de la Nación*, Condamine 478. Good rates, changes Deutschmarks. *Banco Wiese*, Próspero 282. For Mastercard, changes TCs into soles with no commission, rates for cash are not great. There are many money changers on Próspero in the 3 blocks south of Plaza de Armas. Their rates are good on weekdays but not at the weekend. **Communications** Post Office: on the corner of C Arica with Morona, near the Plaza de Armas, open daily 0700-2000. *Telefónica del Perú*, at Arica 276. **Email:** at *Casa de Jaime* restaurant (see above). **Embassies & consulates** Consulates: *Brazil*, Sgto Lores 363, T232081. Open Mon-Fri 0900-1200, 1500-1800, need photo and yellow fever certificate for visa. *Britain*, Mr Lewis Power, Arica 253, T234110 or 234383. *Colombia*, Putumayo 247, T231461. *Spain*, Avda La Marina, T232483. *France*, Napo 346, T232353. *Germany*, Dr Max Drusche, Yavari 660, T232641, F236364. **Hospitals & medical services** Medical services: *Clínica Loreto*, Morona 471, T233752, 24-hr attention. Recommended, but only Spanish spoken. *Hospital Iquitos*, Avda Grau, emergency T231721. *Hospital Regional de Loreto*, 28 de Julio, emergency T235821. *Clínica Ana Stahl*, Avda La Marina 3rd block (taxi drivers know where it is). **Tourist offices** On the Plaza de Armas, in the Municipal building. They have information on all operators offering tours to the jungle and can give good advice. They are very helpful and speak English. They also supply maps and general tourist literature. *Gobierno Regional de Loreto*, Ricardo Palma 113, T233321. Useful town maps, maps of the Quistacocha zoo and literature are available from the main jungle tour operators. You can also get a town map from *Librería Mosquera*, Jr Próspero. *PARD*, Preservation of the Amazon River Dolphin, Pevas 253, T/F(5194)238585. Ask for Roxanne Kremer or Frank Aliaga for information. **Useful addresses** Immigration: Malecón Tarapacá 382. Quick service. **Tourist police:** Sargento Lores 834. Helpful with complaints against tour operators.

Around Iquitos

Bellavista There is a beautiful white, sandy beach at Bellavista, which is safe for swimming and very popular at weekends in summer. Boats can be hired from here to see the meeting of the Nanay and Amazon rivers, and to visit beaches and villages en route. There are lots of food stalls selling typical local dishes. Take a bus from Jr Próspero to 'Bellavista Nanay'; 15 minutes, US$0.40.

Indiana Launches leave Iquitos (from the Mercado de Productores or Bellavista Nanay) for the village of Indiana. Get off at the 'Varadero de Mazán' and walk through the banana plantations to the Río Mazán. A trail leads from the village of Mazán through the secondary jungle to Indiana, where there is a hotel. It's about a two hour walk. If the hotel is full, ask at the mission or municipality for a tent for the night. From Indiana you can do several hikes of between two and four hours to little villages along the Napo river. Catch the launch back to Iquitos at 1300.

Lake Quistococha 13.5 kilometres south of the city, Lake Quistococha is beautifully situated in lush jungle, with a fish hatchery at the lakeside. The Parque Zoológico de Quistococha on the lake gives an example of the local wildlife, though conditions are pretty squalid. At the entrance are pictures and texts of local legends, which are interesting. The ticket office will supply a map of the lake and environs. There's a good two hour walk through the surrounding jungle on a clearly marked trail. See particularly the *paiche*, a huge Amazonian fish whose steaks (*paiche a la loretana*) you can eat in Iquitos' restaurants. There are also bars and restaurants on the lakeside and a small beach. Boats are for hire on the lake and swimming is safe but the sandflies are vicious, so take insect repellent. ■ *Open daily 0900-1700. US$1.30. To get to Quistococha, combis leave every hour until 1500 from Plaza 28 de Julio. The last one back leaves at 1700. Alternatively take a* motocarro *there and back with a one hour wait, which costs US$13. Perhaps the best option is to hire a motorbike and spend the day there. The road can be difficult after rain.*

Santo Tomás On the road to Quistococha, is the turn-off to the village of Santo Tomás, a favourite weekend retreat of inhabitants of Iquitos. Take a left turn just before the airport, and then another left 300 metres further on. Then it's about another four kilometres to the village. There are restaurants open on Sunday and dugout canoes can be hired daily. The village hosts a fiesta on 22-25 September. Trucks go there, taking passengers.

Other excursions can be made to **Rumococha**, an oxbow lake five kilometres from the city. Also to the village of **Santa Clara** and to **Puerto Almendras**, on the new Iquitos-Nauta road. Ask at *Casa de Jaime* restaurant for more details.

Jungle tours from Iquitos

Note that the area within a 50 kilometre radius of Iquitos is too inhabited to support much large wildlife and there is probably no primary rainforest within 100 kilometres of Iquitos. The Napo or Ucayali rivers have more to offer and excursions from Lagunas (see page 462) are more rewarding than those from Iquitos. Similarly with the area around the jungle lodges, however, there is plenty of scope for seeing small fauna and learning about the flora. Trips to visit Yagua Indians are reported to offer little in the way of an authentic cultural experience.

All agencies are under the control of the local office of the Ministry of Tourism. They arrange one day or longer trips to places of interest with guides speaking some English. Package tours booked in Lima are much more expensive than those booked in Iquitos. Some agencies are reported as too easy going about their responsibilities on an organized trip. Take your time before making a decision, shop around, and don't be bullied by the hustlers at the airport. For good advice ask at the Tourist office on the Plaza de Armas, or ask Jaime Acevedo at *Casa de Jaime*, see above, Eating. For an immediate response to any complaints contact *Indecopi*; T(010)80042579, E tour@indecopi. gob.pe. Make sure your guide has a proper licence.

Find out all the details of the trip and food arrangements before paying (about US$40-50 per day). Launches for river trips can be hired by the hour or day. Prices are negotiable, but usually about US$20-30 per hour.

For the birder, two lodges stand out above the rest: *Explorama* and *Explornapo*. They are quite expensive but very comfortable, and *Explornapo* has an excellent canopy walkway, which is superb for observing tree-top birds. Both lodges are excellent for Amazonian birds, particularly for the many species that do not make it south of the Amazon River.

Tour operators and jungle lodges

Explorama Tours, are highly recommended as the most efficient and, after 35 years in existence, certainly the biggest and most established. Their offices are by the riverside docks on Avda La Marina 340, PO Box 446, T(51)94252526/252530, F(51)94252533; in USA, Selective Hotel Reservations, Toll Free, T(800)2236764; MA (617) 5810844, F5813714. E amazon@explorama.com; W www.explorama.com. They have 5 sites: *Explorama Inn*, 40 kilometres (1½ hours) from Iquitos, cold water but comfortable bungalows in a jungle setting, good food, attractive walks, a recommended jungle experience for those who want their creature comforts, US$175 per person for 1 night/2 days, US$75 for each additional night (1-2 people); *Explorama Lodge* at Yanamono, 80 kilometres from Iquitos, 2½ hours from Iquitos, palm-thatched accommodation with separate bathroom and shower facilities connected by covered walkways, US$250 for 3 days/2 nights and US$75 for each additional day (1-2 people); *ExplorNapo Camp* at Llachapa, 160 kilometres (4 hours) from Iquitos, is more primitive, but better for seeing fauna, with an impressive new canopy walkway 35 metres above the forest floor and 500 metres long, set in 105,000 hectares of primary rainforest, "a magnificent experience and not to be missed". *ACEER laboratory* is a scientific research station, only 10 minutes from the canopy walkway; the basic programme costs US$1,000 for 5 days/4 nights (2 people), the first and last nights are spent at Explorama Lodge. A US$25 donation to the Foundation for Conservation of Peruvian Amazon Biosphere (Conapac) is included if visiting the walkway. To spend a night at the ACEER lab is US$55; each extra night to the basic programme costs US$90. Prices include transfers, advance reservations, etc; local rates are much lower. *Explor Tambos*, 2 hours from *ExplorNapo*, more primitive accommodation, 8 shelters for 16 campers, bathing in the river, offers the best chance to see rare fauna. Flight inclusive packages are available from Miami.

Paseos Amazónicos Ambassador, Pevas 246, T/F233110, operates the *Amazonas Sinchicuy Lodge*, US$70 per person per night. The lodge is 1 hour and 15 minutes from Iquitos on the Sinchicuy river, 10 minutes by boat from the Amazon river. The lodge consists of several wooden buildings with thatched roofs on stilts, cabins with bathroom, no electricity but paraffin lamps are provided, good food, and plenty activities, including visits to local villages. Recommended. They also organize visits to Lake Quistacocha.

Amazon Tours and Cruises, Requena 336, T(5194)233931, F231265; in USA, 8700 W Flagler St, suite 190, Miami, FL 33174, T(305)2272266, toll free (800)4232791, F(305)2271880, American-owned company. Various cruises available on the M/V *Arca* Iquitos-Leticía-Iquitos, US$500 per person; and nature cruises on the M/V *Delfín*. They also organize rugged expeditions to various jungle *tambos* (thatched shelters). They are recommended as conscientious and efficient. Contact them for details of *Casa de la Loma*, a new jungle lodge at Pevas, 150 kilometres down-river from Iquitos on the Amazon. The lodge is managed by Judy Balser and Scott Humfeld and has been recommended. It can also be visited independently; F(094)231265.

Anaconda Lara Lodge, Pevas 210, T239147, F232978. 24 kilometres from Iquitos, full day tours US$50, also offers adventure expeditions to the Río Yarapa, 180 kilometres away.

Las Colinas de Zungarococha Amazon Resort, operated by Paucar Tours, Próspero 648-Altos, T235188/232131, or through *Hostal Acosta*, or Ricardo Rivera Navarrete 645E, San Isidro, Lima, T/F4424515. Comfortable lakeside bungalows, swimming pool, watersports, mini-zoo, full day US$40, 1 night/2 days US$70.

Amazon Lodge, Raymondi 382, T237142; Avda Alvarez Calderón 155, Oficina 302, San Isidro, Lima, T(511)2213341, F2210974, 48 kilometres down-river from Iquitos. Recommended as friendly and comfortable; 3 days/2 nights, US$200 per person for 2-4 people, US$50 per person for each additional night.

Albergue Supay is a floating hotel on Supay lake close to the Río Nanay, 2 hours by boat from Iquitos, or taxi and canoe, 1 to 5 day tours from US$60 to US$290 per person, run by Austrian Roland Röggl and Peruvian Luz Elena Montoya; contact Apdo 532, Correo Central, Iquitos, or Jr Próspero 635, T234785; they also have the *hostal* at Fitzcarrald y Nauta 307 (see above).

Yacumama Lodge, Sargento Lores, T/F241022 (Avda Benavides 212, Oficina 1203, Miraflores, Lima). An excellent lodge on the Río Yarapa, 4 days/3 nights, US$389, 6 days/5 nights, US$559 (minimum 2 people), part of the fee is invested in local conservation.

Cumacebo Lodge and Expeditions, Putumayo 263, T/F232229. Tours of 2-8 days to their lodges on the Amazon and Yarapa rivers, good birdwatching guides, 3 days/2 nights for US$120 per person.

See also Tours and tour operators (page 86) for details of *International Expeditions*, who run luxury Amazon cruises.

General information & advice

It is advisable to take a waterproof coat and shoes or light boots on such trips, and a good torch, as well as *espirales* to ward off the mosquitoes at night – they can be bought from drugstores in Iquitos. *Premier* is the most effective local insect repellent. The dry season is from July to September (September is the best month to see flowers and butterflies).

The Southern Jungle

*The southern selva is made up of the Madre de Dios department, created in 1902 and containing the **Manu National Park** (1,532,000 hectares), the **Tambopata-Candamo Reserved Zone** (1,479,000 hectares) and the **Bahuaja-Sonene National Park** (333,000 hectares).*

The forest of this lowland region is technically called Sub-tropical Moist Forest, which means that it receives less rainfall than tropical forest and is dominated by the floodplains of its meandering rivers. The most striking features are the former river channels that have become isolated as ox-bow lakes (*cochas*). These are home to black caiman and giant otter. Other rare species living in the forest are jaguar, puma, ocelot and tapir. There are also capybara, various types of monkey and many hundreds of bird species.

As well as containing some of the most important flora and fauna on Earth, however, the region also harbours gold-diggers, loggers, hunters and oil-men. For years, logging, gold prospecting and the search for oil and gas have endangered the unique rainforest, though fortunately, the destructive effect of such groups has been limited by the various conservation groups working to protect it.

The frontier town of Puerto Maldonado is the starting point for expeditions to Tambopata-Candamo and is only a 30-minute flight from Cusco. Cusco is also the starting point for trips to Manu. The best time to visit is during the dry season when there are fewer mosquitoes and the rivers are low, exposing the beaches. This is also a good time to see birds nesting and to view the animals at close range, as they stay close to the rivers and are easily seen. Note that this is also the hottest time. A pair of binoculars is essential and insect repellent is a must.

The climate is warm and humid, with a rainy season from November to March and a dry season from April to October. Cold fronts from the South Atlantic, called *friajes*, are characteristic of the dry season, when temperatures drop to 15-16°C during the day, and 13° at night. Always bring a sweater at this time.

Birds of Colombia by Steve Hilty and *South American Birds*, by John Dunning, give the best coverage of birds of Peru. Also *Neotropical Rainforest Mammals, A field guide*, by Louise H Emmons. *Tropical Nature*, by Adrian Forsyth and Ken Miyata, gives an explanation of the rainforest. *Manu National Park*, by Kim MacQuarrie and André and Cornelia Bartschi, is a large, expensive and excellent book, with beautiful photographs. *Madre de Dios Packet*, by the South American Explorers Club, gives practical travel advice for the area.

The Ecology of Tropical Rainforests (republished 1999), *Tambopata – A Bird Checklist*, *Tambopata – Mammal, Amphibian & Reptile Checklist* and *Reporte Tambopata* are all published by TReeS (see below under Tambopata-Candamo Reserved Zone for address); they also produce tapes, *Jungle Sounds* and *Birds of Southeast Peru*.

Recommended reading

Amazon Basin

Manu Biosphere Reserve

The Manu Biosphere Reserve covers an area of 2,233,693 hectares (roughly the size of Switzerland) and is one of the largest conservation units on Earth, encompassing the complete drainage of the Manu river, with an altitudinal range from 200 to 4,100 metres above sea-level. No other rainforest can compare with Manu for the diversity of life forms. The reserve is one of the great birding spots of the world (see below). Manu also offers the best chance of seeing giant otters, jaguars, ocelots and several of the 13 species of primates which abound in this pristine tropical wilderness. The reserve is also home to uncontacted indigenous tribes in the more remote areas.

Tourists are not allowed inside the National Park but can visit the adjoining Reserved Zone which is one of the world's great wilderness experiences. The best time to visit is in the dry season from May to the end of October, but trips can also be planned during the rainy season.

The reserve is split into the **Manu National Park** (1,532,000 hectares), where only government sponsored biologist and anthropologists may visit with permits from the Ministry of Agriculture in Lima, the **Reserved Zone** (257,000 hectares), which is set aside for applied scientific research and ecotourism, the **Cultural Zone** which contains acculturated native groups and colonists, and the **Nahua-Kugapakori Reserved Zone** (92,000 hectares), set aside for these two nomadic native groups, where the locals still employ their traditional way of life.

The Cultural Zone is accessible to anyone and several lodges exist in the area (see Lodges in Manu below). The Reserved Zone of the Manu Biosphere Reserve is accessible by permit only. Entry is strictly controlled and visitors must visit the area under the auspices of an authorized operator with an authorized guide. Permits are limited and reservations should be made well in advance. In the Reserved Zone of the Manu Biosphere Reserve the only accommodation is in the comfortable Manu Lodge (see below) or in Safari-style camps.

Birdwatching in Manu

Much of the Manu Biosphere Reserve is completely unexplored and the variety of birds is astounding; over 1,000 species – significantly more than the whole of Costa Rica and over one tenth of all the birds on earth. Although there are other places in the Manu area where you can see all the Manu bird specialities and an astounding variety of other wildlife, the best place for the visiting birder is the Manu Wildlife Centre.

Manu Biosphere Reserve

A typical trip starts in Cusco and takes in the wetlands of Huacarpay Lakes (to the south of the city) where a variety of Andean waterfowl and marsh birds can be seen. Here, the endemic and beautiful Bearded Mountaineer hummingbird can be seen feeding on tree tobacco. Then the route proceeds to the cloud forest of the eastern slopes of the Andes. Driving slowly down the road through the cloud forest, every 500 metres loss in elevation produces new birds. This is the home of the Andean Cock-of-the-Rock, and a visit to one of their leks (they are common here) is one of the world's great ornithological spectacles. These humid montane forests are home to a mind-boggling variety of multi-coloured birds, and a mixed flock of tanagers, honeycreepers, and conebills turns any tree into a Christmas Tree! There are two species of quetzal here, too.

Levelling out onto the last forested foothills of the Andes, the upper tropical zone is then reached. This is a forest habitat that in many parts of South America has disappeared and been replaced by tea, coffee and coca plantations. In Manu, the forest is intact, and special birds such as Amazonian Umbrellabird and Blue-headed and Military Macaws can be found.

A good place to be based for upper tropical birding and an introduction to lowland Amazon species is the Amazonia Lodge (see below), on the River Alto Madre de Dios. From here on in, transport is by river and the beaches are packed with nesting birds in the dry season. Large-billed Terns scream at passing boats and Orinoco Geese watch warily from the shore. Colonies of hundreds of Sand-coloured Nighthawks roost and nest on the hot sand.

As you leave the foothills behind and head into the untouched forests of the western Amazon, you are entering forest with the highest density of birdlife per square kilometre on earth. Sometimes it seems as if there are less birds than in an English woodland; only strange calls betray their presence. Then a mixed flock comes through, containing maybe 70-plus species, or a brightly coloured group of, say, Rock Parakeets dashes out of a fruiting tree. For the birder who craves the mysterious and rare, this is *the* site.

This forest has produced the highest day-list ever recorded anywhere on earth, and it holds such little-seen gems as Black-faced Cotinga and Rufous-fronted Ant-thrush. Antbirds and furnarids creep in the foliage and give tantalizing glimpses until, eventually, they reveal themselves in a shaft of sunlight. To get to this forest is difficult and not cheap, but the experience is well worth it.

The best place for lowland birding is the Manu Wildlife Centre, which is located close to a large macaw lick and to ox-bow lakes crammed with birds. This area has more forest types and micro-habitats than any other rainforest lodge in Peru, and it has recorded an astounding 515 species of birds in one year.

A trip to Manu is one of the ultimate birding experiences, and topping it off with a macaw lick is a great way to finish; hundreds of brightly coloured macaws and other parrots congregate to eat the clay essential to their digestion in one of the world's great wildlife spectacles.

To Manu from Cusco

It is possible to visit the lodges in the Cultural Zone under your own steam. The arduous trip over the Andes from Cusco to the end of the road at Shintuya takes about 16-18 hours by local truck (20-40 hours in the wet season). It is long and uncomfortable, but, throughout, the scenery is magnificent. From Cusco you climb up to the pass before **Paucartambo** (three and a half hours), before dropping down to this mountain village at the border between the departments of Cusco and Madre de Dios (for details of accommodation etc in Paucartambo, see page 193). The road then ascends to the second pass (also cold at night), after which it goes down to the cloud forest and then the rainforest, reaching **Pilcopata** at 650 metres (11 hours). On the way, you pass *Manu Cloudforest Lodge* and *Cock of the Rock Lodge* (see below). There are two basic *hostales* in Pilcopata: **F** per person *Gallito de las Rocas* is opposite the police checkpoint and is clean. The other is **G** per person, run by Sra Robella, and very basic. A good restaurant is *Las Palmeras*.

After Pilcopata, the route is hair-raising and breath-taking, passing through **Atalaya**, the first village on the Alto Madre de Dios river, which consists of a few houses. Even in the dry season this part of the road is appalling and trucks often get stuck. In Atalaya, meals are available at the family of Rosa and Klaus (very friendly people), where you can camp. Boats are available here to take you across the river to *Amazonia Lodge* (see below). The route continues to **Salvacción**, where the Park Office entrance is situated. There are basic hostels and restaurants.

The end of the road is **Shintuya**, the starting point for river transport. It is a   **Shintuya** commercial and social centre, as wood from the jungle is transported from here to Cusco. There are a few basic restaurants and you can camp (beware of thieves). The priest will let you stay in the dormitory rooms at the mission. Supplies are expensive. There are two Shintuyas: one is the port and mission and the other is the native village. You can find a boat in the native village; ask for Diego Ruben Sonque or Miguel Visse. **NB** It is not possible to arrange trips to the Reserved Zone of the Biosphere Reserve from Shintuya, owing to park regulations. All arrangements (including permits) must be made in Cusco.

Trucks leave every Monday, Wednesday and Friday from the Coliseo Cerrado in Cusco   **Getting there** at about 1000 (be there by 0800) to **Pilcopata** and **Shintuya** (passing Atalaya); US$7 to Shintuya. The journey takes at least 48 hours and is rough and uncomfortable. They return the following day, but there is no service on Sunday. There is also a bus service which leaves from the same place to **Pilcopata**, on Monday and Friday and returns on Tuesday and Saturday. The journey takes 12 hours in the dry season and costs US$5-6. From Pilcopata there are trucks to Atalaya (one hour, US$5) and Shintuya (three hours, US$8). Trucks leave in the morning between 0600 and 0900. Make sure you go with a recommended truck driver. Only basic supplies are available after leaving Cusco, so take all your camping and food essentials, including insect repellent. Transport can be disrupted in the wet season because the road is in poor condition (tour companies have latest details). Tour companies usually use their own vehicles for the overland trip from Cusco to Manu.

From Shintuya infrequent cargo boats sail down-river to the gold mining   **Boca Colorado** centre of **Boca Colorado** on the Río Madre de Dios, via Boca Manu, and passing *Pantiacolla Lodge* and *Manu Wildlife Centre* (see below). The trip takes around nine hours, and costs US$15. Very basic accommodation can be found here, but it is not recommended for lone women travellers. To Boca Manu is three to four hours, US$12. From Colorado there are plenty of boats to **Laberinto** (six to seven hours, US$20). From here there are regular combis to **Puerto Maldonado** (see below), one and a half hours.

Boca Manu is the connecting point between the rivers Alto Madre de Dios,   **Boca Manu** Manu and Madre de Dios. It has a few houses, an air strip and some well-stocked shops. It is also the entance to the Manu Reserve. The Park Office is located in **Limonal**, 20 minutes by boat from Boca Manu. You need

Amazon Basin

to show your permit here. There are huts available for accommodation and it is possible to camp. There are no regular flights from Cusco to Boca Manu. These are arranged the day before, if there are enough passengers. Contact *Air Atlantic*, at Maruri 228, oficina 208, Cusco, T245440; or check with the tour operators in Cusco.

To the Reserve Zone Upstream on the Río Manu you pass the *Manu Lodge* (see below), on the Cocha Juárez, three to four hours by boat. Visitors are charged an entrance fee of US$5 (taken care of by tour companies). You can continue to Cocha Otorongo, two and a half hours and Cocha Salvador, 30 minutes, the biggest lake with plenty of wildlife. From here it is two hours to **Pakitza**, the entrance to the Park Zone. This is only for biologists with a special permit.

Between Boca Manu and Colorado is **Blanquillo**, a private reserve (10,000 hectares), where jungle trips can be arranged. Bring a good tent with you and all food. Guides are available for around US$6 per person (Rolando is recommended). Wildlife is abundant, especially macaws and parrots at the macaw lick near *Manu Wildlife Centre* (see below). There are occasional boats to Blanquillo from Shintuya; US$10, six to eight hours.

Tours to Manu There are dozens of agencies in Cusco offering tours to Manu. Prices vary considerably, from as little as US$400-500 per person for a 6-day tour up to US$1,000-1,500 per person with the more experienced and reputable companies. The cheaper tours usually travel overland there and back, which takes at least 2 full days (in the dry season), meaning you'll spend much of your time on a bus or truck. Another important factor to consider is whether or not your boat has a canopy, as it can be very uncomfortable sitting in direct sunlight for hours on end. **NB** Beware of pirate operators on the streets of Cusco who offer trips to the Reserved Zone of Manu and end up halfway through the trip changing the route 'due to emergencies', which, in reality means they have no permits to operate in the area. For a full list of all companies who are allowed access to the Reserved Zone, contact the Manu National Park office (address below).

NB You can only enter the Reserved Zone with a recognized guide who is affiliated to a recognized tour company. Take finely-woven, long-sleeved and long-legged clothing and effective insect repellent. Note that for independent travellers, only the Cultural Zone is an option. Lodge reservations should be made at the relevant offices in Cusco as these lodges are often not set up to receive visitors without prior notice.

Travel agencies The agencies listed below are at the more expensive end of the spectrum but recommended as providing a good quality of service. *Manu Nature Tours EIRL*, Avda Pardo 1046, Cusco, T252721, F234793, E mnt@amauta. rcp.net.pe, www.rcp.net.pe/ MANU. Owned by Boris Gómez, they run lodge-based trips and are owners of Manu Lodge, and part owners of Manu Cloudforest Lodge. They own the only lodge in the Reserve Zone (*Manu Lodge*) open all year, situated on an ox-bow lake, providing access to the forest. Guides are available. Activities include river-rafting and canopy-climbing. It is highly recommended for experiencing the jungle in comfort. They offer 8-day trips with flights both ways or with road/boat transport there and plane back, also 4-day trips with plane both ways. At the same address is *Eco-tour Manu*, a non-profit making organization made up of tour operators which assures quality of service and actively supports conservation projects in the area. When you travel with an Eco-tour member you are assuring you support tropical rainforest conservation projects. Eco-tour Manu comprises Manu Expeditions, Manu Nature Tours, Amazonia Lodge, Pantiacolla Lodge and Blanquillo Lodge. Contact Boris Gómez Luna. *Manu Expeditions*, Avda Pardo 895, T226671,

F236706, E Adventure@ManuExpeditions.com, www.ManuExpeditions.com. Owned by ornthologist, TV star and Manchester United fan Barry Walker of the Cross Keys Pub. They run highly recommended 4-9 day trips in Safari camps and lodges and jointly run the Manu Wildlife Centre (see below). They also specialize in birdwatching and horseriding trips. *Pantiacolla Tours*, C Plateros 360, T238323, F252696, E pantiac@mail.cosapidata. com.pe, W www.pantiacolla.com. Run by Marianne Von Vlaardingen. They run tours to the *Pantiacolla Lodge* (see below) and also 8-day camping trips. *InkaNatura Travel* also run tours to Manu Wildlife Centre (see also page 167).

Manu Cloud Forest Lodge, located at Unión at 1,800m on the road from Paucartambo to Atalaya, owned by *Manu Nature Tours*, 6 rooms with 4 beds. *Cock of the Rock Lodge*, on the same road at 1,500m, next to a Cock of the Rock *lek*, 8 double rooms, run by the ACSS group (see below). *Amazonia Lodge*, on the Río Alto Madre de Dios just across the river from Atalaya, an old tea hacienda run by the Yabar family, famous for its bird diversity and fine hospitality, a great place to relax, contact Santiago in advance and he'll arrange a pick-up. In Cusco at C Matará 334, T/F231370, E amazonia@correo.dnet.com.pe. *Pantiacolla Lodge*, 30 minutes down-river from Shintuya. Owned by the Moscoso family. Book through *Pantiacolla Tours* (see above). *Manu Lodge*, situated on the Manu river, 3 hours upriver from Boca Manu towards Cocha Salvador, run by *Manu Nature Tours* and only bookable as part of a full package deal with transport. Has canopy towers for birdwatching. *Manu Wildlife Centre*, 2 hours down the Río Madre de Dios from Boca Manu, situated on an ox-bow lake near the Blanquillo macaw lick and also near a Tapir lick. Book through *Manu Expeditions* or *InkaNatura*. 20 double cabins, most with private bathroom. Also canopy towers for birdwatching (see Birdwatching above). *Erika Lodge*, on the Alto Madre de Dios, 25 mins from Atalaya, is a biological station used by Pronaturaleza (see below), which now accepts a small number of visitors. It offers basic accommodation and is cheaper than the other, more luxurious lodges. Contact *Aventuras Ecológicas Manu*, Plateros 361, Cusco; or Ernesto Yallico, Casilla 560, Cusco, T227765. *Machiguenga Lodge* (not its official name) is being built near Cocha Salvador, upriver from *Manu Lodge*. Machiguenga-style cabins run by local communities with NGO help. Contact InkaNatura Travel (see page 167).

Useful addresses In Lima: *Asociación Peruana para la Conservación de la Naturaleza* (Apeco), Parque José Acosta 187, 2nd Flr, Magdalena del Mar, T616316. *Pronaturaleza*, Avda de los Rosales 255, San Isidro, T426706/426616. In Cusco: *Asociación para la Conservación de la Selva Sur* (ACSS), Avda Sol 821, 2nd Flr (same office as *InkaNatura Travel*), T243408, F226392, E acss@telser.com.pe. Is a local NGO that can help with information and has free video shows about Manu National Park and Tambopata-Candamo Reserve. They are friendly and helpful and also have information on programmes and research in the jungle area of Madre de Dios. Further information can be obtained from the *Manu National Park Office:* Avda Micaela Bastidas 310, Cusco, T240898, E pqnmanu@ cosapidata.mail.com.pe, Casilla Postal 591. Open 0800-1400. They issue a permit for the Reserve Zone which costs US$10.

Lodges in Manu

Puerto Maldonado

Puerto Maldonado is the capital of the Department of Madre de Dios. Overlooking the confluence of the rivers Tambopata and Madre de Dios, it is an important starting point for visiting the rainforest, or for departing to Bolivia. Nothing much happens here, it's a hot, humid and sleepy place, disturbed only by the fleeting visit of tourists heading to or from the jungle lodges.

Population: 25,000
Altitude: 250 metres
Phone code: 084
Coloured map 6, grid A3

The vast majority of people fly (see below for details).

Getting there

Amazon Basin

The road from Cusco The road from the cold of the high Andes to the steamy heat of the Amazon jungle can only be described as a challenge (and is not really recommended). It is expertly described in Matthew Parris' book *Inka-Cola*. From Cusco take a bus to Urcos; 1 hour, US$2.25 (see also page 194). Trucks leave from here for **Mazuko** around 1500-1600, arriving around 2400 the next day; 33 hours, US$6.65. Catch a truck early in the morning from here for Puerto Maldonado, US$4.50, 13-14 hours. It's a painfully slow journey on an appalling road. Trucks frequently get stuck or break down. The road passes through Ocongate and Marcapata, where there are hot thermal springs, before reaching **Quincemil**, 240 kilometres from Urcos (15-20 hours), a centre for alluvial gold-mining with many banks. Accommodation is available in **F** *Hotel Toni*, friendly, clean, cold shower, good meals. Ask the food-carriers to take you to visit the miners washing for gold in the nearby rivers. Quincemil marks the half-way point and the start of the all-weather road. Gasoline is scarce in Quincemil because most road vehicles continue on 70 kilometres to Mazuko, which is another mining centre, where they fill up with the cheaper gasoline of the jungle region.

The journey takes up to 50-55 hours in total. The road is 99% unpaved and the journey is very rough, but the changing scenery is magnificent and worth the hardship and discomfort. This road is impossible in the wet season. Make sure you have warm clothing for travelling through the Sierra. The trucks only stop four times each day, for meals and a short sleeping period for the driver. You should take a mosquito net, repellent, sunglasses, sunscreen, a plastic sheet, a blanket, food and water.

An alternative route from Cusco goes via Paucartambo, Pilcopata and Shintuya, and from there by boat to Puerto Maldonado (see above under Manu Biosphere Reserve).

Essentials

Sleeping
■ *on maps*
Price codes:
see inside front cover

B *Wasai*, Billinhurst opposite the Capitanía, T571864 (or Cusco (084)221826). In a beautiful location overlooking the Madre de Dios river, with forest surrounding cabin-style rooms, a/c, TV, shower, small pool with waterfall, good restaurant if slightly expensive (local fish a speciality). Highly recommended. They can organize local tours and also have a lodge on the Tambopata river (see below).

C *Cabañaquinta*, Cusco 535, T571863, F571890. With bathroom, fan, good restaurant, friendly, lovely garden, very comfortable, airport transfer. Recommended. **C** *Don Carlos*, Avda León Velarde 1271, T571029, T/F571323. Nice view over the Río Tambopata, a/c, restaurant, TV, phone, good.

D *Libertador*, Libertad 433, 10 minutes from the centre, T572661. Comfortable, with pool and garden, good restaurant. Recommended. **D** *Royal Inn*, 2 de Mayo 333, T571048. Modern and clean, the best of the mid-range hotels.

E *Hostal El Astro*, Velarde 617, T572128. With bathroom, basic. **E** *Hostal El Solar*, González Prada 445, T571571. Basic but clean, fan. **E** per person *Hostal Iñapari*, 4 kilometres from centre, 5 minutes from the airport. Run by a Spanish couple Isabel and Javier, price includes breakfast and dinner, excellent food, very relaxing, friendly, clean. Recommended. **E** *Rey Port*, Avda León Velarde 457, T571177. With bathroom, clean, fan, good value, friendly. **E** *Wilson*, Jr González Prada 355, T571086. With bathroom, clean, basic.

F *Hostal Moderno*, Billinghurst 357, T571063. Brightly repainted, clean, quiet, friendly and the best of the cheaper hotels. **F** *Tambo de Oro*, Avda Dos de Mayo 277, T572057. Basic, clean, water 24 hours.

Eating
● *on maps*

The best restaurant in town is at the *Hotel Wasai* (see above). *El Bambu*, Velarde 423. Serves a good and substantial set lunch. *Chez Maggy*, on the plaza. Cosy atmosphere, good pizzas. *Chifa Wa Seng*, Dos de Mayo 353. Chinese. *La Estrella*, Velarde 474. The smartest and best of the *pollos a la brasa* places. *El Joselito*, Velarde 328, and *El Califa*,

Piura 266 (recommended) often have bushmeat, mashed banana and palm hearst on the menu. There are several cafés for snacks and cakes, such as *Cosa Nostra*, Velarde 521, and *Tu Dulce Espera*, at Velarde 469.

El Witite, Velarde 153. A popular and good disco which plays mostly latin music and charges US$1.75 after 2300. *El Che*, on the plaza. A popular pub. There is a billiard hall at Puno 520.

Bars & nightclubs

Motorcycle hire Scooters and mopeds can de hired from *Ocoñita*, on the corner of Puno and G Prado for US$1 per hour or US$10 per day. No deposit is required but your passport and driving licence need to be shown.

Transport

Air To **Lima**, daily with AeroPerú at 1000 and Aero Continente at 1300, both US$60. Both airlines also fly daily to **Cusco**, US$39. Grupo Ocho sometimes fly to Cusco and to Iberia; their office is at the airport. To **Rio Branco** (Brazil), with Air Tafetal on Saturdays, if there is sufficient demand, US$100. A moto-taxi from town to the airport is US$1.50. **NB** A yellow fever vaccination is offered free at the airport on arrival but check that a new needle is used.

Puerto Maldonado

■ Sleeping
1. Cabañaquinta
2. Hostal El Astro
3. Hostal El Solar
4. Hostal Moderno
5. Rey Port
6. Tambo de Oro
7. Wilson
8. Wasai

Amazon Basin

River To **Boca Manu and Shintuya**, via Colorado. Take a combi to Laberinto (see **Jungle tours** below) and take a cargo boat from there to Colorado; several daily, US$12. You can get a daily cargo boat from there to Boca Manu and Shintuya, 9-10 hours, US$15. From Shintuya trucks go to Pilcopata and Cusco (see above under **Manu Biosphere Reserve**).

To **Puerto Heath** (Bolivian border), it can take several days to find a boat going all the way to the Bolivian border. Motorized dugout canoes go to Puerto Pardo on the Peruvian side, 5 hours, US$4.50 per person (no hotels or shops); wait here for a canoe to Puerto Heath. It is fairly hard to get a boat from the border to Riberalta (a wait of up to 3 days is not uncommon), US$15-20. Alternatively, travel to the naval base at América, then fly.

Directory **Airline offices** *Aero Continente*, Velarde 506, T572285. *AeroPerú*, Velarde 543, T573220. *Air Tafetal*, at the aiport. **Banks** *Banco de Crédito*, cash advances with Visa, no commission on TCs. *Banco de la Nación*, cash on Mastercard, quite good rates for TCs. The best rates for cash are at the *casas de cambio* on Puno 6th block, eg *Cárdenas Hnos*, Puno 605. **Communications** Serpost: at Velarde 6th block. **Telefónica**: on Puno 7th block. **Embassies & consulates** Bolivian Consulate: on the north side of the plaza. **Peruvian immigration**: is on Billinghurst, get your exit stamp here.

Trips from Puerto Maldonado

Lago Sandoval The beautiful and tranquil lake is a one hour boat ride along the Río Madre de Dios, and then a 5-kilometre walk into the jungle. There are two jungle lodges at the lake (see under Jungle lodges below). It is possible to see giant river otters early in the morning and several species of monkeys, macaws and hoatzin. At weekends, especially on Sundays, the lake gets quite busy.

Boats can be hired at the port for about US$20 a day – plus petrol – to go to Lago Sandoval, but don't pay the full cost in advance. A recommended boat owner and guide is Romel Nacimiento. (See also Tour agencies below.)

Upstream from Lago Sandoval, towards Puerto Maldonado, is the wreck of the *Fitzcarrald*. A flood swept the steamer from the Madre de Dios to the next river bed, which is said to have inspired German director, Werner Herzog, to make his famous film of the same name.

Other trips For those interested in seeing a gold rush, a trip to the town of **Laberinto** is suggested. There is one hotel and several poor restaurants. combis and trucks leave from Puerto Maldonado, one and a half hours, US$2.50, and returns in the afternoon daily. Boats leave from here to Manu (see Transport above).

At Km 13 on the Cusco road is a pleasant recreational centre with a restaurant and natural pools where it's possible to swim. It gets busy at the weekends. It's US$2 each way by *mototaxi* from town.

Trips can be made to **Lago Valencia**, 60 kilometres away near the Bolivian border – four hours there, eight hours back. It is an ox-bow lake with lots of wildlife. Many excellent beaches and islands are located within an hour's boat ride.

Tour agencies *Turismo de los Angeles*, Jr Puno 657, T571070. Run trips to Lago Sandoval and Lago Valencia. *Luly Tours*, Avda Velarde 620, T572133. Friendly, informative. Reputable guides are Hernán Llave Cortez, who can be contacted through *Hotel Wilson*, and Willy Wither, Avda Leon Velarde 469, T572014, E compured@ compured. limaperu. net. The usual price for trips to Lago Sandoval is US$25 per person per day (minimum of 2 people), and US$35 per person per day for longer trips lasting 2-4 days (minimum of 4-6 people). All guides should have a Ministry of Tourism carnet for Lake Sandoval, which also verifies them as suitable guides for trips to other places and confirms their identity.

Tambopata-Candamo Reserved Zone (TCRZ)

In Puerto Maldonado you can arrange a tour to Tambopata-Candamo, located between the rivers Madre de Dios, Tambopata and Heath. The area was declared a reserve in 1990 and is a very reasonable alternative for those who do not have the time to visit Manu. It is a close rival in terms of seeing wildlife and boasts some superb ox-bow lakes. There are a number of lodges here which are excellent for lowland rainforest birding. Explorers' Inn is perhaps the most famous, but the Tambopata Research Centre and Tambopata Lodge are also very good.

The **Bahuaja-Senone National Park** runs from the Río Heath, which forms the Bolivian border, across to the Río Tambopata, 50-80 kilometres upstream from Puerto Maldonado, covering 330,000 heactares within the TCRZ. The Park is closed to visitors though those visiting the *collpa* (see below) on the Tambopata or river rafting down the Tambopata will travel through it.

The fee to enter the TCRZ is US$2 per person, if staying at a lodge, or US$20 per person if camping.

Essentials

A2 *Sandoval Lodge*, 1 kilometre beyond *Mejía* (see below) on Lago Sandoval, usually accessed by canoe across the lake after a 3 kilometre walk or rickshaw ride along the trail, can accommodate 50 people in 25 rooms, huge bar and dining area, electricity, hot water. There is a short system of trails nearby, guides are available in several languages. Book through *InkaNatura*, Avda Benavides 3634, oficina 301, Lima, T2718156, or in Cusco at Avda Sol 821, 2nd Floor, T226392, E inkanatura@chavin.rcp.net.pe. They

Jungle Lodges

Tambopata Candamo Reserve Zone & Bahuaja-Sonene National Park

Amazon Basin

👉 The future for Tambopata

Research along the Tambopata (Bahauja – in the local Ese'eja language) river over the last 25 years has shown the enormous biodiversity of this area. In 1977 the Tambopata Reserved zone (TRZ), 5,500 ha adjoining the Eplorer's Inn Jungle lodge, was designated to offer some protection to world record numbers of species.

Reserved Zone status in Peruvian law signifies the temporary protection of an area while further studies are undertaken to decide its long-term future. The TRZ was not large enough to offer long-term protection to many of the mammal species found there which roam over far larger territories, and in 1990 the Tambopata-Candamo Reserved Zone (TCRZ) was declared. At 1,479 million ha it is a much more viable potential conservation unit.

Reserved Zones, along with all other protected areas in Peru, are managed by the Instituto Nacional de Recursos Nacionales (INRENA), a sub-division of the Ministry of Agriculture. In the early 1990s a proposal for the zonification and conservation management of the TRZ was produced by INRENA in conjunction with various NGOs. These included the establishment of a National Park, in the upper part of the region and buffer zones in the lower inhabited area. In the latter a variety of sustainable development projects would be created to try to manage effectively the existing forest.

The proposals were submitted in 1993 but were placed on hold once it became apparent that large oil and gas reserves might lie below the upper Tambopata region. It therefore came as a surprise when the Peruvian government suddenly designated part of the proposed Bahuaja-Sonene National Park in July1996. However, the Upper Tambopata region, arguably the most biodiverse part of the Tambopata drainage basin and containing the largest collpa (macaw salt-lick) in the world, was excluded for the present.

This lack of a management plan for the whole TCRZ leaves a vacuum in the remaining Reserved Zone areas with timber extraction along the Puerto Maldonado/Cusco road and gold-mining on the western side of the TCRZ continuing unchecked. Under Reserved Zone status no new concessions are granted for mineral and timber extraction and various other activities, but this does not prevent such activities from taking place.
It now seems likely that the future of one of the most diverse ecosystems on Earth will be held in limbo for several years until the oil companies have completed their studies and know whether exploitable oil and gas deposits are located there.

also have a small lodge on the Río Heath. **E** *Casa de Hospedaje Mejía*, an attractive rustic lodge on Lago Sandoval, with 10 double rooms but basic communal toilets, canoes are available (to book T571428, or just turn up). *Cusco Amazonico Lodge*, 45 minutes by boat down the Río Madre de Dios. Jungle tours available with multi-lingual guides, the lodge is surrounded by its own 10,000 hectares but most tours are to Lago Sandoval, US$160 per person for 3 days/2 nights package, plus US$25 for single room, a naturalists programme is also provided, negotiable out of season, 50 rustic bungalows with private bathrooms, friendly staff, very good food, multi-lingual guides. To book T/F4226574, Lima; Pasaje J C Tello C-13, Urb Santa Monica, Cusco, T235314, E reservas@inkaterra.com.pe. *Explorers Inn*, book through Peruvian Safaris, Garcilaso de la Vega 1334, Casilla 10088, T313047 Lima, or Plateros 365, T235342 Cusco. The lodge is located in the TCRZ, in the part where most research work has been done, 58 kilometres from Puerto Maldonado. It's a 3-hour ride up the Río Tambopata (2 hours return, in the early morning, so take warm clothes and rain gear), one of the best places in Peru for seeing jungle birds (580 plus species have been recorded here), butterflies (1,230 plus species), also giant river otters, but you probably need more than a 2-day tour to benefit fully from the location. The guides are biologists and naturalists from around the world who study in the reserve in return for acting as guides. They provide interesting wildlife-treks, including to the macaw lick (*collpa*). US$180 for 3 days/2 nights, but varies according to the season. *Cuzco Tambo Lodge*, bungalows 15 kilometres out on the northern bank of the Río Madre de Dios. 2, 3 and 4-day jungle programmes available, from US$90 per person in low season, tours visit Lago Sandoval. Book through Cusco-Maldonado Tour, Plateros 351 (T222332), Cusco. *Tambopata Jungle Lodge*, on the Río Tambopata, make reservations at Avda Pardo 705, Cusco, T225701, F238911, E postmast@patcusco.com.pe. Trips usually go to Lake Condenado, some to Lake Sachavacayoc, and to the *Collpa de Chuncho*, guiding mainly in English and Spanish, usual package US$160 per person for 3 days/2 nights, naturalists programme provided. *Wasai Lodge*, on the Río Tambopata, 80 kilometres (4 hours) upriver from Puerto Maldonado, 2 hours return, same owners as *Hotel Wasai* in town; E wasai@telematic.edu.pe. Small lodge with 3 bungalows for 30 people, 15 kilometres of trails around the lodge, guides in English and Spanish. The *Collpa de Chuncho*, one of the biggest macaw licks in the world, is only 1 hour up river; 3 day trips US$110, 7 days US$500. *Eco Amazonia Lodge*, on the Madre de Dios, 1 hour down-river from Puerto Maldonado. Accommodation for up to 80 in basic bungalows and dormitories, good for birdwatching with viewing platforms and tree canopy access. Book through their office in Cusco: Portal de Panes 109, oficina 6, T236159.

Posadas Amazonas Lodge, on the Tambopata river, 2½ hours upriver from Puerto Maldonado. A unique collaboration between a tour agency the local native community of Infierno. 22 large and attractive rooms with bathroom, hot showers, visits to Lakes Cochacocha and Tres Chimbadas, with good birdwatching opportunities including the Tambopata *Collpa*. 3 days/2 nights or 4 days/3 nights packages for US$90 per person per day. Book through *Rainforest Expeditions*, Galeon 120, Lima 41, T4218347, F4218183, E rainforest@amauta.rcp.net.pe. *Casas de Hospedaje*, is a new intiative set up by long-term colonists living along the Tambopata river, 50-75 kilometres upriver from Puerto Maldonado, 5-6 hours by *peque-peque*. Accommodation for up to 10 in basic, rustic facilities, provides an insight into local lifestyles, minimum of 2 nights, from US$20-35 per person, includes transport to/from Tambopata dock, all food, mosquito net and Spanish-speaking guide, take sleeping bag/bedding and check if the package includes a trip to a *collpa*, in which case you'll also need a tent. There are no formal booking arrangements as yet, but there's usually a representative to meet incoming flights at Puerto Maldonado airport. *Sachavaca Inn*, associated with the same scheme, 2 bungalows for up to 20 people, located between *Explorer's Inn* and *Tambopata Jungle Lodge*. To book, T571883, Puerto Maldonado. *Bahuaja Research Centre*, aimed at attracting scientific researchers who will stay at least 3 months, but there are opportunities for tourists who wish to help out for 2 weeks or more. Basic lodging in bungalows, including food, US$30 per day or camping for US$20 per day, prices include transport to/from Puerto Maldonado. Contact Tina Smith, Apurimac 525, Puerto Maldonado, T573348. In UK, J Farquhar, 17 Swansea Road, Norwich, Norfolk NR2 3HU.

Some of the lodges mentioned above also offer guiding and research placements to biology and environmental science graduates. For more details send an SAE to TReeS: UK – J Forrest, 64 Belsize Park, London NW3 4EH. USA – W Widdowson, 5455 Agostino Court, Concord, CA 94521.

To Iberia and Iñapari

A very worthwhile one or two day excursion by motorcycle (see hire rates above) is by boat across the Río Madre de Dios and follow the road towards **Iberia** and **Iñapari** on the border with Brazil. This can only be done in the dry season. Along the road are picturesque *caserios* (settlements) that serve as

Amazon Basin

collecting and processing centres for the Brazil nut. Approximately 70 percent of the inhabitants in the Madre de Dios are involved in the collection of this prized nut. Many trucks, of varying vintage, take this road and will offer lifts for US$10-20.

At **Planchón**, 40 kilometres up the road, there is a hotel, **G**, which is clean, but has no mosquito nets, and two bar/restaurants. **Alegría** at Km 60 has a hotel/restaurant and Mavilla, at Km 80, a bar.

The hotel at **Alerta**, Km 115, is a room with four beds, **G**. The river is safe to swim in. If there is a boat here, it is the quickest route to Brasiléia (Brazil), apart from the plane. US$10-20 per person in a cargo canoe, or *peque-peque*, to Porvenir and then by road to Cobija (Bolivia), across the border from Brasiléia.

At **San Lorenzo**, Km 145, is the *Bolpebra* bar, which serves cheap food and drink and is generally lively.

Iberia, Km 168, has two hotels, the best is **F** *Hostal Aquino*, basic, cold shower, rooms serviced daily.

Iñapari, at the end of the road, Km 235, has one hotel and a restaurant, but **Assis Brasil** across the border is much more attractive. Just wade across the river to get there.

There is a road from Assis Brasil into Brazil and connections to Bolivia. It can be cold travelling this road, so take a blanket or sleeping bag. There are no exchange facilities en route and poor exchange rates for Brazilian currency at Iñapari.

Crossing to Bolivia and Brazil

Ensure that you get an exit stamp in Puerto Maldonado at the Peruvian immigration office or at the PNP. You cannot get an exit stamp in Iberia or Iñapari at the border. Also check that you do not need a consular visa for Brazil or Bolivia; they are not issued at the border.

To Bolivia: take the boat to Puerto Heath (see above) and get a tourist visa at the Bolivian immigration office in Puerto Maldonado.

To Brazil: take a truck to Iñapari or flight to Iberia and a truck from there. Get a tourist visa at the Brazilian immigration in Iñapari.

Background

13

Background

493 History & politics

493 Precolumbian history

496 Moche culture

497 Inca Dynasty

501 Conquest & after

502 Post-independence Peru

504 Political developments

505 1968 coup

506 Peru under Fujimori

509 Land & environment

509 Geography

512 Climate

513 Flora & fauna

517 Culture

517 People

520 Religion

521 Arts & crafts

526 Music & dance

529 Festivals

530 Literature

533 Fine art & sculpture

**537 Government &
the modern country**

537 Government

537 Economy

540 Society

13

History and politics

Precolumbian history

Despite Peru's formidable geographical difficulties and frequent natural disasters, archaeologists have uncovered a precolumbian history of highly advanced societies that prevailed against these awesome odds. The coastal desert from Lambayeque department south to Paracas has revealed an 'American Egypt', although this has meant a bias towards the coastal region and a reliance on the contents of tombs for information. Knowledge of these tombs often only comes to light following their looting by gangs of *huaqueros* (grave robbers), incited by demand from the international antiquities market.

The Incas told the Spaniards that before they established their Tawantinsuyo Empire, the land was overrun by primitives constantly at war with one another. There were, in fact, many other civilized cultures dating back as far as 2000 BC. The most accomplished of these were the Chavín-Sechín (c. 900-200 BC), the Paracas-Nasca (c. 200 BC-500 AD), the Huari-Tiahuanaco (c. 750 BC-1000 AD), and the Moche-Chimú (200 BC-1400 AD).

Early settlement

It is generally accepted that the earliest settlers in Peru were related to people who had crossed the Bering Straits from Asia and drifted through the Americas from about 20,000 BC. However, theories of early migrations from across the Pacific and Atlantic have been rife since Thor Heyerdahl's raft expeditions in 1947 and 1969-70 (see also under Túcume, page 359).

Human remains found in a cave in Lauricocha, near Huánuco, have a radiocarbon date of circa 7500 BC, but the earliest signs of a village settlement in Peru, were found on the central coast at Pampa, dating from 2500 BC. Between these two dates it is thought that people lived nomadically in small groups, mainly hunting and gathering but also cultivating some plants seasonally. Domestication of llamas, alpacas and guinea pigs also began at this time, particularly important for the highland people around the Titicaca basin.

The abundant wealth of marine life produced by the Humboldt Current, especially along the north coast, boosted population growth and settlement in this area. Around 2000 BC climatic change dried up the *lomas* ('fog meadows'), and drove sea shoals into deeper water. People turned more to farming and began to spread inland along river valleys.

Origins of Andean civilization

From the second millennium BC to around the first century BC is known as the Formative Period when the first signs of the high culture of Andean society appeared. During this period sophisticated irrigation and canal systems were developed, farming productivity increased and communities had more time to devote to building and producing ceramics and textiles. The development of pottery also led to trade and cultural links with other communities. Distribution of land and water to the farmers was probably organized by a corporate authority, and this may have led to the later 'Mit'a' labour system developed by the Incas.

Above all, this period is characterized by the construction of centres of urban

Background

concentration that promoted labour specialization and with it the development of cultural expression. The earliest buildings constructed were *huacas*, adobe platform mounds, centres of some cult or sacred power. Huaca Florida was the largest example of this period, near the Río Rimac, later replaced by Huaca Garagay as a major centre for the area. Many similar centres spread along the north coast, most notably Aspero and Piedra Parada.

During this period, however, much more advanced architecture was being built at **Kotosh**, in the central Andes near Huánuco. Japanese archaeological excavations there in the 1960s revealed a temple with ornamental niches and friezes. Some of the earliest pottery was also found here, showing signs of influence from southern Ecuador and the tropical lowlands, adding weight to theories of Andean culture originating in the Amazon. Radiocarbon dates of some Kotosh remains are as early as 1850 BC.

Chavín-Sechín   For the next 1,000 years or so up to c. 900 BC, communities grew and spread inland from the north coast and south along the northern highlands. Farmers still lived in simple adobe or rough stone houses but built increasingly large and complex ceremonial centres, such as at Las Haldas in the Casma Valley. As farming became more productive and pottery more advanced, commerce grew and states began to develop throughout central and North-central Peru, with the associated signs of social structure and hierarchies.

Around 900 BC a new era was marked by the rise of two important centres; **Chavín de Huantar** in the central Andes and **Sechín Alto**, inland from Casma on the north coast.

Chavín takes its name from the site of Chavín de Huantar in the northern highlands. This was the first of several 'horizon styles' that were of the greatest importance in Peru and had very widespread influence. The other later ones, the Huari-Tiahuanaco and the Inca, were pan-Peruvian, affecting all parts of the country. The chief importance of Chavín de Huantar was not so much in its highly advanced architecture as in the influence of its cult coupled with the artistic style of its ceramics and other artefacts. The founders of Chavín may have originated in the tropical lowlands as some of its carved monoliths show representations of monkeys and felines.

Objects with Chavín traits have been found all along the coast from Piura to the Lurin valley south of Lima, and its cult ideology spread to temples around the same area. Richard L Burger of Yale University has argued that the extent of Chavín influence has been exaggerated. Many sites on the coast already had their own cult practices and the Chavín idols may have been simply added alongside. There is evidence of an El Niño flood that devastated the north coast around 500 BC. Local

Section of the wall at Sechín

cults fell from grace as social order was disrupted and the Chavín cult was snatched up as a timely new alternative.

Chavín cult

The Chavín cult was paralleled by the great advances made in this period in textile production and in some of the earliest examples of metallurgy. The origins of metallurgy have been attributed to some gold, silver and copper ornaments found in graves in Chongoyape, near Chiclayo, which show Chavín-style features. But earlier evidence has been discovered in the Andahuaylas region, dating from 1800-900 BC. The religious symbolism of gold and other precious metals and stones is thought to have been an inspiration behind some of the beautiful artefacts found in the central Andean area. The emergence of social hierarchies also created a demand for luxury goods as status symbols.

Sechín The cultural brilliance of Chavín de Huántar was complemented by its contemporary, Sechín. This huge granite-faced complex near Casma, 370 kilometres north of Lima, was described by JC Tello as the biggest structure of its kind in the Andes. According to Michael Moseley of Harvard University, Chavín and Sechín may have combined forces, with Sechín as the military power that spread the cultural word of Chavín, but their influence did not reach far to the south where the Paracas and Tiahuanaco cultures held sway.

Upper Formative Period

The Chavín hegemony, which is also known as the Middle Formative Period, broke up around 300 BC. The 'unity' of this period was broken and the initial phase of the regional diversification of Andean cultures began. The process of domestication of plants and animals culminated in the Upper Formative Period. Agricultural technology progressed leading to an economic security that permitted a considerable growth in the centres of population. Among the many diverse stylistic/cultural groups of this period are: the Vicus on the north coast; Salinar in the Chicama valley; Paracas Necrópolis on the south coast; and Huarás in the Ancash highlands.

Paracas Necrópolis This was the early phase of the Nasca culture and is renowned for the superb technical quality and stylistic variety in its weaving and pottery. The *mantos* (large, decorated cloth) rank amongst the world's best, and many of the finest examples can be seen in the museums of Lima. The extreme dryness of the desert here has preserved the textiles and ceramics in the mummies' tombs which have been excavated.

Paracas Necrópolis is, in fact, a cemetery located on the slopes of Cerro Colorado, in the Department of Ica, from which 429 funerary bundles were excavated (see page 258). Each bundle is a mummy wrapped in many fine and rough textiles. Paracas Necrópolis corresponds to the last of the 10 phases into which Paracas ceramics have been divided. The previous ones, known as Paracas Cavernas, relate to the Middle Formative Period and were influenced by the Chavín cult.

Nasca culture

The Regional Development Period up to about 500 AD, was a time of great social and cultural development. Sizable towns of 5-10,000 inhabitants grew on the south coast, populated by artisans, merchants, government administrators and religious officials.

One of the most famous cultures of this period, or indeed of precolumbian history was the Nasca. The famous Nasca Lines are a feature of the region. Straight lines, abstract designs and outlines of animals are scratched in the dark desert surface forming a lighter contrast that can be seen clearly from the air. There are many theories of how and why the lines were made but no definitive explanation has yet been able to establish their place in Peruvian history (see Nasca Lines, page 269). There are similarities between the style of some of the line patterns and that

*War-scene depicted
on a Moche vessel
(AD 200-750)*

of the pottery and textiles of the same period. It is clear from the sheer scale of the lines and the quality of the work that, whatever their purpose, they were very important to the Nasca culture.

In contrast to the quantity and quality of the Nasca artefacts found, relatively few major buildings belonging to this period have been uncovered in the southern desert. Dos Palmas is a complex of rooms and courtyards in the Pisco Valley and Cahuachi in the Nasca Valley is a large area including adobe platforms, a pyramid and a 'wooden Stonehenge' cluster of preserved tree trunks. As most of the archaeological evidence of the Nasca culture came from their desert cemeteries, little is known about the lives and social organization of the people. Alpaca hair found in Nasca textiles, however, indicates that there must have been strong trade links with highland people.

Moche culture

Nasca's contemporaries on the north coast were the militaristic Moche who, from about 100-800 AD built up an empire whose traces stretch from Piura in the north to Casma, beyond Chimbote, in the south. The Moche built their capital in the middle of the desert, outside present day Trujillo. It features the huge pyramid temples of the Huaca del Sol and Huaca de la Luna (see page 346). The Moche roads and system of way stations are thought to have been an early inspiration for the Inca network. The Moche increased the coastal population with intensive irrigation projects. Skilful engineering works were carried out, such as the La Cumbre canal, still in use today, and the Ascope aqueduct, both on the Chicama river.

The Moche's greatest achievement, however, was its artistic genius. Exquisite ornaments in gold, silver and precious stones were made by its craftsmen. Moche pottery progressed through five stylistic periods, most notable for the stunningly lifelike portrait vases. A wide variety of everyday scenes were created in naturalistic ceramics, telling us more about Moche life than is known about other earlier cultures, and perhaps used by them as 'visual aids' to compensate for the lack of a written language (see also page 344).

Sipán A spectacular discovery of a Moche royal tomb at Sipán was made in February 1987 by Walter Alva, director of the Brüning Archaeological Museum, Lambayeque. Reports of the excavation in the *National Geographic* magazine (October 1988 and June 1990), talked of the richest unlooted tomb in the New World (see page 357). The find included semi-precious stones brought from Chile and Argentina, and seashells from Ecuador (the Moche were also great navigators).

The cause of the collapse of the Moche Empire around 600-700 AD is unknown, but it may have been started by a 30-year drought at the end of the sixth century, followed by one of the periodic El Niño flash floods (identified by meteorologists from ice thickness in the Andes) and finished by the encroaching forces of the Huari Empire. The decline of the Moche signalled a general tipping of the balance of power in Peru from the north coast to the southern sierra.

Huari-Tiahuanaco The ascendant Huari-Tiahuanaco movement, from c. 600-1000 AD, combined the religious cult of the Tiahuanaco site in the Titicaca basin, with the military dynamism of the Huari, based in the central highlands. The two cultures developed

Background

independently but, as had occurred with the Chavín-Sechín association, they are generally thought to have merged compatibly.

Up until their own demise around 1440 AD, the Huari-Tiahuanaco had spread their empire and influence from Cajamarca and Lambayeque in the north and across much of southern Peru, northern Bolivia and Argentina. The Huari introduced a new concept in urban life, the great walled urban centre, the best example of which is their capital city, 22 kilometres north of Ayacucho (see page 441). They also made considerable gains in art and technology, building roads, terraces and irrigation canals across the country.

The Huari-Tiahuanaco ran their empire with efficient labour and administrative systems that were later adopted and refined by the Incas. Labour tribute for state projects had been practised by the Moche and was further developed now. But the empire could not contain regional kingdoms who began to fight for land and power. As control broke down, rivalry and coalitions emerged, and the system collapsed.

After the decline of the Huari Empire, the unity that had been imposed on the Andes was broken. A new stage of autonomous regional or local political organizations began. Among the cultures corresponding to this period were the Kuelap, centred in the Chachapoyas region (see page 394), and the Chimú.

Chimú culture

The Chimú culture had two centres. To the north was Lambayeque, near Chiclayo, while to the south, in the Moche valley near present-day Trujillo, was the great adobe walled city of Chan Chán. Covering 20 square kilometres, this was the largest pre-Hispanic Peruvian city (see page 345).

Chimú has been classified as a despotic state that based its power on wars of conquest. Rigid social stratification existed and power rested in the hands of the great lord *Siquic* and the lord *Alaec*. These lords were followed in social scale by a group of urban couriers who enjoyed a certain degree of economic power. At the bottom were the peasants and slaves. In 1450, the Chimú kingdom was conquered by the Inca Túpac Yupanqui, the son and heir of the Inca ruler Pachacuti Inca Yupanqui.

Inca Dynasty

The origins of the Inca Dynasty are shrouded in mythology. The best known story reported by the Spanish chroniclers talks about Manco Capac and his sister rising out of Lake Titicaca, created by the Sun as divine founders of a chosen race. This was in approximately AD 1200. Over the next 300 years the small tribe grew to supremacy as leaders of the largest empire ever known in the Americas, the four territories of Tawantinsuyo, united by Cusco as the umbilicus of the Universe. The four quarters of Tawantinsuyo, all radiating out from Cusco, were: 1 Chinchaysuyo, north and northwest; 2 Cuntisuyo, south and west; 3 Collasuyo, south and east; 4 Antisuyo, east.

At its peak, just before the Spanish Conquest, the Inca Empire stretched from the Río Maule in central Chile, north to the present Ecuador-Colombia border, containing most of Ecuador, Peru, western Bolivia, northern Chile and northwest Argentina. The area was roughly equivalent to France, Belgium, Holland, Luxembourg, Italy and Switzerland combined (980,000 square kilometres).

The first Inca ruler, Manco Capac, moved to the fertile Cusco region, and established Cusco as his capital. Successive generations of rulers were fully occupied with local conquests of rivals, such as the Colla and Lupaca to the south, and the Chanca to the northwest. At the end of Inca Viracocha's reign the hated Chanca were finally defeated, largely thanks to the heroism of one of his sons, Pachacuti Inca Yupanqui, who was subsequently crowned as the new ruler.

From the start of Pachacuti's own reign in 1438, imperial expansion grew in earnest. With the help of his son and heir, Topa Inca, territory was conquered from the Titicaca basin south into Chile, and all the north and central coast down to the Lurin Valley. The Incas also subjugated the Chimú, a highly sophisticated rival empire who had re-occupied the abandoned Moche capital at Chan Chán. Typical of the Inca method of government, some of the Chimú skills were assimilated into their own political and administrative system, and some Chimú nobles were even given positions in Cusco.

Perhaps the pivotal event in Inca history came in 1527 with the death of the ruler, Huayna Capac. Civil war broke out in the confusion over his rightful successor. One of his legitimate sons, Huáscar, ruled the southern part of the empire from Cusco. Atahualpa, Huáscar's half-brother, governed Quito, the capital of Chinchaysuyo. In 1532, soon after Atahualpa had won the civil war, Francisco Pizarro arrived in Tumbes with 179 *conquistadores*, many on horseback. Atahualpa's army was marching south, probably for he first time, when he clashed with Piazarro at Cajamarca.

Francisco Pizarro's only chance against the formidable imperial army he encountered at Cajamarca was a bold stroke. He drew Atahualpa into an ambush, slaughtered his guards, promised him liberty if a certain room were filled with treasure, and finally killed him after receiving news that another Inca army was on its way to free him. Pushing on to Cusco, he was at first hailed as the executioner of a traitor: Atahualpa had ordered the death of Huáscar in 1533, while himself a captive of Pizarro, and his victorious generals were bringing the defeated Huáscar to see his half-brother. Panic followed when the *conquistadores* set about sacking the city, and they fought off with difficulty an attempt by Manco Inca to recapture Cusco in 1536.

Inca society The people we call the Incas were a small aristocracy numbering only a few thousand, centred in the highland city of Cusco, at 3,400 metres. They rose gradually as a small regional dynasty, similar to others in the Andes of that period, starting around 1200 AD. Then, suddenly, in the mid-1400s, they began to expand explosively under Pachacuti, a sort of Andean Alexander the Great, and later his son, Topa. Less than a hundred years later, they fell before the rapacious warriors of Spain. The Incas were not the first dynasty in Andean history to dominate their neighbours, but they did it more thoroughly and went further than anyone before them.

Empire building Enough remains today of their astounding highways, cities and agricultural terracing for people to marvel and wonder how they accomplished so much in so short a time. They seem to have been amazingly energetic, industrious and efficient – and the reports of their Spanish conquerors confirm this hypothesis.

They must also have had the willing cooperation of most of their subject peoples, most of the time. In fact, the Incas were master diplomats and alliance-builders first, and military conquerors only second, if the first method of expansion failed. The Inca skill at generating wealth by means of highly efficient agriculture and distribution brought them enormous prestige and enabled them to 'out-gift' neighbouring chiefs in huge royal feasts involving ritual outpourings of generosity, often in the form of vast gifts of textiles, exotic products from distant regions, and perhaps wives to add blood ties to the alliance. The 'out-gifted' chief was required by the Andean laws of reciprocity to provide something in return, and this would usually be his loyalty, as well as a levy of manpower from his own chiefdom.

Thus, with each new alliance the Incas wielded greater labour forces and their mighty public works programmes surged ahead. These were administered through an institution known as *mit'a*, a form of taxation through labour. The state provided the materials, such as wool and cotton for making textiles, and the communities provided skills and labour.

Mit'a contingents worked royal mines, royal plantations for producing coca leaves, royal quarries and so on. The system strove to be equitable, and workers in such hardship posts as high altitude mines and lowland coca plantations were given correspondingly shorter terms of service.

Organization

Huge administrative centres were built in different parts of the empire, where people and supplies were gathered. Articles such as textiles and pottery were produced there in large workshops. Work in these places was carried out in a festive manner, with plentiful food, drink and music. Here was Andean reciprocity at work: the subject supplied his labour, and the ruler was expected to provide generously while he did so.

Aside from *mit'a* contributions there were also royal lands claimed by the Inca as his portion in every conquered province, and worked for his benefit by the local population. Thus, the contribution of each citizen to the state was quite large, but apparently, the imperial economy was productive enough to sustain this.

Another institution was the practice of moving populations around wholesale, inserting loyal groups into restive areas, and removing recalcitrant populations to loyal areas. These movements of *mitmakuna*, as they were called, were also used to introduce skilled farmers and engineers into areas where productivity needed to be raised.

Communications

The huge empire was held together by an extensive and highly efficient highway system. There were an estimated 30,000 kilometres of major highway, most of it neatly paved and drained, stringing together the major Inca sites. Two parallel highways ran north to south, along the coastal desert strip and the mountains, and dozens of east-west roads crossing from the coast to the Amazon fringes. These roadways took the most direct routes, with wide stone stairways zig-zagging up the steepest mountain slopes and rope suspension bridges crossing the many narrow gorges of the Andes.

Every 12 kilometres or so there was a *tambo*, or way station, where goods could be stored and travellers lodged. The *tambos* were also control points, where the Inca state's accountants tallied movements of goods and people. Even more numerous than *tambos*, were the huts of the *chasquis*, or relay runners, who continually sped royal and military messages along these highways.

The Inca state kept records and transmitted information in various ways. Accounting and statistical records were kept on skeins of knotted strings known as *quipus*. Numbers employed the decimal system, and colours indicated the categories being recorded. An entire class of people, known as *quipucamayocs*, existed whose job was to create and interpret these. Neither the Incas nor their Andean predecessors had a system of writing as we understand it, but there may have been a system of encoding language into *quipus*.

Archaeologists are studying this problem today. History and other forms of knowledge were transmitted via songs and poetry. Music and dancing, full of encoded information which could be read by the educated elite, were part of every major ceremony and public event information was also carried in textiles, which had for millennia been the most vital expression of Andean culture.

Background

Textiles

Clothing carried insignia of status, ethnic origin, age and so on. Special garments were made and worn for various rites of passage. It has been calculated that, after agriculture, no activity was more important to Inca civilization than weaving. Vast stores of textiles were maintained to sustain the Inca system of ritual giving. Armies and *mit'a* workers were partly paid in textiles. The finest materials were reserved for the nobility, and the Inca emperor himself displayed his status by changing into new clothes every day and having the previous day's burned.

Most weaving was done by women, and the Incas kept large numbers of 'chosen women' in female-only houses all over the empire, partly for the purpose of supplying textiles to the elite and for the many deities, to whom they were frequently given as burned offerings. These women had other duties, such as making *chicha* – the Inca corn beer which was consumed and sacrificed in vast quantities on ceremonial occasions. They also became wives and concubines to the Inca elite and loyal nobilities. And some may have served as priestesses of the moon, in parallel to the male priesthood of the sun.

Religious worship
The Incas have always been portrayed as sun-worshippers, but it now seems that they were just as much mountain-worshippers. Recent research has shown that Machu Picchu was at least partly dedicated to the worship of the surrounding mountains, and Inca sacrificial victims have been excavated on frozen Andean peaks at 6,700 metres. In fact, until technical climbing was invented, the Incas held the world altitude record for humans.

Human sacrifice was not common, but every other kind was, and ritual attended every event in the Inca calendar. The main temple of Cusco was dedicated to the numerous deities: the Sun, the Moon, Venus, the Pleiades, the Rainbow, Thunder and Lightning, and the countless religious icons of subject peoples which had been brought to Cusco, partly in homage, partly as hostage. Here, worship was continuous and the fabulous opulence included gold cladding on the walls, and a famous garden filled with life-size objects of gold and silver. Despite this pantheism, the Incas acknowledged an overall Creator God, whom they called Viracocha. A special temple was dedicated to him, at *Raqchi*, about 100 kilometres southeast of Cusco. Part of it still stands today.

Military forces
The conquering Spaniards noted with admiration the Inca storehouse system, still well-stocked when they found it, despite several years of civil war among the Incas. Besides textiles, military equipment, and ritual objects, they found huge quantities of food. Like most Inca endeavours, the food stores served a multiple purpose: to supply feasts, to provide during lean times, to feed travelling work parties, and to supply armies on the march.

Inca armies were able to travel light and move fast because of this system. Every major Inca settlement also incorporated great halls where large numbers of people could be accommodated, or feasts and gatherings held, and large squares or esplanades for public assemblies.

Inca technology is usually deemed inferior to that of contemporary Europe. Their military technology certainly was. They had not invented iron-smelting, and basically fought with clubs, palmwood spears, slings, wooden shields, cotton armour and straw-stuffed helmets. They did not even make much use of the bow and arrow, a weapon they were well aware of. Military tactics, too, were primitive. The disciplined formations of the Inca armies quickly dissolved into melees of unbridled individualism once battle was joined.

This, presumably, was because warfare constituted a theatre of manly prowess, but was not the main priority of Inca life. Its form was ritualistic. Battles were suspended by both sides for religious observance. Negotiation, combined with displays of superior Inca strength, usually achieved victory, and total annihilation of the enemy was not on the agenda.

Architecture
Other technologies, however, were superior in every way to their 16th century counterparts: textiles; settlement planning; and agriculture in particular with its sophisticated irrigation and soil conservation systems, ecological sensitivity, specialized crop strains and high productivity under the harshest conditions. The Incas fell short of their Andean predecessors in the better-known arts of ancient America – ceramics, textiles and metalwork – but it could be argued that their

supreme efforts were made in architecture, stoneworking, landscaping, roadbuilding, and the harmonious combination of these elements.

These are the outstanding survivals of Inca civilization, which still remain to fascinate the visitor: the huge, exotically close-fit blocks of stone, cut in graceful, almost sensual curves; the astoundingly craggy and inaccessible sites encircled by great sweeps of Andean scenery; the rhythmic layers of farm terracing that provided land and food to this still-enigmatic people. The finest examples of Inca architecture can be seen in the city of Cusco and throughout the Sacred Valley.

The ruling elite lived privileged lives in their capital at Cusco. They reserved for themselves and privileged insiders certain luxuries, such as the chewing of coca, the wearing of fine vicuña wool, and the practice of polygamy. But they were an austere people, too. Everyone had work to do, and the nobility were constantly being posted to state business throughout the empire. Young nobles were expected to learn martial skills, besides being able to read the *quipus*, speak both Quechua and the southern language of Aymara, and know the epic poems.

Ruling elite

The Inca elite belonged to royal clans known as *panacas*, which each had the unusual feature of being united around veneration of the mummy of their founding ancestor – a previous Inca emperor, unless they happened to belong to the *panaca* founded by the Inca emperor who was alive at the time. Each new emperor built his own palace in Cusco and amassed his own wealth rather than inheriting it from his forebears, which perhaps helps to account for the urge to unlimited expansion.

This urge ultimately led the Incas to overreach themselves. Techniques of diplomacy and incorporation no longer worked as they journeyed farther from the homeland and met ever-increasing resistance from people less familiar with their ways. During the reign of Wayna Capac, the last emperor before the Spanish invasion, the Incas had to establish a northern capital at Quito in order to cope with permanent war on their northern frontier. Following Wayna Capac's death came a devastating civil war between Cusco and Quito, and immediately thereafter came the Spanish invasion. Tawantisuyo, the empire of the four quarters, collapsed with dizzying suddenness.

Conquest and after

Peruvian history after the arrival of the Spaniards was not just a matter of *conquistadores* versus Incas. The vast majority of the huge empire remained unaware of the conquest for many years. The Chimú and the Chachapoyas cultures were powerful enemies of the Incas. The Chimú developed a highly sophisticated culture and a powerful empire stretching for 560 kilometres along the coast from Paramonga south to Casma. Their history was well-recorded by the Spanish chroniclers and continued through the conquest possibly up to about 1600. The Kuelap/ Chachapoyas people were not so much an empire as a loose-knit 'confederation of ethnic groups with no recognized capital' (Morgan Davis *Chachapoyas: The Cloud People*, Ontario, 1988). But the culture did develop into an advanced society with great skill in roads and monument building. Their fortress at Kuelap was known as the

LAVILLADECALLAV

Callao in the early 17th centruy drawn by Huaman Poma de Ayala

most impregnable in Tawantinsuyo. It remained intact against Inca attack and Manco Inca even tried, unsuccessfully, to gain refuge here against the Spaniards.

In 1535, wishing to secure his communications with Spain, Pizarro founded Lima, near the ocean, as his capital. The same year Diego de Almagro set out to conquer Chile. Unsuccessful, he returned to Peru, quarrelled with Pizarro, and in 1538 fought a pitched battle with Pizarro's men at the Salt Pits, near Cusco. He was defeated and put to death. Pizarro, who had not been at the battle, was assassinated in his palace in Lima by Almagro's son three years later.

For the next 27 years each succeeding representative of the Kingdom of Spain sought to subdue the Inca successor state of Vilcabamba, north of Cusco, and to unify the fierce Spanish factions. Francisco de Toledo (appointed 1568) solved both problems during his 14 years in office: Vilcabamba was crushed in 1572 and the last reigning Inca, Túpac Amaru, put to death.

For the next 200 years the Viceroys closely followed Toledo's system, if not his methods. The Major Government – the Viceroy, the *Audiencia* (High Court), and *corregidores* (administrators) – ruled through the Minor Government – Indian chiefs put in charge of large groups of natives – a rough approximation to the original Inca system.

Towards independence

The Indians rose in 1780, under the leadership of an Inca noble who called himself Túpac Amaru II. He and many of his lieutenants were captured and put to death under torture at Cusco. Another Indian leader in revolt suffered the same fate in 1814, but this last flare-up had the sympathy of many of the locally-born Spanish, who resented their status, inferior to the Spaniards born in Spain, the refusal to give them any but the lowest offices, the high taxation imposed by the home government, and the severe restrictions upon trade with any country but Spain.

Help came to them from the outside world. José de San Martín's Argentine troops, convoyed from Chile under the protection of Lord Cochrane's squadron, landed in southern Peru on 7 September, 1820. San Martín proclaimed Peruvian independence at Lima on 28 July, 1821, though most of the country was still in the hands of the Viceroy, José de La Serna. Bolívar, who had already freed Venezuela and Colombia, sent Antonio José de Sucre to Ecuador where, on 24 May, 1822, he gained a victory over La Serna at Pichincha.

San Martín, after a meeting with Bolívar at Guayaquil, left for Argentina and a self-imposed exile in France, while Bolívar and Sucre completed the conquest of Peru by defeating La Serna at the battle of Junín (6 August, 1824) and the decisive battle of Ayacucho (9 December, 1824). For over a year there was a last stand in the Real Felipe fortress at Callao by the Spanish troops under General Rodil before they capitulated on 22 January, 1826. Bolívar was invited to stay in Peru, but left for Colombia in 1826.

Post-independence Peru

Following independence Peru attempted a confederation with Bolivia in the 1830s but this proved temporary. Then, in 1879 came the disastrous War of the Pacific, in which Peru and Bolivia were defeated by Chile and Peru lost its southern territory.

Economic change

Peru's economic development since independence has been based upon the export of minerals and foodstuffs to Europe and the United States. Guano, a traditional fertilizer in Peru and derived from the manure of seabirds, was first shipped to Europe in 1841. In the three decades that followed it became an important fertilizer in Europe and by the early 1860s over 80 percent of the Peruvian government's revenues were derived from its export. Much of this income, though, went to pay off interest on the spiralling national debt. By the 1870s the richer deposits were exhausted and cheaper alternatives to guano were being discovered. One of these was nitrates, discovered in

The War of the Pacific

One of the major international wars in Latin America since independence, this conflict has its roots in a border dispute between Chile and Bolivia. The frontier between the two in the Atacama desert was ill-defined.

There had already been one conflict, in 1836-1839, when Chile defeated Peru and Bolivia, putting an end to a confederation of the two states. The discovery of nitrates in the Atacama only complicated relations, for in the Bolivian Atacama province of Antofagasta nitrates were exploited by Anglo-Chilean companies.

In 1878 the Bolivian government, short of revenue, attempted to tax the Chilean-owned Antofagasta Railroad and Nitrate Company. When the company refused to pay, the Bolivians seized the company's assets. The Chilean government claimed that the Bolivian action broke an 1874 agreement between the two states. When Peru announced that it would honour a secret alliance with Bolivia by supporting her, the Chilean president, Aníbal Pinto, declared war on both states.

Control of the sea was vital, and this was where Chile concentrated her efforts. Following a successful naval campaign, the Chileans invaded the southern Peruvian province of Tarapacá and then landed troops north of Tacna, seizing the town in May 1880 before capturing Arica, further south. The Chilean armies were hot stuff, and in January 1881 they seized control of Lima.

Despite these defeats and the loss of their capital, Peru did not sue for peace, although Bolivia had already signed a ceasefire, giving up her coastal province. Under the 1883 peace settlement Peru gave up Tapapacá to Chile. Although the provinces of Tacna and Arica were to be occupied by Chile for 10 years, it was not until 1929 that an agreement was reached under which Tacna was returned to Peru, while Chile kept Arica. Apart from souring relations between Chile and her two northern neighbours to this day, the war gave Chile a monopoly over the world's supply of nitrates and enabled her to dominate the southern Pacific coast.

the Atacama desert, but Peru's defeat by Chile in the War of the Pacific ensured that she would lose her share of this wealth.

After the decline of guano Peru developed several new exports. In the 1890s the demand in Europe and USA for Amazonian rubber for tyres and for use in electrical components led to a brief boom in both the Brazilian and Peruvian Amazon, the Peruvian industry being based on the Amazon port of Iquitos. This boom was short-lived as cheaper rubber was soon being produced from plantations in the East Indies.

Peru's colonial mineral exports, gold and silver, were replaced by copper, although ownership was mainly under control of foreign companies, particularly the US-based Cerro de Pasco Copper Corporation and Northern Peru Mining. Oil became another important product, amounting to 30 percent of Peruvian exports by 1930. Further exports came from sugar and cotton, which were produced on coastal plantations (see also the Economy section, page 537).

Social change

Independence from Spanish rule meant that power passed into the hands of the Creole elite with no immediate alternation of the colonial social system. The *contribución de indíginas*, the colonial tribute collected from the native peoples was not abolished until 1854, the same year as the ending of slavery.

Until the 1970s land relations in the sierra changed very little, as the older landholding families continued to exert their traditional influence over 'their' peones. The traditional elite, the so-called '44 families', were still very powerful, though increasingly divided between the coastal aristocracy with their interests in plantation agriculture and trade, and the serrano elite, more conservative and inward-looking.

The pattern of export growth did, however, have major effects on the social structure of the coast. The expansion of plantation agriculture and mining led to the growth of a new labour force; this was supplied partially by Chinese indentured labourers, about 100,000 of whom arrived between 1855 and 1875, partly by the migration of Indians from the sierra and partly by the descendants of black slaves.

Political developments

19th century For much of the period since independence Peruvian political life has been dominated by the traditional elites. Political parties have been slow to develop and the roots of much of the political conflict and instability which have marked the country's history lie in personal ambitions and in regional and other rivalries within the elite.

The early years after independence were particularly chaotic as rival caudillos (political bosses) who had fought in the independence wars vied with each other for power. The increased wealth brought about by the guano boom led to greater stability, though political corruption became a serious problem under the presidency of José Rufino Echenique (1851-1854) who paid out large sums of the guano revenues as compensation to upper class families for their (alleged) losses in the Wars of Independence. Defeat by Chile in the War of the Pacific discredited civilian politicians even further and led to a period of military rule in the 1880s.

Early 20th century Even though the voting system was changed in 1898, this did little to change the dominance of the elite. Voting was not secret so landowners herded their workers to the polls and watched to make sure they voted correctly. Yet voters were also lured by promises as well as threats. One of the more unusual presidents was Guillermo Billinghurst (1912-1914) who campaigned on the promise of a larger loaf of bread for five cents, thus gaining the nickname of "Big Bread Billinghurst". As president he proposed a publically-funded housing programme, supported the introduction of an eight hour day and was eventually overthrown by the military who, along with the elite, were alarmed at his growing popularity among the urban population.

The 1920s This decade was dominated by Augusto Leguía. After winning the 1919 elections Leguía claimed that Congress was plotting to prevent him from becoming president and induced the military to help him close Congress. Backed by the armed forces, Leguía introduced a new constitution which gave him greater powers and enabled him to be re-elected in 1924 and 1929. Claiming his goal was to prevent the rise of communism, he proposed to build a partnership between business and labour. A large programme of public works, particularly involving building roads, bridges and railways, was begun, the work being carried out by poor rural men who were forced into unpaid building work. The Leguía regime dealt harshly with critics: opposition newspapers were closed and opposition leaders arrested and deported. His overthrow in 1930 ended what Peruvians call the "Oncenio" or 11 year period.

The 1920s also saw the emergence of a political thinker who would have great influence in the future, not only in Peru but elsewhere in Latin America. Juan Carlos Mariátegui, a socialist writer and journalist, argued that the solution to Peru's problems lay in the reintegration of the Indians through land reform and the breaking up of the great landed estates. (See also the section on Literature.)

The formation of APRA Another influential thinker of this period was Víctor Raúl Haya de la Torre, a student exiled by Leguía in 1924. He returned after the latter's fall to create the Alianza Popular Revolucionaria Americana, a political party which called for state control of the economy, nationalization of key industries and protection of the middle classes, which, Haya de la Torre argued, were threatened by foreign economic interests.

In 1932 APRA seized control of Trujillo; when the army arrived to deal with the rising, the rebels murdered about 50 hostages, including 10 army officers. In reprisal the army murdered about 1,000 local residents suspected of sympathizing with APRA. APRA eventually became the largest and easily the best-organized political party in Peru, but the distrust of the military and the upper class for Haya de la Torre ensured that he never became president.

A turning point in Peruvian history occurred in 1948 with the seizure of power by General Manuel Odría, backed by the coastal elite. Odría outlawed APRA and went on to win the 1950 election in which he was the only candidate. He pursued policies of encouraging export earnings and also tried to build up working class support by public works projects in Lima. Faced with a decline in export earnings and the fall in world market prices after 1953, plus increasing unemployment, Odría was forced to stand down in 1956.

In 1962 Haya de la Torre was at last permitted to run for the presidency. But although he won the largest percentage of votes he was prevented from taking office by the armed forces who seized power and organized fresh elections for 1963. In these the military obtained the desired result: Haya de la Torre came second to Fernando Belaúnde Terry. Belaúnde attempted to introduce reforms, particularly in the landholding structure of the sierra; when these reforms were weakened by landowner opposition in Congress, peasant groups began invading landholdings in protest.

At the same time, under the influence of the Cuban revolution, guerrilla groups began operating in the sierra. Military action to deal with this led to the deaths of an estimated 8,000 people. Meanwhile Belaúnde's attempts to solve a long-running dispute with the International Petroleum Company (a subsidiary of Standard Oil) resulted in him being attacked for selling out to the unpopular oil company and contributed to the armed forces' decision to seize power in 1968.

The 1968 coup

This was a major landmark in Peruvian history. Led by General Juan Velasco Alvarado, the Junta had no intention of handing power back to the civilians. A manifesto issued on the day of the coup attacked the 'unjust social and economic order' and argued for its replacement by a new economic system 'neither capitalist nor communist'. Partly as a result of their experiences in dealing with the guerrilla movement, the coup leaders concluded that agrarian reform was a priority.

Wide-ranging land reform was launched in 1969, during which large estates were taken over and reorganized into cooperatives. By the mid-1970s, 75 percent of productive land was under cooperative management. The government also attempted to improve the lives of shanty-town dwellers around Lima, as well as attempting to increase the influence of workers in industrial companies.

At the same time attempts were made to reduce the influence of foreign companies. Soon after the coup, IPC was nationalized, to be followed by other transnationals including ITT, Chase Manhattan Bank and the two mining giants Cerro de Pasco and Marcona Mining. After a dispute with the US government, compensation was agreed.

Understandably, opposition to the Velasco government came from the business and landholding elite. The government's crack-down on expressions of dissent, the seizure of newspapers and taking over of TV and radio stations all offended sections of the urban middle class. Trade unions and peasant movements found that, although they agreed with many of the regime's policies, it refused to listen and expected their passive and unqualified support.

As world sugar and copper prices dropped, inflation rose and strikes increased. Velasco's problems were further increased by opposition within the armed forces and by his own ill-health. In August 1975 he was replaced by General Francisco

Morales Bermúdez, a more conservative officer, who dismantled some of Velasco's policies and led the way to a restoration of civilian rule.

Belaúnde returned to power in 1980 by winning the first elections after military rule. His government was badly affected by the 1982 debt crisis and the 1981-1983 world recession, and inflation reached over 100 percent a year in 1983-1984. His term was also marked by the growth of the Maoist guerrilla movement **Sendero Luminoso** (Shining Path) and the smaller **Túpac Amaru** (MRTA).

Initially conceived in the University of Ayacucho, Shining Path gained most support for its goal of overthrowing the whole system of Lima-based government from highland Indians and migrants to urban shanty towns. The activities of Sendero Luminoso and another guerrilla group, Túpac Amaru (MRTA), frequently disrupted transport and electricity supplies, although their strategies had to be reconsidered after the arrest of both their leaders in 1992. Víctor Polay of MRTA was arrested in June and Abimael Guzmán of Sendero Luminoso was captured in September and sentenced to life imprisonment. Although Sendero did not capitulate, many of its members in 1994-5 took advantage of the Law of Repentance, which guaranteed lighter sentences in return for surrender, and freedom in exchange for valuable information. Meanwhile, Túpac Amaru was thought to have ceased operations (see below).

APRA victory In 1985 APRA, in opposition for over 50 years, finally came to power. With Haya de la Torre dead, the APRA candidate **Alan García Pérez** won the elections and was allowed to take office by the armed forces. García attempted to implement an ambitious economic programme intended to solve many of Peru's deep-seated economic and social problems. He cut taxes, reduced interest rates, froze prices and devalued the currency. However, the economic boom which this produced in 1986-1987 stored up problems as increased incomes were spent on imports. Moreover, the government's refusal to pay more than 10 percent of its foreign debt meant that it was unable to borrow. In 1988 inflation hit 3,000 percent and unemployment soared. By the time his term of office ended in 1990 Peru was bankrupt and García and APRA were discredited.

Peru under Fujimori

In presidential elections held over two rounds in 1990, **Alberto Fujimori** of the Cambio 90 movement defeated the novelist **Mario Vargas Llosa**, who belonged to the Fredemo (Democratic Front) coalition. Fujimori, without an established political network behind him, failed to win a majority in either the senate or the lower house. Lack of congressional support was one of the reasons behind the dissolution of congress and the suspension of the constitution on 5 April 1992.

President Fujimori declared that he needed a freer hand to introduce market reforms and combat terrorism and drug trafficking, at the same time as rooting out corruption. Initial massive popular support, although not matched internationally, did not evaporate.

In elections to a new, 80-member Democratic Constituent Congress (CCD) in November 1992, Fujimori's Cambio 90/Nueva Mayoría coalition won a majority of seats. Earlier that month a coup designed to remove Fujimori by retired military officers was foiled. Though three major political parties, APRA, Acción Popular and the Movimiento de Libertad, boycotted the elections, they satisfied many aid donor's requirements for the resumption of financial assistance.

A new constitution drawn up by the CCD was approved by a narrow majority of the electorate in October 1993. Among the new articles were the immediate re-election of the president (previously prohibited for one presidential term), the death penalty for terrorist leaders, the establishment of a single-chamber congress, the reduction of the role of the state, the designation of Peru as a market economy

Border dispute with Ecuador

After the dissolution in the 1820s of Gran Colombia (largely present-day Venezuela, Colombia and Ecuador), repeated attempts to determine the extent of Ecuador's eastern jungle territory failed. While Ecuador claimed that its territory has been reduced from that of the old Audiencia of Quito by gradual Colombian and especially Peruvian infiltration, Peru has insisted that its Amazonian territory was established in law and in fact before the foundation of Ecuador as an independent state.

The dispute reached an acute phase in 1941 when war broke out between Ecuador and Peru. The war ended with military defeat for Ecuador and the signing of the Rio de Janeiro Protocol of 1942 which allotted most of the disputed territory to Peru. Since 1960 Ecuador has denounced the Protocol as unjust (because it was imposed by force of arms) and as technically flawed (because it refers to certain non-existent geographic features).

According to Peru, the Protocol demarcated the entire boundary and all the features are provable to US aerial photographic maps. Ecuador's official policy remains the recovery of a sovereign access to the Amazon. In Peru's view, the Protocol gives Ecuador navigation rights, but does not and cannot return land that Ecuador never had in the first place.

Sporadic border skirmishes continued throughout recent decades and in January 1995 these escalated into an undeclared war over control of the headwaters of the Río Cenepa. Argentina, Brazil, Chile and the USA (guarantors of the Rio de Janeiro Protocol) intervened diplomatically and a ceasefire took effect after six weeks of combat, during which both sides made conflicting claims of military success.

Finally, on 26 October 1998, Peru and Ecuador signed a peace treaty, ending their 60-year-old dispute.

---

and the favouring of foreign investment. As expected, Fujimori stood for re-election on 9 April 1995 and the opposition chose as an independent to stand against him former UN General Secretary, Javier Pérez de Cuéllar. Fujimori was re-elected by a resounding margin, winning about 65 percent of the votes cast. The coalition that supported him also won a majority in Congress.

The government's success in most economic areas did not appear to accelerate the distribution of foreign funds for social projects. Rising unemployment and the austerity imposed by economic policy continued to cause hardship for many, despite the government's stated aim of alleviating poverty.

Dramatic events on 17 December 1996 thrust several of these issues into sharper focus: 14 Túpac Amaru guerrillas infiltrated a reception at the Japanese Embassy in Lima, taking 490 hostages. Among the rebel's demands were the release of their imprisoned colleagues, better treatment for prisoners and new measures to raise living standards. Most of the hostages were released and negotiations were pursued during a stalemate that lasted until 22 April 1997. The president took sole responsibility for the successful, but risky assault which freed all the hostages (one died of heart failure) and killed all the terrorists. By not yielding to Túpac Amaru, Fujimori regained much popularity.

Embassy siege

But this masked the fact that no concrete steps had been taken to ease social problems. It also deflected attention from Fujimori's plans to stand for a third term following his unpopular manipulation of the law to persuade Congress that the new constitution did not apply to his first period in office. His chances of winning looked remote as demands grew for a more open, democratic approach, though opposition to his standing for a third term of office remained fragmented. Ultimately, his chances hinge on the economy, which looked to be improving until the worst El Niño this century hit Peru in late 1997, causing chaos, many deaths and devasting damage.

Background

Following disastrous effects of El Niño, Fujimori suffered another major crisis in July 1998, in the shape of Shell-Mobil's withdrawal from the multi-million dollar Camisea natural gas project. Signed in May 1996 and cited as the 'contract of the century', the project looked set to pull Peru out of its energy deficit. However, Shell-Mobil had been unable to agree with the government on the pricing of gas in Lima and gas export to Brazil. Fujimori, keen to assuage a public which had only put him at 22 percent in opinion polls, quickly made a statement that another company would be found to take the Camisea project to its second stage.

Fujimori's unpopularity was further driven home by a 4,000 person march through Lima on 16 July. A 1.4 million-name petition was presented to the National Electoral Authority, requesting a referendum on whether Fujimori should be allowed to stand for a third term. In spite of the amendment to the constitution following Fujimori's *auto golpe* in 1993, allowing presidents to run for only two successive terms, the president had, in 1996, pushed through congress a law of 'authentic interpretation' of the constitution, allowing him to run for election once more. The umbrella opposition grouping, Foco Democratico, submitted a draft bill repealing the 'authentic interpretation' law, but the bill was defeated in congress.

Land and environment

Geography

Peru is the third largest South American country, the size of France, Spain and the United Kingdom combined, and presents formidable difficulties to human habitation. Virtually all of the 2,250 kilometres of its Pacific coast is desert. From the narrow coastal shelf the Andes rise steeply to a high plateau dominated by massive ranges of snow-capped peaks and gouged with deep canyons. The heavily forested and deeply ravined Andean slopes are more gradual to the east. Further east, towards Brazil and Colombia, begin the vast jungles of the Amazon basin.

Geology

The geological structure of Peru is dominated by the Nasca Plate beneath the Pacific Ocean, which stretches from Colombia in the north southwards to mid Chile. Along the coastline, this Plate meets and dives below the mass of the South American Plate which has been moving westwards for much of the Earth's geological history. Prior to the middle of the Tertiary Period, say 40 million years ago, marine sediments suggest that the Amazon basin drained west to the Pacific, but from that time to the present, tectonic forces have created the Andes range the whole length of the continent, forming the highest peaks outside the Himalayas. The process continues today as shown by the earthquakes and active volcanoes and, in spite of erosion, the mountains are still growing higher.

Coast

The coastal region, a narrow ribbon of desert 2,250 kilometres long, takes up 11 percent of the country and holds 44 percent of the population. It is the economic heart of Peru, consuming most of the imports and supplying half of the exports. When irrigated, the river valleys are extremely fertile, creating oases which grow cotton throughout the country, sugar-cane and rice in the north, and grapes, fruit and olives in the south. At the same time, the coastal current teems with fish, and Peru has on occasion had the largest catch in the world.

Not far beyond the border with Ecuador in the north, there are mangrove swamps and tropical rainforest, but southwards this quickly changes to drier and eventually desert conditions. South of Piura is the desert of Sechura, followed by the dry barren land or shifting sands to Chimbote. However, several rivers draining the high mountains to the east more or less reach the sea and water the highly productive 'oases' of Piura, Cajamarca and Chimbote.

South of Chimbote, the Andes reach the sea, and apart from a thin strip of coastland north of Lima, the coastal mountains continue to the Chilean border at Arica. This area receives less rain than the Sahara, but because of the high Andes inland, over 50 Peruvian rivers reach the sea, or would do naturally for at least part of the year. As in the north, there are oases in the south, but mostly inland at the foot of the mountains where the river flow is greatest and high sunshine levels ensure good crop production.

The climate of this region depends almost entirely on the ocean currents along

Background

the Pacific coast. Two bodies of water drift northwards, the one closest to the shore, known as the Humboldt Current, is the colder, following the deep sea trench along the edge of the Pacific Plate. The basic wind systems here are the South-East Trades crossing the continent from the Atlantic, but the strong tropical sun over the land draws air into Peru from the Pacific. Being cool, this air does no more than condense into mist (known as the *garúa*) over the coastal mountains. This is sufficient to provide moisture for some unusual flora but virtually never produces rain, hence the desert conditions. The mixing of the two cold ocean currents, and the cloud cover which protects the water from the strongest sunlight, creates the unique conditions favourable to fish, notably sardines and anchovy, giving Peru an enormous economic resource. In turn, the fish support vast numbers of seabirds whose deposits of guano have been another very successful export for the country. This is the normal situation; every few years, however, it is disrupted by the phenomenon known as '*El Niño*' (see page 512).

Highlands   The Highlands, or *la sierra*, extend inland from the coastal strip some 250 kilometres in the north, increasing to 400 kilometres in the south. The average altitude is about 3,000 metres and 50 percent of Peruvians live there. Essentially it is a plateau dissected by dramatic canyons and dominated by some of the most spectacular mountain ranges in the world.

Mountains   The tallest peaks are in the Cordillera Blanca (Huascarán; 6,768 metres) and the neighbouring Cordillera Huayhuash (Yerupajá; 6,634 metres). Huascarán is often quoted as the second highest point in South America after Aconcagua, but this is not so; there are some five other peaks on or near the Argentina-Chile border over 6,770 metres.

The snowline here, at nine degrees south, is between 4,500 metres and 5,000 metres, much lower than further south. For example, at 16° south, permanent snow starts at 6,000 metres on Coropuna (6,425 metres).

The reasons for this anomaly can be traced again to the Humboldt current. The Cordillera Blanca is less than 100 kilometres from the coast, and the cool air drawn in depresses temperatures at high altitudes. Precipitation comes also from the east and falls as snow. Constant high winds and temperatures well below freezing at night create an unusual microclimate and with it spectacular mountain scenery, making it a mecca for snow and ice mountaineers. Dangers are heightened by the quite frequent earthquakes causing avalanches and landslides which have brought heavy loss of life to the valleys of the region. In 1970, 20,000 people lost their lives when Yungay, immediately west of Huascarán, was overwhelmed.

Canyons   Equally dramatic are the deep canyons taking water from the high mountains to the Pacific. The Colca Canyon, about 100 kilometres north of Arequipa, has been measured at 3,200 metres from the lower rim to the river, more than twice as deep as the Grand Canyon. At one point it is overlooked by the 5,227 metres Señal Yajirhua peak, a stupendous 4,150 metres above the water level. Deeper even than Colca is the Cotahuasi Canyon, also in Arequipa Department, whose deepest point is 3,354 metres. Other canyons have been found in this remote area yet to be measured and documented.

In spite of these ups and downs which cause great communications difficulties, the presence of water and a more temperate climate on the plateau has attracted people throughout the ages. Present day important population centres in the Highlands include Cajamarca in the north, Huancayo in central Peru and Cusco in the south, all at around 3,000 metres. Above this, at around 4,000 metres, is the 'high steppe' or *puna*, with constant winds and wide day/night temperature fluctuations. Nevertheless, fruit and potatoes (which originally came from the *puna* of Peru and Bolivia) are grown at this altitude and the meagre grasslands are home to the ubiquitous llama.

Volcanoes

Although hot springs and evidence of ancient volcanic activity can be seen almost anywhere in Peru, the southern part of the *sierra* is the only area where there are active volcanoes. These represent the northernmost of a line of volcanoes which stretch 1,500 kilometres south along the Chile-Bolivia border to Argentina. Sabancaya (5,977 metres), just south of the Colca canyon, is currently active, often with a dark plume downwind from the summit. Beyond the Colca canyon is the Valle de los Volcanes, with 80 cinder cones rising 50-250 metres above a desolate floor of lava and ash. There are other dormant or recently active volcanoes near the western side of Lake Titicaca – for example Ubinas – but the most notable is El Misti (5,822 metres) which overlooks Arequipa. It is perfectly shaped, indicating its status as active in the recent geologic past. Some experts believe it is one of the most potentially dangerous volcanoes in South America. Certainly a major eruption would be a catastrophe for the nearby city.

Lake Titicaca

The southeastern border with Bolivia passes through Titicaca, with about half of the lake in each country. It is the largest lake in South America (ignoring Lake Maracaibo in Venezuela which is linked to the sea) and at 3,812 metres, the highest navigable body of water in the world. It covers about 8,300 square kilometres, running 190 kilometres northwest to southeast, and is 80 kilometres across. It lies in a 60,000 square kilometres basin between the coastal and eastern Andes which spread out southwards to their widest point at latitude 18° south.

The average depth is over 100 metres, with the deepest point recorded at 281 metres. 25 rivers, most from Peru, flow into the lake and a small outlet leaves the lake at Desaguadero on the Bolivia-Peru border. This takes no more than five percent of the inflow, the rest is lost through evaporation and hence the waters of the lake are slightly brackish, producing the *totora* reeds used to make the mats and balsa boats for which the lake dwellers are famed.

The lake is the remnant of a vast area of water formed in the Ice Age known as Lake Ballivián. This extended at least 600 kilometres to the south into Bolivia and included what is now Lake Poopó and the Salar de Uyuni. Now the lake level fluctuates seasonally, normally rising from December to March and receding for the rest of the year but extremes of five metres between high and low levels have been recorded. This can cause problems and high levels in the late 1980s disrupted transport links near the shoreline. The night temperature can fall as low as -25°C but high daytime temperatures ensure that the surface average is about 14°C.

Eastern Andes and Amazon basin

Almost half of Peru is on the eastern side of the Andes and about 90 percent of the country's drainage is into the Amazon system. It is an area of heavy rainfall with cloudforest above 3,500 metres and tropical rainforest lower down. There is little savanna, or natural grasslands, characteristic of other parts of the Amazon basin.

There is some dispute on the Amazon's source. Officially, the mighty river begins as the Marañon, whose longest tributary rises just east of the Cordillera Huayhuash. However, the longest journey for the proverbial raindrop, some 6,400 kilometres, probably starts in southern Peru, where the headwaters of the Apurímac (Ucayali) flow from the snows on the northern side of the Nevado Mismi, near Cailloma.

With much more rainfall on the eastern side of the Andes, rivers are turbulent and erosion dramatic. Although vertical drops are not as great – there is a whole continent to cross to the Atlantic – valleys are deep, ridges narrow and jagged and there is forest below 3,000 metres. At 1,500 metres the Amazon jungle begins and water is the only means of surface transport available, apart from three roads which reach Borja (on the Marañon), Yurimaguas (on the Huallaga) and Pucallpa (on the

El Niño

> Anyone who tuned into a weather forecast during late 1997 now knows about the climatic effect called El Niño, which means "Christ child". El Niño was so named by Peruvian fishermen who noticed the warming of the waters of the eastern Pacific around Christmas time.
>
> Every 3-7 years, for some inexplicable reason, the trade winds that usually blow west from South America subside. So the warm waters of the Pacific – a giant pool the size of Canada – drift eastwards towards South America. The result is worldwide weather chaos.
>
> In 1997 El Niño made its third visit of the decade – one that made everyone sit up and take notice. The eastern Pacific heated faster than at any time in recorded history to become the most devastating climatic event of the century, surpassing
>
> even the 1982-83 El Niño, which killed thousands and caused almost US$14 billion in damage.
>
> The 1997 El Niño caused drought in Australia, New Zealand, Thailand, Malaysia and Papua New Guinea, the forest fires in Indonesia, famine in North Korea, hurricanes along the US Pacific coast and the failure of the fish harvest in Peru (causing the seabird population to fall dramatically). El Niño also sparked epidemics of cholera, encephalitis and bubonic plague.
>
> But despite being implicated in all these weather crimes, scientists appear to know very little about it. The 1997 El Niño was the first major one to have been forecast. It used to arrive every 5-8 years, but recently it's been coming every 3-5 years.

Ucayali), all at about 300 metres above the Atlantic which is still 4,000 kilometres or so downstream. The vastness of the Amazon lowlands becomes apparent and it is here that Peru bulges 650 kilometres northeast past Iquitos to the point where it meets Colombia and Brazil at Leticia. Oil and gas have recently been found in the Amazon, and new finds are made every year, which means that new pipelines and roads will eventually link more places to the Pacific coast.

Climate

Coast On the coast summertime is from December to April, when temperatures range from 25° to 35°C and it is hot and dry. Wintertime is May-November, when the temperature drops a bit and it is cloudy.

The coastal climate is determined by the cold sea-water adjoining deserts. Prevailing inshore winds pick up so little moisture over the cold Humboldt current, which flows from Antarctica, that only from May to November does it condense. The resultant blanket of cloud and sea-mist (called *garúa*) extends from the south to about 200 kilometres north of Lima. The other major factor to affect the coastal climate periodically is *El Niño*, described above.

Sierra From April to October is the dry season. It is hot and dry during the day, around 20°-25°C, and cold and dry at night, often below freezing. From November to April is the wet season, when it is dry and clear most mornings, with some rainfall in the afternoon. There is a small temperature drop (18°C) and not much difference at night (15°C).

Selva April-October is the dry season, with temperatures up to 35°C. In the jungle areas of the south, a cold front can pass through at night. November-April is the wet season. It is humid and hot, with heavy rainfall at any time.

Flora and fauna

Peru is a country of great biological diversity. The fauna and flora are to a large extent determined by the influence of the Andes, the longest uninterrupted mountain chain in the world, and the mighty Amazon river, which has by far the largest volume of any river in the world.

Natural history

This diversity arises not only from the wide range of habitats available, but also from the history of the continent. South America has essentially been an island for some 70 million years joined only by a narrow isthmus to Central and North America. Land passage played a significant role in the gradual colonization of South America by species from the north. When the land-link closed these colonists evolved to a wide variety of forms free from the competitive pressures that prevailed elsewhere. When the land-bridge was re-established some four million years ago a new invasion of species took place from North America, adding to the diversity but also leading to numerous extinctions. Comparative stability has ensued since then and has guaranteed the survival of many primitive groups like the opossums.

Coast

The coastal region of Peru is extremely arid, partly as a result of the cold Humboldt current (see Climate above). The paucity of animal life in the area between the coast and the mountains is obviously due to this lack of rain, though in some areas intermittent *lomas*, which are areas of sparse scrubby vegetation caused by moisture in the sea mist. The plants which survive provide ideal living conditions for insects which attract insectivorous birds and humming birds to feed on their nectar. Cactuses are abundant in northern Peru and provide a wooded landscape of trees and shrubs including the huarango (*Prosopis juliflora*). Also common in the north is the algorrob tree - 250,000 hectares were planted in 1997 to take advantage of the El Niño rains.

Andes

From the desert rise the steep Andean slopes. In the deeply incised valleys Andean fox and deer may occasionally be spotted. Herds of llamas and alpacas graze the steep hillsides. Mountain caracara and Andean lapwing are frequently observed soaring, and there is always the possibility of spotting flocks of mitred parrots or even the biggest species of hummingbird in the world (*Patagonia gigas*).

The Andean zone has many lakes and rivers and countless swamps. Exclusive to this area short-winged grebe and the torrent duck which feeds in the fast flowing rivers, and giant and horned coots. Chilean flamingo frequent the shallow soda lakes.

The *puna*, a habitat characterized by tussock grass and pockets of stunted alpine flowers, gives way to relict elfin forest and tangled bamboo thicket in this inhospitable windswept and frost-prone region. Occasionally the dissected remains of a *Puya* plant can be found; the result of the nocturnal foraging of the rare spectacled bear. There are quite a number of endemic species of rodent including the viscacha, and it is the last stronghold of the chinchilla. Here also pumas roam preying on the herbivores which frequent these mountain – pudu, Andean deer or guemal and the mountain tapir.

Tropical Andes

The elfin forest gradually grades into mist enshrouded cloud forest at about 3,500 metres. In the tropical zones of the Andes, the humidity in the cloud forests stimulates the growth of a vast variety of plants particularly mosses and lichens. The cloud forests are found in a narrow strip that runs along the eastern slopes of the spine of the Andes. It is these dense, often impenetrable, forests clothing the steep slopes that are important in protecting the headwaters of all the streams and

The debonair dolphin

The Amazonian river dolphin is a strange creature indeed. Part myth, part real, this beast can change its skin colour from a pale grey to a bright, luminescent pink.

The indigenous people of the Amazon have passed down stories from generation to generation about this strange animal, which they call the bufeo. They believe that the dolphins live in an underwater city in Lake Caballococha, downriver from Iquitos, near the Peru-Colombia border. Also that, by night, the bufeo can transform itself into a suave gentleman in a white linen suit and prey on unsuspecting local women. Even today, unwanted pregnancies within Indian communities are sometimes blamed on this magical animal with an impressive line in seduction techniques.

These pink river dolphins were, until recently, a forgotten species, considered extinct. All that remained was the skeleton of one in Paris, brought back from South America as a gift to Napoleon, and a few vague scientific papers dating from the 19th century in the Natural History Museum in London. The bufeo was re-discovered by a British expedition in 1956, but then forgotten again. Until 1987, when Jacques Cousteau astounded TV viewers around the world with the first ever pictures of pink dolphins frolicking in the waters of the Amazon.

Now the adventurous traveller can see the bufeo in the flesh – be it grey or pink, or even dressed in a white suit. But women travellers should beware any charming, smartly-dressed gentlemen in these parts.

rivers that cascade from the Andes to form the mighty Amazon as it begins its long journey to the sea.

This is a verdant world of dripping epiphytic mosses, lichens, ferns and orchids which grow in profusion despite the plummeting overnight temperatures. The high humidity resulting from the two metres of rain that can fall in a year is responsible for the maintenance of the forest and it accumulates in puddles and leaks from the ground in a constant trickle that combines to form a myriad of icy, crystal-clear tumbling streams that cascade over precipitous waterfalls.

In secluded areas flame-red Andean Cock-of-the-Rock give their spectacular display to females in the early morning mists. Woolly monkeys are also occasionally sighted as they descend the wooded slopes. Mixed flocks of colourful tanagers are commonly encountered, and the golden-headed quetzal and Amazon umbrella bird are occasionally seen.

Amazon basin At about 1,500 metres there is a gradual transition to the vast lowland forests of the Amazon basin, which are warmer and more equable than the cloud forests clothing the mountains above. The daily temperature varies little during the year with a high of 23-32°C falling slightly to 20-26°C overnight. This lowland region receives some two metres of rainfall per year most of it falling from November to April. The rest of the year is sufficiently dry, at least in the lowland areas to inhibit the growth of epiphytes and orchids which are so characteristic of the highland areas. For a week or two in the rainy season the rivers flood the forest. The zone immediately surrounding this seasonally flooded forest is referred to as *terre firme* forest.

The vast river basin of the Amazon is home to an immense variety of species. The environment has largely dictated the lifestyle. Life in or around rivers, lakes, swamps and forest depend on the ability to swim and climb and amphibious and tree-dwelling animals are common. Once the entire Amazon basin was a great inland sea and the river still contains mammals more typical of the coast, eg manatees and dolphins.

Here in the relatively constant climatic conditions animal and plant life has evolved to an amazing diversity over the millennia. It has been estimated that 3.9 square kilometres of forest can harbour some 1,200 vascular plants, 600 species of tree, and 120 woody plants. Here, in these relatively flat lands, a soaring canopy some 50 metres overhead is the power-house of the forest. It is a habitat choked with strangling vines and philodendrons among which mixed troupes of squirrel monkeys and brown capuchins forage. In the high canopy small groups of spider monkeys perform their lazy aerial acrobatics, whilst lower down, cling to epiphyte-clad trunks and branches, groups of saddle-backed and emperor tamarins forage for blossom, fruit and the occasional insect prey.

The most accessible part of the jungle is on or near the many great meandering rivers. At each bend of the river the forest is undermined by the currents during the seasonal floods at the rate of some 10-20 metres per year leaving a sheer mud and clay bank, whilst on the opposite bend new land is laid down in the form of broad beaches of fine sand and silt.

A succession of vegetation can be seen. The fast growing willow-like *Tessaria* first stabilizes the ground enabling the tall stands of caña brava *Gynerium* to become established. Within these dense almost impenetrable stands the seeds of rainforest trees germinate and over a few years thrust their way towards the light. The fastest growing is a species of *Cercropia* which forms a canopy 15-18 metres over the caña but even this is relatively short-lived. The gap in the canopy is quickly filled by other species. Two types of mahogany outgrow the other trees forming a closed canopy at 40 metres with a lush understory of shade tolerant *Heliconia* and ginger. Eventually even the long-lived trees die off to be replaced by others providing a forest of great diversity.

The meandering course of the river provides many excellent opportunities to see herds of russet-brown capybara – a sheep-sized rodent – peccaries and brocket deer. Of considerable ecological interest are the presence of ox-bow lakes, or *cochas*, since these provide an abundance of wildlife which can easily be seen around the lake margins.

Jungle wildlife

The best way to see the wildlife, however, is to get above the canopy. Ridges provide elevated view points from which you can enjoy excellent views over the forest. From here, it is possible to look across the lowland flood plain to the very foothills of the Andes, possibly some 200 kilometres away. Flocks of parrots and macaws can be seen flying between fruiting trees and noisy troupes of squirrel monkeys and brown capuchins come very close.

The lowland rainforest of Peru is particularly famous for its primates and giant otters. Giant otters were once widespread in Amazonia but came close to extinction in the 1960s owing to persecution by the fur trade. The giant otter population in Peru has since recovered and is now estimated to be at least several hundred. Jaguar and other predators are also much in evidence. Although rarely seen their paw marks are commonly found along the forest trails. Rare bird species are also much in evidence, including fasciated tiger-heron and primitive hoatzins.

The (very) early-morning is the best time to see peccaries, brocket deer and tapir at mineral licks (*collpa*). Macaw and parrot licks are found along the banks of the river. Here at dawn a dazzling display arrives and clambers around in the branches overhanging the clay-lick. At its peak there may be 600 birds of up to six species (including red and green macaws, and blue-headed parrots) clamouring to begin their descent to the riverbank where they jostle for access to the mineral rich clay. A necessary addition to their diet which may also neutralize the toxins present in the leaf and seed diet. Rare game birds such as razor billed curassows and piping guans may also be seen.

A list of over 600 bird species has been compiled. Particularly noteworthy species are the black-faced cotinga, crested eagle, and the spectacular Harpy eagle, perhaps the world's most impressive raptor, easily capable of taking an adult monkey from the canopy. Mixed species flocks are commonly observed containing from 25 to 100+ birds of perhaps more than 30 species including blue dacnis, blue-tailed emerald, bananaquit, thick-billed euphoria and the paradise tanager. Each species occupies a slightly different niche, and since there are few individuals of each species in the flock, competition is avoided. Mixed flocks foraging in the canopy are often led by a white-winged shrike, whereas flocks foraging in the understorey are often led by the bluish-slate antshrike. (For more information on the birds of Peru, see Birdwatching, page 69.)

Culture

People

Peruvian society today is a melting pot of Native Andeans, Afro-Peruvians, Spanish, immigrant Chinese, Japanese, Italians, Germans and, to a lesser extent, indigenous Amazon tribes, who have lived together for so long that many Peruvians can claim to have mixed blood.

The first immigrants were the Spaniards who followed Pizarro's expeditionary force. Their effect, demographically, politically and culturally, has been enormous. They intermarried with the indigenous population and the children of mixed parentage were called *mestizos*. The Peruvian-born children of Spanish parents were known as *criollos*, though this word is now used to describe people who live on the coast, regardless of their ancestry, and coastal culture in general.

Criollos & mestizos

Peru's black community is based on the coast, mainly in Chincha, south of Lima, and also in some working-class districts of the capital. Their forefathers were originally imported into Peru in the 16th century as slaves to work on the sugar and cotton plantations on the coast. Though small – between two and five percent of the total population – the black community has had a major influence on Peruvian culture, particularly in music and dancing (see page 526) and cuisine (see page 56).

Afro-Peruvians

There are two main Asian communities in Peru, the Japanese and Chinese. Large numbers of poor Chinese labourers were brought to Peru in the mid-19th century to work in virtual slavery on the guano reserves on the Pacific coast and to build the railroads in the central Andes. The culinary influence of the Chinese can be seen in the many *chifas* found throughout the country.

Asian immigrants

The Japanese community, now numbering some 100,000, established itself in the first half of the 20th century. The normally reclusive community gained prominence when Alberto Fujimori, one of its members, became the first president of Japanese descent outside Japan anywhere in the world. During Fujimori's presidency, many other Japanese Peruvians have taken prominent positions in business, central and local government. Despite the nickname 'chino', which is applied to anyone of Oriental origin, the Japanese and Japan are respected for their industriousness and honesty.

Like most of Latin America, Peru received many emigrés from Europe seeking land and opportunities in the late 19th century. The country's wealth and political power remains concentrated in the hands of this small and exclusive class of whites, which also consists of the descendants of the first Spanish families. There still exists a deep divide between people of European descent and the old colonial snobbery persists.

Europeans

Peru's indigenous people

Peru has a substantial indigenous population, only smaller as a percentage of the total than Bolivia and Guatemala of the Latin American republics. The literacy rate

Background

👉 *Day of the dead*

One of the most important dates in the indigenous people's calendar is the 2 November, the 'Day of the Dead'. This tradition has been practised since time immemorial. In the Incaic calendar, November was the eighth month and meant Ayamarca, or land of the dead. The celebration of Day of the Dead, or 'All Saints' as it is also known, is just one example of religious adaptation in which the ancient beliefs of ethnic cultures are mixed with the rites of the Catholic Church.

According to ancient belief, the spirit (athun ajayu) visits its relatives at this time of the year and is fed in order to continue its journey before its reincarnation. The relatives of the dead prepare for the arrival of the spirit days in advance. Among the many items necessary for these meticulous preparations are little bread dolls, each one of which has a particular significance. A ladder is needed for the spirit to descend from the other world to the terrestrial one. There are other figures which represent the grandparents, great grandparents and loved ones of the person who has 'passed into a better life'. Horse-shaped breads are prepared that will serve as a means of transport for the soul in order to avoid fatigue.

Inside the home, the relatives construct a tomb supported by boxes over which is laid a black cloth. Here they put the bread, along with sweets, flowers, onions and sugar cane. This latter item is an indispensable part of the table as it symbolizes the invigorating element which prevents the spirit from becoming tired on its journey towards the Earth. The union of the flowers with the onion is called tojoro and is a vital part of the preparations. It ensures that the dead one does not become disoriented and arrives in the correct house.

The tomb is also adorned with the dead relative's favourite food and drink, not forgetting the all-important glass of beer as, according to popular tradition, this is the first nourishment taken by the souls when they arrive at their houses. Once the spirit has arrived and feasted with its living relatives, the entire ceremony is then transported to the graveside in the local cemetery, where it is carried out again, beside the many other mourning families.

This meeting of the living and their dead relatives is re-enacted the following year, though less ostentatiously, and again for the final time in the third year, the year of the farewell. It does not continue after this, which is just as well as the costs can be crippling for the family concerned.

of the indigenous population is the lowest of any comparable group in South America and their diet is 50 percent below acceptable levels. The highland Indians bore the brunt of the conflict between Sendero Luminoso guerrillas and the security forces, which caused thousands of deaths and mass migration from the countryside to provincial cities or to Lima. Many indigenous groups are also under threat from colonization, development and road-building projects. Long after the end of Spanish rule, discrimination, dispossession and exploitation is still a fact of life for many native Peruvians.

Quechua　According to Inca legend, the Quechuas were a small group who originally lived near Lake Titicaca. They later moved to Cusco, from where they expanded to create the Inca Empire. Their language and culture soon spread from Quito in the north through present-day Ecuador, Peru and Bolivia to northern Chile.

Predominantly an agricultural society, growing potatoes and corn as their basic diet, they are largely outside the money economy. Today, there remain two enduring legacies of Inca rule; their magnificent architecture and their unwritten language, Quechua, which has given its name to the descendants of their subjects. About two million Indians speak no Spanish, their main tongue being Quechua, but there are many more descendants of the Quechua who now speak only Spanish. Though recognized as an official language, little effort is made to promote

Quechua nationally. It is only the remoteness of many Quechua speakers which has preserved it in rural areas. This isolation has also helped preserve many of their ancient traditions and beliefs. See also Festivals, on page 529.

High up in the Andes, in the southern part of Peru, lies a wide, barren and hostile **Aymara** plateau, the *altiplano*. Prior to Inca rule Tiahuanaco on Lake Titicaca was a highly-organized centre for one the greatest cultures South America has ever witnessed: the Aymara people. Today, the shores of this lake and the plains that surround it remain the homeland of the Aymara. The majority live in Bolivia, the rest are scattered on the south-western side of Peru and northern Chile. The climate is so harsh on the *altiplano* that, though they are extremely hard-working, their lives are very poor. They speak their own unwritten language, Aymara.

The Aymaras are a deeply religious people whose culture is permeated with the idea of the sacred. They believe that God, the Supreme Being, gives them security in their daily lives and this God of Life manifests him/herself through the deities, such as those of the mountains, the water, the wind, the sun, the moon and the *wa'qas* (sacred places).

As a sign of gratitude, the Aymara give *wax'ta* (offerings), *wilancha* (llama sacrifices) and *ch'alla* (sprinkling alcohol on the ground) to the *achachilas* (the protecting spirits of the family and community), the *Pachamama* (Mother Earth), *Kuntur Mamani* and *Uywiri* (protecting spirits of the home).

The remote mountains of the bleak altiplano are of particular importance for the Aymara. The most sacred places are these high mountains, far from human problems. It is here that the people have built their altars to offer worship, to communicate with their God and ask forgiveness. The community is also held important in the lives of the Aymara. The *achachila* is the great-great grandfather of the family as well as the protector of the community, and as such is God's representative on earth.

The offerings to the sacred mountains take place for the most part in August and are community celebrations. Many different rituals are celebrated: there are those within the family; in the mountains; for the planting and the harvest; rites to ask for rain or to ask for protection against hailstorms and frosts; and ceremonies for Mother Earth.

All such rituals are led by Aymara *Yatiris*, who are male or female priests. The *Yatiri* is a wise person – someone who knows – and the community's spiritual and moral guide. Through a method of divination that involves the reading of coca leaves, they guide individuals in their personal decision-making

Before the arrival of the Europeans, an estimated six million people inhabited the **Amazonian** Amazon basin, comprising more than 2,000 tribes or ethnic-linguistic groups who **peoples** managed to adapt to their surroundings through the domestication of a great variety of animals and plants, and to benefit from the numerous nutritional, curative, narcotic and hallucinogenic properties of thousands of wild plants.

It's not easy to determine the precise origin of these aboriginal people. What is known, however, is that since the beginning of colonial times this population slowly but constantly decreased, mainly because of the effect of western diseases such as influenza and measles. This demographic decline reached dramatic levels during the rubber boom of the late 19th and early 20th centuries, as a result of forced labour and slavery.

Today, at the basin level, the population is calculated at no more than two million inhabitants making up 400 ethnic groups, of which approximately 200-250,000 live in the Peruvian jungle. Within the basin it is possible to distinguish at least three large conglomerates of aboriginal societies: the inhabitants of the *varzea*, or seasonally flooded lands alongside the large rivers (such as the Omagua, Cocama and Shipibo people); the people in the interfluvial zones or firm lands

Andean mysticism

In the 1990s Andean shamanism and mysticism have attracted increasing attention, though they have always played an important part in the lives of indigenous people.

In highland cities, especially, it is common to engage a ritual specialist, called an altomisayoq, to perform a pago, or offering, when laying the foundations of a house or starting a business venture. Ritual objects for use in these ceremonies are sold at specialized stands in the local markets. Another type of ritualist, called a curandero, is summoned when someone is ill.

Some of these healers are experts in the use of dozens of medicinal plants, while others invoke spirit powers to expel illness. Sometimes eggs or guinea pigs are passed over the patient's body, and then cracked, or killed, in order to read the innards and diagnose the illness. Inevitably this field has its share of charlatans, but there are also curanderos who have many attested cures to their credit.

One thing shamans from all the Andean regions have in common is the use of a mesa – a layout of ceremonial power objects – which is thought to attract spirit power and channel it to the shaman. Another feature running through all strains of Andean mysticism, despite the usual presence of Christian elements, is a living connection, via innumerable practices and associations, to Peru's precolombian past.

Those ritualists who seek to communicate with 'the other side' in their ceremonies often use psychoactive plants. These vary according to the region. On the coast, curanderos often take an infusion of the San Pedro cactus, a form of mescaline. The highland shamans invariably chew coca leaf, a much milder psychoactive, but with broader uses. Coca is burned with every offering, and many ritualists cast the leaves to read the fortunes of their clients. These shamans usually invoke the power of the mountain deities in their ceremonies. In the rainforest regions shamans use the powerful psychedelic vine, ayahuasca (vine of the dead – so called because it is believed to transport the user to the spirit world), as they have for millennia.

(such as the Amahuaca, Cashibo and Yaminahua) and those living in the Andean foothills (such as the Amuesha, Ashaninka and Matsigenka).

The Amazonian natives began to be decimated in the 16th century, and so were the first endangered species of the jungle. These communities still face threats to their traditional lifestyles, notably from timber companies, gold miners and multinational oil giants. There appears to be little effective control of deforestation and the intrusion of colonists who have taken over native lands to establish small farms. And though oil companies have reached compensation agreements with local communities, previous oil exploration has contaminated many jungle rivers, as well as exposing natives to risk from diseases against which they have no immunity.

Religion

The Inca religion (described on page 500) was displaced by Roman Catholicism from the 16th century onwards, the conversion of the inhabitants of the 'New World' to Christianity being one of the stated aims of the Spanish conquistadores. Today, official statistics state that 92.5 percent of the population declares itself Catholic.

One of the first exponents of Liberation Theology, under which the Conference of Latin American Bishops in 1968 committed themselves to the 'option for the poor', was Gustavo Gutiérrez, from Huánuco. This doctrine caused much consternation to orthodox Catholics, particularly those members of the Latin American church who had traditionally aligned themselves with the oligarchy. Gutiérrez, however, traced the church's duty to the voiceless and the marginalized

Is there a Witchdoctor in the house?

Forget courses of antibiotics or the psychiatrists' couch, many Peruvians prefer to employ the services of a curandero, or curer, a person skilled in the use of herbs and potions to heal bodily ailments and fend off those potentially troublesome evil spirits. Such curers performed similar functions in Moche times and methods have remained virtually unchanged since then.

The place where it all takes place bears little resemblance to your average doctor's surgery. Take the human skull sitting proudly centre stage. Human skulls are ever-present at these consultations as participants believe the spirit of the skull will protect them, as well as the curer, from sorcery or even from the evil spells of rival curers.

The session usually starts just before midnight and lasts most of the night. It all happens in total darkness. In order to get around this slight inconvenience, the curer, in his one concession to modern technology, will use a flashlight to identify the various potions, herbs and charms that cover his table. Potions are often made out of perfume mixed with such items as lime juice, sugar and holy water. They also use a hallucinogenic brew made from the San Pedro cactus.

As this ancient practice proceeds into the night the Maestro (curer) will even take a sword and fence with harmful spirits to keep them away from the sufferer. How many doctors would be prepared to do that on behalf of their patients these days?

back to Fray Bartolomé de las Casas (see The Peru Reader, pages 293-96; reference under Further reading, page 83).

The Catholic Church faced a further challenge to its authority when President Fujimori won the battle over family planning and the need to slow down the rate of population growth. Its greatest threat, however, comes from the proliferation of evangelical Protestant groups throughout the country. 5.5 percent of the population now declare themselves Protestant and one million or more people belong to some 27 different non-Catholic denominations.

Although the vast majority of the population ostensibly belongs to the Roman Catholic religion, in reality religious life for many Peruvians is a mix of Catholic beliefs imported from Europe and indigenous traditions based on animism, the worship of deities from the natural world such as mountains, animals and plants. Some of these ancient indigenous traditions and beliefs are described throughout this section.

Arts and crafts

Peru is exceptionally rich in handicrafts. Its geographic division into four distinct regions – coast, mountains, valleys and Amazon basin – coupled with cultural differences, has resulted in numerous variations in technique and design. Each province, even each community, has developed its own style of weaving or carving.

The Incas inherited 3,000 years of skills and traditions: gold, metal and precious stonework from the Chimu; feather textiles from the Nasca; and the elaborate textiles of the Paracas. All of these played important roles in political, social and religious ceremonies. Though much of this artistic heritage was destroyed by the Spanish conquest, the traditions adapted and evolved in numerous ways, absorbing new methods, concepts and materials from Europe while maintaining ancient techniques and symbols.

Woven cloth was the most highly-prized possession and sought after trading commodity in the Andes in precolumbian times. It is, therefore, not surprising that ancient weaving traditions have survived.

Textiles & costumes

A belt for every occasion

The belt plays a particularly important role in the lives of the indigenous peoples. The Incas developed a range of belts, or chumpis, of ritual and spiritual significance which are still used today.

Chumpis are believed to have protective and purifying qualities. In the Cusco area, some communities place chumpis on sacred mountain tops, or apus, in order to communicate with the gods. Traditionally women give birth lying on a chumpi and the baby is wrapped in a softer version, known as a walt'ana, which ensures he or she will grow up properly. From adolescence, women wear a chumpi under their skirt to encourage a lover or deter an unwanted suitor. It is even common practice for the bridegroom to lasso his bride with one. And the age-old tradition of burying the dead with the family chumpi is still occasionally observed.

In the ninth century BC camelid fibre was introduced into weaving on the south coast. This allowed the development of the textiles of the Paracas culture which consist of intricate patterns of animalistic, supernatural and human forms embroidered onto dark backgrounds. The culture of the Chancay valleys cultivated cotton for white and beige dyed patterned cloth in preference to the camelid fibres used by the Paracas and Nasca cultures.

The Incas inherited this rich weaving tradition. They forced the Aymaras to work in *mitas* or textile workshops. The ruins of some enormous *mitas* can be seen at the temple of Raqchi, south of Cusco (see page 195). Inca textiles are of high quality and very different from coastal textiles, being warp-faced, closely woven and without embroidery. The largest quantities of the finest textiles were made specifically to be burned as ritual offerings – a tradition which still survives. The Spanish, too, exploited this wealth and skill by using the *mitas* and exporting the cloth to Europe.

Prior to Inca rule Aymara men wore a tunic (*llahua*) and a mantle (*llacata*) and carried a bag for coca leaves (*huallquepo*). The women wore a wrapped dress (*urku*) and mantle (*iscayo*) and a belt (*huaka*); their coca bag was called an *istalla*. The *urku* was fastened at shoulder level with a pair of metal *tupu*, the traditional Andean dress-pins.

The Inca men had tunics (*unkus*) and a bag for coca leaves called a *ch'uspa*. The women wore a blouse (*huguna*), skirts (*aksu*) and belts (*chumpis*), and carried foodstuffs in large, rectangular cloths called *llicllas*, which were fastened at the chest with a single pin or a smaller clasp called a *ttipqui*. Women of the Sacred Valley now wear a layered, gathered skirt called a *pollera* and a *montera*, a large, round, red Spanish type of hat.

Textiles continue to play an important part in society. They are still used specifically for ritual ceremonies and some even held to possess magical powers. One of the most enduring of these traditions is found among the Aymara people of Taquile island on Lake Titicaca.

Textile materials & techniques The Andean people used mainly alpaca or llama wool. The former can be spun into fine, shining yarn when woven and has a lustre similar to that of silk, though sheep's wool came to be widely used following the Spanish conquest.

A commonly used technique is the drop spindle. A stick is weighted with a wooden wheel and the raw material is fed through one hand. A sudden twist and drop in the spindle spins the yarn. This very sensitive art can be seen practised by women while herding animals in the fields.

Spinning wheels were introduced by Europeans and are now prevalent owing to increased demand. In Ayacucho and San Pedro de Cajas, centres of the cottage textile industry, the wheel is the most common form of spinning. Precolumbian looms were often portable and those in use today are generally similar. A woman will herd her animals while making a piece of costume, perhaps on a backstrap loom, or waist loom, so-called because the weaver controls the tension on one side with her waist with the other side tied to an upright or tree. The precolumbian looms are usually used for personal costume while the treadle loom is used by men for more commercial pieces.

Spanish overseer and an indigenous weaver, from a 16th century chronicle by Felipe Guaman Poma de Ayala

Dyeing The skills of dyeing were still practised virtually unchanged even after the arrival of the Spanish. Nowadays, the word *makhnu* refers to any natural dye, but originally was the name for cochineal, an insect which lives on the leaves of the nopal cactus. These dyes were used widely by precolumbian weavers. Today, the biggest centre of production in South America is the valleys around Ayacucho. Vegetable dyes are also used, made from the leaves, fruit and seeds of shrubs and flowers and from lichen, tree bark and roots.

Symbolism

Symbolism plays an important role in weaving. Traditionally every piece of textile from a particular community had identical symbols and colours which were a source of identity as well as carrying specific symbols and telling a story. One example is on the island of Taquile where the *Inti* (sun) and *Chaska* (Venus) symbols are employed as well as motifs such as fish and birds, unique to the island.

Animal figures dominated the motifs of the Chavín culture and were commonly used in Paracas textiles. Specimens of cotton and wool embroidery found in Paracas graves often show a puma as a central motif. Today, this and other precolumbian motifs are found on many rugs and wall-hangings from the Ayacucho region. Other symbols include Spanish figures such as horses and scenes depicting the execution of Túpac Amaru.

Pottery

The most spectacular archaeological finds in South America have been made in Peru. The Nasca culture (100 BC-AD 900) excelled in polychrome painting of vessels with motifs of supernatural beings, often with strong feline characteristics, as well as birds, fish and animals. Many of the Nasca ceramic motifs are similar to those found in Paracas textiles.

Moche or Mochica vessels combined modelling and painting to depict details of Moche daily life. Human forms are modelled on stirrup spout vessels with such precision that they suggest personal portraits. The Moche also excelled in intricate linear painting often using brown on a cream base. (For a fuller description, see page 344.)

Inca ceramic decoration consists mainly of small-scale geometric and usually symmetrical designs. One distinctive form of vessel which continues to be made and used is the *arybola*. This pot is designed to carry liquid, especially chicha, and is secured with a rope on the bearer's back. It is believed that *arybolas* were used mainly by the governing Inca élite and became important status symbols. Today, Inca-style is very popular in Cusco and Pisac.

With the Spanish invasion many indigenous communities lost their artistic traditions, others remained relatively untouched, while others still combined Hispanic and indigenous traditions and techniques. The Spanish brought three innovations: the potter's wheel, which gave greater speed and uniformity; knowledge of the enclosed kiln; and the technique of lead glazes. The enclosed kiln made temperature regulation easier and allowed higher temperatures to be maintained, producing stronger pieces. Today, many communities continue to apply prehispanic techniques, while others use more modern processes.

Jewellery & Some of the earliest goldwork originates from the Chavín culture – eg the *Tumi*
metalwork knife found in Lambayeque. These first appeared in the Moche culture, when they were associated with human sacrifice. Five centuries later, the Incas used *Tumis* for surgical operations such as trepanning skulls. Today, they are a common motif.

The Incas associated gold with the Sun. However, very few examples remain as the Spanish melted down their amassed gold and silver objects. They then went on to send millions of Indians to their deaths in gold and silver mines.

During the colonial period gold and silver pieces were made to decorate the altars of churches and houses of the élite. Metalworkers came from Spain and Italy to develop the industry. The Spanish preferred silver and strongly influenced the evolution of silverwork during the colonial period. A style known as Andean baroque developed around Cusco embracing both indigenous and European elements. Silver bowls in this style – *cochas* – are still used in Andean ceremonies.

False filigree   This was practised by some pre-Hispanic cultures. The effect of filigree was obtained with the use of droplets or beads of gold. True filigree work developed in the colonial period. Today, there are a number of centres. Originally popular in Ayacucho, the tradition continues in the small community of San Jerónimo de Tunan, near Huancayo. Here, silversmiths produce intricate filigree earrings, spoons and jewellery boxes among other things. Catacaos near Piura also has a long tradition of filigree work in silver and gold.

Seeds, flowers and feathers   These continue to be used as jewellery by many Amazonian peoples. Prehispanic cultures also favoured particular natural materials;

The traditional arybola and plate used by the Incas to carry chicha (fermented corn beer)

From Pagan ritual to folk art

Retablos – or St Mark's boxes, as they were originally known – were introduced to Latin America by the Spanish in the 16th century. These simple, portable altars containing religious images were intended to aid in the task of converting the native population to Catholicism. Early examples often contained images of St James, patron saint of the Spanish army.

The retablos were made from a variety of materials and two distinct styles evolved to suit different needs. Those of clay, leather and plaster were destined for the native rural population, while those for use by the colonial hierarchy were made of gold and silver, or the famous alabaster of Ayacucho, known as Huamanga stone.

Traditional retablos had two floors inside a box. On the top floor were the patron saints of animals: St Mark, patron saint of bulls; St Agnes, patron saint of goats; and St Anthony, patron saint of mules, among others. On the lower floor was a scene of a cattle thief being reprimanded by a landowner.

From the 17th century onwards, the native rural population used the retablo in ceremonies accompanying cattle branding. During August, a ritual believed to have its roots in pagan fertility festivals took place in which the retablo was placed on a table and surrounded by offerings of food and coca leaves. People danced round and sang in front of the box, asking for protection for their animals and celebrating their well-being.

In the 1940s the first retablo reached Lima, by which time the art of making them had virtually disappeared. However, with the new-found outside interest a revival began. The traditional elements began to be varied and the magical or ritualistic value was lost as they became a manifestation of folk art. The artist Joaquín López and his family created the early examples, but today they are made in many workshops.

The figures are made from a mixture of plaster and mashed potato, modelled or made in moulds, sealed with glue, then painted and positioned inside the brightly painted box. Some miniature versions are made in chiclet boxes or egg shells, while, at the other end of the scale, some have 5 floors and take months to complete.

---

eg the sea shell spondylus was highly revered by the Chavín and Moche. It was found only along part of the Ecuadorean coast and must have been acquired through trade. The western fashion for natural or ethnic jewellery has encouraged production, using brightly-coloured feathers, fish bones, seeds or animal teeth.

Woodcarving

Wood is one of the most commonly used materials. Carved ceremonial objects include drums, carved sticks with healing properties, masks and the Incas' keros – wooden vessels for drinking chicha. Keros come in all shapes and sizes and were traditionally decorated with scenes of war, local dances, or harvesting coca leaves. The Chancay, who lived along the coast between 100 BC and AD 1200, used keros carved with sea birds and fish. Today, they are used in some Andean ceremonies, especially during Fiesta del Cruz, the Andean May festival.

Glass mirrors were introduced by the Spanish, although the Chimú and Lambayeque cultures used obsidian and silver plates, and Inca chasquis (messengers) used reflective stones to communicate between hilltop forts. Transporting mirrors was costly, therefore they were produced in Lima and Quito. Cusco and Cajamarca then became centres of production.

In Cusco the frames were carved, covered in gold leaf and decorated with tiny pieces of cut mirror. Cajamarca artisans, meanwhile, incorporated painted glass into the frames.

Gourd-carving

Gourd-carving, or máte burilado, as it is known, is one of Peru's most popular and traditional handicrafts. It is thought even to predate pottery – engraved gourds

A growing tradition

One of Peru's most popular and traditional handicrafts is gourd carving, or *máte burilado*. During the colonial period gourd carving decreased dramatically but limited carving continued and new European styles were developed. After independence a new style developed which incorporated traditional and narrative scenes. This made gourds more commonplace as objects and more meaningful to more people since the motifs had relevance to their own lives.

The gourds come from a creeping plant, Lagenria Vulgaris, which grows only in warm, dry regions, such as the coastal valleys. The decoration is produced by a combination of carving and burning. The outlines are carved freehand by skilled craftspeople and a red-hot stick is used to burn and blacken areas of the surface. It is a slow, laborious process and some carvers can take as long as 6 months to finish a large, finely-carved gourd.

Today, carving is centred around the small communities of Cochas Grande and Chico, near Huancayo, having spread there from the earlier centres of Huanta and Mayoc in Ayacucho. The carvers now sell their art in Huancayo as well as Lima, from where it is exported.

Máte burilado

found on the coast have been dated to some 3,500 years ago. During the Inca empire gourd-carving became a valued art form and workshops were set up and supported by the state.

Gourds were used in rituals and ceremonies and to make *poporos* – containers for the lime used while chewing coca leaves. Today, gourd-carving is centred around the small communities of Cochas Grande and Chico, near Huancayo.

The information on arts and crafts in this Handbook has been adapted from *Arts and Crafts of South America*, by Lucy Davies and Mo Fini, published by Tumi, 1994. Tumi, the Latin American Craft Centre, specializes in Andean and Mexican products and produces cultural and educational videos for schools: at 8/9 New Bond St Place, Bath BA1 1BH, T01225-462367, F01225-444870, 23/2A Chalk Farm Rd, London NW1 8AG, F0171-4854152; Little Clarendon St, Oxford OX1 2HJ, T/F01865-512307; 82 Park St, Bristol BS1 5LA, T/F0117-9290391. Tumi (Music) Ltd specializes in different rhythms of Latin America.

Music and dance

The music of Peru can be described as the very heartbeat of the country. Peruvians see music as something in which to participate, and not as a spectacle. Just about everyone, it seems, can play a musical instrument or sing. Just as music is the heartbeat of the country, so dance conveys the rich and ancient heritage that typifies much of the national spirit. Peruvians are tireless dancers and dancing is the most popular form of entertainment. Unsuspecting travellers should note that once they make that first wavering step there will be no respite until they collapse from exhaustion.

Each region has its own distinctive music and dance that reflects its particular lifestyle, its mood and its physical surroundings. The music of the sierra, for example, is played in a minor key and tends to be sad and mournful, while the music of the lowlands is more up-tempo and generally happier. Peruvian music divides at a very basic level into that of the highlands ('Andina') and that of the coast ('Criolla').

When people talk of Peruvian music they are almost certainly referring to the music of the Quechua- and Aymara-speaking Indians of the highlands which provides the most distinctive Peruvian sound. The highlands themselves can be very roughly subdivided into some half dozen major musical regions, of which perhaps the most characteristic are Ancash and the north, the Mantaro Valley, Cusco, Puno and the Altiplano, Ayacucho and Parinacochas.

Highlands

Musical instruments Before the arrival of the Spanish in Latin America, the only instruments were wind and percussion. Although it is a popular misconception that Andean music is based on the panpipes, guitar and *charango*, anyone who travels through the Andes will realize that these instruments only represent a small aspect of Andean music. The highland instrumentation varies from region to region, although the harp and violin are ubiquitous. In the Mantaro area the harp is backed by brass and wind instruments, notably the clarinet. In Cusco it is the *charango* and *quena* and on the Altiplano the *sicu* panpipes.

The *Quena* is a flute, usually made of reed, characterized by not having a mouthpiece to blow through. As with all Andean instruments, there is a family of *quenas* varying in length from around 15 centimetres to 50 centimetres. The *sicu* is the Aymara name for the *zampoña*, or panpipes. It is the most important prehispanic Andean instrument, formed by several reed tubes of different sizes held together by knotted string. Virtually the only instrument of European origin is the *Charango*. When stringed instruments were first introduced by the Spanish, the indigenous people liked them but wanted something that was their own and so the *charango* was born. Originally, they were made of clay, condor skeletons and armadillo or tortoise shells.

Highland dances The highlands are immensely rich in terms of music and dance, with over 200 dances recorded. Every village has its fiestas and every fiesta has its communal and religious dances.

Comparsas are organized groups of dancers who perform for spectators dances following a set pattern of movements to a particular musical accompaniment, wearing a specific costume. These dances have a long tradition, having mostly originated from certain contexts and circumstances and some of them still parody the ex-Spanish colonial masters.

One of the most notable is the comical *Auqui Auqui* (auqui is Aymara for old man). The dance satirizes the solemnity and pomposity of Spanish gentlemen from the colonial period. Because of their dignified dress and manners they could appear old, and a humped back is added to the dancers to emphasize age. These little old men have long pointed noses, flowing beards and carry crooked walking sticks. They dance stooped, regularly pausing to complain and rub aching backs, at times even stumbling and falling.

Many dances for couples and/or groups are danced spontaneously at fiestas throughout Peru. These include indigenous dances which have originated in a specific region and ballroom dances that reflect the Spanish influence.

One of the most popular of the indigenous dances is the **Huayno**, which originated on the Altiplano but is now danced throughout the country. It involves numerous couples, who whirl around or advance down the street, arm-in-arm, in a 'Pandilla'. During fiestas, and especially after a few drinks, this can develop into a kind of uncontrolled frenzy.

Two of the most spectacular dances to be seen are the **Baile de las Tijeras** ('scissor dance') from the Ayacucho/Huancavelica area, for men only and the pounding, stamping **Huaylas** for both sexes. Huaylas competitions are held annually in Lima and should not be missed. Also very popular among Indians and/or Mestizos are the Marinera, Carnaval, Pasacalle, Chuscada (from Ancash), Huaylas, Santiago and Chonguinada (all from the Mantaro) and Huayllacha (from Parinacochas).

Urban and other styles Owing to the overwhelming migration of peasants into the barrios of Lima, most types of Andean music and dance can be seen in the capital, notably on Sundays at the so-called 'Coliseos', which exist for that purpose. This flood of migration to the cities has also meant that the distinct styles of regional and ethnic groups have become blurred. One example is **Chicha music**, which comes from the *pueblos jóvenes*, and was once the favourite dance music of Peru's urban working class. Chicha is a hybrid of Huayno music and the Colombian Cumbia rhythm – a meeting of the highlands and the tropical coast.

For singing only are the mestizo *Muliza*, popular in the Central Region, and the soulful lament of the *Yaraví*, originally Indian, but taken up and developed early in the 19th century by the poet and hero of independence Mariano Melgar, from Arequipa (see page 530).

Coast **Música Criolla**, the music from the coast, could not be more different from that of the Sierra. Here the roots are Spanish and African. The immensely popular **Valsesito** is a syncopated waltz that would certainly be looked at askance in Vienna and the **Polca** has also undergone an attractive sea change.

Reigning over all, though, is the **Marinera**, Peru's national dance, a splendidly rhythmic and graceful courting encounter and a close cousin of Chile's and Bolivia's Cueca and the Argentine Zamba, all of them descended from the Zamacueca. The Marinera has its 'Limeña' and 'Norteña' versions and a more syncopated relative, the Tondero, found in the northern coastal regions, is said to have been influenced by slaves brought from Madagascar.

All these dances are accompanied by guitars and frequently the *cajón*, a resonant wooden box on which the player sits, pounding it with his hands. Some of the great names of 'Música Criolla' are the singer/composers Chabuca Granda and Alicia Maguiña, the female singer Jesús Vásquez and the groups Los Morochucos and Hermanos Zañartu.

Afro-Peruvian Also on the coast is the music of the small but influential black community, the 'Música Negroide' or 'Afro-Peruano', which had virtually died out when it was resuscitated in the 1950s, but has since gone from strength to strength, thanks to Nicomedes and Victoria Santa Cruz who have been largely responsible for popularizing this black music and making it an essential ingredient in contemporary Peruvian popular music. It has all the qualities to be found in black music from the Caribbean – a powerful, charismatic beat, rhythmic and lively dancing, and strong percussion provided by the *cajón* and the *quijada de burro*, a donkey's jaw with the teeth loosened.

Its greatest star is the Afro-Peruvian diva Susana Baca. Her incredible, passionate voice inspired Talking Head's David Byrne to explore this genre further and release a compilation album in 1995, thus bringing Afro-Peruvian music to the attention of the world. Another notable exponent is the excellent Peru Negro, one of the best music and dance groups in Latin America.

Some of the classic dances in the black repertoire are the Festejo, Son del Diablo, Toro Mata, Landó and Alcatraz. In the last named one of the partners dances behind the other with a candle, trying to set light to a piece of paper tucked into the rear of the other partner's waist.

Background

Festivals

Fiestas (festivals) are a fundamental part of life for most Peruvians, taking place up and down the length and breadth of the country and with such frequency that it would be hard to miss one, even during the briefest of stays. This is fortunate, because arriving in any town or village during these inevitably frenetic celebrations is one of the great Peruvian experiences.

While Peru's festivals can't rival those of Brazil for fame or colour, the quantity of alcohol consumed and the partying run them pretty close. What this means is that, at some point, you will fall over, through inebriation or exhaustion, or both. After several days of this, you will awake with a hangover the size of the Amazon rainforest and probably have no recollection of what you did with your backpack.

Peruvian festivals also involve widespread fighting with balloons filled with water, bags of flour and any other missile guaranteed to cause a mess. In the Amazon region various petroleum by-products are favoured ingredients, which can be bad news for smokers. Some travellers complain that they are being picked on, but to someone from the Altiplano, a six-foot tall, blond-haired gringo makes an easier target. So, don't wear your best clothes, arm yourself with plenty water bombs, get into the spirit and have some fun!

There are too many festivals to mention them all. The main national ones are described in Holidays and festivals, on page 72, and details of local *fiestas* are given under the listings for each town.

Among the most notable celebrations are Carnival week in Cajamarca – a raucous and messy affair, even by Peruvian standards – and the fiesta of the Virgen de la Candelaria, which takes place in the first week in February along the shores of Lake Titicaca near the Bolivian border and features dance groups from all around the region. The most famous Holy Week is held in Ayacucho, when many thousands of fervent devotees participate in daily processions. On the coast, the Spring festival in Trujillo in September is an opportunity to see the Marinera dancers, while in the black communities of Chincha, south of Lima, you can enjoy the best of Afro-Peruvian music and dance (see Music and dance above).

It is only when they don their extravagant costumes and masks and drink, eat and dance to excess that the Peruvian Indians show their true character. The rest of the time they hide behind a metaphorical mask of stony indifference as a form of protection against the alien reality in which they are forced to live. When they consume alcohol and coca and start dancing, the pride in their origins resurfaces. The incessant drinking and dancing allows them to forget the reality of poverty, unemployment and oppression and reaffirms their will to live as well as their unity with the world around them.

Meaning of fiestas

The object of the fiesta is a practical one, such as the success of the coming harvest or the fertility of animals. Thus the constant eating, drinking and dancing serves the purpose of giving thanks for the sun and rain that makes things grow and for the fertility of the soil and livestock, gifts from Pachamama, or Mother Earth, the most sacred of all gods. So, when you see the Aymara spill a little *chicha* (maize beer) every time they refill, it's not because they're sloppy but because they're offering a *ch'alla* (sacrifice) to Pachamama.

The participants in the dances that are the central part of the fiesta are dressed in garish, outlandish costumes and elaborate masks, each one depicting a character from popular myth. Some of these originate in the colonial period, others survive from the Inca Empire or even further back. Often the costumes caricature the Spanish. In this way, the indigenous people mock those who erased their heritage.

Background

Literature

Quechua The fact that the Incas had no written texts in the conventional European sense and that the Spaniards were keen to suppress their conquest's culture means that there is little evidence today of what poetry and theatre was performed in pre-conquest times. It is known that the Incas had two types of poet, the *amautas*, historians, poets and teachers who composed works that celebrated the ruling class' gods, heroes and events, and *haravecs*, who expressed popular sentiments. There is strong evidence also that drama was important in Inca society.

Written Quechua even today is far less common than works in the oral tradition. Although Spanish culture has had some influence on Quechua, the native stories, lyrics and fables retain their own identity. Not until the 19th century did Peruvian writers begin seriously to incorporate indigenous ideas into their art, but their audience was limited. Nevertheless, the influence of Quechua on Peruvian literature in Spanish continues to grow.

Colonial Period In 16th-century Lima, headquarters of the Viceroyalty of Peru, the Spanish officials concentrated their efforts on the religious education of the new territories and literary output was limited to mainly histories and letters.

Chroniclers such as Pedro Cieza de León (*Crónica del Perú*, published from 1553) and Agustín de Zárate (*Historia del descubrimiento y conquista del Perú*, 1555) were written from the point of view that Spanish domination was right. Their most renowned successors, though, took a different stance. Inca Garcilaso de la Vega was a mestizo, whose *Comentarios reales que tratan del origen de los Incas* (1609) were at pains to justify the achievements, religion and culture of the Inca Empire. He also commented on Spanish society in the colony. A later work, *Historia general del Perú* (1617) went further in condemning Viceroy Toledo's suppression of Inca culture. Through his work, written in Spain, many aspects of Inca society, plus poems and prayers have survived.

Writing at about the same time as Inca Garcilaso was Felipe Guaman Poma de Ayala, whose *El primer nueva corónica y buen gobierno* (1613-15) is possibly one of the most reproduced of Latin American texts (eg on T-shirts, CDs, posters and carrier bags). Guaman Poma was a minor provincial Inca chief whose writings and illustrations, addressed to King Felipe III of Spain, offer a view of a stable pre-conquest Andean society (not uniquely Inca), in contrast with the unsympathetic colonial society that usurped it.

In the years up to Independence, the growth of an intellectual elite in Lima spawned more poetry than anything else. As criollo discontent grew, satire increased both in poetry and in the sketches which accompanied dramas imported from Spain. The poet Mariano Melgar (1791-1815) wrote in a variety of styles, including the *yaraví*, the love-song derived from the precolumbian *harawi* (from *haravek*). Melgar died in an uprising against the Spanish but played an important part in the Peruvian struggle from freedom from the colonial imagination.

After Independence After Independence, Peruvian writers imitated Spanish *costumbrismo*, sketches of characters and life-styles from the new Republic. The first author to transcend this fashion was Ricardo Palma (1833-1919), whose inspiration, the *tradición*, fused *costumbrismo* and Peru's rich oral traditions. Palma's hugely popular *Tradiciones peruanas* is a collection of pieces which celebrate the people, history and customs of Peru through sayings, small incidents in mainly colonial history and gentle irony.

Much soul-searching was to follow Peru's defeat in the War of the Pacific. Manuel González Prada (1844-1918), for instance, wrote essays fiercely critical of the state of

Mario Vargas Llosa

The best known of Peru's writers is Vargas Llosa, born in 1936 in Arequipa and educated in Cochabamba (Bolivia), from where his family moved to Piura. After graduating from the Universidad de San Marcos, he won a scholarship to Paris in 1958 and, from 1959 to 1974, lived first in Paris then in London in voluntary exile. Much has been written about his personal life, and his political opinions have been well documented, but, as befits an author of the highest international standing and one of the leading figures in the so-called 'Boom' of Latin American writers in the 1960s, it is for his novels that Vargas Llosa the writer is best known.

The first three – La ciudad y los perros (1963), La casa verde (1966) and Conversación en la Catedral (1969) – with their techniques of flashback, multiple narrators and different interwoven stories, are an adventure for the reader. Meanwhile, the humorous books, like Pantaleón and La tía Julia cannot be called lightweight. La guerra del fin del mundo marked a change to a more direct style and an intensification of Vargas Llosa's exploration of the role of fiction as a human necessity, extending also to political ideologies.

Vargas Llosa has always maintained that in Peruvian society the writer is a privileged person who should be able to mix politics and literature as a normal part of life. This drive for authenticity led to his excursion into national politics. He stood as a presidential candidate in 1990, losing to Alberto Fujimori. He has since taken up Spanish citizenship and now lives in Spain.

the nation: *Páginas libres* (1894), *Horas de lucha* (1908). José Carlos Mariátegui, the foremost Peruvian political thinker of the early 20th century, said that González Prada represented the first lucid instant of Peruvian consciousness. He also wrote poetry, some Romantic, some, like his *Baladas peruanas*, an evocation of indigenous and colonial history, very pro-Indian, very anti-White.

Mariátegui himself (1895-1930), after a visit to Europe in 1919, considered deeply the question of Peruvian identity. His opinion was that it could only be seen in a global context and that the answer lay in Marxism. With this perspective he wrote about politics, economics, literature and the Indian question (see *Siete ensayos de interpretación de la realidad peruana*, 1928).

20th century

Other writers had continued this theme. For instance Clorinda Matto de Turner (1854-1909) intended to express in *Aves sin nido* (1889) her "tender love for the indigenous people" and hoped to improve their lot. Regardless of the debate over whether the novel achieves these aims, she was the forerunner by several years of the 'indigenist' genre in Peru and the most popular of those who took up González Prada's cause.

Other prose writers continued in this vein at the beginning of the 20th century, but it was Ciro Alegría (1909-67) who gave major, fictional impetus to the racial question. Like Mariátegui, Alegría was politically committed, but to the APRA party, rather than Marxism. Of his first three novels, *La serpiente de oro* (1935), *Los perros hambrientos* (1938) and *El mundo es ancho y ajeno* (1941), the latter is his most famous.

Contemporary with Alegría was José María Arguedas (1911-1969), whose novels, stories and politics were also deeply-rooted in the ethnic question. Arguedas, though not Indian, had a largely Quechua upbringing and tried to reconcile this with the hispanic world in which he worked. This inner conflict was one of the main causes of his suicide. His books include *Agua* (short stories – 1935), *Yawar fiesta* (1941), *Los ríos profundos* (1958) and *Todas las sangres* (1964). They portray different aspects of the confrontation of Indian society with the changing outside world that impinges on it.

In the 1950s and 1960s, there was a move away from the predominantly rural and indigenist to an urban setting. At the forefront were, among others, Mario Vargas Llosa, Julio Ramón Ribeyro, Enrique Congrains Martín, Oswaldo Reynoso, Luis Loayza, Sebastián Salazar Bondy and Carlos E Zavaleta. Taking their cue from a phrase used by both poet César Mora and Salazar Bondy (in an essay of 1964), "Lima, la horrible", they explored all aspects of the city, including the influx of people from the Sierra. These writers incorporated new narrative techniques in the urban novel, which presented a world where popular culture and speech were rich sources of literary material, despite the difficulty in transcribing them.

Many writers, such as Vargas Llosa, broadened their horizons beyond the capital. His novels after *La ciudad y los perros* encompassed many different parts of the country. An additional factor was that several writers spent many years abroad, Vargas Llosa himself, for instance, and Ribeyro (born 1929). The latter's short stories, though mostly set in Lima, embrace universal themes of delusion and frustration. The title story of *Los gallinazos sin pluma* (1955), a tale of squalor and greed amid the city's rubbish tips, has become a classic, even though it does not contain the irony, pathos and humour of many of his other stories or novels.

Other writers of this period include Manuel Scorza (1928-83), who wrote a series of five novels under the general title of *La guerra silenciosa* (including *Redoble por Rancas, El jinete insomne, La tumba del relámpago*) which follow the indigenist tradition of the Indians' struggle, and also emphasize the need to defend indigenous society with growing militancy if necessary.

Alfredo Bryce Echenique (born 1939) has enjoyed much popularity following the success of *Un mundo para Julius* (1970), a satire on the upper and middle classes of Lima. His other novels include *Tantas veces Pedro* (1977), the two-volume *Cuaderno de navegación en un sillón Voltaire* (1981, 1985), *La última mudanza de Felipe Carrillo* (1988), *No me esperen en abril* (1995) and various collections of short stories. Another contemporary writer of note is Sergio Bambarén, whose 1995 debut novel, *The Dolphin - story of a dreamer,* was written in English and became a bestseller when published in Spanish.

20th century poetry At the end of the 19th century, the term Modernism was introduced in Latin America by the Nicaraguan Rubén Darío, not to define a precise school of poetry, but to indicate a break with both Romanticism and Realism. In Peru one major exponent was José Santos Chocano (1875-1934), who labelled his poetry "mundonovismo" (New Worldism), claiming for himself the role of Poet of South America. He won international fame (see, for example, *Alma América*, 1906), but his star soon waned.

A much less assuming character was José María Eguren (1874-1942) who, feeling alienated from the society around him, sought spiritual reality in the natural world (*Simbólicas*, 1911; *La canción de las figuras*, 1916; *Poesías*, 1929). It has been said that with Eguren the flourishing of Peruvian 20th century poetry began.

César Vallejo Without doubt, the most important poet in Peru, if not Latin America, in the first half of the 20th century, was César Vallejo. Born in 1892 in Santiago de Chuco (Libertad), Vallejo left Peru in 1923 after being framed and briefly jailed in Trujillo for a political crime. In 1928 he was a founder of the Peruvian Socialist Party, then he joined the Communist Party in 1931 in Madrid. From 1936 to his death in Paris in 1938 he opposed the fascist takeover in Spain. His first volume was *Los heraldos negros* in which the dominating theme of all his work, a sense of confusion and inadequacy in the face of the unpredictability of life, first surfaces.

Trilce (1922), his second work, is unlike anything before it in the Spanish language. The poems contain (among other things) made-up words, distortions of syntax, their own internal logic and rhythm, graphic devices and innovative uses of sounds, clichés and alliterations. *Poemas humanos* and *España, aparta de mí este cáliz* (written as a result of Vallejo's experiences in the Spanish Civil War) were both published posthumously, in 1939.

In the 1960s writers began to reflect the broadening horizons of that increasingly liberal decade, politically and socially, which followed the Cuban Revolution. One poet who embraced the revolutionary fervour was Javier Heraud (born Miraflores 1942). His early volumes, *El río* (1960) and *El viaje* (1961) are apparently simple in conception and expression, but display a transition from embarking on the adventure of life (the river) to autumnal imagery of solitude. In 1961 he went to the USSR, Asia, Paris and Madrid, then in 1962 to Cuba to study cinema. He returned to Peru in 1963 and joined the guerrilla Ejército de Liberación Nacional. On 15 May 1963 he was shot by government forces near Puerto Maldonado.

Other major poets who began to publish in the 1960s were Luis Hernández (1941-77), Antonio Cisneros (born 1942), Rodolfo Hinostroza (born 1941) and Marco Martos (born 1942).

In the 1970s, during the social changes propelled by the Velasco regime (1968-75), new voices arose, many from outside Lima, eg the Hora Zero group (1970-73 – Enrique Verástegui, Jorge Pimentel, Juan Ramírez Ruiz), whose energetic poetry employed slang, obscenities and other means to challenge preconceptions. Other poets of the 1970s and after include José Watanabe, Tulio Mora, Abelardo Sánchez León, Giovanna Pollarda (poet and screenwriter) and Carmen Ollé.

Fine art and sculpture

The Catholic Church was the main patron of the arts during the colonial period. The innumerable churches and monasteries that sprang up in the newly-conquered territories created a demand for paintings and sculptures, met initially by imports from Europe of both works of art and of skilled craftsmen, and later by home-grown products.

An essential requirement for the inauguration of any new church was an image for the altar and many churches in Lima preserve fine examples of sculptures imported from Seville during the 16th and 17th centuries. Not surprisingly, among the earliest of these are figures of the crucified Christ, such as those in the Cathedral and the church of La Merced by Juan Martínez Montañés, one of the foremost Spanish sculptors of the day, and that in San Pedro, by his pupil Juan de Mesa of 1625. Statues of the Virgin and Child were also imported to Lima from an early date, and examples from the mid-16th century survive in the Cathedral and in Santo Domingo by Roque de Balduque, also from Seville although Flemish by birth.

Colonial period

Sculptures were expensive and difficult to import, and as part of their policy of relative frugality the Franciscan monks tended to favour paintings. In Lima, the museum of San Francisco now houses an excellent collection of paintings imported from Europe, including a powerful series of saints by Zubarán, as well as other works from his studio, a series of paintings of the life of Christ from Ruben's workshop and works from the circles of Ribera and Murillo (see Lima Churches, page 101).

The Jesuits commissioned the Sevillian artist Juan de Valdés Leal to paint a series of the life of St Ignatius Loyola (1660s) which still hangs in San Pedro. The Cathedral museum has a curious series from the Bassano workshop of Venice representing the labours of the monks and dating from the early 17th century. Another interesting artistic import from Europe that can still be seen in San Pedro (see Lima Churches) are the gloriously colourful painted tile decorations (*azulejos*)

Background

on the walls of Dominican monastery, produced to order by Sevillian workshops in 1586 and 1604.

Painters and sculptors soon made their way to Peru in search of lucrative commissions including several Italians who arrived during the later 16th century. The Jesuit Bernardo Bitti (1548-1610), for example, trained in Rome before working in Lima, Cusco, Juli and Arequipa, where examples of his elegantly Mannerist paintings are preserved in the Jesuit church of the Compañía (see Arequipa Churches, page 225).

Another Italian, Mateo Pérez de Alesio worked in the Sistine Chapel in Rome before settling in Peru. In Lima the Sevillian sculptor Pedro de Noguera (1592-1655) won the contract for the choirstalls of the Cathedral in 1623 and, together with other Spanish craftsmen, produced a set of cedar stalls decorated with vigorous figures of saints and Biblical characters, an outstanding work unmatched elsewhere in the Viceroyalty.

Native artists European imports, however, could not keep up with demand and local workshops of creole, mestizo and Indian craftsmen flourished from the latter part of the 16th century. As the Viceregal capital and the point of arrival into Peru, the art of Lima was always strongly influenced by European, especially Spanish models, but the old Inca capital of Cusco became the centre of a regional school of painting which developed its own characteristics.

A series of paintings of the 1660s, now hanging in the Museo de Arte Religioso (see Cusco Museums, page 151), commemorate the colourful Corpus Christi procession of statues of the local patron saints through the streets of Cusco. These paintings document the appearance of the city and local populace, including Spanish and Inca nobility, priests and laity, rich and poor, Spaniard, Indian, African and mestizo. Many of the statues represented in this series are still venerated in the local parish churches. They are periodically painted and dressed in new robes, but underneath are the original sculptures, executed by native craftsmen. Some are of carved wood while others use the pre-conquest technique of maguey cactus covered in sized cloth.

A remarkable example of an Andean Indian who acquired European skills was Felipe Guaman Poma de Ayala whose 1,000 page letter to the King of Spain celebrating the Andean past and condemning the colonial present contained a visual history of colonial and precolonial life in the Andes (see also above, page 530).

One of the most successful native painters was Diego Quispe Tito (1611-1681) who claimed descent from the Inca nobility and whose large canvases, often based on Flemish engravings, demonstrate the wide range of European sources that were available to Andean artists in the 17th century. But the Cusco School is best known for the anonymous devotional works where the painted contours of the figures are overlaid with flat patterns in gold, creating highly decorative images with an underlying tension between the two- and three-dimensional aspects of the work. The taste for richly-decorated surfaces can also be seen in the 17th and 18th century frescoed interiors of many Andean churches, as in Chinchero, Andahuaylillas and Huaro, and in the ornate carving on altarpieces and pulpits throughout Peru.

Andean content creeps into colonial religious art in a number of ways, most simply by the inclusion of elements of indigenous flora and fauna, or, as in the case of the Corpus Christi paintings, by the use of a specific setting, with recognizable buildings and individuals.

Changes to traditional Christian iconography include the representation of one of the Magi as an Inca, as in the painting of the Adoration of the Magi in San Pedro in Juli (see Puno Excursions, page 210). Another example is that to commemorate his miraculous intervention in the conquest of Cusco in 1534, Santiago is often depicted triumphing over Indians instead of the more familiar Moors. Among the most remarkable 'inventions' of colonial art are the fantastically over-dressed archangels carrying muskets which were so popular in the 18th century. There is no direct European source for these archangels, but in the Andes they seem to have served as a painted guard of honour to the image of Christ or the Virgin on the high altar.

Political independence from Spain in 1824 had little immediate impact on the arts of Peru except to create a demand for portraits of the new national and continental heroes such as Simón Bolívar and San Martín, many of the best of them produced by the mulatto artist José Gil de Castro (d. Lima 1841). Later in the century another mulatto, Pancho Fierro (1810-1879) mocked the rigidity and pretentiousness of Lima society in lively satirical watercolours, while Francisco Laso (1823-1860), an active campaigner for political reform, made the Andean Indian into a respectable subject for oil paintings. **Independence and after**

It was not until the latter part of the 19th century that events from colonial history became popular. The Museo de Arte in Lima (see Lima Museums, page 104) has examples of grandiose paintings by Ignacio Merino (1817-1876) glorifying Columbus, as well as the gigantic romanticized 'Funeral of Atahualpa' by Luis Montero (1826-1869). A curious late flowering of this celebration of colonial history is the chapel commemorating Francisco Pizarro in Lima cathedral which was redecorated in 1928 with garish mosaic pictures of the conqueror's exploits.

Of the modern movements Impressionism arrived late and had a limited impact in Peru. Teofilo Castillo (1857-1922), instead of using the technique to capture contemporary reality, created frothy visions of an idealized colonial past. Typical of his work is the large 'Funeral Procession of Santa Rosa' of 1918, with everything bathed in clouds of incense and rose petals, which hangs in the Museo de Arte, in Lima. Daniel Hernández (1856-1932), founder of Peru's first Art School, used a similar style for his portraits of Lima notables past and present.

During the first half of the 20th century, Peruvian art was dominated by figurative styles and local subject matter. Political theories of the 1920s recognized the importance of Andean Indian culture to Peruvian identity and created a climate which encouraged a figurative *indigenista* school of painting, derived in part from the socialist realism of the Mexican muralists. José Sabogal (1888-1956) is the best known exponent of the group which also included Mario Urteaga (1875-1957), Jorge Vinatea Reinoso (1900-1931), Enrique Camino Brent (1909-1960), Camilo Blas (1903-1984) and Alejandro González (1900-1984). **20th century**

The Mexican muralist tradition persisted into the 1960s with Manuel Ugarte Eléspuru (1911) and Teodoro Núñez Ureta (1914), both of whom undertook large-scale commissions in public buildings in Lima. Examples of public sculpture in the indigenist mode can be seen in plazas and parks throughout Peru, but it was in photography that indigenism found its most powerful expression. From the beginning of the century photographic studios flourished even in smaller towns. Martín Chambi (1891-1973) is the best known of the early 20th century Peruvian photographers but there were many others, including Miguel Chani (1860-1951) who maintained the grandly named *Fotografía Universal* studios in Cusco, Puno and Arequipa.

From the middle of the century artists have experimented with a variety of predominantly abstract styles and the best-known contemporary Peruvian painter, Fernando de Szyszlo (1925) has created a visual language of his own, borrowing

Background

from Abstract Expressionism on the one hand and from precolumbian iconography on the other. His strong images, which suggest rather than represent mythical beings and cosmic forces, have influenced a whole generation of younger Peruvian artists.

Other leading figures whose work can be seen in public and commercial galleries in Lima include Venancio Shinki, Elda di Malio, Ricardo Weisse, Julia Nabarrete and Leoncio Villanueva. With the more stable economic and political conditions of recent years, young artists have been encouraged to stay in Peru rather than head for Miami. Art schools are flourishing in a number of provincial centres and although quality is variable the future looks bright.

Government and the modern country

Government

Under a new constitution (approved by plebiscite in October 1993), a single chamber, 80-seat congress replaced the previous, two-house legislature. Men and women over 18 are eligible to vote, and registration and voting is compulsory until the age of 60. Those who do not vote are fined. The President, to whom is entrusted the Executive Power, is elected for five years and may, under the constitution which came into force on 1 January 1994, be re-elected for a second term.

In 1987 Congress approved a change in the administration of the country, proposing a system of 13 Regions to replace the 24 Departments (divided into 150 Provinces, subdivided into 1,321 Districts). The proposal remained nothing more than that until 1990, when it was renewed. It has still not been implemented.

Economy

Farming & fishing

Agriculture, forestry and fishing account for only seven percent of gdp, but employ about a third of the labour force. In 1995 a new agriculture law abolished the land reform law imposed by the military régime and eliminated limits on land holding. It is hoped to encourage large scale investment in agroindustry and export crops.

The coast is the most productive area of the country and has traditionally been the dominant economic region. Occupying 11 percent of the total land area, most of the export crops are grown here, with excellent crops of cotton, rice, sugar and fruit where the coastal desert is irrigated. Irrigation is, however, costly and the Government is hoping to substitute luxury fruit and vegetables for export instead of the thirsty sugar cane and rice.

Most food production is in the Sierra, where revitalization of agriculture is a government priority, with the aim of returning to the self-sufficiency of Inca times. Pacification in the highlands and good weather have helped food supply, and there have been improvements in living standards, although two thirds of the inhabitants of the Sierra still live in poverty.

Fishing suffered a dramatic decline in 1983 as the Niño current forced out of Peruvian waters the main catch, anchovy, whose stocks were already seriously depleted by overfishing in the 1970s. Peru lost its position as the world's leading fishmeal exporter to Chile, but by the 1990s was exporting high quality fishmeal again, helped by rising fish catches and the abolition of the state monopoly, which encouraged private investment in new technology. Pescaperú began selling its assets in 1994 and seven fishmeal plants were sold in a year. However, the devasting El Niño of 1997 was a major setback for the recovering fishing industry.

Manufacturing

Manufacturing contributes 28 percent of gdp. After high growth rates in the early 1970s, manufacturing slumped to operating at 40 percent of its total capacity as

Background

purchasing power was reduced and the cost of energy, raw materials and trade credit rose faster than inflation. A consumer-led recovery in 1986 led to most of manufacturing and the construction industry working at full capacity, but the boom was followed by a severe slump in 1988-90. Growth returned in the 1990s and the areas of greatest expansion were food processing, fishmeal and transport equipment, while those sectors still adjusting to increased competition from imports, such as electrical appliances, remained stagnant or declined.

Mining   Although mining has traditionally been important in Peru since pre-Conquest times, the sector contracted sharply in the 1980s because of poor world prices, strikes, guerrilla activity in mining areas, rising costs and an uncompetitive exchange rate. The Fujimori Government passed a new Mining Law in 1992 to attract private investment, both domestic and foreign, and growth in mining has boomed in the 1990s with over 80 mining companies operating in the country. Copper and iron deposits are found on the south coast, but the Sierra is the principal mining area for all minerals, including silver, gold, lead and zinc.

Centromín and Mineroperú, the state mining companies, are having their assets sold off to private mining companies. Mines sold to US companies include Tintaya,

Peru Departmental

a high-grade copper deposit between Cusco and Arequipa, and Cerro Verde, an open pit copper mine in the south. Many under-capitalized Peruvian mining companies have joined forces with foreign companies to develop concessions. The largest locally-controlled company is Compañía de Minas Buenaventura, which in a joint venture owns the largest gold mine in Latin America, Yanacocha, in Cajamarca, which produces 554,000 ounces a year.

The US-owned Southern Peru Copper Corporation (SPCC) was the only major mining company not to be nationalized by the military in the 1970s, and it now produces some two thirds of all Peru's copper at its Cuajone and Toquepala mines. The company invested over US$500 million in the early 1990s in modernization and environmental improvements after fierce public criticism for its lack of pollution control and the need for greater efficiency and competitiveness.

Official estimates for exploration, development and expansion of existing projects start at investment of US$8.7 billion in 1993-2003. New projects will push up investment still further and call for spending on energy generation, roads and other infrastructure, together with housing, health and education facilities for employees. In the same period the value of metals production is forecast to rise from US$2 billion to US$5 billion a year with exports doubling to US$4 billion. Both copper and gold output are also forecast to increase by 100 percent.

Oil comes from the northeastern jungle, although some is produced on and off the **Oil production** north coast. No major new reserves have been found since 1976 and proven oil reserves have declined to 380 million barrels. Oil output fell from a peak of 195,000 barrels per day (b/d) in 1982 to about 130,000 b/d in the mid-1990s. However, the Camisea gas and condensates field in the southeastern jungle is huge, with reserves estimated at the equivalent to 2.4 billion barrels of oil, more than six times current reserves.

The field was discovered by Royal Dutch Shell in the 1980s and development of the field by the company was close to agreement in 1996. However, recent negotiating problems led to their withdrawal in 1998 (see above). Since the passing of new legislation in 1993, several contracts have been signed with private oil companies for exploration and development. The privatization of the state oil company, Petroperú, began piecemeal in 1996.

Growing fiscal deficits in the 1980s led to increasing delays in payments to **Recent trends** creditors and the IMF declared Peru ineligible for further loans in 1986. By 1987 the free-spending policies had pushed the country into bankruptcy and inflation soared as the Government resorted to printing money.

President Fujimori inherited an economy devastated by financial mismanagement and isolationist policies, with Peruvians suffering critical poverty, high infant mortality, malnutrition and appalling housing conditions. His Government had to deal with hyperinflation, terrorism and drug trafficking, compounded in 1991 by a cholera epidemic which affected hundreds of thousands of people, cut food exports and sharply curtailed tourism revenues.

An economic austerity package introduced in 1990 raised food and fuel prices and was the first stage of sweeping reforms. Monetary and fiscal control was accompanied by liberalization of the financial system, reform of labour laws and privatization of state companies. Successful negotiations with creditors reinstated Peru in the international community and investors returned, but the *auto golpe* in 1992 rocked confidence and international aid was suspended until after the elections at the end of the year.

Arrears to the IMF and World Bank were repaid in 1993 and the Paris Club of creditor governments rescheduled debts due in 1993-94. The reform programme remained on course with emphasis put on control of inflation and tight control of

Background

Things go better with coca

Peru produces most of the raw material for cocaine. 60 percent of all coca leaf is grown in Peru, mainly in the tropical Huallaga valley. But though it has been grown in Peru for some 4,000 years, awareness of coca in the First World is rather more recent.

In 1862 German chemists had taken coca leaves brought by an Austrian scientific expedition from Peru and isolated an alkaloid, or nitrogen-based compound which they labelled cocain. By around 1880, it was being tried as a cure for opium addiction and alcoholism. The young Dr Sigmund Freud, reading of its effect on tired soldiers, took some himself and pronounced it a "magical substance", which was "wonderfully stimulating". Today, there is a huge demand for this drug from the millions of North Americans and Europeans who sniff, smoke or inject it.

Supply on this scale is not a problem. Making cocaine hydrochloride is as easy as baking bread. The leaves go into a plastic pit with a solution of water and a little sulphuric acid where they are left to soak for a few days. Then follows a succession of mixing and stirring with more chemicals until the liquid turns milky-white and then curdles, leaving tiny, ivory-coloured granules. This cocaine base is then transported to Colombia, where it is refined into the familiar white powder,

before being shipped abroad. The costs involved to produce a kilo of the stuff are around US$5,000. The return on this investment can be as much as US$50,000.

Cocaine also has its legal uses. Patent medicines containing cocaine were popular – for hay fever, sinusitis and as a general tonic. Today, it is still used in hospitals world-wide as a local anaesthetic. Another legal use of cocaine is in soft drinks. The most famous soft drink in the world doesn't actually contain cocaine, but has something from the coca plant in it. Coca leaves from Peru and Bolivia are shipped to the USA where cocaine is extracted for medical use. From what's left comes a flavouring agent which goes into Coca-Cola, enjoyed in practically every country around the globe.

Easily grown at altitudes ranging from 300-2,000 metres, coca can be harvested four times a year and provides a relatively good return. This may strike some as unethical, but to the campesinos living in grinding poverty and desperate to provide a better future for their children, cocaine is just a business. It may cause addiction, misery, and even death at the end of the line, but the painful truth is that cocaine means economic growth for entire regions in Peru and economic survival for many, as well as massive profits for some.

the money supply. Exports and imports grew strongly and the new economic and political stability also encouraged foreign tourists to return.

In 1994 Peru registered the highest economic growth rate in the world, as gdp expanded by 12.7 percent. An agreement with commercial bank creditors was signed in 1995 when Peru became the last major Latin American debtor nation to convert loans at a discount into bonds, known as Brady bonds. Servicing of the new debt was deemed possible because of a steep rise in tax receipts. Although the pace of privatization was slowed because of fears of overheating and inflation, it was planned that no state companies would remain by the end of the decade.

Society

The most remarkable thing about Peru is its people. For most Peruvians life is a daily struggle to survive in the face of seemingly insurmountable problems. But most people do get by, through a combination of ingenuity, determination and sheer hard work. Many hold down two jobs to make ends meet, others work full time and study at night school and those without work invent their own jobs.

A way of life

Coca leaves have long been used by the people of the Andes as a tonic. As casual as a coffee-break and as sacred as Communion, coca chewing is an ancient ritual.

The coca leaves are chewed with a piece of cal, or lime, which activates with the saliva. Some cocaine is absorbed into the bloodstream through the mouth , providing a slight numbing of cheek and tongue and more is absorbed in the stomach and intestinal tract. The desired effect is to numb the senses, which helps stave off hunger pangs and exhaustion, and to help people live at high altitude with no ill-effects.

As well as being a prerequisite for manual workers, such as miners, coca is also taken in a social context. The native population used to deny this because, in the eyes of their Spanish bosses and clergy, an increase in labour productivity was the only permissible reason for tolerating consumption of 'the devil's leaf'. The only places where coca is not chewed is in church and in the marital bed. The masticated leaves are spat out at the bedside.

Coca is also used in various rites, such as in offerings to Pachamama, or Mother Earth, to feed her when she gets hungry. Various items such as flowers and sweets, along with the coca leaves, are put together in bundles called pagos and burned on the mountains at midnight. In Andean markets different pagos are sold for different purposes: to put into the foundation of a new house; for help in matters of health, business or love; or for magic, white or black. The leaves are also used for fortune-telling.

Peru may not be the poorest country in South America, but recent estimates put the number of poor at 49 percent of the population, while almost a fifth of people live in extreme poverty. Over a third of homes have no electricity or running water and a third of children suffer from chronic malnutrition.

Health

There have been major improvements in health care in recent years, but almost a third of the population have no access to public health services. The infant mortality rate is high – 50 deaths per 1,000 births – and the figure rises steeply in some rural areas where one in ten infants die within a year of birth.

Though health services are free, people still have to pay for prescribed medicines, which are very expensive, and so rarely finish a course of treatment. Lack of health education and limited primary health care also means that many women die in childbirth. Abortion is illegal in Peru, but those with cash can always find a private doctor. Those without the means to pay for a doctor run the risk of death or infection from botched abortions.

Education

Education is free and compulsory for both sexes between six and 14. There are public and private secondary schools and private elementary schools. There are 32 state and private universities, and two Catholic universities. But resources are extremely limited and teachers earn a pittance. Poorer schoolchildren don't have money to buy pencils and notebooks and textbooks are few and far between in state schools. Furthermore, many children have to work instead of attending school; a quarter of those who start primary school don't finish. This is also due to the fact that classes are taught in Spanish and those whose native tongue is Quechua, Aymara or one of the Amazonian languages find it difficult and give up.

Migration

The structure of Peruvian society, especially in the coastal cities, has been radically altered by internal migration. This movement began most significantly in the 1950s and 1960s as people from the Highlands sought urban jobs in place of work on the land. It was a time of great upheaval as the old system of labour on large estates was threatened by the peasant majority's growing awareness of the imbalances

Background

between the wealthy cities and impoverished sierra. The process culminated in the agrarian reforms of the government of General Juan Velasco (1968-75). Highland-to-city migration was given renewed impetus during the war between the state and Sendero Luminoso in the 1980s. Many communities which were depopulated in that decade are now beginning to come alive again.

Footnotes

14

Footnotes

547 Basic Spanish for travellers

550 Shorts

551 Index

555 Map index

560 Advertiser index

563 Coloured maps

Basic Spanish for travellers

No amount of dictionaries, phrase books or word lists will provide the same enjoyment as being able to communicate directly with the people of the country you are visiting. Learning Spanish is an important part of the preparation for any trip to Peru and you are encouraged to make an effort to grasp the basics before you go. As you travel you will pick up more of the language and the more you know, the more you will benefit from your stay. The following section is designed to be a simple point of departure.

General pronunciation
The stress in a Spanish word conforms to one of three rules: 1) if the word ends in a vowel, or in **n** or **s**, the accent falls on the penultimate syllable (*ventana, ventanas*). 2) if the word ends in a consonant other than **n** or **s**, the accent falls on the last syllable (*hablar*); 3) if the word is to be stressed on a syllable contrary to either of the above rules, the acute accent on the relevant vowel indicates where the stress is to be placed (*pantalón, metáfora*). Note that adverbs such as *cuando*, 'when', take an accent when used interrogatively: *¿cuándo?*, 'when?'

Vowels

a	not quite as short as in English 'cat'
e	as in English 'pay', but shorter in a syllable ending in a consonant
i	as in English 'seek'
o	as in English 'shop', but more like 'pope' when the vowel ends a syllable
u	as in English 'food'; after 'q' and in 'gue', 'gui', **u** is unpronounced; in 'güe' and 'güi' it is pronounced
y	when a vowel, pronounced like 'i'; when a semiconsonant or consonant, it is pronounced like English 'yes'
ai, ay	as in English 'ride'
ei, ey	as in English 'they'
oi, oy	as in English 'toy'

Unless listed below **consonants** can be pronounced in Spanish as they are in English.

b, v	their sound is interchangeable and is a cross between the English 'b' and 'v', except at the beginning of a word or after 'm' or 'n' when it is like English 'b'
c	like English 'k', except before 'e' or 'i' when it is as the 's' in English 'sip'
g	before 'e' and 'i' it is the same as **j**
h	when on its own, never pronounced
j	as the 'ch' in the Scottish 'loch'
ll	as the 'g' in English 'beige'; sometimes as the 'lli' in 'million'
ñ	as the 'ni' in English 'onion'
rr	trilled much more strongly than in English
x	depending on its location, pronounced as in English 'fox', or 'sip', or like 'gs'
z	as the 's' in English 'sip'

Greetings, Courtesies

hello *hola*
good morning *buenos días*
good afternoon/evening/night *buenas tardes/noches*
goodbye *adiós/chao*
see you later *hasta luego*
how are you? *¿cómo está?/¿cómo estás?*
pleased to meet you *mucho gusto/encantado/encantada*
please *por favor*
thank you (very much) *(muchas) gracias*
yes *sí*
no *no*
excuse me/I beg your pardon *permiso*
I do not understand *no entiendo*
please speak slowly *hable despacio por favor*
what is your name *¿cómo se llama?*
Go away! *¡Váyase!*

Basic questions

where is_? *¿dónde está_?*
how much does it cost? *¿cuánto cuesta?*
how much is it? *¿cuánto es?*
when? *¿cuándo?*
when does the bus leave? *¿a qué hora sale el autobus?*
    - arrive?   - *llega* -
why? *¿por qué?*
what for? *¿para qué?*
what time is it? *¿qué hora es?*
how do I get to_? *¿cómo llegar a_?*
is this the way to the church? *¿la iglesia está por aquí?*

Basics

bathroom/toilet *el baño*
police (policeman) *la policía (el policía)*
hotel *el hotel (la pensión,el residencial, el alojamiento)*
restaurant *el restaurante*
post office *el correo*
telephone office *el centro de llamadas*
supermarket *el supermercado*
bank *el banco*
exchange house *la casa de cambio*
exchange rate *la tasa de cambio*
notes/coins *los billetes/las monedas*
travellers' cheques *los travelers/los cheques de viajero*
cash *el efectivo*

breakfast *el desayuno*
lunch *el almuerzo*
dinner/supper *la cena*
meal *la comida*
drink *la bebida*
mineral water *el agua mineral*
soft fizzy drink *la gaseosa/cola*
beer *la cerveza*
without sugar *sin azúcar*
without meat *sin carne*

Getting around

on the left/right *a la izquierda/derecha*
straight on *derecho*
second street on the left *la segunda calle a la izquierda*
to walk *caminar*
bus station *la terminal (terrestre)*
train station *la estación (de tren/ferrocarril)*
bus *el bus/el autobus/ la flota/el colectivo/ el micro etc*
train *el tren*
airport *el aeropuerto*
aeroplane/airplane *el avión*
first/second class *primera/segunda clase*
ticket *el boleto*
ticket office *la taquilla*
bus stop *la parada*

Accommodation

room *el cuarto/la habitación*
single/double *sencillo/doble*
with two beds *con dos camas*
with private bathroom *con baño*
hot/cold water *agua caliente/fría*
noisy *ruidoso*
to make up/clean *limpiar*
sheets *las sábanas*
blankets *las mantas*
pillows *las almohadas*
clean/dirty towels *toallas limpias/sucias*
toilet paper *el papel higiénico*

Health

Chemist *farmacia*
(for) pain *(para) dolor*
stomach *el estómago*
head *la cabeza*
fever/sweat *la fiebre/el sudor*
diarrhoea *la diarrea*
blood *la sangre*

altitude sickness *el soroche*
doctor *el médico*
condoms *los preservativos*
contraceptive (pill) *anticonceptivo (la píldora anticonceptiva)*
period/towels *la regla/las toallas*
contact lenses *las lentes de contacto*
aspirin *la aspirina*

Time

at one o'clock *a la una*
at half past two/ two thirty *a las dos y media*
at a quarter to three *a cuarto para las tres* or *a las tres menos quince*
it's one o'clock *es la una*
it's seven o'clock *son las siete*
it's twenty past six/six twenty *son las seis y veinte*
it's five to nine *son cinco para las nueve/ son las nueve menos cinco*
in ten minutes *en diez minutos*
five hours *cinco horas*
does it take long? *¿tarda mucho?*
Monday *lunes*
Tuesday *martes*
Wednesday *miercoles*
Thursday *jueves*
Friday *viernes*
Saturday *sábado*
Sunday *domingo*
January *enero*
February *febrero*
March *marzo*
April *abril*
May *mayo*
June *junio*
July *julio*
August *agosto*
September *septiembre*
October *octubre*
November *noviembre*
December *diciembre*

Numbers

one *uno/una*
two *dos*
three *tres*
four *cuatro*
five *cinco*
six *seis*
seven *siete*
eight *ocho*
nine *nueve*

ten *diez*
eleven *once*
twelve *doce*
thirteen *trece*
fourteen *catorce*
fifteen *quince*
sixteen *dieciseis*
seventeen *diecisiete*
eighteen *dieciocho*
nineteen *diecinueve*
twenty *veinte*
twenty one, two *veintiuno, veintidos*
thirty *treinta*
forty *cuarenta*
fifty *cincuenta*
sixty *sesenta*
seventy *setenta*
eighty *ochenta*
ninety *noventa*
hundred *cien or ciento*
thousand *mil*

Key verbs

To Go *ir*
I go *voy;* you go (familiar singular) *vas;* he, she, it goes, you (unfamiliar singular) go *va;* we go *vamos;* they, you (plural) go *van.*

To Have (possess) *tener*
tengo; tienes; tiene; tenemos; tienen (also used as To Be, as in 'I am hungry' *tengo hambre*)
(NB *haber* also means to have, but is used with other verbs, as in 'he has gone' *ha ido. he; has; ha; hemos; han. Hay* means 'there is'; perhaps more common is *No hay* meaning 'there isn't any')

To Be (in a permanent state) *ser*
soy (profesor - I am a teacher); *eres; es; somos; son*

To Be (positional or temporary state) *estar*
estoy (en Londres - I am in London); *estás; está (contenta -* she is happy); *estamos; están.*

This section has been compiled on the basis of glossaries compiled by André de Mendonça and David Gilmour of South American Experience, London, and the Latin American Travel Advisor, No 9, March 1996.

Shorts

Special interest pieces on and about Peru

129 Airline offices in Lima
520 Andean mysticism
239 Appeasing the Gods
522 belt for every occasion, A
289 blooming century, A
507 Border dispute with Ecuador
238 Camelid fibre
345 Chimú culture, The
27 Cost of living
147 Cusco: visitors' Tickets
518 Day of the dead
514 debonair dolphin, The
46 Domestic airlines
259 economic mess, An
512 El Niño
132 Embassies & consulates in Lima
39 Environmental organizations & Publications
99 fashion for passion, A
160 festival of Inti Raymi, The
525 From Pagan ritual to folk art
488 future for Tambopata, The
473 General hints for river travel
526 growing tradition, A
107 Guilt by inquisition
441 Huari influence, The
94 Impressions of Lima
521 Is there a Witchdoctor in the house
192 last Incas of Vilcabamba, The
213 lasting tradition, A
357 legend of Naymlap, The
430 Lima-Huancayo railway
96 Lima street names
205 load of bulls, A
461 Lope de Aguirre
271 Maria Reiche - Guardian of the lines
531 Mario Vargas Llosa
171 market for beads, A
74 Medical supplies

458 mighty Amazon, The
292 Mining the mountains
344 Moche culture, The
26 Money matters
215 Mother Earth
436 officer and a not-so-gentle nun, An
358 old Lord of Sipán, The
371 old man and the marlin, The
258 Paracas Necropolis Culture, The
22 Peru embassies and consulates
263 Pisco: a history in the making
209 Pot luck
469 rubber boom, The
212 sacred lake, The
317 stone gods of Chavín, The
463 symbolic art form, A
360 tale of demons and fish, A
540 Things go better with coca
34 Touching down
36 Useful addresses
410 Valley of the Whites, The
503 War of the Pacific, The
541 way of life, A

Index

Note: Coloured map references are given in italics. Thus 'Aguas Calientes *M5A5*' will be found on coloured map 5 in square A5.

A

Abancay *M5A5* 444
accommodation 43
  camping 45
  hotels 43
  See also under
    individual towns
  youth hostels 45
Acobamba *M3C5* 446
Acomayo *M3B4* 194
adventure tourism 21
Agallpampa 384
Aguas Calientes *M5A5*
  187
Aguas Verdes 379
Aguaytía *M3A4* 462
Ahuac 430
AIDS 80
air travel 45
  air passes 27
  airline offices 129
  airport information
    33
  domestic airlines 46
  prices and discounts
    28
  See also transport
Alegría 490
Alerta 490
altitude 77
Alto de Toroya 201
Amantaní Island *M6B2*
  214
Amazon River 458
Ambo *M3B4* 451
Anco 434
Ancón *M3C3* 140
Andagua 248
Andahuaylas *M5A4* 443
Andahuaylillas 194
Anta *M3B2* 196
Aplao *M5C5* 245
Apurlec 361
Aramango *M1B3* 416
architecture 500
Arequipa *M5C6* 224
  essentials 228
  sights 225
Arica, Chile 284
art 533
arts and crafts 521
Aspero 330
Atalaya *M3B6* 481
Atico *M5C4* 273

Aucayacu *M3A4* 460
Ayabaca *M1B2* 368
Ayacucho *M5A4* 434
Ayaviri *M6B2* 219
Aylambo 391
Azángaro *M6B2* 203

B

Bagua Grande *M1B3*
  415
Bagua *M1B3* 416
Bahuaja-Senone
  National Park 487
Ballestas Islands *M5B2*
  259
Barranca *M3B2* 330
Barranco
  See under Lima
bars 58
  See under individual
    towns
Batán Grande 359
before you travel 22
Bellavista 474
birdwatching 69
Blanquillo 482
boat travel
  See transport
Boca Coloado 481
Boca Manu 481
bodegas 253
Bolivia frontier 215
buses
  See transport
business hours 34

C

Cabanaconde 243
Cabo Blanco 371
Cahuachi 267
Cailloma *M5B6* 241
Cajabamba *M1C4* 385
Cajamarca *M1C3* 386
Cajamarquilla 140
Cajatambo *M3B3* 324
Calca *M5A5* 171
Caleta La Cruz 374
Callalli 240
Callao *M3C3* 110
Callejón de Conchucos
  317
Camaná *M5C5* 273

camping
  See accommodation
Cancas 374
Canchaque *M1B2* 368
Cañete *M3C4* 252
Canta *M3C4* 449
canyons 510
car
  See transport
Caraz *M3A2* 307
Carhuaz *M3B2* 302
Casapalca 423
cash machines
  See money
Casma *M3B3* 331
Catac *M3B3* 314
Catacaos *M1B1* 366
cave diving
  See sport
Celendín *M1C4* 392
Cerro Baúl 278
Cerro de Pasco *M3B4*
  449
Cerro Olán 405
Cerros de Amotape
  National Park 378
Chacas *M3A3* 319
Chachapoyas *M1C4* 396
Chachas 248
Chala *M5C4* 272
Chamaya *M1B3* 416
Chan Chán *M3A1* 345
Chancay *M3C3* 328
Chanchamayo 447
Chancos *M3B3* 301
Chasquitambo *M3B3*
  331
Chaupa 245
Chavín de Huantar 316
Chavín *M3B3* 315
Checacupe *M5B6* 195
Chepén *M1C2* 356
Chichucancha 314
Chicla 423
Chiclayo *M1C2* 350
Chiguata 201
Chilca *M3C4* 252
children
  health 73
  travelling with 37
Chile frontier 284
Chilete *M1C3* 386
Chimbote *M3A2* 334
Chimú culture 345
Chincha 254

Chinchero *M5A5* 175
Chincheros *M5A4* 442
Chiquián *M3B3* 324
Chira 274
Chivay *M5B6* 241
Choco 244
Chongoyape *M1C2* 358
Chosica *M3C3* 422
Chucuíto *M6B2* 210
Chulucanas *M1B2* 367
Chupaca 430
Chuquibamba *M5B5*
  245
Chuquitanta 140
Churín *M3B3* 329
Cieneguilla *M3C3* 139
climate 512
  See when to go
climbing
  See sport
clothing 38
Cochas Chico 431
Cochas Grande 431
Cohechan 411
Coina 385
Colán *M1B1* 367
Colca Canyon 238
Colcabamba *M5B4* 306
cold 78
colectivos 48
  See transport
Concepción *M3C5* 425
Conococha *M3B3* 331
consulates 22, 85
Contumazá *M1C3* 386
Copacabana, Bolivia
  216
Coporaque 241
Cordillera Huayhuash
  M3B3 321
Cordillera Negra 311
Corire *M5C5* 245
Corongo *M3A2* 321
cost of living 27
Cotahuasi Canyon 245
Cotahuasi *M5B5* 246
Coya 171
credit cards
  See money
Cruz del Cóndor 243
Cueva Guitarreros 303
cultural tourism 69
culture 517
Cumbe Mayo *M1C3* 392

currency
  See money
Cusco *M5A5* 143
  directory 164
  eating 157
  essentials 152
  Sacsayhuamán 151
  sights 147
  sleeping 152
Cusichaca 178
Cusipata *M5B6* 194
customs 23, 38
cycling
  See transport

D

dance 526
Desaguadero *M6C3* 216
Deustua *M6B2* 201
disabled travellers 37
diseases 79
diving
  See sport
drink 58
driving
  See under transport,
  cars
drugs 41
Duraznopampa 405
duty free allowance 23

E

economy 537
Ecuador frontier 379
education 541
El Brujo 347
El Misti 228
El Olivar 108
El Silenco 252
electricity 34
email 55
embassies 22, 85
entry requirements 22
  See also vaccinations
equipment 24
etiquette 38
exchange
  See money
export ban 23

F

Ferreñafe *M1C2* 356
festivals 21, 72, 529
  See also under
  individual towns
fishing
  See sport
flora and fauna
  See wildlife
food 56

G

gay travellers 37
geography 509
getting around
  See transport
getting there 26
  See transport
government 537
Gran Vilaya 404
Guadalupe *M5B2* 261
Guayabamba Valley 410
guide books 36

H

hang gliding
  See sport
health 73, 541
  children 73
  vaccinations 24
heat 78
Hemingway, Ernest 371
hepatitis 81
history 493
hitchhiking
  See transport
holidays 72
  See also under
  individual towns
hotels
  See accommodation
Huacachina 264
Huacarpay 193
Huaccana 443
Huacho *M3B3* 329
Hualahoyo 431
Hualhuas 431
Huallanca *M3A2* 336
Huallay 449
Huamachuco *M3A2* 384
Huambutío *M5A6* 193
Huancabamba *M1B2*
  368
Huancabamba *M3B4*
  448
Huancacalle 189
Huancané *M6B2* 218
Huancas 399
Huancavelica *M3C5* 432
Huancayo *M3C5* 425
Huanchaco *M3A1* 348
Huánuco *M3B4* 451
Huaquillas, Ecuador 380
Huaral *M3C3* 328
Huarautambo 451
Huaraz *M3B3* 293
Huari influence 441
Huari *M3B3* 318
Huaripampa *M3A2* 312
Huarmey *M3B2* 331
Huaro 194
Huascarán National Park
  M3B3 288
Huaura *M3B3* 330

Huayllabamba *M5A5*
  172
Huayllay 450
Huayna Picchu 180
Huaytará 261
Huayucachi 430

I

Iberia *M4C6* 490
Ica 261
Ichupampa 241
IDD code 34
Ilave *M6B2* 211
Ilo *M5C6* 279
immunisation
  See health
Iñapari *M4C6* 490
Inca trail 183
  short 187
Incas 497
Incawasi 253
Indiana *M2B3* 474
Infiernillo 423
Ingenio 425
insects 78
internet 55
  See also under
  individual towns
Intihuatana 441
Iquitos *M2B3* 467
Izcuchaca 431

J

Jaén *M1B3* 416
Jalca Grande 405
Jauja *M3C5* 424
Juli *M6B3* 210
Juliaca *M6B2* 201
Junín *M3B4* 449

K

kayaking
  See sport
Kiteni 192
Kuelap *M1C4* 402

L

La Marca 178
La Merced *M3B2* 447
La Morada *M3A4* 460
La Oroya *M3C4* 423
La Punta 110
La Quinua 441
La Tina-Macará 380
La Unión *M3B3* 454
Laberinto *M6A2* 486
Lago Parón 310
Lago Sandoval 486
Laguna de los Cóndores
  408
Lagunas *M1B6* 462
Lagunillas 258

Huayllabamba *M5A5*
Lake Titicaca *M6B2* 199
Lamas *M1C5* 415
Lambayeque *M1C2* 354
Lampa 203
Lamud *M1C4* 410
language 54
  words and phrases
  547
Lari 241
Las Arenas 372
Las Guaringas 368
lesbian travellers 37
Levanto *M1C4* 399
Leymebamba *M1C4*
  405
Lima *M3C3* 91
  Barranco 109
  directory 130
  eating 116
  essentials 111
  Miraflores 109
  sights 96
  sleeping 111
  San Isidro 108
literature 530
Llacanora *M1C4* 392
Llamellín *M3A3* 318
Llanganuco 305
Llanguat 394
Loma de Lachay
  National Reserve 330
Lope de Aguirre 461
Los Baños del Inca 391
Los Organos 372
Lucre 193
Luisiana 442
Lunahuaná *M3C4* 252
Luya 411

M

Maca 243
Macará, Ecuador 380
Machu Picchu *M5A5*
  179
Madrigal 241
magazines 55
Mala *M3C4* 252
Máncora *M1B1* 372
Mancos *M3A2* 303
Manglares de Tumbes
  Santuario Nacional
  378
Manu Biosphere Reserve
  478
maps 36
Maras 175
Marcará *M3B2* 301
Matacoto 304
Matahulo Muquiyauyo
  431
Matarani *M5C6* 276
Matucana *M3C4* 423
Mayocc *M3C5* 434
Mazuko *M6A2* 484
media 55
medical insurance
  See health

medicines
See health
Medio Mundo 330
Mejía *M5C6* 275
Mendoza 409
migration 541
Miraflores
See under Lima
Moche culture 344
Moho *M6B2* 218
Molinopampa *M1C4* 409
Mollendo *M5C6* 275
money 25
Monsefú *M1C2* 356
Monterrey *M3B3* 300
Montevideo 405
Moquegua *M6C1* 276
Moray *M5A5* 175
Moro 336
Morococha 423
Mórrope *M1C2* 356
motorcycling
See transport
mountain biking
See sport
Moyobamba *M1B5* 413
Musho 303
music 526

N

Nasca Lines *M5B3* 269
Nasca *M5B3* 265
National Vicuña Reserve 240
Naymlap legend 357
Nazareth *M1B3* 416
Nevado Ausangate 194
newspapers 55
Nueva Cajamarca 412

O

Ocoña *M5C5* 273
Ocongate *M5A6* 194
official time 34
Ollantaytambo *M5A5* 176
Olleros *M3B3* 312
Olmos *M1C2* 361
Omate *M6C1* 279
Oracuza *M1B3* 416
Orcopampa *M5B5* 248
Oropesa *M5A6* 193
Otusco *M3A2* 384
Oxamarca *M1C4* 393
Oxapampa *M3B5* 448
Oyón *M3B3* 323

P

Pacarijtambo 195
Pacasmayo *M1C2* 349
Pacatnamú 349
Pacaya-Samiria Reserve 462

Pachacámac *M3C3* 139
Pachacoto *M3B3* 314
Pacucha 443
Paita *M1B1* 366
Palcamayo *M3B4* 446
Palmira *M1C4* 405
Palpa *M5B3* 264
Pampagrande 358
Pampamarca 247
Paracas *M5B2* 257
Paracas Necropolis 258
Paramonga *M3B2* 331
parapenting
See sport
Pariacaca 303
Pariacoto *M3B2* 332
Pasacancha *M3A2* 320
passports
See entry requirements
Pataz 385
Pati *M6B1* 201
Pativilca *M3B2* 330
Paucartambo *M3B4* 480
Paucartambo *M5A6* 193
Pedro Ruíz 411
people 517
Pichingoto 173
Pilcopata *M5A6* 481
Pimentel *M1C2* 356
Pinchollo 243
Pinculluna 178
Pipus 409
Piquillacta 194
Pisac *M5A5* 170
Pisco *M5B2* 255
Piscobamba *M3A3* 320
Piura *M1B1* 362
Planchón 490
planning your trip 19
Playa Tortugas 333
police 42
See also under individual towns
politics 537
Pomabamba *M3A3* 320
Pomachaca 318
Pomata *M6B3* 211
postal services 54
Pozuzo *M3B4* 448
Pucallpa 463
Pucara *M6B2* 203
Pucusana 252
Pucusana *M3C4* 140
Pueblo Libre *M3A2* 310
Puente Santo Tomás 405
Puerto Acosta 218
Puerto Bermúdez *M3B5* 448
Puerto de Lomas 272
Puerto Delfus *M1B4* 416
Puerto Etén *M1C2* 356
Puerto Inca 273
Puerto Maldonado *M6A3* 483
Puno *M6B2* 204
Punta Sal Grande 373
Puruchuco 140

Putina *M6B2* 203

Q

Quebrada Honda 319
Quebrada Rurec 312
Quechualla 247
Quercos 315
Quichuas 434
Quilca *M5C5* 274
Quillabamba *M5A5* 189
Quincemil *M6A1* 484
Quiruvilca *M3A2* 384
Quistococha 474

R

radio 55
rafting
See sport
Raqchi *M6A1* 195
Raura 321
reading, further 83
Recuay *M3B3* 312
Reiche, Maria 271
religion 520
Repartición *M5C6* 275
responsible tourism 39
Rioja 412
road travel
See transport
rubber 469
rules
See etiquette

S

Sacaco 272
Sacsayhuamán
See Cusco
safety 40
Salinas 173
Salvacción 481
Sameriza 416
San Agustín de Cajas 431
San Antonio *M1C5* 410
San Bartolo 252
San Bartolomé 423
San Francisco 467
San Francisco *M3C6* 442
San Ignacio *M1B3* 418
San Isidro
See under Lima
San Jacinto 336
San Jerónimo *M5A6* 431
San Juan de Iris 422
San Juan *M5B3* 272
San Lorenzo *M4C6* 490
San Luis de Shuaro *M3B5* 447
San Luis *M3A3* 319
San Marcos *M1C4* 385
San Marcos *M3B3* 318
San Mateo *M3C4* 423
San Pedro 366, 431
San Pedro de Cajas 446

San Pedro de Casta 422
San Pedro de Utac 405
Saña *M1C2* 356
Santa Clara 467
Santa Inés *M3C5* 434
Santa Lucía *M6B2* 201
Santa María 252
Santa Rosa 356
Santiago de Chuco *M3A2* 384
Santo Tomás 474
Santo Tomás *M1C3* 405
Satipo *M3B5* 447
Sayán *M3B3* 329
sculpture 533
Sechín 333
Sechura Desert *M1B2* 361
Sechura *M1B1* 366
Shapaja *M1C5* 415
Shelby *M3B4* 449
Shintuya *M5A6* 481
Shipata 411
shopping 58
See also under individual towns
Shorey *M3A2* 384
Sibayo 240
Sicaya 430
Sicuani *M5B6* 219
Siguas *M3A2* 275
Sillustani *M6B2* 211
Simbal *M3A1* 384
Sipán 357
skiing
See sport
sleeping
See accommodation
society 517, 540
Spanish
See language
sport
cave diving 68
climbing 60
diving 68
fishing 68
hang gliding 67
kayaking 66
mountain biking 67
parapenting 67
rafting 62
skiing 62
surfing 68
swimming 68
trekking 61
yachting 68
student travellers 37
Sullana *M1B1* 369
sunburn 78, 79
surfing
See sport
swimming
See sport

T

Tacna *M6C2* 281
Talara *M1B1* 370

Tambo Colorado 260
Tambopata-Candamo 487
Tantamayo 453
Tapay 244
Taquile Island *M6B2* 214
Tarabamba 173
Tarapoto *M1C5* 414
Taricá 301
Tarma *M3C4* 444, 445
taxis
    See transport
Tayabamba *M3A3* 385
telephones 54
    See also under individual towns
terrorism 41
Ticlio 423
Tincopalca 201
Tingo *M1C4* 401
Tingo María *M3A4* 458
Tinqui *M6A1* 194
Tinta *M6A1* 195
Tiobamba 176
Tipón 193
tipping 39
Tocache *M3A3* 460
toilets 44
Toquepala *M6C2* 281
Torata *M6C2* 278
Toro Muerto 245
tour operators 85
tourist board 35
tourist information 35
tourist police 34
train
    See transport
transport 26
    air 26, 45
    boat 32
    bus 47
    car 48
    cars 31
    colectivos 48
    cycling 52
    hitchhiking 53
    international buses 31
    motorcycling 51
    river 473
    road 47
    taxis 48
    train 46
    trucks 48
    See also under individual towns
trekking
    See sport 242
Tres de Diciembre 430
Trita 411
trucks
    See transport
Trujillo *M3A1* 336
Túcume *M1C2* 359
Tulumayo 460
Tumbes *M1A1* 375
Tumbes Zona Reservada 378
Tuti 240

U

Ubilón 404
Ulta valley 303
Urcos *M6A1* 194
Uros Island *M6B2* 213
Urubamba *M5A5* 173
Urubamba Valley 169
useful addresses 85
useful websites 88

V

vaccinations
    See health
Vaquería 306
Velinga 247
Ventanillas de Combayo 392
Ventanillas de Otusco 392
Vicos 301
Vilcashuamán 440
Viques 430
visas
    See entry requirements
Vischongo 441
Vitcos 189
Vitór *M5C6* 275
volcanoes 511
voltage 34

W

water 76
weights & measures 34
what to take 24
when to go 20
where to go 19
where to stay
    See accommodation
wildlife 513
Willkawain 300
women travellers 42

Y

yachting
    See sport
Yacila 366
Yanahuanca *M3B4* 451
Yanama *M3A3* 319
Yancabamba 384
Yanque 242
Yauri *M6B1* 220
Yerbabuena *M1C4* 405
youth hostels
    See accommodation
Yucay *M5A5* 172
Yungay *M3A2* 304
Yunguyo *M6B3* 216
Yura 227
Yurimaguas *M1B5* 461

Z

Zepita *M6C3* 211
Zorritos *M1B1* 374
Zungaro 467

Maps

188	Aguas Calientes	**200**	Lake Titicaca
229	Arequipa	**92**	Lima
224	Arequipa, area	**98**	Lima centre
437	Ayacucho	**115**	Central Lima & Breña
118	Barranco	**112**	Miraflores
387	Cajamarca	**306**	Llanganuco to Santa Cruz Trek
391	Cajamarca, around	**253**	Lunahuaná
290	Callejón de Huaylas	**180**	Machu Picchu
308	Caraz	**479**	Manu Biosphere Reserve
332	Casma	**277**	Moquegua
393	Celendín	**266**	Nasca
450	Cerro de Pasco	**177**	Ollantaytambo
397	Chachapoyas	**312**	Olleros to Chavín Trek
400	Chachapoyas, sites around	**257**	Paracas Peninsula
315	Chavín	**1**	Peru
351	Chiclayo	**538**	Peru departmental
355	Chiclayo, area	**170**	Pisac
334	Chimbote	**255**	Pisco
323	Cordilleras Huayhuash & Raura	**363**	Piura
246	Cotahuasi Town	**464**	Pucallpa
148	Cusco	**485**	Puerto Maldonado
154	Cusco centre	**206**	Puno
407	Gran Vilaya Region	**369**	Sullana
432	Huancavelica	**283**	Tacna
426	Huancayo	**487**	Tambopata Candamo Reserve
452	Huánuco		Zone
295	Huaraz	**445**	Tarma
262	Ica	**144**	The Sacred Valley
280	Ilo Viejo	**459**	Tingo María
184	Inca Trail	**340**	Trujillo
470	Iquitos	**346**	Trujillo, around
417	Jaén	**376**	Tumbes
202	Juliaca	**174**	Urubamba
402	Kuelap	**190**	Vilcabamba

Footnotes

Will you help us?

We try as hard as we can to make each Footprint Handbook as up-to-date and accurate as possible but, of course, things always change. Many people write to us - with corrections, new information, or simply comments.

If you want to let us know about an experience or adventure - hair-raising or mundane, good or bad, exciting or boring or simply something rather special - we would be delighted to hear from you. Please give us as precise information as possible, quoting the edition number (you'll find it on the front cover) and page number of the Handbook you are using.

Your help will be greatly appreciated, especially by other travellers. In return we will send you details about our special guidebook offer.

Sales & distribution

Footprint Handbooks
6 Riverside Court
Lower Bristol Road
Bath BA2 3DZ
T 01225 469141
F 01225 469461
E Mail handbooks@
footprint.cix.co.uk

Australia
Peribo Pty
58 Beaumont Road
Mt Kuring-Gai
NSW 2080
T (02) 9457 0011
F (02) 9457 0022

Austria
Freytag-Berndt Artaria
Kohlmarkt 9
A-1010 Wien
T 01 533 2094
F 01 533 8685

Belgium
Craenen BVBA
Mechelsesteenweg 633
B-3020 Herent
T 016 23 90 90
F 016 23 97 11

Canada
Ulysses Travel Publications
4176 rue Saint-Denis
Montréal
Québec H2W 2M5
T (514) 843 9882
F (514) 843 9448

Caribbean
Kingston Publishers
10, LOJ Industrial Complex
7 Norman Road
Kingston CSO
Jamaica
T 001876 928 8898
F 001876 928 5719

**Europe – Central
& Eastern**
Michael Timperley
MTM
E Mail 100421.2070@
compuserve.com
T +852 2525 6264
F +852 2918 1034

**Europe – Germany,
Austria, Scandinavia,
Spain, Portugal**
Bill Bailey
16 Devon Square
Newton Abbott
Devon TQ12 2HR.UK
T 01626 331079
F 01626 331080

Denmark
Kilroy Travel
Skindergade 28
DK-1159 Copenhagen K
T 33 11 00 44
F 33 32 32 69

Nordisk Korthandel
Studiestraede 26-30 B
DK-1455 Copenhagen K
T 33 13 26 38
F 33 91 26 38

Scanvik Books
Esplanaden 8B
DK-1263 Copenhagen K
T 33 12 77 66
F 33 91 28 82

Finland
Akateeminen Kirjakauppa
Keskuskatu 1
FIN-00100 Helsinki
T 09 12141
F 09 121 4441

Suomalainen
Kirjakauppa
Koivuvaarankuja 2
01640 Vantaa 64
F 08 52 78 88

France
L'Astrolabe
46 rue de Provence
F-75009 Paris 9e
T 1 42 85 42 95
F 1 45 75 92 51

VILO Diffusion
25 rue Ginoux
F-75015 Paris
T 01 45 77 08 05
F 01 45 79 97 15

Germany
GeoCenter ILH
Schockenriedstrasse 44
D-70565 Stuttgart
T 0711 781 94610
F 0711 781 94654

Brettschneider
Fernreisebedarf
Feldkirchnerstrasse 2
D-85551 Heimstetten
T 089 990 20330
F 089 990 20331

Geobuch Gmbh
Rosental 6
D-80331 München
T 089 265030
F 089 263713

Gleumes
Hohenstaufenring 47-51
D-50674 Köln
T 0221 215650

Globetrotter Ausrustungen
Wiesendamm 1
D-22305 Hamburg
F 040 679 66183

Dr Götze
Bleichenbrücke 9
D-2000 Hamburg 1
T 040 3031 1009-0

Hugendubel Buchhandlung
Nymphenburgerstrasse 25
D-80335 München
T 089 238 9412
F 089 550 1853

Kiepert Buchhandlung
Hardenbergstrasse 4-5
D-10623 Berlin 12
T 030 311880

Greece
GC Eleftheroudakis
17 Panepistemiou
Athens 105 64
T 01 322 2255
F 01 323 9821

India
Roli Books
M-75 GK II Market
New Delhi 110048
T (011) 646 0886
F (011) 646 7185

Israel
Geographical Tours
8 Tverya Street
Tel Aviv 63144
T 03 528 4113
F 03 629 9905

Italy
Librimport
Via Biondelli 9
I-20141 Milano
T 02 8950 1422
F 02 8950 2811

Kenya
Novelty Wholesalers
PO Box 47407
Nairobi
T 2 743157 F 2 743157

Netherlands
Nilsson & Lamm bv
Postbus 195
Pampuslaan 212
N-1380 AD Weesp
T 0294 494949
F 0294 494455

Norway
Narvesen Distribusjon
Bertrand Narvesens Vei 2
Postboks 6219 Etterstad
N-0602 Oslo 6
T 22 57 32 00
F 22 68 24 65

Schibsteds Forlag A/S
Akersgata 32 - 5th Floor
Postboks 1178 Sentrum
N-0107 Oslo
T 22 86 30 00
F 22 42 54 92

Tanum
PO Box 1177 Sentrum
N-0107 Oslo 1
T 22 41 11 00
F 22 33 32 75

Pakistan
Pak-American Commercial
Zaib-un Nisa Street
Saddar
PO Box 7359
Karachi
T 21 566 0419
F 21 568 3611

South Africa
Faradawn CC
PO Box 1903
Saxonwold 2132
T 011 885 1787
F 011 885 1829

South America
Humphrys Roberts
Associates
Caixa Postal 801-0
Ag.Jardim da Gloria
06700-970 Cotia SP
Brazil
T 011 492 4496
F 011 492 6896

Southeast Asia
APA Publications
38 Joo Koon Road
Singapore 628990
T 865 1600
F 861 6438

Spain
Altaïr,Balmes 69
08007 Barcelona
T 93 3233062
F 93 4512559

Bookworld España
Pje Las Palmeras 25
29670 San Pedro
Alcántara,Málaga
T 95 278 6366
F 95 278 6452

Sweden
Hedengrens Bokhandel
PO Box 5509
S-11485 Stockholm
T 8 6115132

Kart Centrum
Vasagatan 16
S-11120 Stockholm
T 8 111699

Lantmateriet Kartbutiken
Kungsgatan 74
S-11122 Stockholm

Switzerland
Artou,8 rue de Rive
CH-1204 Geneva
T 022 311 4544
F 022 781 3456

Office du Livre OLF SA
ZI 3,Corminboeuf
CH-1701 Fribourg
T 026 467 5111
F 026 467 5466

Schweizer Buchzentrum
Postfach
CH-4601 Olten
T 062 209 2525
F 062 209 2627

Travel Bookshop
Rindermarkt 20
Postfach 216
CH-8001 Zürich
T 01 252 3883
F 01 252 3832

USA
NTC/ Contemporary
4255 West Touhy Avenue
Lincolnwood
Illinois 60646-1975
T (847) 679 5500
F (847) 679 2494

Advertiser index

268 Alegría Tours, Peru
165 Amauta Language School, Peru
237 Amazonas Explorer, UK
 54 AmeriSpan, USA
167 APU Expeditions Cultural
    Adventure Travel, Peru
182 Aracari Travel Consulting, Peru
343 Clara Luz Bravo Diaz, Peru
217 Crillon Tours, Bolivia
 61 Dragoman, UK
168 Expediciones Manu, Peru
161 Galeria Latina, Peru
136 Hada Tours, Peru
155 Hostal Arqueologo, Peru
156 Hostal Royal Frankenstein, Peru
267 Hotel Alegría, Peru
236 Ideal Travel, Peru
478 InkaNatura Travel, Peru
 71 International Expeditions, USA
562 International Expeditions, USA
 29 Journey Latin America, London
 32 Ladatco Tours, USA
 33 Last Frontiers, UK
 30 Latin American Travel
    Consultants, Ecuador
114 La Posada del Parque, Peru
 86 Lost World Adventures, USA
167 Manu Nature Tours
153 Posada del Inca, Cusco
113 Posada del Inca, Lima
172 Posada del Inca, Yucay
111 San Antonio Abad Hostal, Peru
136 Servicios Aereos, Peru
 87 Sol International Tour Operator,
    USA
 32 South American Experience,
    London
138 South American Explorers' Club,
    Peru
561 South American Tours,
    Germany
166 Tambo Tours, USA
 87 Wildland Adventures, USA

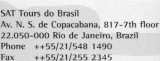

Amazon

The Greatest Voyage in Natural History

Experience a sublime journey into a primordial realm aboard an elegant expeditionary vessel. Explore the mighty Amazon, its frontier tributaries and black water lakes. Our classic riverboats combine style and comfort with superb wildlife viewing, expert naturalists and a true sense of adventure.

Exceptional Wildlife • Expert Naturalists
Private Facilities • Superb Dining • Air Conditioned

8-Day Voyages Depart Monthly
Priced all-inclusive with international airfare from Miami.

Optional extensions to Cusco/Machu Picchu and ACEER Canopy Walkway System

ADVANCED RESERVATIONS REQUIRED.
CONTACT US FOR AVAILABLE DATES AND CURRENT PRICING.

Peru

Altitude in metres
4000
3000
2000
1000
500
200

Neighbouring Country

Paved roads
Unpaved roads
Railway
◆ National Park
International Border

COLOMBIA

ECUADOR

❶

IQUITOS □   *Amazonas*

❷

CHACHAPOYAS □

BRAZIL

□ TRUJILLO

PUCALLPA □

□ HUARAZ

❹

❸

Pacific Ocean

□ HUANCAYO

PUERTO MALDONADO □

LIMA ⟩

□ CUSCO

AYACUCHO □

❺

PUNO □   *L. Titicaca*

BOLIVIA

AREQUIPA □

❻

N

km   100
miles   62

CHILE

Map 1

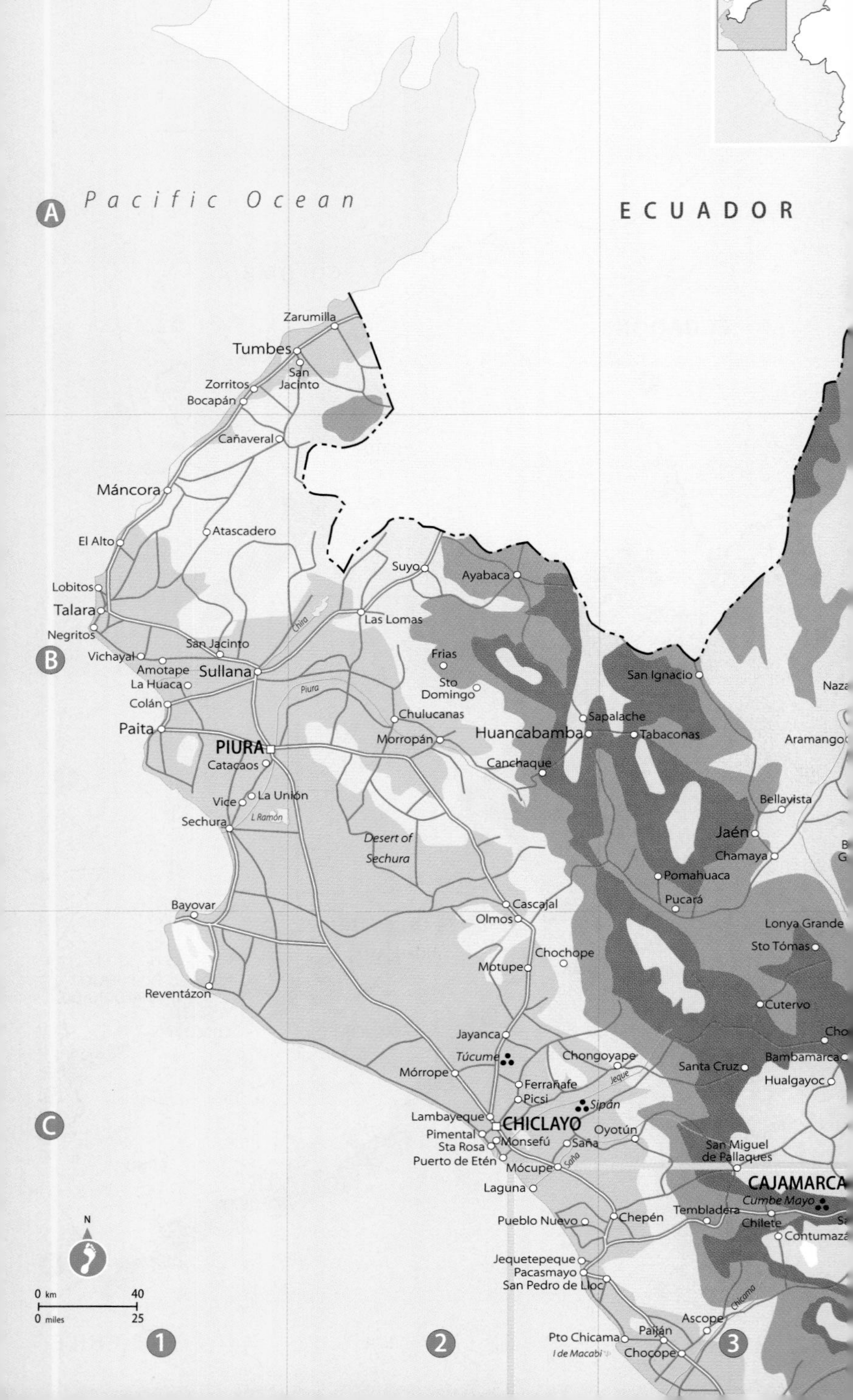

Pacific Ocean

ECUADOR

A

Zarumilla

Tumbes
Zorritos
San
Jacinto
Bocapán

Cañaveral

Máncora

El Alto
Atascadero

Lobitos
Talara
Negritos
Suyo
Ayabaca
Vichayal
San Jacinto
Las Lomas
Amotape
La Huaca
Sullana
Colán
Frias
Paita
Sto
Domingo
Chulucanas
San Ignacio
PIURA
Morropán
Huancabamba
Catacaos
Sapalache
La Unión
Canchaque
Tabaconas
Vice
Aramango
Sechura
Bellavista
Desert of
Sechura
Jaén
Chamaya
Pomahuaca
Bayovar
Pucará
Cascajal
Lonya Grande
Olmos
Sto Tómas
Chochope
Motupe
Cuervo
Reventázon
Jayanca
Túcume
Chongoyape
Bambamarca
Mórrope
Santa Cruz
Hualgayoc
Ferreñafe
Picsi
Sipán
Lambayeque
CHICLAYO
Pimental
Monsefú
Oyotún
San Miguel
Sta Rosa
Saña
de Pallaques
Puerto de Etén
Mócupe
CAJAMARCA
Laguna
Cumbe Mayo
Pueblo Nuevo
Chepén
Tembladera
Chilete
Jequetepeque
Contumazá
Pacasmayo
San Pedro de Lloc
Ascope
N
Pto Chicama
Paiján
0 km 40
I de Macabí
Chocope
0 miles 25

1
2
3

B

C

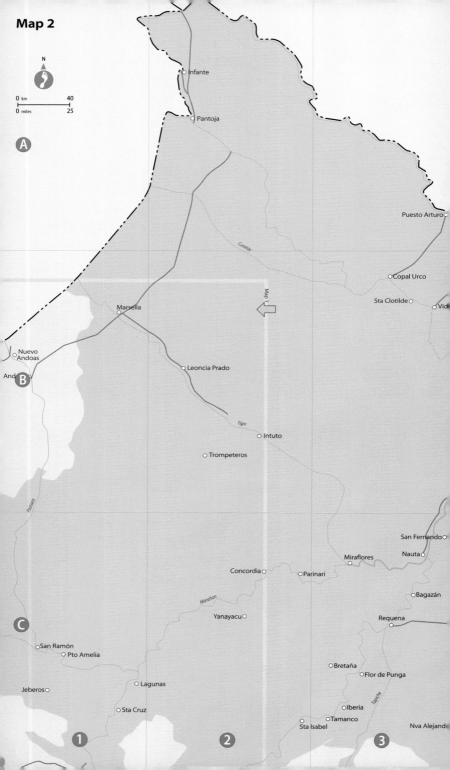

Map 2

N

| 0 km | 40 |
| 0 miles | 25 |

Ⓐ

Ⓑ

Ⓒ

Infante

Pantoja

Puesto Arturo

Cunaroy

Copal Urco

Sta Clotilde

Vid

Marsella

Map

Nuevo Andoas

And

Leoncia Prado

Tigre

Intuto

Trompeteros

San Fernando

Nauta

Miraflores

Concordia

Parinari

Bagazán

Marañon

Yanayacu

Requena

San Ramón

Pto Amelia

Bretaña

Flor de Punga

Jeberos

Lagunas

Iberia

Tapiche

Sta Cruz

Tamanco

Sta Isabel

Nva Alejand

�1

Ⓒ2

Ⓒ3

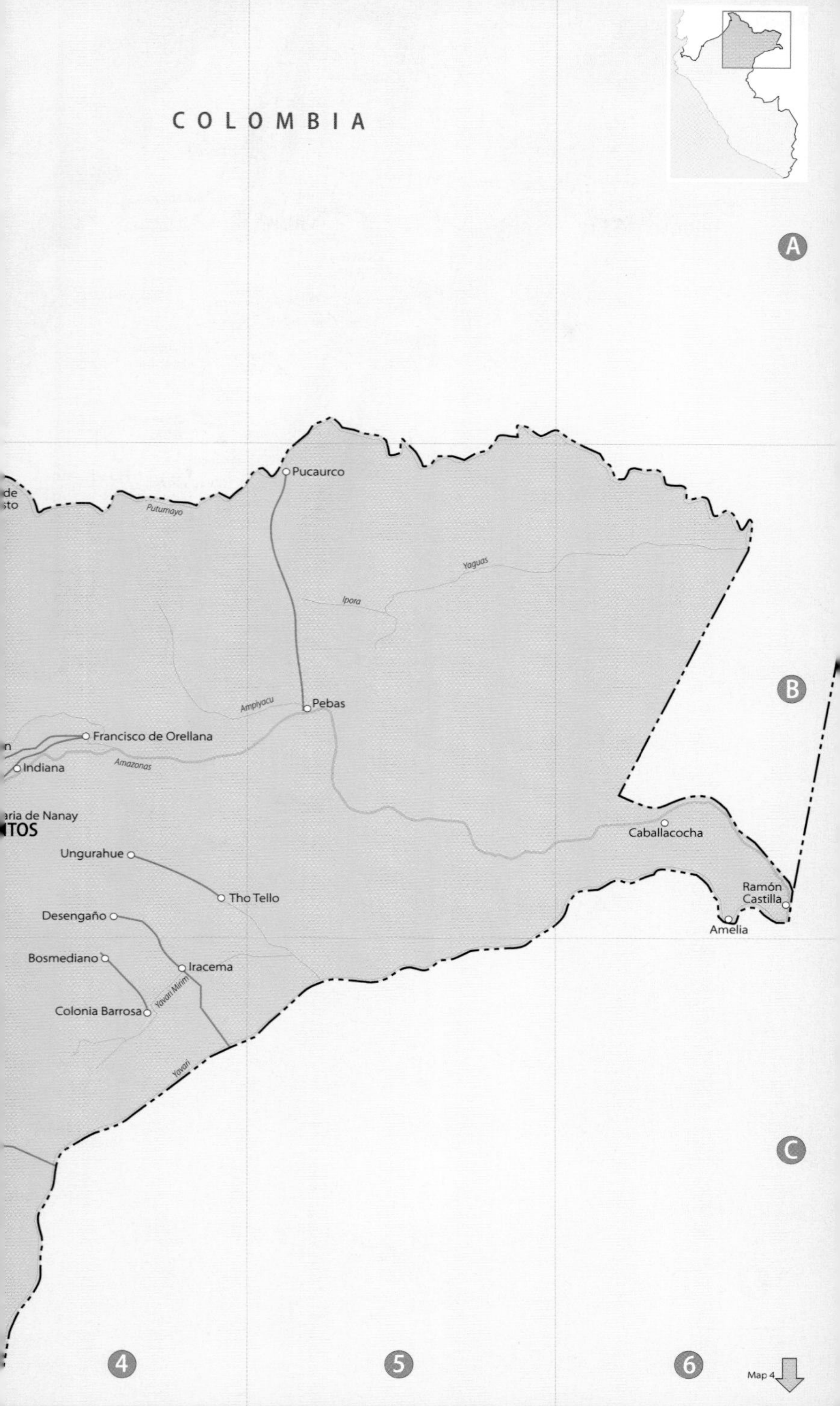

COLOMBIA

Pucaurco

Putumayo

Yaguas

Ipora

Amplyacu

Pebas

Francisco de Orellana

Indiana

Amazonas

aria de Nanay

ITOS

Ungurahue

Caballacocha

Tho Tello

Ramón
Castilla

Desengaño

Amelia

Bosmediano

Iracema

Yavari Mirim

Colonia Barrosa

Yavari

A

B

C

4

5

6

Map 4

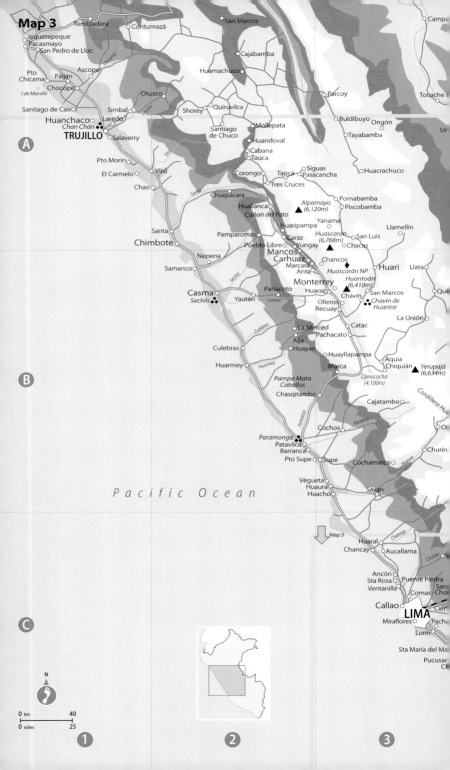

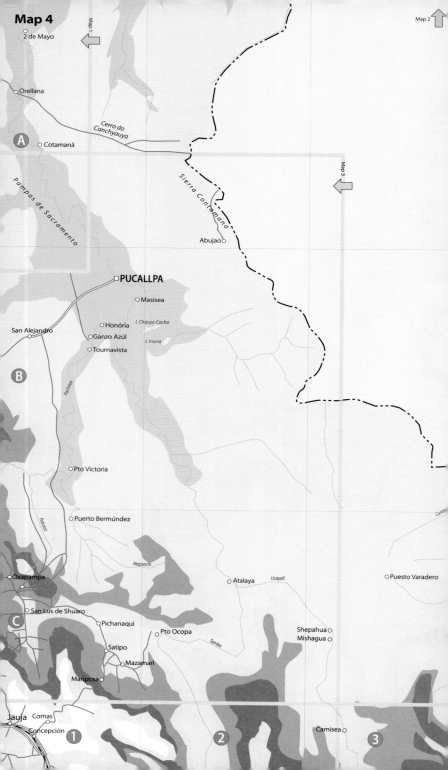

Map 4

Map 1

Map 2

Map 3

2 de Mayo

Orellana

Cerro do
Canchyauya

A

Cotamaná

Pampas de Sacramento

Sierra Contamana

Abujao

PUCALLPA

Masisea

L Chauya Cocha

Honória

San Alejandro

Ganzo Azúl

L Inuria

Tournavista

B

Pachitea

Pto Victoria

Puerto Bermúndez

Palcazú

Neguachi

Ucayali

Curan...

Oxapampa

Atalaya

Puesto Varadero

San Lús de Shuaro

C

Pichanaqui

Pto Ocopa

Shepahua

Mishagua

Satipo

Tambo

Mazamari

Mariposa

Jauja

Comas

Concepción

Camisea

1

2

3

N

0 km 40
0 miles 25

A

BRAZIL

B

Esperanza

Curanja

Iñapari

C

Iberia
San Lorenzo

Las Piedras

Map 5

Madre de Dios

4   Manú   5   6   Map 6

Complete listing

Latin America

Argentina Handbook
1 900949 10 5 £11.99

Bolivia Handbook
1 900949 09 1 £11.99

Brazil Handbook
0 900751 84 3 £12.99

Caribbean Islands Handbook 1999
1 900949 23 7 £14.99

Chile Handbook
0 900751 85 1 £10.99

Colombia Handbook
1 900949 11 3 £10.99

Cuba Handbook
1 900949 12 1 £10.99

Ecuador & Galápagos Handbook
1 900949 29 6 £11.99

Mexico & Central America Handbook 1999
1 900949 22 9 £16.99

Peru Handbook
1 900949 31 8 £11.99

South American Handbook 1999
1 900949 21 0 £22.99

Venezuela Handbook
1 900949 13 X £10.99

Africa

East Africa Handbook 1999
1 900949 25 3 £14.99

Morocco Handbook
1 900949 35 0 £11.99

Namibia Handbook
1 900949 30 X £10.99

South Africa Handbook 1999
1 900949 26 1 £14.99

Tunisia Handbook
1 900949 34 2 £10.99

Zimbabwe Handbook
0 900751 93 2 £11.99

Asia

Cambodia Handbook
0 900751 96 7 £9.99

Goa Handbook
1 900949 17 2 £9.99

India Handbook 1999
1 900949 24 5 £16.99

Indonesia Handbook
1 900949 15 6 £14.99

Laos Handbook
0 900751 89 4 £9.99

Malaysia & Singapore Handbook
1 900949 16 4 £12.99

Myanmar (Burma) Handbook
0 900751 87 8 £9.99

Nepal Handbook
1 900949 00 8 £11.99

Pakistan Handbook
1 900949 37 7 £12.99

Singapore Handbook
1 900949 19 9 £9.99

Sri Lanka Handbook
1 900949 18 0 £11.99

Thailand Handbook
1 900949 32 6 £12.99

Tibet Handbook
1 900949 33 4 £12.99

Vietnam Handbook
1 900949 36 9 £10.99

Middle East

Egypt Handbook
1 900949 20 2 £12.99

Israel Handbook
1 900949 01 6 £12.99

Jordan, Syria & Lebanon Handbook
1 900949 14 8 £12.99

Europe

Andalucía Handbook
1 900949 27 X £9.99

Wexas

Traveller's Handbook
0 905802 08 X £14.99

Traveller's Healthbook
0 905802 09 8 £9.99

What the papers say

"I carried the South American Handbook in my bag from Cape Horn to Cartagena and consulted it every night for two and a half months. And I wouldn't do that for anything else except my hip flask."

Michael Palin

"Of all the main guidebook series this is genuinely the only one we have never received a complaint about."

The Bookseller

"All in all, the Footprint Handbook series is the best thing that has happened to travel guidebooks in years. They are different and take you off the beaten track away from all the others clutching the competitors' guidebooks."

The Business Times, Singapore

"Footprint's India Handbook told me everything from the history of the region to where to get the best curry."

Jennie Bond, BBC Correspondent

"Footprint Handbooks, the best of the best!"

Le Monde, Paris

Acknowledgements

The editor would like to thank the following contributors: Robert and Daisy Kunstaetter hail from Canada and Ecuador respectively. Having lived and travelled throughout Latin America since 1983, they currently make their home in Baños in Ecuador where they edit the Latin American Travel Advisor and produce a travel programme for short-wave radio. Robert and Daisy researched and updated the sections on the Cordillera Blanca, Chachapoyas region and northern Peru, as well as providing additional information for the trekking and climbing sections in adventure sports.

Bill Glick lives and works in Lima as a freelance writer and is a regular contributor to the Peru Handbook. Bill researched and updated Lima as well as providing additional information for the Essentials section.

Canadian-born Janice Davies, of the South American Explorers' Club in Lima, updated the information in the Essentials section.

Mariella Bernasconi and Alberto Mauro, owners of Apu Expediciones in Cusco, provided updated information for the Cusco and Sacred Valley section.

Michael White and Clara Brava live and work in Trujillo as tour guides. They provided updates on Trujillo and the surrounding area.

Efraín Alegría, owner of Alegría Tours and Hotel Alegría, provided updates on Nasca and Pisco.

Cecilia Camiche, owner of Ideal Travels SA in Arequipa, provided updated information for the Arequipa section.

Paul Cripps, co-owner and operator of Amazonas Explorer SA, researched and wrote the river rafting section in adventure sports and also provided updates and additional information on other adventure sports.

John Forrest and Julia Porturas live and work in London. They provided updated information on many areas, in particular, the north coast, south coast, Colca canyon, Puerto Maldonado and Tambopata-Candamo reserve.

The editor would like to thank the following people for their hospitality and assistance: Barry Walker owner of the Cross Keys Pub and Manu Expeditions in Cusco; also Charo and Jessica of Manu Expedions; Italo Molinari and Franco Negri of the Hostal El Balcón in Cusco; Rosario Griffiths of Posada del Inca hotel group; Luz-Marina of Luzma Tours in Cusco; Alberto and Haydée Cafferata of Pony's Expeditions in Caraz; Familia Yomona Díaz, Pedro Ruíz; Carlos and Charo Burga, Hostal Revash, Chachapoyas; Robert Dover, Chachapoyas; Tom Gierasimczuk, Chachapoyas; Steve Abouldahab, Chachapoyas; Vladimiro Hinostrosa, Alojamiento Sol Andino, Huaraz; Manuel and Maruja Quintana, Restaurant Querubín, Huaraz; Felipe Díaz, Heladería El Abuelo, Carhuaz; Karen Martínez, PromPerúoptur, Lima; Eliana Pauca of All Ways Travel, Puno; Jaime Acevedo, Iquitos. Thanks are also due to the many travellers who took the trouble to write in with their experiences and recommendations.